FOURTH EDITION

EXPERIMENTAL PSYCHOLOGY

FOURTH EDITION

EXPERIMENTAL PSYCHOLOGY

Anne Myers

Christine H. Hansen
Oakland University

Brooks/Cole Publishing Company
I⊤P® *An International Thomson Publishing Company*

Pacific Grove • *Albany* • *Belmont* • *Bonn* • *Boston* • *Cincinnati* • *Detroit* • *Johannesburg* • *London*
Madrid • *Melbourne* • *Mexico City* • *New York* • *Paris* • *Singapore* • *Tokyo* • *Toronto* • *Washington*

Sponsoring Editor: Jim Brace-Thompson
Marketing Team: Gay Meixel, Romy Taormina
Editorial Assistant: Terry Thomas
Production Editor: Nancy L. Shammas
Production Service: Matrix Productions
Manuscript Editor: Vicki Nelson
Permissions Editor: Cathleen S. Collins
Interior Design: Cynthia Bogue

Interior Illustration: LM Graphics
Cover Design: Laurie Albrecht
Cover Photo: ©David Bishop/Phototake
Photo Editor: Kathleen Olson
Typesetting: GTS Graphics, Inc.
Cover Printing: Phoenix Color
  Corporation, Inc.
Printing and Binding: Quebecor/Fairfield

For more information, contact:

BROOKS/COLE PUBLISHING COMPANY
511 Forest Lodge Road
Pacific Grove, CA 93950
USA

International Thomson Editores
Seneca 53
Col. Polanco
México, D.F., México
C.P. 11560

International Thomson Publishing Europe
Berkshire House 168-173
High Holborn
London WC1V 7AA
England

International Thomson Publishing GmbH
Königswinterer Strasse 418
53227 Bonn
Germany

Thomas Nelson Australia
102 Dodds Street
South Melbourne, 3205
Victoria, Australia

International Thomson Publishing Asia
221 Henderson Road
#05-10 Henderson Building
Singapore 0315

Nelson Canada
1120 Birchmount Road
Scarborough, Ontario
Canada M1K 5G4

International Thomson Publishing Japan
Hirakawacho Kyowa Building, 3F
2-2-1 Hirakawacho
Chiyoda-ku, Tokyo 102
Japan

Printed in the United States of America

10   9   8   7   6   5   4   3

Library of Congress Cataloging-in-Publication Data

Myers, Anne.
    Experimental psychology / Anne Myers, Christine H. Hansen.—
4th ed.
          p.   cm.
    Includes bibliographical references and index.
    ISBN 0-534-33979-4
    1. Psychology, Experimental.   I. Hansen, Christine H.   II. Title.
BF181.M85   1996
150'.724—dc20
                                                                    96-5045
                                                                    CIP

To my Dad, for many postcards.
A.M.

To R.D.H., my favorite colleague.
C.H.

PREFACE

Goals of the Text

Experimental Psychology, Fourth Edition, is an introduction to the basic principles of research in psychology. It explains the key principles of research, particularly experimental research, clearly and within the context of concrete examples. It teaches students how to design and execute an experiment, analyze and interpret the results, and write a research report. Although the main focus is on experimentation, alternative approaches are discussed as important complements to controlled laboratory experiments.

This text was designed to be as comprehensive as possible—without overwhelming the beginning researcher. The principles of experimentation and the skepticism of the scientific approach are concepts that are new to students and run counter to their commonsense notions about causal inference; for most psychology students, mastering experimental methods requires making a quantum leap from their original ideas about psychology as well as challenges them to learn an entirely new language. This text has been designed to address these issues and provide practical solutions to them. It was written with flexibility in mind for the instructor as well. Each chapter can stand on its own, and instructors can select text assignments to match individual course content.

Special Features of the Text

This text introduces the experimental process in a structured way that allows students to gain a thorough grasp of the scientific method. First, it is organized to carry students through the entire process of conducting an experiment. The major sections—Introduction, Method, Results, and Discussion—parallel the major sections of the research report in order to clarify the relationship among designing, conducting, and reporting the experiment. The *Publication Manual of the American Psychological Association,* Fourth Edition (1994), includes a number of changes and additions along with new requirements and recommendations. Throughout the text we have included new material that incorporates these changes.

Second, many practical aids are provided. Research ethics are discussed in detail, as are specific techniques for developing a research hypothesis. In presenting research methods, we have stressed the integral relationship among the experimental hypothesis, the research design, and the statistical analysis. The process of selecting a design has been broken down into basic steps to provide structure for the student. A detailed chapter on report writing includes a sample journal article to illustrate the most current reporting conventions. (To aid students in producing an APA-style report, the manuscript version of this article is reproduced in Appendix C.) The rationale behind all procedures is explained to help students apply them. Important terms are introduced in boldface type throughout the text and are listed at the end of each chapter. Each chapter also includes a summary and review and study questions. At the end of the book, a random number table (Appendix B), glossary, and index are included.

Third, examples are drawn from a variety of research areas to emphasize the importance of experimental procedures throughout psychological research. The examples, both classic and current, provide clear, concrete illustrations of the concepts under discussion. The eclectic choice of examples gives instructors the freedom to supplement the text with content-oriented readings in areas of their choice.

Statistical material is included to help students interpret research findings. The results section of the text provides students with a conceptual overview of the process of statistical inference and step-by-step instructions for selecting and carrying out some of the tests commonly used in simple experiments. Basic terms are reviewed and statistical tables are included (Appendix B) so that all the required information is available in this single source. The process of interpreting statistical results is discussed in detail.

Organization of the Fourth Edition

Those who used the text in its third edition will find that the overall plan and focus of the book remain unchanged. Many interesting new examples have been included throughout. Some topics have been updated and expanded in response to reviewer and user feedback. New topics have been added. Chapter 1, for example, now includes examples of common pitfalls of nonscientific inference and commonsense psychology. Ethics has been moved to Chapter 2. Chapters 3 and 4 contain broadened coverage of nonexperimental approaches (including survey techniques) and new discussions of popular correlation-based and quasi-experimental methods. Chapter 5 now includes an expanded, practical section on searching the literature, with a greater focus on the use of computer databases.

The chapters on basic experimental designs (Chapters 7, 8, 9, and 10) have been reorganized slightly. Between-subjects experiments with one independent variable have been consolidated into a single chapter (Chapter 7). Between-subjects factorials are now the sole focus of Chapter 8, allowing for more discussion of main effects and interactions. Chapter 9 now includes within-subjects designs, mixed designs, and counterbalancing techniques. Small N designs are now a single, brief chapter (Chapter 10). Control procedures for physical, social, and other extraneous variables are now combined in Chapter 11. New information about experimenter and subject characteristics and some practical tips for recruiting subjects have been added. More classic methodology from Cook and Campbell[1] is included in many of the chapters, including a stronger focus on the relationship between research methods and internal and external validity.

The chapters on statistics, well received in previous editions, have been updated with new examples. The concepts of hypothesis testing, measures of central tendencies, and variability are now presented jointly in Chapter 12. Chapter 13 concentrates on the selection and interpretation of statistics for two-group designs. Coverage of statistics for repeated measures designs has been broadened. As requested by readers, more discussion of chi square is now included, and a statistical table of critical values has been added to Appendix B. The chapter also includes more discussion of computer data analysis. Chapter 14 focuses on one- and two-way analysis of variance. The greater availability of statistical computing programs has made the use of more sophisticated ANOVA techniques commonplace; we have updated the chapter to accommodate this trend. We have added more information about repeated measures, mixed designs, and a brief discussion of multivariate and covariate techniques. Our basic philosophy toward statistics, however, has not changed. We continue to emphasize the importance of *understanding* the statistical techniques that are being used (and we demonstrate what happens when students use statistics they don't really understand). Chapters 13 and 14 both have an added emphasis on interpreting the results of statistical tests.

Chapter 15 now includes even more practical information for students about interpreting findings and evaluating experiments. For example, we have included more about the meaning of significant and nonsignificant statistical results (and the meaning of marginally significant results). Reporting effect sizes (strongly recommended in the new *APA Publication Manual*) is discussed, and a sample calculation is included. Chapter 16 has been completely updated to include changes in the *APA Publication Manual*, such as reporting estimates of variability and the new references style. Chapter 16 has a new sample article ("Gender Differences in Masking Negative Emotions: Ability or Motivation?"), by Teresa L. Davis, which is annotated in detail to help students write their own report. We think you will find the Fourth Edition even more comprehensive than before—but as user friendly as ever.

---

[1]Cook, T. D., & Campbell, D. T. (1979). *Quasi-experimentation: Design and analysis for field settings.* Chicago: Rand-McNally.

Acknowledgments

Many people contributed to the development of this manuscript. We would like to thank our colleagues and students, who offered comments, suggestions, and encouragement. We are especially grateful to Robert D. Nye, who served as an untiring sounding board. Howard Cohen, James Halpern, David Schiffman, Mark Sherman, and Jodi Solomon deserve special mention for reading portions of the original manuscript. Phyllis Freeman, Joanne Green, Zanvel Liff, Barbara Novick, David Morse, Robert Presbie, Richard Sloan, and Carol Vazquez were also helpful.

Special thanks to Dave Carroll, Donna Gerard, Deanna Hall, Andrea Kozak, Mark Hoheisel, Garth Preuthun, Cindy Shantz, and Jane Youngs, who read and commented on the current edition from a student's and teaching assistant's point of view. To Cindy Shantz and Jo Ann Swaney, our sincere gratitude for the numerous literature searches you conducted. Thanks, also, to three methodological wizards—Bill Crano, Randy Hansen, and Larry Messé—as well as Don Campbell and his colleagues, who have taught so many generations of students. We are also deeply indebted to the many researchers whose work inspired much of this text and to the many authors and publishers who permitted reproduction of portions of their works. They are cited throughout the text. Particular thanks to Robert A. Baron, Teresa Davis, and Robert Rosenthal, whose work fills so many pages, and especially to Robert Zajonc, *cher ami*, for his good humor. We are grateful to the literary executor of the late Sir Ronald A. Fisher, F.R.S., to Dr. Frank Yates, F.R.S., and to the Longman Group UK, Ltd. for permission to reprint portions of tables III and XXXIII (Tables B2 and B1 in our Appendix B) from their *Statistical Tables for Biological, Agricultural, and Medical Research* (6th edition, 1974).

We gratefully acknowledge the contributions of Robert Cowan, Northeast Missouri State; Warren Fass, University of Pittsburgh at Bradford; William Frederickson, University of Central Oklahoma; Timothy Goldsmith, University of New Mexico; Paul Koch, St. Ambrose University; Michael Renner, West Chester University of Pennsylvania; Charles Samuelson, Texas A&M University; Allen Shoemaker, Calvin College; and Roland Siiter, Montclair State University who reviewed this fourth edition. Their constructive suggestions improved the book considerably. We remain indebted to Roland Siiter, who has reviewed all three revisions, for his many helpful recommendations.

We would also like to thank the people at Brooks/Cole Publishing Company for their careful handling of the revision, particularly Jim Brace-Thompson, Acquisitions Editor, Nancy Shammas, Production Editor; Cat Collins, Permissions Editor; Kathleen Olson, Photo Coordinator; and Kelly Shoemaker, Cover Coordinator. Finally, we would like to acknowledge our gratitude to Merrill Peterson and Matrix Productions Inc. for deciphering our myriad notes, accepting our quirks, and getting the book into production with speed and care.

—Anne Myers, Christine Hansen

BRIEF CONTENTS

CONTENTS

P A R T   T W O
METHOD   137

PART FOUR

DISCUSSION   415

INTRODUCTION

C H A P T E R   1

EXPERIMENTAL PSYCHOLOGY AND THE SCIENTIFIC METHOD

Psychology is the science of behavior. As psychologists, we take a scientific approach to understanding behavior; our knowledge about psychological processes is based on scientific evidence accumulated through research. As scientists, we rely on scientific methods when we conduct psychological research such as specifying the conditions under which we make our observations, observing in a systematic or orderly way, and accepting or rejecting alternative explanations of behaviors on the basis of what we observe. In short, research about the psychological processes underlying behavior is known as psychological science.

The word **science** comes from the Latin word *scientia,* which simply means knowledge. As the word is used today, however, it has two connotations—content and process. The *content* of science is *what* we know, such as the facts we learn in our psychology or chemistry courses. But science is also a *process*— that is, an activity that includes the systematic ways in which we go about gathering data, noting relationships, and offering explanations. Explaining the process of psychological science is the principal aim of this text.

In the chapters that follow, we will examine some of the basic tactics of research in psychology. We will study **methodology,** the scientific techniques used to collect and evaluate psychological **data** (the facts and figures gathered in research studies). All areas of psychology use scientific research methods. For example, researchers investigating perception collect data in formal laboratory experiments designed to provide the most precise information. Psychologists interested in understanding attitudes and social behaviors sometimes gather data under controlled laboratory conditions; at other times they conduct surveys in the community or observe and record people's behavior in natural settings. Psychologists studying human development might observe young children's reactions under different conditions in the laboratory or in real-world settings. Clinicians may collect data by administering a variety of tests or by observing personality functioning during sessions with patients. Whether the data come from laboratory experiments, real-world settings, psychological testing, or treatment sessions, all psychologists use scientific criteria to evaluate their data.

THE NEED FOR SCIENTIFIC METHODOLOGY

In our daily lives, all of us collect and use psychological data to understand the behavior of others and to guide our own behavior. When you notice that your roommate is in a bad mood, you don't ask for a favor. You do not invite Pat and Terry to the same party because you know they don't like each other. You dress up when you are going for a job interview because you know first impressions are important. You can probably think of many more examples of situations in which you used psychological data to predict the behavior of others and to guide your own behavior. The kind of everyday, nonscientific data gathering that shapes our expectations and beliefs and directs our behavior toward others has been called **commonsense psychology** (Heider, 1958). It seems to work well enough for us most of the time. We may be quite successful finding the best time to ask our roommate for a favor or choosing the right outfit for an interview.

At other times though, nonscientific data gathering can leave us up in the air. Suppose, for example, that your significant other has just announced that she has been accepted for a summer program at the Sorbonne in Paris. Should you be worried? Some of the nonscientific data you gather about absent partners is reassuring ("absence makes the heart grow fonder"), but some is not ("out of sight, out of mind"). Most of your data seems to support the former conclusion, so you see her off at the airport in good spirits. On the drive home, you remember all the stories you have heard about Paris nightlife and sexy Parisian men. . . . Without knowing which outcome is *really* more probable in this specific situation, you are likely to spend an anxious summer. An understanding of the characteristics and limitations of commonsense psychology might not help with dilemmas like this one, but it may help you become a better psychological scientist—if only because it clearly demonstrates the need for a more scientific approach to understanding and predicting behavior.

As commonsense psychologists, we find that our ability to gather data in a systematic and impartial way is constrained by two very important factors: the sources of psychological information and our inferential strategies. Commonsense beliefs about behavior are derived from data we collect from our own observations and experiences and what we have learned from others. The data we collect in our everyday lives have been generated from a very small sample of behaviors, and the conclusions we draw from them are subject to a number of inherent tendencies, or biases, that limit their accuracy and usefulness. Frequently, the sources of our untutored beliefs about behavior can be unreliable, and the explanations and predictions that we derive from them are likely to be imperfect. Do birds of a feather flock together? Or do opposites attract? Our language is filled with these kinds of conflicting, commonsense adages, and commonsense psychology does not help us to know which one to use to predict behavior in any single instance. Let us look briefly at a few of the problems encountered by the commonsense psychologist before we turn to the scientific approaches used in psychological science.

Nonscientific Sources of Data

Some of the data we gather as commonsense psychologists come from sources that *seem* credible and trustworthy—friends and relatives, people in authority, people we admire, reports from the media, books we have read, and so forth—but, in fact, these sources are not always very good ones for obtaining valid information about behavior. Nevertheless, psychological information, particularly when it is offered by people we like, respect, or admire, is typically accepted without question. These beliefs tend to become stable because we rarely, if ever, test them. Once we believe we know something, we tend to overlook instances that might disconfirm our beliefs, and we seek, instead, confirmatory instances of behavior. If you believe that the full moon brings out psychotic behavior (the word *lunacy* comes from the Latin word for "moon"), you will notice and remember instances when people acted abnormally while the moon was full, and you will ignore the many, many more instances in which no unusual behavior occurred.

It is also unlikely that anyone can completely avoid assimilating some myths, superstitions, and pop psychology explanations of behavior. Remember "pyramid power"? The idea that positive energy from the universe could be concentrated in our bodies if we sat under a pyramid-shaped tent probably seems silly now, but how do you feel about crystals? Do you ever read your horoscope? Do you believe in ESP? Do you feel a bit anxious on Friday the 13th? Interestingly, only the latter superstition—fear of Friday the 13th—has produced any supportive scientific documentation (see Box 1-1).

Research has shown that we are more likely to believe information if it comes from certain kinds of individuals: People who are popular, attractive, high in status, seemingly expert, or who appear highly confident are more powerful sources of information than others. But other people are not our sole source of data about psychological processes. We gather a lot of information about behavior from our own observations and interactions with others and the conclusions we draw from them. Children learn very early that their smiles are rewarded and that touching a hot stove can have negative consequences. We learn to predict consequences and direct our behavior toward desired goals. Frequently, we use our beliefs and feelings about how things operate to explain behavior—our own as well as that of others.

Researchers have discovered that we are not always privy to our own decision-making processes (Nisbett & Wilson, 1977). In fact, we are very often unaware of why information feels so persuasive. When we uncritically accept information from an attractive source, for example, we are unlikely to be aware of what actually persuaded us. If someone were to ask us, we would probably believe that the information must have been extremely persuasive. We would be unlikely to realize that we were really persuaded because the person who communicated the information was highly attractive.

We frequently use data from our own experiences to come up with commonsense assumptions about cause and effect—but, if we were to rely only on commonsense psychology, we would frequently be wrong. The inferential

B O X   1 - 1

THE POWER OF NEGATIVE THINKING

Friday the 13th has a mythical history of being unlucky, and if Friday falls on the 13th of the month, the superstition often comes to mind (or someone reminds us!). Do you feel a moment of anxiety when you realize it's Friday the 13th? Have you ever wondered whether it is really unlucky? Apparently it is, but probably not because of any dark and powerful, unseen force that exerts its will upon us. A study conducted in West Sussex in Great Britain and reported in the *British Medical Journal* (Scanlon, Luben, Scanlon, & Singleton, 1993) found that Friday the 13th did appear to be an unlucky day for drivers. When researchers compared each Friday the 13th with each Friday the 6th since 1989, looking at the number of emergency room visits from automobile accidents, more accident victims (as many as 52% more) were treated on Friday the 13th even though fewer cars were driven that day. According to the researchers, the higher accident rate for Friday the 13th was probably caused by increased trepidation about the date; anxiety caused reduced attention to driving, and more accidents occurred. Whether their reason is the correct one or not, it makes sense to be extra cautious if you are driving that day, because *other* drivers might be more anxious and accident-prone than usual.

strategies we use when we process data are sometimes too simple to be completely accurate. Let's look at a few areas in which the commonsense psychologist is likely to make errors.

Nonscientific Inference

One of the first kinds of data we collect about others comes in the form of traits we assign to them. Commonsense psychologists are trait theorists—at least when it comes to explaining the behavior of others. When we understand other people's behavior, there is a strong bias to overlook situational data in favor of data that substantiate trait explanations (Ross & Nisbett, 1991). When we notice that Michelle is sporting another new designer outfit, we conclude that she is vain about her appearance. We tend to miss or ignore other important causally related data about the situation (for instance, that Michelle's mother gets free samples because she designs for the manufacturer).

FIGURE 1-1 Do you believe the gambler's fallacy? Barbara Alper/Stock, Boston

Clearly, perceiving others in terms of their traits can be useful for pre-dicting their behavior, but it can also lead to overestimations of the likeli-hood that they will act in trait-consistent ways in a wide variety of situations. In fact, the research literature suggests that people may overestimate this kind of cross-situational behavioral consistency by as much as a factor of ten. And, apparently, this bias is hard to overcome, even with training. In one amus-ing study (Kunda & Nisbett, 1986), it was discovered that a group of trained research psychologists was not much better at estimating the actual predic-tive power of traits than were people in general—even when they were reminded of the bias by the presence of a very well-known personality researcher.

A related problem of nonscientific inference is illustrated by the process of stereotyping. Once we know that Carol is a librarian, we automatically assume that she is probably also serious because that characteristic is part of a librarian stereotype (Hamilton & Rose, 1980). And, similar to what can happen to individuals who believe the full moon myth, stereotypic expecta-tions can lead us to seek confirmatory instances of behavior: "See! She is so serious, she *always* has her nose in a book." (Of course she does! It's her job!)

Additional problems in prediction occur because people are not very good at using data to estimate the true probabilities of events. The well-known "gambler's fallacy" is a good example of this problem. When we see that a cer-tain slot machine has not paid off in a long time, we tend to believe that it is overdue for a payoff. In reality, it makes no difference whether the machine has recently paid off or not (unless the machine is rigged). Each spin is entirely random and independent, so your odds of a jackpot this time are identical to your odds on any other try.[1]

Finally, compounding our inferential shortcomings is a phenomenon known as the "overconfidence bias." Our predictions, guesses, and explanations tend to *feel* much more correct than they actually are, and the more data we have available (accurate or not), the more confidence we have in our judgments about behavior (Dunning, Griffin, Milojkovic, & Ross, 1990). These and many other inferential biases exist in human information processing. They are believed to be the brain's way of coping with an immense volume of information. They are shortcuts, and most of the time they allow us to function well enough. However, if we want to be able to rely on our conclusions and use them as general principles to predict behavior across many settings and conditions, we need to proceed more systematically and objectively—in other words, scientifically. The steps scientists take to gather and verify information, answer questions, explain relationships, and communicate this information to others are known as the **scientific method.** We will now turn to several important characteristics of the scientific method.

THE CHARACTERISTICS OF MODERN SCIENCE

The Scientific Mentality

The psychologist's goal of prediction rests on a simple, but important, assumption: Behavior must follow a natural order; therefore it can be predicted. This elementary assumption lies at the heart of what Alfred North Whitehead called the "scientific mentality." Whitehead was a philosopher of science who traced the development of science in his now classic book *Science and the Modern World* (1925). He postulated that "faith" in an organized universe is essential to science. If no inherent order existed, there would be no point in looking for one and no need to develop methods for doing so. Research psychologists share the belief that there are specifiable (although not necessarily simple or obvious) reasons for the way people behave and that these reasons can be discovered through research.

Gathering Empirical Data

Whitehead traced the beginnings of modern science to the works of Aristotle, the fourth-century B.C. Greek philosopher. Like contemporary scientists, Aristotle assumed that order exists in the universe, and he set about describing that order in a systematic way by collecting *empirical* data—that is, data that are observable or experienced. Aristotle advocated systematic observation and

---

[1]Calculating the true odds is easy if you know the number of wheels and the number of items on each wheel. If the machine has three wheels, and each wheel has five fruits, your chances of getting three cherries (or three of any fruit) for a payoff are $1/5 \times 1/5 \times 1/5 = 1/125$ or 0.8%; and the probability is identical for any single play.

careful classification of naturally occurring events. From his observations, he argued that heavy objects fall faster than light objects because their "natural" place is down. Later observations by Galileo (1564–1642), however, led to the inescapable conclusion that if we set up the proper testing condition (a vacuum), light objects will fall just as fast as heavy ones. Clearly, gathering empirical data in a systematic and orderly way is preferable to commonsense data collection, but it cannot guarantee that the correct conclusions will be reached.

Seeking General Principles

Modern scientists go beyond cataloging observations to proposing general principles—laws or theories—that will explain them. We could observe endless pieces of data, adding to the content of science, but our observations would be of limited use without general principles to structure them. When these principles have the generality to apply to all situations, they are called **laws.** For example, astronomer Tycho Brahe painstakingly gathered observations of the stars for nearly a lifetime. But it was Johannes Kepler who made these observations useful by explaining them through a system of equations now known as Kepler's laws.

Typically, we do not have enough information to state a general law. We may then propose an interim explanation, commonly called a **theory.** Theories pull together, or unify, diverse sets of facts into an organizing scheme, such as a general principle or set of rules, that can be used to predict new examples of behavior. Theories can explain many, but not all, instances of a situation or behavior—the more a theory can explain, the better it is. Sir Karl Popper, a modern philosopher of science, wrote that science progresses only through progressively better theories (Popper, 1963). Old theories are replaced by new theories with greater explanatory power. Since laws are seldom determined outside the physical sciences, the behavioral sciences like psychology largely progress by developing better and better theories.

Theories also guide the course of future observations: "We must remember that what we observe is very much determined by what theory suggests should be observed; and we must remember also that the way in which

"IT'S UNIFIED AND IT'S A THEORY, BUT IT'S NOT THE UNIFIED THEORY WE'VE ALL BEEN LOOKING FOR."

observation will be reported and interpreted is a function of the theory that is in the observer's mind" (Schlegel, 1972, p. 11). Theory-based expectancies can cause us to pay more attention to behavioral information that is predicted by the theory and to overlook nonpredicted behaviors. The next characteristic of the scientific method, good thinking, is essential to offset a predisposition to find only what we are seeking.

Good Thinking

A central feature of the scientific method is **good thinking**. Our approach to the collection and interpretation of data should be systematic, objective, and rational. The scientist avoids letting private beliefs or expectations influence observations or conclusions. Good thinking includes being open to new ideas and avoiding *woodenheadedness*. Woodenheaded thinking is "assessing a situation in terms of preconceived fixed notions while ignoring or rejecting any contrary signs" (Tuchman, 1984, p. 7). Good thinking also follows the rules of logic. Conclusions will follow from the data, whether they are in agreement with our expectations or not.

Another important aspect of good thinking is the **principle of parsimony,** sometimes called *Occam's razor.* William of Occam was a fourteenth-century philosopher who cautioned us to stick to a basic premise: Entities should not be multiplied without necessity. What Occam had in mind was simplicity, precision, and clarity of thought. We must avoid making *unnecessary* assumptions to support an argument or hypothesis. When two explanations are equally defensible, the simplest explanation is preferred until it is ruled out by conflicting data.

Lewis (1978) applied the idea of parsimony to some developmental findings in an interesting way. He reported that infants in poor families spent more time in their mothers' laps than middle-class infants did. Infants in poor families also tended to vocalize less than infants in middle-class families. We could speculate on all sorts of differences in attitudes, cultural factors, or parental expectations that might lead to differences in mothers' behaviors, which in turn might affect infant development. But Lewis's more parsimonious explanation made a compelling case for a simpler environmental difference:

> Even though the mother's lap is the most frequent place for the infant, the child is less likely to make sounds there than in any other situation. Mothers tend to vocalize more with their children in their arms and their vocalization inhibits their infants from making sounds. Surprisingly, some of the least frequent situations—such as in the playpen and the floor—account for the highest percentage of infant vocalization.
>
> When we analyzed the data by social class, the importance of situational differences became even more clear. . . . No low-income mother ever put her infant on the floor, but middle-class babies spent three percent of their time there. Why? If, for example, the floors of the poor are unsafe—cold, lacking rugs, and with the added danger of attacking rodents—a poor mother would be unlikely to allow her child to play on the floor. Therefore, if infant vocalization is greater when the child is out of the mother's arms, then social class differences in infant vocalization may not be a function of different attitudes or desires of mothers of different classes, but of situational differences as mundane as what shape the floor is in. (p. 22)[2]

It is more parsimonious, or *simpler,* to explain the findings in terms of the physical conditions in poor homes than in terms of the attitudes or desires of different classes.

Self-Correction

Modern scientists accept the uncertainty of their own conclusions. The content of science changes as we acquire new information and old information

---

[2]From "A New Response to Stimuli," by M. Lewis, 1978, *Readings in Psychology 78/79 Annual Editions.* Copyright ©1978. This article is reprinted by permission of *THE SCIENCES* and is from the May/June 1977 issue. Individual subscriptions are $21.00 per year. Write to: The Sciences, 2 East 63rd Street, New York, NY 10021 or call 1-800-THE NYAS.

is reevaluated in light of new facts. Changes in scientific explanations and theories are an important part of scientific progress. Popper argued that theories can best be tested through attempts at **falsification**—not verification. What this means is that scientists challenge existing explanations by testing hypotheses that follow logically from them. If the test shows a hypothesis is false, the original explanation should be modified or abandoned for one that explains the new findings. (We will discuss some of the details of this hypothesis-testing process in later chapters.) Hypotheses that have not been proven false are not, however, necessarily true. Perhaps our testing methods are not sufficiently sensitive to accomplish this critical test. Science can only demonstrate that, at a given point in time, a hypothesis is not false. Experience favors a "weight-of-evidence" approach: The more evidence that accumulates to support a particular explanation or theory, the more confident we can be that the theory is correct. Old explanations often give way simply because the weight of supporting evidence tips the scales in favor of a different scientific explanation.

Publicizing Results

Because of its dynamic nature, modern science has become a highly public activity. Scientists meet frequently through professional and special-interest groups and attend professional conferences to exchange information about their current work. The number of scientific papers published each year in scientific journals is growing, and new publications are constantly being added in specialized disciplines. This continuous exchange of information is vital to the scientific process. It would do little good for scientists to work in isolation. The opportunity to incorporate the most recent findings of others would be missed. There would be much wasted effort as researchers duplicated failures as well as successes.

Replication

Replication is another important part of the scientific approach. It should be possible to repeat our procedures and get the same results again if we have gathered data objectively and if we have followed good thinking. Findings that can be obtained by only one researcher have only limited scientific value. For example, people sometimes report dreams that seem to predict the future. A woman dreams of a stranger and meets him the following day; a man dreams of a car accident and then hears of the fatal crash of a friend. Have these people seen into the future through their dreams? We cannot provide a scientific answer to that question. It is impossible to recreate the original conditions that led to these events, so we cannot replicate these experiences. It is also difficult to evaluate them objectively, since the dreamer is the only observer of the dream.

   In contrast, a researcher predicts that children will hit a doll after they have seen an adult hitting the doll. The prediction is confirmed. In this instance we can apply scientific criteria to the researcher's findings. We can replicate the findings by setting up the same or similar conditions and observing whether the outcome is the same. Replication of research findings by others can be important; we have a great deal more confidence that we have explained something if the predicted effects are repeatable by other researchers.

Generally, replication is more common in the physical than in the behavioral sciences. For example, a few years ago investigators in Texas reported that they had created nuclear fusion in the laboratory without heat (a monumental scientific discovery). The report led to worldwide attempts to replicate their experiment in other laboratories. To date, the claim for cold fusion has not been substantiated by other researchers. As in other sciences, published replications of psychological research are more common when the reported findings either have important implications or when reported results directly contradict current conventional wisdom.

THE TOOLS OF PSYCHOLOGICAL SCIENCE

By now you are familiar with the scientific approach to research: We gather information objectively and systematically, and we base our conclusions on the evidence we obtain. Let us now begin to look at the three main tools of the scientific approach: observation, measurement, and experimentation. These are also the basic tools of the psychological scientist. The research example described in Box 1-2 is a good illustration of observation, measurement, and experimentation.

Observation

The first tool, **observation**, is the systematic noting and recording of events. Only events that are observable can be studied scientifically. At this point it may seem as though we are restricting what we can study in psychology to a very narrow range of events. Many behaviors are observable (smoking, smiling, talking), but what about internal processes such as feelings, thinking, or problem solving? How can we explore those areas? The key is the way we apply the scientific method. It is perfectly legitimate to study events that take place inside a person, such as thinking and feeling—if we can develop observable signs of these events.

The key to studying internal processes is defining them in terms of events that can be observed: the time it takes a person to solve a problem; a person's answers to a mood questionnaire; the amplitude of someone's palmar skin conductance responses. (Finding a suitable definition is one of the problems we will discuss in Chapter 6.) In the experiment described in Box 1-2, Baron and his colleagues needed to observe people's moods. Moods, however, cannot be observed directly in any systematic manner. It is not possible to gauge a person's mood reliably just by looking; instead, researchers like Baron typically ask people to report on their own moods by using questionnaires or other instruments.

B O X   1 - 2

AN EXPERIMENTAL EXAMPLE: WHAT'S IN THE AIR?

Warm, dry, seasonal winds, like the sirocco in the southern Mediterranean or the Santa Ana winds in California, have been blamed for everything from insomnia to homicide, and there is some research evidence that seems to support this. These winds increase air temperature, reduce humidity, and alter the atmosphere's electron balance, splitting electrons into positively and negatively charged particles, called *ions*. During these seasonal winds, there is a slightly higher concentration of positive ions in the air, and a small amount of research evidence suggests that positive ions can produce negative mood shifts. Could negative ions have the opposite effect, making people feel better? Robert A. Baron and his colleagues (Baron, Russell, & Arms, 1985) tested the latter hypothesis in an interesting laboratory experiment. (The actual experiment was more complex than this, and we will return to it again in later chapters.)

To set up the conditions for testing, the researchers used a machine that generates negative ions (as some electronic air cleaners do) to

FIGURE 1-2 Robert A. Baron. Courtesy of Robert Baron

change the air in a laboratory room so that the concentration of negative ions was either low (normal ambient), moderate, or high. In each session a male undergraduate was led to believe he was involved in an experiment about learning. His task during the session involved training another undergraduate to reduce his heart rate with biofeedback. The "learner" was actually a trained confederate of the researchers, and his performance was completely scripted in advance. Sessions were set up so that half of the volunteers were intentionally angered by nasty comments from the "learner" during the session; the other half were not. Each volunteer's mood was measured at the end of the session.

The results were not quite what Baron and his colleagues had predicted. Instead of inducing more positive moods in everyone, higher concentrations of negative ions seemed to increase the strength of *whatever* mood the volunteers reported—good or bad. At the end of the session, nonangered volunteers who had been exposed to higher levels of negative ions reported that they felt less angry, less depressed, and less fatigued than the nonangered volunteers exposed to normal levels. In contrast, the angered volunteers ended up feeling more angry if they had been exposed to higher levels of negative ions than if they had been exposed to normal levels. One explanation is that negative ions may be physiologically arousing, and arousal may increase the strength of whatever emotions people are feeling.

Within the scientific framework, observations also must be made systematically—once the researcher has devised a system for observing, the same system must be applied consistently to each observation. For example, the same mood questionnaire would be given to each person in the study. Of equal importance, observations must be made objectively; another objective observer must be able to obtain the same record of these events. And, clearly, we must avoid distorting data by allowing our preconceived notions of the nature of events to alter our records. Baron and his colleagues recorded and reported their subjects' exact responses to the questionnaires even though the responses did not quite match what the researchers had predicted.

Measurement

Measurement is assigning numerical values to objects or events or their characteristics according to conventional rules. When we do research, we assign numbers to different sizes, quantities, or qualities of the events under observation. We are all familiar with such conventional physical dimensions as length, width, and height. Rather than relying on global impressions ("It was really big!"), we use standardized units, agreed-upon conventions that define such measures as the minute, the meter, and the ounce.

Standards are not always as clear-cut for dimensions of human behavior. We use standardized intelligence tests and a variety of standardized personality measures, but very often our standards are determined by the context of a particular study. We often wish to describe the behaviors of individuals in a predetermined situation (How much did they talk with others in a stressful situation?). Other times, we want to measure individuals' reactions to the situation we have created (How depressed did they feel after a stressful situation?). Or we may wish to quantify their evaluations of an object or another person (In a stressful situation, is a stranger judged more favorably on dimensions such as attractiveness and intelligence?). When Baron and his colleagues measured each volunteer's mood, they designed their mood questionnaire using numbered scales to represent progressively higher levels of anger, depression, and so forth.

As in Baron's experiment, we are typically interested in comparing the behavior of individuals exposed to different sets of conditions. Our measurements must be consistent across each set of conditions. If measurement is inconsistent, we cannot compare our measured observations directly (it's like comparing oranges and apples). The same unit of measurement needs to be used each time we measure our observations; we would not use ounces one day and teaspoons the next. And, to be consistent, we need to use the same instruments and procedures each time the event is observed. In Baron's investigation, for example, the questionnaires, as well as the way they were administered, were identical in each session. Because we use statistics to evaluate research findings, we need numbers, or scores to represent different levels or amounts of the behavior of interest. As you will see in upcoming chapters, we often compare the average scores of all subjects exposed to one set of conditions with scores from other groups of subjects exposed to different conditions.

Experimentation

Experimentation is a process undertaken to show that certain kinds of events are predictable under certain, specifiable situations. Experimentation is used by psychologists to demonstrate the conditions under which a particular behavior can be expected to occur with regularity. When we experiment, we systematically manipulate aspects of a setting to verify our predictions about observable behavior under specific conditions. Experimentation is not always possible. To do an experiment, our predictions must be **testable.** Two minimum requirements must be met: First, we must have procedures for manipulating the setting. Second, the predicted outcome must be observable. Suppose we have predictions about the observable effects on human travelers of making a 20-year journey through outer space. Our predictions are not testable because we do not yet have the technology to make that long a journey. Some hypotheses that cannot be tested now may become testable in the future. Baron's prediction was testable because he could manipulate the setting to create the conditions he wanted to investigate, and he could observe the outcome.

Experimentation must also be objective. Ideally, we do not bias our results by setting up situations in which our predictions can always be confirmed. We do not stack the deck in our favor by giving subjects subtle cues to respond in the desired way. (We will have more to say about this in Chapter 11.) Nor do we prevent them from responding in the nonpredicted direction.

Sometimes experimentation is possible, but it cannot be carried out for ethical reasons. For example, we would not test the effects of smoking on fetal development in pregnant women by asking a group of nonsmoking women to smoke during their pregnancy. We would not peep through windows to study people's sexual behavior. We would not change students' exam grades to learn about how people respond to success and failure. In a moral society, there are many experiments that should never be conducted because it would be unethical to do so. (We will explain ethical guidelines in the next chapter.) This is not to say that these things cannot be studied by psychologists; it simply means we must study them in ethical ways. Sometimes this is done by using nonexperimental methods (Chapters 3 and 4) or by designing experiments that pose less risk to participants (Chapter 6).

SCIENTIFIC EXPLANATION IN PSYCHOLOGICAL SCIENCE

Identifying Antecedent Conditions

In a scientific context, explanation means specifying the antecedent conditions of an event or behavior. **Antecedent conditions,** or antecedents, are the circumstances that come before the event or behavior that we wish to explain. In Baron's experiment, for example, different concentrations of negative ions were the specified antecedent conditions, and mood was the behavior explained by these conditions. If we can identify all the antecedents of a behavior, we can explain that behavior in the following way: When XYZ is the set of antecedent conditions, the outcome is a particular behavior. This explanation allows us to make predictions about future behaviors. If the XYZ set of antecedents occurs again, we expect the same outcome. (See Box 1-3 for an example of *pseudoscientific* explanation.)

Comparing Treatment Conditions

In psychology, it would be virtually impossible to identify all the antecedents that affect the behavior of research participants (also called **subjects**) at a particular time. But although we cannot identify all the antecedent conditions, we may focus on particular antecedents that we believe have an effect on behavior. In the psychology experiment, we create specific sets of antecedent conditions that we call **treatments.** We compare different treatment conditions so that we may test our explanations of behaviors systematically and scientifically. Keep in mind that the word *treatment,* as used in experimentation,

BOX 1-3

PHRENOLOGY: PSEUDOSCIENCE OF THE NINETEENTH CENTURY?

Pseudoscience means "false science." Some past and present endeavors on the fringes of psychology fall into this category: parapsychology, (so-called *Psi* abilities, such as ESP, telepathy, and psychokinesis), astrology (birth signs as determinants of personality), and palmistry (using lines on the hand to predict fortunes), among others. Each can appear to resemble a science, but the appearance is only superficial—we call them *pseudopsychologies*. They have not been submitted to controlled tests (or if they have, as in the case of ESP, tests have failed to support the predictions), and they have served as the basis for many outright frauds. The popularity of different branches of pseudopsychology waxes and wanes. We mentioned pyramid power and crystals earlier. One of the more interesting

FIGURE 1-3 A phrenology chart. Coco McCoy/Rainbow

pseudopsychologies to come and go in the early 1800s was phrenology. Phrenologists claimed they could assess personality by feeling the bumps on a person's head. Supposedly, different traits resided in particular areas of the brain, and bumps formed in the skull to accommodate high levels of certain traits. Phrenologists measured personality by feeling the bumps and mapping them to areas located on phrenological charts (Pogliano, 1991). Phrenologists claimed that understanding the bumps on one's head was the key to happiness, health, and success.

does not necessarily mean that we must actively do something to "treat" each subject (although it can mean this in some experiments). Rather, it means that we *treat some subjects differently than we do others*. We expose them to different antecedent conditions. Sometimes, as Baron and his colleagues did, we test our explanations of behavior by creating treatment conditions in which some people are exposed to one set of antecedent conditions and others are exposed to a different set of antecedents, and we compare the effects of these different antecedents on a particular behavior. When we are able to specify the antecedents, or treatment conditions, that lead to a behavior, we have essentially explained that behavior.

The Psychology Experiment

A **psychology experiment** is a controlled procedure in which at least two different treatment conditions are applied to subjects. The subjects' behaviors are then measured and compared in order to test a hypothesis about the effects of those treatments on behavior. Note that we must have at least two different treatments so that we can compare behavior under varied conditions and observe the way behavior changes as treatment conditions change. Note also that the procedures in the psychology experiment are carefully controlled. Control is necessary so we can be sure we are *measuring what we intend to measure*. For this reason, characteristics of subjects receiving different treatments are also controlled by special techniques (Chapter 7). We want to ensure that people who receive one kind of treatment are *equivalent* (as similar as possible) to subjects receiving a different treatment. If subjects who received one treatment had different characteristics than subjects who received another treatment, we would have no way of knowing whether we were measuring behavioral differences produced by differences in the antecedent conditions we had created or whether we were just measuring behavioral differences that already existed. Control is a critical feature of psychology experiments.

When you were a child, did anyone ever ask you: "Which falls faster, a feather or a rock?" If so, you probably said, "A rock." And of course, you would have been right if the test were made under uncontrolled conditions. Rocks *do* fall faster than feathers, unless we control the effects of air currents and air resistance by measuring how fast they fall in a vacuum. As Galileo discovered, the acceleration due to gravity is really the same for all objects.

We achieve the greatest degree of control with experiments that are run in the laboratory. In a laboratory, the psychologist can insulate subjects from factors that could affect behavior and lead to incorrect conclusions. However, many people feel that laboratory experiments are too artificial. Critics argue that laboratory situations can be unrealistic and that laboratory results might not be applicable to everyday life. After all, not many rocks fall to earth in a vacuum. We sometimes sacrifice a certain amount of realism and generalizability to gain precision.

Establishing Cause and Effect

The greatest value of the psychology experiment is that, within the experiment, we can infer a **cause and effect relationship** between the antecedent conditions and the subjects' behaviors. If the XYZ set of antecedents is always linked with a particular behavior, whereas other treatments are not, we infer that XYZ *causes* the behavior. For example, with all other factors constant, Baron and his colleagues demonstrated that high concentrations of negative ions altered moods. In Chapter 12, however, we will discover that our inferences about cause and effect relationships are stated in the form of probabilities—never certainties.

The type of cause and effect relationship we establish through experiments is called a *temporal* relationship. There is a time difference that holds in the relationship: The treatment conditions come before the behavior. We look for differences in behavior *after* subjects are exposed to the treatment—not before. In fact, if you got differences before the treatments, you would need to look for another cause! We expose subjects to different levels of negative ions, for example, *then* we see how they feel. Temporal relationships are built into our experiments. We give subjects various instructions, then see how they behave. We show children various cartoons, then observe their play.

Other kinds of relationships can suggest cause and effect, but they are less convincing to the scientist because other potential causal explanations are never completely ruled out. Let's look at examples of two other types of relationships that people use: spatial and logical. A very large and rambunctious Labrador retriever and a very tiny, but affectionate, Himalayan cat reside with one of the authors. The cat is much more fond of the dog than he is of her. When the dog runs out of patience, he will chase her around the house. One day, the author heard a crash coming from the living room and ran in to see what happened. A prized figurine was in pieces on the floor next to the coffee table, and the cat was sitting on the edge of the table looking down interestedly at the pieces—the cat and the broken figurine had a *spatial* relationship. Naturally, the author scolded the cat. But was the cat the real culprit? (If so, why was the dog slinking away with his tail between his legs?) Using spatial relationships to infer cause and effect can be compelling—but not always correct.

Sometimes we use *logical* relationships to establish cause and effect. On another occasion, the same author discovered a small hole in the wall above the sofa. She identified the dog, rather than the cat, as the culprit, because of a logical relationship. At about 4:30 every afternoon, the dog sprints at full speed around the house, carrying as many of his prized, wolf-sized, plastic bones as he can fit into his mouth. Running across the sofa is part of this ritual. Most of the time, he runs the course with great agility, but he *has* been known to run into walls, furniture, or people who happen to be in his way. Logically, then, although other causes might be possible, he seemed the most likely perpetrator.

As we search for cause and effect relationships through our research, we generally look for temporal relationships. Of course, the simple fact that one event precedes another is not sufficient, alone, to establish a causal relationship. The Scottish philosopher David Hume (1711–1776) argued that we can never establish causality in this way. (According to Whitehead, the logical conclusion of Hume's philosophy is that there can be no science. For that reason, scientists are not Hume's disciples!) Hume's objections were based on the argument that just because one event precedes another, it does not necessarily mean that the first causes the second. For example, in 16 out of 18 years, the stock market rose in years when an original NFL team won the Super Bowl and fell in years when an original AFL team won (*Wall Street Journal Report,* 1984). Few people would want to say that stock prices are set on the football field. Obviously, many other factors could have had an impact on the economy. The advantage of the experiment in bringing us closer to establishing cause and effect relationships is that in the experiment only *one* factor is allowed to change. If every year were the same except for the team that won the Super Bowl, investors might have to pay closer attention to the gridiron!

Necessary versus Sufficient Conditions

As we seek cause and effect relationships in science and psychology, we try to identify the conditions under which events will occur. We distinguish between *necessary* and *sufficient* conditions. Cutting down on fat intake may be a sufficient condition to produce weight loss. But is it a necessary condition? No. We also could lose weight by increasing our activity level, so reducing fat intake is not a necessary condition. In contrast, a snowmobile will not run without fuel. Therefore fuel is a necessary condition for running a snowmobile.

The cause and effect relationships established through scientific research commonly involve identifying sufficient conditions. For example, a number of psychological studies have shown that being in a good mood increases our willingness to help others (Isen, 1987). However, many other factors (characteristics of the person who needs help, the number of other potential helpers, and so on) can also determine whether we will help or not (Latané & Darley, 1970). Being in a good mood is not a necessary condition to increase helpfulness—but it is sufficient.

When we seek causes, we rarely seek conditions that are *both necessary and sufficient*. To do so would involve a search for the first or primary cause— Cause with a capital C! Given the complexity of our universe, we would make slow progress in our search for order if we refused to settle for anything less than causes that were both necessary and sufficient. Researchers who study helpfulness would probably still be trying to trace the Cause of altruistic behavior—right down to the molecular chain that produces the biochemical changes associated with helping. How that chain got there, the Cause's Cause, would lengthen their search even further. The scientific approach to causality is more practical, relying on sufficient causes as explanations for events.

THE ORGANIZATION OF THE TEXT

You may be required to design and conduct a research project in the course for which you are reading this text. Writing a research report of your findings may also be a required part of the course. You will find that this text is divided into four major parts: Introduction, Method, Results, and Discussion. These parts parallel both the process of conducting an experiment and the corresponding sections of a research report. Part I, Introduction, gives an overall orientation to the field of research methods, much as a literature review gives an overall picture of the state of research in a particular content area. Research ethics are covered first. Later chapters focus on the differences between experimental and other research methods in psychology to help develop your understanding of true experiments. This section of the book ends with a chapter on formulating a testable hypothesis. In short, Part I will provide you with all the information you need to begin thinking about an experiment in a particular area and will provide you with report-writing tips along the way.

Part II, Method, includes all the basic procedures used in conducting simple experiments, including information on selecting subjects and collecting data in a scientific way. It includes chapters on controlling for potential problems. Part III, Results: Coping with Data, reviews the common statistical procedures used to analyze data. Examples of experiments and actual computations are included to help you understand how these procedures are used and what they mean. Part IV, Discussion, looks at the major issues involved in drawing conclusions from data. It examines problems of generalizing from a laboratory experiment to the real world. The chapter on report writing includes information on how each section of a research report is organized and written. Appendix C shows what your finished report should look like. Before we begin learning about the research process, it is important to understand the ethical principals that apply to all research in psychology—and this is the topic of Chapter 2.

SUMMARY

Our knowledge about psychological processes is based on scientific evidence accumulated through research, and, as scientists, we rely on scientific *methodology* when we conduct psychological research. The alternative, *commonsense psychology,* is nonscientific and subject to many kinds of errors. Psychological science shares the key features of all modern science: an emphasis on gathering observable, objective data and the search for general *laws* or *theories* to organize and explain the relationships among isolated bits of data.

The scientific approach requires *good thinking,* thinking that is objective, organized, and rational. Our explanations of behavior should be *parsimonious*—that is, as simple as possible. Scientists constantly engage in *self-correction,* challenging their findings through tests of new hypotheses that follow logically from them. The results of science are communicated through journals and professional meetings, stimulating *replication.* It should be possible to repeat our procedures and obtain the same findings again. Other researchers should be able to do the same.

The scientific approach is applied through observation, measurement, and experimentation. Observation is the systematic noting and recording of events. We can only make a scientific study of events that are observable. To make a scientific study of internal processes like feeling and thinking, we must be able to define those events in terms of observable signs. Measurement is quantifying an event or behavior according to generally accepted rules. We try to measure in standardized units so that our measurements will be meaningful. We keep our measurements consistent. Experimentation is a process undertaken to demonstrate that already observed events will occur again under a particular set of conditions. Objectivity is essential in all phases of the scientific process; we cannot allow our personal feelings or expectations to influence the data we record. One criterion for objectivity is that impartial observers can produce the same record.

A scientific explanation specifies the *antecedent conditions* of an event or behavior. If we can specify all the circumstances that come before a behavior, we say that we have explained that behavior, and we can predict the outcome when the same set of antecedents occurs again.

In the *psychology experiment,* we create specific sets of antecedents called *treatments.* The psychology experiment is a controlled procedure in which at least two different treatment conditions are applied to research participants, or *subjects.* The subjects' behaviors are then measured and compared in order to test a hypothesis about the effects of those treatments on behavior. We may also infer a *cause and effect relationship* between the antecedent treatment conditions and the subjects' behaviors; we may say that the particular treatment causes the behavior. Psychologists generally look for the sufficient conditions that explain behavior rather than the ultimate causes of behavior.

As experimental psychologists, we begin the experimental process with a review of the research literature to suggest a hypothesis about behavior. Next, we design a procedure to test that hypothesis in a systematic way. We use statistical procedures to analyze our observations and to decide whether the data support the hypothesis. We then reevaluate our procedures and write a research report of the findings.

KEY TERMS

Antecedent conditions All circumstances that occur or exist before the event or behavior to be explained; also called *antecedents.*

Cause and effect relationship The relation between a particular behavior and a set of antecedents that always precedes it—whereas other antecedents do not—so that the set is inferred to *cause* the behavior.

Commonsense psychology Everyday, nonscientific collection of psychological data used to understand the social world and guide our behavior.

Data Facts and figures gathered from observations in research. (*Data* is the plural form of the Latin word *datum*.)

Experimentation The process undertaken to discover something new or to demonstrate that events that have already occurred will occur again under a specified set of conditions; a principal tool of the scientific method.

Falsification To challenge an existing explanation or theory by testing a hypothesis that follows logically from it and demonstrating that this hypothesis is false.

Good thinking Organized and rational thought, characterized by open-mindedness and objectivity, and including application of the principle of parsimony; a principal tool of the scientific method.

Laws General scientific principles that explain our universe and predict events.

Measurement The systematic estimation of the quantity, size, or quality of an observable event; a principal tool of the scientific method.

Methodology The scientific techniques used to collect and evaluate psychological data.

Observation The systematic noting and recording of events; a principal tool of the scientific method.

Principle of parsimony An aspect of good thinking, stating that the simplest explanation is preferred until ruled out by conflicting evidence; also known as *Occam's razor*.

Psychology experiment A controlled procedure in which at least two different treatment conditions are applied to subjects whose behaviors are then measured and compared to test a hypothesis about the effects of the treatments on behavior.

Replication The process of repeating research procedures to verify that the outcome will be the same as before; a principal tool of the scientific method.

Science The systematic gathering of data to provide descriptions of events taking place under specific conditions, enabling researchers to explain, predict, and control events.

Scientific method Steps scientists take to gather and verify information, answer questions, explain relationships, and communicate findings.

Subject The scientific term for an individual who participates in research.

Testable Capable of being tested; typically used in reference to a hypothesis. Two requirements must be met in order to have a testable hypothesis: procedures for manipulating the setting must exist, and the predicted outcome must be observable.

Theory A set of general principles that attempts to explain and predict behavior or other phenomena.

Treatment A specific set of antecedent conditions created by the experimenter and presented to subjects to test its effect on behavior.

REVIEW AND STUDY QUESTIONS

1. What is science?

2. Why do we need scientific methods?

3. a. What is commonsense psychology?
   b. Give an example of how you used it within the past week.

4. What are the characteristics of modern science?

5. What do we mean by objectivity? How does objectivity influence each aspect of the scientific method?

6. a. Define an experiment.
   b. Make up an experiment to test the saying, "Absence makes the heart grow fonder."
   c. Make up your own experiment.

7. Suppose, for instance, that a researcher believed that firstborn children have higher IQs than their later born sisters and brothers because the mother's ova are younger when firstborns are conceived. This hypothesis would not be testable. Give two reasons why and explain them.

8. What are antecedent conditions and how are they used in scientific explanation?

9. Professor Hall made the following statement on the first day of class: "To pass this course, you must attend every class and receive a minimum grade of 75 on each exam." Is class attendance a necessary or sufficient condition for a passing grade?

10. What are treatment conditions?

11. What is the purpose of using at least two treatment conditions in an experiment?

12. For each of the following examples, state which basic principles of the scientific method have been violated, and explain why each principle was violated:
    a. Deanna wanted to do an experiment on gas mileage to see whether the name brands give better mileage. She filled her tank with Fuel-Up one week and with a well-known brand the following week. At the end of that time, she thought things over and said, "Well, I didn't notice much difference between the brands. I filled the car with Fuel-Up on a Tuesday and needed gas again the following Tuesday. It was the same story with the big-name brand, so they must be about the same."
    b. Mike has been telling all his friends that his 2-year-old daughter, Laura, can read. One evening Mike invites some of his friends over for coffee and offers to give a demonstration of his daughter's remarkable skill. Laura then appears to read a small storybook that Mike keeps on the coffee table. One of the friends is not convinced and asks the little girl to read a page from a different but equally simple storybook. Laura remains silent. Mike explains Laura's behavior by saying, "She's just shy with strangers."

c. An author advocates the use of large doses of vitamin C to prolong life. In an interview he says he has tried this treatment only on himself.

d. A researcher reports that flowers will move away from someone who tries to cut them off. Others try unsuccessfully to duplicate this finding. The researcher argues that skeptical critics are just insensitive to the plants' responses.

13. Name and describe each of the four main sections of the experimental report.

RESEARCH ETHICS

Any research project involves decisions about the subjects who will participate in the study. Who will they be and how will we study them? In Chapter 1 we discussed the general concept of objective, data-based science. Science deals with facts, with truth seeking, and with understanding our universe. Science is commonly thought of as *amoral;* from a scientific point of view, facts discovered through science are neither moral nor immoral—they just happen to exist. As scientists, it is our responsibility to report our findings truthfully (whether we like them or not).

Thus science per se does not include values. As researchers, however, we do bring our values, ethics, morals, and sense of right and wrong to the work we do. We have to deal with the ethical and moral questions that arise: Is it right to discover ways to build more efficient weapons? Is it right to postpone death by artificial means? Is it right to study ways to create more perfect offspring through behavioral eugenics? Is it right or prudent to investigate techniques that could be used to brainwash people? Do we have the right to perform any experiment imaginable just for the sake of new knowledge?

In this chapter we will focus on the last question. We will discuss the ethics of the researcher's relationship with human and nonhuman subjects and the researcher's responsibilities in every experiment.

RESEARCH ETHICS

The researcher's foremost concern in recruiting and using subjects is treating them ethically and responsibly. Whether we work with animals or humans, we must consider their safety and welfare. Responsible psychological research is not an attempt to satisfy idle curiosity about other people's innermost thoughts and experiences. Rather, responsible research is aimed at advancing our understanding of feelings, thoughts, and behaviors in ways that will ultimately benefit humanity. But the well-being of the individual research participant is no less important than the search for general knowledge: Research that is harmful to subjects is undesirable even though it may add to the store of knowledge. For instance, early experience is an important aspect of child development—but we would not raise children in isolation just to assess the effects of deprivation. There is no way we can justify such a study, no matter how important the knowledge we might gain.

A researcher is also legally responsible for what happens to the subjects of a study. He or she is liable for any harm that comes to subjects, even if it occurs unintentionally. This means a researcher could be sued for damages if an experiment hurt someone, whether the injury was physical or psychological, intentional or accidental. To protect the subjects of psychological research, legal and ethical guidelines have been formulated. From a legal standpoint, human subjects are protected by a federal law (Title 45, Section 46.106[b]).

This law requires each institution engaging in research to set up a review committee, called an **institutional review board,** or **IRB,** to evaluate every

B O X   2 - 1

A TERRIFYING RESEARCH EXPERIENCE

Consider this example of research conducted before the establishment of IRBs and formal ethical guidelines for psychological research. Campbell, Sanderson, and Laverty (1964) established classical conditioning in a single trial through the use of a traumatic event. Classical conditioning, first studied in Pavlov's laboratory, involves the pairing of an initially neutral conditioned stimulus (CS) with an unconditioned stimulus (UCS) that always leads to a specific unconditioned (unlearned) response (UCR). After repeated pairings, the originally neutral conditioned stimulus will lead to a response that resembles the unconditioned response. This response is known as the *conditioned response* (CR), since its occurrence is dependent upon the success of the conditioning procedure.

Campbell, Sanderson, and Laverty used a drug, succinylcholine chloride dihydrate (Scoline), to induce temporary paralysis and cessation of breathing in their subjects. Although the paralysis and inability to breathe were not painful, according to subjects' reports, the experience was "horrific"; "all the subjects in the standard series thought they were dying" (p. 631). Not surprisingly, the effect of the drug (UCS) led to an intense emotional reaction (UCR). The drug was paired with a tone (CS). Subjects became conditioned to the tone in just one trial. After a single pairing of the tone with the drug, the tone alone was sufficient to arouse emotional upset (CR) in most subjects. The emotional reaction persisted (that is, failed to extinguish) and actually increased with repeated presentations of the tone. Would you have wanted to be in this study? Do you think the researchers could have demonstrated classical conditioning in another way?

proposed study. Both laypersons and researchers serve on these committees to guarantee that the views of the general community, as well as those of scientists, are taken into consideration. The primary duty of a review board is to ensure that the safety of research participants is adequately protected (see Box 2-1). Their first task is to decide whether the proposed study puts the subjects *at risk*. According to the regulations,

"subject at risk" means any individual who may be exposed to the possibility of injury, including physical, psychological, or social injury, as a consequence of participation as a subject in any research, development, or related activity which departs from the application of those established and accepted methods necessary to meet his needs, or which increases the ordinary risks of daily life, including the risks inherent in a chosen occupation or field of science. (U.S. Department of Health, Education, and Welfare, 1975, p. 11,854)

In essence, the regulations say that a subject **at risk** is one who is more likely to be harmed in some way by participating in the research. It is up to the IRB to determine that any risks to the individual are outweighed by potential benefits or the importance of the knowledge to be gained. This is called a **risk/benefit analysis.** An understanding of research design is critical to such an analysis, and at least some members of a review board must be skilled in research methodology. As we will see in the following chapters, there are important differences in the kinds of conclusions that can be drawn from different research designs, and research that is improperly designed has few benefits. Psychologist Robert Rosenthal (1994) has given three important reasons why poorly designed research can be unethical:

1. Students', teachers', and administrators' time will be taken from potentially more beneficial educational experiences.
2. Poorly designed research can lead to unwarranted and inaccurate conclusions that may be damaging to the society that directly or indirectly pays for the research.
3. Allocating time and money to poor-quality science will serve to keep those finite resources from better-quality science.

Another very important task of an IRB is to safeguard the rights of individuals by making certain that each subject at risk gives informed consent to participate. **Informed consent** means that the subject agrees to participate after having been fully informed about the nature and purpose of the study. Several aspects of informed consent are particularly relevant to psychological research. First, individuals must give their consent freely, without the use of force, duress, or coercion. Second, they must be free to drop out of the experiment at any time. Third, researchers must give subjects a full explanation of the procedures to be followed and offer to answer any questions about them. Fourth, researchers must make clear the potential risks and benefits of the experiment. If there is any possibility of pain or injury to subjects, researchers must explain this in advance, so that subjects know what they are getting into. Finally, researchers must provide assurances that all data collected from individuals will remain private and confidential.

Consent should be obtained in writing, and subjects should receive a copy to keep. When the subject is a minor or is impaired, researchers should obtain consent from a parent or legal guardian. Even in these cases, however, subjects should still be given as much explanation as they can understand and be allowed to refuse to participate, even though permission has been given by the parent or guardian.

Box 2-2 shows an example of the kind of written *informed consent form* typically used in psychological experiments. The consent form provides sub-

B O X   2 - 2

SAMPLE CONSENT FORM FOR PARTICIPATION OF UNDERGRADUATES IN PSYCHOLOGICAL RESEARCH

Informed Consent for Participation of Human Subjects in a Research Project

Name of Participant: Project Title: I voluntarily agree to participate in this study. I understand that I can terminate my participation at any point and that termination will in no way jeopardize my standing at (name of university).

The investigation has been described to me by the experimenter, who has answered all my questions. I hereby authorize this person to measure certain aspects of my person. I understand that I will be asked to (specific procedures of study).

My participation is subject to the following conditions:

1. That adequate safeguards be provided to maintain the privacy and confidentiality of my responses.
2. That my name and my family's name not be used to ultimately identify said material; instead, code numbers are to be used.
3. That my individual scores not be reported; that data be reported as aggregate or group scores.

_____   _____
(participant's signature)   (investigator's signature)

jects with information relevant to their participation in the experiment: the nature of the experiment, an overview of the procedures that will occur, and what they will be required to do. The specific hypothesis of the experiment, however, is typically not disclosed on the form. If subjects are made aware of the researcher's expectations, their reactions during the experiment may be unintentionally or intentionally altered by this information. (We will talk about this and other demand characteristics in Chapter 11.) The purpose of informed consent is to give subjects enough information about the experiment so that they can make an *informed decision* about whether they want to participate.

THE AMERICAN PSYCHOLOGICAL ASSOCIATION GUIDELINES

Although the law contains specific provisions for the way research is to be conducted, questions may still arise in actual situations. For this reason, the American Psychological Association (APA) publishes its own set of ethical standards (1992).[1] The code applies to psychologists *and students* who assume the role of psychologists by engaging in research or practice. Psychologists conducting research are responsible for maintaining ethical standards in all research conducted by them or by others they supervise. The APA standards include the same general requirements for ensuring subjects' welfare as set forth in civil law.

Whenever any question arises about the ethics of an experiment or procedure, the researcher should seek advice from an IRB or from colleagues and employ all possible safeguards for the research participants. The standards also require IRB approval of each study before it is performed. (You can check with your instructor or supervisor to clarify the procedures that apply in your institution. Always obtain approval for an experiment from an instructor or review board before you begin.) Keep in mind that even after procedures have been approved, the individual researcher has the final responsibility for carrying out the study in an ethical way. Obtaining informed consent is considered especially important.

Fully-informed consent is required from all subjects who are at risk because of the nature of the research. In some cases subjects are considered to be **at minimal risk.** The law defines minimal risk as "risk that is no greater in probability and severity than that ordinarily encountered in daily life or during the performance of routine physical or psychological examinations or tests" (Title 45, Section 46.102[g]). Basically, this means that the research does not alter the participants' odds of being harmed. For example, a study of what proportion of the population uses soap and water to wash their hands in a public restroom would be considered minimal-risk research; the participants are engaging in a public activity in a public place. Whether or not their behavior is recorded as part of a study is unlikely to affect them in any way. There is a small chance they could be injured during the study (for example, by falling on a slippery floor). However, the research does not increase the chances of this happening.

Observations of public behavior, anonymous questionnaires, and certain kinds of archival research (discussed in Chapter 3) fall in the minimal-risk category. Informed consent is not mandatory in minimal-risk research. As a safeguard, however, it is usually desirable to obtain informed consent whenever possible, and many institutions now require it as a matter of course in all research using human subjects. The APA standards for informed consent are reprinted in Box 2-3.

---

[1] The current guidelines are the second revision of the original APA guidelines published in 1971. The first APA committee on ethics was set up in 1952, but it was not until 1966 that the society began wide discussions for a formal code.

B O X   2 - 3

APA STANDARD 6.11: INFORMED CONSENT TO RESEARCH*

a. Psychologists use language that is reasonably understandable to research participants in obtaining their appropriate informed consent, except as provided in Standard 6.12, Dispensing with Informed Consent (discussed in the text as "minimal-risk" studies). Such informed consent is appropriately documented.

b. Using language that is reasonably understandable to participants, psychologists inform participants of the nature of the research; they inform participants that they are free to participate or to decline to participate or to withdraw from the research; they explain the foreseeable consequences of declining or withdrawing; they inform participants of significant factors that may be expected to influence their willingness to participate (such as risks, discomfort, adverse effects, or limitations in confidentiality, except as provided in Standard 6.15, Deception in Research); and they explain other aspects about which the prospective participants inquire.

c. When psychologists conduct research with individuals such as students or subordinates, psychologists take special care to protect the prospective participants from adverse consequences of declining or withdrawing from participation.

d. When research participation is a course requirement or opportunity for extra credit, the prospective participant is given the choice of equitable alternative activities.

e. For persons who are legally incapable of giving informed consent, psychologists nevertheless (1) provide an appropriate explanation, (2) obtain the participant's assent, and (3) obtain appropriate permission from a legally authorized person, if such substitute consent is permitted by law.

*From "Ethical Principles of Psychologists and Code of Conduct," 1992, *American Psychologist, 47*, 1597–1611. Copyright ©1992 American Psychological Association. Reprinted with permission.

The responsibilities of both subject and experimenter must be agreed upon in advance, and the experimenter must honor all commitments made to subjects. Commitments include promises to pay subjects, to give them credit in courses, to maintain confidentiality, and to share the results of the study with them.

Deception and Full Disclosure

The relationship between researcher and participants should be as open and honest as possible. In many psychological studies, however, the true purpose of the study is disguised. Currently, some form of deception is used in approximately 60% of psychological studies (Christensen, 1988). Remember the negative ion study described in the first chapter (Baron, Russell, & Arms, 1985)? Besides merely testing the effects of different levels of ionization on subjects' moods, the researchers wanted to know if different levels of negative ions also would affect aggressive behavior (as the seasonal winds are believed to do). To test this hypothesis in the kind of controlled laboratory conditions necessary to manipulate ion levels, they needed to use deception to create a situation where aggressiveness could occur and where they could measure it systematically.

To accomplish this goal, the researchers enlisted the help of a *confederate* (in this case, a student accomplice). When one of the male subjects showed up for a session, the confederate was already there, posing as another subject. The experimenter explained that the experiment involved learning to decrease heart rate using biofeedback. One subject was to be the "teacher," the other the "learner." They drew slips of paper to select roles—but the drawing was rigged, and the subject was always the "teacher." During the "training session," the "learner" made mistakes. Every time he made a mistake, the "teacher" was supposed to punish him by pushing a button on a machine that (supposedly) sent an unpleasant, but not dangerous, burst of heat to a cuff on the "learner's" wrist. The ten buttons on the machine were labelled from very low to very intense, and the "teacher" was told to select any level he wanted. During the course of the session, the "teacher" had 20 opportunities to punish (i.e., display aggression toward) the "learner."

Of course, no real heat was ever delivered in this experiment, although subjects believed that they were punishing the "learner." The intensity levels selected by each subject, however, were recorded. (In addition, you will recall, half the subjects were angered by this confederate. Before the "learning" trials began, he provoked the real subject through a series of scripted nasty comments. These, of course, were part of the deception, too.) The entire ruse was thoroughly explained to each subject at the end of the session.

How do research subjects feel about being deceived in this way? Many studies have actually been conducted to determine the answer to this question. In a recent review of these studies, Christensen (1988) reports that most research subjects are apparently not bothered by deception.

This review of the literature, which has attempted to document the impact of deception on research participants, has consistently revealed that research participants do not perceive that they are harmed and do not seem to mind being

B O X   2 - 4

APA STANDARD 6.15: DECEPTION IN RESEARCH*

a. Psychologists do not conduct a study involving deception unless they have determined that the use of deceptive techniques is justified by the study's prospective scientific, educational, or applied value and that equally effective alternative procedures that do not use deception are not feasible.

b. Psychologists never deceive research participants about significant aspects that would affect their willingness to participate, such as physical risks, discomfort, or unpleasant emotional experiences.

c. Any other deception that is an integral feature of the design and conduct of an experiment must be explained to participants as early as is feasible, preferably at the conclusion of their participation, but no later than at the conclusion of the research.

*From "Ethical Principles of Psychologists and Code of Conduct," 1992, *American Psychologist, 47,* 1597–1611. Copyright ©1992 American Psychological Association. Reprinted with permission.

misled. In fact, evidence exists suggesting that deception experiments are more enjoyable and beneficial than nondeception experiments. (p. 668)

Interestingly, Christensen also reports that research professionals are much more bothered by deception than subjects. The consensus among researchers, however, seems to be that the use of deception is justified by the knowledge that is gained (Suls & Rosnow, 1988). Many important psychological problems cannot be studied without the use of deception, and it may be argued, as Christensen has, that failing to study important problems is even less justifiable. The standards covering the use of deception are shown in Box 2-4.

Sometimes a small omission, or outright deception, is necessary to make an appropriate test of the experimental hypothesis. How can this be reconciled with the principles of informed consent? The answer is in APA standard 6.15(b), shown in Box 2-4. The deception must not influence a subject's decision to take part in the research—any deception that is used must be such that subjects would not refuse to participate if they knew what was really happening. For instance, it would not be ethical to recruit subjects for a learning experiment without telling them that we intend to punish their incorrect responses by exposing them to the sound of scratching nails on a blackboard. Since many subjects might decline to participate in such a study, our deception would be unethical. In contrast, as far as we know, Baron and colleagues' subjects would probably have consented to participate in the experiment even if they knew that they were *not* really punishing the "learner's" errors. Furthermore, the researchers adhered to the principle of full disclosure required by APA standard 6.15(c), shown in Box 2-4, by completely **debriefing** subjects at the end of the experiment—that is, explaining the true nature and purpose of the study.

Even if subjects are debriefed, will the explanation completely undo the effects of deception? Perhaps not. Bramel's (1963) study of projection is an example of an experiment in which debriefing may have been insufficient. Bramel was interested in studying *attributive projection,* which is the process of projecting traits onto another person. The traits projected are traits the person is consciously aware of having, making this phenomenon different from the classical *projection* that Freud described. (In classical projection, the traits projected are those the person is not consciously aware of possessing.) To ensure that subjects were aware of possessing a trait they might project, Bramel employed a procedural deception. Male subjects were shown photographs of males in various stages of nudity. Subjects were given false feedback about their degree of sexual arousal to the pictures, which led them to believe they possessed homosexual tendencies. Bramel then tested the subjects for projection of sexual arousal onto others. He asked them to estimate how aroused other people would be when they saw the pictures. Bramel found that subjects projected arousal onto people who were similar to themselves (other students) but not onto people who were unlike themselves (criminals).

Of course, Bramel debriefed all his subjects at the end of the experiment; he told them the feedback had been false and that there was no indication of homosexual tendencies in their responses, since this was not even being measured. But was the explanation sufficient? It is possible that for subjects who had doubts about their sexual identity the bogus feedback aroused considerable anxiety and discomfort. It is also possible that subjects may have doubted Bramel's final full disclosure. If he admitted deceiving them about the feedback, perhaps he was also deceiving them about their real responses. At the very least, subjects may have felt somewhat foolish at having been duped by the experimenter. Whether the effects of deception can ever be fully reversed by debriefing remains a serious ethical question. Regardless of any later explanation, the subjects' anxiety and discomfort during the experiment were real. Once done, these experiences cannot be undone.

Since we cannot always reverse our experimental effects, it makes sense to avoid using procedures that are potentially harmful, painful, or upsetting to subjects whenever possible. In addition to their dubious ethical standing, such procedures often add little to our understanding of behavioral processes. For instance, we already know that high anxiety has debilitating effects on many behaviors. What would it add to our understanding of the thinking process to find that subjects learn nursery rhymes or solve riddles less efficiently after they are made extremely afraid by a noxious laboratory procedure?

Some kinds of important research will have unavoidably negative consequences for subjects (because negative consequences are precisely the effect being investigated). In cases like this, special steps need to be taken to remove any harmful effects. Experiments on the effects of violent pornography are a good example. When subjects, typically male undergraduates, are exposed to high levels of violent pornography in psychology experiments, they become more accepting of the "rape myth" than nonexposed men (Donnerstein, Linz, & Penrod, 1987). They are more likely to report callous attitudes toward women, as reflected in such statements as "Women really want to be raped." They are also more likely to say that they would consider raping a woman if they knew they would not be caught. Unfortunately, once established, these attitudes do not seem to disappear quickly on their own. Researchers discovered that a simple debriefing at the end of the experiment was not enough to erase the negative effects produced by the experimental treatment. Instead, extensive postexperimental debriefings that detail the unreality of the themes and images in violent pornography are necessary. In one experiment designed to assess the impact of extensive debriefings, a follow-up study was conducted two to four months after men had participated in a violent pornography study. The researchers found that extensive debriefings helped to remove the harmful beliefs created by the films. Two to four months later, men who had not yet been debriefed showed significantly more accepting attitudes about the rape myth than men who had received extensive debriefings (Donnerstein & Berkowitz, 1981).

Anonymity and Confidentiality

Maintaining anonymity and confidentiality is another important consideration for researchers. It is our responsibility to protect the privacy of research participants. When possible, data should be collected anonymously and identified only by code numbers. Practically, we do not need to identify subjects by name—most psychological research uses *aggregated* or group data and reports results as average scores for each treatment group (these procedures will be covered in later chapters). Data collected are kept confidential. They must be stored in a secure place, and they may not be used for any purpose not explained to the subject. They do not become items of gossip to be shared with friends. When shared with colleagues, data must also be treated with discretion and subjects' identities protected. Fictitious names or numbers (such as subject 17) are used. Identifying details are disguised if there is a chance that a subject will be recognizable.

PROTECTING THE WELFARE OF ANIMAL SUBJECTS

The principles governing informed consent, debriefing, anonymity, and confidentiality are clearly important aspects of ethical research involving human subjects. There are other standards that protect **animal welfare**—the humane care and treatment of animals. The care and treatment of animals in research

FIGURE 2-1 A close relationship can develop between researchers and their non-human subjects. UPI/Bettmann

is regulated by the Animal Welfare Act of 1966, as amended in 1970 (Public Law 91-579). The Animal Welfare Act deals with general standards for animal care. The act was recently reamended by Congress (*Federal Register,* February 15, 1991) to include new regulations that address the psychological well-being of higher animals. It requires, for example, that all dogs receive exercise and that primates are housed along with others of their species. As is the case with research using human subjects, institutions engaged in animal research have review boards, called *institutional animal care and use committees,* to evaluate experiments before they are conducted.

Several professional organizations around the country encourage ongoing monitoring of care of laboratory animals through self-policing by members of the scientific community. The American Association for Laboratory Animal Science (AALAS), for example, publishes detailed training manuals that include information on adequate housing, sanitation, and nutrition for all animals used in research. The American Association for Accreditation of Laboratory Animal Care (AAALAC) also promotes uniform standards. AAALAC uses the U.S. Department of Health, Education, and Welfare's (1978) *Guide for the Use and Care of Laboratory Animals* as its principal set of guidelines. That publication provides specific standards for cage sizes, food and bedding, waste disposal, drugs and anesthesia, and many other aspects of animal care. It also addresses issues of safety and sanitation for the benefit of animal handlers

B O X   2 - 5

APA STANDARD 6.20: CARE AND USE OF ANIMALS IN RESEARCH*

a. Psychologists who conduct research involving animals treat them humanely.

b. Psychologists acquire, care for, use, and dispose of animals in compliance with current federal, state, and local laws and regulations, and with professional standards.

c. Psychologists trained in research methods and experienced in the care of laboratory animals supervise all procedures involving animals and are responsible for ensuring appropriate consideration of their comfort, health, and humane treatment.

d. Psychologists ensure that all individuals using animals under their supervision have received instruction in research methods and in the care, maintenance, and handling of the species being used, to the extent appropriate to their role.

e. Responsibilities and activities of individuals assisting in a research project are consistent with their respective competencies.

f. Psychologists make reasonable efforts to minimize the discomfort, infection, illness, and pain of animal subjects.

g. A procedure subjecting animals to pain, stress, or privation is used only when an alternative procedure is unavailable and the goal is justified by its prospective scientific, educational, or applied value.

h. Surgical procedures are performed under appropriate anesthesia; techniques to avoid infection and minimize pain are followed during and after surgery.

i. When it is appropriate that the animal's life be terminated, it is done rapidly, with an effort to minimize pain, and in accordance with accepted procedures.

*From "Ethical Principles of Psychologists and Code of Conduct," 1992, *American Psychologist, 47,* 1597–1611. Copyright ©1992 American Psychological Association. Reprinted with permission.

working in the labs. APA's Committee on Animal Research and Ethics (CARE) has been influential in establishing national guidelines for animal welfare. APA includes standards for animal care among its ethical principles (see Box 2-5).

As with human subjects, our concern about animal welfare involves avoiding any *unnecessary* pain or risk to the subject. Research involving any procedure that might be painful to the animals, such as surgery, drug use, or shock, must be closely supervised by a researcher specially trained in the field. Despite the existence of legal and ethical guidelines, some critics have argued that animals have been abused in some psychological studies—a violation of ethical principles. In his book *Animal Liberation* (1975), Peter Singer chronicled numerous cases of animal abuse. Many of the examples dealt with studies involving electric shock or food deprivation. (However, an even greater portion of the book dealt with the treatment of animals being raised for food or used to test consumer products.) Let's look at one of Singer's examples.

This case comes from the work of Joseph V. Brady (1958). For several years Brady studied the emotional behavior of rhesus monkeys. The monkeys were kept in restraining chairs; these allowed them to move their heads and limbs but not their bodies (see Figure 2-2). They were placed in the chairs so that they could be trained through various conditioning procedures involving electric shock. The experimental setup, according to Brady, seemed to be highly stressful for the animals. Many of them died during the preliminary study. Autopsies showed that many of the dead subjects had developed ulcers, which are unusual in laboratory animals. Restraint alone was not the explanation; some animals had been kept in the restraining chairs for 6 months, received no shock, and did not develop ulcers. Therefore, in subsequent work Brady explored the effect of the conditioning procedures. Brady trained two monkeys, designating one an executive and one a control. Both monkeys were given brief shocks on the feet. However, the executive monkey could prevent shock by pressing a lever. Unless the executive acted appropriately, it (and its partner, the control monkey) would be shocked on the feet once every 20 seconds.

The monkeys were exposed to alternating 6-hour periods of shock avoidance and rest (no shock). This procedure continued for 23 days, after which the executive monkey collapsed and was sacrificed. Subsequent experiments were conducted with different pairs of monkeys and with different time intervals.

There are several ethical objections to this line of research. First, the use of the restraining chairs alone is probably extremely distressing to the animals. (Bear in mind that some animals spent 6 months in these chairs.) Second, the use of electric shock concerns many critics of animal research. Brady's original article (1958) does not contain the specific level of shock used in the experiment. We are told only that the shocks were brief. Most of us try to avoid electric shock of any magnitude, no matter how brief. Monkeys apparently share this preference, since they quickly learn to work to avoid shock. Some of the animals were so distressed physiologically by Brady's experiment that they actually developed ulcers and other gastrointestinal problems. Many died or were sacrificed so that their tissues could be studied for signs of ulcers. Third, ethical objections also can be raised because the study was poorly designed. Brady's findings were of diminished benefit because of the way the executive and control monkeys were selected in the experiment. (We will return to this issue in Chapter 7.) Thus, in this case, it seems that Singer's

FIGURE 2-2 Rhesus monkeys being kept in restraining chairs.
S. Paul Klien/Walter Reed Army Hospital. Used with permission of Walter Reed
Research Institute, Washington, D.C.

criticisms were probably justified—although, in fairness, it should be pointed
out that Brady's work predates the ethical guidelines that currently apply to
research psychologists.

But what about more recent allegations of animal abuse? Psychologists
Coile and Miller (1984) conducted a study to evaluate some extreme allegations of abuse. They reviewed all 608 articles reporting animal research that
appeared in the major psychology journals between 1979 and 1983. Table
2-1 summarizes a portion of their findings. Overall, the psychology research
literature for this 5-year period simply does not support the claims of extreme
critics like Singer. Although shock and food deprivation were used in some
studies, the manipulations were by no means as extreme as reported by the

TABLE 2-1 Accusations of animal abuses by psychologists and the percentage of articles in which such treatments and/or results were reported

Allegation	Percentage of Articles in Which Reported
"Animals are given intense repeated electric shocks which they cannot escape, until they lose the ability to even scream in pain any longer."	0.0%
"They are deprived of food and water to suffer and die slowly from hunger and thirst."	0.0%
"They are put in total isolation chambers until they are driven insane, or even die, from despair and terror."	0.0%
"They are subjected to crushing forces which smash their bones and rupture their internal organs."	0.0%
"Their limbs are mutilated or amputated to produce behavioral changes."	0.0%
"They are the victims of extreme pain and stress, inflicted upon them out of idle curiosity, in nightmarish experiments designed to make healthy animals psychotic."	0.0%

NOTE: Adapted from "How Radical Animal Activists Try to Mislead Humane People" by D. C. Coile and N. E. Miller, 1984, *American Psychologist, 39,* pp. 700–701. Copyright ©1984 American Psychological Association. Adapted with permission.

critics of animal research. In fact, not a single one of the specific extreme allegations was supported by the literature. Shock was used in 10% of the studies; inescapable shocks stronger than .001 ampere[2] were used in 3.9% of all the studies and in just 0.2% of the studies involving monkeys, dogs, or cats. The longest period of food or water deprivation reported was 48 hours. Less than 1% of the deprivation studies left animals without food or water for more than 24 hours. Most used 24 hours of deprivation, which corresponds to feeding once a day as is recommended for most house pets.

Nor were any studies done out of idle curiosity, as critics had alleged. As Coile and Miller (1984) noted: "Experiments involving inescapable shock . . . were aimed at understanding mechanisms believed likely to be involved in human depression, a condition that often causes its victims such intense suffering that they are driven to suicide. For young adults, suicide is the third leading cause of death" (p. 700). Abuses may occur occasionally, but they are by no means encouraged or condoned by the vast majority of psychological researchers.

The Animal Rights Movement

The basic premise of the APA guidelines for animal research is that animal research is acceptable in order to further the understanding of behavioral prin-

[2]"A strength that most experimenters can easily endure on their fingers" (Coile & Miller, 1984, p. 700).

ciples and to promote the welfare of humans.[3] However, the position that the best interests of humans should automatically take precedence over the rights of animals is hotly debated. Some of the most vocal critics of animal research have been advocates of the concept of **animal rights**—the idea that all sensate species, particularly those who can feel pain, are of equal value and have equal rights. Questions about the rights of animals are not new. Evans, addressing the issue in 1898, summarized one extreme position:

> Animals have no more rights than inanimate objects, and it is no worse from an ethical point of view to flay the forearm of an ape or lacerate the leg of a dog than to rip open the sleeve of a coat or rend a pair of pantaloons. (p. 99)

Clearly, few if any contemporary researchers would agree either with this position or with the activities of some radical animal rights activists.

Nevertheless, the essence of this debate was highlighted on October 26, 1984, when the heart of a healthy baboon was transplanted into a dying newborn baby. Do humans have the right to take the life of another animal? Most of us, consciously or not, make the decision that we do have that right. We decide yes every time we eat a steak or a drumstick (Regan, 1983). We also decide yes every time we open a can or a bag of pet food (Herzog, 1991). Although we might not want to give up our pets or become vegetarians, we may still question whether animals suffer needlessly. Singer made a strong case for this point of view. Other writers share his opinion:

> Many research projects are pointless, gratuitously repetitive, fatally flawed, or concerned with the obvious or the trivial. If animal suffering is of any significance whatsoever, its infliction can only be justified for clearly-defined goals. But many experiments are ill-conceived or actually unconceived in that no hypothesis has been formulated before conducting the experiment. One or a very few repetitions of an experiment may be needed to confirm the results, but some experiments are repeated time and again with no epistemological[4] justification. (Miller & Williams, 1983, p. 326)

The animal rights movement has gained momentum in this country. As an indication of the numbers of people who consider themselves to be involved in the movement for animal rights, 24,000 people attended a rally in Washington, D.C. in June 1990. In a survey of 574 highly committed activists attending the rally, Plous (1991) found that approximately 85% of them would like to see a total ban on the use of animals for research; the comparison figure from a sample of 54 nonactivists (people who just happened to be walking by the protest) was only 17%. Sixty-one percent of the activists surveyed also said they favored laboratory break-ins, whereas only 14% in the nonactivist sample favored them. Clearly, most people see some benefits in animal research.

There is little doubt that humans (and animals) have benefited from such research. Miller has pointed out that psychological experiments with animals

---

[3]Keehn (1977) noted that many animal studies benefit animals, too.
[4]*Epistemological* refers to the gathering of knowledge.

have led to treatments of many psychological problems (such as depression, obsessive-compulsive disorder, enuresis [bedwetting], and anorexia nervosa). A policy statement by AALAS (October 26, 1984) presents the case for continued experimentation using animals this way:

> The use of experimental animals has been shown to be essential to the development of an understanding of many biochemical, behavioral, physiological, and disease processes. Many of the factors that affect both animal and human life can only be studied in intact animal systems by systematically manipulating specific research variables. Given an incomplete knowledge of biological systems, it is inconceivable that animal experimentation can be replaced, in the foreseeable future, by mechanical models or other incomplete biological systems.

The charges of animal rights activists, although exaggerated and overly dramatic at times, do serve to heighten our awareness of the issues. And they have affected the amount of animal research that is conducted: Fewer animals are being used in research each year (Rowan & Andrutis, 1990). However, Johnson (1990) argues that "the animal rights movement has misled the lawmakers and citizens of the country into sacrificing human lives for animal lives. That is the stark reality" (p. 214).

Certainly, as long as animal experimentation continues, researchers have an obligation to behave responsibly. The situations causing the grievances of the past cannot be undone, but the picture for the future of animal welfare is hopeful. Before 1987, the E in CARE stood for "experimentation." It now stands for "ethics." The challenge to contemporary researchers is to ensure that each human or animal subject contributes something worthwhile to scientific knowledge. In the chapters that follow, we will return to ethical questions about human and animal subjects in our examples of actual research projects.

FRAUD IN SCIENCE

So far, we have discussed the ethical concerns of researchers designing experiments involving human or animal subjects. Reporting on research is a necessary part of the scientific process. It is also an ethical matter. We report our procedures and findings honestly and accurately. When we think of **fraud** in science, we typically think about researchers publishing false data. Data falsification is a breach of the ethical principles stated in APA standard 6.21a, "Psychologists do not fabricate data or falsify results in their publications." As well as individual ethics, several important safeguards are built into the public process of scientific reporting that help to keep fraud in check.

First, with very few exceptions, research articles submitted for publication are reviewed by the editor of the periodical and by several experts in the field before they can be accepted for publication. This procedure, called *peer review,* is an important part of the reporting process. The reviewers' task is to assess the worth of a submission; reviewers go over each submission with a fine-tooth comb, looking for problems and suggesting improvements. If there is

"THAT'S IT? THAT'S PEER REVIEW?"

something strange about the findings, expert reviewers are likely to discover it. (Only about 15% to 20% of all articles submitted for publication in psychological journals ever make it into print.) Reviewers make recommendations about publication to the editor of the journal, who makes the final decision. The reviewers and the editor, then, are a first line of defense against data falsification.

Replication is the second line of defense. Researchers often attempt to replicate the published findings of others, particularly if those findings are surprising, novel, or important. If data have been falsified, it is unlikely that the experiment will be successfully replicated!

Third, the competitive nature of academic psychology works against fraud (even though it may also be the primary cause!). Tenure and promotion within academic departments of psychology are partly based on research productivity. You have probably heard the saying, "Publish or perish." There is strong pressure on researchers to publish, and the pressure is probably strongest on those whose work has resulted in a series of failures. Fabricating some impressive data might seem very tempting when keeping one's job depends on publishing the results of a successful experiment. However, competition among colleagues for limited research resources can be a strong deterrent to fraud. As federal funding sources become increasingly scarce, the competition stiffens; as resources become more limited, other researchers in the same area will be on the alert for fraud. Despite these safeguards, fraud does occur from time to time.

One of the most spectacular cases involved the famous English psychologist Sir Cyril Burt, who was awarded APA's prestigious Thorndike Award for distinguished service to educational psychology shortly before he died in 1971 (Green, 1992). Burt had achieved fame for his published studies on the inheritability of IQ in identical twins and fraternal twins who were raised apart (Burt, 1966, 1972). His data showed that the IQ scores of identical twins (twins whose genes are exactly the same) were almost identical even though they had been exposed to very different life experiences; conversely, the IQ scores of fraternal twins (twins who share only a fraction of their genes) could differ greatly. This was very important research in its time. Eventually, other researchers noticed that some of the statistical values he reported in different articles were exactly the same even though Burt had reported using different numbers of twins. Statistically speaking, this is a highly improbable, if not impossible, event. It is widely believed that Burt falsified his results, although his defenders argue persuasively that he was merely "sloppy" about reporting his data (which he had actually stopped collecting in 1939). They make the point that if Burt had intended fraud, "he would have done a better job of it" (Green, 1992, p. 330).

A more recent case involved data falsification in studies of the treatment of hyperactivity in children with stimulant drugs. In the 1980s, a psychologist named Stephen Breuning admitted fabricating data showing that stimulants such as Ritalin and Dexedrine could dramatically reduce hyperactivity. He received a large federal grant from NIMH (National Institute of Mental Health) on the basis of false data. One of his colleagues suspected that Breuning had falsified his data, and reported these suspicions to NIMH. After a three-year *scientific misconduct* investigation conducted by NIMH, Breuning admitted in a plea bargain that he had falsified his data on two occasions in return for NIMH dropping perjury charges (Byrne, 1988).

Breuning's case, among others, has resulted in national discussions about the definition of scientific misconduct used by the two major granting agencies, NIMH and NSF (National Science Foundation). The current definitions are vague and subjective; for example, NSF describes misconduct as "fabrication, falsification, plagiarism, or other serious deviation from accepted practices in proposing, carrying out, or reporting results from activities funded by NSF" (NFS [45CFR Part 689.1 (a)(1)]). Whatever definition is used, the consequences of scientific misconduct can be severe indeed for a researcher, ranging from suspension or firing by the university to a prison term if convicted in court. Universities can be penalized as well; they can be forced to return monies and can be excluded from future funding. In Breuning's case, his university was required to return over $135,000 in funds to NIMH, and Breuning no longer has a research career! In almost all cases, funding from federal grants like Breuning's is actually given to universities, not to individual researchers. The university controls and monitors all spending. However, you have probably read recent newspaper accounts of cases in which several universities have been investigated on charges of spending government research funds frivolously. As funding becomes even scarcer, more frequent investigations and tighter controls are expected.

PLAGIARISM

Let us turn to what is probably a more common kind of fraud, plagiarism. We must be careful in the way we draw upon the work of others in our presentation. To **plagiarize** means to represent someone else's ideas, words, or written work as your own. Plagiarism is a serious breach of ethics and can result in legal action. It is not only "borrowing" facts and figures from someone else; plagiarism includes using someone else's ideas without giving proper credit. A well-known author was sued by a former professor who claimed the ideas in the author's best-selling book came directly from his lectures. The professor won his suit and now receives a share of the author's royalties.

Although some forms of plagiarism are intentional, others occur through simple oversights. It would be a rather large oversight to forget to give authors credit for direct quotations used, but what about paraphrasing their work—using their ideas but changing the words around? Paraphrasing without giving credit is representing someone else's idea as your own; it is also plagiarism. Even if you believe that the information you wish to use is "common knowledge," if you have read it in someone else's book, give the author credit. If you have done a thorough review of the literature, your research report should contain many *citations*.[5] This way the reader will know that you have read the important research in your topic area.

Unfortunately, it is easy to plagiarize without being aware of it. We read many things, jot down notes, and later forget where we got the information. If we use that information elsewhere, we may inadvertently forget or be unable to name the source. In preparing a research report, you should follow several guidelines to avoid the possibility of plagiarism (these guidelines also apply to works that are unpublished or not yet published).

1. Take complete notes, which include a complete citation of the source: author's name, title of article, journal name, volume number, year of publication, and page numbers. For books, include the publisher's name and city.

---

[5]The citation given for Regan's (1983) idea that eating meat and poultry is a decision that goes against the best interests of animals is a good example of this. Everyone has probably heard this argument (and so have we), but we came upon Regan's published article while reviewing the literature on ethics and cite this source because it gave us the idea to write about it.

2. Within your report, identify the source of any ideas, words, or information that are not your own.

3. Identify any direct quotes by quotation marks at the beginning and end of the quotes and indicate where you got the quotes.

4. Be careful with paraphrasing (restating someone else's words). There is a great temptation to lift whole phrases or catchy words from another source. Use your own words instead or use quotes. Be sure to give credit to your source.

5. Include a complete list of references at the end of the report. References should include all the information listed in item 1.

6. If in doubt about whether a citation is necessary, cite the source anyway. You will do no harm by being especially cautious.

Throughout this book you will find figures, passages, and photographs used with the written permissions of the original authors, artists, and publishers.

SUMMARY

A well-planned experiment includes careful treatment of the subjects who participate. Today some aspects of psychological research are regulated by federal law. An institution must, for example, have an *institutional review board (IRB)* to approve each study. The IRB's main tasks are to ensure the safety of human subjects and to conduct a *risk/benefit analysis,* and many of the law's provisions are reflected in the ethical guidelines of the American Psychological Association. Most important is obtaining the *informed consent* of all those who will be subjects in an experiment. This consent must be given freely, without force or coercion. The person must also understand that he or she is free to drop out of the experiment at any time. In addition, subjects must be given as much information about the experiment as possible so that they can make a reasonable decision about whether to participate.

Sometimes a researcher may need to disguise the true purpose of the study so that subjects will behave naturally and spontaneously. In experiments that require some deception, subjects must be *debriefed.* But because simply debriefing subjects does not guarantee that we can undo any upset we caused them, researchers try to avoid exposing subjects to any unnecessary pain or risk. When possible, data should be collected anonymously and identified only by code numbers. Data collected are kept confidential; they may not be used for any purpose not explained to the subject. When they are reported, data should be identified by code numbers or fictitious names to protect subjects' identities.

Ethical principles apply in research with animals, too. Researchers have the responsibility to look out for the welfare of their animal subjects. Animals must receive adequate physical care to stay healthy and comfortable. If drugs, surgery, or any potentially painful procedures are involved, animals must be closely supervised by a researcher who is specially trained in the field. Despite allegations by critics of animal research, there is little evidence to support accusations of widespread abuse in psychological research. Some critics advocate *animal rights,* the position that all species are equally valued and have equal rights, and the animal rights movement has recently gained momentum. Most people, however, see a need for animal experimentation because of its benefits for human welfare.

Fraud in science is typically thought of as falsifying or fabricating data; clearly, fraud is unethical. The peer review process, replication, and scrutiny by colleagues work to hold fraud in check, but the "publish or perish" pressure exists. *Plagiarism,* representing someone else's work as your own, is a serious breach of ethics and is also considered a type of fraud. Researchers must be careful to give proper credit to others who contributed words and ideas to their work.

KEY TERMS

Animal rights The concept that all sensate species who feel pain are of equal value and have rights.

Animal welfare The humane care and treatment of animals.

At minimal risk The subject's odds of being harmed are not increased by the research.

At risk The likelihood of a subject's being harmed in some way because of the nature of the research.

Debriefing The principle of full disclosure at the end of an experiment; that is, explaining to the subject the nature and purpose of the study.

Fraud The unethical practice of falsifying or fabricating data; plagiarism is also a form of fraud.

Informed consent A subject's voluntary agreement to participate in a research project after the nature and purpose of the study have been explained.

Institutional review board (IRB) An institutional committee that reviews proposed research to safeguard the safety and rights of subjects.

Plagiarism The representation of someone else's ideas, words, or written work as one's own; a serious breach of ethics that can result in legal action.

Risk/benefit analysis A determination, made by an institutional review board, that any risks to the individual are outweighed by potential benefits or the importance of the knowledge to be gained.

REVIEW AND STUDY QUESTIONS

1. What are the tasks of an institutional review board (IRB)?
2. What is informed consent?
3. What is the principle of full disclosure?
4. At the end of the semester, all students in a general psychology course

are told they will not receive credit for the course unless they take part in the instructor's research project. Students who refuse to participate are given incompletes and do not get credit for the course. Is this unethical? Which principles of the APA guidelines have been violated?

5. An experimenter studying the effects of stress gave subjects a series of maze problems to solve. The subjects were led to believe that the problems were all quite easy. In fact, several had no solution. Some of the subjects were visibly upset by their inability to solve the problems. At the end of the study, the experimenter gave no explanation of the procedures. What ethical principles apply in this case? What *should* the experimenter have done?

6. In a study of sexual attitudes, a student experimenter finds that Pat, a friend's spouse, has responded yes to the question, "Have you ever had an extramarital affair?" The student is sure that the friend is unaware of Pat's behavior. The student decides to show Pat's answers to the friend. What ethical principles have been violated? How could this situation have been avoided?

7. Have you ever been a subject in a research project? If so, how were ethical principles applied in that study?

8. What ethical principles apply when we do research with animals?

9. Explain the concepts of animal welfare and animal rights.

10. In order to study the effect of a new drug to reduce depression, researchers must sacrifice animal subjects and dissect their brains. Discuss the ethical pros and cons of this line of research.

11. What is fraud? Describe the external pressures that can produce fraud. Describe the safeguards that keep it in check. What are the possible penalties for scientific misconduct?

12. Lee had put off doing a lab report until the end of the term. He was badly pressed for time. His roommate said, "No problem. I took that course last year. You can use my report. Just put your name on it." Lee decides it is all right to use the paper since he has the author's consent. Do you agree? Why or why not?

CHAPTER 3

ALTERNATIVES TO EXPERIMENTATION: NONEXPERIMENTAL DESIGNS

In the traditional psychology experiment, we *create* specific sets of antecedent conditions, or treatments, to test a hypothesis about behavior. To use the experimental approach, the researcher must be able to set up these conditions for *any* individual who ends up as a subject in the experiment. Many times this requirement cannot (and sometimes should not) be met. For example, we may wish to study characteristics of the participants (such as gender or personality) to see how they affect behavior. Because we cannot create the antecedent conditions in these situations, we need to gather data in other ways. Sometimes the conditions a researcher wants to study (such as pregnancy or smoking) cannot be created for ethical reasons.

Nonexperimental approaches are used in situations in which an experiment is not feasible or desirable. They are also used whenever testing a hypothesis in an existing real-life situation is necessary or important. Nonexperimental methods are used to study behaviors in natural settings (children playing, chimps parenting, or life in a gang); to explore unique or rare occurrences (a case of multiple personality, the O. J. Simpson trial); or to sample personal information (attitudes, opinions, preferences). Because each of these nonexperimental approaches can provide useful data, either from single individuals or from large groups of people, it is important to understand how they are applied in psychological research.

As we discussed in Chapter 1, the primary purpose of an experiment is to establish a causal relationship between a specified set of antecedent conditions (treatments) and the subsequent observed behavior. The degree to which a research design allows us to make causal statements is called the **internal validity** of the design. Research is high in internal validity if we can conclude that the antecedents caused the observed differences in behavior among the various groups of subjects in the experiment. Laboratory experiments are popular with researchers in part because they are potentially high in internal validity. (We say "potentially" because there are a variety of ways in which experiments may fall short of this goal. These pitfalls will be discussed in later chapters.) Nevertheless, experiments are frequently criticized—in the media, by students, by laypersons, and by seasoned professionals—for being artificial and unrealistic, and to some extent this criticism may be justified. True experiments often seem to lack **external validity**—that is, *generalizability* or applicability to situations outside the research setting. When observations can be generalized to other settings and other people, they are high in external validity. Nonexperimental designs are often preferred because they may have greater external validity; their generalizability to the real world may be more apparent. There is, however, some trade-off. What we gain in external validity we may lose in internal validity. A study that is fetchingly realistic may bring us no closer to the "truth" than one that seems painfully contrived.

DESCRIBING RESEARCH ACTIVITIES

All approaches to research can be described along two major dimensions: (1) the degree of manipulation of antecedent conditions, and (2) the degree of imposition of units (Willems, 1969). The degree of manipulation of antecedents theoretically varies from low to high, from letting things happen as they will to setting up carefully controlled conditions. For example, a study could involve simply tracking behavior along with subjects' normal diets (low manipulation of antecedents). Or, at the other extreme, we could place subjects on fixed diets where all meals are provided (high manipulation of antecedents). Selecting a high degree of manipulation has its pros and cons: We could then vary meals in predetermined ways and evaluate subsequent changes in behavior, but we would be imposing on subjects artificial conditions that may have little meaning in real life. Experiments are typically high in degree of manipulation; nonexperiments are usually low.

The *degree of imposition of units* is an equally important dimension. This term refers to the extent to which the researcher constrains, or limits, the responses a subject may contribute to the data. In a study of teenagers, for example, we might simply watch a group of teenagers and record whatever they say or do (low imposition of units). With such a plan, we would be imposing relatively little constraint on the teens' behaviors. But suppose that instead we were interested only in a single behavior, such as the amount of time they listen to rock music. We might then limit our subjects' responses to the answer to the question, "How much time do you spend listening to rock music each day?" Our study would then score high on the dimension of imposed units. As you will see in later chapters, most experiments limit subjects' inputs to a narrow range of responses, placing such experiments high on the scale of imposed units. Nonexperimental designs, as you will discover in this chapter and the next, can vary from low to high imposition of units.

Antecedent conditions and imposed units can change independently, and we can represent the various research approaches visually as shown in Figure 3-1. As the figure illustrates, a range of possible research approaches exists. Laboratory experiments, which tend to fall in the high-high range, represent only one approach. As we discuss nonexperimental designs, we will refer to this figure again.

NONEXPERIMENTAL APPROACHES

Let us now discuss four common nonexperimental approaches used by psychologists: (1) phenomenology, (2) case studies, (3) field studies, and (4) survey research. Together, these approaches form an important source of data on human as well as animal behavior. They permit us to gather information and gain understanding when experimentation is not possible or desirable.

Phenomenology

So far we have discussed the scientific method in terms of observing and recording events that are assumed to be external to the observer. An important supplement to the scientific method is the phenomenological approach.

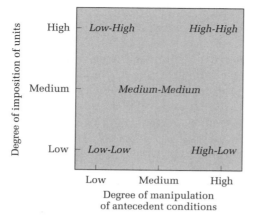

FIGURE 3-1 A space for describing research activities. From "Planning a Rationale for Naturalistic Research," by E. P. Willems. In E. P. Willems and H. L. Raush (Eds.), 1969, *Naturalistic Viewpoints in Psychological Research*. Copyright ©1969 Holt, Rinehart and Winston. Reprinted by permission.

Phenomenology is the description of one's own immediate experience; rather than looking at behaviors and events that are external to us, we begin with our own experience as a source of data.

As a research approach, phenomenology often falls near the low-low end on our graph of research activities (Figure 3-1). Antecedents are not manipulated, and the data may consist of any immediate experience; no constraints are imposed. Much early work in psychology was based on the phenomenological approach. Boring (1950) cites Purkinje as a good example of the phenomenologically based researcher. Purkinje was interested in the physiology of vision and noticed that colors seemed to change as twilight deepened; reds appeared black, and blues retained their hue. This observation (now called the **Purkinje phenomenon**) eventually led to our understanding of the spectral sensitivity of the rods and cones of the eye.

William James (Figure 3-2) also used the phenomenological approach. In his *Principles of Psychology* (1950, original 1890), James dealt with basic psychological issues, including habits, emotions, consciousness, and the stream of thought. James approached many ideas from the perspective of his own experience. One of his most appealing passages deals with his own difficulty in getting up in the morning. He pointed out that our resistance to getting up inhibits our movement. While we concentrate on the pleasure of warm sheets and the dread of a cold floor, we are paralyzed. Said James, "If I may generalize from my own experience, we more often than not get up without any struggle or decision at all. We suddenly find that we have got up" (p. 524). Therefore, if we don't resist, we ought to be able to rise without effort.

FIGURE 3-2 William James (1842–1910). National Library of Medicine

The phenomenological approach precludes experimental manipulation. Comparison of behaviors under different treatment conditions is not required. When using this approach, we simply attend to our own experience. As Boring (1950) explained:

> Since phenomenology deals with immediate experience, its conclusions are instantaneous. They emerge at once and need not wait upon the results of calculations derived from measurements. Nor does a phenomenologist use statistics, since a frequency does not occur at an instant and cannot be immediately observed. (p. 602)

Thus the phenomenological approach is applied to a small sample of subjects—a sample of one. We cannot be sure that the process we are observing in ourselves is not altered in some way by our attention to it. Since the observer is also the person whose process is observed, we may not be able to achieve the degree of accuracy and objectivity through phenomenology that we might achieve through other methods. Nor are our private experiences observable in public; it will be difficult for others to replicate our experiences and apply scientific criteria to our findings. Without replication, it cannot be known if others would have the same experiences. If Purkinje had been color blind, his experience at sundown would have been very different from that of most people.

Phenomenology cannot be used to understand the causes of behavior. Purkinje could not be certain that his experience of altered color was caused by an external change (a change in the amount of light) that would affect all observers in a similar manner. Had he not been a scientist, he might have explained his experience in terms of a demon that had taken possession of his sense organs. In the absence of further evidence, one explanation would have been as good as the other.

Phenomenology may lead us into areas of discovery that might otherwise go unnoticed. It can be a useful source of information that may lead us to formulate hypotheses (we will return to this issue in Chapter 5), but experimentation is still required to determine which antecedent conditions produce the behavior or experience. Elements of phenomenology are frequently combined with other research methods, however. In fact, that is probably one of the most common uses of the approach today. Experimentation, for example, often relies on phenomenological, or *self-report,* data to study the effects of various experimental manipulations. Recall that in the experiment by Baron and his colleagues (1985) cited in Chapter 1, subjects reported on their own moods. Our next method, the case study, makes extensive use of self-reports.

Case Studies

Like phenomenology, the case study method involves no manipulation of antecedent conditions. The **case study**[1] is a descriptive record of an individual's experiences and/or behaviors kept by an outside observer. Such a record may be produced by systematically recording experiences and behaviors as they have occurred over time. Clinical psychology, in particular, has relied heavily on case studies.

There are generally few restrictions on the type of data to be included in a case study. Thus, case studies would be expected to fall in the low-low portion of our graphic scheme. The exact procedures used to produce a case study will depend on the purpose of the study. Sometimes, as in the clinical case, we may work from a record made after the fact; the client or other knowledgeable source provides information concerning events in the client's life and the client's reactions and behaviors. An excerpt from a clinical case is presented in Box 3-1 to illustrate the kind of information that may be found in a case study.

Kazdin (1992) has argued that case studies serve five major purposes:

1. They are a source of inferences, hypotheses, and theories.
2. They are a source for developing therapy techniques.
3. They allow the study of rare phenomena.
4. They provide exceptions, or counterinstances, to accepted ideas, theories, or practices.
5. They have persuasive and motivational value.

Let us look at each point in turn.

---

[1]As the term is commonly used in reference to methodology, research produced by any of the various research methods is called a *study.* Only true experiments, however, are accurately called *experiments.*

B O X   3 - 1

CASE STUDY: AN EXAMPLE OF INVOLUTIONAL PARANOID REACTION

A. S. was admitted to the hospital at the age of 59. The patient was born in Latvia. Little is known about her childhood experiences and the emotional climate of the home. She came to the United States at the age of 19 to marry a man who had preceded her to this country. She and her husband returned to Latvia, where the husband took over his father's farm and attained considerable success and status. At this point the farm buildings were destroyed by fire, and the patient was so seriously burned that she required hospital care for three months. They returned to the United States and the husband established an upholstering business in which the patient assisted until this business failed. The husband then began to drink, and he committed suicide by hanging, a casualty discovered by the patient.

When she was approximately 54 years of age, the patient began to complain that people were talking about her, that her son-in-law was maritally unfaithful, that nearly all persons, especially the clergy of a different religious faith, were sexually immoral. She expressed a fear that she would be "signed away for experimental purposes." She stated that a physician who had treated her at the menopause had given her cancer. Finally, after having complained to the police on several occasions that her food was being drugged and that a "society of science" was plotting against her, she was committed.

Following the patient's admission to the hospital, her daughter, in describing her mother's personality pattern, reported that she had always been a meticulous, hardworking person who was critical, suspicious, stubborn, uncompromising, and domineering. The daughter described her mother as an immaculate housekeeper who also did "beautiful sewing."

On arrival at the hospital, her sensorium was clear and she was fully oriented. She was suspicious, and when her abdominal reflexes were tested, she asked if the physician was going to operate on her. At times she became quite agitated and hostile and insisted that she be permitted to leave. Someone, she said, was trying to secure possession of her home and to kill her; she must therefore appeal to the police to help her. She complained that the nurses tried to compel her to perform unpleasant tasks because they were members of a religious organization that was persecuting her.

(continued)

(*continued*)

Because of an electrocardiogram suggestive of coronary involvement and myocardial damage, it was decided not to give the patient electroshock treatment. After seven months of hospital residence, the patient became much less tense, was pleasant and cooperative, and was regarded as one of the most faithful and capable workers in the hospital cafeteria. Within a year after her admission, she was given freedom of the hospital grounds and was to spend weekends with friends. Unless questioned, she expressed no delusional ideas. Upon inquiry, however, it was found that there had been no fundamental change in her paranoid ideation. Fifteen months after her admission the patient was permitted to leave the hospital. A year later her employer wrote: "Mrs. S. is cheerful and pleasant and I am very satisfied with her work."

So little is known about this woman's emotional relations with parents and siblings during childhood and any early traumatizing experiences that it is not easy to construct a desirably complete genetic-dynamic formulation of her psychotic personality disturbance. Her daughter's report that the patient was a meticulous, critical, suspicious, stubborn, dominating, and uncompromising person suggests that, because of a basic feeling of insecurity, she had developed these personality characteristics to serve as defenses. In spite of a long series of threats, these defenses proved adequate for many years until the involutional period, with its various accompanying psychological factors, became so menacing that lifelong traits were no longer able to control anxiety-producing threats. As a further defense, therefore, the patient resorted to projection to a reality-sacrificing, or psychotic, degree.

Although the problems that the patient had found too difficult to meet must remain a matter of speculation, one suspects, in view of the nature of her personality traits and the character of her delusions, that a deeply seated hostility, the fear of economic insecurity, and a weakening in the repression of instinctive sex drives may have been important ones.*

First, we may use a case study to make inferences about the impact of life events, the origin of disorders, or developmental processes. For example, this approach provided the first systematic data on the development of children's motor, cognitive, and linguistic abilities. By making extensive records of the behaviors of individual children, early researchers like Velten (1943) and Piaget (1954) arrived at descriptions of normal developmental sequences. Psychodynamic development has been inferred from case studies. Freud's case of Little Hans (Freud, 1933) is an example of the way in which an individual case may suggest a developmental process. Hans was afraid of horses. Freud's analysis of Hans's conversations with his father and the dreams he reported suggested that the fear of horses was a symbol for Hans's fear of his father and anxiety about castration. Such case studies led to Freud's formulation of the theory of the Oedipus complex.

The case study provides information about the impact of significant events in a person's life. We may evaluate whether changes occurred in the individual's adjustment following such critical events as loss of a job or birth of a child. Knowledge about these events may lead to a better understanding of the psychodynamics of experience. For example, the fact that an early loss, like the death of a parent, is associated with depression in later life is indicated by many cases (Jacobson, 1971).

Second, as we understand the impact of such events more fully, we may be able to devise more appropriate treatment techniques, as well as preventive measures. The "talking cure" in psychotherapy, for instance, began as a result of treatment of "hysterical" symptoms in Anna O., one of Freud's early cases (Breuer & Freud, 1957). The case of a fearful boy named Peter (Jones, 1924) formed the basis of today's behavioral therapy techniques.

Third, the case study is a perfect forum for the investigation of unique cases or rare problems. Some variants of paraphilia (cross-dressing and sexual masochism, for instance) are very rarely diagnosed in clinical settings; here, case studies can be useful sources of information.

Fourth, case studies can provide evidence that casts doubt on theories or generally accepted practices. For example, the psychoanalytic notion that it could be harmful to treat overt symptoms of dysfunction without treating their base causes was negated as counterinstances accumulated. Simply treating outward symptoms with behavioral therapy techniques is often very effective.

Fifth, case studies are sometimes a dramatic way to illustrate abstract concepts. Seeing can be believing; hence, advertisers frequently use case studies (highly selective ones) to sell products. Because they are so compelling, however, case studies can excite interest and bring about new research.

Furthermore, the case study is used in clinical work to evaluate an individual's overall level of psychological functioning. We compare our case against some hypothetical standard of "normal" behavior. Based on this comparison, we may suspect some form of psychopathology. We may then compare our case against other cases to assess the degree of similarity or difference. This is the process underlying psychological diagnosis. The development of standard diagnostic criteria for categories of mental disorders appearing in the *Diagnostic and Statistical Manual of Mental Disorders,* 4th ed. (1994; abbreviated as *DSM-IV*) reflects groupings of many different patients' case histories. Clinicians have noted similarities among patients which permit their problems to be classified into groups. The records of persons previously diagnosed with "antisocial personality disorder," for example, have certain important similarities (see Box 3-2).

The **deviant case analysis** (Robinson, 1976) is an extension of the evaluative case study discussed earlier. Here cases of deviant and normal individuals are compared for significant differences. These differences may have

B O X   3 - 2

ANTISOCIAL PERSONALITY DISORDER

It is estimated that about 3% of adult American men and 1% of adult American women could be diagnosed as having an antisocial personality disorder. These individuals were formerly called "psychopaths" or "sociopaths." Diagnosis requires that the individual meet several criteria. The diagnostic criteria were determined by the clinical judgments of experts in psychiatry and psychology and evolved from many, many case studies. The terms *psychopath* or *sociopath* bring convicted serial killers like Ted Bundy or Jeffrey Dahmer to mind. However, psychologists Davison and Neale (1986) described an important fact about people with an antisocial personality disorder—they can be found anywhere! "Business executives, politicians, and physicians, plumbers, salespeople, carpenters, and bartenders—they are to be found in all walks of life. Prostitutes, pimps, confidence men, murderers, and drug dealers are by no means the only sociopaths" (p. 233).

It can be said that some individuals with aspects of antisocial personality disorder are quite a bit more successful at managing not to break the law than others. What all these people have in common are personal histories that reflect similar kinds of behaviors and life events. Antisocial personality always begins in childhood or adolescence with occasions of truancy, aggression, vandalism, stealing, lying, physical cruelty, or other antisocial behaviors. Before the age of 18, such individuals would be diagnosed as having a "conduct disorder." Their behavior rarely goes unnoticed; they often find themselves in trouble with the authorities.

After age 18, a diagnosis of antisocial personality disorder is made if individuals fulfill specific behavioral criteria associated with the disorder. Individuals with the disorder carry over the pattern of childhood antisocial behavior into adulthood, where they are seen to engage in repeated instances of behaviors that are assaultive, destructive, irresponsible, or illegal. In addition, these individuals do not suffer from (true) remorse for their actions. From collections of case studies, several predisposing childhood factors have also been identified: inconsistent parental discipline, substance abuse, attention deficits, and hyperactivity, for example. Sociopathy is also more likely if one or both parents had the disorder.

DSM-IV is the standard for diagnosing mental disorders, but not all experts agree with the diagnostic criteria. For example, many psychologists believe that sociopaths are also characterized by a great deal of charm that can make them exceptionally charismatic. Underneath it all, though, they feel little or nothing for others (Cleckley, 1976). Part of the problem with compiling information from case studies on individuals diagnosed with antisocial personality disorder is that generally the individuals available for study are the extreme cases—typically incarcerated criminals or psychiatric patients. One can argue, as have Davison and Neale, that the database for sociopathy probably lacks valuable information about the most successful sociopaths.

important implications for the etiology, or origin, of the psychopathology in question. Mednick and his colleagues have used this procedure to study the etiology of schizophrenia (Mednick, 1969; Mednick, Schulsinger, & Venables, 1981). They found, for example, that the autonomic systems of normal and schizophrenic children function differently. Someday it may be possible to use this difference to predict which children will become schizophrenic.

Clearly, the case study is a useful source of information. It is especially useful when we cannot experiment because of practical or ethical reasons. (Obviously, we would not subject an individual to a stressful life experience, such as loss of a parent, simply to observe the outcome.) However, this approach has several limitations. First, working with only one or perhaps a few subjects, we cannot be sure the people we are evaluating are representative of the general population; we would obtain a very distorted picture of language development if we studied one exceptional child. Second, if we are not able to observe an individual directly all the time, we cannot be sure that we are aware of all the relevant aspects of that person's life. Third, subjects or others providing data for case studies may neglect to mention important information, either because they believe it is irrelevant or because they find it embarrassing.

An even more severe problem is that case studies frequently rely on retrospective data. **Retrospective data** are data collected in the present that are based on recollections of past events. Information collected long after the fact is apt to be inaccurate for several reasons. First, people often cannot accurately remember all that happened at a particular point in time. We also know that human memories become altered or "reconstructed" over time by the cognitive system. Retrospective data can also be easily biased by the situation in which the data are collected. The mood of the data provider, for example, will affect recollections; we tend to recall more positive events when we are in a good mood and more negative events when we are in a bad mood.

In addition, particular kinds of recollections can be triggered by aspects of the situation. Something that seems as innocuous as a reproduction of da Vinci's *Mona Lisa* on a therapist's wall might bring to mind past experiences with enigmatic, dark-haired women that otherwise would not have been recalled at all. Even unintended hints from a researcher that certain kinds of

Copyright ©1996 by Sidney Harris

data are more interesting than others can bias the kind of information that is brought to mind. For these reasons, reliance on retrospective data is a short-coming. Records made at the time of an event are always much preferred. The use of retrospective data is not limited to case studies but frequently occurs in this research method. Finally, because we have not created the antecedent conditions in case studies, we cannot make cause and effect statements about the behaviors we observe. For example, we cannot say that an early loss causes later depression; we can merely say that there seems to be a relationship between the two occurrences. It is just as plausible that some related factor, such as moving or changing schools because of a parent's death, might explain later depression.

Field Studies

Field studies are nonexperimental approaches used in the field or in real-life settings. Researchers doing field studies often combine various types of data gathering to capitalize on the richness and range of behavior found outside the laboratory. Antecedent conditions are not manipulated in field studies, but the degree of constraint on responses varies considerably from study to study. Depending on the measurements used, field studies may fall anywhere along the continuum of low-low to low-high in our graphic scheme (see Figure 3-1). Let us look next at some different types of field studies.

Naturalistic Observation

Naturalistic observation is the technique of observing behaviors as they occur spontaneously in natural settings. It is a *descriptive* method: Like phenomenology and the case study method, naturalistic observation involves no manipulation of antecedent conditions. Subjects' responses are free to vary. Because few constraints are imposed by the researcher (Sackett, 1978), naturalistic observation would be considered low-low in Figure 3-1. The naturalistic observation approach has been used most extensively in animal behavior research, or ethology, but it is often applied to human behavior as well. During naturalistic observation, observers attempt to remain unobtrusive (for example, behind a duck blind) so that the behaviors observed are not altered by their presence. Every attempt is made to keep the setting as natural as possible, so that the naturally occurring events will not be altered in any way: "The primary feature of such research is that human perceptual and judgmental abilities are necessary to extract quantitative data from the flow of responses" (Sackett, 1978, p. 2). This element creates special challenges for the field study. In a typical laboratory experiment, the researcher has only a small set of behaviors to record. In contrast, researchers who conduct field studies must contend with a vast array of responses, often including unanticipated, unconventional responses. Deciding who and when to observe and what to record and analyze draws heavily on both the researcher's judgment and observational skills.

The use of direct naturalistic observation is often essential and even preferable to experimentation. Psychological phenomena are rarely simple; a researcher can fail to take all the important antecedent conditions of an experiment into account. Years of experiments on helpfulness are a case in point. As discussed in Chapter 1, so many factors influence our willingness to help others that it would be impossible to manipulate all of them in a single experiment so that we could look at their combined effects. The field researcher accepts the larger challenge of dealing with data as they occur in real-life settings. Imposing a great deal of constraint on subjects' responses is not always desirable, either. Allowing subjects to behave as they usually would provides a much richer picture of the complex, multiple relationships among behaviors, and results from these studies may have more external validity, or generalizability, than laboratory demonstrations.

In an example of naturalistic observation, Wheeler (1988) spent a year observing Chinese residents of Hong Kong and noted many interesting differences between these Chinese and typical Americans. For example, he observed that during construction of the new headquarters of the Hong Kong and Shanghai Bank (one of the most expensive buildings in the world), traditional *fung shui* (wind and water) experts had to be consulted all along the way. These experts ensured, for instance, that the building was not constructed "on the back of the dragon." Without the guidance of these experts in safely situating the building, people would not have used the bank!

Frequently, a naturalistic observation is designed to answer specific questions. Yepez (1994), for example, wanted to investigate whether teachers in English as a Second Language courses gave equal amounts of attention to their male and female students. With permission of the teachers (but without explaining her hypothesis beforehand), she observed and recorded the number of classroom interactions between four different teachers and their pupils. Each teacher was observed six times. Years of past research have shown that gender inequities are often found in the classroom. Male students tend to be given more attention by teachers. Surprisingly, in Yepez's observation, she found that only one of the four teachers seemed to give more attention to the men than to the women.

Yepez recorded behaviors in the classes using a special coding system, called INTERSECT, developed for scoring various kinds of teacher-student interactions (Sadker & Sadker, 1982). It allowed her to collect data in a more objective and systematic manner. Many such coding systems have been developed for observational research in a wide variety of situations. These systems allow observations to be quantified, permit statistical analyses, and allow researchers to compare results across different studies that used the same coding system.

When she used INTERSECT, Yepez was engaging in the technique of **systematic observation.** In systematic observation, the researcher uses a prearranged strategy for recording observations in which each observation is recorded using specific rules or guidelines, so that observations are more objective. For example, INTERSECT provides guidelines for scoring four kinds of responses teachers are likely to use when interacting with students: positive reinforcement, acceptance, remediation, and criticism. Each type has been carefully defined in a scoring manual, and many examples for coding behaviors are provided (Sadker & Sadker, 1982). Observers need to learn and practice the coding system thoroughly before they can actually use the system in a research setting, and the results should be reproducible by different trained observers. In Yepez's study, for instance, she and an assistant coded practice responses until they consistently generated identical coding results. (We will come back to this idea later.)

Occasionally, naturalistic observation is carried out in the laboratory. At times it is necessary to compare laboratory findings with behavior in natural settings to confirm the usefulness of the laboratory setting for a particular research topic. Because some behaviors may be distorted by bringing them into the laboratory setting, such behaviors are best observed where they occur naturally. Naturalistic observation provides a wealth of descriptive information, but this research method does not lend itself to testing causal antecedents of behavior. We would not know, for example, why the single teacher in Yepez's study treated men somewhat differently than women.

A further limitation of naturalistic observation is that we are dealing with specific samples of time that may or may not contain the behaviors we wish to observe. If we bring our study into the laboratory, we may be able to create conditions to elicit the behavior of interest within a very circumscribed time and space. But when we do this, we must be aware of the possibility that behaviors in the laboratory setting may not be the same as they are in the real world. We may find that behaviors become very different when the subjects know they are being watched. This effect, the tendency of subjects to alter their behavior or responses when they are aware of the presence of an observer, is known as **reactivity.** We may even find that subjects try to guess the purpose of the study so that they may either confirm the researcher's expectations or sabotage the results. (We will discuss these issues further in later chapters.)

Clearly, it is important for observers to remain as unobtrusive as possible in field research. Researchers can make themselves less obtrusive by hiding behind a duck blind, by observing from behind a one-way mirror, or by blending in with the social surroundings so that they are not noticed. Many times behavioral indicators can be observed without the subject's knowledge; such indicators are called **unobtrusive measures.** The amount of wear and tear on your textbook, for example, could indicate how much time you spend studying. The number of candy bar wrappers in your garbage could indicate your penchant for sweets. Your physical distance from another person could indicate how much attraction you feel toward that person. Frequently, researchers make inferences about behavior from observations of aspects of the environment. For example, a researcher could study the traffic pattern in a supermarket by assessing the frequency of replacement of floor tiles in each aisle (or even the wear and tear on tiles in different parts of the store). The subjects—shoppers—would never know their behaviors were being measured. Unobtrusive measures are often preferred over conspicuous measurement techniques (obtrusive measures) because unobtrusive measures overcome the potential for reactivity. (Do you know someone who would skip certain aisles at the supermarket, like the junk food or candy aisle, if they knew a researcher was watching? We do!)

Participant-observer Studies

One special kind of field observation is the **participant-observer study.** Here the researcher actually becomes part of the group being studied. Sometimes this is the only method that can be used to study a group—particularly if the group would not reasonably be expected to cooperate voluntarily with a research investigation. Typically, group members are not told that they are part of a study. Clearly, once their presence is known, researchers run the risk that subjects' behavior may change merely because an observer is present. In some groups, disclosure might lead to being ousted (or perhaps worse). Participant-observer studies usually do not include systematic observation or measurement techniques. Instead, the data gathered tend to be *qualitative* (the researcher's impressions are merely described, as they were in Wheeler's study). Participant-observers are typically trying to gather as much information and detail as they can. Where would this kind of study fall in Figure 3-1?

As you might imagine, some very useful information can be gathered using this method. Recent participant-observer studies have centered around such topics as ethnic identity in an urban high school, homelessness, self-actualization in a spiritual community, and urban crack addicts. Clearly, each of these issues would be difficult to study in more typical ways. But the participant-observer needs to remain aware of the strong possibility that the mere presence of an observer can alter subjects' behaviors in unknown ways. And sometimes observers in these studies find it difficult to remain objective and unbiased: Often, particularly if friendships form, it is hard to remain an objective scientist.

It has probably occurred to you that observational studies occasion special ethical concerns, and participant-observer studies are particularly problematic. Therefore, a great deal of thought needs to go into observational research before it is conducted. Are you invading the privacy of others? Is it ethical not to tell people they are being studied? Is it ethical to pretend to be a real group member? Is your observation going to make an important contribution to psychological knowledge? Keep in mind the ethical guidelines from Chapter 2. If you were a subject in your own study, how would you feel about it? When it comes to observational research, opinions from an institutional review board can be especially valuable for weighing these issues objectively.

Conducting a Field Study

The wide range of techniques that may be used in field studies is illustrated by the work of Bechtol and Williams (1977). These researchers were interested in studying California litter. They noticed that unregulated coastline areas attract large numbers of beachgoers, even though the supervised state beaches are considerably cleaner. They set out to determine who were the users of the unregulated beaches, whether there was a pattern to the littering that occurs on such a beach, and how users of the beach felt about sunbathing in the midst of debris. They employed several of the techniques common in field studies.

Bechtol and Williams spent two years observing activities on an unregulated beach in Southern California. They used *naturalistic observation* to determine who used the beach: They simply watched and recorded what sorts of people appeared. They saw that young people were the principal users. By using an *unobtrusive measure* to assess the pattern of littering—collecting and counting all the cans left on the beach—they assessed behavior without their subjects' knowledge. From the number of cans in the sand, they inferred that people litter the beach. There was no need to see anyone litter. As we might expect, Bechtol and Williams found that littering was greatest during the summer, when beach use was greatest.

In addition to observation, Bechtol and Williams approached people on the beach and asked them how they felt about the condition of the beach. At this point the researchers deviated from naturalistic observation. Instead of continuing to remain inconspicuous, the researchers interviewed people to get

FIGURE 3-3 In this setting, thoughts about littering are probably far away.
Bachmann/PhotoEdit

their views. Their findings were intriguing: First, users of the beach reported being disturbed about its littered condition. Second, all the people interviewed reported that *they* always took their own trash with them when they left—although, in two years of observation, the researchers never saw a single person do so. This study is an excellent example of why interviews and questionnaires (discussed below) should be supplemented with objective observations, including unobtrusive measures, whenever possible.

As with the other approaches we have discussed so far in this chapter, the field study does not involve direct manipulation of conditions: Behaviors are observed and recorded as they occur in the natural setting, and subjects may be interviewed in the "wild," where the contaminating effects of a laboratory setting are absent. It is a useful way of gathering many types of data, particularly when the researcher is studying behavior like littering, which we might not see in the laboratory. Note that a field study is not to be confused with a *field experiment*. A field experiment is a true experiment (the antecedent conditions are manipulated) that is conducted outside the laboratory. A clever example of a field experiment is described in Box 3-3.

Survey Research

We are all familiar with surveys because we are exposed to them all the time: telephone surveys, election polls, television ratings, product surveys.

BOX 3-3

A FIELD EXPERIMENT IN CHICAGO

An example of a field experiment conducted in seven suburban Chicago-area bars is provided by Cunningham (1989). Cunningham trained several college students to approach opposite-sex bar patrons at random, delivering one of several different kinds of conversation-starters ("lines"). The positivity of each patron's response to the line was surreptitiously measured. Cunningham discovered that women were much more sensitive to the kind of line an opposite-sex person delivered than were men. Women responded more positively to lines that were either self-disclosing or ordinary, like a simple "Hi," than they did to a flippantly delivered line like, "You remind me of someone I used to date," or "Bet I can outdrink you." Men, however, did not appear to care which kind of conversational gambit a woman used; they responded equally positively to all three. It is sometimes possible to achieve high degrees of both external and internal validity, as Cunningham did, by conducting actual experiments in the field. We will return to field experiments in later chapters about experimental approaches.

FIGURE 3-4 Could some of these happy-looking people actually be subjects in a field experiment? Spencer Grant/Stock, Boston

Survey research is a useful way of obtaining information about people's opinions, attitudes, preferences, and experiences simply by asking them. Surveys can allow us to gather data about experiences, feelings, thoughts, and motives that are hard to observe directly. Survey data can be useful for making inferences about behavior, although they do not allow us to test hypotheses about causal relationships directly. They are used in conjunction with many kinds of research designs, in the field and in the laboratory (we will see many applications of surveys throughout the text), but they can be particularly important in field research.

Surveys can allow us to gather large amounts of data efficiently. Surveys, of course, are low in the manipulation of antecedents (in Figure 3-1), but they are considered high in the imposition of units. In surveys, we limit subjects' inputs to a very narrow range of responses; we only allow them to answer the questions we pose to them. Written questionnaires and interviews are the two most common survey techniques in psychology research. *Questionnaires* can be handed out or sent through the mail; *interviews* can be face-to-face or over the telephone. The generalizability of survey and interview results is determined in large part by the procedures we use to select our subjects, so we will go into detail about alternative sampling procedures later in the chapter.

Interviews and Questionnaires

Interviews and questionnaires are important techniques for field research. The kinds of interviews and questionnaires used in field studies commonly include an assortment of open-ended and closed questions. *Closed questions* take the form of "Do you smoke?" "Should there be a ban on nuclear energy?" and "On a scale from 1 to 10, how much do you like Madonna?" Closed questions must be answered by one of a limited number of alternatives. *Open questions* solicit information about opinions and feelings by asking the question in such a way that the person must respond with more than a yes, no, or 1–10 rating. Examples of open questions are "Why do you prefer powdered detergents over liquids?" and "What made you decide to come for treatment now?"

By asking a combination of questions, the researcher can gather a great deal of useful information. Open questions can often be used to clarify or expand upon answers to closed questions. Let's look at an example. In a questionnaire or interview designed to study attitudes of 11-year-olds toward cartoon violence, you might begin by asking a closed question: "On the average, how much time do you spend watching Saturday morning cartoons?" You could allow the children to respond to one of the following options: "Less than an hour"   "Between one and two hours"   "Between two and four hours"   "More than four hours." This could be followed up with one or more open questions: "Why do you like to watch cartoons?" "What do you think about characters who hit each other?" "What kinds of things might cause you to hit someone?" However, unless you are simply going to describe people's responses verbatim, you will need to quantify the answers in some way.

Answers to closed questions are much simpler to quantify than open questions. For example, you could simply report the number (or percent) of children who gave each of the four possible responses to the closed question about cartoon viewing time. (Statistical analysis has further measurement and scaling requirements; see Chapter 6.) To quantify answers to open questions, however, a system must be designed to evaluate and categorize the content of each answer. This process, called **content analysis,** is similar to coding behaviors using systematic observational techniques. In a content analysis, responses are assigned to categories according to objective rules or guidelines.

Suppose that the children's responses to the open question, "What kinds of things might cause you to hit someone?" appeared to fall into six categories: (1) Someone looked at me funny, (2) Someone said something to me that I didn't like, (3) Someone wouldn't give me what I wanted, (4) Someone took something away from me, (5) Someone hit me first, and (6) Other responses. You could evaluate each response and code it into the proper category; then you could report the frequency of each kind of response. You can probably think of other categorization schemes that could be constructed for the children's responses: low, moderate, or strong provocation; physical or nonphysical provocation; the number of provocations mentioned by each child; and so forth.

Constructing items properly can take a great deal of skill; there are books devoted entirely to this topic.[2] Here are some tips for getting started: Keep items simple, and keep people involved. Many problems come about because subjects do not understand the meaning of a certain question. Maybe you used words they did not understand. Perhaps your sentences were too complex and included several ideas at once. Ambiguous or incomprehensible questions cannot generate useful data. Get subjects involved right away by asking interesting questions. If you are collecting demographic information (people's vital statistics), consider placing those questions later.

Make sure your questions are not value laden. Do not word your questions in ways that would make a positive (or negative) response seem embarrassing or undesirable. Consider how different the following two questions sound, even though both were designed to measure attitudes toward abortion:

Version 1: Do you believe doctors should be allowed to kill unborn babies during the first trimester of pregnancy?

Version 2: Do you believe doctors should be allowed to terminate a pregnancy during the first trimester?

Clearly, a person unopposed to abortion would find it much more difficult to answer yes to the first question simply because of the way it is worded. Be sure to keep the ethical guidelines in mind when you write survey questions.

If you are using a written questionnaire, be sure the instructions are simple and clear. If you are sending a questionnaire in the mail, be sure to include a polite and professional cover letter (and include a stamped, self-addressed envelope). Make sure your questionnaire and return procedures protect sub-

---

[2]Dillman's book, *Mail and Telephone Surveys: The Total Design Method* (1978), is a rich source of information on all aspects of designing and using questionnaires.

jects' anonymity. Unless you have contacted people in advance about your survey and they have agreed to fill it out, do not expect that everyone will fill out and return your questionnaire. Always keep track of the number of people who do not return the questionnaires; you will need to report it.

If the nonreturn rate is high, interpreting your results can be difficult indeed. Suppose you designed a questionnaire to gather data about drug use and only 40% of the subjects returned it. Suppose, also, that 99% of the returned questionnaires were from people who reported they had never smoked marijuana (one or two said they had smoked, but never inhaled). Would it be reasonable to conclude that 99% of people had never smoked pot? Probably not. On sensitive issues, some subjects just won't answer, particularly if their answer would indicate they had engaged in socially undesirable, deviant, or illegal activities. Individuals will differ in their willingness to give socially undesirable responses (Crowne & Marlowe, 1964). (We will talk more about this issue in Chapter 6.) Any time that nonreturn rates are high, be aware that the people who returned the questionnaire may be different in some way from the ones who did not. You will need to be extremely cautious here in drawing conclusions.

If you are handing out your questionnaire in person, consider the possibility of reactivity. If possible, let subjects fill out the questionnaire in private. Weigh the pros and cons of group sessions. Even though it is a lot easier to collect data from many people at once, subjects may not take your survey as seriously in a group setting. Also consider whether sensitive questions would cause more embarrassment in group sessions. And unless the group consists of complete strangers, you are likely to find that your subjects spend as much time talking to each other as they do filling out your questionnaire.

Response Styles

Sometimes subjects' own personal characteristics may inadvertently alter the way they answer questions, and this creates a special problem whenever we gather data through interviews, questionnaires, or other written tests to which the individuals can respond selectively. **Response styles** are tendencies to respond to questions or test items in specific ways, regardless of the content (Cronbach, 1950; Rorer, 1965). For example, people differ in response styles, such as willingness to answer, position preferences, and yea-saying and nay-saying. These response styles need to be considered and, if possible, controlled for when designing questions.

First, be aware that people differ in their **willingness to answer** questions they are unsure about. Willingness to answer comes into play whenever questions require specific knowledge about facts or issues. When unsure, some people will leave questions blank; others will take a guess. An unwillingness to answer is often a problem in questionnaire or survey research. Subjects may omit answers to key questions, making both scoring and interpretation difficult. Some researchers attempt to control for this factor by explicitly telling subjects to guess if they are not sure of the answer to a question. Other researchers say nothing—and hope for the best. There is no

TABLE 3-1 Possible Items on a Personality Scale

1. I feel happy most of the time.
2. I enjoy being with other people.
3. I dislike paying attention to details.
4. When I can, I avoid noisy places.
5. Sometimes I feel frightened for no apparent reason.

hard-and-fast rule; each researcher must think this through and decide how best to handle it.

If your questions are multiple choice, response styles can influence the selection of answers. When in doubt about the right answer on a multiple-choice exam, perhaps you always answer *b*. This is an example of a **position preference**.[3] Because of position preferences, sophisticated test builders vary the arrangement of correct answers throughout a test. Most questionnaires and interviews are not tests with right or wrong answers, but you need to keep position preference in mind anyway as you design your questions. In a multiple-choice survey gathering data about attitudes toward abortion, for instance, do not always put "pro-choice" responses as option *b*.

A third kind of response style shows up in answers to statements like those in Table 3-1. Would you say that each is true or false for you? The items are similar to ones you might find on the Minnesota Multiphasic Personality Inventory (MMPI), a test made up of a long series of items of this type. The way you answer the items on the test can tell a psychologist various things about your personality—for instance, whether you are anxious or depressed. At first glance, the way people answer such questions seems straightforward; a person who feels happy ought to answer "True" to the first item. We would expect subjects to respond to the **manifest content** of the questions, the plain meaning of the words that actually appear on the page. When we give a questionnaire or other paper-and-pencil test, we are usually interested in the manifest content of the items. "Have you ever visited another country?" means just that; the manifest content of the item is simply foreign travel. Most people would answer based on their actual travel histories. However, researchers have noticed that some interesting things can happen when subjects fill out questionnaires—especially when the questionnaires ask about feelings or attitudes. Some subjects seem to respond to questions in a consistent way: They will answer "Yes" or "True" to most items, or they will say "No" or "False" to most items. Some subjects are yea-sayers; others are nay-sayers. **Yea-sayers** are apt to agree with a question regardless of its manifest content. **Nay-sayers** tend to disagree no matter what they are asked.

---

[3]Even rats learning to run mazes are known to show position preferences. For example, if a food reward always requires a right turn into a white corridor, animals with a preference to turn right will have an advantage. Researchers control for this effect by varying the position of the white corridor so that the animal must sometimes go left, sometimes right.

TABLE 3-2 The Unfounded Optimism Inventory

Version A: No Control for Response Style			Version B: Controlling for Response Style*		
1. I know that everything will be all right.	<u>Yes</u>	NO	1. I know that everything will be all right.	<u>Yes</u>	NO
2. I can pick the fastest line at the bank.	<u>Yes</u>	NO	2. I always stand in the slowest line at the bank.	YES	<u>No</u>
3. I often smile at nothing.	<u>Yes</u>	NO	3. I rarely smile, even when provoked.	YES	<u>No</u>
4. If I lose money, I expect it to be returned.	<u>Yes</u>	NO	4. If I lose money, I expect it to be returned.	<u>Yes</u>	NO

*The yes/no responses are also counterbalanced to control for order effects.

Clearly, a yea-saying or nay-saying response style can pose a question about validity: Are we really measuring what we set out to measure? How can we avoid this problem? One way is by designing questions that force the subject to think more about the answer (Warwick and Lininger, 1975). For instance, think about the difference between these two items:

Do you agree or disagree that the cost of living has gone up in the last year?

In your opinion have prices gone up, gone down, or stayed about the same the past year, or don't you know?

When we phrase questions to have simple yes/no or agree/disagree answers, we make it easy for subjects to respond based on response style. By building some specific content into the options, we encourage subjects to give more thought to each choice.

If we must use yes/no questions, we can still take some precautions. Table 3-2 shows two versions of the Unfounded Optimism Inventory (UOI). The "optimistic" choice is underlined for each item. All the items in version *A* are written so that the optimistic response is a yes response. Subjects who are yea-sayers would score high on unfounded optimism—even if they happen to be somewhat pessimistic. Now look at version *B*. To get a high unfounded optimism score, a subject would have to give both yes and no answers. Using version *B* would give more valid answers; subjects who turned up high on unfounded optimism are probably not pessimistic yea-sayers.

If you decide to ask questions in face-to-face interviews, there are two more important things to keep in mind: establishing rapport and maintaining interviewer consistency. The interviewer's appearance and bearing can affect the ways subjects will respond. The more sensitive the questions, the more important the interviewer's demeanor becomes. To get honest answers to sensitive questions, the interviewer will need to spend time first winning the subject's confidence and establishing trust. Remember that even subtle changes in the interviewer's behavior or tone of voice can influence subjects' responses; your questions must be asked the same way each time. To achieve the necessary consistency requires a lot of practice. You will also need to decide whether your interview will be structured, unstructured, or a little of both. In a structured interview, the same questions are asked in precisely the same way each time—deviations from this structure are not permitted. Structured interviews provide more usable, quantifiable data. Unstructured interviews are more free flowing; the interviewer is free to explore interesting issues as they come up, but the information may not be usable for a content analysis or statistics.

Sampling

Regardless of how you conduct your survey, one of the most critical issues is **sampling.** Selecting subjects is an important part of any research regardless of its design, and it is a particularly critical issue in survey research. First, the researcher must decide who or what the subjects will be. (See Box 3-4 for an interesting approach.) Ideally, when we conduct research, we would include all the members of the population we wish to study. The **population** consists of all people, animals, or objects that have at least one characteristic in common—for example, all undergraduates form one population; all nursing home residents form another; all jelly beans form still another. Clearly, it is almost never possible to study the entire population; instead we rely on samples.

A **sample of subjects** is a group that is a *subset* of the population of interest. Data collected from samples can be used to draw inferences about a population without examining all its members. In this way pollsters like Gallup are able to make predictions about the outcome of important elections. Different samples may produce very different data. How accurately we can generalize our findings from a given sample to a population depends on its **representativeness,** or how closely the sample mirrors the larger population—more precisely, how closely the *sample responses* we observe and measure reflect those we would obtain if we could sample the entire population. We would be very wrong about the percentage of votes going to a candidate if we based our predictions on a preelection sample that included only Democrats! There are two general sampling approaches: probability sampling and nonprobability sampling.

Probability Sampling

Probability refers to the study of the likelihood of events. What are your chances of rolling a 7 with a pair of dice? What are your chances of winning the lottery today? What are your chances of being selected for a survey sample? Probability is a quantitative discipline; to study probabilities, we must be able to count events and possible outcomes. From a theoretical standpoint, some form of probability sampling is the preferred means of selecting subjects for research. **Probability sampling** involves selecting subjects in such a way that the odds of their being in the study are known or can be calculated. We

B O X   3 - 4

ARCHIVAL STUDIES

Many opportunities for field research can be found in survey data that have been collected for other purposes and stored in data archives. A wealth of statistical data is collected by government and private agencies, hospitals, businesses, schools, and so on. Information about such things as crime and death rates, education levels, salaries, housing patterns, and disease rates are accessible to researchers. There are also archives housing data from scientific research surveys, some using large probability samples. In addition to demographic information, some of these surveys include information collected about people's attitudes. This information can be used to analyze societal trends or to gather information about population subgroups. A university librarian is a good place to begin if you want to use archival data. There may be a charge to use them, but it can be well worth the investment. It is also possible to conduct archival research on popular culture at low cost by using other kinds of existing materials (films, newspapers, and magazines, for instance).[4]

In an interesting use of archival data, Bowman (1992) studied some controversial issues about African-American men—namely, documented discouragement over barriers to employment and problems with family roles—from a positive perspective. His study looked at factors related to facilitative, adaptive coping mechanisms in a sample of 372 African-American men who were responsible husbands and fathers. To gather data, he accessed a national data bank archived at the University of Michigan. Data were originally collected in 1979–1980 by face-to-face interviews with 2107 African Americans residing in different parts of the United States. Bowman found that kinship bonds and religious beliefs were stronger in men who were happy in their family roles, and he suggested that family closeness and religion *might* help to mediate family role difficulties. Because this was a correlational study (discussed in Chapter 4), causal inferences cannot be justified. However, valuable information for further study on these important issues was gained (without the great expense of finding the kind of subjects he wanted and traveling all across the country to interview them) by accessing and reanalyzing information from existing data archives in a creative new way.

---

[4]To find out more about archival research, see Judd, Smith, and Kidder, *Research Methods in Social Relations* (1991).

begin by defining the population we wish to study. For example, our target population might be all women born in 1965 and now living in Seattle, Washington. (It would take time, but we could count them and establish each woman's odds of being in the sample.) A second condition for probability sampling is that the researcher must use an unbiased method for selecting subjects (such as flipping a coin or drawing a number out of a hat). This process is called **random selection,** meaning that the outcome of the sampling procedure cannot be predicted ahead of time by any known law (Kerlinger, 1973). Random selection is also a common assumption of the statistical tests used most often to analyze data. Now let us look at *three* types of probability samples—simple random sample, stratified random sample, and cluster sample.

Simple Random Sampling

The most basic form of probability sampling is the **simple random sample,** whereby a portion of the whole population is selected in an unbiased way. Huff (1954) described the basic procedure in these colorful terms:

> If you have a barrel of beans, some red and some white, there is only one way to find out exactly how many of each color you have: Count 'em. However, you can find out approximately how many are red in much easier fashion by pulling out a handful of beans and counting just those, figuring that the proportion will be the same all through the barrel. (p. 13)

Through random sampling we can find out about what the population is like without studying everyone. To obtain a simple random sample, *all members of the population being studied must have an equal chance of being selected.* If there are 1 million people in the population, the chance of any particular person being selected should equal one in a million. Even then, using random selection procedures does not guarantee that our sample will be truly representative of the whole population. Suppose someone put all the white beans into Huff's barrel first. If he took his sample from the top, he might conclude incorrectly that the barrel contained only red beans. Random sampling yields an *estimate* of what is likely to be true.

Stratified Random Sampling

When the population is known to contain distinct subgroups, researchers often prefer another variation of probability sampling known as stratified random sampling. A **stratified random sample** is obtained by randomly sampling from people in each subgroup in the same proportions as they exist in the population. Here is an example. A particular factory is made up of 10% managers and 90% production workers. If you wanted to measure employee morale in this plant, it would be desirable to use stratified random sampling. Managers and production workers may not have the same feelings about the company. If you wanted a stratified sample of 100 employees, you could randomly select 90 production-line workers (90%) and 10 managers (10%). Then your sample would reflect the makeup of the entire staff. A simple random sample could result in a sample that included only production-line workers. By using stratified random sampling to include management, you ensure that their views are represented in the data.

A researcher conducting a survey of urban attitudes might use stratified random sampling to mirror ethnic differences. A market researcher might use it to represent various age and income groups more accurately. There are two advantages to stratified sampling: First, the subsets are sampled separately so that important minorities or subgroups are represented in the total. Second, different procedures can be used with different subgroups to maximize the utility of the data (Warwick & Lininger, 1975). This strategy is desirable when the various subgroups are likely to respond differently.[5]

Cluster Sampling

When the population of interest is very large, it is often too costly or impractical to randomly select subjects one by one. In such cases researchers may use another form of probability sampling called **cluster sampling.** Instead of sampling individuals from the whole population or from subgroups, they sample entire *clusters,* or naturally occurring groups, that exist within the population. As with all forms of probability sampling, participants are randomly selected, but whole groups of people are selected rather than individuals. Suppose you wanted to survey attitudes about the education system in Connecticut. It would be very expensive and time consuming to randomly sample all 28 million people. Instead you could randomly select clusters that already exist, such as zip code areas, school districts, cities, or counties. If you selected six counties at random, then everyone in those six counties would be surveyed.

The main advantage of cluster sampling is that the researcher can sample data efficiently from relatively few locations. A potential disadvantage of this approach is that subjects within clusters may resemble one another. The people in one county, for instance, may be quite similar in economic status, education, race, and even age. For that reason, it is desirable to sample many clusters and to obtain as large a sample as possible.

Some form of probability sampling is generally preferred for research purposes because it increases the external validity of the study. Probability samples are more representative of the population, so research conclusions have greater generalizability. There are, however, other ways of selecting samples, which fall under the heading of nonprobability samples.

Nonprobability Sampling

It is sometimes impossible to use the kinds of procedures we have just described, despite their advantages. Even though random selection of subjects

---

[5]When conducting surveys, researchers need to be particularly sensitive to cultural differences among subgroups in the population. Will questions be equally understandable and have the same meaning for all subgroups? Are there language problems or other barriers to communication that need to be overcome? Cross-cultural researchers have emphasized that unless researchers are very familiar with each subgroup, their survey items may not be assessing what they intend (e.g., Lonner, 1990).

is accepted as a cornerstone of good research, many surveys and other kinds of studies are based on nonprobability samples. As the name implies, in **nonprobability sampling** the subjects are not chosen at random. Let us look at two common examples of nonprobability samples—quota and convenience.

Quota Sampling

In **quota sampling,** researchers select samples through predetermined quotas that are intended to reflect the makeup of the population. Samples can reflect the proportions of important subgroups, but the individuals are not selected at random. For example, a newspaper may wish to document campus attitudes toward nuclear arms. A reporter is sent to a university with instructions to interview 40 students, half male, half female, since the student body is roughly half men, half women. There are no constraints on how the reporter selects people to interview as long as the quota is filled. Because the selection is not random, the resulting sample may or may not be a good representation of the college community. The reporter, for example, may arrive early in the morning and approach students gathered around the vending machines in the student union building. There are many sources of potential bias in this approach—students who have late classes are missing; those who have money for the vending machines may be overrepresented; the reporter may want to approach only those who appear most friendly and cooperative. Such samples have human interest value and are sometimes used in public opinion polls. However, quota sampling lacks the rigor required in scientific research and is low in external validity.

> The operation of a poll comes down in the end to a running battle against sources of bias, and this battle is conducted all the time by all reputable polling organizations. What the reader of the reports must remember is that the battle is never won. No conclusion that "sixty-seven per cent of the American people are against" something should be read without the lingering question, Sixty-seven per cent of which American people? (Huff, 1954, p. 22)

Convenience Sampling

Convenience sampling is obtained by using any groups who happen to be available—for example, a church choir, a psychology class, a bowling league, or a supermarket checkout line. This is considered a weak form of sampling because the researcher exercises no control over the representativeness of the sample. Despite this drawback, convenience sampling (also called *accidental sampling*) is probably done more often than any other kind. It is convenient, it is certainly less expensive than sampling the whole population at random, and it is usually faster. However, researchers who rely on accidental samples must be cautious in the conclusions they draw from their data. Accidental samples greatly limit any study's external validity. Whatever qualities distinguish choir members, classmates, or bowlers from the rest of the population may also lead to atypical research findings. It may not be valid to generalize observations beyond the group studied. Through random selection we have our best chance of obtaining a sample that is representative of the whole population (see Box 3-5).

B O X   3 - 5

USING RANDOM SELECTION

Suppose we want to collect data on beliefs about the relationship between regular exercise and "quality of life" among older persons. The population we are interested in studying is people over age 75. Clearly, we cannot study the entire population; what we want is a random representative sample. In practice, we often find that this goal cannot be achieved. We may, for example, only have access to the residents of one nursing home. Thus the "population" available for study is already a select group. Although we would ultimately like to make statements about the general population of older people, our sample must be taken from this smaller group.

Suppose there are 32 residents over age 75, but we only want to interview 20 subjects. Assuming that all the residents are willing to be interviewed, how do we decide which 20 will take part? We could simply ask everyone over 75 to report to the interview room and allow the first 20 arrivals to be in the study. But some residents may arrive later than others for a variety of reasons. Those who are new to the home might not know their way around the grounds and might take more time to find the correct room. General health may be a factor. Individuals who do not feel well may not want to walk to the interview room. Furthermore, there may be significant personality differences between those who get up early and those who sleep late. Thus, a sample of subjects based on arrival time may not be representative of the group as a whole; it would be biased to include a disproportionate number of healthy early risers who know their way around the building.

We can get a fairly good random sample of the nursing home residents if we write all the prospective subjects' names on small pieces of paper, put them into a hat, mix well, and draw them out one by one until we have as many as we need. The hat method is usually adequate, but it is not foolproof: A small variation in the size of the papers may bias the selection. The papers may not be mixed enough, so you draw out only names beginning with the letters M through Z, or only the last numbers you wrote. A better procedure might be to use the **random number table** (see Appendix B), a table of numbers generated by a computer so that every number to be used has an equal chance of being selected for each position in the table. Unlike the hat method, the computer-generated table is totally unbiased.

(continued)

(continued)

How do we use the random number table? We begin by assigning code numbers to all members of our subject pool. At the nursing home, we might simply number the subjects in the order they appear on an alphabetical list. If there are 32 people available, we assign them numbers 1 through 32. If we need only 20 subjects, we go through the random number table in an orderly manner (such as by reading vertically down each successive column of numbers) to find the first 20 numbers between 1 and 32 that appear in the table. Look at Appendix B, Table B1. Beginning at the top of the first column and reading down, we find the numbers 03, 16, and 12. All are between 1 and 32. So subjects 3, 16, and 12 will be in our sample. (The numbers 97 and 55 also appear in the first column, but since they are greater than 32, we ignore them.) We continue going through the table systematically until we have a total of 20 subjects. This group of 20 is a random sample of the 32 people available for the experiment. The starting point for each study should be decided in a blind manner. For instance, you might close your eyes and put your finger on a part of the table. You would begin your selection there.

Reporting Samples

The way a sample is chosen influences what can be concluded from the results. The research report must explain the type of sample used and how subjects were recruited, so that the results can be interpreted properly. After all, in many circumstances college students might respond differently than nursing home residents, and results obtained from one convenience sample might not be expected to generalize to everyone. So we need to tell the reader exactly how the sample was obtained. This includes identifying the specific population sampled (for example, college students), as well as giving an exact description of where and how subjects were obtained (for example, "The subjects were 60 undergraduates, 30 men and 30 women, at the University of Oregon who responded to an ad in the college newspaper"). Include gender, age, and other important demographic characteristics (education level, racial and ethnic heritage, socioeconomic status, etc.) *if* they could be important in interpreting the results.

Any details that might have influenced the type of subject participating in the study must be included. If subjects were paid for participating or students' participation fulfilled a course requirement, readers should be told that, too. Any limitations on who could participate should also be noted. In the nursing home example from Box 3-5, we might say:

The subjects were 20 (6 male and 14 female) randomly selected residents of the Valley Nursing Home in Elmtown, Ohio. To participate, subjects needed to be at least 75 years old and in good health. The average age was 77.3 years; the ages ranged from 75.2 years to 83.4 years.

Note that this statement immediately tells readers that, although we are discussing attitudes about the values of exercise in healthy older persons, our subjects were drawn at random from a very small pool. It also tells readers that we studied both men and women who fell within a particular age range.

Occasionally, some subjects who are selected are not included in the report: They dropped out, their data were discarded because they could not follow the instructions, and so on. These facts should also be reported. This may seem like a lot of information to report, but details about your sample are a critical component of all research, and they are of major importance in survey research. They give the reader the information necessary to evaluate the generalizability of the results or to compare the results of different studies. They are also necessary for replication. In the next chapter, we will learn about other nonexperimental designs—correlational and quasi-experimental designs—that provide additional techniques for describing relationships among behaviors and for investigating individual differences in attitudes, behavior, and personality.

SUMMARY

Research activities may be described along two dimensions: degree of manipulation of antecedent conditions and degree of constraint on subjects' responses. Laboratory experiments tend to fall at the high end of both dimensions, representing only a small portion of the possible research options. Nonexperimental designs tend to be low on the first dimension but vary from low to high on the second. This chapter covers four major nonexperimental approaches to data collection: phenomenology, case studies, field studies, and survey research. These approaches may be higher in *external validity* than laboratory experiments, but they are probably lower in *internal validity*.

Phenomenology is the description of one's own immediate experience. Rather than looking out at behaviors in the world, the phenomenological approach requires us to begin with our own experience as a source of data. Phenomenological data are limited in three major respects: Since we do not compare subjects under different conditions, we cannot make cause and effect statements about our experience. We have no way of knowing whether attending to our experience alters it; it may not be completely accurate or objective. Our experiences may or may not be generalizable to others.

The *case study* is used to study individuals. It is a descriptive record made by an outside observer of an individual's experiences and/or behaviors. Case studies are a useful source of ideas; they can lead to therapy techniques; they allow the study of rare phenomena; they demonstrate counterinstances; they can lead to more research. The record may be made systematically over a period of time or after the fact, as is often the case in clinical practice. This approach enables us to study a variety of life events we would not study experimentally.

Field studies are studies done in real-life settings. They allow us to explore behavior that we probably would not see in the laboratory. But these studies cannot be used to make inferences about cause and effect relationships. Field studies include a variety of techniques for collecting data. *Naturalistic observation,* the technique of observing events as they occur in their natural setting, is a common component of field research. During naturalistic observation, the observer remains unobtrusive so that the behaviors being observed are not altered by the presence of an intruder. This approach reduces subjects' *reactivity* and allows study of behaviors that would be distorted or absent in the laboratory. In another field technique, the *participant-observer study,* the researcher may interact with subjects as well as observe them to obtain information; this method is infrequently used.

Surveys (*questionnaires* and *interviews*) are frequently used in field studies, but can be part of many research designs. When designing questions, the researcher needs to consider *response styles,* such as *willingness to answer, position preference,* and *yea-saying/nay-saying. Sampling procedures* can be particularly important for studies using surveys. Some form of *probability sample* is preferred, but *convenience samples* are more frequently used.

KEY TERMS

Case study The descriptive record of an individual's experiences and/or behaviors kept by an outside observer.

Cluster sampling A form of probability sampling in which a researcher samples entire *clusters,* or naturally occurring groups, that exist within the population.

Content analysis A system for quantifying responses to open questions by categorizing them according to objective rules or guidelines.

Convenience sampling A convenience sample is obtained by using any groups who happen to be convenient; considered a weak form of sampling because the researcher exercises no control over the representativeness of the sample (also called *accidental sampling*).

Deviant case analysis An extension of the evaluative case study in which deviant individuals are compared with those who are not to isolate the significant variations between them.

External validity The degree to which research observations are generalizable or applicable to other settings and other people.

Field study A nonexperimental research method used in the field or in a real-life setting, typically employing a variety of techniques including naturalistic observation and unobtrusive measures or survey tools, such as questionnaires and interviews.

Internal validity The degree to which a researcher is able to state a causal relationship between antecedent conditions and the subsequent observed behavior.

Manifest content The plain meaning of the words or questions that actually appear on the page.

Naturalistic observation A descriptive, nonexperimental method of observing behaviors as they occur spontaneously in natural settings.

Nay-sayers People who are apt to disagree with a question regardless of its manifest content.

Nonprobability sampling Sampling procedures in which subjects are not chosen at random; two common examples are quota and convenience samples.

Participant-observer study A special kind of field observation in which the researcher actually becomes part of the group being studied.

Phenomenology A nonexperimental method of gathering data by attending to and describing one's own immediate experience.

Population All people, animals, or objects that have at least one characteristic in common.

Position preference When in doubt about answers to multiple-choice questions, some people always select a response in a certain position, such as answer *b*.

Probability sampling Selecting samples in such a way that the odds of any subject being selected for the study are known or can be calculated.

Quota sampling Selecting samples through predetermined quotas that are intended to reflect the makeup of the population; they can reflect the proportions of important population subgroups, but the particular individuals are not selected at random.

Random number table A table of numbers generated by a computer so that every number has an equal chance of being selected for each position in the table.

Random selection An unbiased method for selecting subjects in such a way that the outcome of the sampling procedure cannot be predicted ahead of time by any known law.

Reactivity The tendency of subjects to alter their behavior or responses when they are aware of the presence of an observer.

Representativeness The extent to which the sample responses we observe and measure reflect those we would obtain if we could sample the entire population.

Response style Tendency for subjects to respond to questions or test items in a specific way, regardless of the content.

Retrospective data Data collected in the present based on recollections of past events; apt to be inaccurate because of faulty memory, bias, mood, and situation.

Sample of subjects A selected subset of the population of interest.

Sampling Deciding who or what the subjects will be and selecting them.

Simple random sampling The most basic form of probability sampling whereby a portion of the whole population is selected in an unbiased way.

Stratified random sampling A form of probability sampling in which subjects are selected by randomly sampling from people in each important population subgroup in the same proportion as they exist in the population.

Survey research A useful way of obtaining data about people's opinions, attitudes, preferences, and experiences that are hard to observe directly; data may be obtained using questionnaires or interviews.

Systematic observation A system for recording observations; each observation is recorded using specific rules or guidelines, so observations are more objective.

Unobtrusive measure A procedure used to assess subjects' behaviors without their knowledge; used to obtain more objective data.

Willingness to answer The differences among people in their style of responding to questions they are unsure about; some people will leave these questions blank, whereas others will take a guess.

Yea-sayers People who are apt to agree with a question regardless of its manifest content.

REVIEW AND STUDY QUESTIONS

1. Describe each of these nonexperimental approaches and give an example of how each might be used:
   a. Phenomenology
   b. Case study
   c. Field study
   d. Survey research

2. What is meant by external validity? Why are nonexperimental studies often higher in external validity than true experiments?

3. What is meant by internal validity? Why are nonexperimental studies often lower in external validity?

4. What is retrospective data? Why is the use of retrospective data considered a shortcoming in scientific research?

5. What are unobtrusive measures?

6. Devise an unobtrusive measure to establish each of the following:
   a. Which professor at the university is the most popular?
   b. What are the most popular library books?
   c. Do people prefer to sit on the left or the right side of the theater when they go to the movies?
   d. If people find addressed letters with stamps on them, will they mail them?

7. Describe the difference between open and closed questions. How are open questions quantified?

8. Name three response styles and give an example of each. Explain how you would go about controlling for them when designing questions.

9. Explain the difference between probability sampling and nonprobability sampling and describe the different forms of each.

10. For each of the research topics listed here, indicate the type of nonexperimental approach that would be most useful and explain why. (You may find more than one approach potentially useful for some topics.)
    a. Pushing ahead in line
    b. Daydreaming
    c. Locating the most popular painting in an art gallery
    d. Sibling rivalry

    e. Studiousness in college students

    f. Determining whether a particular patient has improved with psychotherapy

11. For each of your answers to question 10, explain whether an experiment would generate more useful information than the nonexperimental method you selected. Would it be possible to set up experiments to explore all these problems? If not, why not?

12. Discuss the logic behind random selection and why it is important in research.

13. For each of the following populations, outline three different sampling approaches that would yield random samples:

    a. College seniors

    b. Readers of *Time* magazine

    c. Assembly-line workers

    d. Computer owners

14. Evaluate each of the following as a technique for obtaining a random sample of subjects.

    a. An experimenter obtains subjects by asking every third driver stopping at the stoplight on the corner of Hollywood and Vine streets in Los Angeles to be in an experiment.

    b. A researcher places an ad in a local paper asking for volunteers for a psychology experiment.

    c. An experimenter calls every fourth number in the phone book and asks for volunteers for a research project.

    d. A wealthy graduate student posts signs on the university bulletin boards offering $5 per hour for participating in a 2-hour perception experiment.

15. What is a random number table? How do you use it?

16. Using Table B1, the random number table in Appendix B of this book, select a random sample of 10 subjects from a subject pool of 20.

C H A P T E R   4

ALTERNATIVES TO EXPERIMENTATION: CORRELATIONAL AND QUASI-EXPERIMENTAL DESIGNS

In this chapter, we continue our discussion of nonexperimental designs. We will focus on two categories of nonexperimental research methods: correlational designs and quasi-experimental designs. Correlational designs are used to establish relationships among preexisting behaviors and can be used to predict one set of behaviors from others (such as predicting your college grades from your entrance examinations). They can show relationships between sets of antecedent conditions and behavioral effects (the relationship between smoking and lung cancer in humans, for instance), but, as you will see, the antecedents are preexisting. They are neither manipulated nor controlled by the researcher. Advanced correlational methods, however, such as path analysis and cross-lagged panel designs, can be used to *propose* cause and effect relationships by developing causal models. As with all nonexperimental methods, however, it is much more difficult to establish cause and effect relationships conclusively using correlational techniques.

When subjects cannot be randomly assigned to different treatment groups as they are in true experiments, researchers frequently select a quasi-experimental design. A quasi-experimental design can be used to demonstrate behavioral differences associated with different types of subjects (e.g., normal or schizophrenic children), naturally occurring situations (e.g., being raised in a one- or two-parent home), or a wide range of common or unusual events (e.g., the birth of a sibling or surviving a hurricane) that cannot be manipulated by an experimenter. In cases such as these, the experimenter wishes to study a set of preexisting antecedent conditions. Subjects are selected and placed into groups on the basis of the characteristic or circumstance that the experimenter wants to investigate; thus, the "treatments" are either selected life events or preexisting characteristics of individuals.

As you already know, manipulating antecedent conditions is frequently *not* an option for researchers. A behavior such as childhood schizophrenia certainly falls into the category of behaviors that may never lend themselves to true experimentation. We may never be able to fully explain behavioral disorders such as schizophrenia, but quasi-experimentation can increase our understanding of its associated environmental, biological, cognitive, and genetic characteristics, as well as its symptoms and manifestations. Quasi-experimentation often allows the researcher more systematic control over the situation than the designs from Chapter 3 and can be used in a wide variety of research settings—both in the field and in the laboratory.

Experimenters also use quasi-experimental designs whenever subjects cannot be assigned at random to receive different experimental manipulations or treatments. Suppose, for example, that a researcher wanted to compare the effects of fluorescent and incandescent lighting on worker productivity in two manufacturing companies. The researcher could manipulate the lighting conditions, installing fluorescents in Company A and incandescent light bulbs in Company B, but subjects would already by preassigned to receive a particular treatment. As the prefix *quasi-* implies, quasi-experimental designs can "almost seem like" experiments, but they are not because subjects have not been randomly assigned to the different treatment conditions of the experiment. If the researcher found that productivity differed in the two lighting conditions, it would be difficult to establish with certainty that the lighting treatments were the true cause—the workers themselves may have differed; or other working conditions influencing productivity may have differed dramatically in the two manufacturing plants. Quasi-experiments can seem to have all the trappings of a true experiment, but unless other antecedents that can influence productivity are carefully controlled, the experiment will not be high in internal validity.

Recall from the last chapter that *internal validity* is our ability to establish a causal relationship between a specified set of antecedent conditions (treatments) and the subsequent observed behavior. It is the degree to which a research design allows us to make cause and effect statements. Research is high in internal validity if we can conclude with a high degree of confidence that the specified set of antecedents—and not something else, such as differences in the subjects—caused the observed differences in behavior among the various groups of subjects in the experiment. Using quasi-experiments, the researcher can explore consistent differences between preexisting groups of people or compare treatments in nonrandom groups of subjects, but the cause of behavioral differences cannot be established with confidence. As a group, correlational designs and quasi-experiments tend to be higher in *external validity,* or generalizability, than laboratory experiments. But external validity must be assessed on a case-by-case basis.

Returning to the two-dimensional scheme we used in the last chapter (in Figure 3-1), we could say that correlations are low in the manipulation of antecedents. As our examples have shown, quasi-experiments will vary in the degree of manipulation of antecedents, but without random assignment they are not considered high. Both correlational and quasi-experimental designs, however, tend to be high in the imposition of units. They restrict, or limit, the responses subjects may contribute to the data being collected. In both types of designs, researchers are typically interested in obtaining only specific kinds of information from each subject. Both methods rely on statistical data analyses, which allow the significance, or meaningfulness, of results to be evaluated objectively. Some of these designs use correlational analyses; others use inferential statistics (like the *t* tests and analyses of variance covered in Chapters 13 and 14). Some designs (like path analysis), use sophisticated correlational techniques to create causal models, although each has limited internal validity. Let us begin with correlational designs first.

CORRELATIONAL DESIGNS

Frequently, we wish to go beyond describing our observations to provide a statistical summary of what we have seen. There are a great many ways to describe the data of nonexperimental studies. One approach, correlation, is so common in nonexperimental studies that it is discussed as a research method in its own right. Correlation can be used with both laboratory and field data.

Correlation

You already know that some questions cannot be answered experimentally for practical and ethical reasons. Questions such as, "What are the long-term effects of TV violence on aggressiveness?" fall into this category. To find the answer experimentally, it would be necessary for researchers to manipulate childrens' exposure to TV violence for many years while controlling for other potential influences on aggressiveness—clearly an impossible (and unethical) task. Instead, you might consider conducting a correlational study.

A **correlational study** is one that is designed to determine the **correlation**, or degree of relationship, between two traits, behaviors, or events. When two things are correlated, changes in one are associated with changes in another. Researchers often use correlational studies to explore behaviors that are not yet well understood. By measuring many behaviors and seeing which go together, we begin to see possible explanations for behaviors. With the widespread availability of computers, researchers can measure and analyze the relationships among countless numbers of variables in a single study. (Incidentally, a *variable* is any observable behavior, characteristic, or event that can vary or have different values.) Although this shotgun approach is not always the most elegant research strategy, it may have *heuristic* value, aiding us in the discovery of important influences on behavior. Correlational data may serve as the basis for new experimental hypotheses, as we shall see in Chapter 5.

In a correlational study, selected traits or behaviors of interest are measured first. Numbers (i.e., scores) are recorded that represent the measured variables. Next, the degree of relationship, or correlation, between the numbers is determined through statistical procedures. However, correlation is really a technique for summarizing data that could be used in studies falling in any portion of our graphic scheme. In the correlational study, the researcher measures events without attempting to alter the antecedent conditions in any way; she or he is simply asking how well the measures go together. Correlational studies thus fall in the low-high portion of Figure 3-1 in Chapter 3. Once the correlation is known, it can be used to make predictions. If we know a person's score on one measure, we can make a better prediction of that person's score on another measure that is highly related to it. The higher the correlation, the more accurate our prediction will be.

Suppose a researcher wonders whether there is a relationship between television viewing and the size of people's vocabularies. The researcher could gather data to determine whether such a relationship exists. First, he or she would devise an objective measure of vocabulary. Depending on time, resources, and the subjects' patience, either a standardized test or an improvised procedure might be used. For instance, the researcher might ask subjects to go through a dictionary and check off all the words that are familiar. The researcher would also carefully measure daily television viewing time. The degree of relationship, or correlation, between the two measures would then be assessed through statistical procedures.

Relationships between pairs of scores from each subject are known as *simple correlations.* The Pearson Product-Moment Correlation Coefficient (r) is the most commonly used procedure for calculating simple correlations; you will see the Pearson r reported in most correlational studies. When r is computed, three general outcomes are possible: a positive relationship, a negative relationship, or no relationship.[1] These are illustrated in Figure 4-1. Because of the way the statistic is computed, *the values of a correlation coefficient can only vary between* −1.00 *and* +1.00. The sign (plus or minus) tells us the positive or negative *direction* of the relationship; the absolute value of r (the unsigned value) tells us the *strength* of the relationship. Correlation coefficients can be depicted on a number line going from −1.00 to +1.00 (we always carry correlation coefficients out to two decimal places).

You will notice that a collection of dots is shown in each section of Figure 4-1. These dots illustrate what researchers call **scatterplots** (or scattergrams), visual representations of the scores belonging to each subject in the study. Each dot stands for one subject, and each subject has two scores—one for TV viewing time and one for vocabulary. One score is used to place the dot along the X (horizontal) axis. The second score is used to place the dot along the Y (vertical) axis.

Scatterplots are often the researcher's first step toward analyzing correlational data. As you can see, the arrangement of dots gives a rough indication of both the direction and strength of relationship that has been measured. Figure 4-1 depicts three possible correlational outcomes for the TV viewing and vocabulary study. In Figure 4-1(a), the scatterplot shows that as viewing increased, vocabulary also increased (a positive relationship). In Figure 4-1(b), as viewing increased, vocabulary declined (a negative relationship). In Figure 4-1(c), the dots form no particular pattern (no strong relationship). This is reflected in the value of the computed r, which is quite small (+.02).

The lines drawn on the scatterplots are called **regression lines,** or lines of best fit. They illustrate the mathematical equation[2] that best describes the

---

[1] This discussion is limited to linear, or straight-line, relationships. The Pearson r does not measure nonlinear relationships.

[2] These equations, called *regression equations,* can be used as formulas to predict one score from the other.

FIGURE 4-1 Some hypothetical relationships between size of vocabulary and length of daily TV viewing: (a) a positive (direct) relationship; (b) a negative (inverse) relationship; (c) no strong relationship.

relationship between the two measured scores. The direction of the line corresponds to the direction of the relationship. As you can see, the position of the line changes as the correlation changes.

When the computed value of r is positive, there is a **positive correlation** between vocabulary and TV viewing time; the more a person watches television, the larger his or her vocabulary. This is also called a *direct relationship*. The absolute (unsigned) value of r tells us how strong the relationship is. If $r = +1.00$, we have a perfect positive correlation, and we can predict the value of one measure with complete accuracy if we know a subject's score on the other measure. Positive values of r that are less than $+1.00$ (for example, $+.52$) tell us there is a direct relationship between our two measures, but we cannot predict the value of one from the other with complete accuracy because the relationship between them is imperfect. If the value of r is relatively small (for example, $+.02$), our prediction may be no more accurate than any random guess. In that event the correlation would not be very useful.

A second possibility is a **negative correlation** between vocabulary and TV viewing time (that is, r is negative). This would mean that the more a person watches television, the smaller his or her vocabulary. This is also called an *inverse relationship.* One of the most difficult concepts to grasp about correlations is that *the direction of the relationship (positive or negative) does not affect our ability to predict scores.* We could predict vocabulary just as well from a negative correlation as from a positive one, provided that the strength of the relationships was the same. You will recall that the strength of the relationship is indexed by the absolute (or unsigned) value of r. A correlation of $r = -.34$ actually represents a stronger relationship than $r = +.16$. The sign merely tells us whether the relationship is direct or inverse; the absolute value tells us how strong it is. As the absolute value gets larger, we can make more and more accurate predictions of a person's score on one measure when we know the person's score on the other.

A third possibility is no relationship between vocabulary and TV viewing time (r is near zero). In that event we would not learn anything about a person's vocabulary through knowledge of his or her television habits.

It is easy to see that correlations provide information that can be quite useful. The reason that universities ask for SAT or ACT scores from entering freshmen is that these scores show a positive correlation with college grades. Students with higher admissions test scores tend to also get better grades in college. But obviously the predictive power is not perfect—you may even know someone with outstanding SAT scores whose college course grades are only mediocre (or worse).

Because they are so useful and are relatively easy to conduct, correlational studies are used by researchers in every branch of psychology. They have become indispensible in many areas that cannot be investigated using experimental approaches. For example, the link between smoking and many serious health problems was revealed from correlational studies. Correlational data, though, have one serious drawback.

When we are dealing with correlational data, we cannot make causal inferences: *Correlation does not prove causation.* In other words, even though a relationship exists between two measures, we cannot say that one causes the other, even when such a statement appears reasonable. Even a perfect correlation ($+1.00$ or -1.00), if it were obtainable, does not indicate a causal relationship. The fact that two measures are strongly related does not prove that one is responsible for the occurrence of the other. For example, Bowman's archival study from Chapter 3 produced high positive correlations between family closeness and satisfaction with family roles (and also between religiousness and satisfaction with family roles), but it did not prove that family closeness (or religious beliefs) caused greater satisfaction. Over the last hundred years, there has probably been a positive correlation between the number of automobiles and the number of airplanes in the world. But it would be illogical to say that automobiles cause airplanes or vice versa.

Another look at the earlier example of studying the effects of TV violence on aggressiveness illustrates the limitations of trying to explain the cause of behavior from correlational studies. It would not be difficult to correlate the amount of time a person spends watching television violence with some measure of trait aggressiveness (indeed, similar studies have been done many times since the advent of TV!). Let us imagine that we actually carried out this study and found that exposure to TV violence and aggressiveness were strongly related. Can we say that violent TV causes aggressiveness? No.

No matter how reasonable this hypothesis sounds, we have not established that TV violence causes aggression. Why not? Because the *causal direction* cannot be determined by simple correlations: We cannot be certain which behavior is the cause and which is the effect—nor, as you will see, can we be certain that there is a causal relationship at all between the measured behaviors. Along with our hypothesis that aggression is produced by exposure to TV violence, there are three alternative possibilities.

First, innate aggressiveness may determine a preference for violent TV—not the other way around. More aggressive people could simply gravitate toward more violent programs. A second alternative is also plausible. It is possible that innate aggressiveness results in more exposure to TV violence, but at the same time the more exposure a person has, the more aggressive he or she becomes. The behaviors may affect each other. This is known as *bidirectional causation.*

Finally, some third agent may actually be causing the two behaviors to appear to be related. (Could this explain the automobile/airplane relationship?) This is known as the *third-variable problem.* It is also plausible that a preference for violent TV and a tendency toward aggressiveness both result from an unknown or unmeasured variable, such as underactive autonomic nervous system functioning. Violence produces negative arousal in many individuals, and so does aggressiveness, but it may be that some people are less adversely affected than others. Less arousable individuals may be able to both watch more violent TV and behave more aggressively.

Because any of these alternatives is possible, inferring that TV violence is the cause of aggression would have been an unjustified conclusion. *Keep in mind that these three types of plausible alternative explanations hold for all correlational studies.* But even though a causal statement is not justified, it *would* be appropriate to predict an individual's aggressiveness by how much violent TV the person watched.

Sometimes we wish to see whether there is a relationship among a number of measured behaviors (as in Box 4-1). Intercorrelations among three or more behaviors can be computed with a statistic known as **multiple correlation,** represented by R. Conceptually, R is quite similar to r. Multiple correlations are particularly useful to augment information gained from simple correlations. For example, let us say that we took three measurements (age, amount of television viewing, and vocabulary) for a large sample of children, whose ages varied from a few days old to 10 years old. We might find that a large multiple correlation was obtained ($R = +.61$), showing that age, television viewing, and vocabulary are all interrelated. This is not too surprising, really, because infants do not watch TV or know any words, but as children get older they watch more TV and also learn more words. But this multiple correlation would tend to put a damper on a hypothesis that watching TV increases vocabulary, wouldn't it? More likely, both television time and

B O X   4 - 1

FACTOR ANALYSIS

A common correlational procedure that is used when individuals are measured on a large number of items is called *factor analysis.* Factor analysis allows us to see the degree of relationship among many traits or behaviors at the same time. Such complicated statistical procedures have become common now that computers are available for statistical data analysis. When measurements of many behaviors are taken, those measurements that are most strongly intercorrelated are grouped together by the analysis as *factors.* Factor analysis is commonly used in personality research. Over the years, hundreds of trait dimensions (warm/cold, shy/sociable, dominant/submissive) have been measured by researchers, but factor analysis routinely groups them into only a few basic factors (Cattell, 1946), such as sociability, agreeableness, conscientiousness, emotionality, and culture. Many researchers now believe that a few basic factors underlie all human personality structure.

Factor analysis can identify the important dimensions underlying a large number of responses. Using factor analysis, Conway and Rubin (1991), for example, ascertained that six different dimensions (i.e., factors) seemed to underlie people's motivation for watching TV. In one part of a larger study, they asked subjects to respond to a questionnaire containing 27 motivational statements that had been synthesized from the results of past research on why people like to watch television. Results of the factor analysis are shown in Figure 4-2.

Numbers reported in the factor analysis represent *factor loadings.* Factor loadings are statistical estimates of how well an item correlates with each of the factors (they can range from -1.0 to $+1.0$, like other correlational statistics). The factor analysis determines the factors and sorts items according to their groupings in the different factors, allowing the researcher to identify items belonging in each factor. We have boxed the items in each factor to make them easy to see at a glance. Notice that the items with high factor loadings (these researchers selected a cutoff of .60) are grouped together, showing that subjects' scores on these items are all strongly interrelated. The factor analysis also sorts the factors in order of importance: Factor 1 is the most important because it can account for more variation in all of the subjects' scores. (We will return to variation in Chapter 12.)

I watch television . . .	Viewing Motive Factors					
	Pass Time	Enter-tainment	Infor-mation	Escape	Relax-ation	Status Enhancement
Factor 1: Pass Time						
Passes the time away, especially when I'm bored.	.75	.21	.07	.13	.11	.04
When I have nothing better to do.	.73	−.02	−.03	.18	−.02	−.11
Something to occupy my time.	.70	.27	.06	.15	.14	.16
No one else to talk to or be with.	.70	.00	.07	.06	.27	.12
Just because it's on.	.69	−.06	.00	.24	−.07	−.02
Factor 2: Entertainment						
It's enjoyable.	.00	.79	.15	.06	.17	.01
It entertains me.	.10	.70	.11	−.07	.21	−.09
Just like to watch.	.27	.69	.07	.23	−.05	.00
It amuses me.	.03	.69	.10	.14	.19	.28
Factor 3: Information						
Learn how to do things.	.01	.19	.78	.06	.01	.02
Learn what might happen to me.	.01	.05	.72	.24	−.02	.15
Know others have the same problems.	.17	.02	.72	.08	.16	.17
Learn about myself and others.	−.12	.12	.69	.01	.12	.09
Factor 4: Escape						
Get away from what I'm doing.	.33	.03	.06	.68	.26	.03
Get away from the rest of the family and others.	.35	.02	.07	.64	.12	.28
Something to do when friends come over.	.24	.19	.07	.60	.00	.24
Factor 5: Relaxation						
It relaxes me.	.13	.16	.08	−.06	.75	.15
It allows me to unwind.	.12	.34	.13	.18	.70	−.03
Factor 6: Status Enhancement						
Feel more important than really am.	.19	.15	.21	.25	.02	.70
Impress people.	.14	.01	.33	.27	.06	.68

FIGURE 4-2 Viewing motives: primary factor loadings. Adapted from "Psychological Predictors of Television Viewing Motivation," by J. C. Conway & A. M. Rubin, 1991, *Communication Research, 18* (4), 443–463. Copyright ©1991 Sage Publications, Inc. Adapted with permission of Sage Publications, Inc.

vocabulary are age-related changes.[3] The multiple correlation does not explain why the three measures are related, but it suggests the hypothesis that age is an important third variable that could be explored in subsequent research.

In an experiment we are able to establish causality by setting up at least two different treatment conditions and evaluating their effects on behavior. If we can specify exactly the conditions that will lead to a particular behavior, we have explained the occurrence of that behavior and may say that a particular set of conditions caused that behavior. This is not possible in the correlational study because we do not manipulate the conditions under which we are testing; we simply measure what occurs and ask whether the dimensions are related to each other. It is important to remember that correlational studies are limited by the way data are obtained—not by the statistical methods used to analyze them. Advanced correlational methods are extremely sophisticated. Let us proceed to designs that use correlational techniques to create causal models from sets of related behaviors.

Causal Modeling

As computer statistics programs become widely available, more sophisticated research designs based on advanced correlational techniques have become increasingly frequent in the literature. One inherent drawback of all correlational designs, of course, is the problem of the direction of cause and effect, discussed earlier. For example, we know that time spent watching violent TV is positively correlated with aggressiveness levels, but simple correlational designs do not provide information about the direction of the cause and effect sequence, if it exists. Even if experimentation is not possible, we would like to be able to design and conduct research that allows us to speculate about whether watching TV violence causes aggressiveness, or whether more aggressive people just naturally gravitate toward programs containing more violent content. Researchers have tools for **causal modeling** in correlation-based designs, such as a cross-lagged panel design and path analysis.

Path Analysis and Multiple Regression

Path analysis is an important nonexperimental research method that can be used when subjects are measured on several related behaviors. In path analysis, the researcher creates models of possible causal sequences. For example, Serbin and her colleagues (Serbin, Zelkowitz, Doyle, Gold, & Wheaton, 1990) were interested in trying to explain differences between boys' and girls' academic performance in elementary school. They suspected that different things could influence girls and boys. Through path analysis, they confirmed that the best models to predict school performance differed for boys and girls. Socioeconomic and parental education factors were important for predicting success in all the children. Beyond these factors, girls' performance in the

---

[3]We could test this prediction by computing another statistic, a *partial correlation*. This analysis allows the statistical influence of one measurement to be held constant while computing the correlation between the other two.

lower grades seemed to be better accounted for by social responsiveness and willingness to follow directions. Boys' academic performance, however, was better predicted by their level of visual/spatial skills. Clearly, path analysis is another descriptive method, but it generates important information for prediction and can generate experimental hypotheses. Path analysis is limited, however, in an important way. The models can only be constructed using the behaviors that have been measured. If a researcher omits an important behavior, it will be missing in the model, too.

Path analysis, a sophisticated type of correlational study, uses multiple correlation (R) techniques to test one or several possible causal models. You will recall from our discussion of simple correlations (r) that a *regression equation* generated from the correlational analysis can be used for prediction. This technique is called **regression analysis.** If two behaviors are strongly related, the regression equation allows the researcher to estimate a score on one of the measured behaviors from a score on the other. If we knew, for example, that time spent watching TV and scores on a vocabulary test were correlated, we could plug someone's viewing time into the formula; solving the equation would give us an estimate of what their performance should be on the vocabulary test. The stronger the correlation, the better the prediction, in general.

When more than two related behaviors are measured, a **multiple regression analysis** (from multiple correlation, or R) can be used to predict the score on one behavior from scores on the others. Multiple regression analyses are very common in the literature. We could use multiple regression analysis, for example, to predict vocabulary scores from TV viewing time and age if all three were intercorrelated. Logically, we might imagine that age would be more important in predicting vocabulary than viewing time; if so, the regression equation would "weight" age more heavily than viewing time. Regression equations determine the weight of each predictor, and we could simply report these weights (called *beta weights*) in a research report. Or we could use the weights in a path analysis to construct *path models,* outlining possible causal sequences for the related behaviors (one is shown in Figure 4-3). Computers can easily compare many regression equations testing different paths, looking for the best model. Finally, the selected model can be further tested for "goodness of fit" to the actual data.

Path models can be very complex. When there are many interrelated characteristics and behaviors to be considered, each path may have many steps. Some models include multiple paths to the same predicted "effect." It is not difficult to find path analyses in the literature that include multiple sets of interweaving paths linking as many as a dozen or more predictors (e.g., Pedersen, Plomin, Nesselroade, & McClearn, 1992). Figure 4-3 shows a simpler path model, constructed by Schwartz, Lerman, Miller, Daly, and Masny (1995). These health psychologists were interested in constructing a path model to predict psychological distress in women who were at increased risk for ovarian cancer. Past research had demonstrated a three-step model. In the three-step model, *monitoring* (a style of extreme vigilance to threat cues in the environment) predicted the number of intrusive thoughts people had, and these thoughts predicted psychological distress. Schwartz and colleagues

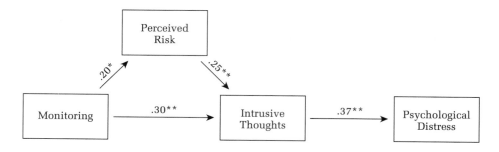

*p < .05,   **p < .01

FIGURE 4-3 Path model predicting psychological distress adjusted for age and objective risk factors of the first degree relative and age and stage of the index patient. From Schwartz, Lerman, Miller, Daly, and Masny (1995).

wanted to test the idea that the model was missing an important component. Perhaps, they speculated, the path from monitoring to intrusive thoughts is not direct—perhaps monitoring increases people's perception of being at risk, and that perception leads to intrusive thoughts. Their path analysis showed that both paths to distress fit the data obtained from subjects. Monitoring might lead to intrusive thoughts either directly or indirectly via perceived risk, and instrusive thoughts could then lead to distress.

Researchers who use this approach are always very careful *not* to frame their models in terms of causal statements. Can you figure out why? We hope you reasoned that the internal validity of a path analysis is low because it is based on correlational data. The direction from cause to effect cannot be established with certainty, and "third variables" can never be ruled out completely. Nevertheless, causal models can be extremely useful for generating hypotheses for future research and for predicting potential causal sequences in instances where experimentation is not feasible.

Cross-lagged Panel Design
Another method used to create causal models is called a **cross-lagged panel.** This design uses relationships measured over time to suggest the causal path. In a cross-lagged panel design, subjects are measured at two separate points in time on the same pair of related behaviors or characteristics (the time "lag" can be quite a few years). Then the scores from these measurements are correlated in a particular way, and the pattern of correlations is used to infer the causal path. The most famous cross-lagged panel study was done by Eron, Huesmann, Lefkowitz, and Walder (1972). Their study looked at the correlation between a preference for violent TV and aggressiveness in kids as they grew to young adulthood. The researchers measured aggressiveness levels and preferences for violent TV among a large group of youngsters. Subjects were assessed once in the third grade and

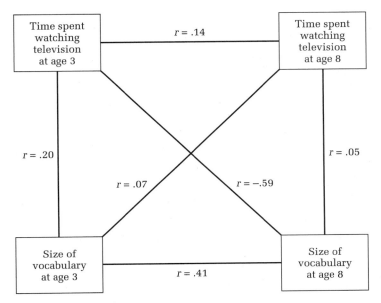

FIGURE 4-4 Results of a hypothetical cross-lagged panel design.

again ten years later. The results of the cross-lagged panel indicated that it was more likely that TV violence caused aggressiveness than the other way around.

Let us explore the logic of this design. Figure 4-4 shows the pattern of correlational results from a hypothetical cross-lagged panel study of two related behaviors—TV viewing time and vocabulary scores. Imagine that we made observations of 70 boys and girls at two different times, at ages 3 and 8. At each observation, we measured the TV viewing time and vocabulary of each subject. Then we computed six r values, one for each of the six possible paths between them. Let's assume that r values below $r = .20$ are not high enough to indicate a strong relationship (the idea of *statistical significance* can wait until later chapters).

In a cross-lagged panel design, the correlations along the two diagonals are the most important for determining the causal path because they represent effects across the time lag. On one hand, if vocabulary size is the cause of TV viewing, we would expect that vocabulary size at age 3 and the amount of time spent watching TV at age 8 should be strongly correlated. Are they? No. The r value is only .07. On the other hand, if time spent watching TV at age 3 determined vocabulary size at age 8, there should be a strong relationship between them. And there is. The r value is $-.59$, a very strong correlation. In a cross-lagged panel, we are looking for the largest diagonal correlation to indicate the causal direction. In our hypothetical example, then, we would infer that the most likely path from cause to effect is the one from viewing time to vocabulary size. Note, however, that the correlation is negative! If TV viewing time influences vocabulary size, what kind of influence does it have according to our hypothetical cross-lagged panel? (We would have to say that watching a lot of TV appears to decrease—not increase—the size of a child's vocabulary!)

But we also need to examine the rest of the panel. Does it all make sense? What else can it tell us? Notice, for example, the moderate correlation between viewing time and vocabulary size at age 3 ($r = .20$). It is positive, indicating that for the 3-year-olds, more time watching TV is related to a *larger* vocabulary. If watching television is related to a larger vocabulary at age 3, why is the correlation close to zero ($r = .05$) when the children are age 8? (Perhaps influences on vocabulary change with age. Or, perhaps the initial relationship was *really* produced by something else—a third variable, such as curiosity?). Also notice that our panel shows a strong positive correlation between vocabulary size at age 3 and vocabulary size at age 8 ($r = .41$). How might you interpret that? (Perhaps verbal skills are relatively stable.) You can see that carefully exploring the relationships in a cross-lagged panel design can lead to many new ideas and new questions. Keep in mind that a cross-lagged panel design can only suggest the possible direction of a cause and effect relationship between two behaviors. Evidence from this design is never conclusive. For instance, bidirectional causation and the third variable problem cannot be ruled out. Let us move on from causal models to quasi-experimental designs, which are sometimes used to measure changes over time.

QUASI-EXPERIMENTAL DESIGNS

Quasi-experimental designs are used when subjects cannot be randomly assigned to receive different treatments. Quasi-experiments can be used to explore the effects of different experimental manipulations on preexisting groups of subjects or to investigate the same kinds of naturally occurring events, characteristics, and behaviors that we measure in correlational studies. In the simplest quasi-experiments, we form *quasi-treatment* groups based on the particular event characteristic, or behavior, whose influence we want to investigate. Our statistical analyses are based on aggregated data from each group. For example, we could use a quasi-experimental design to look at gender differences in the kinds of toys boys and girls prefer. By observing the kinds of toys the children select, we might discover that, on the average, they tend to select gender-stereotyped toys (Carter & Levy, 1988). But can we say for sure that children's toy preferences are caused by their gender? Does merely being born male or female determine the kinds of toys children will like to play with? Of course not. There are many outside influences (such as the kinds of toys adults buy for them) that help to determine toy preferences. There may even be other influences internal to the children (such as their aggressiveness levels) that play a role in the kinds of toys they prefer. (This is the same third variable problem we encountered with correlation.) The point to remember is that when we conduct quasi-experiments, we can never know for certain what causes the effects we observe—so, relative to true experiments, we say these designs are low in internal validity.

In some quasi-experiments, subjects are exposed to different treatments (as they are in true experiments), but the experimenter cannot exert control over who receives which treatment because random assignment is not possible. An important difference between experiments and quasi-experiments is the amount of control the researcher has over the subjects who receive treatments. In an experiment, the researcher randomly assigns subjects to receive different treatments so that the only conditions that will systematically influence behavior are the treatment(s) being tested. Without random assignment, other individual differences between members of different treatment groups may produce misleading effects on behavior.

Recall the example of a quasi-experiment to test lighting in two different companies that was used earlier in the chapter. Suppose the researcher had installed fluorescent lighting in Company A and incandescent lighting in Company B. After workers had used the lights for three months, productivity was measured and the researcher found that workers with incandescent lighting were more productive. How confident could we be that the lighting actually produced the difference in productivity? Not as confident as we would like to be, because there are any number of other potential causes (third variables). For instance, the workers in Company B might be more productive even without the incandescent lights (or Company A's workers might be less productive). In this example, other conditions within the two companies also might have altered the productivity of subjects in one or both groups (a bonus from Company B, threats of a layoff in Company A, and so forth). In true experiments, other outside influences are carefully controlled, so the only systematic effect on behavior results from the treatment(s)—not from anything else. In the remainder of the chapter we will take a closer look at several kinds of quasi-experimental designs.

Ex Post Facto Studies

Often, researchers are interested in the effects of traits, behaviors, or naturally occurring events that cannot or should not be manipulated by a researcher. In those cases the researcher may choose to do an **ex post facto study**—that is, a study in which the researcher systematically examines the effects of subject characteristics (often called **subject variables**) but without actually manipulating them. The researcher forms treatment groups on the basis of differences that already exist between subjects (Kerlinger, 1973).

Ex post facto means "after the fact." In effect, the researcher capitalizes on changes in the antecedent conditions that occurred before the study. The result is a study that looks a great deal like an experiment, with the important exception that the antecedent conditions have not been manipulated by the experimenter. The experimenter also has no direct control over who belongs to each of the treatment groups of the study. These studies generally fall in the low-high portion of Figure 3-1.

Preexisting differences define membership in different treatment groups in the study: Shirley's father died last year, so Shirley is placed in a group of subjects who have experienced the loss of a parent. Subjects come into an ex post facto study with attributes that already differ from one subject to another. The differences are used as the basis for separating them into groups (for example, extroverts, introverts), and the researcher then looks for differences in behavior that are related to group membership.

The ex post facto approach has some special advantages. Like the correlational study, it deals with things as they occur. There is no manipulation of the conditions that interest the researcher. However, the ex post facto study allows a researcher to zero in on those occurrences in a more systematic way; instead of studying the whole range of people along a particular dimension (like extremely introverted to extremely extroverted), the focus can be on a carefully chosen subset. Typically, the ex post facto researcher studies the extremes, the subjects who rank highest and lowest on the dimension of interest. This focus increases the likelihood that the researcher will be able to see the effects of changes along that dimension more clearly.

Ex post facto studies are also generally done with many of the same rigorous control procedures used in experiments. The researcher makes a prediction in advance and attempts to test it in the most objective way. Systematically forming groups based on differences in preexisting characteristics is a critical feature of an ex post facto study, but it also prevents such a study from being classified as a true experiment.

In a true experiment, there should be no systematic differences between people in different treatment conditions. As we will see in the next chapter, guarding against these kinds of systematic differences is an important benchmark of true experiments. Experimenters typically use a method known as *random assignment of subjects* to create treatment groups in which any preexisting differences in people are distributed evenly across all the treatment groups. In an ex post facto study, those preexisting differences become the "manipulation," and measuring the effects they produce is the objective of the research.

Franklin, Janoff-Bulman, and Roberts (1990) were interested in studying the potential effects of divorce on attitudes and beliefs of children. Using an ex post facto design, they assessed whether college-age children of divorced parents held different beliefs about themselves and other people than college students who came from intact families. Franklin and colleagues were interested in measuring these subjects' beliefs about the world in general, about people in general, about their own self-worth, and about interpersonal relationships. Interestingly, they found no differences between the two groups of college students on any of the first three kinds of beliefs. Both groups reported similar beliefs about the world, others, and themselves. Differences *were* found, though, on beliefs about relationships—especially on issues related to love and marriage. As a group, the students from divorced families reported more accepting attitudes toward divorce and more pessimistic beliefs about their own success in a marriage. Students with divorced parents believed that they were less likely to have a long and successful marriage than the students whose parents had stayed together. Using an ex post facto design, the researchers were able to demonstrate that a life event, the divorce of parents, does not *seem* to have global, negative effects on children's belief systems.

Instead, divorce *seemed* to influence only a narrow range of beliefs, those related to the possibility of divorce in their own future.

A strong word of caution. Results of ex post facto studies can be easily misinterpreted (see Box 4-2). Because the kinds of effects Franklin and colleagues (1990) found greatly resembled the event used to classify subjects into groups, it would be tempting to make a causal inference—to say that divorce *alters* beliefs about marriage and divorce. However, because the researchers did not create the group differences but instead relied on a naturally occurring event, there is no way to be certain that the effects were actually produced by the *ex post facto variable* and not by something else. It is always possible that something other than divorce was the actual cause: Perhaps the parents held similar pessimistic attitudes about marriage before the divorce. The parents' negative expectations may have caused both the divorce and their children's pessimistic attitudes about marriage. You may have noticed that this is the same problem that we encountered with correlational studies—that nemesis of nonexperimental designs, the third variable. All ex post facto studies are low in internal validity because there is always the possibility that other differences between the groups of subjects were the true cause of the effects. Because of this, we cannot explain behavior from an ex post facto study. We can, however, learn a great deal of useful information.

In addition to studying personal attributes (such as gender or handedness) and life events (such as divorce or the loss of a limb), researchers often use ex post facto studies to learn more about the behavioral ramifications of individual differences in psychological functioning and personality processes. As you can probably guess, we cannot study mental illness or personality in a strictly experimental manner. How would we go about manipulating antisocial personality disorder, Type A behavior, or agoraphobia to create the tendency we want to study? If we *could* devise procedures that would accomplish that goal, would we really want to use them?

The ex post facto approach enables us to explore many dimensions that we could not or would not choose to study experimentally. For that reason, it is a very useful source of information. For example, using an ex post facto design, researchers discovered that a person's coping style when faced with a negative experience could be important in the treatment of cancer patients (Ward, Leventhal, & Love, 1988). Ward and colleagues studied cancer patients who had been identified as either repressors or nonrepressors. Repressors are individuals who minimize negative emotional experiences. (You may remember the theory of repression from studying Sigmund Freud.) A repressive or nonrepressive coping style can be reliably identified by a personality questionnaire.

Using interviews and questionnaires to measure the patients' symptom-related behavior, the researchers found important differences between the two kinds of people. Repressors were much less likely than nonrepressors to report awareness of either cancer treatment side effects or symptoms of their illness. Even though these differences cannot be explained, the information may be very important for the prevention and treatment of cancer. As the researchers noted, repressors may be less likely to notice cancer symptoms and seek early

BOX 4-2

ARE BIG CARS SAFER THAN SMALL CARS?

For people who do not understand research designs, interpreting the results of an ex post facto study present a serious challenge. All too frequently, results of these studies are misinterpreted in media reports. Here is one of our favorites (even though the models change slightly from year to year, the interpretation reported in newspapers, in magazines, and on TV news does not!). The headline typically reads something like this:

WHICH VEHICLES ARE THE SAFEST?

The article begins with statements like this one from a recent newspaper report:*

Large passenger vehicles—vans, station wagons and luxury-model cars—are safer than small vehicles according to a new study by the Insurance Institute for Highway Safety. The study looked at the number of driver deaths in the 1988–92 models of 184 vehicles during the years 1989–93. Following are the dozen safest passenger vehicles, with the number of actual driver deaths per 100,000 vehicles of the make and model registered in the U. S. during those years. (The average rate for all vehicles was 11 driver deaths.)

Ranking	Type of Car	Number of Deaths
1	Volvo 240 4-door, midsize luxury car	0.00
2	Volvo 740/760 4-door midsize luxury car	1.85
3	Plymouth Voyager, large passenger van	2.23
4	Mercedes 190 D/E, midsize luxury car	3.06

. . . and so on.

The highest death rates were for small cars, sport utility vehicles and small pickup trucks. The worst record: the Chevy Corvette, with 36 driver deaths per 100,000 vehicles. . . . Incidentally, a driver's side air bag was in 10 of the 12 vehicles with the lowest death rates. Air bags were absent in nine of the 11 vehicles with the highest death rates.

*From "Which Are the Safest Vehicles?," *Parade Magazine*, Nov. 17, 1994. Reprinted with permission from Parade, copyright ©1994.

Let's look at their conclusion a little more carefully. The researchers used an ex post facto design to select groups based on different kinds of vehicles, and then they compared death rates. Do you believe that they have proven their case that large cars are safer than small cars? Do you think that the size of the car is the only reason that drivers of, let's say, Volvo 240 4-door, midsize luxury cars have many fewer deaths per 100,000 than drivers of compact cars and Chevy Corvettes? (Small, inexpensive cars are usually at the bottom along with Corvettes.) Do you think the lower death rates in the cars at the top are really attributable to air bags?

What else is going on here that they have failed to mention? *What about the kinds of people who typically drive these different cars?* How are Volvo and Corvette drivers likely to differ? (age, gender, risk-taking . . . ?) How are Volvo (or Plymouth Voyager, Mercedes 190D/E, etc.) and Ford Escort drivers likely to differ? (age, wealth . . . other factors?) There are probably many differences between the owners of cars in the large and small categories. These differences are likely to play a large role in the death rate differences—but these reports never mention it. The same can be said about the implied role of air bags in safety: Is it the air bags, or is it the people who drive the more expensive, larger vehicles? Clearly, we cannot rule out either car size or air bags as having some part in the safety statistics, but they are certainly not the only cause of statistics such as these, are they?

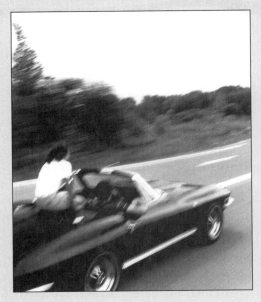

FIGURE 4-5 Could this be one reason why small cars can be unsafe?
Frank Siteman/Stock, Boston

treatment. Once the disease is diagnosed, however, repressors may actually cope better with cancer treatment.

Despite its limitations, the ex post facto approach is an extremely useful technique that allows us to demonstrate that certain predictable relationships exist. We can establish, for instance, that gender, or personality traits, or mental disorders are associated with particular patterns of behavior. In some respects, ex post facto studies are more useful than certain kinds of experiments because the information they provide helps us to understand the kinds of complex behaviors that occur in real life. They have greater external validity because they focus on naturally occurring events. Even though we cannot draw conclusions about cause and effect, ex post facto studies provide more realistic data that can be applied in practical ways. Often, researchers will include subject variables in their experiments to see whether their treatments produce different effects on different kinds of subjects (see Box 4-3).

Longitudinal Designs

Psychologists also use quasi-experiments to measure the behaviors of the same subjects at different points in time and look to see how things have changed. Here the specific question is often one of the influence of time on behaviors, rather than how different behaviors are related, as we saw in the cross-lagged panel design. These long-term studies employ **longitudinal designs.** Longitudinal designs are used in all areas of psychology, but they are particularly important for psychologists studying human (and animal) growth and development. Stewart, Mobley, Van Tuyl, and Salvador (1987) conducted an interesting longitudinal study to assess behavioral changes in first-born children after the birth of a second child. They observed and interviewed 41 middle-class families five different times: one month before the birth of the second child, and at one, four, eight, and twelve months after the birth. One of the behaviors they were interested in was regression.

Regression, in psychoanalytic theory, is a way of escaping the reality of a stressful situation by reverting to more childlike patterns of behavior. More cognitively oriented developmentalists see it as a child's falling back to an earlier cognitive stage as a way of learning to cope with new, and more complex, situations. Previous work had suggested that after the birth of a sibling, firstborns sometimes showed more independent, "grown-up" behavior (in language, feeding, toileting, etc.); other times, they seemed to regress or become more infantile. These researchers found some evidence for regressive behavior in the firstborns, particularly when they were measured one month after the birth. Interestingly, though, there were more regressive behaviors if the firstborn and the new baby were the same sex! One explanation is that the behaviors they were seeing might be imitation, not regression. Firstborns might have been *imitating* behaviors of the new baby as a way of trying to direct maternal attention away from the newborn toward themselves; imitating a same-sex sibling might be more natural than imitating an opposite-sex sibling. (Incidentally, the imitation strategy seemed to have been abandoned by the 12-month interview.)

B O X   4 - 3

NEGATIVE IONS AND TYPE A BEHAVIOR

You will remember the study by Baron, Russell, and Arms (1985) from Chapters 1 and 2. These researchers found that a high concentration of negative ions increased the intensity of people's good and bad moods. Negative mood shifts were reported by subjects who had been intentionally angered by a confederate; positive mood shifts were reported by nonangered subjects. Besides testing the effects of different concentrations of negative ions, their study also included a subject variable. They used subjects who were Type A and Type B personalities (Jenkins, Zyzanski, and Rosenman, 1979) to see whether ionization would have different effects on these two types of people. Type A people have characteristically high levels of irritability, a sense of time urgency, and strong reactions to stressors; Type B people are low in all three traits.

Part of the subjects' (supposed) task in this experiment was to punish all of the "learners'" errors with a painful burst of heat to the wrist. Each time they delivered the heat punishment, the subjects selected how intense it would be (the 10 buttons on the machine were labeled from "very low" to "very intense"). The intensities chosen by subjects represented a measure of aggressive behavior toward the "learners." Interestingly, even though the negative ions affected the moods of both Type As and Type Bs in similar ways, the negative ions impacted differently on the aggressiveness of the two types of subjects. For Type B subjects, ion levels produced no effect at all on the intensity of the bursts. But for Type A subjects, there was a dramatic effect—both moderate and high levels of negative ions significantly enhanced the aggressiveness of the Type A subjects. The intensity of the bursts used to punish the "learners'" errors got much higher, particularly if they had been angered. Even though this design does not allow the researchers to state with certainty that the differences in effects produced by ionization were caused by the subjects' Type A or Type B personality, the results are clearly useful for predicting different kinds of behaviors for Type As and Type Bs!

Cross-Sectional Studies

Longitudinal studies are time consuming and hard to conduct. Retaining subjects over a long period of time can be very difficult. Often researchers use another method that approximates results from a longitudinal study. Instead of tracking the same group over a long span of time, subjects who are already at different stages are compared at a single point in time using a **cross-sectional study**. For example, instead of following the same group of subjects for more than a year, Stewart and his colleagues could have observed groups of families who were already at each of the five different stages: They might have observed one group of families expecting a second child in a month, another group whose second child was a month old, another group whose child was four months old, and so on. Then they could have compared the amount of "regressive" behavior among firstborns in the five different groups to see whether it differed.

There are trade-offs to consider when choosing between the two designs. On one hand, the longitudinal study takes much longer to complete. On the other hand, a cross-sectional study will require more subjects; the more groups to be compared, the more subjects needed. The statistical tests needed to analyze effects across different groups are typically less powerful than those used to verify the same kind of effects within one group of subjects. And using different groups of subjects runs the risk that people in these groups might differ in other characteristics that could influence the behaviors you want to investigate. (In this respect, a cross-sectional design is similar to an ex post facto design, discussed earlier.) In a longitudinal study, the same people are observed each time. Important information about changes across the lifespan can be gained from both of these designs, but neither can be used to infer cause and effect—potentially, many influences could have produced the changes in behavior. Clearly, antecedents are not manipulated in either type of study; however, imposition of units is generally high.

Pretest/Posttest Design

Sometimes we want to assess whether the occurrence of an event increases or decreases the existing level of a behavior. Does aversion therapy reduce the number of self-abusive behaviors? Do attitudes toward a product become more positive after a new TV commercial airs? Does the President's approval rating go up after the State of the Union address? We can measure the level of behavior before and after the event and compare these levels using a **pretest/ posttest design**—one of the most frequently used quasi-experimental designs in the social sciences (Cook & Campbell, 1979). It is often used to assess the effects of naturally occurring events when a true experiment is not possible; sometimes such a design is used in laboratory studies, but it has a number of problems that reduce its internal validity.

Let's look at an example. Suppose a school counselor wanted to assess the effectiveness of a preparation course for college admissions tests that she had developed for college-bound students. Sixty students have signed up to take the course from her. Optimally, she would like to be able to give the training to only half these students so she could compare admissions test scores of students who received the training with scores of those who did not. But she feels it might be unethical to deny training to some students who want it. She considers using another group of students who did not sign up as a comparison group, but she decides against it because she is worried that the two groups of students might have different characteristics.[4] She decides to use a pretest/posttest design.

The first day of the course, she gives all 60 students in the course a pretest—a practice SAT—to establish a baseline score for each student. She is hopeful that at the end of the six-week preparation course, students will get higher scores than they did the first time around. At the end of the course, she tests them again. She finds that, on the average, their scores improved by 20 points. Should she keep the training program? This is an internal validity question. How confident can she be with this design that her training program caused the improvement? Not as confident as she would like.

In a pretest/posttest design, there are simply too many other things that could have caused the improvement. In this design, the possibility of *practice effects* (also called *pretest sensitization*) cannot be ruled out. Anastasi (1958), for example, has shown that people do better the second time they take an intelligence test—even without any special training in between! Simple familiarity with a test can improve performance. Test takers may be less anxious the second time around. They also may have learned new information (in their other classes, reading the paper, or watching TV) that improves their scores. Or they may think about their answers on the pretest, and this can influence how they answer the second time around. And without a group that receives no training to control for other things that may occur with the passage of time, it is clear that a pretest/posttest design lacks internal validity. Even so, it has been widely used in situations, particularly outside the laboratory, where a comparison group is impossible or unethical.

A pretest/posttest design is often used to test the effects of forseeable real world events, such as attitude or behavior changes after a series of public service announcements about "safe sex" airs on television, or ticket sales before and after renovations are made to a concert hall. When there is a long time between the pretest and the posttest, the researcher needs to be aware that the event being assessed may not be the only cause of differences before and after the event. Any number of uncontrolled, outside influences also may be affecting the results. A pretest/posttest study of this kind is very low in internal validity.

From time to time, a pretest/posttest design is used in circumstances where the treatment time is short, as in a single laboratory session. A researcher who wants to test the benefits of subliminal self-help tapes designed to increase self-esteem could use a pretest/posttest design. He might test 30 subjects, one at a time. Using a standard test, he could measure self-esteem

---

[4]Actually, this option has been used when researchers cannot randomly assign subjects to treatment or comparison groups for practical or ethical reasons. Threats to internal validity present in the pretest/posttest design can be *partially* controlled by comparing subjects who received treatment with another group of subjects who did not. Subjects in the comparison group receive no treatment, but they are measured (pretest and posttest) according to the same time schedule as the treatment group. Threats to internal validity are not completely controlled because the comparison group is taken from another population and is unlikely to be equivalent to the treatment group; this design is called a *nonequivalent control group design*.

when subjects first arrive at the laboratory. Subjects could listen to the 45-minute tape, and the researcher could measure self-esteem again. If all other potential influences had been carefully controlled during all 30 experimental sessions, we would be *somewhat* more confident that an increase in self-esteem after the treatment was really attributable to the tape. However, we still could not be certain that the rise in self-esteem was not brought about by practice with the test,[5] because people *also* seem to get better scores on personality and adjustment tests with practice (Windle, 1954).

Sometimes this design is used with one or more comparison groups that attempt to control for these internal validity issues. *If subjects can be randomly assigned to different groups* by the experimenter, some of these problems can be attenuated by adding comparison or control groups. (We will cover control groups in Chapter 6.) But you would need a number of comparison groups: (1) a group that took both the pretest and posttest but was not exposed to the "treatment," (2) a group that received the treatment and took only the posttest, and (3) a posttest-only group. When all four groups are included in the design, it is called a *Solomon 4-group design* (Campbell & Stanley, 1963). But, it should be pointed out that when a researcher has this much flexibility, it is usually better to do without the pretest and select, instead, one of the experimental designs covered in the following chapters.

Despite their limitations, quasi-experimental approaches are clearly very important adjuncts to experimentation. They can be extremely useful for showing relationships and for predicting behavioral differences among people. At times, they are the only approaches available to us. In addition, the quasi-experimental approaches may lack the artificiality that is sometimes criticized in experimental research. Finally, they are often used as the sources of experimental hypotheses that lead to further research. Formulating a research hypothesis just happens to be the topic of our next chapter.

SUMMARY

In this chapter, we continued our discussion of nonexperimental designs, focusing on two categories of nonexperimental research methods: correlational and quasi-experimental designs. Because antecedents are not manipulated, it is much more difficult to establish cause and effect relationships conclusively using these techniques, but they can be high in external validity. *Correlational studies* may be run in the laboratory or in the field. A correlational study is done to determine the *correlation,* or degree of relationship, between two traits, behaviors, or events. First, the variables of interest are measured; then the degree of relationship between them is established through statistical procedures. When two measures are strongly correlated, we can more accurately

---

[5]In fact, this explanation is quite plausible. Greenwald, Spangenbert, Pratkanis, and Eskenazi (1991) used a more complex pretest/posttest design to test subliminal self-help tapes. After replicating the study on three different subject samples, they concluded that the tapes had no effect on self-esteem. With or without the tapes, posttest self-esteem scores were somewhat higher than pretest scores.

predict the value of one if we know the value of the other. But we cannot infer cause and effect from a correlation. Relationships between three or more measures can also be investigated by computing a *multiple correlation.*

Researchers can use sophisticated correlational tools to create causal models using a *cross-lagged panel design* or *path analysis.* Causal models can suggest cause and effect relationships, but they cannot establish these relationships conclusively because other potential influences and causal directions cannot be entirely ruled out.

As the prefix *quasi-* implies, *quasi-experimental designs* "almost seem like" experiments, but they are not. Quasi-experimental designs are used when subjects cannot be randomly assigned to receive different treatments. Quasi-experiments can be used to explore the effects of different experimental manipulations on preexisting groups of subjects or to investigate the same kinds of naturally-occurring events, characteristics, and behaviors that we measure in correlational studies. Researchers often use an *ex post facto study* to examine the effects of subject characteristics (often called "subject variables") systematically without actually manipulating them. Here the researcher forms groups on the basis of differences that already exist between subjects and measures behavioral differences between the groups.

Some quasi-experiments look for changes or differences over time. *Longitudinal studies* follow the same group of subjects and take measurements at different points in time. *Cross-sectional studies* select groups of subjects who are already at different stages and compare them at a single point in time. A *pretest/posttest design* can be used to assess whether the occurrence of an event alters behavior, but the design is low in internal validity. Pretest sensitivity and the possibility that outside influences may affect results are particular problems.

Correlational and quasi-experimental designs can be used to show relationships and predict behavior. They may result in research hypotheses that can be tested in future research.

KEY TERMS

Causal modeling Creating and testing models that may suggest cause and effect relationships among behaviors.

Correlation The degree of relationship between two traits, behaviors, or events, represented by r.

Correlational study A study designed to determine the correlation between two traits, behaviors, or events.

Cross-lagged panel design A method in which the same set of behaviors or characteristics are measured at two separate points in time (often years apart); six different correlations are computed, and the pattern of correlations is used to infer the causal direction.

Cross-sectional study A method in which different groups of subjects who are at different stages are measured at a single point in time; a method that looks for time-related changes.

Ex post facto study A study in which a researcher systematically examines the effects of preexisting subject characteristics (often called subject variables) by forming treatment groups based on these naturally occurring differences between subjects.

Longitudinal study A method in which the same group of subjects is followed and measured at different points in time; a method that looks for changes across time.

Multiple correlation Statistical intercorrelations among three or more behaviors, represented by R.

Multiple regression analysis A correlation-based technique (from multiple correlation) that uses a regression equation to predict the score on one behavior from scores on the other related behaviors.

Negative correlation The relationship existing between two variables such that an increase in one is associated with a decrease in the other; also called an *inverse relationship*.

Path analysis An important correlation-based method in which subjects are measured on several related behaviors; the researcher creates (and tests) models of possible causal sequences using sophisticated correlation techniques.

Positive correlation The relationship between two measures such that an increase in the value of one is associated with an increase in the value of the other; also called a *direct relationship*.

Pretest/posttest design A research design used to assess whether the occurrence of an event alters behavior; scores from measurements made before and after the event (called the *pretest* and *posttest*) are compared.

Quasi-experimental designs Nonexperimental designs that "almost seem like" experiments (as the prefix *quasi-* implies) but are not because subjects are not randomly assigned to treatment conditions.

Regression analysis A correlation-based technique that uses a regression equation to estimate a score on one measured behavior from a score on another behavior.

Regression line The line of best fit; represents the equation that best describes the mathematical relationship between two variables measured in a correlational study.

Scatterplot A graph of data from a correlational study, created by plotting pairs of scores from each subject; the value of one variable is plotted on the X (horizontal) axis and the other variable on the Y (vertical) axis.

Subject variable The characteristics of the subjects in an experiment or quasi-experiment that cannot be manipulated by the researcher; sometimes used to select subjects into groups.

REVIEW AND STUDY QUESTIONS

1. Define the term *quasi-experiment* and discuss the pros and cons of quasi-experimentation.

2. What is a correlation? When can it be used?

3. A researcher found that variable X and variable Y are strongly correlated. She claimed that variable X causes variable Y to occur. Why can't this statement be made? (What else may be going on?)

4. Dean just computed the Pearson Product Moment Correlation Coefficient for two sets of data. He got $r = +2.3$. Dean is thrilled, marveling at what a large relationship he found. What can he conclude from his findings?

5. A college administrator has located a new aptitude test that is correlated with academic achievement ($r = -.54$). The admissions committee of the college now uses a screening test also correlated with academic achievement, but the correlation is $r = +.45$. Which test would be a better choice if the admissions committee is interested in predicting how well prospective students would do at the school?

6. How is multiple regression analysis used to construct paths in a path analysis?

7. What does a cross-lagged panel design attempt to do? What two things cannot be ruled out as alternatives to any cause and effect model found with a cross-lagged panel design?

8. Explain the pros and cons of longitudinal versus cross-sectional studies.

9. Claire conducted an ex post facto study comparing attitudes of a group of rap music fans and a group of classical music buffs. She found that the rap group had more sexist attitudes about women than the other group. She claimed that rap music causes people to become sexist. Can she say that from the results of her study? Why not?

10. What influences do the three added groups control for in the Solomon 4-group design?

11. Design a quasi-experiment to test each of the following:
    a. If hot weather is associated with higher rates of violence in the streets
    b. If rap music causes people to become more sexist (rather than the other way around)
    c. If childhood schizophrenia can be predicted from cognitive deficits, genetic predisposition, and autonomic arousal in childhood
    d. If older persons exercise less than middle-aged persons
    e. If a college education increases people's SAT scores

12. For each quasi-experiment you designed for question 12, list all the reasons you can think of that explain why your study would be low in internal validity.

FORMULATING THE HYPOTHESIS

The term *hypothesis* has appeared a number of times in the preceding chapters. Most psychological research is designed to test hypotheses. We will look first at the differences between experimental and nonexperimental hypotheses and then turn our attention to hypotheses for experimental designs—the major focus of this chapter. We will look at the characteristics of the experimental hypothesis and discuss several ways of arriving at hypotheses suitable for experimental study: induction, deduction, building on prior research, serendipity, and intuition. Then we will see how the hypothesis forms the basis of a research report, beginning with the Introduction section.

The hypothesis represents the end of the long process of thinking about a research idea. The **hypothesis** is the thesis, or main idea, of an experiment. It is a statement about a predicted relationship between at least two variables. Some nonscientific synonyms are *inkling, conjecture, guess,* and *hunch.*

The statement of a research hypothesis is designed to fit the type of research design that has been selected. You know from Chapters 3 and 4 that nonexperimental designs are used to demonstrate relationships between sets of behaviors, but they may not be used to infer a cause and effect relationship between them. For this reason, a **nonexperimental hypothesis** is a statement of your predictions of how events, traits, or behaviors might be related—not a statement about cause and effect. In a true experiment, the hypothesis predicts the effects of specific antecedent conditions on some behavior that is to be measured.

Some nonexperimental designs, particularly those that do not restrict subjects' responses, do not typically include a hypothesis. Phenomenology, case studies, naturalistic observation, and surveys, for instance, are primarily intended to explore and describe behaviors as they occur naturally. And it would be difficult to make guesses about behaviors or events that may or may not occur.

Other nonexperimental designs, such as correlational and ex post facto studies, generally include hypotheses about predicted relationships between variables. The following sentences are examples of nonexperimental hypotheses: "The amount of television viewing will be directly related to vocabulary size." "College grades should be related to subjects' SAT scores." "Repressors will report fewer treatment-related side effects than nonrepressors." Nonexperimental hypotheses are straightforward predictions of the relationships the researcher expects to find between variables.

THE CHARACTERISTICS OF AN EXPERIMENTAL HYPOTHESIS

Every experiment has at least one hypothesis. Complicated experimental designs that compare several treatments at the same time may test various hypotheses simultaneously. Each **experimental hypothesis** is a tentative explanation of an event or behavior. It is a statement that predicts the effects of specified antecedent conditions on a measured behavior.

By the time you are ready to formulate your hypothesis, you have already thought a great deal about a behavior. You may have discarded several improbable explanations of it and are ready to propose one explanation that seems plausible.

Suppose you began to make a list of all the conditions that could affect a behavior. Say the behavior is the speed at which you are reading this book. The factors that affect your reading speed include the style in which this text is written and your average reading speed. Your pace might also be affected by the amount of noise outside, the amount of light in the room, and whether or not you have eaten lunch. Perhaps it is even affected by the number of people who are now singing in Tibet or the number of shrimp in the ocean. Clearly, an enormous number of factors might affect your behavior at any given time. Before doing an experiment to determine which factors are critical to your reading speed, you would obviously want to narrow down the possibilities.

Things far removed from one another are not likely to be causally related. Thus we would not consider the shrimp population as a likely explanation for reading speed. Similarly, we would not spend much time on the people in Tibet. However, factors such as writing style, your normal reading speed, and lighting probably do determine your speed. If you have not had lunch, your images of food will certainly reduce your speed.

This process of whittling away at the number of possible factors affecting your reading speed is the key to formulating a hypothesis. Now that we have selected a small, finite number of possibilities, we are ready to propose an explanation for your reading speed. We are ready to state a hypothesis.

To be scientific, each hypothesis should meet certain basic criteria. As you will see, the criteria have very little to do with personal beliefs or attitudes. Believing that something is true or interesting is not enough to make it a useful hypothesis. Hypotheses must be synthetic statements that are testable, falsifiable, parsimonious, and (we hope) fruitful.

Synthetic Statements

Synthetic statements are those that can be either true or false. Psychologists have borrowed the terminology from the field of logic. Each experimental hypothesis must be a synthetic statement so that there can be some chance it is true and some chance it is false. "Hungry students read slowly" is a synthetic statement that can be supported or contradicted. An experiment designed to test the statement will yield information we can use to decide between the two possibilities.

Nonsynthetic statements should be avoided at all costs. These fall into two categories: analytic or contradictory. An **analytic statement** is one that is always true; for example, "I am pregnant or I am not pregnant." Clearly, even the best constructed experiment could not disprove that statement because the statement itself can explain all possible outcomes. Sometimes we inadvertently generate analytic statements by failing to state our predictions adequately. For example, the prediction, "The weight of dieters will fluctuate" is essentially an analytic statement because it is sufficiently vague to be true for everyone. Everyone's weight fluctuates a bit, whether dieting or not. When stating a hypothesis, we want to be concise enough to be proven wrong. Similarly, we want to avoid making **contradictory statements**—that is, statements with elements that oppose each other—because contradictory statements are always false. "I have a brother and I do not have a brother" is an example of a contradictory statement. Since analytic statements are always true and contradictory statements are always false, we do not need to conduct experiments to test them: We already know what the outcome will be. To ensure that a hypothesis is a synthetic statement, we must evaluate its form. A hypothesis meets the definition of a synthetic statement when it can be stated in what is known as the "If . . . then" form. This form is another way of expressing the potential relationship between the antecedents and the behaviors to be measured:[1] "If you look at an appealing photograph, then your pupils will dilate" is such a hypothesis. It expresses a potential relationship between a particular antecedent condition (being shown an appealing photograph) and a behavior (pupil dilation). The statement can be true or false.

Testable Statements

An experimental hypothesis must also be **testable**—that is, the means for manipulating antecedent conditions and measuring the resulting behavior must exist. There are many interesting hypotheses that are currently of no scientific use because they do not meet this criterion. For example, have you ever wondered whether your dog dreams? Many dogs make movements and sounds in their sleep that resemble the way they behave when they are awake

---

[1]Ex post facto hypotheses can also be stated in this form, as illustrated by the following: "If people are repressors, then they report fewer treatment side effects."

and engaging in familiar activities—if its legs move and it barks just like it does when it chases the cat, maybe it's dreaming about chasing the cat. And some people hypothesize that dogs dream because they exhibit behaviors that correspond to behaviors associated with dream reports in humans—rapid eye movements, muscle twitches, even occasional vocalizations. Suppose we propose a research hypothesis in the "If . . . then" form: "If dogs display muscle twitches and vocalizations during sleep, then they must be dreaming."

We now have a hypothesis in proper form. But how do we proceed to test it? We could manipulate any number of antecedents to encourage sleep. We might start with a simple comparison of dogs fed warm food versus those fed food at room temperature. Some might sleep more than others. But how will we know if they are dreaming? We can ask them, of course, although we cannot expect any useful answers. The difficulty here is that we have an interesting but, alas, untestable hypothesis. The means for observing and recording the behavior of interest—namely, dreaming in dogs—does not exist.

Still, untestable hypotheses are not necessarily useless. Scientists who speculated on what it would be like to walk on the moon probably generated quite a few untestable hypotheses at the start. But there is always the hope that new technology will open new areas of discovery. Someday perhaps dreams will be projected on television screens. We will then know not only whether dogs dream but—if they do—what they are dreaming about. In the meantime, if you are reading this book as part of a course assignment, it will be to your advantage to work with hypotheses you can test.

Falsifiable Statements

Statements of research hypotheses must be **falsifiable** (disprovable) by the research findings. Hypotheses need to be worded so that failures to find the predicted effect must be considered evidence that the hypothesis is indeed false. Consider the following (purely illustrative) "If . . . then" statement: "If you read this book carefully enough, then you will be able to design a good experiment." Suppose you carefully read the book, spending hours on each chapter, and after you finish we ask you to design an experiment. You come up with an experiment, but your design is not very good. Given the wording of the statement (it contains the qualifier *enough*), would we be willing to accept this evidence that our book did not teach experimental methods very well? More likely, we would be tempted to say that you simply did not read it carefully *enough*. As the hypothesis was worded, it simply is not falsifiable, because any failures to produce the predicted effect can be explained away by the researcher.

Parsimonious Statements

A research hypothesis should also be **parsimonious**. You will recall from Chapter 1 that parsimony means that the simplest explanation is preferred. Thus a simple hypothesis is preferred over one that requires many supporting assumptions. The hypothesis, "If you look at an appealing photograph,

"Hey! I think you've hit on something there! Sheep's clothing! Sheep's clothing! . . . Let's get out of these gorilla suits!"

then your pupils will dilate" would be preferred over "If you look at an appealing photograph, then your pupils will dilate if it is a warm Saturday in June."

Fruitful Statements

Ideally, a hypothesis is also **fruitful;** that is, it leads to new studies. It is often difficult to know in advance which hypotheses will be the most fruitful. There is some indication that a hypothesis is fruitful when we can think of new studies that will become important if the hypothesis is supported. An example of a fruitful hypothesis is Watson and Rayner's 1920 study of classical conditioning. These researchers hypothesized that fear of otherwise neutral objects could be acquired through learning. Their hypothesis might be stated in the "If . . . then" form as follows: "If a child, Albert, is repeatedly exposed to a loud, cry-inducing noise in the presence of a harmless furry animal, then Albert will begin to cry at the sight of the animal alone." This hypothesis and its confirmation led to a multitude of studies on classical conditioning in human subjects that continues today.

We have considered what may seem like an overwhelming number of criteria for a good hypothesis. The good hypothesis is a synthetic statement of the "If . . . then" form. It is testable, falsifiable, parsimonious, and fruitful.

With so many criteria and so many areas of research, how does an experimenter ever arrive at a hypothesis? According to Bertrand Russell (1945), "As a rule, the framing of hypotheses is the most difficult part of scientific work, and the part where great ability is indispensable. So far, no method has been found which would make it possible to invent hypotheses by rule" (p. 545).

Even so, a number of general approaches can describe the way in which hypotheses are most often formed. Although there are no rules that can be used to generate hypotheses, an understanding of these approaches will help you to think about the psychological issues you might like to study experimentally.

THE INDUCTIVE MODEL

The **inductive model** of formulating a hypothesis, the process of reasoning from specific cases to more general principles, is often used in science and mathematics. By examining individual instances, we may be able to construct an overall classification scheme to describe them.

Has something like this ever happened to you at a party? A stranger comes over to you and says: "You must be a Libra. I can tell by your beautiful clothes, your meticulous grooming, and the birthstone ring you're wearing." The stranger has tried a somewhat overworked conversation starter—but it illustrates the basics of inductive thinking. He or she has taken certain specific facts about you (your style of dress and your manner) and used them to reach a more general conclusion about you—your birth sign. A person familiar with astrology may take certain specific facts about you and arrive at a hypothesis about your birth sign through induction.

Research hypotheses often come from the use of inductive reasoning. While standing in line at the dorm cafeteria, you may have noticed many instances of athletes (who tend to wear clothes advertising their sport) cutting to the front of the food line. You also notice that no one seems to challenge their behavior. You come up with your own explanation for this: Being identified as an athlete allows a person privileges not available to nonathletes. This is a hypothesis that came about through induction. You observed several specific instances of behavior and used these instances to form a general principle to explain the behavior. You may be able to come up with an interesting idea for testing it experimentally.

B. F. Skinner (1904–1990) was a convincing advocate for inductive research in psychology. Skinner (see Figure 5-1) extensively studied operant conditioning in rats and pigeons. In *operant conditioning,* the organism is reinforced or rewarded when it produces a particular response, such as bar pressing, which has been selected by the experimenter for reinforcement. Skinner studied many variations of the basic operant procedures, keeping careful records of what happened to behavior under various conditions. He tried giving reinforcement on some but not all occasions when the animal emitted the required response. He tried new reinforcement contingencies based solely on the number of responses emitted (one pellet of food for each three bar presses) or on the elapsed time (one pellet of food per minute for one or more bar

FIGURE 5-1 B. F. Skinner (1904–1990).
Brooks/Cole photo

presses). He tried withholding reinforcement after the response was well established. From the results of numerous experiments, Skinner developed the concepts of partial reinforcement and extinction, along with reliable descriptions of the way intermittent reinforcement alters behavior (Ferster & Skinner, 1957). Concepts essential to understanding the learning process grew out of Skinner's inductive approach.

Induction is the basic tool of theory building. A *theory* is a set of general principles that can be used to explain and predict behavior. Through induction, researchers construct theories by taking bits of empirical data and forming general explanatory schemes to accommodate those facts. While we may not put much faith in it, the 12 astrological signs represent a theory of behavior. Some scientific theories have been constructed on the work of a single researcher, such as Skinner. Other times, theories come about by assimilating the research of many experimenters into general explanatory principles. For instance, the theory of the *mere exposure effect* came about as a result of reviewing the published results of many past experiments that seemed to zero in on the same conclusion: The more we are exposed to something, the more we like it (Zajonc, 1966). Over the years Zajonc and his students have refined the theory through experimentation, and its success can be seen by how often the theory is used as the basis of advertising and political campaigns.

THE DEDUCTIVE MODEL

The **deductive model** of formulating a hypothesis is the converse of the inductive model. Deduction is the process of reasoning from general principles to make predictions about specific instances. The deductive model is most useful when we have a well-developed theory with clearly stated basic premises. Then it is possible to deduce predictions about what should happen in new situations in which the theory would apply. Testing such predictions provides a test of the value of the theory.

An excellent example of the deductive method in psychology is research that stemmed from predictions generated by *equity theory* (Walster, Walster, & Berscheid, 1978). These psychologists were not the first to consider equity (or perceived fairness) an important determinant of behavior in human relationships. Philosophers like Aristotle also believed it was important. But Walster, Walster, and Berscheid provided a comprehensive and useful theory of equity in interpersonal situations. They proposed that the behavior of individuals could be predicted by three simple propositions:

1. Individuals will try to optimize their outcomes (outcomes = rewards minus costs).
2. When individuals believe they are in an inequitable relationship, they will feel distress in direct proportion to the perceived degree of inequity.
3. The more distress they feel, the harder they will work to restore equity.

Equity theory has been used by many researchers to predict behavior. It has successfully predicted outcomes in a great number of interpersonal circumstances: victimization, helping, employment, and love are a few. Apparently, whether we feel overbenefited or underbenefited in a relationship, we will do what we can to restore a sense of fairness. For example, Pritchard, Dunnette, and Jorgenson (1972) found that workers who *felt* they were overpaid relative to others doing the same job actually worked harder than other workers who believed they were paid less than others. (In actuality, the researchers manipulated the antecedent conditions so that everyone was being paid the same wage.)

COMBINING INDUCTION AND DEDUCTION

We have looked at induction and deduction as two separate approaches to formulating a hypothesis. In practice, these approaches are not so neatly separated. As you might imagine, theorists like Walster, Walster, and Berscheid did not formulate equity theory without some reference to specific cases. They formulated the theory on the basis of their own and others' observations. In fact, the list of references used for the book describing their theory included over 500 such observations, which were used as evidence for the theory. Thus their propositions were formed initially through induction from specific cases.

Later tests of the propositions were based on predictions derived through deduction. Box 5-1 illustrates the importance of these processes in the work of the chemist Dmitri Mendeleyev.

Both induction and deduction are important in research, and both are useful in formulating hypotheses for study. Through induction we devise general principles and theories that can be used to organize, explain, and predict behavior until more satisfactory principles are found. Through deduction we rigorously test the implications of those theories.

BUILDING ON PRIOR RESEARCH

So far we have discussed global approaches that can be applied to a variety of research topics. Now we will look at how the researcher narrows down the field of possibilities enough to formulate a single hypothesis. The most useful way of finding hypotheses is by working from research that has already been done. The nonexperimental studies we discussed in Chapters 3 and 4, for example, are good sources of ideas for experimentation. Nonexperimental studies can *suggest* cause and effect explanations that can be translated into experimental hypotheses. We will look briefly at some examples of the way in which this might be done.

The Bechtol and Williams (1977) study of California litter (discussed in Chapter 3) was a field study. Bechtol and Williams observed people on an unregulated beach in California to see who would litter and concluded that everyone littered. One explanation for littering suggested by Bechtol and Williams was that there were no trash baskets on the unregulated beach. From this observation we may state a testable hypothesis about littering: "If there are no trash baskets, then people will litter." We could set up different antecedent conditions to test the hypothesis experimentally. We set up one beach with trash baskets and an identical beach without trash baskets. Let us assume that the people who use the two beaches are comparable. Given our hypothesis, we would expect to find less litter on the beach that has trash baskets. If trash baskets have no effect on littering, we would find the same amount of litter accumulating on both beaches. If the predicted difference in litter for the two beaches occurs, we conclude that the lack of trash baskets causes littering.

The other nonexperimental approaches may also lead to experimental hypotheses. One very important example is the research on cigarette smoking and cancer. At first, only correlational and ex post facto data were available. Researchers noted a positive correlation between smoking and lung cancer. In ex post facto studies, smokers had higher rates of lung cancer than nonsmokers. This finding suggested the hypothesis that smoking causes cancer. Stated in the "If . . . then" form: "If people smoke, then they will get cancer." Experimenters test the hypothesis under controlled conditions. Because of ethical issues, the subjects in these experiments are animals rather than humans: If smoking really does cause cancer, scientists would not want to expose human subjects to smoking. The experiments begin with the creation of different antecedent conditions—groups of rats are exposed to varying amounts of

BOX 5-1

DMITRI MENDELEYEV AND THE PERIODIC TABLE

The work of Dmitri Mendeleyev illustrates the use of induction to generate scientific hypotheses. Mendeleyev was a 19th-century chemist interested in devising a meaningful classification scheme for all 66 elements known at that time. He reviewed the atomic weight (the weight of a single atom as compared to a standard) and the typical properties of all the elements. Mendeleyev saw a pattern, a general relationship now known as the periodic law: When arranged according to their atomic weights, the elements show a periodical change in properties. From the patterns he observed, Mendeleyev was able to predict the discovery of a number of elements as well as their properties (Partington, 1964). Although his classification scheme has been revised to incorporate newly discovered elements (there are now 112 in all), Mendeleyev's basic work remains a cornerstone of chemistry and physics.

Although we have discussed Mendeleyev as an example of an inductive thinker, his work also illustrates the complementary nature of induction and deduction. Mendeleyev saw a pattern in the atomic numbers of the elements and their properties. However, he also saw that some elements did not exactly fit this pattern. Having arrived at the general pattern through induction, Mendeleyev deduced that some of the atomic numbers on record were inaccurate. The probable course of Mendeleyev's thinking is represented schematically by Figure 5-2.

cigarette smoke. If rats that "smoke" develop higher rates of cancer than rats that do not, the conclusion is that smoking causes cancer. Again, the systematic manipulation of the antecedent conditions permits us to make cause and effect inferences that cannot be made on the basis of nonexperimental data alone.

Prior experimental research is another excellent source of hypotheses. If you do not already have a specific hypothesis in mind, you will find the experimental literature useful in focusing your thinking on important issues. As you read more and more studies in an area, you may begin to see points that other researchers have missed or new applications for previously tested hypotheses. These may form the basis for new experiments. For instance, if you are interested in equity theory, reading what others have done can trigger ideas for new applications of the theory—perhaps feelings about the fairness of course grades would predict how many hours students are willing to put into a course. Other

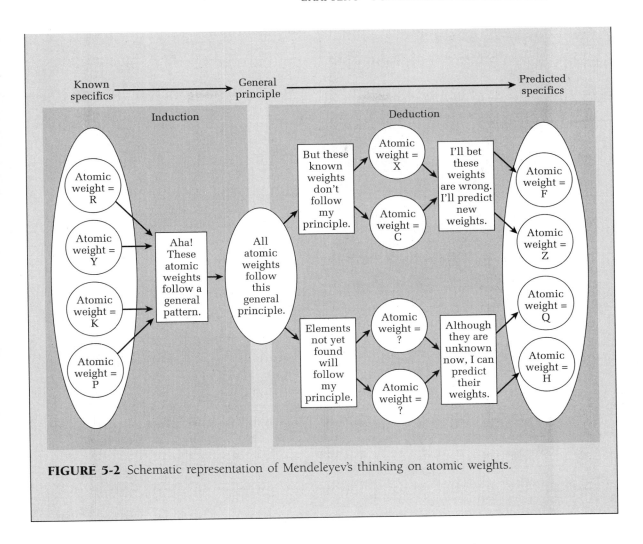

FIGURE 5-2 Schematic representation of Mendeleyev's thinking on atomic weights.

times, past research will suggest additional variables that could mediate an effect demonstrated in an experiment—perhaps littering is not directly caused by the availability of trash baskets, but instead is mediated by the amount of alcohol consumed by the sunbathers. By reading prior studies, you will also see the kinds of problems others have had in researching a topic. This will help you to anticipate difficulties you might not have thought of alone.

A thorough search of the literature available on your topic is important in designing a good experiment and essential to writing an effective report, as we will see at the end of this chapter. Regardless of where an experimental hypothesis originates, reviewing the literature is still a necessary component of report writing. An important goal of report writing is to integrate your findings into existing facts. A good literature review will also help you avoid duplicating someone else's work when a replication is not what you had in mind.

FIGURE 5-3 Ivan Pavlov (1849–1936).
National Library of Medicine

SERENDIPITY AND THE WINDFALL HYPOTHESIS

All the approaches we have looked at so far are purposeful; the experimenter is usually looking for a new hypothesis on which to base an experiment. However, at times a discovery has been made where none was intended; such discoveries may be attributed to serendipity. The word comes from the 18th-century tale "The Three Princes of Serendip" by Horace Walpole, which describes the adventures of three princes who found many valuable things they were not seeking. **Serendipity** is the knack of finding things that are not being sought. Discoveries through serendipity have been made in the physical sciences as well as in psychology.

An element of serendipity appeared in the work of Ivan Pavlov (1927), a Russian physiologist whose main interest was the digestive glands (Figure 5-3). His studies involved feeding dogs and observing the changes that occurred in their stomach secretions. Through his work Pavlov became interested in salivation. He asked such questions as, "If I feed the dog, how long will it be before the dog begins to salivate?" The questions seemed straightforward enough until Pavlov began to notice some distracting things. As the dogs became familiar with the bread Pavlov fed them, they began to salivate even before they were actually fed. Seeing the food seemed to produce salivation. Indeed, in a short while the dogs began to salivate as soon as he entered the room. Pavlov found these observations so interesting that he began to study the "psychic secretions" that he hypothesized were the result of the dogs' mental activity. His unplanned observations pulled him in a most unexpected direction.

What Pavlov observed was the phenomenon of classical conditioning. Initially, salivation was elicited only by eating the food. After repeated pairings, the sight of the food, as well as the sight of Pavlov, elicited salivation. Pavlov won the Nobel Prize for his work on digestion, but he also made an unplanned contribution to the psychological study of learning.

Are such happy accidents really achievements? Didn't animal trainers and many parents know about conditioning already? Couldn't anyone have made the same contribution as Pavlov, if not with salivation, then with some other response? The answer is probably, "No." What distinguishes a scientist like Pavlov is that he was able to distinguish between a commonplace incident and something of great importance. Another person might have abandoned the salivation research as hopeless. Pavlov continued his research, performing many new experiments and offering unique interpretations of his findings. Serendipity can be useful in generating new hypotheses only when we are open to new possibilities (remember woodenheadedness?). The good scientist takes note of all potentially relevant observations and analyzes and evaluates them: Are they interpretable? Do they explain something that was previously unexplained? Do they suggest a new way of looking at a problem? Serendipity is not just a matter of luck; it is also a matter of knowing enough to use an opportunity.

INTUITION

Intuition, another approach we will examine here, is not discussed in most experimental psychology texts. Psychology is a science, and as such it should be governed by formal, logical rules. But using intuition is not necessarily unscientific; rather, the inferences drawn from intuition can sometimes violate scientific criteria.

Intuition may be defined as knowing without reasoning. As such, it is probably closest to phenomenology. We acquire phenomenological knowledge simply by attending to our own experience. However, intuition may take us beyond mere apprehension of our own experiences. We may feel by intuition that a close relative has died. Because what the feeling is cannot be specified in observable, quantifiable terms, it seems out of place in a scientific context.

Although it is difficult to be concrete about what we mean by intuition, intuition is probably a very common basis for experimentation. We have a hunch about what might happen in a particular situation, so we set up an experiment to test it. Intuition guides what we choose to study. Of course, our experiments are still conducted in the context of prior research. We review the experimental literature to avoid carrying out experiments that are pointless given what is already known. For example, we may believe intuitively that dogs can see colors, but a review of the prior work on perception shows that they cannot.[2] Knowing this, we would not begin a new series of tests to check color vision in dogs.

---

[2]Dogs are able to discriminate brightness. Such discriminations sometimes appear to be based on color, but dogs do not have color vision.

When is intuition likely to be most helpful? According to Herbert Simon (1967), a psychologist and computer scientist who won the Nobel Prize, intuition is most accurate if it comes from experts. He believes that good hunches are really an unconscious result of our own expertise in an area—not a form of clairvoyance at all! The more we know about a topic, the better our intuitive hypotheses are likely to be.

We must be careful to remain within the bounds of science when we use our intuition. By intuition, we may have a tentative explanation for behavior or events. But such an explanation is truly tentative. It cannot be accepted as valid until it has been translated into a hypothesis and subjected to empirical tests. (Also keep in mind the discussion from Chapter 1 about the kinds of cognitive and judgment errors people tend to make.)

Intuition is just that—and it should not be confused with fact. If we were going on vacation and knew only by intuition that the plane leaves at noon, it would be risky to go to the airport without first checking to verify the flight schedule. Furthermore, intuition should not turn into woodenheadedness and destroy objectivity. Even though we believe intuitively that something is true, we must be prepared to change our thinking if the experimental evidence does not confirm our belief. Unless we find flaws in the experiment that would account for why our expectations were not confirmed, the observable data take precedence over intuition. Box 5-2 contains an example of some results that don't match what our intuition tells us.

WHEN ALL ELSE FAILS

If you are reading this text as part of a course requirement, you may be required to design an experiment of your own. You realize by now that you must have a hypothesis. Perhaps you also realize that our discussion of the ways in which others derive hypotheses has not been particularly helpful. As Russell said, there are no rules that can be used to generate hypotheses. If you feel completely at sea, here are some suggestions that have helped other students.

You are least likely to come up with a hypothesis by trying to think about everything you know about psychology. Begin by focusing on one or two broad areas that interest you. Perhaps you like learning and memory. If so, that is the place to start.

Once you select some broad areas of interest, take out a general psychology text and reread the sections on these areas. You may now be able to narrow down the number of possible topics even further. Perhaps you are most interested in the work on learning lists of words. Now locate the latest research that has been done in this area. You may have to do quite a bit of reading before you can derive a hypothesis of your own. Try to structure your reading in terms of the approaches we have discussed. Do you find any specific instances that suggest general principles? Is there a study that sets out a theory leading to deductions that are testable? Were there nonexperimental studies that can be redone as experiments to test cause and effect inferences? You

B O X   5 - 2

THE HOME FIELD DISADVANTAGE*

Sports fans often mention the *home field advantage* when predicting the chances of their favorite team in a sports championship. We typically assume that playing at home gives a team the edge. The presence of the cheering fans spurs players on to do their best. Or does it? Baumeister and Steinhilber (1984) put the question to an empirical test through a creative application of the ex post facto approach.

The researchers read through the sports archives and analyzed data on home and away victories during each World Series from 1924 through 1982. They found that the home team enjoyed a clear advantage during the early games of a series. However, during decisive last or seventh games (pressure situations), the visitors won significantly more often. The results are summarized in Table 5-1.

Similar results were found for fielding errors committed during World Series games. Analysis of basketball (NBA) championship and semifinal playoff series showed comparable patterns.

Baumeister and Steinhilber had predicted these findings on the basis of prior research on self-presentation and self-attention. The self-presentation model suggests that thinking about our image distracts us from doing what needs to be done: "To give a crude but relevant example, the [baseball] shortstop who is busy imagining himself celebrated as a World Series hero in a victory parade may misjudge the ball bouncing toward him and make a fielding error" (p. 86).

The self-attention model suggests that paying too much attention to

TABLE 5-1 World Series game results 1924–1982

| Games | Winners | | Home % |
	Home	Visitor	
1 and 2	59	39	.602
Last game	20	29	.408
7	10	16	.385

NOTE: Tabulations exclude ten Series in which the same team won all the games.

(continued)

(continued)

skills that have become automatic may disrupt them and hamper performance: "The shortstop who monitors the arm and hand muscle movements by which he throws the baseball to first base, after years of doing it automatically, may alter the skillful execution and make an error" (p. 86). Baumeister and Steinhilber did not try to determine which explanation works better for their findings. It is clear, however, that contrary to popular belief, the home field advantage is nothing to cheer about.

*Table 5-1 and quotes from "Paradoxical Effects of Supportive Audiences on Performance Under Pressure: The Home Field Disadvantage in Sports Championships," by R. F. Baumeister and A. Steinhilber, 1984, *Journal of Personality and Social Psychology, 47*, 85–93. Copyright ©1984 American Psychological Association. Reprinted with permission.

may hit upon something by accident, or you may develop a hunch about what might happen in a slightly new experimental setting.

Here is another suggestion: Try observation. Some very good hypotheses come from observing how people behave in public places. In graduate school an early class assignment of one of the authors was to go to a public place and observe people until a testable experimental hypothesis was found. It worked. Forming hypotheses about the kinds of antecedent conditions that affect people's behavior comes naturally—we do it all the time. These hypotheses are called *causal attributions* (Kelley, 1971). We search for a cause to which we can attribute someone's behavior. Has the following ever happened to you? You are driving behind a slow automobile on a one-lane road, and it seems to you that the driver speeds up whenever it is legal to pass and slows down in the no-passing areas. You can form a hypothesis about this behavior (and you probably will). You may decide that the cause of the slowing down is *internal* (dispositional)—the person is a bad driver, or worse, a real blockhead. Or you could decide that the cause is *external* (situational)—the no-passing lanes are always on hills, and some cars have trouble maintaining their speed on hills. Either causal attribution could be turned into a research hypothesis.

Finally, if all else fails, turn your attention to a real-world problem and try to figure out what causes it. An added benefit of this approach is that once the cause can be determined, a solution often suggests itself. A psychologist studying vision noticed that the elderly have more trouble than others reading road signs. He hypothesized that the problem was caused by the spatial frequency of letters and numbers typically placed on the signs. Experimentation confirmed this hypothesis and led to subsequent research to find a spatial frequency (width of line contours) that was more easily read by all drivers (Schieber, 1988). Attempting to discover causes of littering, vandalism, or shoplifting would be other examples of real-world problems to explore.

Since there are no rules, it is usually impossible to predict how long it will take to develop a good hypothesis. Remember that the work you will do in a single course is not expected to alter the course of psychology. Set realistic goals for yourself. Work from hypotheses that can be tested in the time frame you have available. You will probably need all the time you can get, which means that it is not a good idea to wait until the last minute to begin thinking about a hypothesis—or to begin searching the literature, the topic of the next section.

SEARCHING THE RESEARCH LITERATURE

Getting Started

Conducting a thorough literature search is an important part of conducting research, and it is necessary for writing a research report. In searching the literature, you are looking for important research that has already been done on your topic. Thousands of research articles are published each year in **psychological journals,** periodicals that publish individual research reports and integrative research reviews (up-to-date summaries of what is known about a specific topic). If your literature search is thorough, you are bound to be able to locate work done to test your hypothesis or one that is closely related. Published research reports on your topic can also help you to get good ideas for procedures to use in your own experiment, and they are full of tips for measuring your observations.

Conducting a literature search is bound to seem daunting at first, because there are simply so many sources available. Besides journal articles, entire books may have been written on the topic that interests you. Be on the lookout for edited volumes that contain chapters written by experts in your topic area; they can be a particularly good place to start because they summarize the most important recent work. (You may find a few useful references in psychology textbooks, too.) Research reviews, whether they come from journals or books, give you an overview of a topic area, and they are an invaluable source of references as well. If an experiment is summarized that seems like it might be relevant to your experiment, you can use the reference to look up and read the original research report.

A particularly good source of information is a *meta-analysis* conducted on your topic, which can be found in either journals or edited volumes. Meta-analysis is a statistical reviewing procedure that utilizes data from many similar studies to summarize research findings about individual topics. A meta-analysis has the added benefit of quantification of past findings—it uses special statistical procedures to measure how strong the cause and effect relationship between the antecedent conditions and measured behaviors appears to be. And because they are statistically derived, conclusions from a meta-analysis can be more objective than review articles. In general, it is best to skip popular books written by nonresearchers, essays, and sources from popular media, such as popular magazines and newspapers. While they may be a source of interesting hypotheses, these are not considered reliable or scientific sources of information (remember the safety report about car size?).

Writing the Report

Published research reports from psychological journals will form the bulk of the reading you are expected to do as background for writing a research report. The **Introduction** section of a research report consists of a *selective review* of relevant, recent research. (Only if your topic has a long history would you include early articles.) We say the review is selective because the writer selects only the articles that are directly related to the research *hypothesis*—not everything that has ever been done on the topic. The specific studies cited in the Introduction should provide empirical background for your experiment and guide the reader toward your research hypothesis. (Specific tips on writing can be found in Chapter 16.)

Another goal of a research report is to integrate your experiment into the existing body of knowledge: to show how your research advances knowledge, increases generalizability of known effects, or contradicts past findings. In order to do this, you may need to refer to specific past work in the **Discussion** section of your research report as well. (You can read more on this in Chapter 16.) The implications of your findings—what the results mean—go in this section. If your findings are inconsistent with past results reported by other researchers, you will need to explain that here as well by contrasting your study with theirs.

Finding the Articles You Need

Fortunately, there are many library aids to help you find the journal articles you need. The most important resource for psychologists is *Psychological Abstracts,* published by the American Psychological Association. Each month, APA publishes abstracts (summaries) of research that has been published on your topic in the major psychological journals worldwide. You can search the abstracts by hand, using the set of published index volumes, but this is an extremely time-consuming process. Almost all university libraries now have on-line computer literature searches available for students. Usually, you can do this yourself; if not, your library will conduct one for you (but there may be a charge for this). You can type in key words (by subject or by author) to call up abstracts and references on your topic, and the computer will generate a printout for you. In some facilities, you can copy the information onto a diskette. However, you still have to select the abstracts that seem most relevant, locate the journal articles, and read them.[3]

---

[3]Unless your university library is very large (and heavily endowed), do not expect it to have all the journals you want. However, unavailable articles can be easily ordered through interlibrary loan services, and you can usually get them within a few days. Nowadays, some libraries even have fax service available.

(a)   PC-SPIRS 3.30   Journal Articles 1/74–12/89

No.	Records	Request
#1	394	BARON
#2	2095	RUSSELL
#3	2	#1 and #2
#4	503	ARMS
#5	1	#3 and #4

(b)   PC-SPIRS 3.30   Journal Articles 1/74–12/89

No.	Records	Request
#1	202	IONS
#2	4223	MOOD
#3	10	#1 and #2
#4	16926	MEMORY
#5	1	#3 and #4

FIGURE 5-4 PsycLIT searches for Baron, Russell, and Arms (1985) by authors (panel a) and by key words (panel b).

PsycLIT, a CD-ROM based program for personal computers, is the most widely available computerized abstract retrieval service. You will need to learn a few commands, but once you master them, the program is relatively user-friendly (PsycLIT has its own tutorial). For example, it allows you to use several key words at once to narrow down your topic precisely, so that abstracts only peripherally related to your topic are skipped. Start with the most recent abstracts. Remember that journal articles contain lists of references that can be used to go farther back into a problem if necessary. We have found that the biggest problem with PsycLIT is discovering the correct key words to use for the search. The *Thesaurus of Psychological Index Terms,* published by APA, is a useful guide to key word terminology. PsycLIT also allows a search by author as you identify key people in your area of interest.

Figure 5-4 shows how we searched PsycLIT for information about the negative ion study by Baron, Russell, and Arms (1985) cited in Chapters 1, 2, and 4. The first search was by authors; the second by key words. Notice how using several names or words narrows down the number of potential articles from hundreds or, in some cases, thousands to the single article we want in only a few steps. The information actually retrieved by PsycLIT is shown in Figure 5-5.

Another good source of journal articles (after you have identified key people) is the *Social Science Citations Index.* Here you will find each author's publications listed and, after each publication, a list of other authors who have used those publications in their research reports. Generally, these newer reports are articles about research on a closely related topic.[4]

---

[4]The sources listed here are the major ones for psychology; however, many more abstract retrieval services are available. There are other sources in psychology, and all major disciplines (education, sociology, medicine, and so forth) have their own. Should you wish to use one or more of these, ask your librarian what is available in your library.

FIGURE 5-5 Information about Baron, Russell, and Arms (1985) retrieved from PsycLIT

SUMMARY

Every experiment is designed to test a hypothesis about the effects of different treatment conditions on behavior. Every experiment must have a hypothesis. The *hypothesis* represents the end of the process of thinking about a behavior and zeroing in on one particular explanation that seems plausible.

The *experimental hypothesis* has several characteristics. First, it must be a *synthetic statement*. A hypothesis meets the definition of a synthetic statement if it can be stated in the "If . . . then" form. Second, the experimental hypothesis must be *testable:* The means for manipulating the antecedent conditions and measuring the resulting behavior must exist. The hypothesis must be disprovable or *falsifiable.* The hypothesis must also be *parsimonious;* the simplest hypothesis is preferred until it is ruled out by conflicting evidence. Ideally, the hypothesis is also *fruitful* and will lead to new research.

Hypotheses may be found through induction, deduction, prior research, serendipity, or intuition. *Induction* is the process of reasoning from specific cases to more general principles. *Deduction* is the process of reasoning from general principles to predictions about specific instances. In practice, induction and deduction are often used together. Through induction we may devise general principles, or theories, that may be used to organize, explain, and predict behavior until more satisfactory principles are found. Through deduction, we may rigorously test the implications of a premise or theory.

Regardless of which method we use, we are generally *building on prior research.* Ex post facto and other nonexperimental studies may suggest experiments to test cause and effect relationships. Hypotheses occasionally grow out of *serendipity,* the knack of finding things that are not being sought. Researchers occasionally make unexpected observations that lead them in surprising directions. *Intuition* may also lead to hypotheses. We may have a hunch that something is true and carry out an experiment to test that notion.

Hypotheses may also arise out of systematic searches through the research in specific areas of interest. Finally, hypotheses may come from *everyday observation* of behaviors and real-world problems.

The first step in designing research and writing a research report is to conduct a thorough literature search. The *Psychological Abstracts* are the most important source for locating the journal articles you will need. A computer search of the abstracts, using key word searches, is available through PsycLIT. The articles you select provide the basis for the *Introduction* section of the report and can also be used in the *Discussion* section to integrate your experiment into the body of literature.

KEY TERMS

Analytic statement A statement that is always true.

Contradictory statement A statement that is always false.

Deductive model The process of reasoning from general principles to specific instances; most useful for testing the principles of a theory.

Discussion Concluding section of the research report, used to integrate the experimental findings into the existing body of knowledge; showing how the current research advances knowledge, increases generalizability of known effects, or contradicts past findings.

Experimental hypothesis A statement that predicts the effects of specified antecedent conditions on a measured behavior.

Falsifiable statement A statement that is worded so that it is falsifiable, or disprovable.

Fruitful statement A statement that leads to new studies.

Hypothesis The thesis, or main idea, of an experiment consisting of a statement that predicts the relationship between at least two variables.

Inductive model The process of reasoning from specific cases to more general principles to form a hypothesis.

Introduction Beginning section of a research report that guides the reader toward your research hypothesis; includes a selective review of relevant, recent research.

Intuition The development of ideas from hunches; knowing directly without reasoning from objective data.

Nonexperimental hypothesis A statement of predictions of how events, traits, or behaviors might be related, but not a statement about cause and effect.

Parsimonious statement A statement that is simple and does not require many supporting assumptions.

Psychological journal A periodical that publishes individual research reports and integrative research reviews, which are up-to-date summaries of what is known about a specific topic.

Serendipity The knack of finding things that are not being sought.

Synthetic statement A statement that can be either true or false, a condition necessary to form an experimental hypothesis.

Testable statement A statement that can be tested because the means exist for manipulating antecedent conditions and for measuring the resulting behavior.

REVIEW AND STUDY QUESTIONS

1. What is a hypothesis?
2. What are the characteristics of a good hypothesis?
3. Which of the following are synthetic statements? Why?
   a. If I am cold, then it is December.
   b. Out of sight, out of mind.
   c. Virtue is its own reward.
   d. A statement that is always true is always true.
4. Explain what is meant by induction and deduction. How are they different?
5. What is serendipity?
6. Is a discovery made through serendipity just a matter of luck?
7. a. What is the role of intuition in research?
   b. Is intuition scientific?
   c. Why are our hunches often correct?
8. Before you set up an experiment, you should make a review of the research literature. What is the purpose of such a review?
9. Dr. P. has just completed a study that shows a correlation between the amount of time children watch television and their attention span. Assume the correlation was $-.34$. State an experimental hypothesis based on this finding and devise a simple procedure for testing it.
10. Explain the way in which an ex post facto study could be used to generate an experimental hypothesis.
11. Mary is lost: She just cannot think of a hypothesis. Give her some advice on how to proceed.
12. Select one of the research areas listed below. Review some of the prior work in that area and formulate a new experimental hypothesis based on your review.
    a. Paired-associate learning
    b. The influence of a set in problem solving
    c. Solving anagrams (scrambled words)
    d. Bystander apathy
    e. The mere exposure effect
13. Sit in a public place and observe people for an hour. Write down all the hypotheses that come to mind to explain their behaviors.

C H A P T E R   6

THE BASICS OF EXPERIMENTATION

Once you have formulated a hypothesis, the next step is to design a procedure to test it. As you saw in Chapters 3 and 4, there are many useful nonexperimental approaches to research. Each demands special skills, and each could form the basis of an entire text. The remainder of this book, however, deals primarily with experimentation. Much of the research currently done in the field of psychology is experimental. Moreover, an understanding of the principles of experimentation strengthens any researcher's potential for success.

When it is feasible, psychologists prefer experiments over other research methods because a properly conducted experiment allows us to draw causal inferences about behavior. When an experiment is well conducted, it is high in internal validity. To review briefly, the psychology experiment has these main features: We manipulate the antecedent conditions to create at least two different treatment conditions. At least two treatments are required so that we can make statements about the impact of different sets of antecedents; if we used only one treatment, there would be no way to evaluate what happens to behaviors as the conditions change. We expose subjects to different treatment conditions so that we can measure the effects of those conditions on behavior. We record the responses or behaviors of subjects under various conditions and then compare them. We can then assess whether our predictions are confirmed.

Doing an experiment allows us to draw causal inferences about behavior. If behavior changes as the antecedent conditions change, we may say that the differences in antecedent conditions caused the difference in behavior. However, such an inference is justified only when a carefully controlled test of our predictions has been made. A researcher must consider a number of influences that can threaten an experiment's internal validity. The chapters in this section of the text deal with the basic methods and problems involved in planning a good experiment.

In this chapter you will begin to see how researchers move from the general idea expressed in a hypothesis to the specific actions required to carry out an experiment. For the purposes of scientific research, the experimenter must clearly define what is being studied, and how, so that the research can be evaluated as well as replicated.

By the end of this chapter, you will be familiar with the basic components of experiments: the independent variable, the dependent variable, operational definitions, and control. We will examine these concepts in the context of specific experiments. We will also discuss some issues involved in evaluating definitions and experiments: reliability, validity, and confounding. We will take a look at some classic threats to internal validity. The concepts presented in this chapter are fundamentals of experimental design that we will return to again and again throughout the book.

INDEPENDENT AND DEPENDENT VARIABLES

An experimental hypothesis states a potential relationship between two variables: If *A* occurs, then we expect *B* to follow. Variables are aspects of an experiment that vary, things that can take on different values along some dimension. To be more precise, the experimental hypothesis expresses a potential relationship between two kinds of variables, the independent and the dependent variable. We will begin with some textbook definitions of these terms and then look at some concrete examples from actual research.

An experiment's **independent variable (IV)** is the dimension that the experimenter intentionally manipulates; it is the antecedent the *experimenter* chooses to vary. This variable is "independent" in the sense that its values are created by the experimenter and are not affected by anything else that happens in the experiment. Independent variables are often simply aspects of the physical environment that can be brought under the experimenter's direct control; we call these **environmental variables.** Illumination (bright or dim), typeface size (large or small), and noise levels (loud or soft) are some examples. Aspects of a given task may also become independent variables; we call these **task variables.** Complexity (easy, moderate, or difficult), mode of presentation (auditory versus visual), and meaningfulness (nonsense syllables versus real words) are examples of task variables.

At least two different treatment conditions are required to meet the definition of an experiment; thus the IV must be given at least two possible values in every experiment. The researcher decides which values of the IV to use. These values are called the **levels of the independent variable** in the experiment. The researcher varies the IV by creating different treatment conditions within the experiment. Each treatment condition represents one level of the IV. If the IV is to have two levels, there must be two different treatment conditions; if three values of the IV are to be used, there must be three different treatment conditions, and so on. Be careful not to confuse the levels of the IV with the IV itself. For example, suppose a professor tries giving tests on either blue or yellow paper to see if the color of the paper influences the scores. Blue and yellow represent two levels of the one IV, color. We could add other levels such as pink, green, and orange. We would still have only one IV—color.

In an ex post facto study (discussed in Chapter 4), the researcher may explore the way behavior changes as a function of changes in variables outside the researcher's control. These are typically **subject variables,** characteristics of the subjects themselves (age, personality characteristics, gender, and so on) that cannot be manipulated experimentally. It is common for researchers to refer to these quasi-experimental variables as independent variables too. Although they are not manipulated by the researcher, they are often independent in the sense that the researcher selects the particular values that will be included in the study. For instance, in their study of cancer patients' reactions to chemotherapy, Ward, Leventhal, and Love (1988) selected patients who showed repressor or nonrepressor coping styles.

In ex post facto and other quasi-experimental studies, researchers behave as if they were doing true experiments; they have treatments and measured observations (Cook & Campbell, 1979). However, in these kinds of studies the independent variable is not manipulated the way it is when we study something under our direct control, such as a drug dose or the brightness of a light. In quasi-experiments, the researcher *selects* rather than creates the levels of the IV by assigning subjects to treatment groups on the basis of a subject variable. In an ex post facto study, individuals in various treatment groups are supposed to differ on a subject variable because the subject variable is the one we are testing.

In a true experiment, we test the effects of a manipulated independent variable—not the effects of different kinds of subjects. Therefore, in a true experiment, we have to make certain that our treatment groups do not consist of people who are different on a preexisting characteristic. If we simultaneously varied *both* a subject variable and a manipulated independent variable, there would be no way of knowing whether effects we observed were due to differences between subjects or to the IV. For example, if we gave introverts their exams on blue paper and extroverts their exams on yellow paper, we would not know whether differences in their exam grades were caused by the color of the paper or personality differences. This problem is known as *confounding,* and we will return to it later in the chapter.

How will we know whether changes in the levels of the IV have altered behavior? We measure the dependent variable to determine whether the independent variable had an effect. The **dependent variable (DV)** is the particular behavior we expect to change as a result of our experimental intervention; it is the behavior we are trying to explain. Sometimes it helps to think of it this way: In an experiment, we are testing effects of the IV *on* the DV. Because we manipulate the IV and measure its effects on the DV, dependent variables are sometimes called *dependent measures.*

If the hypothesis is correct, different values of the independent variable should produce changes in the dependent variable. The dependent variable is dependent in the sense that its values are assumed to depend on the values of the independent variable: As the independent variable changes value (as

"THEN, AS YOU CAN SEE, WE GIVE THEM SOME MULTIPLE CHOICE TESTS."

we look at behavior under different treatment conditions), we expect to see corresponding changes in the value of the DV.

Selecting appropriate independent and dependent variables is an important part of setting up every experiment. If we expect to understand the causes of behavior, we need to focus on the relevant antecedents. Remember, if we can specify the antecedents that lead to a particular behavior, we have explained that behavior from a scientific viewpoint.

We also need to assess accurately the impact of our treatment conditions. In an experiment we cannot rely solely on our overall impression about whether the independent variable has some effect. We need more precision: We need an objective measure of the effect of the independent variable. We do not want the evaluation of the experiment's outcome to depend on our subjective judgment, which might be somewhat biased. In addition, our findings will have more widely understood meaning if they are presented in terms of an observable dimension that can be measured again and again. By clearly defining the way we are measuring the effect of the independent variable, we make it easier for others to replicate our research. Let us turn now to some specific examples of independent and dependent variables in the research literature.

Some Research Examples

Schachter

Consider this hypothesis, tested in an experiment by Schachter (1959): If people are anxious, then they will want to affiliate, or be, with others. Put another way, misery loves company. The hypothesis states a potential relationship between two variables—anxiety and affiliation. To test the hypothesis, Schachter did the following experiment: Subjects were brought into a room with an experimenter wearing horn-rimmed glasses and a white laboratory coat. The experimenter introduced himself as Dr. Gregor Zilstein of the Departments of Neurology and Psychiatry. He explained that this was an experiment on the effects of electric shock. The subjects were split into two groups. One group was shown some elaborate electrical equipment and led to expect painful shocks: "These shocks will hurt, they will be painful. As you can guess, if, in research of this sort, we're to learn anything at all that will really help humanity, it is necessary that our shocks be intense" (p. 13). The other group received instructions leading them to believe they would feel no pain: "Do not let the word 'shock' trouble you; I am sure that you will enjoy the experiment. . . . I assure you that what you feel will not in any way be painful. It will resemble more a tickle or a tingle than anything unpleasant" (p. 13).

Thus both groups were told that they would receive electric shock, but one group expected pain whereas the other did not. Clearly, the group that expected pain was expected to be more anxious than the group that did not. The experimenter then explained that there would be a delay while the experiment was being set up and asked the subjects to indicate on a questionnaire whether they preferred to wait for the next part of the experiment alone, with other subjects, or had no preference. Based on the hypothesis, those subjects who were more anxious would be more likely to want to wait with others. This was the end of the experiment. The real purpose of the study was then explained, and no one ever actually received electric shock.

In his hypothesis Schachter stated a potential relationship between two variables, anxiety and affiliation: If subjects are anxious, then they will want to affiliate with others. The hypothesis expresses the relationship between the independent and the dependent variables.

The independent variable in any experiment is the antecedent condition (the treatment) deliberately manipulated by the experimenter. Its values are represented by the various treatment conditions of the experiment. Schachter created two levels of anxiety (high and low) by using different sets of instructions. He manipulated anxiety by giving subjects varying instructions, leading

FIGURE 6-1 Stanley Schachter. Courtesy of Stanley Schachter/Columbia University

them to believe that they either would or would not be exposed to painful shock; anxiety was the independent variable in this experiment. The variable was independent in the sense that its values were set by Schachter; it was not affected by anything else that occurred in the experiment.

The dependent variable is the variable measured to determine whether the independent variable had the expected effect on behavior. It was dependent in the sense that its values were assumed to depend on the values of the independent variable. In Schachter's experiment the dependent variable was affiliation. According to the hypothesis, whether subjects choose to wait alone or with others depends on how anxious they are: Anxious subjects will be less likely to want to wait alone. If anxiety has no effect on affiliation, all the subjects, whether anxious or not, will be equally willing to wait alone. In fact, Schachter's experiment supported his hypothesis; he found that the subjects who expected painful shocks were less likely to want to wait alone.

Hess

Let us look at another research example of testing the effects of an independent variable on a dependent variable. Hess (1975) tested the following hypothesis: Large pupils make people more attractive. Throughout history there has been popular support for this notion. Women once used belladonna to make themselves more beautiful; one of the drug's effects is dilation (widening) of the pupils. Candlelight dinners seem to flatter everyone; aside from masking minor imperfections, dim light also causes pupils to dilate.

To test his hypothesis, Hess asked male subjects to rate four photographs of two women. The photographs were retouched so that each woman had small pupils in one photograph and large pupils in another. (Examples resembling Hess's photographs are shown in Figure 6-2.) Subjects were asked to select which woman in a series of pairs of these photographs appeared to be more friendly, charming, and so on.

The independent variable in this experiment was pupil size. Hess deliberately varied the size of the pupils in order to test the effects of pupil size on attractiveness. The two treatment conditions were two different values, or levels, of the independent variable: large and small pupils. The dependent variable, of course, was attractiveness. If the hypothesis is correct, measures of attractiveness should depend on size of pupils. And in fact, Hess found that his subjects were likely to attribute more of the attractive traits to the women with large pupils. Later, Neidenthal and Cantor (1986) replicated Hess's findings using both male and female subjects. These researchers also showed that similar attractiveness effects on impressions were produced by photos of both men and women whose pupil sizes were enlarged artificially.

Identifying Variables

You will have little difficulty identifying the independent and dependent variables in an experiment if you take the time to think about what the experimenter did. Ask yourself the following questions: What did the experimenter manipulate? Is this the independent variable? What was used to assess the effect of the independent variable? Is this the dependent variable? Suppose we are designing an experiment to test our own hypothesis. How will we identify the independent and dependent variables? Since the experiment has not been done, we cannot examine the procedures that were used. There is no simple rule for deciding which variable is the independent variable in a hypothesis. To make this determination, we must think about the hypothesis and the way we would go about testing it.

When you are working with your own hypothesis, you must ask the same types of questions you ask about an experiment that has already been done: What will you manipulate or vary to test the hypothesis? (This is your independent variable.) What behavior are you trying to explain; what will you measure to find out whether your independent variable had an effect? (This is your dependent variable.) Keep in mind that if you do not need to manipulate the antecedent conditions by creating different treatment conditions (if you will simply measure behaviors as they occur), you do not have an experimental hypothesis.

Suppose this is your hypothesis: People learn words faster when the words are written horizontally than when they are written vertically. You have come to this hypothesis through your review of research on the effects of practice.

FIGURE 6-2 Photographs of a woman retouched so that she has small pupils in one photograph and large pupils in the other. Brooks/Cole photo

Since English-speaking people customarily see words printed horizontally, you suspect that words oriented vertically might seem more unfamiliar and thus be harder to learn. What are the independent and dependent variables in this hypothesis?

First, what will be manipulated? To test the hypothesis, you must manipulate the way the words are oriented when you present them. You must present some words vertically and some horizontally. The independent variable is *word orientation*. You could run the experiment with two treatment conditions, horizontal orientation and vertical orientation. Note again the distinction between the IV and its levels. The IV is the general dimension that is manipulated—in this case, word orientation. There are a great number of possible word orientations along the many diagonal lines that could be drawn between horizontal and vertical. We have, however, selected to use only two of the possible values. Horizontal and vertical are our two levels of the single IV, word orientation.

What will you measure to evaluate the effect of word orientation? According to the hypothesis, the orientation of the words will affect the rate of learning. So, *rate of learning* is the dependent variable. If the hypothesis is correct, subjects will learn words faster if they are presented horizontally. You are predicting that the rate of learning depends on the way the words are presented.

The independent variable in one experiment may function as the dependent variable in another. Whether a particular variable is an independent variable, a dependent variable, or neither depends on the hypothesis being tested.

In Schachter's experiment, the independent variable was anxiety and the dependent variable was affiliation. Schachter found that subjects who were anxious wanted to wait for the next part of the experiment with others.

Based on Schachter's findings, we might suggest a new hypothesis. Perhaps people want to be with others when they are anxious because being with others causes them to become less anxious. How would we go about testing this hypothesis? We might place subjects in one of two conditions. In one condition, subjects are asked to spend 20 minutes waiting alone in a room. In another condition, they are asked to spend 20 minutes waiting in a room with another person. At the end of the waiting period, the subjects' anxiety levels are measured. If the hypothesis is correct, subjects who wait alone should be more anxious than subjects who wait with another person. The independent variable in *this* experiment is affiliation. We manipulate affiliation by assigning subjects to wait either alone or with others. The dependent variable is anxiety. According to the hypothesis, anxiety level depends on whether subjects wait alone or with another person. In Schachter's original experiment, anxiety was the independent variable, and affiliation was the dependent variable. As you can see, we changed the status of these variables when we turned to another hypothesis.

OPERATIONAL DEFINITIONS

So far we have talked about IVs primarily in everyday language. We all have a conceptual notion of what we mean by "brightness" or "rate of learning," for example. However, because one criterion of science is replicability, it is not enough to have only conceptual definitions. Earlier we talked about color as an IV and blue and yellow as treatment levels. For scientific purposes, we would have to be much more precise in our designation of these colors. There are many shades and hues of blue and yellow (one source—Judd and Kelly, 1965—identified 7500 different colors). In our experiment we would have to specify which blue we are using by giving a standardized definition. Psychologists use the Munsell color chart, developed by Albert Henry Munsell, that describes colors by hue, saturation (purity), and lightness or brightness.

Similarly, what one person means by "anxiety" may actually be quite different from what another person means. And so, in addition to giving conceptual, everyday labels to our variables, we also need to specify what they mean in the context of each experiment.

The definition of each variable may change from one experiment to another. When we run an experiment, we naturally want to be sure that others will understand what we have done. Many concepts have more than one meaning, and those meanings are often vague. If we study variables without defining them exactly, the meaning of our findings will be unclear. As scientists, we also want to be sure that our procedures are stated clearly enough to enable other researchers to replicate our findings.

Thus each IV and each DV has two definitions—one conceptual definition that is used in everyday talk and one **operational definition** that is used in carrying out the experiment. An operational definition specifies the precise meaning of a variable within an experiment: It defines a variable in terms of observable operations, procedures, and measurements. It is called an operational definition because it clearly describes the *operations* involved in manipulating or measuring the variables in an experiment. Operational definitions are statements of operating procedures, sets of instructions that tell others how to carry out an experiment. They are essential because many variables of interest to psychologists cannot be observed directly, and operational definitions describe variables in terms of observable reality. We include operational definitions in written reports of experiments so that other researchers will understand exactly what was done and will be able to replicate it.

Operational definitions are quite different from ordinary dictionary definitions. A dictionary may define anxiety as "a state of concern or painful uneasiness about a future or uncertain event," or learning as "acquiring skill or knowledge." Although both definitions may be adequate for everyday use, neither will do in the context of an experiment because they do not tell us how to produce different levels or values of the variables. They do not give us procedures we could follow to make people feel anxious or nonanxious or to have more or less learning. Similarly, they contain no information on how to measure or quantify the variables. How would we determine who has more anxiety or more learning? Operational definitions provide both of those types of information.

Defining the Independent Variable: Experimental Operational Definitions

We can distinguish between two kinds of operational definitions, experimental and measured (Kerlinger, 1973). **Experimental operational definitions** explain the meaning of independent variables; they define *exactly* what was done to create the various treatment conditions of the experiment. An experimental operational definition includes all the steps that were followed to set up each value of the independent variable. Schachter gave experimental operational definitions of high and low anxiety. The high-anxiety condition was defined in terms of the electronic equipment set up in the room, the ominous behavior of Dr. Zilstein, and the explicit statement that the subjects should expect painful shocks. The low-anxiety condition was defined by the absence of equipment, Dr. Zilstein's more relaxed manner, and the explicit statement that the shocks would not be painful. If we were to replicate Schachter's experiment, we would be able to follow all these procedures in setting up each of the two treatment conditions. Note that if Schachter had merely said, "I set up a high-anxiety condition and a low-anxiety condition," we would not know how to go about repeating his experiment. We would also have difficulty interpreting his findings, since we would have no way of judging just how "anxiety producing" his conditions may have been.

If we were constructing an experiment to test our hypothesis about the learning of words presented horizontally or vertically, we would need to specify the precise nature of the experimental procedures and stimuli. For others to evaluate our procedures and replicate our work, we would need to provide a detailed description of how we set up our treatments: the procedure used to present the words; the size of the words; the type of printing; the level of illumination in the room; the distance and location of words in the subject's visual field; and the duration of word presentation.

In the case of quasi-experimental studies, the experimental operational definition is somewhat different. It is essentially the procedure used to select subjects who fit the required levels of the independent variable. In the Ward, Leventhal, and Love (1988) study described earlier, the researchers selected subjects on the basis of a written test of repressive coping style. A description of the test and the cut-off scores used to place people into different groups make up the operational definition of the quasi-independent variable used in the study.

Defining the Dependent Variable: Measured Operational Definitions

Dependent variables are defined by **measured operational definitions,** which describe what we do to measure the variables. Measured operational definitions of the dependent variable describe exactly what procedures we follow to assess the impact of different treatment conditions. They include exact descriptions of the specific behaviors or responses recorded. They also explain how those responses are scored. If we are using scores on a standardized test to measure our dependent variable, we identify the test by name: "scores on the Wechsler Adult Intelligence Scale," not simply "scores on an intelligence test." If our dependent measure is not standardized, we describe it in enough detail to allow other researchers to repeat our procedures. In Schachter's experiment the dependent variable, affiliation, was given a measured operational definition. Schachter scored the desire to affiliate by having subjects check off their preferences on a questionnaire. The questionnaire is described in detail in his report. Again, it would be easy to replicate his procedures for measuring affiliation: We would simply administer the same questionnaire in the same way.

Defining Constructs Operationally

The need for operational definitions becomes easily apparent when we zero in on variables, like anxiety, that are actually **hypothetical constructs,** or concepts, which are unseen processes postulated to explain behavior. Many psychological variables are hypothetical constructs; that is, constructs that cannot be observed directly. We infer their existence from behaviors that we can observe: An ordinarily good student panics and does poorly on an important exam. An actor has stage fright and forgets his lines. From these observations, we infer the existence of "anxiety." We could say that "anxiety" is a peculiar feeling of queasiness that inhibits behavior. Unfortunately, that definition also neatly fits the first time one of the authors ate raw clams. She was not anxious, but she was definitely queasy, and she has not eaten clams since. Furthermore, what we mean by "anxiety" may be quite different if we are talking about a person's experience before taking a test compared to waiting in line for a rollercoaster ride. Clearly, just labeling the variable "anxiety" would be much too vague without a precise operational definition.

Researchers often formulate different definitions for the same construct variable when it is used in different experiments. Schachter's experiment illustrated one kind of operational definition for anxiety. In effect, Schachter said that "high anxiety" is the feeling experienced in a particular kind of situation—namely, one in which the person expects pain. In the low-anxiety condition, the subjects saw no equipment and did not expect pain. By definition, the feeling they experienced in this setting is "low anxiety." You may or may not agree with Schachter's decision to define anxiety in this way, but you do know what definitions apply in this particular experiment.

Operational definitions for constructs like anxiety are also important for another reason—namely, *effects produced on behavior may differ from one operational definition to another.* When anxiety is defined in another way, its effects on the desire to affiliate may be very different. Another research example shows that this is indeed the case. Sarnoff and Zimbardo (1961) conducted a study in which anxiety was operationally defined in a very different way. Undergraduate men were told that they would be participating in a study of sensory stimulation of the skin around the mouth. Subjects in a "high-anxiety" condition were told that the procedure would require them to suck for 2 minutes on various objects while physiological sensations around the mouth were being measured. An experimenter showed them several different objects they would be sucking on: things like baby bottles, oversized nipples, pacifiers, and breast shields (sometimes worn over a woman's breast while nursing). They were also shown vivid slides of a man demonstrating the sucking procedure on each of the objects. You may have guessed by now that Sarnoff and Zimbardo were trying to create a different sort of high anxiety than that manipulated by Schachter! In a "low-anxiety" condition, a similar procedure was used; but subjects were told instead that they would be placing objects (whistles, kazoos, and the like) in their mouths for 10 seconds while their skin sensations were recorded. To make the waiting period seem natural, all subjects were told that they would need to wait in another room while their pre-experimental (*baseline*) physiology was recorded. As in the Schachter experiment, they were given the option of waiting alone or with others. Do you think the high-anxiety men in this experiment wanted to wait with others or alone? Not surprisingly, men exposed to the high-anxiety condition showed much *less* desire to affiliate than did men in the low-anxiety condition—a reversal of what Schachter had found. You can see from this amusing example how important an experimental operational definition is for defining construct variables.

Similarly, we need a measured operational definition when a construct variable like anxiety is a dependent variable. There are many possible measured operational definitions of anxiety, too. One such definition might be "a heartbeat in excess of 120 beats per minute following 5 minutes rest on a sofa." This definition could be used to explain what we mean by "anxiety" in a particular experiment. Notice that the components of the definition are observable dimensions; we can readily determine a person's pulse. We would expect to get good agreement on whether or not a person is "anxious" according to this definition.

We can also define anxiety by a score on a written test like the Taylor Manifest Anxiety Scale, or TMAS (Taylor, 1953). This test includes a variety of items that are assumed to index different degrees of anxiety, such as the frequency of nightmares, fear of spiders, worries about work, and so on. In using the test, we assume that people who express many of these concerns are more anxious than those who express few of them. We use predetermined cut-off scores to determine who is anxious and who is not. Again, we have an objective, observable set of measures (the subjects' responses to a series of test items) to define anxiety. To say that anxiety is "feeling queasy" is not acceptable. We cannot observe queasiness directly, nor can we be sure that subjects will know what we mean if we simply ask them whether they are "anxious."

Learning is also a construct. Like anxiety, it cannot be observed directly; it must be operationally defined by objective criteria. We can define learning in terms of performance on a written test, in a maze, or on a bicycle. We can count up the number of correct responses or errors. We can also use the time taken to complete a task as an index of learning. In an experiment to test our word-orientation hypothesis, we can define learning as the number of words that subjects are able to remember and write down, or as their scores on a written recognition test that we devise. Although the operational definitions vary, they all specify learning in observable terms. We cannot measure learning directly, but we can infer its occurrence from these objective measures— and we can state our procedures clearly enough to permit other researchers to measure learning in the same way.

Defining Nonconstruct Variables

It is easy to see why operational definitions are required when we are dealing with constructs. Something that cannot be seen must be defined by observable dimensions before we can deal with it scientifically. However, operational definitions are equally important when we are working with variables that can be observed more directly. Suppose we wish to test the effects of lighting on newborn babies. We may wish to compare crying among babies in light rooms versus crying in dark rooms, as did Irwin and Weiss in 1934. The comparison seems straightforward enough, but before it can be made we must operationally define what we mean by "light" versus "dark" rooms. Is a "light" room as bright as a sunny day? Is a "dark" room completely shielded from any source of light, or one in which the shades are drawn? To make a legitimate comparison, we must define what we mean by "light" and "dark" as objectively as possible, ideally by the use of a photometer or light meter.

The dependent variable, "crying," must also be defined. It must be done in such a way that independent observers would reliably agree on its occurrence. Do intermittent sounds constitute "crying," or must the sound be sustained for a given period of time? Is a whimper also a cry or must the sound reach a certain level of intensity (some decibel level)? All these decisions must be made before the experiment is conducted. Otherwise, the results may not mean anything to anyone except the experimenter.

Defining Scales of Measurement

In setting up experiments and formulating operational definitions, researchers also consider the available **scales of measurement** for each variable. You may have noticed that in our examples of independent variables, some of the levels we specified were simply comparative labels (bright or dim illumination, large versus small typeface). However, it might have been possible to make them precise quantitative measurements, such as 50 versus 100 luxes (standard units of illumination) and 10-point versus 14-point typeface.

Many variables can be measured in more than one way. The measurement alternatives differ in the degree of information they provide. Setting treatment levels at 5 versus 10 milligrams of a drug, for example, is more precise than dividing subjects simply on the relative basis of low versus high doses. Stating the level of room illumination in luxes is going to allow other researchers to evaluate and replicate an experiment more thoroughly than knowing only that a room was bright or dim.

Dependent variables can also be measured in more than one way, and the amount of information provided will depend on how the variable is measured. The two experiments that tested the effects of "anxiety" on affiliation used the same dependent variable (desire to affiliate), but the way affiliation was measured differed somewhat. In the Schachter (1959) experiment, subjects simply stated whether they wished to wait with others, alone, or had no preference. But Sarnoff and Zimbardo (1961) had subjects rate the intensity of their preference on a scale from 0 (very weak preference) to 100 (very strong preference). The second type of measurement provides the researcher with additional information and uses a different level of measurement.

The **level of measurement** is the kind of scale used to measure a variable. There are four levels of measurement: nominal, ordinal, interval, and ratio. The simplest level of measurement is called a **nominal scale,** which classifies items into two or more *distinct* categories on the basis of some common feature. A nominal scale groups items together into categories that can be named (the term *nominal* comes from the Latin word for "name"). But it does not quantify the items in any way. Classifying subjects' answers to a true/false test uses the nominal level of measurement. Subjects can circle "true" or "false" for an item, but not both. Nominal scaling is sometimes called the lowest level of measurement because it provides no information about magnitude. For some subject variables, however, it is the only type of scale that can be used. Political affiliation is a commonly used nominal measurement.

FIGURE 6-3 An example of nominal scaling. Drawing by Koren; ©1982 The New Yorker Magazine, Inc. Reprinted with permission.

You may be a Democrat, Republican, Independent, or Other. There is no difference in magnitude among these categories; you are not more or less affiliated if you belong to one party rather than another.

In Schachter's (1959) experiment, a nominal scale was used to assess affiliation. Subjects selected a response item from one of three categories: wait alone, with others, or no preference. (See Figure 6-3 for another example.) Nominal scales place responses into categories but do not provide the researcher with any information about differences in magnitude between the items.

The next level of measurement is called an **ordinal scale,** which is a rank ordering of items. The magnitude of each value is measured in the form of ranks. Placing first, second, or third in a track event is an example of an ordinal scale. The winner's time is faster than the runner-up's time; the runner-up's time is faster than the time of the third-place finisher. Here, an ordinal scale gives us some idea about the *relative* speed of the three racers, but it does not tell us the precise speed of any single racer. A researcher interested in studying the effects of violent cartoons on children's aggressiveness might rank order different cartoons in terms of how violent they are. "Teenage Mutant Ninja Turtles" might be ranked higher than "New Kids on the Block," but we would not know *how much* higher. To quantify the magnitude of differences between events, we turn to higher levels of measurement.

An **interval scale** measures magnitude or quantitative size using measures with equal intervals between the values. However, an interval scale has no true zero point. The Fahrenheit and centigrade temperature scales are interval scales. Although both have zero points, neither has an absolute zero. Neither 0° F nor 0° C represent true zero points (the absence of *any* measurable temperature): Temperatures below zero are possible on both scales. For that reason, we cannot say 40° is twice as hot as 20°. But because the intervals between values (between degrees) are equal, we can say that the difference between 40° and 20° is the same as the difference between 20° and 0°.

Sarnoff and Zimbardo's (1961) 0–100 scale is an example of the type of interval scale commonly used by researchers to measure a dependent variable. Some statisticians question whether number scales like this truly meet the criteria for an interval scale, but the value of the information that can be obtained from them and their common acceptance among psychologists argue strongly for using them. Some common methods of constructing interval-scale questions are described in Box 6-1.

The highest level of measurement is called a **ratio scale,** which has equal intervals between all values *and* a true zero point. Measures of physical properties, such as height and weight, are variables whose quantity or magnitude can be measured using ratio scales. Time (measured in seconds, minutes, or hours) is another common ratio-scaled variable. The values of a ratio scale are expressed by numbers such as 3 feet, 18 kilograms, or 24 hours. Clearly, the intervals between scale values (feet, kilograms, hours) are equal. Measures of feet, kilograms, and hours also have a true zero point—values of 0 feet, 0 kilograms, and 0 hours represent the true absence of height, weight, or time. These attributes enable us to express relationships between values on these scales as ratios: We can say 2 meters are twice as long as 1 meter.

As we move from lower to higher scales of measurement, we gain more precise information about the magnitude of variables or their quantitative size. Ordinal scales provide more information than nominal scales. Knowing that each of three racers placed first, second, or third (ordinal scale), for example, is more informative than just knowing that each of three racers won or lost (nominal scale), but neither provides as much information about the differences between racers as knowing their actual times (ratio scale).

Selecting Levels of Measurement

Variables may be measured by using one of the four types of scales. At times it is possible to measure a variable by more than one of these scales. Hamburgers, for example, could be categorized by fast-food restaurant (nominal data), ranked in order of taste (ordinal data), or measured for exact calorie counts (ratio data). The best type of scale to use will depend on two things: the nature of the variable you are studying and how much measurement precision you desire. The level of measurement needs to "fit" the variable being measured. Sometimes a nominal scale is sufficient. If we were interested in measuring marital status, for example, knowing whether someone is unmarried or married (nominal data) may be all the information that we need. A different kind of study might require knowing how many years subjects have been married (ratio data).

Often, psychological variables lend themselves to different levels of measurement because they represent a **continuous dimension.** Traits, attitudes,

BOX 6 - 1

SCALING TECHNIQUES: INTERVAL SCALES OF MEASUREMENT

If we wanted to discover people's attitudes about scientific research, how could we go about measuring them? Well, we could just ask them an open-ended question, "What do you think about scientific research," and let them answer in their own words. But, as we discussed in Chapter 3, we would have to analyze the content of each response and come up with a system for assigning each one a numerical value. For example, imagine that one person answered, "Well, it's okay, I suppose," and another said, "I don't have a real strong opinion about that." Do these people have the same or a different opinion? Is one more favorable than the other? If so, how much more favorable?

Because it is much more convenient, psychologists who solicit attitudes standardize both the questions asked and the answers available to the respondents. *Scaling* is an example of this practice. There are many different scaling techniques, but we are going to focus on the two most common: semantic differential and Likert scales.

The semantic differential was devised by Osgood, Suci, and Tannenbaum (1957). If we were to use their semantic-differential technique for measuring people's attitudes toward scientific research, we would ask respondents to indicate their attitude by evaluating it on a number of dimensions. Each dimension would consist of two adjectives separated by a scale, usually consisting of 7 points. The adjectives on each scale are antonyms (having opposite meanings), so the semantic differential is comprised of *bipolar adjective scales*. Our semantic differential might look like the following example:

Scientific Research

Positive	___	___	___	___	___	___	___	Negative
Worthless	___	___	___	___	___	___	___	Valuable
Wise	___	___	___	___	___	___	___	Foolish
Unethical	___	___	___	___	___	___	___	Ethical
Helpful	___	___	___	___	___	___	___	Destructive

(continued)

(continued)

We would ask our subjects to indicate their attitude toward scientific research by placing a check mark on each scale. To quantify each person's attitude, we could score each scale from 1 (most negative) to 7 (most positive) and then sum the person's score across all the scales.

The Likert scaling procedure (Likert, 1932) takes a different approach. If we were to use this technique to measure attitudes toward scientific research, we would present people with some positively worded statements and some negatively worded statements about scientific research. We would arrange the possible responses to each statement in a multiple-choice format. Most often, researchers give respondents five answer options: "strongly disagree," "disagree," "undecided" (or "neutral"), "agree," and "strongly agree." With this technique we could ask people to indicate the degree of their agreement or disagreement with each of the following statements:

Scientific research has produced many advances that have significantly enhanced the quality of human life.

_____ strongly disagree

_____ disagree

_____ neutral

_____ agree

_____ strongly agree

Scientific research has frequently produced confusing results, based on statistics that are biased in the direction of the researcher's beliefs.

_____ strongly disagree

_____ disagree

_____ neutral

_____ agree

_____ strongly agree

We would quantify each person's attitude by scoring each question and then summing their scores across all the questions. We want higher numbers to indicate more positive attitudes, so we would have to make strong *agreement* with a *positively* worded statement (for example, the first question above) worth 5 points. We also would make strong *dis*agreement with a *negatively* worded statement (for example, the second question above) worth 5 points. Strong disagreement with a positively

worded statement or strong agreement with a negatively worded statement would each be worth 1 point.

A slightly different Likert-type technique is also employed to assess
individuals' evaluations of people, ideas, or things. If you were asked to
rate the value of scientific research on a scale from 0–10 (0 is your least
positive rating and 10 your most positive), a researcher would be measuring your answer using a common Likert-type scale. This type of rating scale can also be used to measure the strength of either the positive
or negative attitudes an individual holds toward scientific research, as
in the following example:

How do you feel about scientific research? (Circle a number on the scale
below.)

Strongly Against	Somewhat Against	Neutral	Somewhat For	Strongly For
−2	−1	0	+1	+2

and preferences can be viewed as continuous dimensions, and each individual may fall at any point along each dimension. The trait of sociability, for
example, can be conceptualized as a continuous dimension that ranges from
very unsociable to very sociable—each person falls somewhere on that dimension. Attitudes can range from strongly negative to strongly positive, and preferences from very weak to very strong. Multiple scales are possible for these
dimensions. Attitudes toward issues like animal experimentation, for example, could be measured using a nominal scale ("for" or "against") or an interval scale ("On a scale of 1–10, how strongly do you favor using animals in
psychological research?").

Researchers generally use the following rule for selecting a level of measurement: When different levels of measurement will "fit" equally well, choose
the highest level possible because it provides more information about a variable. In subsequent chapters we will also learn that various levels of measurement are analyzed with different statistical techniques, and the statistical
tests we can use for interval or ratio data are more *powerful* than those for
nominal and ordinal data. Thus ratio and interval scales tend to be preferred
by researchers over ordinal and nominal measurements.

EVALUATING OPERATIONAL DEFINITIONS

Since there may be many definitions for the same variable, how is it possible
to know which definition is best? This question has no hard and fast answers.
As with many other aspects of experimentation, what works well in one

experiment may simply not be appropriate in another. Our definition must be objective and precise so that others can evaluate and duplicate the procedures. There are more general criteria as well, which can be grouped under the general headings of reliability and validity.

Reliability

Reliability means consistency and dependability. Good operational definitions are reliable: If we apply them in more than one experiment, they ought to work in similar ways each time. Suppose we have specified all the operations that must be performed to create two treatment conditions, "hungry" and "not hungry." If our operational definition is reliable, every time we apply the definition (each time we create these two conditions), we should obtain similar consequences. Subjects in the "hungry" condition should consistently show signs of hunger—increased activity, food-seeking behavior, or a verbal report of hunger if our subjects are people. If our "hungry" subjects show signs of hunger only occasionally, our operational definition is not reliable. The procedures we have specified to define the various levels of the independent variable work haphazardly: Sometimes we produce hunger and sometimes not. Better definitions are needed.

Measured operational definitions should also be reliable. If we took several sets of measurements according to our operational definition of the dependent variable, we should get the same results each time. When possible, we select measuring instruments, like standardized tests, that have been shown to be reliable. When we are not using standardized measures, we make sure our measurement procedures are clearly and simply defined. The more accurate they are, the more likely they are to be reliable. There are several procedures for checking the reliability of measurement techniques.

Interrater Reliability

One way to assess reliability of measurement procedures is to have different observers take measurements of the *same* responses; the agreement between their measurements is called **interrater reliability.** Typically, this method is used in a content analysis, when the qualitative content of subjects' responses must be scored by raters (for example, several raters might score all subjects' essays for "assertiveness"). When two or more raters score each response, scores given by different raters can be statistically compared.[1] If there is little agreement between them, the chances are good that the measuring procedure is not reliable. There are other types of measurement reliability that can be assessed through statistical techniques.

---

[1]Statistical tests of reliability provide reliability coefficients (similar to correlation coefficients) that range from 0.0 (only chance levels of agreement) to 1.0 (perfect agreement). For a more detailed presentation of methods for assessing reliability and validity, see Crano & Brewer (1986). *Principles and methods of social research.* Newton, MA: Allyn & Bacon.

Test-retest Reliability

Reliability of measures can also be checked by comparing scores of people who have been measured twice with the same instrument. They take the test once, then they take it again (after a reasonable interval). This is called **test-retest reliability.** Reliable measures should produce very similar scores each time the person is measured. If people consistently get about the same scores on a personality test, the test is considered reliable. Standardized intelligence tests, like the Wechsler Adult Intelligence Scale, have been shown to have fairly good test-retest reliability; people's scores do not change very much from one testing session to another.

Interitem Reliability

A third way of checking the reliability of measurement procedures is to assess the degree to which different items measuring the same variable attain consistent results, called **interitem reliability.** Scores on different items designed to measure the same construct should be highly correlated. This type of interitem reliability is called *internal consistency*. A test of internal consistency is most often used when a researcher has created a multiple-item questionnaire to measure a construct variable like intelligence, need for achievement, or anxiety. The individual items on a standardized test of anxiety, such as the TMAS (Taylor, 1953), will show a high degree of internal consistency if they are reliably measuring the same variable.

Validity

A second important problem in formulating definitions is stating definitions that are valid. **Validity** in experiments refers to the principle of actually studying the variables that we wish to study. How valid were Schachter's and Sarnoff and Zimbardo's experimental operational definitions of anxiety? Did they really manipulate anxiety in their subjects as they claimed? If the answer to this last question is yes, then we can say their definitions were valid. We can formulate precise, objective definitions that may even be reliable, but if they are not valid, we have not accomplished the goals of our experiment.

Often, several procedures can be used to manipulate the same variable, like "anxiety." But which is the most valid? Which represents what we want to call "anxiety"?

One approach to the problem is a comparison of the consequences of the various procedures. If they all produce "anxiety," they should all lead to the same observable signs of anxiety: heartrate acceleration, sweaty palms, self-reported anxiety, and so on. Researchers make these kinds of comparisons to develop the best procedures. Comparing all the available procedures is not always feasible, particularly in the course of a single experiment. However, it should be clear that we need to evaluate the validity of our experimental manipulations. We must ask whether we really manipulated what we intended to manipulate. Validity can be determined in several ways.

Face Validity

Validity of operational definitions is least likely to be a problem with variables that can be manipulated and measured fairly directly. For instance, in studying the effects of pupil size, it is reasonably easy to know whether we are using a valid experimental operational definition of pupil size. We simply use a standard measuring device—for instance, a ruler—to define the treatment conditions. Defining pupil size by the marks on a ruler has **face validity.** The procedure is self-evident; we do not need to convince people that a ruler measures width. Face validity is the least stringent type of validity.

Similar issues arise in evaluating definitions of the dependent variable. The validity of a measured operational definition centers around the question of whether we measured what we intended to measure. As with experimental definitions, there should be some consensus that our procedures yield information about the variable we had in mind when we started the experiment. But because many psychological variables require indirect measures, the validity of a measured definition may not be self-evident—but it may still be a good measure. Response time is considered to be a valid measure of attitude importance (judgments about important attitude objects are made more quickly), even though the connection between time and attitude strength is not readily apparent (Fazio, 1990). Two other kinds of validity are of greater importance as we develop measures: content validity and predictive validity. Measures that appear to have face validity do not necessarily meet these criteria.

Content Validity

Content validity depends on whether we are taking a fair sample of the quality we intend to measure. When we evaluate **content validity,** we are asking: Does the content of our measure fairly reflect the content of the thing we are measuring? The questions students might raise about an exam are often questions of content validity. An exam is supposed to measure what students have learned. However, students sometimes feel an exam includes *only* questions about the things they did not understand. Winston Churchill (1930) had the same feeling when he wrote the following:

> I had scarcely passed my 12th birthday when I entered the inhospitable regions of examinations, through which, for the next seven years, I was destined to journey. These examinations were a great trial to me. The subjects which were dearest to the examiners were almost invariably those I fancied least. I would have liked to be examined in History, Poetry, and writing essays. The examiners, on the other hand, were partial to Latin and Mathematics. And their will prevailed. Moreover, the questions which they asked on both these subjects were almost invariably those to which I was unable to suggest the satisfactory answer. I should have liked to be asked to say what I knew. They always tried to ask what I did not know. When I would willingly have displayed my knowledge, they sought to expose my ignorance. This sort of treatment had only one result: I did not do well in examinations.

Whether a particular measure has content validity is often a matter of judgment. Teachers and students sometimes disagree on whether particular tests or particular questions are fair representations of the course material. For experimental purposes, however, we try to obtain some consensus on the content validity of our measures. For areas in which a great deal of research is conducted, like intelligence, content validity of measures is often the topic of books by experts (Lutey, 1977).

Suppose you have devised a questionnaire to measure racial attitudes. You have a series of questions about whether people would live in integrated neighborhoods, whether they would help a person of another race who was in trouble, and so on. You could simply administer the questionnaire, but you would have a better idea of whether your questionnaire had content validity if you obtained ratings of the items from objective judges. Each judge would be asked to rate each item for its measurement of racial attitudes. You would then have the opportunity to include items that are most representative of that variable, according to the raters' judgments. If the raters do not agree on the items, you will have to rework the questionnaire.

The degree of content validity we can achieve depends on the variable we want to measure. The more specific the variable, the easier it will be. Clearly, it would be relatively easy to define weight gain in a way that would have high content validity. Measuring the size of a mental image poses more difficult problems. Other times, it is difficult to attain high content validity because the circumstances you wish to measure are very infrequent. Researchers studying the content validity of tests used to assess combat readiness in the military, for example, find it difficult to achieve a high level of content validity because most tests are simulations conducted in peacetime (Vineberg & Joyner, 1983).

Predictive Validity

We can also ask whether our measures of the dependent variable have **predictive validity.** Do our procedures yield information that enables us to predict actual behavior or performance? They should, if we are measuring what we intend to measure. Schachter (1959) defined the desire to affiliate in terms of subjects' responses to a questionnaire. You will recall that they were asked to indicate whether they preferred to wait alone, with others, or had no preference. This definition has face validity. It seems to have something to do with people's desire to be together. It seems to have content validity too; part of the desire to affiliate is a wish to be with other people. When we raise the question of predictive validity, however, we are asking this: Can we use people's responses to this questionnaire to predict how they will actually behave? If people have the desire to affiliate, it is reasonable to predict that they will stay near others when they have the opportunity. In Schachter's study we could evaluate the predictive validity of the affiliation measure by changing the procedures slightly. Instead of telling subjects that the experiment was over after they completed the questionnaire, we could take them all into a large waiting room. If the affiliation measure has predictive validity, the subjects who said they wanted to wait with others will seat themselves closer together and perhaps talk to each other more than subjects who preferred to wait alone. If we do not observe these overt signs of the desire to affiliate, we may have to conclude that the written measure does not have predictive validity: It does not predict what people will do.

Construct Validity

The fourth, and perhaps most important, aspect of validity is **construct validity.** Somewhat different from the other forms of validity we have discussed, construct validity deals with the transition from theory to research application. We start with a general idea of the qualities that characterize the construct we wish to test; then we seek to find ways of putting our idea to an empirical test. The issue of construct validity arises when we ask: "Have I succeeded in creating a measuring device that measures the construct I want to test? Are my operational definitions tapping only the construct I want to test?"

The specific modern methods for evaluating construct validity are largely statistical and highly theoretical. Basically, researchers ask whether the data make sense in the context of the overall theoretical framework in which they operate. One way of doing this is to see whether the data follow expected patterns in relation to other concepts. Although we cannot look at the details of how a construct validity analysis might be done, a description of two simple applications will help clarify the essence of what is involved.

Suppose we wish to study intelligence. Depending on our hypothesis, intelligence could be either a *quasi*-independent or dependent variable. If intelligence were the IV, we might separate subjects into groups on the basis of high or low intelligence test scores. Or if intelligence were the DV, we might introduce some environmental change (for example, better nutrition) and observe its impact on subsequent IQ scores. In either case we would want to be sure that our intelligence test truly measures only "intelligence," and that we have not inadvertently measured another construct.

From a scientific standpoint, we are faced with a construct validity question. Does the test we use actually measure the hypothetical construct we call "intelligence"? Perhaps the test measures something else, such as test-taking skills, cultural background, or motivation. There is extensive research literature dealing with such issues, and testing experts have tried to create tests that minimize the influence of these other factors. The Ravens Progressive Matrices Test is one example of a test that is considered relatively culture fair. Figure 6-4 illustrates the type of item found on such a test.

As a student, you are unlikely to be heavily involved in construct validation. The experts who have created standardized intelligence tests have already addressed the problem for you. Your task would be to select the most appropriate test on the basis of the research literature. In constructing tests, experts work with many sources of data as they assess validity. Computer applications have made much of this work feasible. To the extent that the tests measure intelligence, test scores ought to show certain predictable relationships with other related variables, such as school achievement and reading level. Test results should also correlate highly with scores on other intelligence tests. A valid intelligence test should also be able to appropriately classify known groups of people with high and low levels of intelligence. It should

Choose one to complete the relationship.

FIGURE 6-4 Example of item found on a *culture-fair* intelligence test.

have no trouble discriminating between members of Mensa (a society admitting only high-IQ individuals) and mentally retarded individuals. Thus the validation process focuses on *how well* the test scores fit in an overall theoretical network of understanding how the concept of intelligence works in human functioning.

There are many other examples of construct validity in the psychological literature. Researchers do not always have standardized tests to work with and therefore have to solve their own validation problems. How they go about establishing construct validity is illustrated in an article by Marsh and Parker (1984). They assessed the construct validity of the Self Description Questionnaire (SDQ), an instrument that was intended to measure self-concept. Sample items from the 76-item questionnaire are shown in Table 6-1.

As in the case of intelligence testing, Marsh and Parker looked for predictable relationships between SDQ scores (presumably self-concept) and other variables. They were able to do that through sophisticated statistical procedures, including factor analysis and path analysis. They evaluated the relationships between SDQ scores and other variables, such as teacher ratings of student self-concept and academic achievement. They were able to show that self-concept, as measured by the SDQ, actually has two distinct components—academic and nonacademic self-concept.[2]

Basically, how people perform in school does not necessarily affect the way they view their abilities in other areas. Winston Churchill probably would have agreed.

EVALUATING THE EXPERIMENT: INTERNAL VALIDITY

So far we have focused on the notion of validity in connection with operating procedures. We want to develop procedures that define our variables in valid ways. However, a more general evaluation is also required: Is the experiment valid? Have we made valid measurements of the effects of the

---

[2]Paradoxically, they also found that students in educationally disadvantaged schools had higher self-concepts than those in better schools. Although students in better schools achieved more academically, Marsh and Parker raised the question of whether it is preferable "to be a relatively large fish in a small pond even if you don't learn to swim as well."

TABLE 6-1 Selected items for the Self Description Questionnaire

	False	Mostly False	Sometimes False, Sometimes True	Mostly True	True
I like the way I look	☐	☐	☐	☐	☐
I get good marks in all SCHOOL SUBJECTS	☐	☐	☐	☐	☐
My parents like me	☐	☐	☐	☐	☐
I do lots of important things	☐	☐	☐	☐	☐
I am dumb at READING	☐	☐	☐	☐	☐

From *Selected Items for the Self Description Questionnaire,* by H. W. Marsh and I. D. Smith. Copyright ©1981 H. W. Marsh and I. D. Smith, The University of Sydney. Reprinted with permission.

independent variable? (Box 6-2 presents an important measurement validity issue to consider.) We can talk about two kinds of validity when we look at the experiment as a whole. The first is **internal validity**—the degree to which a researcher is able to state a causal relationship between antecedent conditions and the subsequent observed behavior. Later in the book we will discuss external validity, how well the findings of the experiment generalize or apply to situations that were not tested directly (for example, real life). But before we can think about the external validity of an experiment, we must first evaluate its internal validity.

When we set up an experiment, we plan procedures to measure the effects of various treatment levels. We are trying to assess the impact of the independent variable. We can ask whether we have achieved that goal in the context of the experiment: *An experiment is internally valid if we can be sure that the changes in behavior observed across the treatment conditions of the experiment were actually caused by the independent variable* (Campbell, 1957). If other explanations are possible, the experiment is not internally valid; we cannot identify the impact of the independent variable with certainty. We cannot make any correct generalizations from an experiment that is not internally valid. In the following sections we will look at three important concepts that are tied to the problem of internal validity: extraneous variables, threats to internal validity, and confounding. These important factors affect our ability to understand and interpret the effects of our treatment conditions.

Extraneous Variables and Confounding

From an experiment we can draw a causal inference about the relationship between the independent and dependent variables. If the value of the dependent variable changes significantly as the independent variable changes, we

B O X   6 - 2

THE SOCIAL DESIRABILITY RESPONSE SET

Remember the various response styles (willingness to answer, position preference, yea-saying and nay-saying) from Chapter 3? Response styles can reduce the validity of our dependent measures if subjects are not responding to the *manifest content,* the plain meaning, of our questions in the way we intend. A different problem occurs when subjects ignore manifest content and, instead, answer questions based on **latent content,** the "hidden" meaning behind the question. People frequently shape their responses to latent content with a particular goal in mind. That goal can be a **response set**—a picture we want to create of ourselves. An excellent example of a response set is behavior during a job interview. Unless we don't want the job, we answer the interviewer's questions with the goal of appearing qualified and hard working. Few prospective applicants would say they want to work as little as possible (even though many people probably fantasize about winning the lottery and never working again!). Instead, most applicants try to put their best foot forward.

In psychological research, we frequently worry that subjects will respond based on what they believe their answers say about them. Crowne and Marlowe (1964) developed a 33-item true/false questionnaire, which is used widely to test whether subjects have the response set called "social desirability." To look good on many of the items, subjects would have to lie. Table 6-2 lists a few of the items designed to measure social desirability. For example, few of us would find it easy to get along with "loud-mouthed, obnoxious people," although it is socially desirable, or nice, to be able to get along with everyone. People who respond "True" to these items are most likely distorting the truth.

What can we do about response sets? A person with a response set will answer based on the latent content of questions. Some subjects may try to give the most socially desirable response; others might try to give a deviant response. To counteract a response set, we can develop alternative questions that have the same latent content. For example, which statement in each pair best describes your attitudes toward pets?

Everyone should have a pet.
I think pets are a waste of time.
or
Pets are fun but not everyone wants the responsibility.
Pets make good companions.

(continued)

(continued)

TABLE 6-2 The Marlowe-Crowne Social Desirability Scale Personal Reaction Inventory[*]

Listed below are a number of statements concerning personal attitudes and traits. Read each item and decide whether the statement is true or false as it pertains to you personally.

1. Before voting I thoroughly investigate the qualifications of all the candidates. (T)

2. I never hesitate to go out of my way to help someone in trouble. (T)

3. It is sometimes hard for me to go on with my work if I am not encouraged. (F)

4. I have never intensely disliked anyone. (T)

5. On occasion I have had doubts about my ability to succeed in life. (F)

6. I sometimes feel resentful when I don't get my way. (F)

7. I am always careful about my manner of dress. (T)

8. My table manners at home are as good as when I eat out in a restaurant. (T)

9. If I could get into a movie without paying and be sure I was not seen, I would probably do it. (F)

10. On a few occasions, I have given up doing something because I thought too little of my ability. (F)

11. I like to gossip at times. (F)

12. There have been times when I felt like rebelling against people in authority even though I knew they were right. (F)

13. No matter who I'm talking to, I'm always a good listener. (T)

14. I can remember "playing sick" to get out of something. (F)

15. There have been occasions when I took advantage of someone. (F)

16. I'm always willing to admit it when I make a mistake. (T)

17. I always try to practice what I preach. (T)

18. I don't find it particularly difficult to get along with loud-mouthed, obnoxious people. (T)

19. I sometimes try to get even, rather than forgive and forget. (F)

20. When I don't know something, I don't at all mind admitting it. (T)

21. I am always courteous, even to people who are disagreeable. (T)

22. At times I have really insisted on having things my own way. (F)

23. There have been occasions when I felt like smashing things. (F)

24. I would never think of letting someone else be punished for my wrongdoings. (T)

25. I never resent being asked to return a favor. (T)

26. I have never been irked when people expressed ideas very different from my own. (T)

27. I never make a long trip without checking the safety of my car. (T)
28. There have been times when I was quite jealous of the good fortune of others. (F)
29. I have almost never felt the urge to tell someone off. (T)
30. I am sometimes irritated by people who ask favors of me. (F)
31. I have never felt that I was punished without cause. (T)
32. I sometimes think when people have a misfortune they only got what they deserved. (F)
33. I have never deliberately said something that hurt someone's feelings. (T)

*The responses shown are the socially desirable ones. From *The Approval Motive,* by D. P. Crowne and D. Marlowe. Copyright ©1964 John Wiley & Sons, Inc. Reprinted with permission.

You can see how the implications of the choices differ. In the first pair, one answer seems to be more socially desirable than the other. Some people would feel pressured to pick the first choice so that they would appear to be animal lovers. In the second pair, the choices are about equally acceptable. People can show that they like animals by selecting either item. They can also express feeling that pets can be a nuisance without worrying that the response will stigmatize them in some way. The second set of alternatives is more likely to lead to valid data.

may say that the independent variable *caused* changes in the dependent variable.[3] But this inference is justified only when the experiment is well controlled. Many things other than the independent and dependent variables may be changing throughout an experiment—time of day, the experimenter's level of fatigue, the particular subjects who are being tested. Such variables are called **extraneous variables;** they are factors that are not the main focus of the experiment. They are neither intentionally manipulated independent variables nor dependent variables measured as indexes of the effect of the independent variable. They can include differences among subjects, equipment failures, inconsistent instructions—in short, anything that varies. Extraneous variables can affect results: Experimental subjects may be tired if they are in an experiment at the end of the day; equipment breakdowns can change the results produced by an independent variable during a treatment

---

[3]Significance is a statistical term we will return to many times. In an experiment, there is *always* some probability that observed effects were produced by chance, rather than our treatment. A significant effect is one in which statistics have determined that the odds of the observed effect occurring by chance are quite small (usually 5% or less).

FIGURE 6-5 Don't let this happen to your experiment. PhotoDisc/Robert Western

session; differences in the way instructions are presented can alter subjects' responses.

In a well-controlled experiment, we attempt to recognize the potential for extraneous variables and use procedures to control them. Realistically, though, even the most well-controlled experiment will be influenced from time to time by extraneous variables that cannot be controlled in advance. As long as these influences are infrequent, *random* events, they do not necessarily invalidate an experiment. However, random influences from extraneous variables do introduce errors into the scores obtained from subjects, so it is important to control them as carefully as possible. These influences will obscure the effects we are really interested in and make it more difficult to detect significant treatment effects.

The real gremlin that wreaks havoc on an experiment is an extraneous variable that changes in a *systematic* way along with the independent variable. In a well-controlled experiment, the variation in the independent variable must be the only systematic variation that occurs across treatment conditions. If an extraneous variable occurs in one treatment condition but not another, an experiment cannot be internally valid. If uncontrolled extraneous variables are allowed to change along with the independent variable, we may not be able to tell whether changes in the dependent variable were caused by changes in the independent variable or by extraneous variables that also changed value across conditions.

When the value of an extraneous variable changes systematically across different conditions of an experiment, we have a situation known as **confounding.** Box 6-3 presents a hypothetical experiment in which confounding is a serious problem. When there is confounding, experimental results cannot be interpreted with certainty. Causal relationships between the independent and dependent variables cannot be inferred. In effect, confounding sabotages the experiment because the effects we see can be explained equally well by changes in the extraneous variable or in the independent variable. Our experiment is not internally valid. In subsequent chapters we will study some of the basic techniques used to avoid confounding. Our goal is always to set up an experiment in such a way that the independent variable is the only variable (besides the dependent variable) that changes value across conditions. To draw causal inferences about the effects of the independent variable, we must be sure that no extraneous variables change along with the independent variable.

What's wrong with this experiment? Suppose a researcher was interested in the effects of age on communicator persuasiveness. She hypothesized that older communicators would be more persuasive than younger communicators—even if both presented the same arguments. She set up an experiment with two experimental groups. Subjects listened to either an 18-year-old man or a 35-year-old man presenting the same 3-minute argument in favor of gun control. After listening to one of the communicators, subjects rated how persuaded they were by the argument they had just heard. As the researcher predicted, subjects who heard the older man speak were more persuaded. Would she be justified in stating that a speaker's age influences persuasiveness? Hopefully, you identified this as a confounded experiment. Too many extraneous variables could have changed along with the independent variable (age): The older speaker may have seemed more attractive, better educated, more intelligent, or more self-confident (all these variables can influence our persuasibility). Even though the researcher believed she was manipulating only the age of the speaker, several other extraneous variables may also have systematically varied along with the IV. Clearly, we could not say with assurance that age (and not one of the other variables) influenced persuasion. What might she have done to control for these potential sources of confounding?

Classic Threats to Internal Validity

Psychologist Donald Campbell (Campbell, 1957; Campbell & Stanley, 1966; Cook & Campbell, 1979) identified eight kinds of extraneous variables that can threaten the internal validity of experiments and quasi-experiments. Since that time, Campbell's listing of these potential sources of confounding has

B O X   6 - 3

CONFOUNDED EXPERIMENT

With the increasing concern about food additives, we might hypothe-size that the average consumer would now be more likely to select a product with fewer food additives than a similar one with more addi-tives. Suppose we set up an experiment to be conducted in a local super-market.

We approach every third customer who enters the market and ask that person to participate in a study of consumer preferences. We show the subject two containers of potato chips. The first container (labeled "Crunchy Chips" in bright, cheerful colors) lists the following ingredi-ents: potatoes, oil, salt. The second container (labeled "Sludgy Chips" in dull, unattractive colors) lists these ingredients: potatoes, oil, salt, monosodium glutamate, calcium silicate, disodium inosinate, disodium guanylate, polymorphosperversinate, artificial flavor, and artificial color. We now ask our subjects to examine both packages and indicate the one they would be more likely to buy, assuming the price of the two items is equal.

Suppose that of the 236 shoppers who agree to participate, 232 select the first as the product they would be most likely to buy. May we conclude that, consistent with our original hypothesis, shoppers prefer products with less additives? Definitely not.

This experiment contains two confounding variables! The indepen-dent variable is the number of additives listed on the food package. The dependent variable is desirability, measured by the subjects' reports of which product they would be more likely to purchase. Based simply on reported preferences, we might be tempted to conclude that shoppers avoid foods that contain many additives. However, in addition to the number of additives, two other factors also varied systematically across conditions: the names of the products and the attractiveness of the pack-ages. The name "Crunchy Chips," which suggests a crispy product, may be more appealing than "Sludgy Chips." The package also differed across conditions—"Crunchy Chips" had a more attractive package than "Sludgy Chips." Since the names of the products and their packaging as well as the ingredients are different, we cannot conclude with certainty that subjects chose one product over the other because of the ingredi-ents and not the names or the packaging.

To establish that subjects prefer one product over another on the basis of ingredients, we must eliminate the names of the products and the packaging.* We might relabel both products simply "Potato Chips." We would also want to use two packages of the same color and size, keep the price of the two items constant, and refrain from smiling as subjects examine the labels. With all other factors held constant across conditions, if subjects still showed a clear preference for one product over the other, we might then conclude that subjects preferred one to the other because of the ingredients.

*In Chapter 8 you will learn about factorial designs, in which it is possible to explore the effects of both the names and the ingredients at the same time.

become required course material for successive classes of experimental psychology students; hence, they have become known as the *classic threats to internal validity.*

You will recognize some of these classic threats from the previous chapters covering nonexperimental and quasi-experimental designs. All quasi-experimental designs contain one or more classic threats to internal validity—in fact, that is the reason they are not true experiments; they are potentially confounded. As you are learning the classic threats, see if you can recognize which threats are inherent to each of the quasi-experimental designs from Chapter 4: longitudinal, cross-sectional, ex post facto, and pretest/posttest designs.

Remember that a confound is an extraneous variable that *varies systematically* along with experimental conditions. An extraneous variable that pops up randomly across conditions is not a confound—it simply increases the amount of variance in the scores that we call error, making it harder to detect a significant treatment effect. Designs using different subjects in each treatment group may be confounded if an extraneous variable affects some experimental groups but not others with regularity. (These are called between-subjects designs, and we will proceed to them in the next chapter.) Other designs in which subjects are measured multiple times may be confounded if an extraneous variable is present only in certain experimental conditions but not in others. (These are called within-subjects designs, and we will deal with them in Chapter 9.)

Whenever you design or evaluate experimental research, you must consider each of these eight classic threats to internal validity. In Chapter 7, we will begin learning about the various types of experimental designs. Controlling for extraneous variables that might confound experiments is one of the most important elements of research design. If one or more of these threats are present, the experiment will lack internal validity, and you can never be sure that the effects produced on the dependent variable were really due to the experimental manipulation.

History

The first threat is called **history,** and it refers to the history of the experiment. Ask yourself whether the experimental effects could have been caused by any outside event or occurrence rather than the independent variable. (It need not be a great historical event, although it could be.) History is most often a problem when a whole group of individuals are tested together in the same experimental condition. Some outside event that occurred prior to their group testing session could influence responses of the entire group, and effects produced by the event could be mistaken for effects of the IV. History effects can be problematic.

Suppose you were testing two different weight-loss programs in which subjects were exposed to your treatment during daily group meetings. You assessed the benefits of the program by measuring how much weight each person lost at the end of a seven-day program. After weighing subjects in both groups, you discover that individuals who received treatment *B* lost an average of 2 pounds that week; whereas the average for treatment *A* was 4 pounds. You want to make sure that the "history" of both groups prior to weighing was the same. Imagine the confound in your experiment if individuals in group *B* were weighed right after lunch, but the subjects in group *A* were weighed just before lunch. You would not know if the differences you observed were caused by your diet program or by the fact that one group had just eaten and the other had not.

Maturation

The second classic threat, **maturation,** refers to any internal (physical or psychological) changes in subjects that might have affected scores on the dependent measure (not just "maturing" in the way we typically think of it; although it could be). The kinds of internal changes that we usually worry about in experimentation are things like boredom and fatigue that can occur during a single testing session. Boredom or fatigue are more likely in within-subjects designs that require lengthy testing sessions. You will learn that there are techniques for balancing out the order of treatments subjects receive (Chapter 9), so that whatever boredom or fatigue exists will be spread evenly across all the conditions of the experiment.

It should be obvious that maturation effects can also be a problem in studies that take months or even years to finish. For example, maturation must be considered in longitudinal studies, such as the one by Stewart, Mobley, Van Tuyl, and Salvador (1987) that observed first-born children's behavior before and after the birth of a sibling. Young children can make cognitive and physical leaps during certain ages, so researchers need to consider that effects might be produced by these changes, rather than the event being studied. For example, Stewart and colleagues found that the number of imitative behaviors at one month postpartum were positively correlated with the firstborn's age.

Another kind of maturation can occur even in brief experiments whenever university students are the subjects. Just as you are now more sophisticated about research than you were when you first opened your textbook, other students are gaining knowledge over the course of the semester, too. In psychology experiments, the subjects are often students taking a course in introductory psychology, and they may be much more sophisticated about correctly guessing your hypotheses later in the semester than they are in the beginning. You would not want to run treatment condition *A* in September and October and leave condition *B* for November and December!

Testing

A **testing** threat refers to effects on the dependent variable produced by a previous administration of the same test or other measuring instrument (remember what we said about the pretest/posttest design?). It is not uncommon to measure subjects on a dependent variable (anxiety, depression, extroversion) at the beginning of the experiment and then remeasure them using the same test after a treatment is given. Unfortunately, this procedure introduces a testing threat, because individuals frequently perform differently the second time they are tested—even without any intervening experimental treatment. This is one reason that *test-retest reliability* can be an important piece of information for a researcher. Low test-retest reliability can mean that the researcher can expect large differences in scores from one testing session to the next even without any experimental manipulation. Even the most reliable tests that psychologists use—standardized intelligence tests like the Wechsler Adult Intelligence Scale–Revised—do not have perfect test-retest reliability. Performance tends to improve somewhat with practice even without any special treatment.

Instrumentation

Whenever some feature of the measuring instrument itself changes over the course of the experiment, the researcher is faced with the possibility of an **instrumentation** threat to internal validity. The example most often used to illustrate this concept is the case of the rubber ruler. Imagine that your dependent measure was the length of a line drawn by subjects. To measure it, you use the only ruler you have—a rubber ruler. Unknown to you, it stretches a bit every time you use it. Each consecutive measurement is a little more inaccurate, and successive measurements tend to underestimate line length. If you measure lines drawn by subjects in one treatment condition before you measure lines drawn in a different condition, your measurements in one group will systematically underestimate line length to a greater extent than your measurements in another group.

We are certain you will never use a rubber ruler to measure your dependent variable, but instrumentation threats are not always this obvious. Mechanical measuring instruments can break or become less accurate. A speedometer could falter at high speeds but not at low, underestimating how fast subjects are pedaling an exercise bike in your "high-motivation" condition.

Instrumentation is also a potential problem whenever human observers are used to record behavior, score questionnaires by hand, or perform content analyses. For example, the behavior of subjects in one condition can be inherently more interesting than in another, and observers might pay much less attention in a particular condition, making more errors in recording. Or raters doing a content analysis might find their judgments changing a little as the analysis goes on and they become more familiar with the procedure.

Instrumentation of a different sort can be a problem when you administer written instruments to subjects. Are all your questions equally easy to read in all conditions? Are the intervals you typed on all the scales really equal? When you ran out of questionnaires, were your new copies as good as the first set? Did you allow subjects in all conditions the same amount of space to write stories? Such seemingly small things can alter subjects' responses; if they vary systematically with your treatment conditions, your experiment is confounded.

Statistical Regression

The threat of **statistical regression** (also called **regression toward the mean**) can occur whenever subjects are assigned to conditions on the basis of extreme scores on a test. Statistically, extreme scores tend to have less test-retest reliability than moderate scores (those closer to the mean, or average). If the same extreme scorers are retested, their scores are likely to be closer to the mean the second time around. Extreme high scores tend to go down a bit, and extreme low scores tend to rise somewhat; scores at both extremes typically get closer to the mean *without any treatment at all.*

Selection

Whenever the researcher does not assign subjects randomly to the different conditions of an experiment, a **selection** threat is present. In experimentation, we control for individual differences in each subject's characteristics by assigning subjects to different conditions of the experiment using randomization procedures. In this way, we attempt to balance out differences among subjects across all the conditions of the experiment so that the subjects in one condition are not different from the subjects in another condition in any *systematic* way. Random assignment is an important feature of true experiments that will be discussed in detail in Chapter 7.

Always consider how members of the treatment groups were chosen. If nonrandom assignment procedures were used (or if random assignment failed to balance out differences among subjects), the subjects in one treatment condition may begin the experiment with different characteristics than the subjects in another condition. And there is always a chance that these characteristics—not your IV—might be the cause of observed effects on the DV. This would clearly be a problem in any experiment that included a subject or ex post facto variable.

Subject Mortality

Always consider the possibility that more subjects dropped out of one experimental condition than another. If so, **subject mortality** threatens internal validity. Dropout rates should always be stated in a research report, so that the reader can be on the lookout for this threat. Whenever the dropout rate in a particular treatment condition is high, it should be a red flag: Something about the treatment could be making subjects drop out. Often it means that the treatment is frightening, painful, or distressing. If the dropout rate is very high, it can mean that the treatment is sufficiently obnoxious that *typical* subjects would choose to leave, and the ones who remain could be unusual in some respect. You have to ask yourself: "Why did so many subjects drop out?" (Maybe the experimental tasks were too repetitious or the weight-loss regimen was too difficult.) "What does this tell me about the subjects who finished this condition of the experiment?" (They were probably more patient than most people or they were more motivated than most dieters.) Your answers are likely to uncover a confounding variable. Effects on the dependent measure might have been produced by this characteristic, not by the independent variable.

Selection Interactions

The last threat is really a family of threats. A selection threat can combine with another threat to form a **selection interaction**. If subjects were not randomly assigned to groups (or if random assignment failed to balance out differences among subjects), any one of the other threats may have affected some experimental groups but not others. Selection can interact with history, maturation, mortality, and so on to produce effects on the dependent variable. Suppose that your two groups of dieters were selected nonrandomly from among patrons of two different gyms and, as a result, your dieters in condition *A* were much more body conscious than those in condition *B*. And, since joining the experiment, many of the group *A* subjects had succumbed to those TV commercials showing what their bodies could look like after only a few minutes a day on a cross-country ski machine—many had bought one and were using it. The subjects in group *B* never even considered buying one. Not surprisingly, subjects in the *A* group lost a lot more weight over the course of their program than the other subjects did. Could you say that treatment *A* was really better? Of course not. Clearly, this experiment would not be internally valid. Here you would be faced with a selection-by-history threat: a history threat that *combined* with other characteristics of only one of your treatment groups to produce a confound.

You can see that it is difficult to control all the sources of possible confounding in an experiment. We must often compromise in setting up our experimental design by focusing on the variables most likely to affect the dependent variable we are measuring. For example, in a study of learning in the classroom, we would be more concerned about finding classes of comparable intelligence than classes containing equal numbers of brown- and blue-eyed students. Just as we narrow down the number of possible independent variables we want to explore, we narrow down the number of extraneous variables we choose to control. The rule is: *Control as many variables as possible.* If a variable can be held constant in an experiment, it makes sense to do so even when any impact of that variable on the results may be doubtful. In the hypothetical persuasion experiment, for example, the researcher did control some potential confounds (sex of the speaker and content of the speech). However, we often find that as we control one variable, another changes value and is out of control. Many of the design problems you will face can be described as "finding the least worst alternative." Ways to achieve control using between-subjects designs will be a major focus of Chapter 7.

PLANNING THE METHOD SECTION

The **Method** section of the research report is the place to describe your experiment (who, what, when, and how). It needs to be detailed enough that another researcher could read it and replicate what you did. Typically, the Method section is divided into labeled subsections: Participants, Apparatus or Materials, and Procedure, but some flexibility is allowed to accommodate specific experiments. More detailed information about style and content is given in Chapter 16. An overview at this point will help you to plan the report as you are planning your experiment.

First, you will need to describe your subjects ("Participants"). The information about reporting samples (in Chapter 4) is relevant to describing experimental subjects, but you probably will not need as much detail as survey researchers put in their reports. It is a good idea, however, to track the genders and ages of your subjects, as well as how many participated because you are expected to report this minimal amount of information about them. Any other information that you feel might limit the *generalizability* of your results should also be included. For example, if the participants came from a highly selective university or from your church group, the subjects might have special characteristics that could affect the *external validity* of results from certain kinds of experiments. (Ask yourself: Would your results generalize just as well to people with fewer academic skills or different religious values?) Report, also, how subjects were recruited and anything tangible they received in return for participation.

Second, you will need to describe any equipment used in the study. If it is specialized equipment, record the name, manufacturer, model number, and so on. If it was custom designed, you may need a diagram. Items presented to subjects (films, questionnaires, stories, and so forth) also must be described in detail (except for standardized tests and measures). Depending upon your experiment, this information will be needed for the subsection called Apparatus or Materials, whichever is most appropriate. In Box 6-4, you will find more details about this subsection. Finally, keep careful notes about the procedures used in your experiment, including any verbal instructions given to subjects. If you used verbal instructions to manipulate the independent variable, you will need to report them verbatim. Make sure you have a record of the chronological order of events, because that is often the simplest way to present this information in the Procedures subsection.

B O X   6 - 4

THE APPARATUS SECTION

In the Method section of many journal articles, you will find a subsection headed Apparatus. This subsection contains a description of the equipment used to conduct the experiment. The technology of stimulus generation and response recording has become more sophisticated across the field of psychology. These advances have been documented across the years in the Apparatus sections of journal articles. Today participants in experiments are shown digitized visual images that have been generated or manipulated with computers running sophisticated software. Computer-controlled event recorders track complex human and animal behaviors and can measure micromomentary differences in response times.

This does not mean, however, that every scientific report written must have an Apparatus section. Sometimes it is appropriate, sometimes not. Remember that the purpose of the Method section is to provide enough information about the experiment that it can be evaluated and reconducted by another researcher. An Apparatus section, then, is particularly appropriate in the description of an experiment that was conducted with unique or specialized equipment or equipment with capabilities that are important for the reader to know in order to evaluate or reconduct the experiment.

Imagine we had conducted an experiment in which people watched a videotape on a television set. We are now writing a report that we will submit to a scientific journal. Should our report include an Apparatus section? Maybe not. It probably would not be necessary to provide an extensive description of the videotape machine and the television set. If any VCR and television set would do, one or two sentences describing the important features of the equipment (such as the size of the television set) would probably be sufficient. But imagine instead that we had conducted an experiment in which we showed people a series of visual images. We very carefully controlled the length of time each image was shown using shutters mounted on slide projectors, operated by a computer. In this case, we would probably want to include an Apparatus section in which we described all of the equipment: the shutters, the slide projectors, the computer, and even the software used to operate the shutters. Many times, this turns out to be easier than it seems. For example, equipment is often known to most researchers who would be interested in the experiment. We could give these researchers almost everything they needed to know by simply providing the name of the

(continued)

FIGURE 6-6 Microprocessor-based laboratory equipment for computer acquisition of psychophysiological data. Jay Damiano

(continued)

manufacturer and the model number of each item. We have explained how we presented the visual images to the people in our experiment. But we might also have to describe the equipment we used to obtain the measurements we took while the people in our experiment were watching the visual images.

Suppose we measured the electrical activity of each person's brain while each image was shown. To do this, we placed electrodes at specific sites on their heads, amplified the signal with a polygraph, and had our computer record the signal from the polygraph. (This technique is called electroencephalography—EEG for short—and it is a psychophysiological measure. Its designation as a psychophysiological measure means that we are looking for evidence of a psychological process in a physiological event.) Our Apparatus section just got longer! We must now describe the electrodes, the polygraph, and the computer software we used to make our measurements.

When you write a report, you must decide what is appropriate. Just remember the rule that guides what is needed: You must provide enough information for another researcher to reasonably evaluate or reconduct the experiment.

SUMMARY

In this chapter we have examined a number of basic experimental concepts. The *independent variable* is the antecedent condition (the treatment) that is deliberately manipulated by the experimenter to assess its effect on behavior. We use different values or levels of the independent variable in order to determine how changes in the independent variable alter the value of the dependent variable, our index of behavior. The *dependent variable* is an indicator of change in behavior. Its values are assumed to depend on the values of the independent variable.

Both independent and dependent variables must be defined operationally. An *operational definition* specifies the precise meaning of a variable within an experiment: It defines the variable in terms of observable operations, procedures, and measurements. Operational definitions establish what operations and procedures constitute each of the different values needed to test the effect of the independent variable. They also specify the procedures used to measure the impact of the independent variable.

The researcher must define the *level of measurement* of each variable. There are four levels of measurement: nominal, ordinal, interval, and ratio. A *nominal scale,* the lowest level of measurement, measures a variable by establishing categories, which are not measures of size but are mutually exclusive: An item cannot belong to more than one nominal category at the same time. An *ordinal scale* reflects differences in magnitude by rank ordering values of a variable. An *interval scale* has magnitude, equal intervals between values of a variable, but no absolute zero point. A *ratio scale,* the highest level of measurement, has magnitude, equal intervals between its values, and an absolute zero point. We generally use the highest level of measurement that is feasible.

Operational definitions are developed according to criteria of *reliability* and *validity.* Reliable procedures have consistent and dependable outcomes. Valid definitions are sound and sensible. If our definitions are valid, we will be manipulating and measuring the variables we intend to study. *Face validity* is the simplest criterion for evaluating validity. We may also evaluate the *content* and *predictive validity* of our dependent measures. Researchers are also concerned with *construct validity,* the fit between data and theory.

An experiment is *internally valid* if we can be sure that the changes in behavior that occurred across treatment conditions were caused by the independent variable. Ideally, only the independent and dependent variables will change value in the different treatment conditions of the experiment. However, sometimes we find that *extraneous variables,* variables that are neither independent nor dependent variables in the experiment, also change across conditions. When extraneous variables change value from one treatment condition to another along with the independent variable, we have a situation known as *confounding.* When there is confounding, we cannot say for sure whether the changes we see in the dependent variable from one condition to another were caused by the changes in the values of the independent variable or by an extraneous variable that was also changing: The experiment is not internally valid.

Campbell and his colleagues have identified eight classic threats to the internal validity of experiments and quasi-experiments: *history, maturation, testing, instrumentation, statistical regression, selection, subject mortality,* and the set of *selection interactions.*

Tips for planning the *Method* section of the research report include keeping careful notes about gender, age, and number of subjects, any equipment and written or other materials, and the procedure you used in the experiment.

KEY TERMS

Confounding An error that occurs when the value of an extraneous variable changes systematically along with the independent variable in an experiment; an alternative explanation for the findings.

Construct validity The degree to which an operational definition accurately represents the construct it is intended to manipulate or measure.

Content validity The degree to which the content of a measure reflects the content of what is measured.

Continuous dimension The concept that traits, attitudes, and preferences can be viewed as continuous dimensions, and each individual may fall at any point along each dimension; for example, sociability can be viewed as a continuous dimension ranging from very unsociable to very sociable.

Dependent variable (DV) The specific behavior that a researcher tries to explain in an experiment; the variable that is measured.

Environmental variable Aspects of the physical environment that the experimenter can bring under direct control as an independent variable.

Experimental condition A treatment condition in which the researcher applies a particular value of an independent variable to subjects and then measures the dependent variable.

Experimental operational definition The explanation of the meaning of independent variables; defines *exactly* what was done to create the various treatment conditions of the experiment.

External validity How well the findings of an experiment generalize or apply to people and settings that were not tested directly.

Extraneous variable A variable other than an independent or dependent variable; a variable that is not the main focus of an experiment and that may confound the results if not controlled.

Face validity The degree to which a manipulation or measurement technique is self-evident.

History threat A threat to internal validity in which an outside event or occurrence might have produced effects on the dependent variable.

Hypothetical construct Concepts used to explain unseen processes, such as hunger or learning; postulated to explain observable behavior.

Independent variable (IV) The variable (antecedent condition) that the experimenter intentionally manipulates.

Instrumentation threat A threat to internal validity produced by changes in the measuring instrument itself.

Interitem reliability The degree to which different items measuring the same variable attain consistent results.

Internal validity The determination that the changes in behavior observed across treatment conditions in the experiment were actually caused by the independent variable.

Interrater reliability The degree of agreement among different observers or raters.

Interval scale The measurement of magnitude or quantitative size having equal intervals between values but no true zero point.

Latent content The "hidden meaning" behind a question.

Level of measurement The type of scale of measurement used to measure a variable.

Levels of the independent variable The two or more values of the independent variable manipulated by the experimenter.

Maturation threat A threat to internal validity produced by internal (physical or psychological) changes in subjects.

Measured operational definition The description of *exactly* how a variable in an experiment is measured.

Method The section of a research report in which the subjects and experiment are described in enough detail that the experiment may be replicated by others; it is typically divided into subsections, such as Participants, Apparatus or Materials, and Procedures.

Nominal scale The simplest level of measurement; classifies items into two or more distinct categories on the basis of some common feature.

Operational definition The specification of the precise meaning of a variable within an experiment; defines a variable in terms of observable operations, procedures, and measurements.

Ordinal scale A measure of magnitude in which each value is measured in the form of ranks.

Predictive validity The degree to which a measure, definition, or experiment yields information allowing prediction of actual behavior or performance.

Ratio scale A measure of magnitude having equal intervals between values and having an absolute zero point.

Reliability The consistency and dependability of experimental procedures and measurements.

Response set A tendency to answer questions based on their latent content with the goal of creating a certain impression of ourselves.

Scale of measurement The type of precise, quantitative measurement used to measure variables.

Selection interactions A family of threats to internal validity produced when a selection threat combines with one or more of the other threats to internal validity; when a selection threat is already present, other threats can affect some experimental groups but not others.

Selection threat A threat to internal validity that can occur when nonrandom procedures are used to assign subjects to conditions or when random assignment fails to balance out differences among subjects across the different conditions of the experiment.

Statistical regression threat A threat to internal validity that can occur when subjects are assigned to conditions on the basis of extreme scores on a test; upon retest, the scores of extreme scorers tend to regress toward the mean even without any treatment.

Subject mortality threat A threat to internal validity produced by differences in dropout rates across the conditions of the experiment.

Subject variable The characteristics of the subjects in an experiment that cannot be manipulated; an independent variable, in the sense that a researcher can select subjects for their particular values.

Task variable An aspect of a task that the experimenter intentionally manipulates as an independent variable.

Testing threat A threat to internal validity produced by a previous administration of the same test or other measure.

Test-retest reliability Consistency between an individual's scores on the same test taken at two or more different times.

Validity The soundness of an operational definition; in experiments, the principle of actually studying the variables intended to be manipulated or measured.

REVIEW AND STUDY QUESTIONS

1. Define each of the following terms:
   a. Independent variable
   b. Dependent variable
   c. Extraneous variable

2. Identify the independent and dependent variables in each of the following hypotheses:
   a. Absence makes the heart grow fonder.
   b. It takes longer to recognize a person in a photograph seen upside down.
   c. People feel sadder in rooms painted blue.
   d. Smoking cigarettes causes cancer.

3. What is an operational definition?

4. Formulate an experimental operational definition for each independent variable in question 2.

5. Formulate a measured operational definition for each dependent variable in question 2.

6. For each hypothesis in question 2, discuss three extraneous variables that might interfere with making a valid test of that hypothesis.

7. Define and give an example to illustrate each of these terms:
   a. Interrater reliability
   b. Test-retest reliability
   c. Interitem reliability
   d. Content validity
   e. Predictive validity
   f. Construct validity

8. Discuss the requirements of a good operational definition.

9. What is internal validity? Why is it important?

10. Summarize the characteristics of each of the following levels of measurement and give an example of each:
    a. Nominal
    b. Ordinal
    c. Interval
    d. Ratio

11. What type of scale is being used in each of these instances?
    a. A researcher measures the brand of car purchased by subjects who heard one of three advertising campaigns.
    b. A counselor assesses the divorce rate among couples who had marriage counseling.
    c. A seamstress estimates how much fabric will be needed to make a coat.
    d. Three racks of sweaters are labeled "small," "medium," and "large."
    e. In Murphy's Hardware, all the latex paints are on the top shelf; all the oil-base paints are on the bottom shelf.
    f. On a scale from 0–10 (0 = not at all; 10 = extremely), how hungry are you right now?

12. Define each of the eight classic threats to internal validity and give an example of each.

13. List each classic threat to internal validity that is intrinsic to the following designs:
    a. ex post facto study
    b. longitudinal study
    c. pretest/posttest study

C H A P T E R   7

BASIC BETWEEN-SUBJECTS DESIGNS

To test an experimental hypothesis, a researcher must develop a basic plan or design for the experiment. The **experimental design** is the general structure of the experiment. It is like the floor plan of a building, which specifies how many rooms there are and how they are connected but says nothing about what is inside the rooms and how they are used. Just as a floor plan describes rooms that can serve many purposes, an experimental design can be used to answer many kinds of research questions. Experiments that test different hypotheses may have the same design. Or, alternatively, the same hypothesis may sometimes be approached through more than one design. The design is simply the *general structure* of the experiment, not its specific content; it is made up of things like the number of treatment conditions and whether the subjects in all conditions are the same or different individuals. The design used in an experiment is determined mainly by the nature of the hypothesis. However, prior research, the kind of information the researcher is seeking, and practical problems in running the experiment also influence choice of design.

Although there is an infinite variety of potential hypotheses, the majority of research questions use a few basic designs. Three aspects of the experiment play the biggest part in determining the design: (1) the number of independent variables, (2) the number of treatment conditions needed to make a fair test of the experimental hypothesis, and (3) whether the same or different subjects are used in each of the treatment conditions. We will look at basic research designs in terms of these aspects. In this chapter and the next, we will look at designs in which different subjects take part in each condition of the experiment. These are called **between-subjects designs**. The name is based on the fact that we draw conclusions from between-subjects experiments by making comparisons between the behavior of different groups of subjects. In Chapter 9 we look at within-subjects designs, in which the same subjects take part in more than one treatment condition of the experiment. In those designs we look for changes in behavior within the same group of subjects. But before we discuss the details of specific designs, let us look at the researcher's first important decisions—selecting and recruiting the sample of subjects.

SELECTING AND RECRUITING SUBJECTS

In the context of designing survey research in Chapter 4, you learned about sampling procedures for selecting subjects. In experiments, as in surveys, we rely on samples to test hypotheses. How accurately we can generalize the results of experiments depends on the representativeness of our sample: *The more the sample resembles the whole population, the more likely it is that the behavior of the sample mirrors that of the population.* Clearly, some form of random sampling procedure is highly desirable because it greatly increases an experiment's external validity. Ideally, when we take a random sample, every individual in the population has an equal chance of being selected. In practice, this ideal is rarely achieved.

Practical Limits

Most of the time, our samples must be drawn from subsets of the population, such as the residents of one nursing home in the example from Chapter 4. Typically, we do not have access to all college students. We can sample only the airline passengers at the terminal nearest us. Our nursing home example dealt with a situation in which we have more individuals available than are needed. However, this is not always the case; people are often reluctant to participate in an experiment because they feel it will take too much time.[1] Unfortunately, they also are often wary of psychological research. At times individuals seem fearful that the experimenter will uncover very private information. This attitude stems partly from the popularization of Freud's ideas, especially the idea that every action contains an important hidden meaning known only to the trained psychologist. This makes it especially important that we follow ethical guidelines and keep subjects informed of what we are doing.

Rosnow and Rosenthal (1976) offered some suggestions for encouraging prospective subjects to volunteer: Make your appeal interesting, nonthreatening, and meaningful. Get someone known to the subjects to ask them, preferably a woman of high status. Emphasize the responsibility of people to aid in research that can help others and point out that lots of people do it. Pay them if you can and give token gifts (a stick of gum would do) for taking time to hear you out. Assess whether you should ask for volunteers publicly (show of hands) or privately (fill out a form). Try to put yourself in the other's place and ask what would make you most likely to say yes.

As you recruit subjects, you may find that you have to use procedures that do not guarantee a random sample. You may have to recruit all your subjects from a single class or location, resulting in a convenience sample. Students in our classes have found that the lobby of the college library and out-

---

[1] One of the authors recalls scouting for subjects to take part in a brief, on-the-spot perception experiment that lasted about a minute. Prospective subjects often provided elaborate explanations of why they had no time to participate. Their stories usually lasted longer than the actual experiment.

BIZARRE SEQUENCE OF COMPUTER-GENERATED RANDOM NUMBERS

Copyright ©1996 by Sidney Harris

side the bookstore can sometimes be good places to find willing subjects. In desperation, they have also resorted to asking their friends to participate. However, asking friends is risky on three counts: First, it can dissolve a friendship. Second, friends may not be totally ignorant about the purpose of an experiment that you have been talking about for two weeks. They may also be sensitive to your subtle cues to behave in particular ways. These cues may influence the way they respond in the experiment and may lead to erroneous data. Third and most important, they may feel obliged to participate, which raises ethical questions concerning free choice. But even when we have the time, energy, and resources to do extensive sampling, another difficulty remains. People who volunteer to participate in research may be somewhat different from those who do not (Rosenthal & Rosnow, 1969). (We will come back to this issue in Chapter 11.) Perhaps we would obtain very different data if we tested everyone regardless of personal choice. Without resorting to coercion, there is no way we can ever guarantee a truly random sample.

How Many Subjects?

How many subjects are enough for an experiment? Ten? One hundred? There is no simple answer to this question. In later chapters, we will discuss experiments that require only one or two subjects and others that require many more. Usually, we want to have more than one or two subjects in each treatment condition. Remember that we use samples of subjects to make inferences about the way the independent variable affects the population. Too small a sample can lead to erroneous results. For instance, if we wanted to know the height of the "average" American adult, we would want a large sample. Samples of two or three people would probably be inadequate even if they were randomly selected. We would hesitate to make statements about millions of people on the basis of such a small sample. Similarly, in an experiment we might hesitate to make great claims for our independent variable on the basis of a few subjects.

Of course, if everyone were exactly the same, if everyone behaved exactly the same way, we could use samples of one or two subjects with confidence. We would know that the experimental results reflect what we would find if we tested everyone in the population. But we also know that in reality subjects are not all the same. Different subjects will get different scores. Our independent variable may affect different subjects in different ways. The more responses can vary, the harder it is to get a sample that reflects what goes on in the population. If individuals in the population are all very similar to one another on the dependent variable, small samples are adequate. However, when individuals are likely to be quite different, larger samples are needed. *If we take larger samples, we are more likely to obtain individuals who represent the full range of behaviors on the dependent variable*—some people who score high, some who score low, and some who score in between. Thus a larger sample is more likely to mirror the actual state of the population.

Typically, we get slightly different responses from different subjects in an experiment because of individual differences. Subjects' scores should also differ because of the treatment conditions. We expect the behavior of subjects under different treatment conditions to be noticeably different. We use statistical tests to make comparisons between the behavior of subjects under different treatment conditions. When we discuss test results (Part 3), you will see exactly how these procedures work. As we choose our samples, though, certain general characteristics of the statistical procedures shape our decisions. The statistical procedures we will discuss in this text require computing averages of the results under different treatments. In effect, we ask whether, *on the average,* our independent variable had an effect. We evaluate the effect in terms of the amount of fluctuation we would expect to see among *any* samples measured on our dependent variable. We are not especially interested in the performance of individual subjects in the experiment; we know that individual scores will differ. The question is whether or not we see more of a difference if we look at responses obtained under different treatment conditions.

We use statistical procedures to decide whether the differences we see between responses under different treatment conditions are *significant differences:* Are they larger than the differences we would probably see between *any* groups that we measure on the dependent variable? Are they so unlikely to have happened accidentally that they are noteworthy and require a scientific explanation? From a statistical standpoint, an experiment has less power to detect effects with smaller samples (Cohen, 1988). It is much harder to show that differences between treatment groups are significant when we use a small number of subjects. This is especially true when individual responses are apt to vary a great deal from one subject to another under any circumstances. For that reason, we usually try to have a reasonably large number of subjects in each treatment group. If the effects of the independent variable are strong, we should be able to detect them with about 10 to 20 subjects per group. A moderate size effect should show up with about 20 to 30 subjects per group. Weaker effects may be detected in larger groups. Of course, these are only rough estimates. Other factors besides the number of subjects and the impact of the independent variable influence the outcome; a larger sample is no guarantee that an experiment will turn out as you expect.

Practical considerations also affect the total number of subjects to be used. You may plan to have 50, but if you can only get 30, that may have to do. If the experiment requires lengthy individual testing sessions, it may not be feasible to run large numbers of subjects. You can use the review of prior research as a guide. If other researchers have had success with 20 subjects, that is a reasonable number. As a general rule, it is advisable to have at least 15 subjects in each treatment group. Smaller numbers make it very difficult to detect an effect of the independent variable unless the effect is enormous.

ONE INDEPENDENT VARIABLE: TWO-GROUP DESIGNS

The simplest experiments are those in which there is only one independent variable. As you know, an experiment must have at least two treatment conditions: The independent variable is manipulated in such a way that at least two levels or treatment conditions are created. When only two treatment conditions are needed, the experimenter may choose to form two separate groups of subjects. This approach is known as the **two-group design.** There are two variations of the two-group design: One is the two-independent-groups design, the other is the two-matched-groups design. Both use two treatment conditions, but they differ dramatically in the way the researcher decides *which* subjects will take part in each treatment condition.

TWO INDEPENDENT GROUPS

In the **two-independent-groups design,** randomly selected subjects are placed in each of two treatment conditions through random assignment. The first step is to choose subjects through an unbiased selection procedure, as discussed previously. We may draw names out of a hat or use the random number table to decide which individuals will be in the experiment. Ideally, each member of the population we study should have an equal chance of being selected for our experiment. If it is not possible to select subjects entirely at random, the two-independent-groups design can still be used, but the researcher will have to settle for conclusions with less *external validity.* However, since a two-group design involves two treatment conditions, we also need to make decisions about which individuals will take part in each treatment condition. We do that by using another procedure, random assignment. Even if a researcher cannot use true random selection in deciding who the subjects of an experiment will be, he or she *always* uses random assignment to treatment conditions.

Random Assignment

Random assignment means that every subject has an equal chance of being placed in any of the treatment conditions. When we use an independent-groups design, we use the same unbiased procedures for assigning subjects to groups that are used in random selection of subjects for an experiment. Putting subject 3 in group A should not affect the chances that subject 4 will also be assigned to that group. In an independent-groups design, the groups are "independent" of each other. The makeup of one group has no effect on that of the other.[2]

If subjects are not assigned at random, confounding may occur. We may inadvertently put all our witty subjects in group A and so distort the outcome of the experiment. Random assignment gives us a better chance of forming groups that are *roughly* the same on all the extraneous variables that might affect our dependent variable. Assigning subjects at random controls for the differences that exist between subjects before the experiment. In short, it controls for subject variables. Our separate treatment groups will not consist of identical individuals, of course, but any potential differences will be spread out randomly across the conditions of the experiment. Thus random assignment guards against the possibility that subjects' characteristics will vary *systematically* along with the independent variable. When there are two treatment conditions, as in the two-independent-groups design, assignment may be made by simply flipping a coin. When there are more than two conditions, we may use the random number table. These methods eliminate bias; they reduce the chances that our experiment will be confounded because treatment groups are already different when we start the experiment.

Remember that random selection and random assignment are two separate procedures. It is possible to select a random sample from the population but then assign the subjects to groups in a biased way. The reverse is also possible. We can start out with a nonrandom, biased sample of subjects and randomly assign those subjects to our different treatment groups. But the original sample is still biased and may not represent the population we are trying to study. Nonrandom selection affects the external validity of an experiment—that is, how well the findings can be applied to the population and other situations. Random assignment, however, is critical to internal validity. If subjects are not assigned at random, confounding may occur, a selection threat may be present. The experiment will not be internally valid because we will not be sure that the independent variable caused the differences observed

---

[2]Sometimes we may have to deviate from this ideal plan. For practical reasons, we may want to have equal numbers of subjects in all treatment groups. That may mean that we have to throw our last few subjects into one group to even up the numbers. We call this *random assignment with constraints*. The assignment is random except for our limitations on numbers per group, equal numbers of men and women per group, and so on.

across treatment conditions. It could be that the differences we see were created by the way we assigned the subjects to the groups.

Even though the researcher attempts to assign subjects at random, without objective aids the assignments may be biased in subtle ways. For instance, without being aware of it, the experimenter may put all the subjects he or she dislikes into the control condition because it is the most tedious. The treatment groups would then be different even before the experiment begins. If the groups are already different at the start, it might look as though the experimental manipulation is having some effect, even if it is not. The opposite can also happen. Differences in the treatment groups can mask the effect of the independent variable. Either way, the experiment leads to false conclusions about the effects of the independent variable.

Randomization was important in a classic study by Kelley (1950). Kelley, who was interested in the effects of people's expectations on their impressions of others, carried out a two-independent-groups experiment. Introductory psychology students were given one of two written descriptions of a guest lecturer before he came to class. Half the students were told the visitor was a "warm" person; half were told he was "cold." Kelley was careful to hand out the descriptions of the lecturer at random. The guest came and led a 20-minute class discussion. After that, students were asked to report their impressions of him. Their ratings differed in ways that indicated that students who expected the lecturer to be warm reacted more favorably to him.

Why was it important to hand out the descriptions of the lecturer at random? What might have happened if, say, all the "warm" descriptions were given out first? For one thing, students who sit in different parts of the classroom might be different. If we gave out all the "warm" descriptions first, they might go to all the students who sit in the front of the class. Perhaps these students sit up front because they are more interested in the material or because they arrive earlier. In any case, their reactions to the class may be different from those of people who sit in the back. When it comes time to rate a guest speaker, these attitudes could alter the ratings as much as the descriptions that were given. Again, unless subjects are assigned randomly to different conditions of the experiment, differences among subjects can confound the results of the experiment.

In Box 7-1 we return to Brady's (1958) study of ulcers in monkeys. You will recall from Chapter 2 that this study raised several ethical concerns. It also raised methodological questions, since the researcher failed to assign subjects at random to the two treatment conditions.

Experimental Group–Control Group Design

To assess the impact of the independent variable, we must have at least two different treatment conditions so that we can compare the effect of different values of the independent variable. At times, one condition is an experimental condition and the other is a control condition. In the **experimental condition,** we apply a particular value of our independent variable to the subjects and measure the dependent variable. The subjects in an experimental

B O X   7 - 1

ULCERS IN EXECUTIVE MONKEYS

Brady's (1958) study of ulcers in executive monkeys has received a great deal of publicity. Recall that the monkeys were divided into two groups. An executive group was given control of a button connected to an apparatus that produced electric shock. The executive's task was to prevent a painful electric shock by hitting the control button at least once every 20 seconds. Each nonexecutive was coupled (or yoked) with an executive. If the executive failed to hit the button in time, the nonexecutive would also receive a shock. The nonexecutives had no control over the shock; only the executives could prevent it.

The independent variable in Brady's experiment was control over the shock. The executives had control; the nonexecutives had none. The dependent variable was the development of gastrointestinal ulcers. Brady hypothesized that monkeys that had the responsibility of remaining vigilant and preventing the shock would be more apt to develop ulcers. In other words, their "executive" responsibilities in the experiment would be stressful; they would develop ulcers just as a hard-driving human executive might. After the experimental phase of the experiment ended, Brady sacrificed the monkeys and studied their tissues for signs of ulcers. As predicted, the executives had many ulcers; the nonexecutives did not.

On the face of it, his experimental procedure appears sound. Brady devised a controlled task that would presumably be more stressful to one treatment group than the other. Executives and nonexecutives were coupled together so that both received the same total number of shocks. The only difference was the degree of control the monkeys had over the shocks. Nevertheless, the study has been severely criticized. Weiss (1972) pointed out that Brady's treatment groups were not formed at random. Brady had used a pretest to determine which monkey in each pair could learn to avoid the shock more quickly, and this monkey was then made the executive. Therefore the study was not internally valid; the way the treatment groups were formed introduced a confounding variable. We cannot be sure that the requirements of the executive job produced ulcers. The executive monkeys may have been more sensitive to the shock, or they may have differed in other ways from the nonexecutives before the experiment began. They may, for example, have been more prone to ulcers under any circumstances. In fact, in another study using rats as subjects, Weiss (1972) demonstrated that lack of control over the shocks was apt to be more stressful than being in charge of things—if subjects were assigned to the treatment conditions at random. The number of coping attempts and the amount of appropriate or relevant feedback were also identified as important variables.

condition are called an **experimental group.** The **control condition** is used to determine the value of the dependent variable without an experimental manipulation of the independent variable. The subjects in a control condition are called a **control group.** In the control condition, we carry out exactly the *same* procedures that are followed in the experimental condition, except for the experimental manipulation. Sometimes the control condition is a "no-treatment" condition. We simply measure subjects' responses without trying to alter them in any way. A no-treatment control condition tells us how subjects *ordinarily* perform on the dependent measure. We can use this control condition as a point of comparison; we can see whether subjects' performance in the experimental condition was better, worse, or the same as subjects who were not exposed to our experimental manipulation. For instance, we could compare test performance of students who engaged in 15 minutes of aerobic exercise prior to the exam with the performance of students who did not exercise. Without the no-treatment control group, we cannot say whether the experimental subjects did better or worse than usual.

Often, however, a control group does receive treatment—in the sense that in the control condition, subjects engage in the same behaviors except for some level of the independent variable of interest. An example will explain the difference. Suppose we are interested in the effects of televised violence on kids. We decide to look at violence in music videos to see if it produces the same kinds of increased aggressiveness that other kinds of TV violence appear to produce. Our hypothesis is that violence in music videos will increase aggressiveness. We plan an experiment on the effects of violent music videos on early adolescents' aggressive behavior during their school lunch recess. Naturally, we would need to define both our IV and DV operationally. If we used a no-treatment control condition as one level of the IV, we would show one group of students but not the other a music video that had been rated by objective judges as very violent. Then we would record the aggressiveness of both groups of kids (counting the number of arguments they begin, perhaps). If we found that kids exposed to the violent video were indeed more aggressive, we could say that a violent video caused an increase in aggression.

But did we really construct a good test of our hypothesis about violent content? Perhaps *any* music video increases aggression because the music is physiologically arousing—a reasonable hypothesis. A better control condition for the music video experiment would be to expose the control group to a nonviolent but equally arousing music video and then measure aggressiveness during recess. If we still found that kids who watched the violent music video were more aggressive, then we could say that the increased aggression was caused by the *violent* content of the video (which was really what we set out to demonstrate). A research example illustrating the importance of a control group is given in Box 7-2.

The type of control group you select will depend on what you want to show. If you simply want to compare the presence of a treatment with the absence of a treatment (like the difference between exercise and no exercise), you could use a no-treatment control condition. But a word of caution about no-treatment control conditions: You always need to think about what the subjects in the control group are doing while subjects in the experimental group are being treated. For instance, in the exercise experiment you would need to make sure that the subjects in the no-treatment control condition were not spending their 15 minutes studying for their exam while the other students were exercising! Remember what we said in the beginning of this section: In the control condition, we carry out exactly the *same* procedures that are followed in the experimental condition, except for the experimental manipulation. Very often, control conditions involve carefully arranging conditions that *control* for what control-group subjects are doing. In the exercise experiment, we might decide to create a situation in which the control group is engaged in some (nonaerobic) activity that would not be expected to have any effect on how well they will perform on the upcoming test.

Two-Experimental-Groups Design

It may not always be possible or even desirable to use a treatment condition in which subjects are not exposed to some value of the independent variable. Control-group experiments are most useful in the first stages of experimentation on a variable. But once it has been established that an IV produces some effect not ordinarily present, researchers will often use a **two-experimental-groups design** to gather more precise information. A two-experimental-groups design can be used to look at behavioral differences that occur when subjects are exposed to different values or levels of the IV. For example, we could test whether a highly violent music video produces more aggressiveness than a music video with a low level of violence. Or we could investigate whether 15 minutes of aerobic exercise is better than 10 minutes.

Holloway and Hornstein (1976) carried out a well-designed, two-experimental-groups experiment. These researchers argued that news can influence our view of human nature, and they tested the effects of hearing good or bad news in an experiment. Subjects were brought into a waiting room one at a time. They thought they were waiting for the experiment to begin, but in reality it had already started. While they were in the waiting room, a radio played music for a time. The music was then interrupted by the voice of a newscaster who read one of two "news items." Half the subjects heard the report of a man whose life would be saved because of a kind donor who would provide the organ needed for an emergency kidney transplant. The remaining subjects heard a very different story. This one reported the murder of an elderly woman. The murderer was identified as a respected clergyman and neighbor of the vic-

B O X   7 - 2

A RESEARCH EXAMPLE

Doob and colleagues (1969) were interested in the effect on final sales of the initial selling price of an item. Manufacturers will often introduce new products at special low prices and provide free samples or coupons to induce consumers to try the products. The hope is that shoppers will continue to buy the product. Doob and colleagues tested this notion by introducing new products at low prices in a chain of discount houses. The initial low prices were later raised to the regular selling prices. If the marketers' notion is correct, shoppers should continue to buy the product after the price increases. Several items were tested, including mouthwash, toothpaste, aluminum foil, and light bulbs. In most cases the researchers found that sales dropped off after the price increase but continued at a reasonable level. On the surface it seems that the low price was a useful device to encourage people to try the products, since at least some buyers continued to use them.

Nevertheless, as you can see, the experiment requires a control group. In order to establish normal sales for each product, Doob and colleagues introduced the products at their regular prices in a comparable set of stores. That is, they included a control condition in which there was no price reduction. This is an essential part of the experiment. Without knowing sales levels when a product's initial price is the regular price, we cannot say whether the lower price affects sales at all. Some buyers will try any new product regardless of its price. Thus initial sales might be explained by curiosity. Since a product usually has some merits, at least some buyers will remain after the price increase.

In fact, Doob and colleagues found that the low initial selling price actually reduced overall sales of the products. After periods ranging from 4 to 20 weeks, depending on the product, they found that in stores where the initial price was the usual selling price, sales were higher than in stores where an initially low price was later increased to the normal selling price. They explain their paradoxical findings in terms of cognitive dissonance theory: When customers pay more for a product, they must come to like it more in order to reduce their dissonance, or conflict, over buying the item at that price. Then, because they like it more, they buy it again. On the other hand, a cheap item does not need to be as good to be worth the price; there is little need to justify buying it.

tim. After these reports, the radio returned to music until one of the researchers casually turned it off and ostensibly began the experiment.

In the next part of the experiment, subjects were asked to make ratings about human nature. They were asked questions like "What percentage of people try to apply the Golden Rule even in today's complex society?" Holloway and Hornstein found that "the people who heard the tale of the woman's murder thought much less of their fellows than those who heard the good news about the kidney donor. The former estimated that fewer members of their community were decent, honest, and altruistic" (p. 76).

In this experiment the independent variable was news (good versus bad). The dependent variable was the subjects' opinion of humankind—that is, how honest, decent, and upright the subjects rated other people. The experiment had two independent groups of subjects, those who heard "good news" and those who heard "bad news." Good news was operationally defined as a news story in which one person helps another. Bad news was operationally defined as a news story in which one person harms another. The dependent variable was operationally defined in terms of subjects' answers to a series of questions about the morals and attitudes of others. The Holloway and Hornstein experiment is a well-designed experiment that had no control group. All subjects heard some news, either good or bad. Holloway and Hornstein concluded the following: "The good news produces more favorable views of humanity's general moral disposition than bad news does—despite the fact that the news deals only with certain special cases and not at all with human nature on the grand scale" (p. 76). The conclusion is worded carefully. Since there was no group that received no news at all, Holloway and Hornstein could only make statements about the relationship between the different values of the independent variable that were actually tested—good and bad news.

Still, it is possible that hearing any news will alter people's attitudes or feelings. Folklore tells us, "No news is good news." Does this mean that even good news might produce some negative effects? Perhaps the highest ratings of humanity would be obtained from subjects who heard no news at all. Indeed, we might speculate that although the "good news" story in the Holloway and Hornstein experiment has a happy ending, it is not a particularly good story at all. Both men must endure the pain and risk of major surgery; each will have to function for the rest of his life with only one kidney. This story could cause some subjects to focus on human frailty, which in turn might cast doubt on others' ability to resist temptation and abide by ethical and moral standards. Of course, there is no way of verifying any of these speculations without a control group. *The conclusions that may be drawn from an experiment are restricted by the scope and representativeness of the treatment conditions.*

As you design your own experiments, you will want to focus on the hypothesis you are testing. You must decide in advance which and how many treatment conditions will be necessary to make an adequate test of your hypothesis. Since Holloway and Hornstein focused on the differences produced by good versus bad news, the absence of a control group does not invalidate their study. However, using a control group would have increased the amount of information about the effect of the independent variable. Sometimes deciding whether or not to use a control group becomes an ethical decision (see Box 7-3).

BOX 7 - 3

ETHICAL DILEMMAS IN HUMAN RESEARCH

Researchers use the guidelines provided by law and by APA to guide their ethical decisions. In Chapter 2, we discussed some of the ethical decisions that must be made: whether to use deception; whether the information gained from an experiment justifies the risk of harm to participants, and so on. Sometimes researchers face another kind of ethical decision. In some experiments the need for a control group actually creates an ethical dilemma.

Testing the efficacy of psychotherapeutic procedures and medical and drug treatments often requires a control group so that effects of the treatment can be compared with the absence of treatment. In drug-testing experiments, a special type of control group (called a **placebo group**) is used. The placebo group is the prototype of a good control group: a control condition in which subjects are treated exactly the same as subjects who are in the experimental group, except for the presence of the IV. Subjects in the experimental group get some dosage of a drug, but subjects in the placebo group get something that looks like a drug but is actually a placebo (a pill containing an inert substance or an injection of a saline solution). Physiological effects on both groups of subjects are measured and compared to see whether the drug produced the effects. However, at some time the drug needs to be tested on people who have the medical problem the drug is designed to help. This need creates the ethical dilemma. When the placebo procedure is carried out on people who are actually in need of the benefits expected from the medication, the researcher in effect may be denying treatment to people who need it for the sake of scientific advancement. A partial solution is to compare a new drug with one that is currently being used. If the new drug performs as well or better, then positive results have been obtained.

A similar problem occurs in psychological research. Testing the efficacy of a psychotherapeutic treatment for depression sometimes requires comparing its results against a group of depressed people who have received no treatment. The control group for a psychotherapy study is frequently a *waiting-list control group*—people who are waiting their turn for treatment. If the therapy proves beneficial, does the researcher then have the responsibility to treat the control group as well? It is often argued that the control group would not normally be receiving treatment,

(continued)

(continued)

so they are not being denied a benefit. But this it is an ethical decision the researcher must make.

The AIDS epidemic has brought these kinds of ethical dilemmas to the forefront. Similar questions are being asked both of drug testing and psychological experiments. Kelly, St. Lawrence, Hood, and Brashfield (1989) were faced with this decision when they used a waiting-list control group in an experiment to test a behavioral intervention to reduce risky sexual practices in gay men. A 12-week program that combined education, social support, and assertiveness training to counteract coercive sexual situations was successful in reducing high-risk behaviors when measured in a follow-up eight months later. Without a control group, there would have been no way of knowing whether men receiving the intervention were being helped by it. A much greater dilemma would have been created if the control group had been comprised of people who would ordinarily have been receiving some kind of treatment.

Forming Independent Groups

Let us look a little more closely at the randomization procedures used to form two independent groups in an experiment.

Zajonc, Heingartner, and Herman (1969) tested the hypothesis that cockroaches would run faster through a simple maze when other roaches were present than when they had to run alone. The hypothesis is based on the principle of social facilitation: In the presence of an audience, the performance of some behaviors improves. Cockroaches should do better in some mazes when other roaches are present. We can test this hypothesis ourselves using two independent groups.[3] One group, the experimental group, runs through the maze in the presence of an audience. The control group runs with no one watching. The dependent variable is the average time it takes each group to run the maze. Just like human subjects, the cockroaches must be assigned at random to each condition.

We begin by assembling our roaches for the experiment. As we take each roach out of its cage, we flip a coin to decide whether it goes into the experimental or the control group. By assigning subjects at random, we hope to create two groups that are roughly equivalent on important subject variables that could influence the outcome of the experiment. One such variable is the weight of each individual subject; heavy subjects might run more slowly than light ones under any circumstances. Weight, then, is a potential source of confounding in

---

[3]Zajonc, Heingartner, and Herman's actual experiment had a more complicated design to include a test of the effect of drive level as well as the presence of an audience.

FIGURE 7-1 Robert Zajonc. Courtesy of
Robert Zajonc

this experiment. Table 7-1 shows the hypothetical weights of our subjects assigned at random to the two treatment conditions. As you can see, the weights of individual subjects differ. We would expect this, since subjects differ from one another. If we look at the groups on the whole, however, we find that their *average* weights (represented by $\overline{X}$) are about the same. Even though individual roaches in each group weigh different amounts, the average weight of the groups is about equal. If we chose to, we could evaluate whether the small difference between the groups is statistically significant. We would find that although the groups are not identical, the difference between them is not significant; that is, it is not enough to merit concern. We can accept the groups as *equivalent* enough for our purposes. Assigning our subjects to the groups at random, we created two groups that are equivalent on an important subject variable. We will not have confounding due to weight in this experiment.

When we assign subjects at random, we expect to form groups that are roughly the same on any subject variables that could affect our dependent variable. This is important because we may not always be aware of every variable that should be controlled. Sometimes we are aware of variables but do not have the tools, the time, or the resources to measure them. *Assigning subjects at random controls for differences we have not identified but that might somehow bias the study.*

The more subjects we have available to assign to treatment conditions, the better the chances that randomization will lead to equivalent groups of

TABLE 7-1 Cockroaches randomly assigned to treatment conditions: Hypothetical weights

Experimental Group		Control Group	
Subject Number	Hypothetical Weight (gm)	Subject Number	Hypothetical Weight (gm)
S_1	1.59	S_6	3.52
S_2	1.26	S_7	1.57
S_3	1.34	S_8	2.31
S_4	3.68	S_9	1.31
S_5	2.49	S_{10}	1.18
$N = 5$		$N = 5$	
$\overline{X}_E = 2.072$		$\overline{X}_C = 1.978$	

NOTE: Randomization produced two groups of very similar average weight ($\overline{X}_E$ is about the same as $\overline{X}_C$).

subjects. For example, if we have only two cockroaches available, one light and one heavy (like S_2 and S_4 in Table 7-1), there is no chance at all of forming similar groups. We will always have one heavy group and one light group. With ten cockroaches (as in Table 7-1), our chances of attaining groups with similar weights is increased. As we add additional subjects, the odds are even better that random assignment will produce similar groups. This becomes particularly important when we consider humans. We expect people to differ on many characteristics that could potentially affect their responses on the dependent variable. The more subjects we have, the better our chances of achieving groups that are equivalent on a number of different characteristics.

When to Use a Two-Independent-Groups Design

How do we decide whether the two-independent-groups design is appropriate for an experiment? We begin by looking at the hypothesis. If there is only one independent variable, the two-independent-groups approach may work if the hypothesis can be tested with two treatment conditions. In an experiment such as the one on cockroaches, two groups made sense. We simply wanted to see whether cockroaches would run better with (condition 1) or without (condition 2) an audience. When we run the experiment, we carefully assign subjects to the treatment conditions at random.

When we use the two-independent-groups design, we assume that randomization is successful. We assume that when we start the experiment, the treatment groups are about the same on all the extraneous subject variables that might affect the outcome. Unfortunately, this is not always the way things turn out.

TABLE 7-2 Cockroaches randomly assigned to treatment conditions

Experimental Group		Control Group	
Subject Number	Hypothetical Weight (gm)	Subject Number	Hypothetical Weight (gm)
S_{10}	1.18	S_4	3.68
S_2	1.26	S_6	3.52
S_3	1.34	S_8	2.31
S_9	1.31	S_5	2.49
S_7	1.57	S_1	1.59
$N = 5$		$N = 5$	
$\overline{X}_E = 1.332$		$\overline{X}_C = 2.718$	

NOTE: Randomization produced two groups of very different weights.

In our cockroach experiment, we assigned subjects to the treatment groups at random. As you saw in Table 7-1, the random assignment produced two groups of very similar average weight. But suppose we do the experiment again. We again take the roaches from their cages and flip a coin to decide which group to put them in. The hypothetical weights of these new groups are shown in Table 7-2. What is wrong? We assigned our subjects at random, but the control group looks much heavier than the experimental group. How can this be? Well, you know that random assignment means every subject has an equal chance of being assigned to either treatment condition. There is always a chance that treatment groups will end up being very different on some subject variables, and this is particularly true when we have a small number of subjects in each condition.[4]

Here our random assignment did not produce comparable groups. Just by chance, the control group turned out to be heavy compared to the experimental group. Since the dependent variable in this experiment is running speed, the difference in weight may contaminate the results. The way things turned out here, the weight of the two groups is a confounding variable. If there is a difference in the running speed of the two groups, we cannot be sure whether it is the result of the audience or the difference in weight. The difference in running speed can be explained equally well by either variable.

---

[4]You can test this principle, called *Bernoulli's law of large numbers,* by flipping a coin. The laws of chance predict equal odds (50/50) for heads or tails each time you flip; this means that half your flips should end up heads and half tails. But if you flipped a coin only four times, it would not be unusual to get three heads and one tails or even four heads and zero tails. However, as you increase the number of coin flips, your chances of getting an equal number of heads and tails go up. If you flipped a coin 100 times, your chances of getting an equal number of heads and tails is much better than if you only flipped it four times. The same law applies to random assignment to treatment conditions: The likelihood that treatment groups will be equivalent on extraneous subject variables increases as the number of subjects increases.

TWO MATCHED GROUPS

Randomization does not guarantee that treatment groups will be comparable on all the relevant extraneous subject variables. Researchers therefore sometimes use another two-group procedure, the **two-matched-groups design.** In this design there are also two groups of subjects, but the researcher assigns them to groups by matching or equating them on a characteristic that will probably affect the dependent variable. The researcher forms the groups in such a way that they are sure to be comparable on an extraneous variable that might otherwise produce confounding.

Matching Before and After an Experiment

To form matched groups, subjects must be measured on the extraneous variable that will be used for the matching. Table 7-3 shows the way our cockroaches might be divided into two groups matched on weight. Once the roaches have been weighed, we separate them into pairs. The members of each pair are selected so that they have similar weights. For instance, the first pair is made up of subjects 2 and 10. Subject 2 weighs 1.26 grams; subject 10 weighs 1.18 grams. Although members of each pair are not exactly equal in weight, they are closer to each other than to any other roaches in the sample. *When it is not possible to form pairs of subjects that are identical on the matching variable, the researcher must decide how much of a discrepancy will be tolerated.* A difference of 0.8 grams might be acceptable, but a difference of 2 grams might not. According to Underwood (1966), the decision is arbitrary. However, we obviously want to make good enough matches to ensure that our

TABLE 7-3 Cockroaches assigned to two groups matched on weight

Pair	Experimental Group Subject Number	Hypothetical Weight (gm)	Control Group Subject Number	Hypothetical Weight (gm)
a	S_2	1.26	S_{10}	1.18
b	S_3	1.34	S_9	1.31
c	S_1	1.59	S_7	1.57
d	S_8	2.31	S_5	2.49
e	S_6	3.52	S_4	3.68
	$N = 5$		$N = 5$	
	$\overline{X}_E = 2.004$		$\overline{X}_C = 2.046$	

NOTE: The matched groups have very similar average weights ($\overline{X}_E$ is about the same as $\overline{X}_C$). Within each pair, the members are assigned to the treatment conditions at random. One member of each pair is randomly chosen to be in the control group; the other member is placed in the experimental group.

groups are not significantly different on the matching variable. If there is no suitable match for an individual in the sample, that individual must be eliminated from the study.

After all the pairs have been formed, we randomly assign one member of each pair to a treatment condition. We can do this simply by flipping a coin. It is very important to put the members of each pair into the treatment conditions at random. If we do not, we may create a new source of confounding—exactly what we are trying to avoid.

In our cockroach example, the matching is done before the experiment is run. In some experiments it may not be feasible to do the matching beforehand. Suppose we need to match our subjects on intelligence. We may not be able to give an intelligence test, score it, match and assign subjects to groups, and run the actual experiment in a single block of time. Since we must know the test scores before we can do the matching, we might need a separate testing session just to give the test. In these situations we may proceed differently. We make the initial assignment to conditions at random and run the experiment with two randomly assigned groups of subjects that may or may not be comparable on our matching variable. Our subjects take part in the treatment conditions as usual. However, we also give them the intelligence test (that is, we measure them on the matching variable). When the experiment is over, we use the intelligence test scores to match the subjects across the two groups, discarding those subjects in each group who cannot be matched.

There are three ways to go about doing this. We may use **precision matching,** in which we insist that the members of the matched pairs have identical scores. A more common procedure is **range matching,** in which we require that the members of a pair fall within a previously specified range of scores. The process of range matching subjects after the experiment is run is illustrated in Table 7-4. In the table you can see that subjects are considered matched if their scores fall within 3 points of each other. The choice of range

TABLE 7-4 Matching subjects after the experiment: Pairing of scores on the matching variable, intelligence

Experimental Group		Control Group	
Subject Number	IQ	IQ	Subject Number
S_1	109	91	S_6
S_2	94	100	S_7
S_3	116	111	S_8
S_4	102	(63)	S_9
S_5	(133)	115	S_{10}

NOTE: Connecting lines represent final pairs of subjects. Subjects 5 and 9 must be discarded because there are no suitable matches for them in the sample.

is arbitrary. The smaller the range, however, the more similar the subjects must be on the matching variable. If we set the range at 50 points on an intelligence test, we would obviously gain little through matching.

As you can see from the table, range matching after the experiment is run may create problems. Some subjects will have to be discarded if no match is available, but this could raise questions about the representativeness of the remaining subjects. Subjects who can or cannot be matched may differ in important ways that will affect their scores on the dependent variable. In using matching, it is therefore advisable to sample as many subjects as possible. This tactic will minimize the chances that no match will exist within the sample. If we must discard subjects, the net result is that the total number available for analysis is smaller than we had planned. Having less data reduces the chance of detecting the effect of the independent variable. For this reason, matching before running the experiment is preferable to matching after it.

A third matching procedure, **rank-ordered matching,** is sometimes used. The subjects are simply rank ordered on the basis of their scores on the matching variable. Subjects with adjacent scores then become a matched pair. With rank-ordered matching, we do not specify an acceptable range between members of each pair. The benefit of rank-ordered matching is that unless you have to discard a subject because you have an uneven number of scores, all subjects are typically used. The down side is that there may be unacceptably large differences between members of a pair on the matching variable. This would certainly have been the case if we had used rank-ordered matching to form pairs from subjects in Table 7-4.

When to Use Two Matched Groups

Whether to match at all is another question. The advantages are clear: By matching on a variable that is likely to have a strong effect on the dependent variable, we can eliminate one possible source of confounding. We do not need to *assume* that our treatment groups are comparable on an important extraneous variable; we can make them comparable through matching.

In some cases, matching can also make the effects of the independent variable easier to detect even if random assignment has worked successfully and confounding is not a concern. When we match, we use statistical procedures that differ from those used with independent groups. We will look at these procedures in some detail in Part 3 of the book; it is enough to say here that the matched-groups procedure allows us to make comparisons based on the differences between the members of each of our matched pairs of subjects. Because some of the effects of individual differences are controlled within each pair, the impact of the independent variable is clearer. We are able to compare the responses of rather similar subjects who were tested under different treatment conditions. Procedures for independent groups, however, require that we combine, or "pool," all the data from each treatment group and make comparisons between group averages. This makes it somewhat harder to detect the effect of our independent variable: We are forced to look at treatment effects along with the effects of individual differences. If our independent variable has an effect, we are more likely to detect it in our data if we have used matching.

Matching procedures are especially useful when we have very small numbers of subjects because there is a greater chance that randomization will produce groups that are dissimilar. This risk is not so great when we have large numbers of subjects available. As pointed out before, the larger the treatment groups, the better the chances that randomization will lead to similar groups of subjects and the less need there may be for matching.

Since there are advantages in using the matched-groups design, why not always use it? By matching on a variable such as weight, we can guarantee that our treatment groups will be similar on at least one extraneous variable. Unfortunately, there are potential disadvantages in this procedure. *When we match, it is essential that we match on the basis of an extraneous variable that is highly related to the dependent variable of the experiment.* In an experiment on weight loss, it would make sense to begin by matching subjects on weight. Subjects who are already heavy may be more likely to lose weight during the experiment. It would not make sense to match subjects on weight in an experiment on how to teach spelling to 12-year-olds because it is difficult to see any clear connection between weight and spelling ability. It would be more appropriate to match on another variable, such as intelligence; intelligence does affect the ability to spell. We would want to match on intelligence to avoid getting two groups of subjects with different IQs who would learn spelling at different rates regardless of the teaching method.

Unfortunately, it is not always easy to know what variables are the best to use for matching. If we match on a variable that is *strongly* correlated with the dependent variable, then matching can increase the researcher's ability to detect changes. If we match on a variable that is *not* strongly correlated with the dependent variable, it will be much more difficult to detect the effect of experimental manipulations. This is true because of the special statistical procedures used for data from matched groups (Chapter 13). There is another potential problem when matching is used. Matching on one variable could accidentally result in larger differences in other extraneous variables that could dampen effects produced by the independent variable. For now, Box 7-4 summarizes the guidelines for setting up two-group designs.

MULTIPLE GROUPS

We have seen how we can test a variety of hypotheses by using two groups of subjects. We run subjects through two sets of treatment conditions so that we can see how their behaviors differ when the independent variable has different values. We can use two groups of subjects who are assigned to the treatment conditions at random or are matched on a relevant subject variable.

Sometimes, however, it takes more than two treatment conditions to make a good test of a hypothesis: In an experiment to test the effectiveness of a new drug, we might need to test several different dosages. A simple comparison

USING A TWO-GROUP DESIGN: GUIDELINES

Use a two-group design whenever two values of the independent variable are needed to test a hypothesis. Sometimes one group will be a control or no-treatment group, and the second will be an experimental group that is given some value of the independent variable. Other times, both groups will be experimental groups given different levels of the independent variable. Whenever possible, subjects should be selected at random. However, you must always assign your subjects to the treatment conditions at random: Each subject must have an equal chance of being assigned to each of the two conditions. If subjects are not assigned at random, there may be confounding in the experiment; the two treatment groups may be different before the experiment begins. If they are different to start with, you will not be able to tell whether differences in the dependent variable across conditions are due to the experimental manipulation or to the initial difference between the groups.

To avoid confounding because of subject variables, you can consider forming matched groups of subjects (for example, subjects with similar IQ scores), particularly when only small numbers of subjects are available. Matched groups are used when we do not want to assume that randomization alone was enough to produce two equivalent groups. However, there are potential drawbacks: (1) If you match on an unimportant variable, you will lose sensitivity to detect treatment effects; and (2) it is always possible that matching on one variable will increase differences in subjects on other subject variables, making it harder to detect effects.

We form matched groups by first measuring subjects on the variable that will be used for matching. Then we divide the subjects into pairs. The pairs are formed so that the members are roughly the same on the matching variable. Then we randomly assign one member of each pair to condition 1; the other member of each pair is placed in condition 2. This guarantees that the final groups of subjects are about the same on the matching variable. If we cannot do the matching before the experiment, we can randomly assign the subjects to the treatment conditions first. Then we carry out the experiment and measure the subjects on the matching variable. After the experiment, we form our pairs. But we can lose data this way, so it is a good idea to do the matching before the experiment begins.

between the presence or absence of the drug would be too crude to assess its effects adequately; the amount of a drug makes a difference in how well it works. In situations in which the amount or degree of the independent variable is important, we usually need a **multiple-groups design**—a design in which there are more than two groups of subjects and each group is run through a different treatment condition. Often, one of the treatment conditions is a control condition in which subjects receive the zero value of the independent variable. The most commonly used multiple-groups design is the **multiple-independent-groups design**, in which the subjects are assigned to the different treatment conditions at random. It's also possible to use multiple groups and matched subjects. The basic procedures are the same as those used in the two-matched-groups design, except that there are more than two treatment conditions.

Assigning Subjects

Because most researchers use the randomized approach, we will do the same here. When there are only two treatment conditions, assigning subjects randomly to each condition is a simple matter. But how do we deal with the problem of assigning subjects to several treatment conditions in such a way that no bias results? One way would be to use a random number table. Suppose we are set to run an experiment with three different treatment conditions and 30 subjects. We could first pick a starting point in the random number table (see Appendix B) in an unbiased way, for instance, by closing our eyes and pointing. We then look for the numbers 1, 2, and 3 in the table. Whatever order they appear in (2, 3, 1, 3, for example) would be the order in which we assign subjects to the three treatment conditions. The first volunteer would be assigned to treatment condition 2; the second volunteer would be assigned to treatment condition 3, and so on. We could proceed this way until we have assigned all the available subjects to the conditions of the experiment. (Box 7-5 shows another procedure, *block randomization,* that works well for multiple-groups designs.)

Suppose we want to test the hypothesis that coffee drinking enhances productivity. Everyday experience tells us that some people simply cannot function without a morning cup of coffee. We suspect that some amount of coffee is (temporarily, at least) beneficial—but how much? If one cup of coffee is beneficial, perhaps two or more might be even better. Because we are interested in the effects of different levels of the independent variable, we could test our hypothesis with three groups of subjects—one control group and two experimental groups.

The experiment would be quite simple to conduct. Coffee drinking is our independent variable and productivity is our dependent variable. A cup of coffee could be operationally defined as one level teaspoon of Instant Maxwell House dissolved in one cup of boiling water. The operational definition here is important. The proportion of coffee to water is critical, since the strength of the coffee probably determines its effect. There may be differences between

B O X 7 - 5

BLOCK RANDOMIZATION

Using the random number table works fairly well; however, because we have followed a random sequence, the number of subjects in each treatment group will not necessarily be the same. For a total of 30 subjects, we might find 14 in condition 1, 9 in condition 2, and only 7 in condition 3. In order to obtain equal numbers of subjects in all treatment conditions, psychologists use a sophisticated procedure called **block randomization.** Basically, the researcher begins the process of randomization on paper by creating *treatment blocks*. If there are three different treatment conditions in the experiment, each treatment block contains the three conditions listed in random order. As subjects sign up for the experiment, the researcher fills each successive treatment block. The more blocks she or he can fill, the more subjects there will be in each treatment condition.

Table 7-5 shows a block randomization design created to guarantee five subjects per condition for an experiment with three treatment conditions. Note that there are five blocks, *A*, *B*, *C*, *D*, and *E*, and each of the three conditions is represented once per block. The order of the treatments within each block comes from the random number table. To set up a block, pick a spot at random from the random number table. Look for the number 1, 2, or 3. Whichever occurs first is the first treatment in that block. Continue down the table until you find a different number between 1 and 3. This will be the second treatment in the block. Since each treatment can be used only once per block, the last number is the one we have not used yet. Then create a second treatment block in exactly the same way. Repeat the process for each treatment block.

TABLE 7-5 Example of block randomization in a three-condition experiment

Block A		Block B		Block C		Block D		Block E	
S_1	2	S_4	2	S_7	3	S_{10}	1	S_{13}	2
S_2	1	S_5	1	S_8	2	S_{11}	3	S_{14}	1
S_3	3	S_6	3	S_9	1	S_{12}	2	S_{15}	3

NOTE: Here we have five subjects per condition. To have more subjects per condition, successive blocks are filled as subjects (S_n) sign up for the experiment. The order of treatments within blocks is random.

Every additional block we can fill with subjects adds one subject to each treatment condition. Through block randomization we thus create a scheme by which subjects can be assigned to conditions at random while still ensuring equal numbers across conditions.

Here we have described the process for an experiment with three conditions. However, the same procedures apply for any number of treatment conditions. Simply set up blocks in which each treatment occurs once in a random order. For an experiment with four conditions, each block must contain the four conditions in random order. A five-condition experiment would have five conditions per block, and so on. The total number of blocks determines the number of subjects in each treatment group. The more blocks you fill, the larger your treatment groups.

the effects of brewed versus instant coffee or between Maxwell House and other brands that might need to be explored in the future. Whether we allow subjects to use cream and sugar in their coffee is an issue we would need to consider. Do we want to allow these extraneous variables to exert potential influences on productivity? No. So we will require our subjects to drink the coffee black. Our dependent variable, productivity, can be operationally defined as the number of *os* a subject crosses out on a page of newsprint in 10 minutes.

The control group (C) drinks no coffee; the first experimental group (E_1) drinks one cup; the second experimental group (E_2) drinks two cups. Assume that the hypothesis is confirmed: The more coffee the subjects drink, the more productive they are. Our hypothetical results are illustrated in Figure 7-2, which reflects a gradual increase in productivity as the amount of coffee consumption increases.

We may be convinced that coffee enhances productivity. But let us try just one more experiment. This time we will have four groups, one control and three experimental groups. The hypothetical outcome of this experiment is illustrated in Figure 7-3. Again, we see that moderate amounts of coffee appear to enhance productivity. However, something different seems to be happening to group E_3: It received the largest amount of coffee, but its productivity is *low* relative to the other groups. Although the smaller amounts of coffee seem to increase productivity, the larger amount seems to inhibit it. These fictitious results resemble some actual research findings. Broadhurst (1959), for example, reported that subjects perform best on complicated tasks when they have a moderate amount of drive (that is, motivation). This is paradoxical; when we have little motivation, we do not accomplish much. But too much motivation interferes with performance. Think about taking a test, where the stimulation of a little anxiety helps you to do better. But if you are extremely anxious, you may not remember anything; your mind goes blank, and you do not do very well.

FIGURE 7-2 Productivity as a function of the amount of coffee consumed (fictitious data from a three-group experiment).

Because different values of the same independent variable can produce different effects, researchers often test more than two levels of an independent variable. By using more than two conditions, they can often get a better idea of how the independent variable operates. They need to test such variables across a wide range of values to get an understanding of how the variables work.

Choosing Treatments

What if we decide that we need more than two treatment conditions? How do we know how many to use? Some variables have an infinite number of possible values; we could not test them all even if we wanted to. We might be able to create many different conditions, but using all of them might not make sense. Let us look at an actual experiment that illustrates how an experimenter can zero in on the appropriate number of conditions.

Lassen (1973) was interested in what happens during a patient's initial interview with a therapist. In particular, she thought that seating arrangements might affect the amount of anxiety patients showed during their first session. Lassen used a multiple-groups design to test the hypothesis that patients would show more anxiety with increasing distance from the therapist. Three groups of patients were randomly assigned to each of three experimental conditions. In the first condition, patients were seated 3 feet away from the therapist, in the second condition, patients were seated 6 feet away, and in the third condition they were 9 feet away. The sessions were audiotaped. Later, the tapes were used by raters who evaluated the amount of anxiety displayed by each of the patients during the sessions. Lassen found that patients seated

FIGURE 7-3 Productivity as a function of the amount of coffee consumed (fictitious data from a four-group experiment).

3 feet away from the therapist showed less anxiety than patients seated 6 feet away. Patients who were seated 9 feet away showed the most anxiety. The therapists who ran the sessions, however, unanimously preferred the 6-feet condition, although they adapted to the 3-feet condition "unless a patient was particularly flirtatious, hostile, odorous, or fat" (p. 231). Like their patients, therapists were less comfortable in the 9-feet condition, feeling out of touch.

Lassen's independent variable, the distance between patient and therapist, can take on an infinite number of values. Some, of course, are obviously inappropriate for this experiment. We would not seat patients and therapists in the same chair. A distance of a mile would be just as ridiculous. Still, there are many other real possibilities. Lassen could have placed patients at 1 foot away. She could have used 18 or even 100 feet. Why did she restrict the conditions to 3, 6, and 9 feet? Let us try to imagine some of the thinking that might go into the choice of these three conditions:

> I want to see the effect of different distances between patient and therapist in the first session. Which distances make the most sense? Well, in our culture strangers usually don't stand too close to one another to have a conversation. Most people think it's rude for a stranger to come very close to ask a question—we prefer to have a little distance between us. From what I've seen of people's behavior, 3 feet seems to be about as close as people want to stand when they are talking to someone they don't know very well. Patients and therapists would rarely want to get closer than this. If we look at how furniture is arranged in therapists' offices, the closest chairs seem to be about 3 feet apart. So it makes sense to use 3 feet as the smallest distance I will test.
>
> Now I'll have to decide about the greatest distance. I can eliminate distances over about 20 feet because patient and therapist would probably have difficulty hearing each other if they were that far apart. Anyway, most consultation rooms

aren't that large. What about 20 feet? Even that seems too great. It's just not comfortable to talk to someone that far away. The chairs in consultation rooms seem to be placed no more than 10 feet apart. Since I've decided to use 3 feet as my smallest distance, I'll use 9 feet as my largest distance. That way I'll have two conditions that are proportional to one another: Nine feet is exactly three times as far as 3 feet. I'd also like to test a distance in between these two extremes so that I'll have a better idea of how distance affects patients' behavior. I could use several conditions between 3 and 9 feet, but one is probably enough to give me a good idea of how distance affects anxiety. Since my extremes are 3 and 9 feet, I'll make the middle condition 6 feet. That way I'll have three conditions that are all proportional to one another.

Actually, if you consult Lassen's article, you will find that her decisions were dictated by prior research. She cites Hall's (1966) space dimensions as the source of her choices. Hall described a number of space categories, including personal distance—far (2 1/2 to 4 feet), social distance—close (4 to 7 feet), and social distance—far (7 to 12 feet). As you can see, Lassen set up her treatment conditions to fit these categories. But notice that Lassen chose conditions that are *proportional* to one another. Given Hall's categories, she could have used distances of 3, 5, and 12 feet. Instead she chose to use 3, 6, and 9 feet. Why? You will find that research involving quantitative variables is usually done this way. You may see an experimenter using drug doses of, say, 5, 10, and 15 milligrams. You are less likely to see one in which the experimenter uses randomly chosen doses such as 2, 9, and 14 milligrams. It is possible to do experiments with conditions that are selected at random rather than planned. Sometimes that is the only possible way. However, many researchers prefer to be able to make statements about conditions that are proportional. For instance, Lassen could see very clearly from her study whether doubling the distance between the patient and the therapist also doubled the patient's rated anxiety.

When you think about using a multiple-groups design, always think in terms of the hypothesis you are testing. The principal question you should ask is this: *What will I gain by adding these extra conditions to the experiment?* Lassen was interested in evaluating the usefulness of Hall's categories. Since there were several categories, it made sense for her to use more than two treatment conditions. It is also reasonable from a logical viewpoint. The effect of distance, like motivation or coffee drinking, might be complex. Instead of simply increasing as the distance increases, the patient's anxiety might increase to a point and then decline. For instance, at a very great distance, patients might feel out of touch and uninvolved with their sessions. Using three conditions gave Lassen a better idea of how distance from the therapist works within its usual range of values.

Let us return to an experiment in which the researchers decided *not* to use the multiple-groups approach. Recall that Holloway and Hornstein (1976) used a two-independent-groups design to test "good" versus "bad" news, but they could have used a multiple-groups design instead. What would they have gained by adding more groups? For example, what information would be gained by adding a control group? If the researchers had wanted to know about people's opinions of human nature without any news at all, they could have added a group of subjects who listened to the same music broadcast but without a news interruption. Maybe opinions are the most positive without *any* news (Maybe no news *is* good news!). If so, opinions would have been equally positive for subjects in either the good-news or no-news conditions. With a control condition, we would have gained useful information.

Alternatively, they could have added an intermediate value of news ("neutral" news) to act as a starting point, or baseline, for comparisons with their two conditions. The two-group design allowed the researchers to say that opinions were more positive after good news than after bad news, but it did not tell us whether opinions after good or bad news were any different than opinions after hearing any news at all. It would be more informative if we knew whether good news *increases* positivity over neutral news or whether bad news *decreases* positivity. In general, people have a *positivity bias* toward others (Zajonc, 1968). We tend to think of people as basically good. Maybe any news—except bad news— will produce generally positive evaluations of others.

Holloway and Hornstein could also have included additional levels of bad and good news. For instance, they might have used "super," "very good," "slightly good," "slightly bad," "very bad," and "horrid" as additional treatments. Additional levels could have added to our understanding of the effects of news. But Holloway and Hornstein used only those levels that were critical to *their* hypothesis. Since the hypothesis dealt with the effects of good versus bad news, it was perfectly appropriate to test only these contrasting levels. Other values of the independent variable could be explored in future experiments. Notice that the levels chosen were at opposite ends of the continuum. They used good versus bad rather than good versus very good. Researchers try to use values of a variable that are extreme enough to bring out differences on the dependent variable. They do this to maximize the possibility of seeing a change across conditions. The effects of "good" versus "very good" stories might be about the same. If we test values that are farther apart, we are more likely to find a difference if one exists.

However, researchers also want to use values that are realistic. If Holloway and Hornstein had tested only news that was "horrid" versus "super," their results would have only limited generalizability, because people seldom hear news this extreme in real life. As mentioned in the discussion of Lassen's (1973) experiment, it is possible to use values that are too extreme to be meaningful. But as long as we select appropriate levels of the independent variable, two groups may be all that are necessary to test our hypothesis. Then it is more economical to use a two-group design, even though a multiple-groups design is possible. As a general rule: Select the simplest design that will make an adequate test of your hypothesis.

Practical Limits

As you set up experiments, you will make decisions about which comparisons will provide the most appropriate test of the hypothesis. An experiment that includes several levels of the independent variable can often yield more information than one that includes only two groups. However, practical considerations also affect choice of design. The multiple-groups procedure assumes that treatment groups are formed by random assignment. Thus there will be as many different treatment groups in the experiment as there are levels of the independent variable. If you have five levels of the independent variable, you will need five groups of subjects. It may be difficult to find enough subjects to make this design feasible. Running additional levels also takes more time, and the statistical procedures are more complicated than those used with the two-group design. Thus it makes sense to think through all the advantages and disadvantages of the multiple-groups design before you begin your experiment. A review of the experimental literature in the area should guide you. If prior researchers have consistently used two-group designs to compare only opposite values of the independent variable, you may want to do the same. However, if others have used additional levels to gather information, this may be the most appropriate strategy.

Sometimes researchers conduct a **pilot study** to pretest selected levels of an independent variable before conducting the actual experiment. A pilot study is like a mini-experiment in which treatments are tested on a few subjects to see whether the levels seem to be appropriate or not. Pilot studies are also a good way to work out any bugs in the procedures of an experiment before the real experiment is underway. A pilot study allows you to make changes before you invest the time and resources in a large-scale experiment.

SUMMARY

The *design* of an experiment is its general structure—the experimenter's plan for testing the hypothesis—not the experiment's specific content. The researcher decides on the *experimental design* mainly on the basis of three factors: (1) the number of independent variables in the hypothesis, (2) the number of treatment conditions needed to make a fair test of the hypothesis, and (3) whether the same or different subjects are used in each of the treatment conditions.

A basic assumption behind each experimental design is that subjects in the experiment are typical of the population they represent. After subjects have been selected for the experiment, they are assigned to treatment conditions in various ways. *Between-subjects designs* are those in which different subjects take part in each condition of the experiment; we draw conclusions by making comparisons between the behavior of different groups of subjects. We looked at two types of between-subjects designs with two treatment groups: two independent groups and two matched groups.

The *two-independent-groups design* is used when one independent variable must be tested at two treatment levels or values. Sometimes one of the treatment conditions is a control condition in which the subjects receive the zero value of the independent variable. The other condition is an experimental condition in which the subjects are given some nonzero value of the independent variable. Other times, both groups are experimental groups; each experimental group receives a different (nonzero) value of the independent variable. The independent-groups design is based on the assumption that subjects are assigned at random; we assume that randomization was successful. Sometimes, however, especially when the total number of subjects is small, we do not want to rely on randomization. Even with *random assignment,* treatment groups sometimes start out being different from each other in important ways. If treatment groups are different on a variable related to the dependent variable of the experiment, the result may be confounding.

Instead of relying on randomization, we may want to use the *two-matched-groups design,* in which we select a variable that is highly related to the dependent variable and measure subjects on that variable. For a two-group experiment, we form pairs of subjects having similar scores on the matching variable and then randomly assign one member of each pair to one condition of the experiment. The remaining member of each pair is placed in the other treatment condition. Matching is advantageous because we can guarantee that groups start out the same on variables that matter. If the matching variable is strongly related to the DV, matching can make treatment effects easier to detect statistically. However, there are also disadvantages: We do not always know what we should use as our matching variable. Because of the statistical tests used for matched groups, we have to be sure that our matching variable is really related to our dependent variable. If it is not, matching can actually work against us—making it more difficult to see whether the independent variable had an effect.

In between-subjects designs, a comparison of two values of the independent variable is sometimes not enough; we may need more than two treatment conditions to test an experimental hypothesis. A multiple-groups design serves this purpose. In a *multiple-independent-groups design,* there are more than two levels of the independent variable and subjects are assigned to treatment conditions at random. With several treatment conditions, researchers can look at the effects of different values of the independent variable and see whether low, medium, and high values of a variable produce increasing changes in the dependent variable. They can also detect more complex patterns. For instance, some variables may produce little change at extreme values but a lot of change at middle values. Although we can get additional information from a multiple-groups design, it is not always practical or necessary to do so. For some experimental hypotheses, a comparison of just two values of the independent variable is sufficient.

KEY TERMS

Between-subjects design A design in which different subjects take part in each condition of the experiment.

Block randomization A process of randomization that first creates treatment blocks containing one random order of the condition in the experiment; subjects are then assigned to fill each successive treatment block.

Control condition The determination of the value of a dependent variable without the presence of the independent variable.

Control group The subjects in a control condition.

Experimental condition In an experimental group–control group design, the group that receives some value of the independent variable.

Experimental design The general structure of an experiment (but not its specific content).

Experimental group The subjects in an experimental condition.

Multiple-groups design A between-subjects design with one independent variable, in which there are more than two treatment conditions.

Multiple-independent-groups design The most commonly used multiple-group design in which the subjects are assigned to the different treatment conditions at random.

Pilot study A mini-experiment using only a few subjects to pretest selected levels of an independent variable before conducting the actual experiment.

Placebo group In drug testing, a control condition in which subjects are treated exactly the same as subjects who are in the experimental group, except for the presence of the actual drug; the prototype of a good control group.

Precision matching Creating pairs whose subjects have identical scores on the matching variable.

Random assignment The technique of assigning subjects to treatments so that each subject has an equal chance of being assigned to each treatment condition.

Range matching Creating pairs of subjects whose scores on the matching variable fall within a previously specified range of scores.

Rank-ordered matching Creating matched pairs by placing subjects in order of their scores on the matching variable; subjects with adjacent scores become pairs.

Two-experimental-groups design A design in which two groups of subjects are exposed to different levels of the independent variable.

Two-group design The simplest experimental design, used when only two treatment conditions are needed.

Two-independent-groups design An experimental design in which subjects are placed in each of two treatment conditions through random assignment.

Two-matched-groups design An experimental design with two treatment conditions and with subjects who are matched on a subject variable thought to be highly related to the dependent variable.

REVIEW AND STUDY QUESTIONS

1. Explain the meaning of the terms *experimental design* and *between-subjects design.*

2. Why is it important to assign subjects to each treatment condition at random?

3. You are planning an experiment to test whether students learn better with or without a radio playing while they study.
   a. What will be your independent and dependent variables?
   b. How will you define them operationally?
   c. What type of design will you use?
   d. Is more than one design possible?
   e. What subject variables will you need to control?

4. A researcher wanted to test the effect that riding the subway has on mental health. She formed two groups of subjects, an experimental group and

a control group. The experimental group rode the subway for 60 minutes every morning. The control group jogged for an equal period of time. At the end of one month, both groups were measured on a scale of adjustment and well-being. The control group was found to be better adjusted than the experimental group. Do you accept the conclusion that riding the subway damages mental health? Why or why not?

5. A skeptical student tells you that it's silly to bother with a control group. After all, you're really only interested in what the experimental group does. How would you convince the student otherwise?

6. If people stand closer together, they will communicate better. How would you test this hypothesis? How many treatment conditions would you need? Would it be possible to test this hypothesis with more than one design?

7. People who have known each other for a long time may communicate better than people who have known each other for a short time. Imagine you are carrying out the study suggested in question 6. All your subjects know each other, but for varying lengths of time. How can you make sure that the length of time that subjects have known each other will not be a confounding variable in your study?

8. Describe a matched-groups design. How is the matching done?

9. A watched pot never boils. What design can you use to test this notion? How many treatment conditions do you need?

10. A researcher would like to match subjects on weight for an experiment on weight control. The weights of each subject in the sample are shown in the table below. Match them into pairs and form one experimental and one control group by using random assignment. Carry out the procedure using precision matching, range matching, and rank-ordered matching.

Subject Number	Weight	Subject Number	Weight
S_1	115	S_9	122
S_2	185	S_{10}	160
S_3	163	S_{11}	159
S_4	122	S_{12}	154
S_5	165	S_{13}	143
S_6	183	S_{14}	143
S_7	184	S_{15}	138
S_8	115	S_{16}	137

11. Referring back to question 10, how did the outcomes of precision, range, and rank-ordered matching differ? What are the pros and cons of using each procedure?

12. Describe a multiple-independent-groups design. When do we need this type of design?

13. Explain the advantages of using a multiple-groups design rather than a two-group design.

BETWEEN-SUBJECTS FACTORIAL DESIGNS

In the last chapter, we saw how a variety of hypotheses about a single independent variable can be tested by using two or more groups of subjects. We run different groups of subjects through two or more sets of treatment conditions so that we can see how their behaviors differ when the independent variable has different values. We can use groups of subjects who are assigned to the treatment conditions at random or are matched on a relevant subject variable. In this chapter we will study another type of research design—the factorial design. Like two-group and multiple-groups designs, factorial experiments can be carried out using the between-subjects approach: Different groups of subjects participate in the different treatment conditions of the experiment. When we wish to explore more than one independent variable in the same experiment, we use a factorial design.

MORE THAN ONE INDEPENDENT VARIABLE

All the designs we have examined so far have tested only one independent variable. But in real life variables rarely occur alone. It often seems most appropriate to look at more than one variable at a time. Suppose we wanted to see whether talking to plants actually makes them grow better. Like any other hypothesis, this one would have to be tested in a rigorous, controlled fashion. We could set up a simple experiment in which talking is the independent variable. But we might also want to know whether music is beneficial to plants. We could run another experiment in which music is the independent variable. *This approach is very inefficient;* we may need twice as many plants and perhaps twice as much time to carry out two experiments rather than one. It also has another disadvantage: A relationship may exist between the effects of music and talking. Perhaps plants that get conversation do not need music, or maybe they prefer music to conversation. There is no way to look for these kinds of relationships if we study music and conversation separately. We need another kind of experimental design, one that enables us to look at the effects of more than one independent variable at a time. Because experiments with multiple independent variables are efficient and provide more information than experiments with one independent variable, they are the preferred design of many experimental psychologists.

Designs in which we study two or more independent variables at the same time are called **factorial designs.** The independent variables in these designs are called **factors.** The simplest factorial design has only two factors and is called a **two-factor experiment.** The data we get from a factorial experiment give us two kinds of information: (1) They give us information about the effects of each independent variable in the experiment, called main effects. (2) They enable us to answer this question: How does the operation of one independent variable affect the operation of another in the experiment?

Looking for Main Effects

A **main effect** is the action of a single independent variable in an experiment. When we measure a main effect, we are asking: How much did the changes in this one independent variable change subjects' behaviors? When we look more closely at statistical tests, we will look at this definition again in a more quantitative way. However, keep in mind that a main effect is simply a change in behavior associated with a change in the value of a single independent variable.

When we have only one independent variable in an experiment, we do not usually talk about main effects, although we could. An experiment with one independent variable has only one main effect. When more than one independent variable exists, each one has a main effect. *There are as many main effects as there are factors.* These main effects may or may not be statistically significant. To tell if they are, we need to carry out statistical tests. When we do those tests, we first evaluate the impact of each independent variable in the experiment separately. We test whether each main effect is statistically significant or not.

Our plant study, for example, would have two factors—talking and music. We would want to know about the main effects of *both* factors. A factorial experiment allows us to know if each factor produces a significant effect on behavior or not.

Factor 1: How much did changes in talking affect plant growth?

Factor 2: How much did changes in music affect plant growth?

We would conduct statistical tests to determine if either independent variable or both produced any *significant* main effects. (Notice that this provides us with exactly the same information we would get if we ran two separate experiments on plant growth: one on the effects of talking and another on the effects of music.) However, in addition to determining the main effects for each factor, a factorial experiment also tells us whether the two factors are interdependent.

Looking for Interactions

As well as being more efficient, the factorial design allows us to test for relationships between the effects of different independent variables. Earlier we posed the notion that plants that get conversation might not need music.

Alternatively, of course, plants that get both might show truly spectacular growth. This is one example of how effects produced by two (or more) variables might influence each other. When this kind of relationship exists, we have an interaction.

An **interaction** is present if the effect of one independent variable changes across the levels of another independent variable. For instance, we could suppose that music might be helpful to plants that have not been spoken to at all. But the same music might have no effect on plants that have been exposed to speech. The impact of one independent variable (music vs. no music) might change at different levels of the other (speech vs. no speech). In other words, there could be an interaction between these two variables. Let us look at more realistic examples.

Your roommate sometimes teases you about how dumb you are, and you usually laugh it off or respond in kind. However, if you just received a poor grade on an important exam, you may become angry or depressed by those same teasing remarks. The impact of the teasing is altered by an important variable, your recent exam grade.

A few drinks at a party can make you feel relaxed and happy. If you are upset or anxious, a sleeping pill may help you to sleep. By themselves, a little alcohol or a sleeping pill may not be especially harmful. But take the two together and you may end up dead or in a coma. There is an *interaction* between these two substances: The effect of sleeping pills is altered by the presence of alcohol.

Whenever an interaction is present in a two-factor experiment, we cannot get a complete picture of the results of the experiment without considering both factors *because the effects of one factor will change depending on the levels of the other.* This is an important point that is often missed by beginning researchers. The presence of an interaction between two factors can sometimes tell us that the main effect produced by an individual factor might not always occur. An interaction tells us that there may be limits or exceptions to the effects of one or more factors. Thus, we say that an interaction *qualifies* the main effects.

In our plant example, suppose the two factors (music and speech) did interact. It could mean that while music alone will produce effects on plant growth (a main effect), music might not produce any further growth when speech is also present. Here the interaction tells us that any effects from music will *depend* on whether speech is also present or not. Figure 8-1 depicts this interaction. Notice that the figure shows that music *does* aid plant growth when there is no speech present (left side of graph), but it *does not* have any effect when speech is also present (right side). The interaction tells us that there are limits or qualifications to the effect of music on plant growth.

The number of possible interactions depends on the number of independent variables in the experiment. When two independent variables are present, there is usually only one possible interaction.[1] The two independent

---

[1] The picture is more complicated when we have the same subjects in more than one treatment condition of the experiment.

FIGURE 8-1 Hypothetical results of an experiment showing a music × speech interaction.

variables may interact with each other. When there are more than two independent variables, the picture becomes more complex; we can get **higher-order interactions** that involve more than two variables at a time. In a three-factor experiment, it is possible to get an interaction between all three independent variables. The action of each factor could be influenced by the values of the other two; driver experience, alcohol, and degree of darkness, for example, may interact in causing traffic accidents. In an experiment with three independent variables, it is also possible that any two factors, but not the third, could interact just as they might in a two-factor experiment.

As with main effects, we measure interactions quantitatively through statistical tests—we evaluate their significance. It is possible to run an experiment and find that an interaction between variables is significant even though the main effects are not. We may also get significant main effects with no significant interaction. It is also possible to have an interaction along with one or more significant main effects. All possible combinations of outcomes can occur. We will look at some of these possibilities more closely later in the chapter. Box 8-1 presents an actual research problem that can be approached through a factorial design.

LAYING OUT A FACTORIAL DESIGN

We can use a factorial design to approach the research problem outlined in Box 8-1. We can study the effects of name type and name length in the same study. Type of name is one factor; length of name is another. We will use only two levels (values) of each factor. It helps to look at our design graphically as we set it up. If you can translate your thinking about an experiment into a simple diagram, called a *design matrix,* you will find it easier to understand

BOX   8 - 1

WHAT'S IN A NAME: A FACTORIAL APPROACH

Does the length of your first name say something about you to others? Apparently it can. Mehrabian and Piercy (1993a) conducted an experiment to test whether people assign different kinds of personality characteristics to others based solely on their first name. In one experiment, they had people rate the characteristics of people with various given names or nicknames. Based partly on previous findings from their own work and that of other researchers, they hypothesized that nicknames would receive more favorable judgments than given first names—at least on certain kinds of traits. The researchers predicted that nicknames would be rated more positive in terms of characteristics like warmth, friendliness, and popularity. However, they predicted that given first names would be judged higher in traits related to intelligence and trustworthiness than nicknames. Were they right? Yes. A person with a nickname like Liz, for example, would probably be rated as friendlier and more popular than a person with the given name Elizabeth; but Elizabeth would probably be rated more intelligent and trustworthy.

Mehrabian and Piercy noticed, however, that nicknames were usually shorter than given names. This led them to wonder whether name length, by itself, could have similar effects. In a second experiment (1993b), they used only given names—no nicknames—and asked subjects to infer the characteristics of people with each of 858 given names of various lengths. They predicted that shorter names would be associated with greater warmth and similar traits, but longer names would be judged higher in traits like intelligence and trustworthiness. In general, their hypotheses (particularly for male names) were supported.

What would happen if, instead of conducting two separate experiments, we combined both independent variables in a factorial experiment? We could call one factor "type of name," and compare two levels: given names and nicknames. The other factor could be "name length," and again we could use two levels: short or long. We would need to operationally define each of the variables and select valid names for each condition. Then we could use procedures similar to those of Mehrabian and Piercy and have subjects judge each kind of name on a number of traits.

What would we gain by a factorial experiment? It would be more efficient to do one rather than two separate experiments. We could still

(continued)

(*continued*)

learn whether each factor, independently, produced main effects. In addition, however, we could learn whether the two independent variables interact when they are combined—information we cannot get if we do two separate experiments. Perhaps name length operates differently for given names than for nicknames.

Have you ever noticed that lots of longer nicknames end in the letters *y*, *ie*, or *i*? ("Timmy," "Jeri," "Terry," and "Susie," for instance.) Maybe nicknames that are *diminutive forms* of given names make them seem equally less intelligent as very short nicknames. Perhaps the short nickname "Kim" and the longer "Kimmy" would be judged equally unintelligent—less intelligent than the given name "Kimberly." Maybe the nicknames "Jim," "Jimmy," and even "the Jimster" would be judged equally warm and friendly—more warm and friendly than the short given name "James." You can probably come up with other potential interactions between name type and name length that are just as plausible. The point to be made here is that unless a factorial experiment is conducted, interaction effects will not be discovered.

what you are testing, what kind of design you are using, and how many treatment conditions are required.[2] Figure 8-2 illustrates our two-factor experiment. Your diagram will be more complex if you are working with more than two factors or more than two levels of each factor.

We begin by diagramming the basic components of the design, the two factors (Figure 8-2, step 1). Notice that we label each factor with a number—type of name is factor 1, and length of name is factor 2. These numbers may be used later as a shorthand way of referring to the factors in the final report. We predicted that the type of name has an effect; given names and nicknames will be the two values we select for factor 1. We indicate "given name" and "nickname" in our diagram (Figure 8-2, step 2). We are also planning to use two levels of the length factor. Our question about the effect of name length at this point is simply whether length has any effect on judgments of traits. We may indicate the two levels of the length factor in the diagram simply by "short" and "long" (Figure 8-2, step 3); we can always explore more subtle differences in future studies. We now draw the four separate *cells* of the matrix that represent the four treatment conditions needed in the experiment (Figure 8-2, step 4). If we assign our subjects to the conditions at random, each cell also represents a different group of randomly assigned subjects. Some subjects will rate given names that are short; others will rate given names that are long, and so on.

---

[2]You can use the same diagram later as you do the statistical tests. Values of the dependent variable—for instance, the average ratings for the traits "warm" and "intelligent"—would be recorded in the cells (see also Part 3). This provides a picture of the treatment effects in each condition, making interpretation easier.

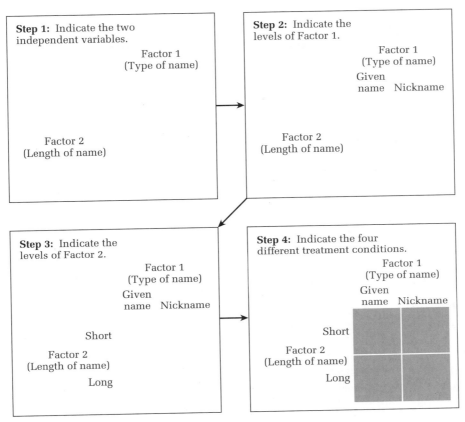

FIGURE 8-2 Diagramming a design matrix for the two-factor experiment described in Box 8-1.

Describing the Design

We know this is a two-factor experiment because it has two independent variables. However, there is another common way of describing factorial designs, a shorthand method that actually gives us more information. This design is called a 2 × 2 (read as "two by two") *factorial design*. This **shorthand notation** tells us several things about the experiment it describes. First, the numbers tell us the number of factors involved. Here there are two numbers (2 and 2); each number refers to a different factor. Hence, this experiment has two factors. The value of each number tells us how many levels each factor has. If we have a 2 × 2 design, we automatically know each of the experiment's two factors has two levels. We also know that the experiment has four different conditions (the product of 2 × 2). Box 8-2 shows other methods used to describe factorial designs.

Although our example involves only two factors, it is possible to design factorial experiments with any number of factors. The number of factors will determine the way the design is labeled—an experiment involving three

B O X   8 - 2

ADDITIONAL METHODS FOR DESCRIBING DESIGN VARIABLES

When factorial designs are described in research reports, the shorthand notation system is often expanded to include the variable names. This system makes it much easier to understand the complete research design at a glance. There are several ways to do this, and you will find examples of each of these methods in the research literature. For simplicity, we will illustrate how the 2 × 2 name experiment would be described using each different method. The same methods can also be used to describe larger factorial designs.

Factor-Labeling Method

The names of each factor are placed in parentheses following the numerical notation. The name of the factor represented by the first digit would be the first name you would list; the name of the second factor would be the second. Just like the shorthand notation, the factor labels are separated by ×. Because different subjects have been assigned to each of the four treatment conditions, the experiment is a between-subjects factorial design.

Example 1: 2 × 2 (Type of Name × Length of Name) between-subjects factorial design

Factor and Levels Methods

There are two procedures for this method, and you can use either. These give the most complete information about the experimental design because they also list the values or levels of each factor. The first method places the factor name and its levels immediately following the shorthand notation for the entire design. This simply extends the factor-labeling method to include the factor levels. The second method places the names for the individual levels of each variable immediately following its number in the shorthand notation.

Example 2: 2 × 2 (Type of Name: given, nickname × Length of Name: short, long) between-subjects factorial design

Example 3: 2 (given name or nickname) × 2 (short or long name) between-subjects factorial design

FIGURE 8-3 Diagram of a 2 × 3 × 2 factorial design. The diagram represents an experiment in which there are three independent variables: the sex of the person delivering a persuasive communication, the attractiveness of that communicator, and the sex of the subjects being exposed to the communication. The hypothesis of this experiment is as follows: Subjects will be more persuaded by a message delivered by a more attractive communicator, but only when the communicator is the opposite sex from the subject.

independent variables, for example, is called a three-factor experiment. The shorthand notation indicates additional information. If an experiment is referred to as a "2 × 3 × 2 factorial design," we immediately know several things about it. Since three digits are mentioned (2, 3, and 2) we know this experiment involves three independent variables. The numerical value of each digit tells us the number of levels of each of the factors. We know that the first factor has two levels, the second has three, and the third has two. We also know that this experiment has 12 separate conditions (the product of 2 × 3 × 2). Figure 8-3 presents a sample diagram of a 2 × 3 × 2 experiment.

A RESEARCH EXAMPLE

Let us take a closer look at an experimental example of a 2 × 2 factorial experiment. This experiment produced one significant main effect along with a significant interaction. Pliner and Chaiken (1990) were interested in the relationship between gender and eating behavior. It is well known that, in our culture at least, young women show a greater concern with eating lightly and being slim than do men. Even though research has shown that young men do not really prefer slim over average-weight women, being thin is a goal that seems to obsess many American women. Anorexia and bulimia, potentially life-threatening eating disorders, can be an end product of this distorted view of the "ideal" female body image.

Pliner and Chaiken believe that thinness and light eating have come to be viewed as appropriate sex-role behaviors for women, making them appear more feminine than their heavy-eating counterparts. If this is the case, women should be especially prone to eat lightly in situations where they want to appear most feminine—when they are with an attractive person of the opposite sex! Young men, the authors argue, don't worry about how much they eat in front of others because it does not affect the kind of impression they will make.

The authors conducted an experiment that tested the following hypothesis: Women will eat less in the presence of an opposite-sex partner than in the presence of another of the same sex, but men's eating behavior will not be influenced by their partner's gender. Pliner and Chaiken predicted that two variables—subject sex and partner sex—would interact in their effects on eating behavior. Let us look at the variables in their experiment.

What must be manipulated to test the hypothesis? First, the behavior of women must be compared with that of men. The first independent variable is the sex of the subject. Notice that this factor is actually a *quasi*-experimental or subject variable. The "manipulation" is simply the selection process; subjects are automatically assigned to an experimental group on the basis of their gender. Second, the sex of the subject's partner must be manipulated. The second independent variable is the gender of a second person with whom the subjects are paired: a partner of the same or opposite sex. Here the experimenters manipulate which type of partner subjects will get.

Individual subjects in the experiment were led to believe that they and a partner were taking part in a study on the effects of hunger on task performance. They had been asked not to eat anything the day of the experiment so that they would be hungry when they arrived. Each subject was told that he or she and the partner had been assigned to the "full" condition of the experiment and would be asked to eat as much as it took for them to feel comfortably full while working on the experimental task. Crackers with various toppings were provided. Early in the session, the subject and partner were interviewed together by the experimenter. This interview was designed to give the subject the impression that her or his partner was single and socially attractive.[3]

The dependent variable in this experiment was eating behavior. The researchers measured eating by counting how many crackers each subject ate. To make sure that the partner's eating did not confound the experiment, the partner always ate 15 crackers (about 315 calories). The researchers' hypothesis would be supported if a significant interaction between the two factors was obtained: if women ate fewer crackers in the presence of an opposite-sex partner than with a same-sex partner, but men's eating did not differ. Their findings are depicted graphically in Figure 8-4. Before we explore an interaction between the factors, however, let us look at the effects produced by each factor alone.

Remember that in a factorial experiment we always look at the effect of each independent variable separately as well as looking for an interaction. These main effects explore each factor by itself, ignoring the other. (These are like the effects we would get if we had conducted two separate experiments— one testing the effect of subject sex on eating and one testing the effect of partner sex on eating.)

---

[3]For simplicity, we are including only effects that occurred when subjects actually perceived their partner to be socially attractive.

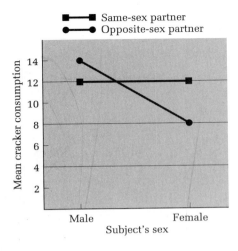

FIGURE 8-4 Cracker consumption by women and men in the presence of a same-sex or an opposite-sex partner. From results reported by Pliner and Chaiken (1990).

Did the first factor, subject sex, produce any effects on eating? Yes. The experiment produced a significant main effect for this factor. If we just consider how many crackers men and women tended to eat in the experiment, we find that men ate more crackers on the average than women (about 13.5 versus 10.9). This is not too surprising; we expect men to eat more than women.

Did the second factor, same- or opposite-sex partner, have any effect by itself on eating? No, it did not. If we combine the data for all subjects in the experiment, we find that, on average, people ate about the same amount of crackers whether their partners were the same sex or the opposite sex. There were a few more men than women in the experiment, which brought the average for the entire group up slightly, so the average number of crackers eaten in the presence of either type of partner was about 12.3.

Finally, we look at the interaction. The interaction describes the effects of one factor (male vs. female subjects) at different levels of the other (same-sex vs. opposite sex partners). The interaction asks whether men's or women's eating habits change with different kinds of partners. Was Pliner and Chaiken's hypothesis supported? Yes, there was a significant interaction between subject sex and type of partner. Men ate about the same amount whether their partner was the same or the opposite sex. But, as expected, women varied their eating depending on the gender of their partner. If their partner was the same sex, they ate more than if their partner was the opposite sex.

Understanding Effects from Factorial Designs

Figure 8-4 illustrates the actual outcome of the experiment done by Pliner and Chaiken (1990). However, a variety of other patterns of results might be observed in a factorial experiment, and each would require a different interpretation. Figures 8-5 to 8-11 present some additional possibilities to help you understand the difference between main effects and interactions. Keep in mind that these figures do not represent actual data.

Key: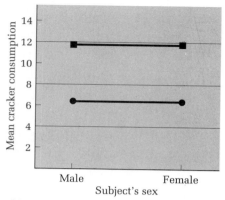

(a) No significant main effects or interaction

(b) Significant main effect for partner's sex

FIGURE 8-5 Hypothetical outcome of Pliner and Chaiken (1990)—no significant main effect or interaction.

FIGURE 8-6 Hypothetical outcome of Pliner and Chaiken (1990)—significant main effect for partner's sex.

In Figure 8-5, the experimental data show no significant main effects or interactions. This is the way the data would look when graphed if the subject's sex had not influenced eating and if subjects ate about the same amount regardless of the type of partner they had. This would mean that the experimenters' hypothesis was wrong or that the procedures used were inadequate to detect the effect.

Figure 8-6 illustrates the outcome if there were a significant main effect for type of partner, but the main effect for subject sex and the interaction were not significant. The figure depicts an outcome in which both male and female subjects ate less in the presence of an opposite-sex partner. And, in fact, this finding was actually reported in an earlier experiment by Mori, Chaiken, and Pliner (1987).[4]

What would the graph look like if a significant main effect for type of partner indicated that both male and female subjects ate less in the presence of a same-sex partner than they did in the presence of an opposite-sex partner? The two lines would be reversed; the line for same-sex partners would be lower than the line for opposite-sex partners.

A significant main effect for sex of subject is illustrated in Figure 8-7. The graph would look like this if men ate more than women regardless of who their partners were. In this graph, neither the main effect for type of partner nor the interaction is significant. What would the graph look like if a main effect for sex of subject showed that women ate more than men? The points on the left would be lower than the points on the right.

[4]In a second experiment reported by Pliner and Chaiken (1990), both men and women ate less in the presence of an opposite-sex partner. The authors suggested that eating can be influenced by the kinds of personal and social motives that are important at the time. Wishing to appear cooperative or similar to their opposite-sex partner or wishing to have their behavior appear "socially desirable" may have reduced eating among men in the presence of women.

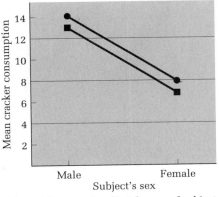

(c) Significant main effect for sex of subject

FIGURE 8-7 Hypothetical outcome of Pliner and Chaiken (1990)—significant main effect for sex of subject.

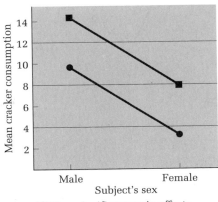

(d) Two significant main effects

FIGURE 8-8 Hypothetical outcome of Pliner and Chaiken (1990)—two significant main effects.

Figure 8-8 shows one possible outcome when there are two significant main effects in the data but no interaction. As shown in the figure, whether a subject is male or female affects how much they eat. However, whether the partner is the same or opposite sex also makes a difference. Men in all conditions eat more than women, *and* everyone eats more with a same-sex partner than when they have an opposite-sex partner. Both independent variables exert an influence on eating, but they do not interact; the influence of one variable does not depend on the level of another.

Figures 8-9 and 8-10 depict two examples of significant interactions in

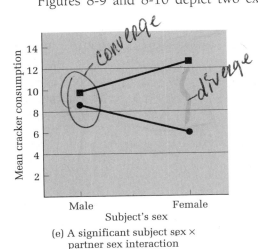

(e) A significant subject sex × partner sex interaction

FIGURE 8-9 Hypothetical outcome of Pliner and Chaiken (1990)—significant subject sex × partner sex interaction.

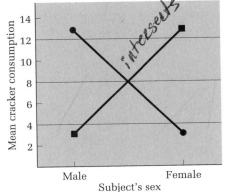

(f) A maximum significant subject sex × partner sex interaction

FIGURE 8-10 Hypothetical outcome of Pliner and Chaiken (1990)—maximum significant subject sex × partner sex interaction.

FIGURE 8-11 Hypothetical outcome of Pliner and Chaiken (1990)—a significant subject sex main effect, a significant partner sex main effect, and a significant subject sex × partner sex interaction.

the absence of any significant main effects. The graphs of data that reflect an interaction always show a characteristic pattern: The lines are not parallel. Graphs showing an interaction can *diverge* (spread out, as in Figure 8-9), *converge* (come together), or *intersect* (as in Figure 8-10 and the earlier Figure 8-4). Notice that the interaction depicted in Figure 8-10 is the maximum possible interaction. The effects of each factor *completely reverse* at each level of the other factor. We call this a *crossover interaction*.

Remember that an interaction can also occur along with any number of significant main effects. (You saw an example of an interaction along with one significant main effect earlier in Figure 8-4.) Figure 8-11 depicts two significant main effects and a significant interaction. In this figure, both the subject's sex and the partner's sex have effects on eating—and the two factors interact. When we were talking about our earlier plant example, we said that interactions *qualified* main effects (Figure 8-1). Figure 8-11 shows a different kind of qualification. Here both factors produce effects on eating, but the *magnitude* of the effects of one factor changes across the levels of the other factor. For example, this graph shows that, in general, women eat less than men, and both eat less in the presence of an opposite-sex partner. And in addition, the interaction tells us that women's eating in front of an opposite-sex partner drops *a great deal more* than a man's eating does.

Measuring interactions is one of the key reasons for doing factorial research. By looking at two (or more) variables together, we can assess whether the effect of one variable depends on the level of another variable. When we have an interaction, knowing the value of just one IV will not necessarily enable us to predict the performance of subjects with any degree of accuracy. For instance, suppose the data came out like those displayed in the graph in Figure 8-9, which represents an outcome in which men ate the same amount regardless of type of partner, but women varied their eating with different partners. Women ate more with a same-sex partner than with an opposite-sex partner. Because there is an interaction, eating depends on both factors. If we want to predict accurately how many crackers would be eaten by any subject, we would need to know both the subject's sex and the type of partner.

This effect is even more apparent in the crossover interaction depicted in Figure 8-10. Here the effect of type of partner on eating is exactly opposite for male and female subjects. To predict for any subject in the experiment, we would need to know whether the subject was male or female and what type of partner the subject had.

From the interaction in Figure 8-11, we can also see that we do not have a complete picture of the effects of the independent variables unless we look at the effects of both factors together because the effects differ in magnitude across the levels of both factors. Main effects and interactions are quantified and evaluated through statistical tests. Chapter 14 contains additional information on these concepts and the procedures required to evaluate them.

CHOOSING A BETWEEN-SUBJECTS DESIGN

As you begin planning your first experiments, you will probably experience the temptation of trying to do everything in one experiment. You may try to set up studies with as many as five or six different factors. But if you try to do too many things at once, you may lose sight of what you are trying to accomplish. A simple set of hypotheses that zeros in on the most important variables is better than a more elaborate set that includes everything from astrological signs to zest for life. Keep your first experiment simple. Although factorial designs make it possible to look at many different variables at a time, do not get carried away. Focus on the variables that are critical. Once again, a review of the experimental literature will be a helpful guide. If other researchers have simply controlled time of day by testing all their subjects together, there is no need to vary time of day in your study so that you can include it as an independent variable—unless you have strong reasons for doing so. You will develop a better understanding of the experimental process by starting with simple designs and working up to more complex ones.

There are several practical reasons for keeping factorial designs simple. First, subjects are usually assigned to each of the treatment conditions at random. This means you will need as many groups of subjects as you have treatment conditions. It is not always easy to find subjects. More treatment conditions also means more time to run the experiment and more time to do the statistical analysis. Moreover, the results of complicated designs may be virtually uninterpretable. It is very difficult to describe the interaction of three factors, let alone explain why it happened (see Box 8-3). A significant three-way interaction (like the outcome predicted for the experiment in Figure 8-3) is rarely a predicted result. Four-way interactions are practically impossible to conceptualize and explain. There is not much point in collecting data that we cannot understand. It is just not practical to include unnecessary factors and conditions. Use your review of prior research in the area to help you decide what variables and what levels to include.

B O X   8 - 3

MULTIPLE INTERACTIONS: THE BARON, RUSSELL, AND ARMS (1985) EXPERIMENT

In a two-factor between-subjects design, there can be only three possible effects: a main effect for each factor and an interaction between the two factors (total = three possible effects). Whenever a factorial expands beyond a two-factor design, the number of possible main effects and interactions increases dramatically. Let's use *A*, *B*, and *C* to represent three factors in an experiment. What kind of significant effects are possible? First, each factor can produce a significant main effect on the dependent variable: a main effect for *A*, a main effect for *B*, and a main effect for *C*. Next, each pair of factors can interact: An interaction between *A* and *B*, between *A* and *C*, and between *B* and *C* are possible. Finally, all three factors can interact at once: an interaction among *A*, *B*, and *C*. If we add up the possible significant effects, the total = 7. (In a four-factor design, the total = 15.) Think about this as you design your experiment!

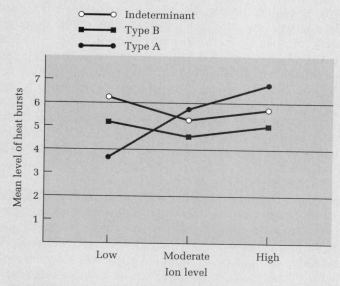

FIGURE 8-12 Hypothetical mean level of aggression as a function of ion level and type A–type B dimension.

Recall the negative ion experiment conducted by Baron and colleagues (1985). In the full design, they had three independent variables: type of subject (type A, indeterminate, or type B); provocation condition (angered or not angered); and ion level (low, moderate, or high). In all, there were 18 different experimental conditions. The results on aggressiveness were very complex; two 2-way interactions were obtained. The 3-way interaction was almost statistically significant, too. The presence of two 2-way interactions made interpretation of the experimental findings extremely difficult. An interaction between the type of subject and the level of negative ions in the air is shown in Figure 8-12.

Statistics done to test for differences between each of the nine experimental conditions (in this case, a Duncan multiple-range test) showed that increasing the level of negative ions only increased aggression in Type A subjects. For Type As, both moderate and high levels of negative ions caused significantly stronger "heat bursts" to be directed toward the confederate than did low levels of negative ions. Notice that the line for Type As shows a distinct upward trend as the ion level is increased. The lines for Indeterminate and Type B subjects are relatively flat across all three ion levels, because increasing the level of negative ions did not produce any significant effects on their aggressive behavior toward the confederate.

So far we have covered four different kinds of between-subjects designs. We looked at two-group designs that had either independent or matched groups. We also looked at multiple-groups designs and factorial designs. You may still feel a bit uneasy about trying to select the appropriate design for your own between-subjects experiment. To make things easier, you should always begin with some basic questions. Your design will be determined to a large extent by the number of independent variables you have and by the number of treatment conditions needed to test your hypothesis. You should also use your literature review to get an idea of the kinds of designs others have used for similar problems. To help make your search more systematic, we summarize the basics of the decision-making process in Figure 8-13 on the following page. Simply begin at the top and work down, answering the questions in terms of your experiment.

In the next chapter, we will look at another important type of experimental strategy—within-subjects designs. In the four designs we have already covered, each subject participates in only one treatment condition and is measured on the dependent variable after the experimental manipulation has taken place. In a within-subjects experiment, subjects participate in more than one treatment condition of an experiment, and a measurement is taken after each treatment is given. Factorial experiments can also be conducted using a within-subjects design. In a within-subjects factorial design, subjects receive all conditions in the experiment instead of receiving only one.

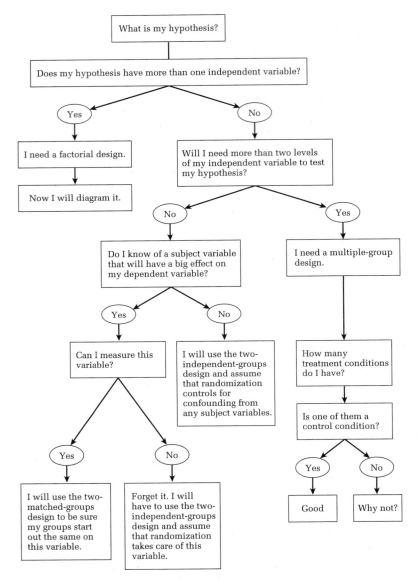

FIGURE 8-13 Questions to ask when designing a between-subjects experiment. (Start at the top and work down.)

SUMMARY

The *factorial design* has two or more independent variables, which are called *factors*. Factorial designs testing two or more factors are more efficient than separate experiments testing the same set of independent variables. By studying more than one factor at a time, we can measure *main effects*—the action of each independent variable in the experiment. We can also measure *interactions*—a change in the effect of one independent variable across the levels of another independent variable. Psychological variables are often complex, and only a factorial design can detect and measure interactions.

Factorial designs are described with *shorthand notation*. If we are told that an experiment has a 3 × 2 × 4 design, we know it has three independent variables because three numbers are given. The value of each number tells us how many levels each factor has. The first factor has three, the second has two, and the third has four levels, or values. We also know there are 24 treatment conditions, the product of 3 × 2 × 4. *Higher-order interactions* can be produced in experiments with more than two factors.

Statistics are used to assess the significance of each effect in a factorial experiment. All combinations of main effects and interactions are possible. For example, Pliner and Chaiken's (1990) 2 × 2 factorial experiment on eating in the presence of same or opposite-sex partners produced one significant main effect along with a significant interaction. However, there are a number of other possible outcomes.

There are practical limitations on using factorial designs: They often require many subjects. They can be time consuming, and they require more complicated statistical procedures than the other designs we have discussed. However, they also provide valuable information that other types of experiments cannot.

KEY TERMS

Factor An independent variable in a factorial design.
Factorial design An experimental design in which more than one independent variable is manipulated.
Higher-order interaction An interaction effect involving more than two independent variables.
Interaction The effect of one independent variable changes across the levels of another independent variable; can only be detected in factorial designs.
Main effect The action of a single independent variable in an experiment; the change in the dependent variable produced by the various levels of a single independent variable.
Shorthand notation A system that uses numbers to describe the design of a factorial experiment.
Two-factor experiment The simplest factorial design, having two independent variables.

REVIEW AND STUDY QUESTIONS

1. What is a factorial design?
2. Explain what we mean by the terms *main effect* and *interaction*.
3. What are the advantages of running experiments with a factorial design?

4. After watching a group of nursery school children, we get the idea that some toys are more popular with children than others. We would like to test the difference in time spent playing with toys that are used for building (for example, blocks) and toys that are not (for example, stuffed animals). Since there are many differences between boys and girls, we would also like to look at sex as an independent variable. What kind of design do we need?

5. Diagram the experiment suggested in question 4.

6. Describe the design in the diagram in question 5 using the factor-labeling method and the factor and level methods.

7. You are told that an experiment has a 3 × 3 × 3 design.
   a. How many independent variables does it have?
   b. How many different treatment conditions does it have?
   c. Make a diagram of it.

8. A researcher decides to run an experiment to study the effects of three independent variables on learning. (1) She will vary background noise by playing or not playing a radio while subjects study a list of words. (2) She will vary smoking: Half the subjects (all regular smokers) will have a cigarette before the experiment and half will not. (3) She will vary the length of the list to be learned: Half the subjects will try to learn a short list; half will try to learn a long list in the same amount of time. The dependent variable is the percentage of words recalled. Take this hypothetical experiment and do the following:
   a. Describe this experiment using shorthand notation for factorial designs.
   b. Diagram the experiment.
   c. In addition to defining the subject population as "regular smokers," what other subject variables might be important to the outcome of this study? How can they be controlled?
   d. Identify three nonsubject variables you think might affect the outcome of this study.

9. What features of an experimental hypothesis are important in selecting a design?

10. In a study of age and recognition of advertised products, Stoneman and Brody (1983) reported that children who saw a video presentation (viewing commercials without hearing the sound track) or audiovisual presentation (TV picture plus sound) recognized more products than children who heard only the sound. They also found that second-grade children later recognized more of the products than kindergarten children did and that kindergarten children scored better than preschoolers.
   a. What is the design of this experiment? Describe it using shorthand notation. Diagram it.
   b. How many main effects were reported?
   c. Using a simple graph, illustrate the pattern of the overall results of this experiment.

C H A P T E R   9

WITHIN-SUBJECTS DESIGNS

We have focused on four main types of designs so far: two independent groups, two matched groups, multiple groups, and factorial designs. All our examples of these designs had one underlying assumption—that the subjects in each of the treatment conditions were different, randomly selected individuals. We assumed that each subject would be in only one treatment condition. These are called *between-subjects designs*. Conclusions are based on comparisons among subjects (that is, among the different groups of the experiment). This approach usually works well, but only in certain cases. Other experiments call for a different type of design, as the following example illustrates.

People seem to smile more when there is an audience to see the smile than when they are alone (Fridlund, 1989). Smiling seems to serve a social and communicative function; it can serve to notify others when we are feeling happy or pleased. Currently, there is a debate in the psychological literature about whether smiles serve mostly to communicate emotions or are automatic manifestations of an inner emotional state. (There is evidence for both sides.) If smiles function to communicate emotions to other people, the behavior of smiling to others would probably be a learned behavior, and researchers have wondered just how early it is learned. Jones and her colleagues have been investigating communicative smiles in infants. In one experiment, they found evidence for an audience effect in 18-month old infants (Jones & Raag, 1989). The infants smiled more at their mothers when the mothers were attending to them than when they were not; when the mothers were not attending, the infants simply smiled at an available stranger who was paying attention to them.

However, 18-month-old infants are already well socialized in many respects and are beginning the *word explosion* period (a time of rapid vocabulary growth and development of an understanding of symbolic communications). Jones wondered if infants might begin the social control of facial expressions, including smiles, even earlier. She set up a laboratory testing situation in which she could observe 10-month-old infants and their mothers (Jones, Collins, & Hong, 1991). The setup of the testing room is shown in Figure 9-1. Each mother spent a minute describing and demonstrating several toys affixed to a pegboard stand, then left the baby next to the toys and sat down in the chair. Two 6-minute segments followed: In one, the mother paid attention to the baby playing; in the other, she read a magazine.[1] The baby was videotaped using the two cameras in the room, and smiles were later scored and recorded by judges who viewed the tapes. Jones and her colleagues made the following prediction: If 10-month-old infants use their smiles to communicate, they should smile much more to their mothers if the mothers are paying attention to them than if they are not. Their hypothesis was strongly supported. The 20 babies smiled at their mothers almost four times as much when the mothers were attending than when they were not.

Suppose we used a between-subjects approach for this research. Each mother and baby would take part in only one of the two 6-minute segments—

---

[1]For half the mother-baby pairs, the attention segment came first; for the other half, the nonattention segment came first.

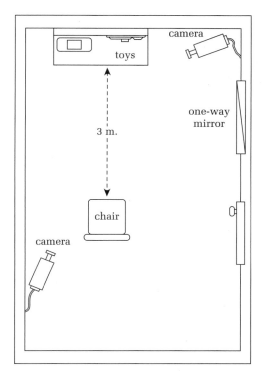

FIGURE 9-1 Experimental setting. From "An Audience Effect in Smile Production on 10-Month-Old Infants," by S. S. Jones, K. Collins, and H-W Hong, 1991, *Psychological Science, 2,* 45–49. Copyright ©1991. Reprinted with the permission of Cambridge University Press.

either attending or not attending—and we would compare the average number of smiles from the babies in each group. We would have a few problems if we tried to do this. First, there is a great deal of variability among 10-month-old infants in terms of the number of smiles they produce. Some only smiled once or twice; others smiled a lot. Such large differences exist in the amount of smiling in babies that a difference between the two groups might not be detectable. Whenever we expect responses from subjects to be extremely dissimilar, finding effects from an independent variable is like looking for a needle in a haystack. Second, we would probably need a much larger sample of mothers and babies if we had to divide them into two groups—and finding mothers with babies just the right age (who are also willing to volunteer for an experiment) can be extremely difficult.

For this kind of research, it is much better to use a **within-subjects design**—a design in which each subject serves in more than one condition of the experiment. By having the same subjects in both attention conditions, Jones and her colleagues improved their chances of detecting differences between the attention and nonattention conditions. From a statistical viewpoint, we refer to this as increasing the power of the experiment. Increased **power** means a greater chance of detecting a genuine effect of the independent variable.

Some hypotheses and research topics naturally require a within-subjects approach: Does a family's perception of itself change over the course of family therapy? Do you improve each time you take the same intelligence test? Do additional reviews of class notes yield better exam scores? Let us turn to another laboratory experiment in which a within-subjects approach was used.

A WITHIN-SUBJECTS EXPERIMENT: PERCEPTUAL BIAS FOR FORWARD MOTION

We can set up a variety of within-subjects designs. The basic principles remain the same: Each subject takes part in more than one condition of the experiment. We make comparisons of the behavior of the same subjects under different conditions. If our independent variable is having an effect, we are often more likely to find it if we use a within-subjects design. In a between-subjects design, the effects of our independent variable can be masked by the differences between the groups on all sorts of extraneous variables. A comparison within each subject is more precise. If we see different behaviors under different treatment conditions, these differences are more likely to be linked to our experimental manipulation. Remember that the whole point of an experiment is to set up a situation in which the independent variable is the only thing that changes systematically across the conditions of the experiment. In a between-subjects design, we change the independent variable across conditions. However, we also use different subjects in the different conditions. We can usually assume that randomization controls for extraneous variables that might affect the dependent variable. But we have even better control with a within-subjects design, because we use the same subjects over and over.

McBeath, Morikawa, and Kaiser (1992; experiment 2) used a within-subjects design to investigate a perceptual bias toward seeing motion in certain kinds of pictures or figures. They predicted that figures facing in a certain direction would sometimes seem to be moving in that direction—even when they really were not. To test this hypothesis, they needed to compare figures that faced in different directions. The researchers were also interested in testing different categories of pictures. They used the set of stimulus figures shown in Figure 9-2. You can see that some of the figures are facing left, some are neutral and some are facing right.

McBeath and his colleagues used a computer to show each figure twice to subjects. One of the figures would be presented for 1 second, then it would be immediately replaced by the same figure in a close location. Half the time the second image was a bit to the right of the first one; half the time it was a bit to the left. This way the figure would seem to move slightly to the right or the left. If the direction the figures were facing made no difference, subjects should be equally accurate at determining which way each pair of images

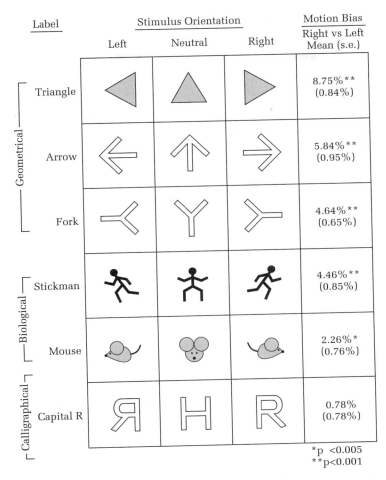

Label	Stimulus Orientation			Motion Bias Right vs Left Mean (s.e.)
	Left	Neutral	Right	
Triangle				8.75%** (0.84%)
Arrow				5.84%** (0.95%)
Fork				4.64%** (0.65%)
Stickman				4.46%** (0.85%)
Mouse				2.26%* (0.76%)
Capital R				0.78% (0.78%)

*p <0.005
**p<0.001

FIGURE 9-2 Stimuli. From "Perceptual Bias for Forward-Facing Motion," by M. K. McBeath, K. Morikawa, and M. K. Kaiser, 1992, *Psychological Science, 3*, 362–367. Copyright ©1992. Reprinted with the permission of Cambridge University Press.

appeared to move. But this is not what happened. Instead, the researchers discovered that people do have a perceptual bias for forward-facing motion. When a figure faces in a particular direction, we apparently expect it to move that way—to move forward—and we sometimes make perceptual errors. For example, even though the computer presented a right-facing stickman so that it should have seemed to move to the left, subjects sometimes believed they saw it moving to the right because that is the direction the stickman was facing.

Using a within-subjects design allowed the researchers to get a more precise picture of how the bias worked. They discovered, for example, that the most forward-facing motion errors occurred with the geometrical figures, followed by the biological figures. No significant bias was found for the letter *R*. McBeath and his colleagues made their data more precise by comparing responses of the same subjects under different conditions, which eliminated the error from differences between subjects. The responses of the same subjects are likely to be more consistent from one measurement to another. Therefore, if responses change across conditions, the changes are more likely to be caused by the independent variable. Because it controls for individual differences between subjects, a within-subjects design also allowed them to use many fewer subjects, making it a more efficient experiment. There were 18 figure conditions in the experiment. But these researchers were able to detect significant differences produced by the figures using only ten subjects!

WITHIN-SUBJECTS FACTORIAL DESIGNS

So far we have talked about within-subjects designs that tested a single independent variable. However, these designs can also be set up as factorial designs. Suppose a researcher was interested in measuring how long it takes to identify different facial expressions. She might decide to show subjects slides of people displaying four different expressions—perhaps anger, fear, happiness, and sadness—and measure how quickly people can recognize each one. She could use a within-subjects design, showing each subject all four kinds of faces and timing how long it takes each subject to identify each expression. Past research suggests that in terms of communicating emotions on their faces, women are generally better "senders" (Fridlund, Ekman, & Oster, 1987), so the researcher also wants to show subjects both male and female faces. In this case, she can use the sex of the person in the slide as an additional within-subjects factor. The design would be a 4 × 2 *within-subjects factorial*; each subject would take part in eight separate conditions (4 × 2 = 8). Subjects would see and identify eight different faces: a man and a woman displaying each of the four expressions.[2] It is easy to see that a within-subjects factorial can require many fewer subjects than a between-subjects factorial design that is testing the same hypothesis.

MIXED DESIGNS

It is also possible to use a factorial design that combines one factor that is manipulated within subjects (such as the four types of expressions) with a between-subjects factor (often a subject variable, such as gender or age, that cannot be manipulated by an experimenter). A design that combines within- and between-subjects variables in a single experiment is called a **mixed design.** Suppose the researcher who conducted the facial expression experiment found that some expressions were indeed identified more quickly than

---

[2]As you will discover later in the chapter, the experimenter would also need to use a special control procedure, called *counterbalancing;* different subjects would see the eight faces in different orders to prevent confounding.

others, but it did not matter whether the person in the slide was male or female. She might continue investigating facial expressions along other lines. For instance, she might wonder whether men or women are faster at identifying these facial expressions. Testing this hypothesis would require a 2 × 4 mixed design. Subjects would be divided into two groups on the basis of their gender; subjects in both groups would see and identify slides of all four different expressions. Mixed designs are common in psychology. The statistical procedures for analyzing mixed designs are more complex than those for within-subjects or between-subjects factorial designs; with computer statistical analysis programs so widely available, however, student experimenters frequently select mixed designs. An example of a mixed design in which all the independent variables were manipulated is shown in Box 9-1.

ADVANTAGES OF WITHIN-SUBJECTS DESIGNS

In within-subjects experiments, we use the same subjects in different treatment conditions. This is a big help when we cannot get many subjects. (As you will see in the next chapter, we can actually run an entire experiment with only one subject if we must.) If we have four treatment conditions and want 15 subjects in each condition, we only need 15 subjects if we run the experiment within subjects. Each of the 15 subjects runs through all four conditions. However, if we run the same experiment between subjects, we need 60 subjects, 15 in each condition.

A within-subjects design can also save us time when we are actually running the experiment. If subjects must be trained, it is more efficient to train each subject for several conditions instead of for just one.

We usually have the best chance of detecting the effect of our independent variable if we compare the behavior of the same subjects under different conditions. The within-subjects design controls for subject variables, the ways in which subjects differ from one another. That way, if we see differences in behavior under different conditions, we know that they are not likely to be simply the differences that occur because the subjects in one group do not act like the subjects in another. From a statistical standpoint, we have a better chance of detecting the effect of our experimental manipulation if we use a within-subjects design. The reasons parallel the reasons we discussed in connection with the matched-groups procedures.

In a sense, the within-subjects design is the most perfect form of matching we can have. The influence of subject variables across different treatment conditions is controlled because the same subjects take part in all the treatment conditions. *Each subject serves as his or her own control in the experiment.*

In a within-subjects design, the subject is measured after each treatment condition; therefore, subjects are measured more than once on the dependent variable. For this reason, this type of design is also called a **repeated-measures design.** We repeat the measurements of the impact of the different values of the independent variable on the same subjects.

B O X   9 - 1

EMOTIONS AND PERCEPTION: A FACTORIAL EXPERIMENTAL APPROACH

Everyday experience tells us that our feelings can influence the way we see the world. When we are happy, everything seems more positive. When we are depressed, the world looks bleak. When we are afraid, everything seems scarier. Our emotions seem to influence the way we perceive things. But does this really happen? In an interesting mixed-factorial experiment, Niedenthal and Setterlund (1994; experiment 1) tested whether our emotions could really influence our perceptions.

The researchers used music to put subjects in either a happy or sad mood.* After the mood induction, subjects were given the task of identifying 60 letter strings as either real words or nonwords (pronouncible strings of letters) as quickly as possible. Six of the words were happy-related (*delight, cheer, joy, humor, harmony,* and *comedy*). Six were sad-related (*weep, despair, regret, hurt, frown,* and *defeat*). If our emotions can influence perception in the way that Niedenthal and Setterlund hypothesized, happy subjects should be significantly faster than sad subjects at identifying happy words as words, and sad subjects should be faster than happy subjects at identifying sad words as words. And that is exactly what happened. Niedenthal and Setterlund believe these findings are highly generalizable. By taking other research and theory into account, they argue that "emotional individuals should perceive all emotion-congruent stimuli more efficiently than other stimuli" (p. 410).

Interestingly, this effect of mood on perception seems to be extremely specific. There were other positive and negative words among the ones presented to subjects, but these words were unrelated to either happiness or sadness (e.g., *charm* was a positive word; *dislike* was a negative word). The moods of the subjects did not influence their ability to detect these words at all; subjects' moods only influenced words that were in exactly the same emotion category as the states (happy or sad) induced by the music.

*The selections were all classical music and included *Eine Kleine Nachtmusik* by Mozart (happy mood) and *Adagio for Strings* by Barber (sad mood). As part of the experiment, each subject's mood was measured after the mood induction to ensure that the manipulation worked as it was supposed to.

Since we are looking at the responses of the same people under different conditions, we expect their responses to be about the same—*unless our treatment conditions affect their behaviors.* If we have the same subjects in all our conditions (or matched subjects who are also somewhat similar), any differences in behavior produced by the experimental intervention will be more apparent. These differences will not be buried among the variability that is created by testing different subjects. We have increased the power of the experiment.

In a within-subjects experiment, we can also get an ongoing record of subjects' behaviors over time. This gives us a more complete picture of the way the independent variable works in the experiment. We have both practical and methodological gains with this approach. Since there are so many advantages to a within-subjects design, why not always use it?

DISADVANTAGES OF WITHIN-SUBJECTS DESIGNS

Practical Limitations

There are several reasons why within-subjects designs do not always work. Sometimes such designs are just not practical. Within-subjects designs generally require each subject to spend more time in the experiment. For instance, the various conditions of an experiment might require the subjects to read and evaluate several stories. A researcher might need to schedule several hours of testing if this experiment is run with a within-subjects design; each subject must spend several hours reading and scoring several stories. The same experiment might be run with a group of subjects in only an hour using a between-subjects design; each individual subject would spend just one hour reading and evaluating one story.

If a procedure involves testing each subject individually, a great deal of time can be taken up by resetting equipment for each condition. That could lead to extra hours of testing per subject. In a perception experiment that requires calibrating several sensitive electronic instruments for each condition, the researcher and subjects are in for some tedious testing sessions. As an alternative, several subjects in a row could be tested in each condition, requiring fewer changes to the equipment.

Experiments can easily become tedious for subjects. Subjects who are expected to perform many tasks may get restless during the experiment and begin to make hasty judgments to hurry the process along—leading to inaccurate data. For the most part, these limitations are really just inconveniences. We can seek out subjects who are willing to invest a lot of time in a study. We can spend an additional 10, 20, or even 100 hours testing subjects if it is essential to the value of the experiment. Sometimes it is, and experimenters may spend hours or even days testing each subject. But more serious problems, linked to the independent variable, limit the within-subjects approach.

Interference Between Conditions

Often each subject can be in only one condition of the experiment. Taking part in more than one condition would be either impossible or useless or would change the effect of later treatments.

Imagine that we are doing a study on car-buying preferences. We hypothesize that the type of car people first learned to drive will influence their own purchasing choices later. For simplicity, let us say that people who learn to drive in small cars (compact or smaller) will be more likely to buy small cars than people who learn to drive in full-sized cars. With the cooperation of a local driving school, we randomly assign half our subjects to each treatment condition (small or full-sized car).

We suspect that car-buying preferences are influenced by a wide range of other factors, too—including financial status, parents' choice of car, advertising, and perhaps even unidentified genetic differences in personality that influence our choices. The numerous makes and models on the market attest to the diversity of tastes. People differ a great deal in what they want in a car. Since so many subject variables are involved, perhaps a within-subjects design would be a better choice.

Actually, in this experiment our choice is simple: We cannot do a within-subjects experiment. Once a person learns to drive in a small car, he or she can never learn to drive in a full-sized car. Even if we put subjects through the same sets of lessons again, they would not respond to them in the same fashion because they are not novices any more. The first training condition would interfere with all later attempts. If one treatment condition precludes another, as it does in this kind of experiment, a between-subjects design is required.

Sometimes it is possible to run all subjects through all treatments, but it does not make sense to do this. What if we want subjects to learn a list of words? In one condition, we tell the subjects to learn the words by forming mental pictures (images) of them. In the other condition, we ask subjects to repeat the words over and over. We want to use the same list in both conditions so that the difficulty of the list will not be a confounding variable. But once the subjects have practiced the list in one condition, they will recall it more easily in the next condition. If they formed pictures of elephants sitting on flagpoles, they will remember elephants and flagpoles. Bower (1972, 1981), a well-known researcher in the field of memory, understood this phenomenon and therefore used between-subjects designs in similar experiments. The interference between different conditions of an experiment is the biggest drawback in using within-subjects designs. If the treatments clash so badly that we cannot give them to the same subjects, we need a between-subjects design.

Whenever we consider a within-subjects design, we also need to consider the possibility that effects on the dependent variable might be influenced by the order in which we give the treatments. Subjects' responses might differ from one treatment to another just because of the position, or order, of the series of treatments. In a within-subjects experiment, order is always a *potential* confound. For instance, if we were asking people to watch a series of television commercials and rate how much they liked each one, the order in which we presented the commercials might affect ratings. The first commercial they saw might always get a higher rating than it deserves simply because it is novel. By the third or fourth one, ratings of any commercial may be lower than they should be because subjects have tuned out. Advertisers know about this kind of order effect and keep their fingers crossed that their commercial will be placed first in any long commercial break. In a within-subjects design, we use special counterbalancing procedures to offset interference and to control for potential order effects between conditions.

CONTROLLING WITHIN-SUBJECTS DESIGNS

Controlling for Order Effects: Counterbalancing

Suppose we want to do some market research on a new brand of cola. We know that people differ a great deal in their preferences for foods and beverages, so we decide to use a within-subjects design. We would like to get people to compare their present brand of cola with our new brand. We will get ratings on how good our cola tastes compared to the old brands. That information will tell us whether we can expect the new product to compete with well-known brands. Our hypothesis is that our new cola will get better ratings than the old brands.

We recruit cola drinkers and bring them to our testing center. For two hours before the taste test, we keep them in a lounge in which they can relax and read magazines—but cannot eat or drink. Then we give each subject a glass of the new cola. After subjects have had time to drink it, we ask them to indicate on a rating scale how much they liked the taste. Since we want to compare subjects' ratings of the new cola with their ratings of their regular brands, we carry out a second condition. We ask all subjects to drink a glass of their favorite cola. After they finish, we get them to rate their favorite drinks on the rating scale. Now we have ratings of the two types of colas, new and old. We can compare the average ratings and see how our product competes.

Would it surprise you to learn that the average rating of our new brand was much higher than the average rating of the old brands? What is wrong with this experiment? The problem, of course, is that *any* cola might taste good after you have had nothing to drink for several hours. The first cola will taste better than the second.

In this experiment we varied the brand of cola that people were asked to drink. There were two conditions, "new brand" and "old brand." Unfortunately, in addition to varying the brand of cola, we varied an important extraneous variable—order. We created confounding by always giving subjects the new cola first. Subjects might have rated the new brand higher because it really is delicious, but the ratings were probably distorted because subjects had not had anything to drink for a full two hours before they tasted the new product. The subjects may have given the old brands lower ratings because they had just had something else to drink and were no longer thirsty.

In this experiment we see that the order in which we presented the treatment conditions (that is, the different colas) may have changed the subjects' responses. We have confounding caused by **order effects,** the changes in performance that occur when a condition falls in different places in a series of treatments.

Order effects are important in within-subjects experiments, which require that each subject be in more than one condition. Subjects will naturally receive some treatments before others. If the order of the treatments alters their effects, we can get some very distorted data. Two kinds of changes can occur when subjects are run in more than one condition. (1) **Fatigue effects** can cause performance to decline as the experiment goes on: Subjects get tired. As they solve more and more word problems, for instance, they may begin to make mistakes. They may also become bored or irritated by the experiment and merely go through the motions until it is over (see Figure 9-2). (2) Other factors may lead to improvement as the experiment proceeds—that is, to **practice effects.** As subjects become familiar with the experiment, they may relax and do a little better. They get better at using the apparatus, develop strategies for solving problems, or even catch on to the real purpose of the study.

All these changes, both positive and negative, are called **progressive error:** As the experiment progresses, results are distorted. The changes in subjects' responses are not caused by the independent variable; they are order effects produced when we run subjects through more than one treatment condition. Progressive error includes any changes in the subjects' responses that are caused by testing in multiple treatment conditions. It includes order effects, such as the effects of practice.

We control for any extraneous variable by making sure it affects all treatment conditions in the same way. We can do that by eliminating the variable completely, by holding it constant, or by balancing it out across treatment conditions. However, in a within-subjects experiment, we cannot eliminate order effects. Neither can we hold them constant, giving all subjects the treatments in the same order, because we are trying to avoid just this kind of systematic effect. But we can balance them out—distribute them across the conditions—so that they affect all conditions equally.

Think about the cola experiment. We did a poor job of setting it up because we let the order of the colas stay the same for all subjects. Everyone tasted the new brand first. How could we redo the experiment so that progressive error would affect the results for both kinds of colas in the same way? We want to be sure that subjects' ratings reflect accurate taste judgments, not merely a difference between the first and second glass of cola. Suppose we modify our procedures a little. We run the first condition the same as before: Subjects do not eat or drink for two hours; then they drink a glass of the new brand of cola and give their ratings. But instead of having them drink the old brand immediately, we have them return to the lounge for another two hours. At the end of that time, we give them the old brand of cola and get the second set of ratings. Does this help? We avoid the problem of having subjects drink the new brand after two hours in the lounge and the old brand when they are not as thirsty. However, our data may still be contaminated by the order of the conditions. When the subjects drink the new brand, they have been in the lounge a total of two hours. When they drink the old brand, they have spent four hours in the lounge. By this time, they may be tired of hanging around. They may be getting hungry. They have also had practice filling out the rating scale, as well as time to think about what they said before.

Fortunately, researchers have worked out several procedures for controlling for order effects. These procedures are called **counterbalancing,** and they all have the same function: to distribute progressive error across the different treatment conditions of the experiment. By using these procedures, we can guarantee that the order effects that alter results on one condition will be offset, or counterbalanced, by the order effects operating on other conditions.

Let us assume that we can actually graph the effects of progressive error in our cola experiment. With each subject, error accumulates as the experiment progresses. Subjects get better at filling out the rating scale, they develop criteria for evaluating taste, and so on. Their responses change relative to their responses on the first trial. Figure 9-3 illustrates what progressive error in an experiment might look like. You can see that it is low in the early part of the experiment and increases gradually as the experiment continues. If everyone tastes the new brand first, there will be less progressive error affecting that condition than any other. The experiment will be invalidated.

Subject-by-Subject Counterbalancing

We can control for progressive error in the cola experiment through one of two general approaches. First, we can control it by using **subject-by-subject counterbalancing.** The idea is to divide up the effects of progressive error so that they will be the same for all conditions that each subject completes. How can we do this? Think carefully about what Figure 9-3 illustrates. The amount of progressive error (that is, the net outcome of fatigue, practice, and so on) in an experiment changes as the experiment continues. We can never expect progressive error to be the same for both conditions as long as we always run one condition first. Progressive error will always be less for the condition we run first. Somehow we have to set up a procedure to make sure both conditions include some trials when progressive error is relatively low and others when it is relatively high.

If we try different ways of presenting two treatments, we will find one effective way to handle progressive error: Present each treatment more than once. We give each subject two glasses of each cola instead of one, but we do it in a particular order. Let us call the new brand "condition A" and the old brand "condition B." We can equalize progressive error for these two conditions by presenting them in the order ABBA. If you refer to Figure 9-3, you can gain some insight into how the ABBA procedure works.

The values of progressive error are depicted on the vertical axis for each of four successive trials. For the first trial, progressive error is equal to 1 unit; for the second trial, 2 units; for the third and fourth trials, 3 and 4 units, respectively. If we run treatment conditions in the ABBA order, we can add up the units of progressive error for condition A and condition B. Progressive error works out to be 5 units for condition A (1 unit plus 4 units) and 5 units

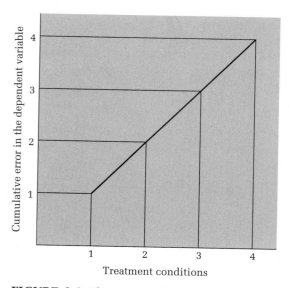

FIGURE 9-3 The impact of progressive error on responses in an experiment. The later trials (conditions) are affected more than the earlier ones.

for condition B (2 plus 3 units). Of course, these numerical quantities are hypothetical, but you can see the logic behind the counterbalancing procedure. Now both conditions contain some trials in which progressive error is relatively high and others in which it is relatively low, but the total units of error are the same for both conditions.

Using subject-by-subject counterbalancing, each subject gets the *ABBA* sequence. This guarantees that progressive error affects conditions *A* and *B* about equally for each subject, assuming progressive error follows the pattern shown in Figure 9-3. If there are more than two treatment conditions, we can counterbalance for each subject by continuing the pattern. With three conditions, each subject gets *ABCCBA*; with four, each subject gets *ABCDDCBA*; and so on.

Progressive error is not necessarily this easy to control completely. Figure 9-3 illustrates error that is *linear*; that is, described by one straight line. But suppose true error has a more complex distribution across trials. Subjects get a little better with practice; they also fatigue to some extent. But on a long series of trials, they may catch their second wind and do a bit better as the experiment draws to a close. Suppose the impact of progressive error looks more like that represented in Figure 9-4. If we use the *ABBA* procedure, progressive error will be 3 units (1 + 2) for condition *A* and 5 units (2 + 3) for condition *B*. This is little better than testing everyone on *A* first, then *B*.

The effects of progressive error are not always linear. They may be *curvilinear* or *nonmonotonic* (changing direction), as in Figure 9-4. In reality, we rarely know precisely what progressive error will look like. Therefore it is

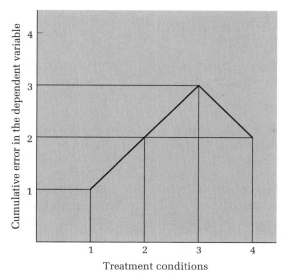

FIGURE 9-4 Nonlinear impact of progressive error in a hypothetical experiment.

especially important to be cautious when planning a design involving repeated measures for each subject. The available control procedures may not be adequate to distribute the effects of progressive error equally across all conditions. We rely on prior research to guide our decisions. Occasionally, progressive error itself must become a variable for study. When we clarify its impact beforehand, we can set up the most effective controls.

Across-Subjects Counterbalancing

One of the drawbacks of counterbalancing within each subject is that we have to present each condition to each subject more than once. As the number of conditions increases, the length of the sequence also increases. Depending on the experiment, the procedures can become time consuming, expensive, or just plain boring for the subjects as well as the experimenter. As an alternative, we can often use another set of procedures, **across-subjects counterbalancing.** These procedures serve the same basic purpose as subject-by-subject counterbalancing: They are used to distribute the effects of progressive error so that, theoretically, the effects will be the same for all conditions of the experiment. We are not always concerned about the individual subject's responses, but we still want to be sure that progressive error affects the various treatment conditions equally. These across-subjects techniques are complete and partial counterbalancing.

Complete Counterbalancing

If we always present treatment conditions in the same order, progressive error will affect some conditions more than others. Complete counterbalancing controls for this effect by using all possible sequences of the conditions and using every sequence the same number of times. If we had only two treatments, *A* and *B*, we would give half the subjects *A* and then *B*. We would give the other subjects *B* first and then *A*. You can see that this is very similar to what we did to control order effects within each subject by giving each subject both sequences, *AB* and *BA*. But when we counterbalance across subjects, we need to give each subject only one sequence. Different subjects are assigned to the sequences at random. Some subjects go through condition *A* without any practice; others go through *B* without any practice. The effects of progressive error should turn out to be about the same for each condition if we pool the data from all subjects.

It is easy to counterbalance when there are only two conditions, but suppose there are more. What if we are testing the hypothesis that people remember happy faces better than sad ones? In our experiment we have three sets of photographs. One set (*A*) shows smiling faces. The second set (*B*) shows frowning faces. The third set (*C*) is used as a control; it shows faces that appear to be neutral. We plan to show subjects each set of photographs once. Then we will ask them to go through another much larger set, say, 100 in all—and pick out the ones they have seen before. The large set will contain faces of all types so that subjects will not be able to select the correct faces simply by picking out all those that are smiling, frowning, or expressionless. Our dependent variable is the number of faces subjects can recognize from each treatment condition. Clearly, we should not show all the happy faces first. We know, for instance, that when subjects are asked to remember things, the ones they learn first may interfere with later items. Thus subjects might recognize the first set of faces more efficiently than later ones. We can control for this kind of error by using complete counterbalancing. We use all the possible sequences of the treatment conditions; we also use each sequence the same number of times.

Table 9-1 shows complete counterbalancing for an experiment with three treatment conditions. There are six possible sequences of orders for the three conditions. For our face recognition experiment, we would need order sequences like happy, neutral, sad (*ACB*) and sad, happy, neutral (*BAC*). To counterbalance completely, we must use all the sequences and use each one the same number of times. For six sequences, we would need at least six subjects. Ideally, we should have more than one subject for each sequence, so we need a number of subjects that is a multiple of 6. Remember that we have to use all the sequences an equal number of times. We can use 6, or 12, or 18 subjects but not 9, 11, or 17 because these are not multiples of 6.

TABLE 9-1 The six sequences of three treatment conditions

A	*B*	*C*	*B*	*A*	*C*
B	*C*	*A*	*C*	*B*	*A*
C	*A*	*B*	*A*	*C*	*B*

Can we tell in advance how many sequences and how many subjects we will need? How can we be sure we did not miss a sequence? You can find the number of possible sequences by computing n factorial, represented by $n!$. We get $n!$ by computing the following product:

$$n! = 1 \times 2 \times 3 \ldots (n - 1)(n)$$

This may look difficult, but it is really very simple. The n stands for the number of conditions we are working with. We begin with 1 and simply multiply each successive number together until we have gone through n. Let us see how it works by computing $4!$:

$$4! = 1 \times 2 \times 3 \times 4 = 24$$

$4!$ is equal to 24. This tells us that when we have four treatment conditions, there are 24 possible orders in which to present them.

Earlier we saw that there are six possible sequences if we have only three conditions. You can verify that by the formula too:

$$3! = 1 \times 2 \times 3 = 6$$

The number of possible order sequences clearly increases very quickly as the number of treatment conditions rises. To counterbalance an experiment completely, we need at least one subject for each possible sequence. That means we need at least four times as many subjects for a four-condition experiment as we do for a three-condition experiment (24 versus 6 possible sequences). We also need to present each sequence an equal number of times. If we want more than one subject per sequence, we will need multiples of 24 for a four-condition experiment—a minimum of 48 subjects.

Partial Counterbalancing

You can see that it is economical to keep the number of treatments to a minimum. If we double the number of conditions from three to six, we increase the minimum number of subjects needed to counterbalance completely from 6 to 720. Of course, it makes sense to omit any condition that is not necessary for a good test of the hypothesis. Still, sometimes six or even more conditions are essential. In those cases we may use **partial counterbalancing** procedures. The basic idea is the same. We use these procedures when we cannot do complete counterbalancing but still want to have some control over progressive error. Partial counterbalancing controls progressive error by using some subset of the available order sequences; these sequences are chosen through special procedures.

The simplest partial counterbalancing procedure is **randomized counterbalancing**. When there are many possible order sequences, we randomly select out as many sequences as we have subjects for the experiment. Suppose we have 120 possible sequences (five treatment conditions) and only 30 subjects. We would randomly select 30 sequences, and each subject would get one of those sequences. You can see that this procedure may not control

TABLE 9-2 Latin square counterbalancing for four treatment conditions

A	B	C	D
B	A	D	C
C	D	A	B
D	C	B	A

for order effects quite as effectively as complete counterbalancing, but it is better than simply using the same order for all subjects. If possible, use complete counterbalancing because it is safer. If you must use partial counterbalancing, be realistic about it. If there are 720 possible order sequences in the experiment, running three subjects just does not make sense. You will not be able to get good control over order effects. *As a general rule, use at least as many randomly selected sequences as there are values of the independent variable.*

Another procedure commonly used to select a subset of order sequences is called **Latin square counterbalancing.** A matrix, or square, of sequences is constructed that satisfies the following condition: Each treatment appears only once in any order position in the sequences. Table 9-2 shows a basic Latin square for an experiment with four treatment conditions. Each row represents a different order sequence. Notice that each of the four treatment conditions appears in the first, second, third, and fourth position only once. This method controls adequately for progressive error caused by order effects because each treatment condition occurs equally often in each position.

Once you have selected your sequences, you would assign subjects at random to receive the different orders. Remember that each sequence is used equally often. With four sequences, you would need to run at least four subjects. If you have more subjects available, it is always better to run more than one subject in each order condition. For the four-condition experiment, any multiple of 4 subjects could be used: 8, 12, 16, and so on.

Using a Latin square to determine treatment sequences will provide protection against order effects, but it cannot control for other kinds of *systematic interference* between two treatment conditions. Notice that some parts of the sequences tend to repeat themselves. For instance, in Table 9-2, condition *A* comes right before *B* in two out of four of the sequences. If exposure to condition *A* affects how subjects will respond to condition *B*, the Latin square will not provide enough control. The experiment can still be confounded. This kind of systematic interference is called a carryover effect.

Carryover Effects

Perry Mason, the great fictional defense attorney, always wins his cases (except once, when the client really was guilty). He always finds a way to get to the truth before the end of the trial. Imagine Perry in court, cross-examining a witness. His large, imposing frame commands respect. A witness has just iden-tified the defendant as the woman who passed close by him in the hallway outside the murder victim's apartment. The witness vividly recalls the defen-dant's rare and expensive perfume. No, he could not be mistaken about it. Perry wants to test the man's ability to identify other scents. He presents the witness with a small vial. "It is essence of lilac," says the witness confidently. The witness sniffs a second vial and correctly states, "This smells like gaso-line!" Now Mason presents the critical test—a vial containing the defendant's perfume. A dismayed and confused witness is unable to identify it. His testi-mony crumbles. He breaks down and confesses to the crime.

A dramatic and fanciful story indeed, but it illustrates another key prob-lem in the within-subjects design. Mason was using a within-subjects approach when he presented the witness with the vials. What the witness did not know was that Mason was playing with **carryover effects:** The effects of some treatments will persist, or carry over, after the treatments are removed. A few whiffs of gasoline spoiled the witness's ability to identify any other scents for a time. The guilty witness panicked and confessed.

On a smaller scale, imagine how carryover effects could sabotage experi-ments. Earlier in the chapter we saw how some combinations of treatments are impossible to administer to the same subjects because one treatment pre-cludes another. For instance, we cannot both do and not do surgery on the same animal. Similarly, we do not want to allow one experimental condition to interfere with a subsequent condition. For example, we do not want to give subjects treatments that will give them clues to what they should do in later conditions. We do not want one experimental treatment to make a later treat-ment easier (or harder). We do not want the effects of early conditions to con-taminate later conditions.

Researchers studying emotions are forced to work around this problem all the time. Suppose we are interested in studying facial muscle movements dur-ing different emotional states. Smiling, for example, is accompanied by move-ment of the *zygomaticus major,* the muscle that lifts up the corners of the mouth; frowning comes about when the *corrugator supercilii* pulls the brows together and down (Ekman, Friesen, & Ancoli, 1980). In this area of research, within-subjects designs are preferred because there are large individual dif-ferences in people's facial muscle activity. A researcher might use a series of film clips to induce different emotions in an experiment, while several pairs of electrodes are connected to the subject's face.

Ordinarily, a very funny film sketch brings on a wide smile in viewers, and a lot of electrical activity is recorded from the pair of electrodes placed above the *zygomaticus.* Conversely, the *corrugator* typically shows a lot of activity during a very sad scene. However, we cannot apply one of these treatment conditions right after another because of carryover effects. A funny scene does not seem nearly as funny as it should if a subject has just watched a tragic death scene. If we were recording the facial muscles, we would find that the activity of the *zygomaticus* was dampened by the previ-ous emotion. When inducing different emotions within subjects, researchers have to take precautions to ensure that one emotion has completely passed before they begin each new treatment. In this case they must wait until all activity from the facial muscles has stopped before they apply a new treatment condition.

Notice that carryover effects differ from order effects in an important way. Order effects emerge as a result of the *position* of a treatment in a sequence. It does not matter what the specific treatment is; if it occurs first in a sequence, subjects will handle it differently than if it occurs last. Carryover, however, is a function of the *treatment* itself. Gasoline will produce changes in the ability to detect odor no matter whether the subject smells it first, second, or last. Feeling sadness will carry over to the next emotion regardless of whether sadness is the first, second, or fourth condition in the experiment.

We can control for carryover effects to some extent. If treatments affect each other about equally, an experimenter can get reasonably good control by using some of the same procedures that control for order effects—counterbalancing. Subject-by-subject counterbalancing and complete counterbalancing will usually control carryover effects adequately by balancing them out over the entire experiment. Control is less assured with randomized counterbalancing, and it may not be controlled at all if Latin square counterbalancing is used.[3]

Choosing Among Counterbalancing Procedures

Every experiment with a within-subjects condition will need some form of counterbalancing. In a within-subjects design with one independent variable or a within-subjects factorial design, you must counterbalance all conditions. If the design is a within-subjects factorial, remember to multiply the levels of each factor together to get the total number of conditions. For instance, our earlier factorial example of comparing slides of men and women displaying four different expressions (a 4 × 2 within-subjects design) has eight conditions that need to be counterbalanced. In a mixed design, only within-subjects factors need to be counterbalanced.

Deciding whether to use subject-by-subject or across-subjects counterbalancing can be a problem in itself. We need to counterbalance for each subject when we expect large differences in the pattern of progressive error from subject to subject. In a weightlifting experiment, we might expect subjects to fatigue at different rates. In that sort of experiment, it makes sense to counterbalance conditions for each person in the study because that would give the most control over order and carryover effects. In some experiments we do not expect large differences in the way progressive error affects each subject. To put it another way, if we could graph progressive error for *each* subject, in some experiments the graphs might look about the same. We do not need to worry about progressive error within each subject when we know the effects will be about the same for everyone.

---

[3]Using mathematical techniques, it is possible to construct special Latin squares (called *balanced Latin squares*) that can control for both systematic treatment effects and order effects. In balanced Latin squares, each treatment condition (1) appears only once in each position in the order sequence, and (2) precedes or follows every other condition an equal number of times. Construction techniques are demonstrated in Elmes, Kantowitz, and Roediger (1995).

There are practical things to consider, too. You may not have the time to run through all the conditions more than once for each subject. You may not have enough subjects to make across-subjects procedures feasible. The same considerations that come into play as you select a within- or between-subjects design can also limit your choice of controls in the within-subjects experiment. Again, you should look at the procedures that have been used in similar experiments. If prior researchers have had success with across-subjects counterbalancing, it is probably all right to use it. Try to avoid randomized and Latin square counterbalancing if you expect carryover effects. When in doubt, counterbalance subject by subject if you can. The worst that can happen is that you may overcontrol the experiment. It is always a good idea to use the procedures that give the most control, simply because you may not know what the extraneous variables are or whether progressive error really will be the same for all subjects.

Although we have talked about counterbalancing mainly in the context of within-subjects designs, counterbalancing procedures can be useful in between-subjects experiments, too. For example, in an experiment on list learning, a researcher might compare two different study conditions on people's ability to memorize a list of ten words. The researcher would want both groups to memorize the same ten words to make sure that the lists were equally difficult in both study conditions. In addition, it might be desirable to use several different random orders of the items on each list and randomly assign some number of subjects in each group to each different list. If just one order were used, the possibility exists that the list contained some logical sequence that was easier to learn under one set of conditions than another. Whenever subjects are presented with an experimental *stimulus* that is really a group of items (words, pictures, stories, and the like), the order of the items should be counterbalanced to avoid confounding. You may find other opportunities to apply the counterbalancing procedures you have learned as you design your own experiments.

Order as a Design Factor

If you are concerned that a partial counterbalancing technique might not be controlling adequately for progressive error or carryover effects, there is a way to test whether treatments are producing similar effects in all order sequences. (Researchers do this fairly routinely if they use a Latin square and have four or less order sequences.) You can simply include treatment order as a factor in the design. Suppose you wanted to conduct the happy (*H*) versus sad (*S*) film clip experiment described earlier. You might be concerned that one type of film produces more carryover than another. It would be a good idea to include order as a factor in your design. With only two treatment conditions, it should be fairly easy to use both possible order sequences: Half the subjects receive the sequence *HS*, and the other half receive *SH*. Your experiment would be statistically analyzed as a 2 × 2 (Order × Film) mixed-factorial design. (Order is always a between-subjects factor.)

If the order factor produced no significant effects, you can feel more confident that your counterbalancing procedure worked. However, if the order of
treatments produced effects, you will know your experiment is confounded!
Effects on the dependent variable may have been produced by the order of
treatments, rather than by the treatments themselves.

Sometimes, as we saw with Perry Mason and the gasoline, you will find
that the effect of one condition *is* much greater than that of others. Gasoline
altered the witness's performance more than lilacs did or onions would. When
one condition has more impact than the others, we say that the carryover
effects are *asymmetrical*—or, more simply, lopsided. When one condition car-
ries over more than the others, control is extremely difficult, if not impossible. In such situations an experimenter should reconsider the design of the
experiment and switch to a between-subjects design if possible.

HOW CAN YOU CHOOSE A DESIGN?

How do you decide whether to use a within-subjects or a between-subjects
design? First, as always, think about the hypothesis of the experiment. How
many treatment conditions do you need to test the hypothesis? Would it be
possible to have each subject in more than one of these conditions? If so, you
may be able to use a within-subjects design. Do your treatment conditions interfere with one another? Yes? Then you ought to use a between-subjects design.

Consider the practical advantages of each approach. Is it simpler to run
the experiment one way or the other? Which will be more time consuming?
If you can get only a few subjects, the within-subjects design may be better.
Remember that there is a trade-off: The longer the experiment takes, the
harder it may be to find willing subjects (and the more likely it is that they
will become fatigued).

You can control subject variables best in a within-subjects design. If there
are likely to be large individual differences in the way subjects respond to the
experiment, the within-subjects approach is usually better.

Remember to review the research literature. If other experimenters have
used within-subjects designs for similar problems, it is probably because that
approach works best. If all other things seem equal, use the within-subjects
design. It is better from a statistical standpoint; you maximize your chances
of detecting the effect of the independent variable.

SUMMARY

Within-subjects designs are designs in which each subject takes part in more
than one condition of the experiment. These designs are advantageous because
they enable us to compare the behavior of the same subjects under different
treatment conditions. We can often get a more precise picture of the effects
of the independent variable from a within-subjects design than we can from
a between-subjects design. Subject variables are better controlled in the

within-subjects experiment. We eliminate the error produced by differences between subjects and thus make a more precise assessment of the impact of the independent variable. *Within-subjects factorial designs* and *mixed designs* can also be used.

However, complicated control problems occur in experiments using within-subjects designs because each subject takes part in more than one condition of the experiment. In these experiments we have to control for two kinds of extraneous variables, order effects and carryover effects.

Order effects are the positive and negative changes in performance that occur when a treatment condition falls in different places in a series of treatments. All these changes, both positive and negative, are called *progressive error*: Results are distorted as the experiment progresses. We looked at three forms of *counterbalancing* procedures for controlling order effects. All have the same basic function, to distribute progressive error across the different treatment conditions of the experiment.

Subject-by-subject counterbalancing controls for progressive error for each individual subject; it consists of presenting all treatment conditions twice, first in one order, then in reverse order. With two treatment conditions, for example, each subject will get the sequence *ABBA. Across-subjects counterbalancing* (complete and partial counterbalancing) can accomplish some of the same goals by pooling all subjects' data together to equalize the effects of progressive error for each condition. *Complete counterbalancing* requires using all the possible sequences that can be formed out of the treatment conditions and using each sequence the same number of times. The number of subjects needed for a completely counterbalanced experiment increases very rapidly as the number of treatment conditions increases. With three conditions, there must be a minimum of 6 subjects (3 factorial, or 3!); with six conditions, there must be a minimum of 720 subjects (6!). When complete counterbalancing is not feasible, we may use a *partial counterbalancing* procedure such as *randomized counterbalancing*. This involves selecting a subset of all the available sequences at random. A second partial counterbalancing technique, *Latin square counterbalancing,* is a particularly effective procedure for controlling order effects.

As well as order effects, there may also be *carryover effects* in a within-subjects experiment. These occur when the treatment conditions affect each other. Most carryover effects can be controlled adequately by using within-subjects counterbalancing or complete counterbalancing. One technique to consider for assessing order or carryover effects is taking treatment order as a factor in the design.

Deciding on the particular form of counterbalancing to use may be difficult. Subject-by-subject counterbalancing offers the most control and should be used whenever possible. If this cannot be used, across-subjects counterbalancing has many practical advantages. Counterbalancing of some form must be used in every experiment that has a within-subjects design. The procedures may also be useful in between-subjects experiments containing series of trials. It is always better to err on the side of controlling too much; there is more danger in failing to control an element of the experiment that could affect the results.

KEY TERMS

Across-subjects counterbalancing A technique for controlling progressive error that pools all subjects' data together to equalize the effects of progressive error for each condition.

Carryover effect The persistence of the effect of a treatment condition after the condition ends.

Complete counterbalancing A technique for controlling progressive error that uses all possible sequences that can be formed out of the treatment conditions and uses each sequence the same number of times.

Counterbalancing A technique for controlling order effects by distributing progressive error across the different treatment conditions of the experiment; may also control carryover effects.

Fatigue effects Changes in performance caused by fatigue, boredom, or irritation.

Latin square counterbalancing A partial counterbalancing technique in which a matrix, or square, of sequences of treatment conditions is constructed to which subjects are assigned at random.

Mixed design A factorial design that combines within-subjects and between-subjects factors.

Order effects Change in subjects' performance that occurs when a condition falls in different positions in a series of treatments.

Partial counterbalancing A technique for controlling progressive error by using some subset of the available sequences of treatment conditions.

Power The chance of detecting a genuine effect of the independent variable.

Practice effect Change in subjects' performance resulting from practice.

Progressive error Fatigue, practice, and other extraneous sequence effects producing changes in subjects' responses during within-subjects experiments.

Randomized counterbalancing The simplest partial counterbalancing procedure in which the experimenter randomly selects as many sequences of treatment conditions as there are subjects for the experiment.

Repeated-measures design A design in which subjects are measured more than once on the dependent variable; same as a within-subjects design.

Subject-by-subject counterbalancing A technique for controlling progressive error for each individual subject by presenting all treatment conditions twice, first in one order, then in reverse order.

Within-subjects design A design in which each subject takes part in more than one condition of the experiment.

REVIEW AND STUDY QUESTIONS

1. What is a within-subjects experiment? How is it different from a between-subjects experiment?

2. Discuss three advantages and three disadvantages of using a within-subjects design.

3. Outline a within-subjects experiment to test this hypothesis: Children who are given weaponlike toys (for example, toy guns and knives) become more aggressive.

4. Mary is very excited about the within-subjects approach. "Now I'll never need to run large numbers of subjects again," she says. What has she forgotten?

5. For each of the following dependent measures, evaluate the pros and cons of using a within-subjects approach:
   a. The taste of a new toothpaste
   b. The cavity-preventing properties of a new toothpaste
   c. The readability of a new typeface
   d. The impact of good and bad news

6. Explain how the levels of your independent variable can influence your decision to use a within- or between-subjects design.

7. What requirements must be met to make the within-subjects approach feasible?

8. You are planning an experiment on anagrams (scrambled words). You want to test whether different scramble patterns lead to different solution rates. For instance, the letter order 54321 might be easier to solve than 41352 (12345 represents the actual word). You want to use the same words in all conditions so that the type of word will not be a confounding variable. People solve anagrams at different rates, so you are thinking about using a within-subjects design.
   a. If you use a within-subjects design for this experiment, will you have to worry about order effects? Why or why not?
   b. Review the three counterbalancing techniques (subject by subject, complete, and partial) for handling order effects discussed in this chapter. Which would help you most in this experiment? Why?
   c. What are carryover effects? Would they be a problem in this experiment? How would you handle them?

9. You have just bought two new pairs of shoes and are wondering which will wear better. Design a within-subjects experiment that would answer your question. What extraneous variables would you want to control? Would counterbalancing be useful in this study? How?

10. A television commercial showed people tasting and choosing between two colas. One was labeled R; the other was labeled Q. The majority of people said they liked cola R better than cola Q. Given what you know about experimental design, would you accept the ad's claim that cola R tastes better than cola Q? Why or why not? How might you change the procedures to get more acceptable data?

11. Explain why (when it is used as a factor in a design) order is always a between-subjects factor.

12. Figure 9-5 illustrates progressive error measured in an experiment on breathing rate during weightlifting. Because of warmup and fatigue effects

FIGURE 9-5 Progressive error in an experiment on breathing rate during weightlifting.

across subjects, progressive error was curvilinear. Based on the figure, what strategy would you recommend for handling progressive error in this experiment and why?

13. Two Latin squares for four treatment conditions (*A*, *B*, *C*, and *D*) are shown here:

```
A  B  C  D        A  B  C  D
B  A  D  C        B  D  A  C
C  D  A  B        C  A  D  B
D  C  B  A        D  C  B  A
```

a. What is each one called?
b. Which one(s) controls for order effects?
c. Which one(s) controls for both order and carryover effects?

WITHIN-SUBJECTS DESIGNS: SMALL *N*

All the experimental designs we have discussed thus far have required manipulating or selecting independent variable(s) and testing a number of subjects. These are called **large N designs** (N stands for the number of subjects needed in the experiment). The large N approach is by far the most common technique used in research design, but it is not the only approach used by contemporary researchers.

SMALL N DESIGNS

Some researchers prefer to use **small N designs,** which test only one or a very few subjects. These researchers argue that large N designs lack precision because they *pool,* or combine, the data from many different subjects to reach conclusions about the effects of independent variables. The conclusions of large N experiments can sometimes be misleading because they obscure the results of individual subjects, who can vary widely in their responses to treatment conditions. Small N researchers argue that aggregate effects are artificial, since they often do not represent what really occurs with any individual subject—instead, large N experiments can reveal only general trends, which might produce dubious conclusions. For example, it is possible to miss the effect of an independent variable in a large N experiment. Responses of different subjects to the same independent variable can vary greatly; sometimes they may even cancel each other out, giving the appearance that no effects at all were produced. The following example will demonstrate how that might happen.

Suppose you used an experimental group–control group design to test the hypothesis that children pay more attention to cartoons that contain violence than they do to control cartoons. You measure attention by tracking the children's eye movements. At the end of the experiment, your statistics show no differences between the two groups. You conclude that children do not pay more attention to violent cartoons—but your conclusion might be erroneous. Your conclusion could be wrong if there are large individual differences in the way children respond to violence. For instance, when cartoons are violent, fearful children might spend *less* time watching the screen, but nonfearful children might spend *more.* In this case, the experimental group's pooled data might look quite similar to data from the control group. Your large N design is simply not sensitive enough to detect two competing kinds of effects.

Small N designs take a very different approach to studying effects of independent variables. Here the behavior of one or a few subjects is studied much more intensely. Typically, the researcher measures the subject's behavior many times. A subject can be studied in one intensive session or over a period of weeks, months, or even years. Small N designs are used in the laboratory and in the field; they can be used to study both human and animal behavior.

Sometimes small N designs are used for practical reasons. In clinical psychopathology research, for example, a psychologist might wish to conduct an experiment to test a new therapy treatment for depressed individuals. It might not be possible for the researcher to find enough depressed individuals to form experimental and control groups for a large N study; however, a small N experiment could be conducted in which the progress of one or a few patients could be studied intensively. (This is one approach to solving the ethical dilemma of untreated control groups that we talked about in Chapter 7.)

Animal researchers very often use small N designs for practical reasons. Research animals, from mice to chimpanzees, are costly to acquire and maintain, and their training often involves months or years. Sometimes animals must be sacrificed so that their brain or other tissues may be studied. In these cases, researchers try to use as few animals as possible; here small N designs make a great deal of sense.

Another area of psychology in which small N designs are common is *psychophysics* (the study of how we sense and perceive physical stimuli). Basic psychophysical processes operate in a very similar way for most individuals, so researchers can obtain a good picture of how these processes operate by testing a very small number of subjects. Small N research of this kind has a venerable history in psychology. In fact, a major component of early experimentation in the United States in the late nineteenth century was the study of psychophysical processes, which relied on the single-subject approach almost exclusively. If additional subjects were tested at all, they were used to replicate effects produced on a single subject. It wasn't until Sir Ronald Fisher invented the statistical technique called analysis of variance in the 1930s (Fisher, 1935) that large N or group designs requiring inferential statistics began to gain in popularity.

Small N designs are used in many areas of psychology, but nowhere are they used more extensively than in experimentation using principles of *Skinnerian conditioning* (named for B. F. Skinner, who was mentioned in Chapter 5), a form of behaviorism that relies on operant conditioning. Skinner thought there was often more to gain by careful, continuous measurement of the behavior of a single subject than by using statistical tests to compare data obtained from different groups of subjects. Skinner's approach uses just one or two subjects and requires special measurement procedures. Let us look at these procedures in a simple hypothetical experiment.

A Small N Design: Talking to Plants

We want to test the notion that talking to a plant makes it grow better. Of course, we want to approach this hypothesis in a rigorous, scientific way. On one hand, we could use a large N design, such as a two-group experiment. We could compare different groups of plants by talking to one group but not to the other. Then we would measure their growth and see how the groups compare. Or we might plan a multiple-groups experiment and use varying amounts of talking as our treatment conditions. We might even choose (as we did in Chapter 9) to look at a second variable, such as music, and set up a factorial design.

On the other hand, instead of sacrificing our entertainment budget for a whole year to purchase enough plant subjects to conduct a large N study, we could use a small N design to do our experiment. First, we carefully choose our subject. Cactus grows too slowly to be of much use; bamboo grows very quickly but needs a temperate climate. After some library research, we settle on the hardy *ficus elastica*, better known as the rubber plant. We begin with the control condition of the experiment (condition A): For a time, we do not talk to the plant at all. During this period—say, three months—we simply chart its growth by measuring it each Monday. This establishes a **baseline** of behavior, a measure of behavior as it normally occurs without the experimental manipulation. In the second phase of the experiment, we introduce the experimental manipulation (condition B): For another three months, we talk to the plant for 2 hours a day. "Talking" is operationally defined as reading aloud from Euell Gibbons's *Stalking the Wild Asparagus* (1970). We continue to chart the plant's growth each Monday throughout this phase of the experiment. If talking aids growth, the plant should grow more during the second part of the experiment. If talking has no effect on growth, the plant should continue to grow about as much as it did in the baseline condition.

So far, this procedure looks very much like what we do when we carry out a two-group design: We use a control group to establish a baseline of behavior, and we compare behavior in the experimental condition with what we see in the control condition. In those respects, the procedures are similar, but there is also an important difference. Since we are using only one subject, we are looking at that subject at different points in time. Our rubber plant is three months older by the time we finish the first set of observations. The season has changed. The plant now gets a different amount of light each day. The humidity has probably changed, too. Of course, some of these extraneous variables can be controlled. We can raise our plant in a laboratory in which light, temperature, and moisture are always the same. But we cannot discount the fact that the plant has aged. Any differences in the amount of growth we see during the experimental manipulation might be caused by natural changes in the growth cycle of this plant (the classic threat called *maturation*). In other words, we may have confounding. For this reason, the small N experiment includes one additional, crucial step. After completing the experimental manipulation, we remove the independent variable and return to the original control condition (A). We do not talk to the subject at all during the last three months of the experiment; we simply continue to monitor its growth (see Figure 10-1).

We can verify the effect of our independent variable in the small N experiment by returning to the original baseline condition. Our hypothesis is that talking to a plant makes it grow faster. Suppose that our plant did grow faster in the second phase of the experiment; compared to the baseline condition, the plant grew faster when we talked to it. If the change in growth rate was produced by some extraneous variable such as maturation, the growth rate will probably not change much after we stop talking to the plant. On the other hand, if talking caused the plant to grow faster, we would expect a decline in the growth rate after we stop. But under some circumstances, the change in behavior caused by an experimental manipulation may persist even after the experimental manipulation has been discontinued. If the target

FIGURE 10-1 Hypothetical growth of a single *ficus elastica* in an *ABA* experiment.

behavior does not return to the baseline level, we cannot automatically rule out the effect of the independent variable. One problem is that no matter how hard we try, we may not be able to recreate the original baseline conditions perfectly. This is especially true in experiments outside the laboratory. In these cases, we may want to repeat the procedures more than once. We can return to the baseline condition and reapply the experimental manipulation many times if we wish. Often we need to do that several times to make sure our findings were not produced by some chance variation in the testing situation.

ABA DESIGNS

The small N experiment on the rubber plant used an **ABA design.** *ABA* (as in Figure 10-1) refers to the order of the conditions of the experiment: *A* (the baseline condition) comes first, followed by *B* (the experimental condition). Finally, we return to the baseline condition (*A*) to verify that the change in behavior is linked to the independent variable. *ABA* designs may only be used if the treatment conditions are reversible; for that reason, they are also called *reversal designs.* Many small N experiments use the *ABA* design. (*ABA* designs are sometimes used with a large N too, as demonstrated in Box 10-1.)

Variations of the *ABA* Format

Frequently, researchers use other variations of the *ABA* format. In one amusing experiment, Hall (1971) reports on the case of a new bride who was

B O X   1 0 - 1

AN EXAMPLE OF AN *ABA* DESIGN USING A LARGE *N*

Pedalino and Gamboa (1974) wanted to study the behavior of workers in a large manufacturing and distribution center. Specifically, they wanted to see how they could get more people to come to work regularly using Skinner's positive reinforcement principle. They hypothesized that attendance would improve if people were rewarded for coming to work. Their independent variable was reinforcement; their dependent variable was absenteeism. For practical reasons, Pedalino and Gamboa decided against using a random groups design. Because the workers were spread over several offices, it would be impossible to monitor and control all the changes in working conditions that could occur during the experiment; for example, supervisors would be rotated; some workers would get raises; some might quit and others take their places. They also wished to see what would happen to the same workers before, during, and after the experimental intervention, so they tested their hypothesis using a large *N*, *ABA* design.

First, they collected baseline data by measuring the amount of absenteeism under the usual working conditions. The experimental condition was a lottery poker game. During this condition, each employee was allowed to pick a card from a deck of playing cards on each day he or she came to work on time. At the end of the five-day work week, the employee with the best poker hand won $20. During the time the lottery was in effect, absenteeism dropped 18%. When the lottery was stopped, people began skipping work more often. Pedalino and Gamboa concluded that the lottery poker game had reduced absenteeism.

You can see that switching back to the baseline condition was essential to test this hypothesis. If the researchers had not returned to the baseline condition, it is possible that their results might have been the result of a *history* threat to internal validity. Something else might have happened about the same time the lottery was started. Maybe everyone had just gotten a raise and felt better about coming to work. Maybe the flu season ended. But we know that the lottery produced a change in attendance because absenteeism rose again when the lottery ended. As a further check, Pedalino and Gamboa started up the lottery again and absenteeism dropped again.

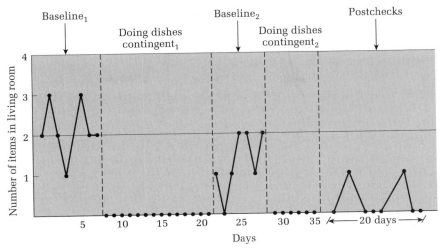

FIGURE 10-2 A record of the number of clothing items left in the living room by a newlywed husband. From "Managing Behavior. 3: Applications in School and Home," by R. V. Hall, S. J. Alley, and L. Cox. Copyright ©1971 PRO-ED, Inc. Reprinted with permission.

having a problem with her husband: "According to the wife, Jim's jacket was a permanent fixture on the back of the couch and his shoes could usually be found close by. Occasionally he would decorate the back of the chair with a sweater" (p. 43). The bride did not want to pick up after Jim or continue nagging him to put his clothes away. The solution was found through a simple behavior-modification experiment. In these kinds of experiments, researchers try to change behaviors by applying various rewards and punishments as the independent variable. Rewards and punishments are presented as a consequence of the target behaviors to be modified. Researchers often use small N designs to do this. Let us look further at Hall's experiment, which used an **ABABA design**.

First, of course, the experimenters needed a baseline of behavior. We need to know how often the husband left his clothes in the living room under the usual circumstances. Each day for a week, records were made of how many items of clothing remained in the living room for more than 15 minutes; the average was two per day. During the experimental phase of the study, husband and wife agreed that whoever left more clothing in the living room during the week would have to do the dishes the following week. Leaving clothing in the living room then had a specific consequence. The husband could avoid that consequence by putting his clothes away. During the two-week experimental period, the husband left no clothing in the living room. (Presumably the tidy wife did the same, so it is not clear who actually did the dishes during that time.) The results are shown in days 8 through 21 of Figure 10-2.

Did the threat of doing the dishes (the independent variable) really produce the change in behavior? Perhaps the husband just became more aware of his wife's concern for the appearance of the house. The wife thought the problem was solved, so she let her husband know that the threat of dishwashing was lifted; nothing more would happen if he left his clothes in the living room. The outcome is illustrated in days 22 through 28 in Figure 10-2. You can see that the husband went back to leaving his clothes in the room when the threat of doing the dishes was removed. It seemed that the threat really did affect his behavior. Still, you can also see from the figure that he did not leave quite as many clothes around as before. It may be that the second baseline period was not exactly identical to the first. For instance, if the weather had warmed up, Jim's jacket may have stayed in the closet during that time. This story had a happy ending. As you can see from the figure, after additional training (doing dishes, contingent$_2$), Jim was much more consistent in putting his clothes away.

It is also possible to use several different experimental conditions in a small N experiment by extending the ABA format. We can proceed using different treatment conditions as follows: AB_1 AB_2 AB_3, and so on. What is important is that we collect baseline data before any experimental intervention and that we return to the baseline condition after each experimental treatment.

The small N design is frequently used to test the effects of positive or negative reinforcement (as well as punishment) on individuals with behavioral problems. The small N approach can be applied to many behavior-modification problems (see Box 10-2).

Up to this point, we have focused on the importance of returning to the baseline conditions to verify the impact of our independent variable. However, in many clinical and behavior modification studies, researchers choose not to return to the baseline condition, even temporarily. Kazdin (1992) explains why:

> If behavior did revert to baseline levels when treatment was suspended temporarily, such a change would be clinically undesirable. Essentially, returning the client to baseline levels of performance amounts to making behavior worse. . . . In most circumstances, the idea of making a client worse just when treatment may be having an effect is ethically unacceptable. (p. 168)

This is clearly true in experiments done to modify self-injurious behaviors. Suppose you were working with a disturbed child who hit his head against the wall, kicked himself, and punched himself with his fists. Tate and Baroff (1966) reported their work with just such a boy. When the boy, Sam, harmed himself, Tate and Baroff stopped talking to him and stopped holding his hand. With these and other interventions, Sam's self-destructive behaviors decreased.

How do we know that not talking to Sam and not holding his hand actually caused the change in behavior? Perhaps the change was just a coincidence. Would we want to find out? Would we want to return to an original set of

B O X   1 0 - 2

AN *ABAB* DESIGN TO IMPROVE CHILDREN'S HOMEWORK PERFORMANCE

Miller and Kelley (1994) designed behavioral interventions to improve children's homework performance. Two boys and two girls (ages 9–11) participated along with a parent who would actually implement the treatment program. The researchers combined two behavioral techniques usually employed alone: goal setting and contingencies. Each parent and child signed a contract similar to the following:

The following materials need to be brought home every day: **homework pad, workbooks, text books, pencils.**

If (child's name) remembers to bring home all of these materials, then he/she may choose one of the following rewards: **gumballs, 10¢.**

However, if (child's name) forgets to bring home some homework materials, then he/she: **does not get a snack before bed.**

(child's name) may choose one of the following rewards if he/she meets 90% to 100% of his/her goals: **late bedtime (by 20 minutes), 2 stickers** or one of these if he/she meets 75% to 89% of her goals: **soda, 1 sticker.**

If (child's name) meets **80%** or more of the goals on at least **3** days this week, he/she may choose one of the following BONUS rewards: **renting a videotape, having a friend from school over to play.**

_____   _____
Child's signature   Parent's signature

The researchers tailored each child's program and contract to include appropriate goals and contingencies, including rewards that ranged from gum balls to trips to the mall. Homework accuracy was one of the dependent measures. An *ABAB* design was used. Baseline levels of homework accuracy were measured first (baseline$_1$). Then, accuracy was measured during a period of treatment (the goals and contracted contingencies were in place). Next, to ascertain whether the intervention was responsible for improvement, the treatment was removed and accuracy was again measured (baseline$_2$). Finally, the intervention was reinstituted, and accuracy was measured again.

Each child's homework performance was better during the treatment periods than during the baseline periods, suggesting that the interventions were successful. Some children, however, improved more than others. Children who showed the fewest behavioral problems, in general,

(continued)

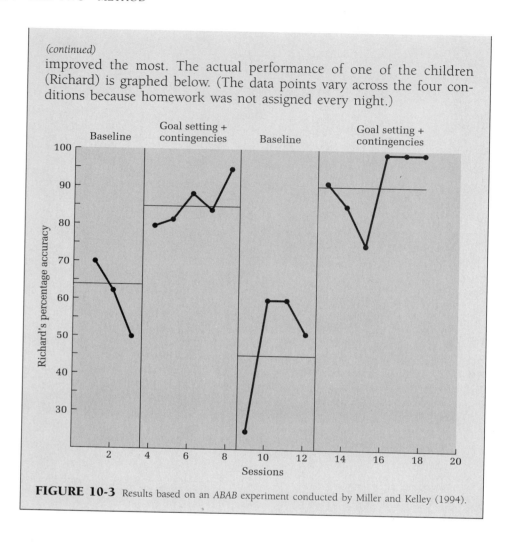

(continued)

improved the most. The actual performance of one of the children (Richard) is graphed below. (The data points vary across the four conditions because homework was not assigned every night.)

FIGURE 10-3 Results based on an *ABAB* experiment conducted by Miller and Kelley (1994).

conditions that might make Sam hurt himself again? No. Even though the experimental procedures require a return to the baseline conditions, psychologists sacrifice some scientific precision for ethical reasons. When we make an intervention that we hope will be therapeutic, our primary goal is helping the patient. If we succeed in changing his or her behavior to something more adaptive using only an **AB design**, we have accomplished that goal.

MULTIPLE-BASELINE DESIGN

In Sam's case, a reversal design might be possible even though we would not wish to use it for ethical reasons. In certain cases, we cannot consider a reversal design for other reasons. For example, when the effects of the treatment

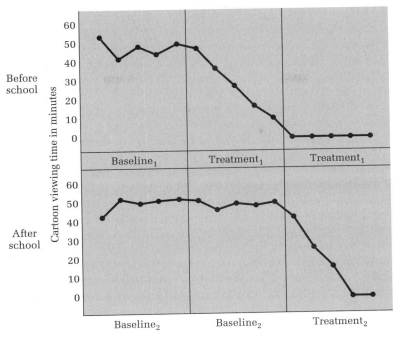

FIGURE 10-4 Hypothetical results of multiple baseline design to reduce cartoon viewing time of a 6-year-old boy.

are not reversible, we cannot use one of the family of reversal, or *ABA*, designs. In other cases, a researcher might want to assess the effects of a treatment on two or more different behaviors. Or a researcher might be interested in testing the effects of an intervention on a behavior that occurs in multiple settings or situations. In all these instances, the researcher has the option of using a **multiple-baseline design**, in which a series of baselines and treatments are compared within the same person, but once it is established, a treatment is not withdrawn.[1]

Let us look briefly at a hypothetical example of one of these designs (shown in Figure 10-4). Imagine that a parent wants to institute a program to decrease the amount of time a 6-year-old boy spends watching television cartoons. The most cartoon viewing occurs in two settings: before school and after school. The parent decides to reward the child when he does something else at these times by awarding him points, which can be accumulated and traded in at the end of each week for toys. To use a multiple baseline design, the parent would collect baseline data for each setting, and institute the reinforcement program at different intervals. Suppose the parent begins with the early morning setting first (treatment₁). After behavior change is established here, the parent can add treatment for the second setting. Now the boy would

[1]A multiple baseline design could also be used to assess the effect of an intervention across different people.

receive reinforcement for both the early morning and after school sessions. Each setting is continuously monitored during the entire period so that the parent can see that cartoon viewing in each of the two settings drops after it is reinforced, but not before, suggesting that the reward program has been successful. If other settings, such as weekend mornings, were also a problem, the parent could have included them in the design as well.

Have you noticed something unusual about the small N experiments you have learned about so far? We have not mentioned statistics at all. That is because most small N experiments do not use them, even though there are statistics that can be used on single-subject and other small N designs.[2] Often it is possible to determine whether the independent variable had an effect simply by looking at the data. In the small N study described earlier, for example, statistics would not be necessary to judge whether the boy's cartoon viewing had dropped. The use of statistics in these designs seems to be increasing, although it remains controversial (Schweigert, 1994). One role of statistics is to allow us to make inferences about the population from our sample. Some argue that it is not reasonable to make generalizations about whole populations from data on a single subject. Also, unless 50 to 100 measurements are taken during each treatment and baseline phase of the experiment, the pattern of data obtained from a single subject may violate the assumptions behind many statistical procedures (these will be discussed further in later chapters). Statistics can be useful, however, when the pattern of data is too ambiguous to interpret just by looking—for instance, when there are frequent ups and downs (i.e., variability) in the behavior of interest.

DISCRETE TRIALS DESIGNS

The designs we have looked at so far have all used baselines to control for behavior as it normally occurs without the experimental manipulation. However, another type of small N design frequently used in psychophysical research is the **discrete trials design**, which does not rely on baselines. Instead, it relies on presenting and averaging across many, many applications of different treatment conditions, and comparing performance on the dependent variable across treatment conditions. Repeated presentation over many trials can provide a reliable picture of the effects of the independent variable. And because individuals' sensory systems are quite similar, the results from a small number of subjects is generalizable to others. An experiment testing auditory perception will demonstrate how the design works.

Ivry and Lebby (1993) wanted to know whether auditory perception of high and low frequency tones would evidence right versus left hemisphere asymmetry. Stated simply, the researchers tested whether the two types of tones were processed more efficiently by different sides of the brain. To find out, they tested four subjects using a discrete trials design. The task of the subjects was to judge whether a set of three different tones was, on the aver-

[2]If you are interested in more information about this, a good place to begin is Schweigert (1994).

age, higher or lower than a target tone (Ivry & Lebby, 1993; experiment 4). The target tones were either high (ranging around 1900 Hz) or low (ranging around 200 Hz) frequency. Each subject participated in four different sessions; two tested high-frequency tones, and two tested low-frequency tones. The tones were presented to either the right or left ear. Discrimination of high-frequency tones was faster and more accurate when the tones were presented to the right ear (the right ear is controlled by the *left* hemisphere of the brain), whereas discrimination of low-frequency tones was faster and more accurate when they were presented to the left ear (controlled by the right hemisphere).

Hemispheric differences were quite small. For example, it took subjects slightly more than 500 msec (half a second) to make each judgment, and the difference between tones presented to the right or left ear averaged only about 20 msec. In this experiment, statistics *were* used to compare tones presented to different ears, showing that the hemispheric asymmetry was significant. Each subject participated in 2688 trials during the four experimental sessions, providing a clear picture of the small, but stable, asymmetry.

WHEN TO USE LARGE N AND SMALL N DESIGNS

The small N design is appropriate when studying a particular subject, such as a disturbed child. It is also useful when very few subjects are available. You can actually carry out an entire experiment with just one subject, although this is not often ideal. A small N study may have little external validity. When we do experiments, we usually want to be able to generalize from our results—we want to be able to make statements about people or pigeons (see Box 10-3) that were not actually subjects in an experiment. Many researchers prefer to do large N studies because they believe that they can generalize from their results more successfully. All other things being equal, an experiment with more subjects has greater generalizability.

In a large N study, we may form separate groups of subjects for each treatment condition. The subjects run through their assigned conditions, and we then measure them on the dependent variable. We pool data from each group and evaluate them statistically to see if the groups behaved differently. In a small N experiment, we watch one or two subjects over an extended period of time. We record baseline data. We introduce the experimental intervention and monitor the changes in the dependent variable throughout the experimental condition. Typically, we take several measurements. We can see whether the effect of the experimental intervention is instant or whether it builds over time. We continue to measure after the intervention is removed. We can verify that the independent variable causes changes in behavior because we can see what happens when that variable is removed. In short, we may get a more complete and accurate picture from a small N study than from a large N study that tests the same hypothesis.

Then why not use a small N design for every experiment? We would certainly save a lot of time recruiting subjects. But is it safe to generalize from a small N study? Small N researchers say yes, as long as we can evaluate how

BOX 10 - 3

TEACHING PIGEONS TO DISCRIMINATE PAINTINGS BY MONET AND PICASSO

Watanabe, Sakamoto, and Wakita (1995) conducted a small *N* experiment using pigeons as subjects, which produced surprising results—pigeons could be trained to discriminate the painting style of Monet from that of Picasso—and even to recognize the painter's style in paintings not seen before. This experiment featured a special form of discrete trials design.

The researchers first selected a set of 20 slides of paintings (10 by Monet and 10 by Picasso). Monet and Picasso were chosen because the styles differed dramatically: Most of the paintings of Monet, an Impressionist, have round contours (as in Figure 10-5); typical paintings by Picasso, considered a Cubist, have sharp contours (as in Figure 10-6). To make sure that the pigeons were not influenced by the different colors favored by the two artists, all slides were black and white. Each day the full set was shown to four separate pigeons in specially constructed cages. Each cage was set up with a special food dispenser, which the pigeon could operate by pecking at a food key. The experimenters set up the food keys to dispense the reward of hemp seeds only in instances when the pigeons correctly performed a discrimination task. In the first part of the experiment, the pigeons were trained to discriminate between the Monets and the Picassos in the slide set.

Two pigeons received a reward if they correctly pecked the food key when a Monet was displayed; two were rewarded for pecking at a Picasso. Each slide set was shown to each pigeon once a day until a criterion of 90% correct responses in two successive sessions was achieved. The number of training sessions needed ranged from six to 24. After each pigeon was trained, it was tested to see if it had learned the artist's style. During the test, each bird was shown a new set of 20 slides: four new paintings by Monet and four by Picasso, along with four each by Renoir, Matisse, and Delacroix. Each of the birds achieved test scores averaging around 90% correct for the new set! It appears they had learned the artist's style. Learning to discriminate a Monet from a Picasso *generalized* to a completely new set of stimuli.

FIGURE 10-5
Round contours.
SuperStock

FIGURE 10-6 Sharp contours. Artists Rights Society

"typical" our small sample is. One *ficus elastica* may be much like another; one pigeon may or may not be. We could compare the behavior of our pigeon during the baseline condition with the records of other pigeons in the research literature. If our pigeon seems to behave about the same as other pigeons, we would probably assume it is a typical subject. However, even if the subject behaves typically in our baseline conditions, we still cannot be sure this particular subject is not unusually sensitive to the independent variable.

Generalizing from the results of one or two subjects is particularly risky when the subjects are people. No two people would be expected to react in exactly the same way. Pooling the responses of many individual subjects makes it more likely that the effects are generalizable to people outside the experiment. Generalizing also depends on the type of process that is being measured. Some psychophysical processes are quite similar in most people. We all react in much the same way to a loud, unexpected sound, such as a gunshot, by displaying a startle reaction. Other psychological processes—such as whether we will laugh in relief or get angry at an experimenter who fired off a gun close to our head—show large individual differences. If we are measuring a process that is relatively *invariant*, the results from a small N experiment would have greater generalizability than if we were measuring a behavior for which we expected large differences among people.

In a small N study, we also cannot be sure that the results are not caused by some unseen accident (a *history threat*). For instance, our plant study could be contaminated by a well-meaning cleaning person who gives fertilizer to our subject just at the time we begin talking to it. For these reasons, it is especially important to replicate the findings of a small N experiment before generalizations are made. An experiment with multiple applications of a treatment and multiple returns to baseline is more convincing than a single application.

It is impossible to say whether small or large N studies always have greater generality. All things rarely are equal. A large N study with a badly biased sample may tell us little about behavior in the population. However, the findings of a well-controlled experiment with a single subject might be successfully replicated again and again on different subjects. By gathering baseline data, applying the experimental manipulation, and then returning to the baseline condition, we can get a very clear idea of the impact of the independent variable.

SUMMARY

The small N design is used to study the behavior of only one or very few subjects. This approach requires very careful control over the conditions of the experiment. A typical small N experiment begins with observing and recording the subject's behavior under the control condition (before the independent variable is introduced). This is called the *baseline*. The experimental intervention is then introduced, and the subject's behavior is monitored throughout the experimental period. This behavior is then compared with the baseline records. To rule out the possibility of confounding by extraneous variables, we return to the original control condition. Multiple applications of the treatment and multiple returns to baseline are most convincing. To increase external validity, small N experiments should be replicated.

Most small N studies use some form of reversal, or *ABA design*. *ABA* refers to the order of the treatment conditions. Sometimes, for ethical reasons, the researcher would not wish to remove treatment; in this case, an *AB* design is used, even though without reversal it cannot be shown that the treatment caused the change in behavior. An *ABAB* design is fairly common in behavior therapy research; it can be more convincing than an *AB* or *ABA* design, and has the benefit of leaving an efficacious treatment in place. We can also use the *ABA* approach or some variation in experiments with groups of subjects as well as with individuals. The main limitation on this approach is that we can use it only with experimental treatments that are reversible.

Sometimes researchers use *multiple-baseline designs* when (1) it is not desirable to reverse a treatment, (2) the researcher wishes to test a treatment across multiple settings, or (3) the researcher wants to assess the effects of a treatment on several behaviors. Another small N approach, called a *discrete trials design*, is particularly popular with researchers testing psychophysical processes. This design does not use baselines, but, instead, relies on averaging the behavior across many, many trials to obtain a stable picture of effects of the experimental manipulation.

Whether to choose a small or large N design depends on several factors. Practical and methodological considerations come into play. A small N design can be used to study the behavior of a single individual in depth, or it can be used when subjects are scarce. For example, psychologists who wish to study the effects of a therapeutic intervention on a client with a particular psychopathology could use a small N design. Clearly, a small N design requires fewer subjects; it is less time consuming when each human or animal subject requires extensive training. Statistics are not typically used in small N experiments, although their use is growing. Some discrete trials designs using more than one subject typically include statistics to compare the behavior of different subjects.

KEY TERMS

AB design A design in which a baseline condition (A) is measured first, followed by measurements during the experimental intervention (B); there is no return to the baseline condition.

ABA design A design in which a baseline condition (A) is measured first, followed by measurements during the experimental condition (B), followed by a return to the baseline condition (A) to verify that the change in behavior is linked to the experimental condition; also called a reversal design.

ABAB design A design in which a baseline condition (A) is measured first, followed by measurements during a treatment condition (B), followed by a return to the baseline condition (A) to verify that the change in behavior is linked to the experimental condition, followed by a return to the treatment condition (B).

ABABA **design** A design in which a baseline condition (A) is measured first, followed by measurements during a treatment condition (B), followed by a return to the baseline measurement condition (A), followed by a return to the treatment condition (B) and a final baseline measurement condition (A) to verify that the change in behavior is linked to the experimental condition.

Baseline A measure of behavior as it normally occurs without the experimental manipulation; a control condition used to assess the impact of the experimental condition.

Discrete trials design A design that relies on presenting and averaging across many, many experimental trials; repeated applications result in a reliable picture of the effects of the independent variable.

Large N design A design in which the behavior of groups of subjects is compared.

Multiple-baseline design A small N design in which a series of baselines and treatments are compared within the same person; once established, however, a treatment is not withdrawn.

Small N design A design in which just one or two subjects are used; typically, the experimenter collects baseline data during an initial control condition; applies the experimental treatment; then reinstates the original control condition to verify that changes observed in behavior were caused by the experimental intervention.

REVIEW AND STUDY QUESTIONS

1. What is a small N design?
2. Discuss the relative advantages and disadvantages of small N versus large N designs.
3. What is an *ABA* design? Why is it really a family of designs?
4. What do we mean by a reversal design?
5. Explain how a baseline condition in a small N experiment is similar to a control group in a large N experiment.
6. Outline a small N experiment to test this hypothesis: Children who are given weaponlike toys (for example, toy guns and knives) become more aggressive.
   a. What are your independent and dependent variables?
   b. How would you operationally define *aggression*?
   c. What procedures would you use to test the hypothesis ?
   d. What are the disadvantages of using a small N design for this experiment?
7. One student is still looking for shortcuts. He says: "Running through the baseline condition of an experiment twice is silly. I'll just run through A

and *B* and draw my conclusions from that." What would you say to him to convince him that carrying out the entire *ABA* design would be a better idea?

8. Give an example of a clinical study in which the student from question 7 would be justified in using an *AB* design.

9. Describe how you would conduct an *ABAB* experiment in which punishment (a squirt bottle containing 9 parts water to 1 part vinegar) was used to control barking in a dog.

10. Why was an *ABAB* design used in question nine rather than an *ABA* design?

11. Draw a graph to illustrate a *successful* multiple baseline experiment to control two problem behaviors (barking and chasing the cat) exhibited by the dog from question 9. Assume the squirt bottle is your intervention.

12. Explain how history and maturation could potentially threaten the internal validity of the study you designed for question eleven.

13. Discuss the benefits of a discrete trials design.

SOLVING PROBLEMS: CONTROLLING EXTRANEOUS VARIABLES

When we experiment, we want to create treatment conditions that will let us clearly see the effects of the independent variables. Our experiments should be internally valid; only the independent variable should change systematically from one condition to another. In the last several chapters, you saw the various ways we can control for some subject variables that may lead to confounding: We can use random assignment to different treatment groups; we can match subjects on variables that are related to the dependent variable before randomly assigning them to groups; and we can run the experiment using a within-subjects design. In this chapter we will look closely at some techniques for handling other types of extraneous variables that can threaten an experiment's internal validity: physical, social, personality, and context variables. In some instances, these variables threaten an experiment's external validity by reducing the generalizability of the findings. Each poses special problems in an experiment. Many can be controlled by the same procedures, but some require special procedures. Let us begin by looking at the first type, physical variables.

PHYSICAL VARIABLES

Poor Janice Johnson was trying to run an experiment on tricky riddles that required a lot of thought. On Thursday, her first day of testing, Janice recruited subjects in the library and tested them on the spot in a quiet reading room. The next day she came back to run the rest of the experiment. To her dismay, Janice found that the reading room closed early on Fridays. The only place she could test her subjects was the building's lobby. It was fairly quiet there, but people walked by now and then, laughing and talking about plans for the weekend. Janice cried, "What a dummy I am! These testing conditions will confound my experiment! Why did I run all my control group subjects yesterday?"

The day of the week, the testing room, the noise, the distractions are all **physical variables**, aspects of the testing conditions that need to be controlled. Janice's experiment was in real trouble because she ran all her control subjects on a Thursday and all her experimental subjects on a Friday (and we all know that Fridays are different!).[1] The control group was tested under quiet conditions; the experimental group was tested in a different place with more noise and distractions. Clearly, there was confounding in Janice's experiment because the testing conditions changed along with the independent variable. Her problems could have been avoided by using one of the three general techniques for controlling physical variables: elimination, constancy of conditions, and balancing. We cannot possibly identify all the extraneous variables that influence the outcome of a study—but we try to find as many as we can. By using control techniques, we increase the chances of an internally valid experiment.

Elimination and Constancy

To make sure that an extraneous variable does not affect an experiment, sometimes we just take it out—we **eliminate** it. If noise might confound the results, we test in a soundproof room. If we do not want interruptions, we hang a sign on the door saying, "Do not disturb. Experiment in progress."

Ideally, we would like to eliminate all extraneous variables from an experiment, but this is easier said than done. Sometimes there is no soundproof room. Factors like the weather, the lighting, and the paint on the walls are simply there; we cannot eliminate them. Instead, we use the second control procedure—constancy of conditions.

Constancy of conditions means simply that we keep treatment conditions as nearly similar as possible. If we cannot eliminate a variable, we try to make sure that it stays the same in all treatment conditions. We cannot take the paint off the walls, but we can test all subjects in the same room. That way we make sure that the pea-green walls offend all subjects equally in all conditions. The same goes for lighting, the comfort of the chairs, the mustiness of the drapes; all stay the same for all the subjects. We also try to keep the mechanics of the testing procedures the same. For instance, it is helpful to write out instructions to subjects before beginning the experiment. The written instructions are then read to subjects to guarantee that all subjects in each condition get exactly the same instructions. Audio- or videotaping them might be even better. Exactly the same amount of time is allowed for each subject to complete each task—unless time is the independent or dependent variable.

Many physical variables such as time of testing, testing place, and mechanical procedures can be kept constant with a little effort. An experimenter may end up controlling some variables that would not have affected the results anyway, but it is better to use the controls than to have regrets later. If some-

---

[1]Many of our colleagues try to avoid running *any* experiments on Fridays. We are not sure if it is because they are worried that subjects will be less motivated to participate or whether they themselves are just looking forward to the weekend.

one can punch holes in the results simply by pointing out that the experimental group had lunch but the control group did not, the experimenter will have a hard time making a strong case for the effects of the independent variable.

Balancing

Sometimes neither elimination nor constancy can be used. Perhaps some variables cannot be eliminated. For example, we would like to test in a soundproof room, but we do not have access to one. We would like to test all subjects together at the same time, but they cannot all come at once. What can we do in these situations? Confounding occurs when something in the experiment changes systematically along with the independent variable. If we cannot eliminate extraneous physical variables or keep them constant throughout an experiment, we can still make sure that they do not confound the results. The key to the problem is the way the variables change. If they change in a way that is *systematically linked to the levels of the independent variable,* we are in trouble because a confound is present. If we test experimental subjects in one room and control subjects in another, we have created an orderly change in many of the variables that make up the testing conditions. We will not be able to tell for sure whether the independent variable or something about the different testing rooms produced changes in the groups. The control group may do better if it is tested in the same sunny room as the experimental group. The key to controlling variables that cannot be eliminated or held constant is the third technique for physical variables, balancing.

We know that ideally we should not test subjects in two different rooms. But perhaps we have no choice; it is two rooms or nothing. We still want to be sure testing conditions do not change in a way that is related to the independent variable. We can do this through **balancing**, distributing the effects of an extraneous variable across the different treatment conditions of the experiment. A way in which we might do this with room assignment is shown in Table 11-1.

We begin by randomly assigning half the subjects to the first testing room. The other half will be tested in the second room. Next, we randomly assign half the subjects *in each room* to the experimental condition; the remaining subjects will be in the control condition. Notice that we have not wiped out the differences between the two testing rooms; they are just as different as ever. However, the hope is that the effects of the rooms are the same, or balanced, for both treatment conditions. For every control subject tested in the green room, an experimental subject is also tested in that room; for every control subject tested in the pink room, an experimental subject is also tested there.

Janice could have salvaged her riddle experiment by using balancing. Instead of testing all control subjects on the first day, she should have randomly assigned each subject to either the experimental or the control condition. Then she would have tested, by chance, roughly half the control subjects

TABLE 11-1 Balancing the effects of the testing room across two treatment conditions, control (C) and experimental (E)

Green Testing Room: Subjects	Pink Testing Room: Subjects
C_1	C_4
C_2	C_5
C_3	C_6
E_1	E_4
E_2	E_5
E_3	E_6

NOTE: Half the subjects are randomly assigned to each testing room. Half the subjects in each room are then randomly assigned to the control condition, half to the experimental condition.

and half the experimental subjects on Thursday. Roughly half the control subjects would have taken part in the quiet reading room along with roughly half the experimental subjects. On the second day, Janice would have continued assigning subjects to the two treatment conditions at random. She would then have tested about half the control subjects and half the experimental subjects in the noisy lobby. Notice that she still would have had subjects who were tested under two different testing conditions. But the effects of these conditions would have been about the same for the two treatments in the experiment, so the testing conditions would not have confounded the results of her experiment.

We can use balancing for many other variables as well. For example, if we cannot test all subjects at the same time of day, we can arrange things so that we test equal numbers of experimental and control subjects before and after lunch. Many physical variables will be balanced across conditions automatically as we assign our subjects to treatment conditions at random. Time of testing, weather conditions, and day of the week are typically controlled in this way. Usually, we do not even think about these sorts of extraneous variables. As long as there is no systematic change in an extraneous variable, things are fine. If we assign subjects to treatment conditions at random, we can be reasonably sure (but not positive) that we will not accidentally test all control subjects on a cool, comfortable day and all experimental subjects on a hot, muggy day. We can, of course, easily improve control by using block randomization (see Chapter 7).

At this point you may be wondering whether there is a limit on the number of extraneous variables that must be controlled. There may indeed be many possibilities, but you can set up a reasonably good experiment by taking these precautions: Eliminate extraneous variables when you can. Keep treatment conditions as similar as possible. Balance out the effects of other variables, such as the testing room, by making sure that the effects are distributed evenly across all treatment conditions. As always, be sure to assign individual subjects to treatment conditions at random. The experimental literature will also help you plan a strategy. If other experimenters have carefully controlled the size of the testing room, you will want to be more cautious with that variable than with some others, such as the day of the week. If you can avoid it, do not let extraneous variables change along with the independent variable. You can never completely rule out the possibility of confounding if you let that happen.

SOCIAL VARIABLES

Besides controlling physical variables that might alter the outcome of the experiment, researchers are concerned about **social variables,** qualities of the relationships between subjects and experimenters that may influence results. Two principal social variables, demand characteristics and experimenter bias, can be controlled through single- and double-blind experiments.

Demand Characteristics

Demand characteristics are aspects of the experimental situation that *demand* that people behave in a particular way. Have you ever walked along a busy street and noticed someone looking up at the sky or at a building? You may have found yourself looking up, too. This is a good example of what we mean by demand characteristics. What we do is often shaped by what we think we are expected to do. When you enter a classroom, even on the first day of the term, you probably walk in and take a seat. When the professor begins talking, you listen. Of course, you are fulfilling a role you learned in your earliest days at school, the role of "good student" in the classroom. The cue of being in the classroom leads you to behave in a predictable way. Most research subjects want to be good subjects. They want to conform to what they think is the proper role of "subject." They may not even be consciously aware of the ways in which they alter their behavior when they come into an experiment. For example, subjects may assume a very active role. They may try to guess the hypothesis of the experiment and adjust their responses accordingly.

Suppose we want to run a perception experiment in which two lights move at the same speed but in different paths: circular or square. We are looking for a difference in the way subjects perceive the movement of these lights. Specifically, we expect subjects to perceive the light in the circular path as moving faster. We ask: "Did the light in the circular path move faster, slower, or about the same as the light in the square path?" If you were a subject in this experiment, what would you think about this question? The experimenter has gone to a lot of trouble to set up these lights and recruit subjects. Suppose you really could not see any difference in the speed of the lights. But why would anyone go to the bother of showing you two lights that move at the same speed and then ask you whether one moved faster? You may begin to suspect that there really was some subtle difference in the speeds and somehow you did not notice it. But you want to be a good subject; you do not want to tell the experimenter that you were not paying attention or that you are not very good at judging speed. So you guess. You say, "Well, maybe the round one really was moving a little faster because it didn't make all those turns. So I'll say the round one was faster even though I'm not sure that's what I saw." Box 11-1 illustrates this problem further.

An experimenter generally wants subjects to be as naive as possible. They should understand the nature and purpose of the experiment but not the exact hypothesis. The reason for this is simple. If subjects know what we expect to find, they may produce data that will support the hypothesis. On the surface that may seem like a good thing. Wouldn't it be wonderful if experiments always confirmed their hypotheses? It would—if the experiments were valid. We want to be able to say that the independent variable caused a change in behavior. If behavior changes simply because subjects think the researcher wants an experiment to turn out in a particular way, the experiment has not measured what it was intended to measure.

Subjects often try to guess the hypotheses. This is a problem, especially in within-subjects experiments; since the subjects take part in more than one treatment condition, they usually have a better chance of guessing the hypothesis. Of course, subjects sometimes guess incorrectly. They may think they are helping by responding in a particular way, but their help produces data that make it impossible to confirm the hypothesis. Occasionally, subjects will actually try to produce data that conflict with the hypothesis. They may guess the hypothesis, disagree with it, and set out to disprove it. Again, they may be wrong; they may actually wind up supporting the predictions. But either way, our problem is that this kind of data is not worth much. We want to set up experiments in which we can test the effect of an independent variable, not the subjects' skill at guessing the experimental hypothesis.

Does this sort of thing really happen? Do subjects' experiences and answers change depending on what they think is supposed to happen in the experiment? Can the demand characteristics of an experiment lead to changes in subjects' behavior? What if subjects simply do what they think they are supposed to do? Orne and Scheibe (1964) devised a clever experiment to evaluate the effects of demand characteristics in research on sensory deprivation.

Traditionally, subjects in sensory-deprivation experiments were isolated from sensory experiences of all kinds. They wore translucent goggles so that they could not see shapes clearly; they were typically restricted to lying on a soft bed; they wore coverings over their arms to minimize sensations from movement and touch. White noise (noise of all frequencies that sounds very much like static on a radio) was played to mask ordinary sounds. With these procedures, prolonged sensory deprivation led to emotional upset, disorientation, and even hallucinations. Orne and Scheibe followed a very different

BOX 11-1

THE "GOOD SUBJECT" PHENOMENON

Martin Orne is well-known for his programmatic research on social variables in the experimental setting. According to Orne (1978), the experimental setting creates a situation of extraordinary control over the behavior of research subjects. He uses the following example to illustrate. If you were simply to ask a casual college acquaintance to get down on the floor right now and do five push-ups, what do you think that person's response would be? When Orne tested it, people's responses tended to be "amazement, incredulity and the question, 'Why?'" But what would happen if you made the same request to another student who was a subject in an experiment? When Orne tested this, the typical response was "Where?" (p. 235) Orne explains the difference in terms of the "good subject" phenomenon.

Certainly, subjects volunteer for experiments for any number of reasons (course requirements, extra credit, money, a hope that the psychologist can make them feel better, etc.), but over and above these reasons, Orne believes that college student subjects share with experimenters the belief that the experiment is important. And even though the experiment may require a lot of effort or even discomfort, the results are worth it. Subjects feel they have a stake in experiments they participate in, and they want to perform well for the experimenter—to be "good subjects." A social desirability response set (from Chapter 7) may play a part, too. And regardless of the true purpose of the experiment, many subjects believe that their psychological adjustment is being judged by the experimenter, so they are extremely cooperative.

Orne demonstrated this phenomenon in an amusing experiment (although it probably was not so amusing for the subjects who endured it!). Subjects were given a task of adding up pairs of adjacent numbers on sheets filled with rows of random digits (just like the random number table in Appendix B). Each subject was given a stack of 2000 sheets, clearly, an impossible task. Subjects' watches were taken away, and they were told simply, "Continue to work; I will return eventually." *Five and a half hours later, the experimenter finally gave up.* Most subjects kept working until the experimenter eventually came back and told them to stop!

The surprised Orne tried to make the task even more frustrating (and completely meaningless) to see if that would reduce compliance.

(continued)

(*continued*)

In the second experiment, subjects were given the same task and instructions, but after they completed each sheet they were told to pick up a card that would tell them what to do next. Each card was identical; it instructed them to tear up the sheet they had just completed into a minimum of 32 pieces and to go on to the next sheet. Orne expected subjects to stop when they realized that each card said the same thing. But, according to Orne, subjects kept at the task for several hours. When he asked them why, they all came up with reasons that made the task seem meaningful (e.g., "It was an endurance test."). They were indeed "good subjects."

procedure. They placed their experimental and control subjects alone in a room that hardly created any deprivation at all. The room was 6 × 7 × 8 feet in size and was furnished with a desk and two chairs. The subjects could easily hear sounds from the hallway and birds chirping outside. They did not wear goggles and so had their normal vision. There was water and a sandwich in case they got hungry. They were given a set of arithmetic problems to work on if they wanted something to do, and they could move around as much as they wanted to within the room.

The difference between the experimental and control groups in this study was the way the experiment was presented to each group. Experimental-group subjects were interviewed by a man in a white medical coat. A tray of drugs and medical instruments, labeled "Emergency Tray," was in the room. Subjects were told that there was an alarm button in the "deprivation chamber." If they became upset, they were advised to press the alarm button. They were also told that a physician was present. Pulse and blood pressure readings were taken. Everything possible was done to create an atmosphere of seriousness and preparation for a possible crisis. Subjects were also read some instructions for reporting their experiences while in the chamber, including possible visual imagery, unusual feelings, and disorientation—the typical sensory-deprivation effects.

Control-group subjects were told that they were control subjects. The experimenter wore regular business clothes. There was no emergency tray or alarm button. Subjects were told that if they wanted to leave the chamber, they could simply knock on the window. They were given the same general instructions to report their experiences, but everything was done to create a relaxed impression. When the blood pressure and pulse readings were made, the control subjects were told that the readings were being taken simply because they had been taken for the experimental subjects.

If we compare the two procedures, we see that Orne and Scheibe manipulated demand characteristics in their experiment. All subjects were placed in the same "deprivation" setting, but the experimental subjects were given every reason to expect that something awful, or at least out of the ordinary, might happen to them. The control group was treated in a more casual way that probably communicated something like, "You'll be in this room for a while." What would you expect to happen in this experiment? Would subjects show the usual effects of sensory deprivation? If we look only at the physical lay-out of this experiment, we can see that there is little reason to expect anyone to become disoriented or show any other unusual symptoms in a short period of time. The subjects had full use of all their senses. Their movements were not restricted, they could eat, and they had a task to do if they got bored.

Orne and Scheibe's findings implicated demand characteristics as a cause of some of the prior sensory-deprivation findings: Their experimental subjects, those led to expect some strange experience, showed significantly more signs of disturbance. Compared to the controls, the experimental subjects gave the "impression of almost being tortured" (p. 11). All the subjects in Orne and Scheibe's experiment experienced the same "deprivation," but only the exper-imental group showed the usual effects of sensory deprivation. For the exper-imental group, the researchers had created the impression that something unusual would happen to them. The subjects' expectations were confirmed; they experienced a variety of changes that did not occur for the control sub-jects, who had a different set of expectations. The changes were varied and at times dramatic: "The buzzing of the fluorescent light is growing alternately louder and softer so that at times it sounds like a jackhammer"; "There are multicolored spots on the wall"; "The numbers on the number sheets are blur-ring and assuming various inkblot forms" (p. 10). Indeed, one subject hit the panic button and listed "disorganization of senses" as one of his reasons for stopping. These findings do not rule out the possibility that some genuine changes occur when subjects undergo an actual restriction of sensory experi-ence. They do, however, illustrate the importance of demand characteristics in shaping the outcome of such studies.

Controlling Demand Characteristics: Single-Blind Experiments

When we run experiments, we try not to give subjects clues to what may hap-pen to them because of the independent variable. We do not want to influ-ence the outcome of the experiment by having subjects know the hypothesis. A good way to control some effects of demand characteristics is through a **single-blind experiment**, an experiment in which subjects do not know which treatment they are getting.

When we do a single-blind experiment, we can disclose some but not all information about the experiment to subjects. We can disclose what is going to happen to them in the experiment; we can also keep them fully informed about the purpose of the study. But we keep them "blind" to one thing: We do not tell them what treatment condition they are in. This approach is very common in experiments with drugs. If we give a subject some substance, the subject might react based on what he or she *expects* the drug to do. For instance, suppose we want to test a new headache remedy. If we give the new drug to several people with headaches, some of them will report that they feel better after taking the medicine. Did the medicine help? We don't know. To

GEO. N. ALLING,
GRAND AVE. cor. STATE ST., NEW HAVEN, CONN.

FIGURE 11-1 An advertisement for Dr. R. C. Flower's Nerve Pills. The success of some patent medicines can be attributed in part to placebo effects. However, a large measure of alcohol in some preparations may have helped, too. National Library of Medicine

answer this question, we need a control group of people who do not receive the drug. Researchers know that if you give a person *any* pill, the person is apt to say the pill helped. We call this the **placebo effect.**

When we test a drug, we give the control group a placebo—a pill, injection, or other treatment that contains none of the actual medication. And, we only disclose partial information. We do not tell subjects which treatment they are receiving. The subject is blind to that aspect of the experiment. We can eliminate some of the effects of demand characteristics by ensuring that subjects do not know exactly what changes (if any) they should expect. They cannot be sure whether they are in the control group or in an experimental group. If we see changes in their behavior, those changes are more likely to be caused by the independent variable. Subjects will not be able to report what they think the experimenter wants to hear (for example, that the new medication made them feel better). They will not know what the experimenter expects because they will not know which treatment they are getting.

However, as Leavitt (1974) points out, subjects typically know they are getting *some kind of treatment,* and so we may rarely be able to measure the actual effects of a drug by itself. Instead, we see the effects of the treatment plus placebo effects that are shaped by the subjects' expectations. We then compare those effects with the effects of the placebo alone on the control group.

In other kinds of experiments we can get placebo effects, too. Suppose we want to conduct a simple learning study; we want to see whether the brightness of a room influences how easily people learn. We hypothesize that people will learn more quickly under bright lighting conditions. We form two groups: an experimental group and a control group. Both groups will be asked to memorize a list of ten nonsense words—like *bragzap* and *crumdip* (in several different random orders, of course). Subjects will be tested individually in the same small office, which is furnished with a desk, chair, and reading lamp. The control group will learn the list under normal illumination conditions (a 75-watt reading light); the experimental group will learn it under brighter-than-normal conditions (a 150-watt light). The length of time it takes subjects to memorize all ten words will be the dependent measure.

We want to conduct a single-blind study. We might tell subjects: "We are investigating the effects of room lighting on learning. We are asking people to learn a list of ten made-up words as quickly as possible. Different people will learn the list under different lighting conditions, and we will see whether lighting makes a difference." We have given subjects information about the purpose of the experiment and have told them what would happen to them during the experiment. Notice that we have not disclosed our expectations about their performance, and we have not told them which condition they are in. But have we structured the situation so that these parameters are fairly simple to figure out? Probably we have. Subjects are quite likely to figure out our hypothesis—and behave accordingly. If they believe the light is normal or even a bit dim, they may take longer to learn the list simply because they expect it to take longer. If the light seems bright, they may learn the list more quickly because they expect the added light makes learning easier. This could confound the experiment because their expectation varies systematically with the independent variable— it would take them longer in the control than in the experimental condition, just as we predicted, but the difference might not be due to the light levels at all.

What alternatives do we have? We could give them less information. We could simply say that we are investigating the influence of different study environments on learning. This might keep them from guessing our true hypothesis or it might not. Perhaps some experimental subjects guess that we are testing quiet versus noisy spaces or different kinds of chairs or different colored walls. Whatever they guess, there is always the possibility that their guess will be confirmed by the way they behave. Whatever they guess may alter the time it would normally take to learn the list. Nevertheless, most researchers would agree that this situation is somewhat better than the first. Chances are that individual subjects would guess different things and behave in different ways, but their behavior would not change systematically along with the independent variable. It would not be a confound, but it would certainly make the impact of the independent variable more difficult to detect. It would introduce large individual differences in responding, which is something we work hard to avoid when we can.

Controlling Demand Characteristics: Cover Stories

There is another alternative for controlling the possibility that subjects may guess the experimental hypothesis—we could use a cover story. When we create an experimental situation, we want subjects to respond as normally as possible. At the very least, we do not want their expectations to alter their responses on the dependent measure. Sometimes the best control over demand characteristics is gained through the use of a **cover story,** which is a plausible but false explanation for the procedures used in the study. It is told to disguise the actual research hypothesis so that subjects will not guess what it is.

Consider the following situation. Wells and Petty (1980) noticed that people nod their heads up and down when they are exposed to something they find agreeable and shake their heads from side to side in the presence of something they find disagreeable. They wondered if this could be reversed. Would people tend to find something agreeable if they were nodding their heads when they were exposed to it? Would they find something disagreeable if they were shaking their heads when exposed to it?

To test their hypothesis, the researchers would have to get some subjects to nod their heads when they were exposed to a stimulus and other subjects to shake their heads when they were exposed to the same stimulus. They could then ask all the subjects how agreeable or disagreeable they found the stimulus. They predicted that subjects who were nodding their heads would find it agreeable and those who were shaking their heads would find it disagreeable.

They could have instructed subjects to nod or shake their heads and told them the experimental hypothesis. But if the results had come out the way Wells and Petty predicted, would you have been convinced? Probably not. What if the researchers did not disclose the hypothesis but simply instructed subjects either to nod or to shake their heads? Would you have been convinced if the data came out as predicted? No, because there is a strong chance that subjects might figure out such a simple hypothesis: "You told me to shake my head because you want me to find this thing disagreeable, so I'll tell you that I find it disagreeable."

How can the researchers get around this problem? They can't instruct subjects to move their heads because the subjects will probably use the instructions to figure out the hypothesis. Yet they must get the subjects to either shake or nod their heads to test the hypothesis. This is the type of situation in which a cover story must be developed. And we have to be clever because the cover story has to give the subjects an explanation for what we want them to do—move their heads—without tipping them off to the hypothesis being tested. Wells and Petty came up with a cover story that was clever indeed. They told subjects they would be listening to a message (the experimental stimulus) through a set of headphones. They told subjects that the purpose of the experiment was to test the headphones—to see whether the headphones worked efficiently if listeners were moving their heads while listening. Their cover story provided subjects with an explanation for the head-moving instructions that had nothing to do with the experimental hypothesis. Given this plausible explanation, subjects would not look for another explanation and would be unlikely to discover the real experimental hypothesis. Wells and Petty explained the real purpose of the head movements to subjects at the end of the experimental session.

Why not always use a cover story such as one devised by Wells and Petty? Quite simply, cover stories involve deception. Deception is a departure from fully informed consent. As we discovered in Chapter 2, researchers must

"WHAT IT COMES DOWN TO IS YOU HAVE TO FIND OUT WHAT REACTION THEY'RE LOOKING FOR, AND YOU GIVE THEM THAT REACTION."

increasingly be concerned about the rights of the participant as the departure from fully informed consent becomes more dramatic. For this reason, cover stories should be used sparingly. Remember that debriefing is required for all subjects in such experiments. If you believe your experiment can have internal validity without a cover story, do not use one.

Experimenter Bias

Perhaps without realizing it, an experimenter can give subjects cues that tell them how he or she would like them to respond. Subjects will often comply with these subtle requests and give the data the experimenter is seeking. Imagine the experimenter running the earlier perception experiment. She asks, "Does the light in the circular path move faster, slower, or at the same speed as the light in the square path?" As she says "faster," she leans forward slightly, raises her eyebrows, and speaks a little louder. Most of her subjects say that the light in the circular path moved "faster."

We call this sort of influence **experimenter bias;** the experimenter does something that creates confounding in the experiment. The experimenter may give a cue to respond in a particular way, or he or she may behave differently in different treatment conditions. Dr. R. might be warm and friendly in the experimental condition, but he may seem indifferent in the control condition. That is all right if the experimenter's demeanor is the independent variable. If it is not, it may confound the results. Subjects might feel more at ease in the experimental condition and so perform better.

Sometimes, as in the case of Dr. R., the nature of the experimental treatment can bring on experimenter bias. Dr. R. may have found the experimental condition much more interesting than the control condition. If so, then Dr. R. probably found it much more fun to run experimental than control sessions, and his preference showed up as increased warmth toward subjects in the experimental condition. But experimenter bias doesn't always work in this way.

Imagine that Dr. R.'s experimental condition was particularly noxious for subjects and Dr. R. knew it. Researchers do not enjoy putting subjects through unpleasant procedures! Every time Dr. R. knew that a subject would be undergoing the noxious procedure, he became somewhat anxious, and he transmitted this anxiety to subjects. As you can imagine, his behavior would be a particular problem if the dependent variable was anxiety. If Dr. R.'s hypothesis was that the noxious procedure would make subjects more anxious than the control procedure, his experiment would be confounded. Subjects could have picked up the cue from Dr. R. that there was something to be anxious about, and so they were. Effects on subjects' anxiety may have had every bit as much to do with Dr. R.'s demeanor as with the independent variable.[2]

So far it seems that experimenter effects can be a problem only with human subjects. After all, a rat will not notice a smile and then learn faster. Probably not, but experimenters may handle rats more and handle them more gently if they think the rats are special.

Experimenter effects can be just as important in animal studies as they are in human ones. Experimenters may treat subjects differently depending on what they expect from them. They may give more time to subjects that have gone through a particular treatment. This outcome is called the **Rosenthal effect** after the man who first reported it (Rosenthal, 1976). (It is also called the *Pygmalion effect,* after the legend in which the sculptor Pygmalion fell in love with his own statue of the perfect woman.) Box 11-2 summarizes some of Rosenthal's key findings. The Rosenthal effect can be another source of confounding in an experiment.

Experimenter bias occurs in other ways, too. The experimenter may also make errors in recording the data from the experiment. He or she may "misread" a scale or score an item incorrectly. Coincidentally, Rosenthal (1978) reported that researchers are more likely to make errors that favor the hypoth-

---

[2]This actually happened to one of the authors in the first experiment she ran in graduate school. The experiment was ruined, but it taught her a valuable lesson—one that both authors hope you will not learn through your own personal experience.

FIGURE 11-2 Robert Rosenthal

esis. In a sample of 21 published studies, he found that about 1% of all observations made were probably wrong. Of those, two-thirds favored the experimenters' hypotheses. By chance, we would expect only about 50% of the errors to support the researchers' hypotheses.

Controlling Experimenter Bias: Double-Blind Experiments

How can we eliminate experimenter effects from research? The first step, of course, is to be aware of them. We want to be sure we do not do anything that will contaminate the data. By following a set of written directions, timing all phases of the experiment, and being as consistent as possible, we can avoid some mistakes. We make our observations as objective as possible. We try to set up experiments to minimize the amount of personal contact between an experimenter and a subject so that unintentional bias does not happen. But sometimes we just cannot anticipate how bias may creep into an experiment.

Let us say we are doing a study of cartoons and children's art. We want to see whether children who have just watched a cartoon will draw more abstract pictures than children who have just watched a filmed version of the same story. The cartoon group sees animated drawings of people; the film group sees actual people acting out the same story. We show the children the cartoon or film, then we ask them to draw pictures.

We have developed a way of scoring the children's drawings for abstractness. Our measure includes a number of specific dimensions, such as whether objects are colored in their true-to-life colors. We will score each child's picture

BOX 11-2

THE ROSENTHAL EFFECT

In a variety of laboratory and nonlaboratory studies, researchers have documented the self-fulfilling prophecy: Expectations can alter the behavior of others, even animals (Rosenthal & Fode, 1963). As Rosenthal explained:

> Fode and I told a class of 12 students that one could produce a strain of intelligent rats by inbreeding them to increase their ability to run mazes quickly. To demonstrate, we gave each student five rats, which had to learn to run to the darker of two arms of a T-maze. We told half of our student-experimenters that they had the "maze-bright" intelligent rats; we told the rest that they had the stupid rats. Naturally, there was no real difference among any of the animals.
>
> But they certainly behaved differently in their performance. The rats believed to be bright improved daily in running the maze—they ran faster and more accurately—while the apparently dull animals did poorly. The "dumb" rats refused to budge from the starting point 29 percent of the time, while the "smart" rats were recalcitrant only 11 percent of the time.
>
> Then we asked our students to rate the rats and to describe their own attitudes toward them. Those who believed they were working with intelligent animals *liked* them better and found them more pleasant. Such students said they felt more relaxed with the animals; they treated them more gently and were more enthusiastic about the experiment than students who thought they had dull rats to work with. Curiously, the students with "bright" rats said they handled them more but talked to them less. One wonders what students with "dull" rats were saying to those poor creatures. (p. 58)

In a later study, Rosenthal and Jacobson (1966) found a similar effect in the classroom. They gave children an IQ test at the start of the school year. Randomly selected children in each class were labeled "intellectual bloomers." "We gave each teacher the names of these children, who, we explained, could be expected to show remarkable gains during the coming year on the basis of their test scores. In fact, the difference between these experimental children and the control group was solely in the teacher's mind" (p. 248). Eight months later, they found greater gains in the IQ scores of the "bloomers" relative to the other children.

Based on this and many other studies, Rosenthal (1973) proposed a fourfold explanation for the phenomenon. People who have been led to expect good things from their students, children, clients, or what-have-you appear to:

> * create a warmer social-emotional mood around their "special" students (climate)
> * give more feedback to these students about their performance (feedback)
> * teach more material and more difficult material to their special students (input)
> * give their special students more opportunities to respond and question (output) (p. 60)
>
> From "The Pygmalion Effect Lives" by R. Rosenthal, in R.E. Schell (Ed.), 1973, *Readings in Developmental Psychology Today, 2nd Ed.,* pp. 247–252.

on the abstractness scale. If our hypothesis is correct, the drawings of the children who saw the cartoon will be more abstract than the drawings of children who saw the film.

As we sit down to score the pictures, we notice different features in the drawings. We may also notice that we tend to score somewhat differently depending on which child drew the picture. Sometimes it is not clear how we should score a particular item. Melanie drew what appears to be a green orange. Oranges really are green before they get ripe, but they are usually orange in pictures. Should we score this picture as "abstract" or not? Scoring the dependent measures is no time to be making subjective judgments. We should have worked out these kinds of issues before running the experiment. But if these questions do arise in scoring, we might find ourselves deciding in favor of the more abstract rating if we were scoring a picture drawn by a child who saw the cartoon. We might distort the scoring a little by being inconsistent; we would bias the data so that they would support our own hypothesis. In doing so, we have created an *instrumentation threat* to the internal validity of the experiment. It is easy to do this without even realizing it.

One of the best ways of controlling for experimenter bias is to run a **double-blind experiment**, one in which the subjects do not know which treatment they are in, and the experimenter does not know, either. The value of the double-blind experiment is this: If the experimenter does not know which treatment the subject is getting, he or she cannot bias the responses in any systematic way. Since the subject is kept in the dark, too, the effects of demand characteristics are controlled along with experimenter bias.

If we are running a nutrition experiment and want to use the double-blind procedure, we ask an assistant to assign subjects to treatment conditions. Experimental subjects receive a dietary supplement (for example, vitamin E). Control subjects receive a placebo. The subjects are not told which treatment they will receive; they only know they are part of an experiment on nutrition and that they may or may not receive a vitamin supplement that is thought to produce various effects. The assistant administers the treatments. When we measure the subjects on the dependent variable (for example, interview them, observe them in a waiting room, or score them on a written test), we also do not know which treatment a subject received. We are "blind" to that information. After the data have been collected and scored, the assistant lets us know who belonged to each treatment group. We can then go on to evaluate the impact of the independent variable.

Wasson and colleagues (1984) followed this same basic procedure in a study of the effects of continuity of outpatient health care in elderly men. They randomly assigned patients to a "continuous" or "discontinuous" condition. In the continuous condition, subjects saw the same health-care provider (physician, nurse practitioner, or physician's assistant) each time they visited the clinic. Subjects in the discontinuous condition were assigned for treatment in such a way that on each visit there was a 33% chance of seeing a different provider, and no provider could be seen more than three consecutive times.

Only 10% of the clinic patients participated in the study. They were not identified to the health-care providers and changes in patient assignments were made gradually so that patients would not suspect the pattern of assignments. Although we can easily question whether patients caught on to the nature of the study, it was in principle a double-blind experiment. The outcome was that patients in the continuous group had fewer hospital admissions, had shorter stays, and perceived that providers were more knowledgeable, competent, and interested in patient education.

In some experiments the subjects always know what treatment condition they are getting. For instance, in our study of cartoons and children's art, each child would know whether he or she saw a cartoon or a film. The children would not know the exact hypothesis of the study. Still, we could not really say that they are "blind" to the treatment conditions. In these experiments we may not be able to use a truly double- or even single-blind procedure. Even so, we can build in some controls for experimenter bias. We can try not to assign subjects to their conditions until after we have finished interacting with them. We can make sure that the person who scores the subjects' responses does not know which treatment each subject received. We might have an independent rater score subjects' drawings. We do not tell the rater which subjects belonged to which group. If we are doing our own scoring, it is more difficult to remain naive. With some planning, however, we can skirt the most serious temptations. We standardize the testing and scoring procedures as much as possible. We try to be consistent in the way we handle the experiment from one subject to another. We avoid giving subjects extraneous clues as to how to behave.[3]

---

[3]When the researcher does know the subject's condition (which happens if there isn't an assistant available), researchers often find a way to standardize the instructions that need to be given to subjects. There are several good ways to do this: You can give subjects written instructions or you can have them listen to the instructions on tape. If you read the instructions to subjects, avoid relying on memory. Remember, it is important that the words *and* your voice stay the same each time.

As you design experiments, you will work very hard to control sources of confounding. If effects on the independent variable are produced by your behavior, the experiment does not have internal validity. Always keep in mind that *you* may be the biggest extraneous variable of all.

Double check your procedure. As you think about your experiment, try to anticipate subjects' reactions. Put yourself in the subject's place. How would you feel about answering your own questions? Would you be inclined to distort your answers because you would be too embarrassed to answer honestly? Would the experimental hypothesis be obvious to you? Think about your own behavior and the design of the experiment. Have you stacked the deck in any way? Do your instructions suggest the changes you expect to observe? Have you taken precautions to keep your own behavior as consistent as possible from one treatment condition to another? Are your instructions written down so that you will follow the same procedures each time? Are you prepared to introduce yourself and interact with all your subjects in the same way? It is always a good idea to make a dry run before you start testing subjects. You might even consider a pilot study so that any bugs in the procedures can be worked out before you actually collect data for the experiment.

PERSONALITY VARIABLES

Experimenters

We saw in the last section that the behavior of the experimenter can be an important extraneous variable in an experiment. You learned that social variables, qualities of the relationships between subjects and experimenters, may influence results if they are not carefully controlled. The personal characteristics, or **personality variables,** that an experimenter brings to the experimental setting can be important, too. An experimenter who is *warm and friendly* can elicit very different responses from subjects than one who is cold and aloof: Subjects sometimes learn better, talk more, get better scores on intelligence and adjustment tests, and are typically more compliant and eager to please when the experimenter acts in a friendly manner (Rosenthal, 1976).

Remember the response set called social desirability from Chapter 6? Apparently, experimenters who score high on the social desirability scale (Crowne & Marlowe, 1964) are particularly good at being likeable experimenters; they are more enthusiastic, more friendly, and smile more at their subjects. Interestingly, experimenters who come across as likeable can alter the kinds of responses, as well as the number of responses, obtained from subjects. For instance, studies on interviewing styles have shown that a likeable interviewer will collect better data, more usable responses, and fewer "I don't know's" from respondents. But keep in mind that an experimenter who improves subjects' performance may attenuate an experiment's external validity; similarly high levels of performance may not be obtained in another setting. Conversely, an experimenter who appeared hostile, aggressive, or authoritarian (demanding obedience) would get less than optimal performance from research subjects (Rosenthal, 1976).

The research setting is a novel one for most subjects, and they are often a bit anxious. We want to establish rapport with subjects so that they will feel at ease, but (unless the experimenter's demeanor is the independent variable) we do not want to make subjects behave in an atypical way. So be pleasant, but remember that you can affect the outcome of your experiment.

It is also important to maintain consistency in your interactions with subjects. Remember that when you act more friendly (or hostile, or anxious, etc.) toward subjects from time to time, you are introducing another source of variability into the experiment. The more you vary your behavior, the more you are likely to produce variability in the responses of your subjects. The more variability in their responses, the harder it will be to detect the effect of the independent variable.

Most important, however you act toward subjects, do it *consistently across all the treatment conditions.*[4] Do not allow your behavior to change systematically along with the conditions of the experiment. If your behavior is different in the experimental and control conditions, for example, the experiment will not have internal validity because *you* are a potential threat. With many personality variables, the influence is unpredictable and can interact with characteristics of particular subjects. There are ways to control for personality variables in your experiment. Some of the control techniques discussed earlier in the chapter will reduce the influence of personality variables.

If possible, use multiple experimenters, and make sure that each experimenter runs about the same number of people in each of the conditions of the experiment (in effect, *balancing* them across the experiment). Some researchers advocate including the experimenters as a factor in the data analysis (McGuigan, 1971). If you do not analyze for experimenter differences, you will never know for certain if they were a problem in your experiment or not. Chances are, your first experiment will have only a single experimenter—you—so you will need to take precautions to keep from influencing your subjects in unknown ways. The best control is to keep face-to-face contact to a minimum, and always adhere strictly to the experimental procedures.

Volunteer Subjects

Do we need to be concerned about the personality characteristics of subjects in the same way that we are about personality variables associated with experimenters? After all, we use random assignment to balance out these kinds of individual differences across all conditions of the experiment. You already know that if the characteristics of subjects vary *systematically* in the different

---

[4]Be especially careful not to treat male and female subjects differently. Studies have found, for example, that male experimenters are apt to be more friendly toward their female subjects than their male subjects.

conditions of an experiment, we have a *selection* threat to the experiment's internal validity. But as long as a sufficient number of subjects are randomly assigned to each treatment group, we can assume that extraneous subject variables are controlled.

When we consider personality variables of experimental subjects, we are generally thinking about the general characteristics shared by typical subjects. We want to know if the subjects in a sample are truly representative of the population. No one has stated the problem better than McNemar (1946) when he said, "The existing science of human behavior is largely the science of the behavior of sophomores" (p. 333). Reading journal articles, you will find that the majority of published experiments are conducted on college students taking introductory psychology courses, because this is the most convenient source of samples for academic researchers. However, the sophomores who volunteer to be research subjects may not be entirely representative even of the general population of sophomores from which they come.

During the 1960s it was popular to conduct studies looking at the kinds of personality variables that discriminated volunteers from nonvolunteers, and the effects are conveniently summarized by Rosenthal and Rosnow (1969). For example, results of personality tests have shown that volunteers are likely to be more sociable and score higher in social desirability (Crowne & Marlowe, 1964) than nonvolunteers. Volunteers tend to hold more liberal social and political attitudes and tend to be less authoritarian than nonvolunteers. Interestingly, people willing to volunteer for experiments also tend to score higher on intelligence tests, on the average, than do nonvolunteers. Whether these differences remain today is an empirical question, but if they do exist, they would suggest that experiments using university samples may have somewhat less external validity than researchers would wish. These differences would be expected to tend to limit the generalizability of some kinds of experiments more than others.

CONTEXT VARIABLES

The preceding sections have covered the most important extraneous variables and ways to control them. In this final section, we will look at another set of extraneous variables, context variables, that can influence the results of experiments. **Context variables** are those that come about from procedures created by the environment, or context, of the research setting. Context variables represent subject recruitment, selection, and assignment procedures, as well as typical problems encountered in research on a university population. Most are easily controlled with some forethought. We will cover two basic kinds of context variables: those occurring when subjects select their own experiments and those produced when experimenters select their own subjects.

When the Subjects Select the Experiment

When you run an experiment using human subjects, you may be allowed to recruit your subjects from a *subject pool* of psychology students. Most departments of psychology in major universities rely on students to serve as research subjects from time to time. (Perhaps you have already had the experience of serving as a subject in someone else's research.) In research universities, psychology students are typically required either to participate in a certain number of experiments or (if they choose not to volunteer) to fulfill a substitute requirement. Frequently, a list of experiments needing subjects is posted in a central location on campus. Sometimes students can sign up for a session on the spot, or other arrangements can be made. Students can often look over what is available, select one that seems interesting, and make an appointment to participate.

Usually, there are two factors involved in the decision: Am I free at a time when subjects are needed? What kind of experiment is it? Often, the only information that potential subjects are given is the name of the experiment. Sometimes these titles can bias your sample, reducing the external validity of your experiment. Suppose students have the following two choices: "The Memory Test Experiment," and "The Heavy Metal Music Experiment." Do you think students who volunteer for the two experiments might be somewhat different? Of course. To avoid getting a biased sample, researchers try to keep the names as neutral as possible, without sounding boring: "The Impression Formation Experiment," "The Close Relationships Experiment." Instead of "The Sexual Practices Survey," it could be called "Contemporary Judgments." A biased sample greatly reduces your ability to generalize your findings; the experiment will have less external validity.

The time for subjects to decide *not* to participate in your experiment, if that happens, is after the experiment has been explained to them at the beginning of the session. Always keep track of any subjects who drop out (and what condition of the experiment they were assigned to) for later reporting; even though it is unlikely that your experiment will include conditions that are noxious enough to produce a *subject mortality* threat. Keep in mind that some subjects who volunteer probably will miss their sessions for a variety of reasons (Friday sessions are notorious for no-shows), so it is always a good idea to plan about 10% more sessions that you actually need.

When the Experimenter Selects the Subjects

You may be required to recruit your own subjects from the university population or from outside. The information you learned about random selection procedures (Chapter 3) is also applicable here. If you do not select your subjects randomly, your sample will be biased, resulting in less generalizability. If you use a convenience sample, your results may not be generalizable beyond these subjects. There are some common pitfalls to avoid when selecting subjects. It is always best to use people you do not know, because the behavior of your friends in your experiment will differ from more typical subjects (Rosenthal, 1976). Once you have chosen a population (perhaps other university students), you cannot recruit only those people who smile and seem friendly and approachable. Control for this possible threat by constructing a procedure for randomly selecting the people you approach *ahead of time,* and stick to it. For instance, if you decide to ask every fifth person who walks by, you must adhere to this procedure even if person 5 is the president of the university or has six rings in each nostril. You must plan out your procedures for acquiring subjects as carefully as you plan your experimental procedures, and you must keep your demeanor uniform throughout the selection process.

Assigning subjects to conditions can have similar pitfalls. If you conduct your experiment in the laboratory using volunteers from the subject pool, you probably will not be tempted very much to deviate from your procedure for determining random assignment to conditions. However, if your experiment is conducted in the field, you can expect to find some subjects a bit aggressive or intimidating. If you had your choice, you would probably prefer to give them the (easier) control condition and send them on their way. Avoid this temptation. What would happen if all your "nice" subjects ended up in the experimental group, while the "nasty" subjects all fell in the control group? The actual effects would depend on what you were testing, but regardless of the experimental outcome, your experiment would be confounded by a *selection threat.* Again, the best way to control for this possibility is to design an assignment procedure, and stick with it.

Some Folklore about Subjects

The conventional wisdom among academic researchers is to beware of data collected from the end-of-the-term subject pool: students who sign up late in the term might be less motivated to participate than those who volunteer early. Rosenthal (1969) puts the problem this way: "In the folklore of psychologists, there is the notion that sometimes, perhaps more often than we would expect, subjects contacted early in an experiment behave differently from subjects contacted later" (p. 190). He argues, though, that changes are just as likely to be caused by changes in the experimenter—namely, *practice* and *fatigue effects.* As you read your instructions over and over to subjects, you become more practiced, more accurate, and faster. Over the course of the experiment, you become more fatigued (i.e., less interested or bored). The first can be controlled, somewhat, if you become highly practiced before you run any subjects; the second is more difficult to counteract. Make sure that your random assignment procedure ensures that one condition is not finished up earlier than another, or you could become an *instrumentation threat.* Again, the best advice is to minimize face-to-face contact, so that you will have less impact on how your subjects behave.

This chapter brings us to the close of the Method section of this text. We have covered many techniques for designing and running solid experiments.

We have discussed control over extraneous variables that can threaten both internal and external validity. In Part 3, we will look at results and our next important question: What do we do with our data once we have them?

SUMMARY

One of the major goals in setting up experiments is to avoid confounding by controlling extraneous variables. The independent variable should be the only thing that changes systematically across the conditions of the experiment. This principle is essential to all good experiments. Several control procedures can be used to handle extraneous *physical variables*—aspects of the testing conditions that need to be controlled, such as the nature of the testing room, the time of day, and the mechanics of running the experiment. The three general techniques for dealing with physical variables are *elimination, constancy of conditions,* and *balancing.*

Uncontrolled *social variables* (demand characteristics and experimenter bias) may threaten the internal validity of an experiment. *Demand characteristics* can create problems in experiments. Just being in an experiment can lead to changes in a subject's behavior that may have nothing to do with the experimental manipulation. Subjects may want to be "good" subjects; they may try to provide data that confirm the hypothesis. Their expectations about what will happen to them in the experiment can also shape their responses. One way of controlling demand characteristics is to run a *single-blind experiment.* Here the experimenter tells subjects everything about the experiment except which treatment they will receive. Because the subjects in a single-blind experiment do not know for sure which treatment condition they are in, they are less likely to provide data that are distorted to conform to their notion of what the researcher expects to find. Another way to reduce demand characteristics is to use a *cover story,* which disguises the real research hypothesis.

Another potential source of error is *experimenter bias.* Without realizing it, an experimenter may give subtle cues that tell subjects how they are expected to behave. If an experimenter smiles at subjects every time they give the predicted response, he or she may not be getting an accurate picture of the way the independent variable operates. One way to control for experimenter bias is the *double-blind experiment,* in which neither the experimenter nor the subjects know which treatment the subjects are getting. This approach enables the experimenter to measure the dependent variable more objectively.

Characteristics of experimenters and volunteer subjects, called *personality variables,* can also affect the results of experiments. Experimenters who are warm and friendly, for example, tend to produce more and better data from subjects than experimenters who are hostile or authoritarian. We control for these variables by strictly adhering to our procedures and minimizing face-to-face contact with subjects. Levels of certain personality variables, like sociability and intelligence, tend to be higher in volunteer subjects than in nonvolunteers. This difference might decrease the external validity, or generalizability, of experiments using college student subjects.

Some extraneous variables, called *context variables,* are created by the experimental context or setting. If subjects are allowed to select their own experiments, the names of experiments can bias the sample when different kinds of subjects volunteer for different-sounding experiments, reducing generalizability further. When the experimenter selects the subjects, there are certain pitfalls to avoid, such as selection or assignment based on how friendly or unfriendly the subject seems. This bias, too, can reduce generalizability or, in extreme cases, can even confound the experiment. Experimenters also need to be aware of the possibility that they can show practice and fatigue effects over the course of running an entire experiment and take precautions to control for them.

KEY TERMS

Balancing A technique used to control the impact of extraneous variables by distributing their effects equally across treatment conditions.

Constancy of conditions A control procedure used to avoid confounding; keeping all aspects of the treatment conditions identical except for the independent variable that is being manipulated.

Context variable Extraneous variable stemming from procedures created by the environment, or context, of the research setting.

Cover story A plausible but false explanation of the procedures in an experiment told to disguise the actual research hypothesis so that subjects will not guess what it is.

Demand characteristics The aspects of the experimental situation itself that demand or elicit particular behaviors; may lead to distorted data by compelling subjects to produce responses that conform to what subjects believe is expected of them in the experiment.

Double-blind experiment An experiment in which neither the subjects nor the experimenter know which treatment the subjects are in; used to control experimenter bias.

Elimination A technique to control extraneous variables by removing them from an experiment.

Experimenter bias Any behavior of the experimenter that can create confounding in an experiment.

Personality variables The personal characteristics that an experimenter or volunteer subject brings to the experimental setting.

Physical variables Aspects of the testing conditions that need to be controlled.

Placebo effect The result of giving subjects a pill, injection, or other treatment that actually contains none of the independent variable but elicits a change in subjects' behavior regardless.

Rosenthal effect The phenomenon of experimenters treating subjects differently depending on what they expect from the subjects; also called the *Pygmalion effect.*

Single-blind experiment An experiment in which subjects are not told which of the treatment conditions they are in; a procedure used to control demand characteristics.

310 PART TWO METHOD

Social variables The qualities of the relationships between subjects and experimenters that may influence the results of an experiment.

REVIEW AND STUDY QUESTIONS

1. What are physical variables in an experiment?

2. How is elimination used as a control procedure? Give two examples of variables that could be controlled by elimination.

3. What is constancy of conditions? Give two examples of variables that could be controlled through constancy of conditions.

4. What is balancing? Give two examples of variables that could be controlled by balancing.

5. You are doing a study at a local school. Because of the way things are scheduled, you can have one small testing room in the morning and another much larger testing room in the afternoon. If you have two treatment conditions (experimental and control), how can you assign subjects to the testing rooms so that the type of room will not lead to confounding in your experiment?

6. What are demand characteristics? How do they affect our data? How can they be controlled?

7. A researcher says, "I want my experiment to be a success. I'm sure my hypothesis is correct. So I'll just give my subjects a couple of hints here and there. You know, maybe a wink now and then if they give a good answer. That way I'll really be able to show that my independent variable had an effect."
   a. How would you convince her that her plan is faulty?
   b. What is a double-blind experiment? Would you recommend that she use it? Why or why not?

8. Dr. L. is planning a large-scale learning experiment. He would like to have 100 rats in the experimental group and another 100 in the control group. Because he needs so many rats, he says, "Well, I can't test all these animals by myself. I'll ask Dr. P. to help me. She can run the animals in the control group while I test the animals in the experimental group."
   a. Knowing what you know about experimenter bias, is Dr. L.'s solution a good one? What may happen if one experimenter tests all the experimental subjects while another tests all the control subjects?
   b. Given what you know about balancing procedures, work out a better plan for Dr. L.

9. When should a cover story be used? When shouldn't one be used? Discuss the ethical problem raised by the use of cover stories.

10. Why is it important that an experimenter behave in the same way toward all subjects in the experiment? What precautions can be taken to ensure that he or she does this?

11. In what ways are volunteer subjects different from nonvolunteers? What difference does it make?

12. Find out the names of several experiments that are being conducted in your department this term. Evaluate each name in terms of its potential to bias the sample.

13. Think of two things an experimenter could do to safeguard against *fatigue effects* during the course of the experiment.

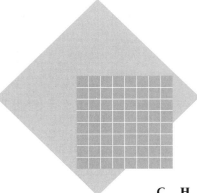

WHY WE NEED STATISTICS

Somehow the word *statistics* brings terror to the eyes of even the most dedicated student—and you may be feeling the same emotion. If you glance through this chapter, however, you will find that only a few basic computations are presented. Instead, the chapter is intended to give you a general understanding of why we use statistics in research. We will cover some of the basic terms you need in order to understand how statistics are applied. We will discuss the principles of statistical inference and the logic behind statistical tests. By the end of this chapter, you will know how to begin organizing and summarizing your data. Selecting data analyses for different research designs (as well as how to conduct them) will be presented in Chapters 13 and 14.

Statistics are quantitative measurements of samples. Through statistics we can quantify the phenomenon we observe. Vesselo (1965) summed it up in this way:

> Loose phrases such as "miles away," "poles apart," "a giant's stride," "minute," "pinpoint," "in a nutshell," though picturesque, are notably inaccurate. Though this is unimportant in conversational or literary activity, these impressions persist; when transferred to fields of serious thought, where important and far-reaching decisions are being made, leading to a choice of alternative lines of actions, or when planning for the future, with a great expenditure of time and money and even life at stake, vague impressions will not do. Accurate measurement and comparison, and estimation in a scientific form are vital. (p. 189)

Many different kinds of statistics can be computed on any given sample. A statistic may be thought of as a numerical index of some characteristic of the data. Each statistic describes something different about the data, much as miles per gallon and compression ratios each tell us something different about our cars. Some statistics can be used to make comparisons between different samples.

We work with statistics because they allow us to evaluate objectively the data we worked so hard to collect. Let us look at a hypothetical murder mystery to demonstrate the kind of evaluation that takes place.

WEIGHING THE EVIDENCE

Ms. Adams has just been arrested for murder. Detective Katz has found the victim's car keys, footprints, and bifocals in Ms. Adams's apartment. Witnesses say the victim and Ms. Adams were having dinner together at the local coffee shop a short time before the crime was committed. Yes, there is evidence against her. But did she actually commit the crime? Detective Katz knows he must establish her guilt beyond a reasonable doubt. Can he do that? Yes, he has the keys, the footprints, and even the bifocals that were found in Ms. Adams's apartment. He has witnesses who will swear they saw the suspect and victim dining calmly on hot pastrami sandwiches a short time before the murder. But is this proof? What Detective Katz has put together is a case based on circumstantial evidence. The evidence suggests that Ms. Adams knew the victim well enough to share pastrami sandwiches and that the victim visited her apartment sometime before the murder. The evidence implicates Ms. Adams in the crime, but it does not *prove* that she did it. Other people may have known the victim well enough to share sandwiches, too. And other people may have committed the murder. Given the evidence, the best Detective Katz can do is attempt to establish Ms. Adams's guilt beyond a reasonable doubt. He can show that Ms. Adams, more than anyone else, is likely to be the murderer.

When we carry out a psychological experiment, we find ourselves in a plight similar to the one Detective Katz is in. Katz has investigated a case; we have run an experiment. Katz has collected evidence; we have gathered some data. Katz would like to prove his suspect committed the crime; we would like to prove our independent variable caused the changes we see in our dependent variable.

Given all you have learned about experimentation, you will not be too surprised to learn that we can never actually *prove* that an independent variable caused the changes we see in a dependent variable. Proving something means establishing the truth of it by presenting evidence and logical arguments. Do you remember doing proofs in geometry? You began with a premise such as this: *In every right triangle, the square of the hypotenuse is equal to the sum of the squares of the legs.* You would then use all the facts you knew about geometry to construct a logical argument that would prove the premise true. Your proof would show that the premise is true because there would be no logical alternative. You would come down to a final step that would look something like this: $AB = AB$.

Unfortunately, outside of mathematics, proving things is not always so straightforward. Detective Katz would like to prove Ms. Adams guilty. He believes she is. But can he develop a proof as airtight as $AB = AB$? No. Since his evidence is circumstantial, the best he can do is show that she is *probably* guilty.

When we evaluate the data from a psychological experiment, we do a very similar thing. We carry out statistical tests to determine whether the independent variable *probably* caused changes in the dependent variable from one treatment condition to another. We cannot really prove that it did. Other fac-

Copyright ©1996 by Sidney Harris

tors such as coincidence or chance can also lead to differences. Nevertheless, we can make some statements about how likely it is that the independent variable had an effect. We base those statements on the statistical tests that we do.

STATISTICAL INFERENCE: AN OVERVIEW

As we evaluate the results of an experiment, we naturally want to be able to come to conclusions about the impact of the independent variable. We could just look at our results and see which groups did better. But that would not be very precise. When we run an experiment, we typically start with a sample of subjects drawn from a population. The population consists of all people, animals, or objects that have at least one characteristic in common, and the sample is a group that *represents* the larger population. Remember that we typically test samples, but we want to be able to make inferences about the entire population we have sampled. Fortunately, the way statistics work allows us to do exactly that.

Within any population, the scores on a dependent variable will differ somewhat. Because the members of a population are different individuals, we do not expect everyone to score exactly the same. The scores of the subjects we sampled will also differ. The question we ask with statistics is this: Are the differences we see between treatment groups significantly greater than what we would expect to see between *any* samples of scores drawn from this population? Answering this question involves a **statistical inference**, making a statement about the population and all its samples based on what we see in the samples we have.

Suppose two groups of students in a class are asked to report their weights. To make a statistical inference about the two groups (samples), we must first calculate the **mean,** or arithmetical average, of each group by adding up the students' weights and then dividing the sum by the total number of weights. The mean weight of the 12 students on the window side of the room is 152 pounds. The mean weight of the 12 students on the opposite side of the room is 147 pounds, an absolute difference of 5 pounds. Would you conclude from these measurements that students on the two sides of the room do not belong to the same population? Perhaps they belong to different species. Or perhaps sitting near the windows causes students to gain weight. More likely, you are thinking that it is silly to make anything of a difference of 5 pounds. After all, not everybody has the same weight; the average weight of any two groups will differ somewhat. You have made a statistical inference based on your knowledge of the weight of these groups. You conclude they probably belong to the same population—even though you have not measured everyone in that population.

Defining Variability

When we measure subjects on any variable, we do not expect everyone to come out with exactly the same score. If we measure two or more groups on almost any dimension, we can expect some variability, or fluctuation, in their scores, just as we would expect that the weights of the 12 individuals in each of the two groups in our example would vary. Variability is one of the most important concepts you need to understand and to analyze the results of experiments. In a commonsense way, **variability** is the amount of change or fluctuation we see in something. The altitude of California varies from its highest point, Mt. Whitney, which is 4418 meters (14,494 feet) high to its lowest point in Death Valley, which is 86 meters (382 feet) below sea level.[1] In between are areas at sea level, inland valleys, and foothills. We could say there is a lot of variability in the altitude of places in California. There is relatively little variability in the altitude of Florida; most of Florida lies very close to sea level. The highest point in Florida is an unnamed place 105 meters (345 feet) high.

When we do a statistical test, we are asking whether our pattern of results is significantly different from what we would expect to see because of the usual variability among different people in the population. Since we are using

---

[1] *National Geographic Atlas of the World* (6th ed.) (1990), pp. 21, 26.

the scientific method, we do not want to answer this question in a subjective way. A researcher may wish to argue that his or her results are obviously significant. You may disagree. Instead of leaving the choice up to the individual, statistical tests have been set up so that we have *standards*—conventions or guidelines about what is significant so that everyone can agree on whether results are significant or not. In law we accept the verdict of the jury as our standard of guilt or innocence. In psychology we accept the outcome of statistical tests to establish whether an independent variable had an effect in a particular experiment. We can summarize the overall process of statistical inference with a few steps. In each experiment, the researcher (1) samples from a population, (2) states a null hypothesis, (3) chooses a significance level, and (4) evaluates the results of the experiment for statistical significance, rejecting or failing to reject the null hypothesis.

Testing the Null Hypothesis

In our legal system, a person is presumed innocent until proved guilty. We assume that the person did not do anything wrong until convincing evidence shows otherwise. We make a similar assumption about the independent variable as we set up statistical tests. Until we can determine otherwise, *we assume an independent variable has no effect.*

We do not actually test the research hypothesis of an experiment directly. Instead, we formulate and test the **null hypothesis (H_0)**, which states that the performance of the treatment groups is so similar that the scores must have been sampled from the same population. In effect, the null hypothesis says that any differences we see between treatments amount to nothing. We assume that a suspect is innocent until the evidence leads us to conclude that he or she is guilty. Similarly, we assume that the data from different treatment groups came from the same population, and any differences between them amount to nothing more than the ordinary variability in scores we would expect in any population. We hold to the assumption that the null hypothesis is correct until the evidence shows the assumption can be rejected.

At this point, you may be feeling a bit confused. "Don't we get our samples from the same population to begin with? Why do we have to assume that the data came from the same population?" Actually, the null hypothesis is not as strange as it seems. We do take our sample of subjects from the same population, at least as far as we know. Ideally, we take random samples and use random assignment to avoid creating treatment groups that differ from each other before the experiment even begins. In the experiment, however, we manipulate the independent variable so that the treatment groups are exposed to different conditions. When the experiment is over, we would like to be able to *reject the null hypothesis* by showing that the effect produced by the independent variable led to real differences in the responses of the groups. We reject the null hypothesis by showing that our treatments produced differences sufficiently large that they are unlikely to be encountered within the same population even if we take normal variability into account. And in a sense, even though we test only a sample, the experiment is testing whether the population of untreated subjects' scores now differs from the population of treated subjects' scores.

We use statistical tests to tell us if we can reject the null hypothesis or not. If we reject the null hypothesis, we are confirming a change between the groups that occurred as a result of the experiment: Our results are **statistically significant.** If we can reject the null hypothesis, we are saying that the data from the treatment groups are now so different that they look as if they came from different populations; the normal *variability* of scores on the dependent measure is not enough to account for our results. However, when we retain the null hypothesis, we are saying that the scores from the treatment groups are still so similar that the experimental manipulation must have had little impact; the pattern could be explained simply by normal variability in a single population.

There is no way to directly test the **alternative hypothesis (H_1)**—the research hypothesis—which states that the data came from different populations. Therefore, we can never really *prove* that our research hypothesis is correct. There is no way to *prove* that the data came from different populations or that the independent variable caused the pattern of results. The best we can do is show it is unlikely that the pattern occurred from chance variation within the population we sampled: We can only show that the null hypothesis is probably wrong.

Let us suppose our experiment deals with the effects of background music on job performance. We form two random groups of subjects and place them in identical testing rooms. We give them sets of purchase invoices and instruct them to write a seven-digit account number on each one, separate out the carbon copies, and order them alphabetically. The task is routine and similar to many office jobs. We want to test the research hypothesis that background music enhances job performance. We can only test this alternative hypothesis *indirectly* by attempting to show that the null hypothesis is probably false. We predict that the experimental group that hears background music will process more invoices in a set period of time than a control group that does not hear background music. So that we will not create experimenter effects during the testing, we operate all our equipment controls from outside the testing rooms. After playing taped instructions over an intercom, we turn on the music for the experimental group by flipping a switch on a control panel. The control group performs in an identical but quiet room.

When the testing hour is over, we return to collect our materials. We debrief the subjects, explaining the purpose of the experiment and what we expected to find. To our dismay, subjects in the experimental group become uneasy. They are concerned about their hearing because it seems they did not hear any music at all. With a little checking, we discover that the control switch is not working. When we thought we turned on the music, nothing happened. The music affected our experimental group as much as it did the control group—not at all.

What do you think would happen if we went ahead and counted up the number of invoices each group processed anyway? Our treatment groups were

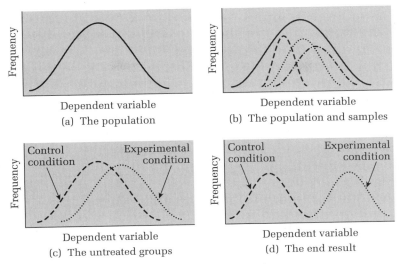

FIGURE 12-1 A schematic representation of statistical inference in an experiment in which the independent variable had a large effect.

randomly selected from the same population and randomly assigned to the two conditions. Thus we would expect both groups to have processed about the same average number of invoices. Our independent variable had no effect on the experimental group, so there is no reason to expect the performance of the two groups to be very different. We expect their performance will continue to look like the performance of two groups drawn from the same population.

When we do a statistical test, we begin by doing essentially the same thing: We formulate the null hypothesis by stating that the performance of the treatment groups is so similar that the groups must belong to the same population. We reject the null hypothesis when the difference between treatments is so large that chance variations cannot explain it. A series of *frequency distributions* in Figure 12-1 illustrates the general way this process works in an experiment in which the independent variable has a large effect.

Process of Statistical Inference

1. Consider the population to be sampled: Because of variability, individual scores on the dependent variable will differ.

2. Consider different random samples within the population: Their scores on the dependent variable will also differ because of normal variability. Assume the null hypothesis is correct.

3. Apply the treatment conditions to randomly selected, randomly assigned samples.

4. After the treatment, the samples now appear to belong to different populations: Reject the null hypothesis.

B O X   1 2 - 1

FREQUENCY DISTRIBUTIONS OF SCORES

We often represent a group of individual scores on a dependent variable by graphing the distribution of scores in the form of frequency distributions. You will be seeing many of these in the pages to come. In graphing a frequency distribution, you should mark off possible values of the dependent variable along the *abscissa*, the X or horizontal axis at the bottom. Frequencies (numbers of individuals) are marked off on the *ordinate*, the Y or vertical axis.

Suppose you have a data set consisting of 38 subjects' scores on a seven-point rating scale—a scale with numbers from 0 to 6 used as the dependent measure. The possible values of the scale would be listed at equidistant points along the abscissa. The leftmost mark along the abscissa would be the smallest possible value—0. This would be followed by a mark for 1, 2, 3, and so on, up to 6.

Frequency would be marked off on the ordinate, beginning with a frequency of 0 near the bottom of the ordinate, then 1, 2, and so on, until you get to the number representing the *maximum frequency* for any score. Let's say that the number 3 on the scale was chosen by more people than any other number and that it was chosen by 10 subjects. The maximum frequency for any score, then, will be 10. So the last value you would mark off near the top of the ordinate is a 10. Now that you have labeled the graph, you simply plot the frequency for each value of the dependent variable as we have done in Figure 12-2.

Because the dependent variable has seven values, you would end up with seven points on the graph. Each point represents the number of individuals (frequencies) that chose each of the seven values: one person chose 0; four people chose 1, and so on. (You can tell the number of individuals by adding up the individual frequencies: $1 + 4 + 7 + 10 + 8 + 6 + 2 = 38$.) Finally, you simply connect the dots. The distribution of your sample data is now represented by a curve, sometimes called a *frequency polygon*. You will notice that the frequency distributions illustrating general concepts rather than actual sets of data look more symmetrical and do not have the abscissa or ordinate completely labeled. Of course, graphs do need to be completely labeled if an actual data set is used.

A frequency polygon makes it easy to examine an entire data set at a glance. You can plot one experimental group or several on the same

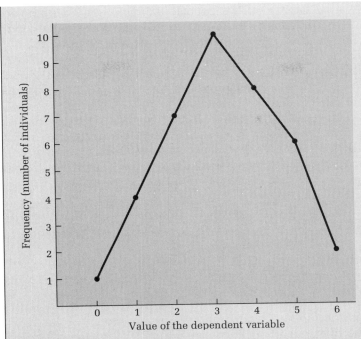

FIGURE 12-2 Hypothetical frequency distribution for a data set from a sample of 38 participants.

graph (see Figure 12-1). You can visually inspect the data to see whether the curve resembles the shape of the normal curve depicted in Figure 12-3. While we will not cover the procedure in this book, statistics courses teach ways that you can *transform* a data set so that it more closely approximates a normal curve. This sometimes makes it easier to reject the null hypothesis.

Whether or not we will reject the null hypothesis depends to a large extent on variability. When there is a great deal of variability in the population, large differences between samples will be common. The more variability there is on the dependent measure, the greater the difference between treatment groups has to be before we may say that the data look like they belong to different populations. *The more variability, the harder it will be to reject the null hypothesis.*

In an experiment we want to be precise; we want to know exactly how much variability there is in the data. Then we can estimate the exact odds that we would see such large differences between treatment groups even if the independent variable had no effect. There is always some chance that the null hypothesis is true; even very large differences can occasionally appear between two samples from the same population.

The reasoning is the same when we evaluate the data from a within-subjects experiment. If the difference in the data from various treatment conditions is large in relation to variability, then we may be able to reject the null hypothesis. We may conclude that the data of subjects under different treatments look like data that probably came from different populations; the odds are that something in the experiment produced a significant change in subjects' behavior from one condition to another. The null hypothesis (H_0) states that the means (average scores) for the treatment conditions come from the same population. Thus the difference we see between two treatments merely reflects chance variation: We have drawn two samples from a population in which there is variability on the dependent measure. Let us turn to another example so we can look at these principles in a more concrete way.

APPLYING STATISTICAL INFERENCE: AN EXAMPLE

Imagine we are running another experiment. This is our hypothesis: Time passes quickly when you are having fun. This is a **directional hypothesis**; it predicts the way the difference between groups will go. We are saying that time will go faster, not slower, for people who are having fun than for people who are not having fun. We have decided to use a two-group, between-subjects design. We operationally define "having fun" as looking at a collection of cartoons. Our experimental group will be given the cartoons and instructed to examine them to see how funny they are. We will not tell subjects that they will be given 10 minutes for the task. The control group will also be given 10 minutes to examine the same cartoons, minus the captions. Control subjects will see the drawings, but they will miss the punch lines and will not have much fun. The independent variable is fun. The dependent variable is subjects' estimates of the amount of time that elapses during the experiment.

A small deception is used in this experiment: We do not tell the subjects the true purpose of the experiment beforehand. After subjects examine the cartoons for 10 minutes, we ask them to estimate the amount of time that has passed since they started. The null hypothesis (H_0) is that the time estimates of the two groups are similar and were sampled from the same population. Note that this is different from the research hypothesis (H_1), which says that the fun group will make shorter estimates.

Suppose we have actually run the experiment and computed the means. The mean estimated elapsed time for the control group is 12.5 minutes. The mean estimated elapsed time for the experimental group is 8.4 minutes. On the face of it, the experimental group really did seem to experience the time as going more quickly than the control group; on average, the members of the experimental group thought that only about 8 minutes had passed. To them it seemed they had been at their task for less time than the actual clock time. The control group on average estimated the elapsed time to be longer than it really was. Can we conclude that fun makes the time pass more quickly?

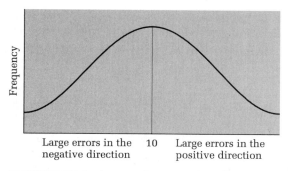

Large errors in the   10   Large errors in the
negative direction   positive direction

FIGURE 12-3 A normal curve: Hypothetical distribution of time estimates of all college sophomores estimating the length of a 10-minute time interval.

No. You know that we have to consider the variability in the data before we can draw any conclusions about the differences we find between two treatment groups. We need to evaluate our data with statistical tests. Our first step was to state a null hypothesis: The time estimates came from the same population. Now if we could measure the population from which our samples were drawn—say, all college sophomores—we would find that ability to estimate elapsed time varies. Some people are very accurate; others are inaccurate. Some overestimate time; others underestimate. If we could somehow test all college sophomores and ask them to estimate the length of a 10-minute interval, we might get a frequency distribution that looks something like the one shown in Figure 12-3. This distribution is a **normal curve**—a symmetrical, bell-shaped curve. The bulk of the scores represented by this distribution fall close to the center. (Most students' estimates will be fairly accurate.) Many of the statistical tests you will do include the assumption that the population you have sampled is normally distributed on the dependent variable. If you could somehow measure everyone in the population on that variable, the frequency distribution of all those measurements would be a normal curve.

Since we are rarely able to measure the whole population we want to study, we make inferences about what goes on in the population. We base those inferences on what we see in our samples. Keep in mind that what we want to know about our data is whether the differences we observe between treatment groups are significant. The means of different samples of subjects will vary when they are measured on just about any variable, but can we reject the null hypothesis? In reality, we are rarely able to work with the normal curve that represents the actual population of interest. However, means of samples have a distribution, too. It is called the *sampling distribution of the mean*. The larger the sample size, the more closely this distribution will resemble a normal curve.

It is also possible to construct the distribution of other statistics, such as the difference between means of samples drawn two at a time from the same population. Because of variability, any two samples will differ from one another. Some will differ a great deal, some very little. The question is whether they differ enough to allow us to conclude that the null hypothesis is not a likely explanation for what we have observed. In our time-passage experiment, the null hypothesis says that although the time estimates of our groups are different, they only reflect chance variations. The greater the variability in the population, the less likely it is that we will be able to reject the null hypothesis. If the population varies greatly, then occasionally we would even expect to see very large differences between samples from that population. Those large differences could occur by chance and would have nothing to do with the independent variable.

The figures we are using to illustrate these relationships are, of course, hypothetical. We cannot measure everyone in the population. So although the figures help us understand the logic of what we expect to happen in an experiment, they do not help us make decisions about our data. Fortunately, mathematicians have worked out other methods.

The test statistics we will cover later are mathematical representations of the relationship between observed differences between groups and variability. Test statistics have known distributions that we *can* use to make inferences about our data. In the next chapter, you will find some examples of how these sorts of inferences are made. The process requires some knowledge of probability theory.

We make our decisions about the null hypothesis on the basis of probabilities. How likely is it that a difference so large occurred just by chance? What are the odds that the usual variability in the population led to treatment groups that differ so much on the dependent variable? We test the null hypothesis (H_0) for two reasons. First, it is the most likely explanation of what has occurred. When we measure different samples, or even the same sample at different times, we expect some variation between them. It would actually be very unusual to get exactly the same data from different groups. So when groups differ, we are most likely observing variations that would occur even if there had been no experimental intervention. Second, there is no way we can directly verify the alternative to the null hypothesis. The alternative hypothesis (H_1) states that the treatment means are so different that they come from distinct populations. H_1 is actually what we would like to show. We would like to be able to say that the treatment groups differ because of our experimental manipulation. Unfortunately, no matter how different the groups are, there is always some chance that the results were caused by sampling error. Like Detective Katz, the best we can do is show that our explanation for what happened is *probably* true.

Choosing a Significance Level

To decide whether the differences between our treatment conditions are significant, we need a **significance level**, a criterion for deciding whether to retain or reject the null hypothesis. How much of a difference between treatments do we require? If the differences between treatments are probably caused by the chance variation in the population, we cannot talk about a treatment effect. You know that there is always a possibility that even extreme differences between treatments occurred by chance.

Now suppose you knew that, by chance, the odds of getting a difference as large as we found are about 2 out of 3. The treatment means were likely to be different—even if the independent variable had no effect at all. Would you be willing to scrap the null hypothesis? If we rejected the null hypothesis against those odds, we would probably be wrong two out of three times. We would be saying that the means came from different populations when they actually came from the same one.

Naturally, we would like to be reasonably sure about our conclusions. If we reject the null hypothesis, we would like to know that our decision is probably correct. How sure we need to be can vary depending on the circumstances: Suppose you are at a sidewalk sale and you find a good-looking, cheap shirt. Because it is a sidewalk sale, however, you cannot try on the shirt, and if you buy it, you cannot return it. You guess there is a 1 in 10 chance that the shirt will not fit. Will you buy it anyway? Your decision will be based on what you stand to lose. If the shirt costs $5, you might risk it. But you might not risk $20. If you are short of cash, you might not be willing to risk anything. Similarly, when we evaluate the results of an experiment, we evaluate the risks involved in making the wrong decision. If we are dealing with life-and-death research on new drug therapies or suicide prevention, we will be much less willing to risk being wrong. We might be somewhat more relaxed in a taste test of a new beverage. What an experimenter does in a particular experiment depends on what he or she is testing. However, there are conventions for deciding whether to accept or reject the null hypothesis. In psychology, by convention, we can generally reject the null hypothesis if the probability of obtaining this pattern of data by chance alone is less than 5%. Then we say the significance level is $p < .05$ (read "p less than .05"). A significance level of $p < .05$ would be appropriate for our time-estimation experiment.

When we choose a significance level of .05, we are saying that we will reject the null hypothesis if we get a pattern of data so unlikely that it could have occurred by chance less than 5 times out of 100. That is actually less than the odds of tossing a coin four times and getting four consecutive heads.[2] It is possible to get four heads in a row—but it is not likely. If we saw it happen, we would probably ask to see the coin. If we see such unlikely differences between treatment groups, we reject the null hypothesis and say that our results are statistically significant.

In some experiments we may want a stricter criterion. We may choose a significance level of $p < .01$. That means the odds of getting such large treatment effects by chance are less than 1 in 100—that is, a little less than the odds of tossing a coin six times and getting six consecutive heads. Pharmaceutical

[2] For the curious reader, the actual probability of four heads in a row is $p = .0675$ ($.5 \times .5 \times .5 \times .5$).

research, for example, generally adopts this criterion. Even stricter criteria, such as $p < .001$ (less than 1 in 1000), might be chosen for some medical research or other projects in which being wrong about a treatment effect could have disastrous human consequences.

To make a valid test of a hypothesis, we must think ahead and decide what the significance level will be before running the experiment. It is not legitimate to collect all the data and then pick the significance level depending on how the results turned out. The experiment would yield significant results—but only because we stacked the deck in our favor. For instance, we might find that the difference between performance of two treatment groups is significant at the .20 level. That would mean a difference this large could have occurred just by chance about 20 times out of 100. We might accept this as a meaningful difference, but we would not be making a very rigorous test of the hypothesis. (And, by convention, p values greater than .05 in psychological research would not be considered statistically significant by other researchers.) Now that precise probability levels can be easily obtained using computer data-analysis programs, many researchers simply report the significance levels of the results they obtained so that readers can evaluate them on their own. Reporting obtained probability levels is also commonly done when the results did not reach the significance level the researcher had chosen.

In the time-estimation experiment, we are testing the notion that time passes quickly when a person is having fun. Assume we had chosen $p < .05$ as the significance level for this experiment. We would evaluate the results against this criterion. If the results could have occurred by chance more than 5% of the time, we could not reject the null hypothesis: The data are too similar to say that they probably came from different populations, and the results are not statistically significant. However, if the results could have occurred by chance less than 5% of the time, we are able to reject the null hypothesis: The data are statistically significant—they look as if they came from different populations. This is just another way of saying that the independent variable apparently had an effect: It altered the behavior of the treatment groups. Our groups started out the same, but their scores on time estimation now look as if they came from different populations.

Figure 12-4 illustrates the way the distributions of sample means from those two populations might look. The figure represents what we would find if we were able to test all possible samples from both populations (people who are having fun and people who are not). Of course, there is variability among the samples drawn from both populations; some samples give more accurate estimates than others. In this idealized situation, however, you can see that the populations do not overlap. On time estimation, people who are having fun are distinctly different from people who are not. On the average, people who are having fun consistently say that time passes more quickly than it does for the control subjects who are not having fun. If that were really so, we would expect to obtain large differences between treatment groups exposed to different levels of the independent variable (fun). We would expect a significant difference between treatment groups if the independent variable had such a large effect on subjects' behaviors.

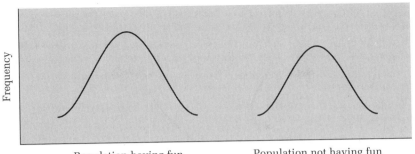

FIGURE 12-4 Hypothetical distributions of populations having fun and not having fun. The independent variable had a large effect on subjects' time estimates.

In reality, the picture is rarely so perfect. Many extraneous variables can affect the outcome of an experiment, and the data may not be a true reflection of the impact of the independent variable. Recall from Chapter 11 that variability also can be produced by the many forms of **experimental errors.** Experimental errors are variations in subjects' scores produced by uncontrolled extraneous variables in the experimental procedure, experimenter bias, or other influences on subjects not related to effects of the independent variable.[3] Also, although the experimental manipulation is effective, its impact may not be as powerful as the one we have drawn here. More typically, we expect some overlap between treatment populations. But we cannot be sure exactly how much overlap there is because we usually cannot measure every possible sample. And because of this overlap, our conclusions about the results may be wrong.

Type 1 and Type 2 Errors

Even though our results were statistically significant, there is always some probability that the null hypothesis could still be true. It could be that we have somehow obtained treatment means that really do belong to the same population. They seem to be significantly different even though the independent variable really had no effect. What are the odds of making that mistake? After all, we reject the null hypothesis only if the treatment groups are very

---

[3]Increased variability in scores from sample data may be caused by any number of uncontrolled factors in an experiment. Some "errors" may be caused by the behavior of the experimenter or deficiencies in the manipulation or measurement procedures; others may be the result of chance differences in subjects at the time of the experiment. For example, suppose the experimenter is having a bad morning, and inadvertently treats one subject in a less friendly manner than usual, making the subject somewhat anxious. This subject's anxiety can alter scores on the dependent variable from what they would have been otherwise, contributing variability to the group's scores. Similarly, subjects may have a bad day or be overtired or sick, affecting their scores and thereby adding variability to the data.

different. Is this really a problem? How serious the error is depends on the actual experiment. If the decision involves a life-and-death issue, the consequences could be very serious. However, from a practical standpoint, making the wrong decision about the null hypothesis is always serious. Why bother to run a carefully controlled experiment only to draw the wrong conclusions at the end?

If we reject the null hypothesis when it really is true, we have made a **Type 1 error:** A Type 1 error occurs when we say that significant differences between treatments were produced by the independent variable even though it really had little or no effect at all. The odds of making a Type 1 error are exactly equal to the value we choose for the significance level. If we are using a .05 significance level, the probability of a Type 1 error is .05. If our significance level is .05, then 5 times out of 100 (or 5% of the time), we will reject the null hypothesis when we should not. There will be 5 times out of 100 when the large differences we see really occurred by chance. If we choose a more extreme .01 significance level, the probability of a Type 1 error is .01, or 1 chance in 100.

Could we minimize the odds of a Type 1 error simply by choosing a more extreme significance level? Yes, but there is a trade-off in doing that. We can make a second kind of error, a **Type 2 error:** We can fail to reject the null hypothesis even though it is really false. When we conclude that the pattern of results was caused by chance variations when it was really caused by the independent variable, we have made a Type 2 error. We have missed a treatment effect that was really present.

The more extreme the significance level, the more likely we are to make a Type 2 error. There is a greater chance of a Type 2 error at $p < .01$ than there is at $p < .05$. But how does a Type 2 error happen? Won't the differences between treatments be so extreme that we will surely find them? Not necessarily. Treatment effects are easier to find when the independent variable has a very dramatic effect (and there is not much variability between subjects on the dependent variable). Then, we might wind up sampling from two completely distinct populations, such as people having fun and people not having fun (as in Figure 12-4), which show no similarity at all. *But more typically, the responses of the populations will overlap.* Figure 12-5 illustrates that possibility for the experiment on time estimation.

When data from two populations look very similar, there is no sure way we can tell that they come from different populations. These are the cases that lead to a Type 2 error. Because there is overlap between the responses we sample, we are sometimes unable to show a significant difference between the treatments, even though the independent variable had some effect. Instead, we retain the null hypothesis. We say that the differences between the treatment means occurred simply by chance.

The probability of making a Type 2 error is affected by the amount of overlap between the populations being sampled. If the responses of people having fun are very similar to those of people not having fun, it will be hard to show that fun altered the responses in any way. The more overlap there is, the harder it is to detect the effect of the independent variable. The proba-

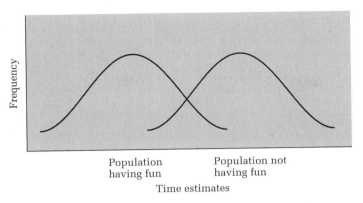

FIGURE 12-5 Hypothetical distribution of populations having fun and not having fun. The independent variable had a moderate effect on subjects' time estimates.

bility of making a Type 2 error is represented by the Greek letter β (beta). We would be able to find the exact value of β only if we could measure all possible samples of both populations. But say we knew that the odds of making a Type 2 error were equal to exactly .75 in our experiment. Then the odds of making a correct decision would be equal to 1 − .75, or .25. If we are likely to be wrong 3 out of 4 times (.75), then we should be right 1 out of 4 times (.25). The odds of correctly rejecting the null hypothesis when it is false are always equal to 1 − β.

This last quantity (1 − β) is also referred to as the *power* of the statistical test.[4] We touched on this concept in Chapter 7 in connection with sample size. Although we cannot measure the precise value of β, we can reduce it by increasing our sample size. We stand a better chance of correctly rejecting H_0 with a sample of 50 than with a sample of 20. As you know, the ability to detect a treatment effect is also related to how much variability there is in the population; therefore we can reduce β by reducing the variability in our sample data (for instance, by controlling extraneous variables or using a within-subjects or matched-groups design). We can also use the more powerful statistical tests, called *parametric tests*. They make certain assumptions about the parameters of the population represented by our samples (e.g., normally distributed data, comparable variability across groups, interval or ratio data). Tests known as *nonparametric tests* are used when these assumptions cannot be met. They are somewhat less powerful. (We will come back to these types of tests in Chapter 13.)

We can also accept a less extreme significance level. We are more likely to detect a difference using a significance level of $p < .05$ than one of $p < .01$.

[4]Even though beta cannot be precisely measured, there are useful charts and tables for estimating statistical power (1 − β). Power charts can be found in many statistics textbooks, but the classic source book is Cohen (1988).

Remember, however, that adopting a less extreme significance level also increases the chance of a Type 1 error.

The probability of making a Type 1 error is always equal to the value chosen as the significance level. This is represented by the Greek letter α (alpha). There is some chance (α) that we will reject the null hypothesis when we should have retained it. There is a $1 - \alpha$ chance that we will fail to reject the null hypothesis when that is the correct decision. Altogether, there are four possible decisions we can make when we evaluate the data from an experiment. These are summarized in Table 12-1.

When we make a Type 2 error, the independent variable has produced an effect, but we are unable to detect it. A Type 2 error is like acquitting a suspect who is guilty; we allow the suspect to go free although he or she really did commit the crime. When we make a Type 1 error, our mistake has greater implications for the suspect. Making a Type 1 error is like putting an innocent person in jail. We attribute a crime to someone who did nothing at all. We reject the null hypothesis and conclude that the differences between treatment means are so great that they confirm our predictions. For instance, we may conclude that the time estimates of people having fun are significantly less than the time estimates of people not having fun. Remember, that does not prove the research hypothesis; it suggests that it is *probably* true. Of course, we are always pleased to confirm our predictions. We can begin to speculate on all the important consequences of having demonstrated a significant effect. But think about what is happening in this case. When we make a Type 1 error, we explain an effect that does not really exist, and this can often be a more serious error than failing to detect an effect. The possibility of making a Type 1 error makes it especially important that we replicate the findings of experiments.

TABLE 12-1 Evaluating results: The four possible outcomes and the odds that they will occur

	Your Decision	
	Not to reject the null hypothesis	**Reject the null hypothesis**
Null hypothesis is true. (The data came from the same population.)	You are correct: $p = 1 - \alpha$	You have made a Type 1 error: $p = \alpha$
The Real Story		
Null hypothesis is false. (The data belong to different populations.)	You have made a Type 2 error: $p = \beta$	You are correct: $p = 1 - \beta$

NOTE: p stands for probability; α represents the significance level of the experiment.

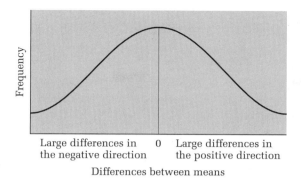

FIGURE 12-6 Hypothetical distribution of the differences between all possible pairs of means drawn from a distribution.

THE ODDS OF FINDING SIGNIFICANCE

Together with choosing and applying a significance level, it is important to understand how the odds of finding significance are affected by two factors: the amount of variability in the data and whether we have a directional or a nondirectional hypothesis. Let us take a closer look at how these factors influence the outcome of an experiment.

The Importance of Variability

Suppose we could somehow measure all possible samples of college sophomores on time estimation. We would see that the distribution of means of those samples is a normal distribution—a symmetrical, bell-shaped curve. Like individual subjects, some samples perform better than others. Most are about average; but some do well and some do poorly. Suppose we could take all possible pairs of samples and find the differences between their means. We would get another distribution. The outcome would resemble Figure 12-6. You can see that many of the differences between sample means fall right around zero. Because time estimation is normally distributed, the means of most samples will be close to the mean of the population on that variable. The differences between those means will be very small. However, some differences are very large; they occur at the extremes of the distribution. They represent differences between means of groups that are far apart on time estimation. As you can see, extreme differences are infrequent. We find fewer and fewer instances as we move away from zero. There is variability in the differences between means just as there is variability between samples.

Some differences between means are more likely than others. For normal distributions, it is possible to calculate the odds that each difference will occur (and statisticians have spent a lot of time calculating these odds for us). The

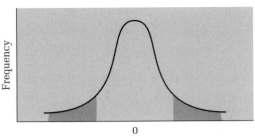

(a) A distribution with low variability

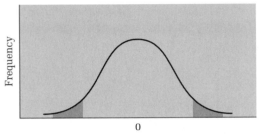

(b) A distribution with moderate variability

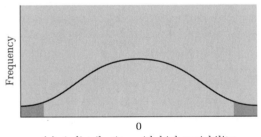

(c) A distribution with high variability

FIGURE 12-7 Three hypothetical distributions of differences between sample means. Shaded areas represent the most extreme 5% of each distribution.

odds of getting very small differences—close to zero—between the means of any two samples are high. Most sample means fall close to the mean of the population, so if you subtract one sample mean from another, the difference will be close to zero. We should not be too surprised if the groups in our experiment turn out to be very close together on the dependent variable. But the odds of seeing much larger differences are less. The exact odds depend on the amount of variability in the population.

Large differences are more likely in populations that have high variability on the dependent measure. Figure 12-7 shows you three distributions of differences between sample means. The distributions are similar except for the amount of variability in the populations sampled. The first distribution shows differences between the means of samples from a population in which the variable that was measured showed little variability. Because the sample means are all relatively close to each other (that is, they showed little variability), the differences between them also tend to be small. The second distribution is based on a population in which the variable measured showed a moderate amount of variability. You can see that the differences between means of samples from this population tend to be larger than the differences in the first distribution. The third distribution is based on a population in which the variable measured showed a great deal of variability. You can see that this distribution is the widest. The differences between the means of the samples from this population tend to be very large because there is a great deal of variability in the population.

The shaded areas of the curves in Figure 12-7 are the **critical regions** ($p < .05$), the parts of each distribution that make up the most extreme 5% of the differences between means. Differences large enough to fall within these areas will occur by chance less than 5% of the time. If our significance level is $p < .05$, we will reject the null hypothesis if the treatment groups differ by amounts that fall within these critical regions. Do you notice anything special about where the cutoffs for the 5% levels are? You will find that they fall in a different place for each distribution. Actually, as the amount of variability in the distribution goes up, the critical regions fall farther from the center of the distribution. *When there is more variability, larger differences are required to reject the null hypothesis.*[5]

Ideally, we want our treatment conditions to be the only source of variability in an experiment. We reduce experimental error by controlling variables such as testing conditions and practice time that might create differences between subjects' scores and therefore introduce unwanted variability. For instance, in the time-estimation experiment, we must be careful to give everyone exactly 10 minutes to look at the cartoons. Remember, we will be making inferences about the population on the basis of the samples we observe. If our samples produce highly variable data, we must assume that the population is also highly variable on the dependent measure. If the population has high variability, finding a statistically significant effect requires very large differences between the scores from different treatment groups in the experiment. Any unnecessary sources of variation in an experiment will not only reduce the chances of rejecting the null hypothesis, they will also increase the chances of a Type 2 error. It will be difficult to get significant results if extraneous variables are not carefully controlled.

---

[5]When there is very little variability, however, statistically significant results can sometimes be obtained from very *small* differences between treatment groups—so small that they can seem trivial. For example, imagine that everyone in our time estimation experiment was a pretty good judge of time, and each subject's estimate was very close to 10 minutes. Suppose that the average score of the experimental group and the control group differed by only .8 seconds. This small difference could be statistically significant, even though it might not be very meaningful in real-life terms.

"Darling, you have made a significant difference in my life ($p < .01$)."

One-Tailed and Two-Tailed Tests

In Figure 12-7 you will also notice that the critical regions of the distributions have been divided up between both ends of the curves. For each curve, the 5% critical region includes 2.5% on the low end and an additional 2.5% on the high end. These curves have been marked to illustrate a **two-tailed test** of a hypothesis: The critical region of the distribution is divided between its two tails.

We use a two-tailed test whenever we have a **nondirectional hypothesis**, one that does not predict the exact pattern of results—the direction of the effect we will produce through the experimental manipulation. For example, cars driven on oil A perform differently from cars driven on oil B. Notice that the hypothesis predicts there will be a difference between the performance of cars driven on two different brands of oil. However, there is no indication of what the pattern of results will be. Will cars driven on A perform better than those driven on B? The researcher has not made a prediction on that. The hypothesis is nondirectional.

You can understand why we use a two-tailed test with such a hypothesis if you think about what we mean by significance level and critical region. We want to know if our pattern of results is so unlikely that it was probably not caused by chance variations in the population; we want to know whether differences between treatment groups fall within the critical region. When a researcher states a nondirectional hypothesis, he or she is willing to accept extreme differences that go in either direction. It does not matter whether A is better than B or vice versa; the researcher has only postulated that the independent variable produces a difference. Since differences in either direction are acceptable, the critical region, the most extreme 5% of the distribution,

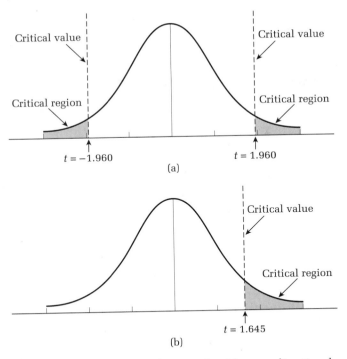

FIGURE 12-8 The critical region for (a) a nondirectional (two-tailed) test and (b) a directional (one-tailed) test.

has to be split between both tails of the curve. Suppose we did not split it, but instead included 5% on each end of the distribution. If we did that, we would be changing the significance level—in fact, we would have doubled it. We would be saying that we would reject the null hypothesis if the difference falls in the most extreme 10% of the distribution.

Often we are able to make a more precise prediction about the effects of the independent variable. These may be based on our own pilot studies or on our review of prior research. A nondirectional hypothesis can often be transformed into one that is directional: for example, that cars driven on oil A perform better than cars driven on oil B. Now we are predicting exactly what we will see when we evaluate the performance of cars driven on oils A and B; we predict that A will fare better than B.

When we have a directional hypothesis, we make a **one-tailed test:** The critical region is located in just one tail of the distribution. The hypothesis that time passes quickly when you are having fun is a directional hypothesis, and it requires a one-tailed test. Figure 12-8 shows the relative locations of the critical regions of the same distribution using a one-tailed and a two-tailed test.[6]

---

[6]The distribution shown depicts locations of critical regions for the t statistic, which will be discussed in Chapter 13.

The advantage of using a one-tailed test is obvious. The size of the critical region is larger and closer to the center of the distribution, making it easier for differences between means to be large enough to fall there. You can see from the figure that the *critical value,* the minimum statistical value needed for significance, will be smaller when we do a one-tailed test. Treatment effects do not need to be as dramatic when we have a directional hypothesis; we can get significant results more easily when we use a directional hypothesis and a one-tailed test.

You may be thinking that it will be easy to get significance now. We can just state our hypothesis in a directional way; then, if the data go in the other direction, we will change the hypothesis and still have significant results. It is a reasonable idea, but unfortunately we cannot handle things that way. Just as you need to choose a significance level in advance, you need to decide on the hypothesis in advance and stick to it. Otherwise, you have not tested anything. If you write a hypothesis to fit results you already have, you are actually describing a set of data after the fact. Of course, there is nothing inherently wrong with offering explanations for observations. That is how we generate new hypotheses. However, we cannot call that experimentation. By definition, when we experiment we make a controlled test of a hypothesis that has already been stated.

So far we have looked at hypothetical distributions based on the means of all the samples that could be drawn from a population. These make wonderful illustrations of the concepts we are discussing. However, to draw these figures, we had to assume we were somehow able to take huge numbers of samples. In the real world, that is nearly always impossible. We do not have the actual distributions of all sample means when we run an experiment; we rarely even know the average score for the whole population. Instead, we have to draw conclusions on the basis of the few samples of subjects that we do have. To do that, we compute inferential statistics.

TEST STATISTICS

Inferential statistics are statistics that can be used as indicators of what is going on in the population. They are also called **test statistics** because they can be used to evaluate results. A test statistic is a numerical summary of what is going on in our data. When we compute a test statistic, we transform the relationship between treatment differences and variability into a simple quantitative measure. Generally speaking, the larger the value of the test statistic, the more likely it is that the independent variable produced a change in subjects' responses. A large test statistic indicates that the differences we see across treatments are large relative to the amount of variability in the data.[7] We are more likely to be able to reject the null hypothesis if we obtain a large test statistic.

You know there is always *some* chance that the null hypothesis really is true. It is always possible that even a large test statistic is within the range of

---

[7]Distributions for some test statistics, such as the chi square test covered in Chapter 13, are not based on population means and variability; they have a different basis for rejecting the null hypothesis.

events that could occur by chance. But think about a throw of the dice. You know that the odds of rolling 7 are greater than the odds of rolling snake eyes. How do you know? You can calculate the odds of each event. There are more ways to make 7 than there are to make 2. Similarly, statisticians have worked hard to calculate just how likely every value of a test statistic would be. Each test statistic has its own distribution of values. For each value, statisticians have calculated the probability that the value could occur just by chance due to random sampling. Those values and probability levels are summarized in tables like the ones you will find at the back of this book.

Although we have anchored our discussion of statistics to examples of particular experiments, we have not dealt with many of the details of doing the actual statistical tests. In the next two chapters, we will look at how we decide which test to use. We will also look closely at the actual procedures used to compute and evaluate test statistics.

ORGANIZING AND SUMMARIZING DATA

Suppose we have actually run an experiment and we have the data. What do we do with them? Where do we begin? There are three basic steps in analyzing any set of data: First, we organize it. Second, we summarize it. Third, we apply a statistical test to interpret our results. We will look at the first two of these steps in the present chapter.

Organizing Data

We start by organizing the data we have collected. Hypothetical data from our time-estimation experiment have been organized in Table 12-2. You can see that these data have been laid out in columns. Subjects' responses are divided into two columns, one for each of the two treatment groups; each subject in each group is listed by number next to his or her datum. Statistical work will go more quickly and be more accurate if you begin by organizing the data

TABLE 12-2 Laying out organized data

Group 1 (Incomplete Cartoons)		Group 2 (Complete Cartoons)	
Subject	Time Estimate (min)	Subject	Time Estimate (min)
S_1	11.2	S_6	13.6
S_2	16.2	S_7	10.9
S_3	13.3	S_8	5.5
S_4	12.1	S_9	8.8
S_5	18.2	S_{10}	9.2

and labeling them in a clear and orderly way. Especially with more complex designs, you will avoid a great deal of confusion if you take the time to prepare data tables. Many students find it easiest to use columnar paper, such as bookkeeping paper. At the very least, do your work on lined paper so you will be sure which datum belongs to which subject. You can simplify the task by preparing an orderly data sheet that you can use to record subjects' responses throughout the experiment.

Summarizing Data: Using Descriptive Statistics

Published articles rarely contain the data obtained from every single subject in the experiment. The data we record as we run an experiment are called **raw data.** Like raw potatoes, they are unprocessed and sometimes hard to swallow.

Whenever we report the results of an experiment, we report **summary data** rather than raw data. Usually readers are not interested in the scores of individual subjects, and neither are we. Rather, we want to compare treatment effects, and we do that by comparing group data. (The only exception is a small N experiment.) When we have group data, we summarize them with **descriptive statistics,** shorthand ways of describing data: They represent standard procedures for summarizing results. For example, when we want to order a window shade, we do not carry the window frame to the hardware store. Instead, we summarize its characteristics using the standard dimensions of length and width. Similarly, we summarize and describe data by using some of the standard descriptive statistics: measures of central tendency (mean, median, and mode) and measures of variability (range, variance, and standard deviation).

Measures of Central Tendency

As you know, statistics are quantitative indexes of the characteristics of our samples. Some of the most commonly computed and reported statistics are **measures of central tendency,** summary statistics that describe what is typical of a distribution of scores. The **mode** is the score that occurs most often. The **median** is the score that divides the distribution in half so that half the scores in the distribution fall above the median, half below. The **mean** is the arithmetic average: Add all the scores together and divide by the total number of scores, and you have the mean. The mean is by far the most commonly reported measure of central tendency, and you will need to report it in your research report. Only the mean can be manipulated algebraically (an important feature in statistical analysis).

Together, the mean, median, and mode are useful indicators of the *shape* of the distribution of values in our data. If the distribution is symmetrical and has only one mode (no scores tied for most frequent), the mean, median, and mode will coincide. Distributions of scores are rarely perfectly symmetrical. More often they are asymmetrical, or *skewed*—one tail of the distribution will be longer than the other, representing more extreme low or high scores. In a skewed distribution, the mean, median, and mode will be different, and each may lead to different impressions about the data. The mean is particularly sensitive to skew; it is pulled in the direction of extreme scores. Consider this set of scores:

3 4 5 6 6 6 7 8 9

These data form a symmetrical distribution. The mean is 6, the mode is 6, and the median is also 6. Suppose we substitute a higher score (18) into the set:

3 4 5 6 6 6 7 8 18

The distribution of scores is no longer symmetrical. Substituting the single extreme score has altered the shape of the distribution; to accommodate the extreme score, one tail is now longer than the other, so the curve has become skewed. The mode and median are still 6. However, the mean is now 7. The mean has increased because of one exceptionally large score. Alternatively, if our distribution had been skewed in the direction of an extreme low score rather than an extreme high score, the mean would have been less than the mode and median.

Even when the means of two distributions are the same, the distributions may be quite different. Reichmann (1961) cited these examples:

a. 5 5 6 6 6 6 7 7
b. 1 2 4 9 10 10

In (a) the mean is 6 and is truly typical of the data because the distribution is symmetrical. In (b) the mean is also 6, but clearly 6 is not a usual score.[8] Note that the mode can be useful to describe distributions that contain many identical scores. The mode of (a) is 6 and the mode of (b) is 10, but obviously the mode would be more representative of (a) than (b).

Clearly, the summary statistic we choose to report can make a difference in the impression we create through our data. Wages are often cited as one category of data that is subject to distortion. The distribution of wages in the United States is not symmetrical but is skewed to the right; lots of people earn relatively small amounts of money, whereas a few earn a great deal. The mean income is thus always higher than the median or the mode because millionaires pull the mean up. Corporate management would prefer to use means in salary negotiations; labor would prefer to talk in terms of median or modal

---

[8]You will need to report means in your report, but there are times when you may also want to include modal or median scores if a complete description of your distribution of values would be helpful to the reader. For example, if almost everyone in the experimental condition had the same value, the mode would be useful information; if your sample data were strongly skewed, the median might be reported along with the mean.

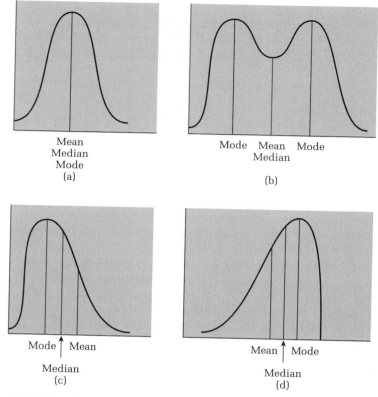

FIGURE 12-9 Mean, median, and mode in different distributions.

salaries. When evaluating any descriptive data, it is important to ask who is reporting what statistic and for what purpose. (Huff's *How to Lie with Statistics* [1954] is a delightful treatise on this topic.) Figure 12-9 depicts the mean, median, and mode of various distributions. Panel (a) illustrates a symmetrical distribution (the mean, median, and mode are the same). Panel (b) illustrates a *bimodal* distribution (two scores are tied for most frequent). Panels (c) and (d) represent two types of skewed distributions in which the mean, median, and mode are three different values.

Measuring Variability

We also use descriptive statistics to measure the amount of variability in data. You will need to report a measure of variability in your research report. So far we have talked about variability in a commonsense way: We say that anything that fluctuates has variability. When we do statistical tests, **variability** has more specific meanings. It is defined numerically by one of several

FIGURE 12-10 Two distributions with the same range (80 points).

descriptive statistics: the range, the variance, and the standard deviation. By using these statistics, we can compare the variability of one sample with that of another. The simplest measure of variability is the **range,** the difference between the largest and smallest scores in a set of data. If the scores on an exam varied from a high of 100 points to a low of 74, we would say that the range is 26. (Just subtract 74 from 100.) If the price of a 6-ounce bag of potato chips varies from 39 cents in one store to 53 cents in another, we would say that the price range is 14 cents. The range is often a useful measure; it can be computed quickly, and it gives a straightforward indication of the spread between the high and low scores in a distribution.

The problem with using the range is that it does not reflect the precise amount of variability in all the scores. Figure 12-10 shows you two distributions of test scores with the same range. You can see that the distributions are really very different from each other. The distribution for class 1 indicates that the test scores varied a great deal from student to student. In class 2, however, most students got similar scores; one extreme score accounts for the relatively large size of the range in this case. Knowing that these distributions have the same range tells us very little about them.

Computing the Variance

When we measure variability, we would like to be able to compare different samples in a more precise way. Computing the statistic we call the variance enables us to do that. Computing the variance is a way of transforming variability into a standard form that provides a good but simple description of how much individual scores differ from one another. By using the variance, we can talk about the variability of all our scores without having to present an entire set of data each time, just as we can order a window shade without carrying the window frame to the shop.

The variance tells us something about how much scores are spread out, or *dispersed,* around the mean of the data. Are they spread out a great deal around some central value, or are they tightly clustered around the mean? This can be useful information. Merchants sometimes use the concept of variance when they select stock for their stores. Let's take the example of figuring out how many pairs of women's shoes to order in a particular style. We know that the average shoe size of American women is $8\frac{1}{2}$. Clearly, an individual woman's shoe size can vary considerably from this mean. But how much do sizes typically vary? Are most women going to wear a size close to an $8\frac{1}{2}$, or will many women wear sizes far away from this average? Knowing how much variability to expect would help a store owner know how many pairs of each size to keep on hand. If shoe size varies only a little, most customers will wear a size close to $8\frac{1}{2}$, and the owner could safely stock only sizes that are close to the average without missing too many sales. But if there is a lot of variance in shoe size, the owner would want to stock some number of all the smaller and larger sizes, too, because it is likely that the next customer who walks through the door could have either very small or very large feet!

The **variance,** then, is the average squared deviation of scores from their mean. The easiest way to explain this is to show you how we get the variance. Table 12-3 shows the steps we follow to compute the variance of the scores of one group of subjects from the hypothetical time estimation data in Table 12-2. The scores are those of the group of subjects who estimated the time that passed while they were looking at a series of cartoons with missing captions. The steps are numbered so that you can follow them more easily. One way or another, you will be computing the variance in just about every statistical test that you do, so it is important to master this concept.

Step 1

We have already listed each subject's score, so step 1 has been completed. Note that each subject's score is represented by X_i.

Step 2

If we have not already done so, we must compute the group mean by first adding together the scores of all the subjects in the group. The total is represented in mathematical notation by the Greek letter *sigma* (Σ).

Step 3

Once you have the total of all the scores in the group, compute the mean. Divide the total of all the scores in the sample (ΣX_i) by the number of scores you have (N). The mean is represented by $\overline{X}$. The mean, an average, gives us an idea of what the overall sample is like. The mean time estimate of this

TABLE 12-3 Computing the variance: Time estimates of subjects who saw incomplete cartoons (in minutes)

Step 1. List each subject's score (X_i):

Subject	X_i
S_1	11.2
S_2	16.2
S_3	13.3
S_4	12.1
S_5	18.2

Step 2. Add the scores together:
$\Sigma X_i = 71.0$

Step 3. Compute the mean:

$$\overline{X} = \frac{\Sigma X_i}{N}$$

$$\overline{X} = \frac{71.0}{5}$$

$$\overline{X} = 14.2 \text{ min}$$

Step 4. Compute the deviation from the mean for each subject ($X_i - \overline{X}$):

$11.2 - 14.2 = -3.0$
$16.2 - 14.2 = 2.0$
$13.3 - 14.2 = -0.9$
$12.1 - 14.2 = -2.1$
$18.2 - 14.2 = 4.0$

Step 5. Square the deviation from the mean for each subject $(X_i - \overline{X})^2$:

$(-3.0)(-3.0) = 9.00$
$(2.0)(2.0) = 4.00$
$(-0.9)(-0.9) = 0.81$
$(-2.1)(-2.1) = 4.41$
$(4.0)(4.0) = 16.00$

Step 6. Add the squared deviations together:
$\Sigma(X_i - \overline{X})^2 = 34.22$

Step 7. Compute the variance:

$$s^2 = \frac{\Sigma(X_i - \overline{X})^2}{N - 1}$$

$$s^2 = \frac{34.22}{5 - 1} \text{ or } 8.6 \text{ min}$$

sample is 14.2 minutes. You can see that some subjects gave estimates that are above the mean and others gave estimates that are below it. In fact, in this sample no subjects' estimates are exactly equal to the mean. The mean is an overall description, but how representative it is of the sample depends on other factors, such as the variance.

Step 4

We now compute the deviations from the mean for each subject. Deviations are differences between what we see and what is typical. If someone behaves in an unusual way, we say that his or her behavior deviates from the norm.

A sample of data has a mean—that is, an average that gives us an idea of what the sample is like. The mean of this particular sample is 14.2 minutes. This tells us that when we added up the estimates of all the subjects in the sample and divided by the number of subjects, we got 14.2 minutes. It does not say that *each* subject estimated 14.2 minutes. Actually, we know that no one in this sample said that exactly 14.2 minutes had passed; all the subjects deviated from the group mean. But by how much? We can find out simply by calculating the difference between each subject's estimate and the group mean. We subtract 14.2 ($\overline{X}$) from the actual estimate each subject gave.

Step 5

Next, we square the deviations from the mean. Remember that when we multiply a negative number (for example, -30) by itself, the result is a positive number. That means that all squared deviations from the mean will be positive numbers even though some of the subjects fell below the mean and so had negative deviations from the mean.

Step 6

Now we add all the squared deviations together to get a total of squared deviations from the mean.

Step 7

Finally, we compute the variance. You can see that we need the results of steps 1 through 6 before we can do step 7. The formula is just a shorthand way of writing all the operations we perform to get the variance. The variance for a sample is represented by s^2. The s comes from the Greek letter sigma, used to represent the variance of a population. The formula tells us that to get the variance of a sample, we must divide the sum of the squared deviations from the mean by $N - 1$. N is the number of scores.

The variance formula actually tells us to compute an average—the *average of the squared deviations from the mean*. That is exactly what we mean by variance. The variance is an indicator of how much variability there is in our data. The more variability, the larger the variance. You may be wondering why the variance formula tells us to divide by $N - 1$, not simply by N: When we compute the mean, we divide by N. When we compute the variance for a sample, we are actually trying to estimate how much variability there is in the population we are sampling. Since we cannot measure the whole population, we draw inferences from samples. Statisticians have shown that samples typically *underestimate* the variance of the population, so we correct for this in the variance formula. We get a more accurate estimate of how much variability there is in the population if we compute the variance of a sample by dividing by $N - 1$ instead of by N.

The variance (s^2) for the subjects who were shown the incomplete cartoons is 8.6 minutes.[9] This tells us that, on average, the *square* of each subject's deviation from the group mean is 8.6 minutes. If we take the *square root* of the variance, we have another useful measure of variability, the **standard deviation,** or *s*. It reflects the average deviation of scores about the mean. We cannot compute that average directly by adding up the deviations; the total of the deviations from the mean is always zero. So we use the square root of the variance to return to the original unsquared units of measurement. The standard deviation of our "no-fun" group means that, on average, we can expect each individual subject to deviate from the group mean by 2.93 min-

---

[9]We have rounded this figure off to the nearest tenth. Remember the conventions used for rounding: Round down if the last digit is less than 5; round up if the last digit is more than 5. If the last digit is 5, we follow this rule: Round up if the digit to be rounded off is an odd number; simply drop the 5 if the digit to be rounded is an even number. Thus 8.35 becomes 8.4, and 4.65 becomes 4.6.

utes. We use the same procedures for each treatment group. To save time, we will tell you that those computations yield a group mean of 9.6 minutes and a variance of 8.8 minutes for the "fun" group, subjects who saw cartoons complete with caption. You may want to verify those figures by working through the formulas on your own.

When we report the results of our experiments, we usually report these summary statistics in place of raw data. Typically, we give the mean and the variance or standard deviation of each treatment group. We may also report the range, although the range is often not given in published reports because of its limited use. We have now completed the first two stages of analyzing our results: We have organized and summarized the data. The third step is to apply a statistical test to interpret our results. We will use the summary data again for computing test statistics in the next chapter.

SUMMARY

In principle, experimenters would like to prove that the independent variable caused the changes observed in the behavior of subjects under different conditions. In practice, however, the best they can do is show that the differences observed were *probably* caused by the experiment. Experimenters carry out statistical tests to determine whether the independent variable probably caused the changes in the dependent variable. They really cannot prove that it did, but they can make statements about how likely it is that the independent variable had an effect.

In a statistical analysis of data, we test the *null hypothesis* (H_0), which states that the differences between treatments amount to nothing more than expected variability in the data. *Variability* is the amount of fluctuation observed in scores on a dependent variable. We assume the null hypothesis is true until the evidence shows it can be rejected. To know whether or not to reject the null hypothesis, an experimenter needs to know how much variability is present on the dependent measure. The more variability there is, the greater the difference between groups has to be before we can say that the data probably came from different populations. Since we cannot actually measure the populations, we make *statistical inferences* from the samples we do measure.

Some differences between treatments are more likely than others, and it is possible to calculate the odds that each difference will occur. The *means* (averages) of most samples are close to the mean of the population. Thus the odds of getting treatment means that are fairly similar are high. The odds of seeing much larger differences are less. The exact odds depend on the amount of variability in the population. We decide whether the differences between treatments are statistically *significant* on the basis of probabilities. In psychology, by convention, we usually reject the null hypothesis if the difference between treatments is so extreme that it could have occurred by chance less than 5 times out of 100. This is called a .05 *significance level*. In effect, it says that the probability of getting so large a difference just by chance is less than .05 ($p < .05$).

If we have chosen a .05 significance level, and the difference between treatments is so large that it could have occurred by chance less than 5% of the time, we reject the null hypothesis. When we reject the null hypothesis, the *alternative hypothesis* (H_1), which states that the treatment data are sampled from different populations, is supported. When we reject the null hypothesis, we are saying that the experiment is the most likely explanation for the differences we have observed.

There are two types of decision errors, Type 1 and Type 2. A *Type 1 error* means the experimenter has incorrectly rejected the null hypothesis: The conclusion is that the differences between treatment means were probably not caused by chance—although, in fact, they were. *Type 2 errors* occur when the independent variable really did have an effect, but the experimenter fails to detect it: The null hypothesis is accepted when the treatment means were actually drawn from different populations.

The decision about the null hypothesis must take variability into account. *Test statistics,* numerical summaries of what is going on in the data, must be computed. For each test statistic, statisticians have calculated the probability of each possible value. Those probabilities are used to judge the significance of the results.

There are three basic steps in analyzing results: (1) organize the data; (2) summarize them; (3) apply the appropriate statistical test to interpret the results. We organize data by making sure that all subjects' responses are labeled clearly and separated by treatment condition. We summarize data by computing *descriptive statistics,* shorthand representations of data. Some commonly used descriptive statistics are the *measures of central tendency* (mean, median, and mode) and *measures of variability* (range, variance, and standard deviation).

The *mean* is the arithmetic average of all scores in a group. The *mode* is the most frequent score. The *median* is the score that divides the distribution in half.

We also want to know how much variability exists among subjects' scores. The *range* is the difference between the largest and the smallest scores in a set of data. Two distributions with the same range can look strikingly different; the range shows only how much the highest and lowest scores differ. The *variance* (s^2) is a more precise indication of the amount of variability. It reflects the amount of variability among all the scores in a distribution, and so it is a more useful indicator than the range. The larger the variance, the more subjects' scores differ from one another. The *standard deviation* is the square root of the variance. It reflects the average deviation of scores about the mean. Finding the standard deviation converts squared deviations back to the original unsquared units of measurement. The larger the standard deviation, the more each individual subject is apt to differ from the group mean.

KEY TERMS

Alternative hypothesis (H_1) A statement that the data came from different populations; the research hypothesis, which cannot be tested directly.

Critical region Portion(s) of the distribution of a test statistic extreme enough to satisfy the researcher's criterion for rejecting the null hypothesis—for instance, the most extreme 5% of a distribution where $p < .05$ is the chosen significance level.

Descriptive statistics The standard procedures used to summarize and describe data quickly and clearly; summary statistics reported for an experiment, including mean, range, and standard deviation.

Directional hypothesis A statement that predicts the exact pattern of results that will be observed, such as which treatment group will perform best.

Experimental error Variation in subjects' scores produced by uncontrolled extraneous variables in the experimental procedure, experimenter bias, or other influences on subjects not related to effects of the independent variable.

Inferential statistics Statistics that can be used as indicators of what is going on in a population; also called *test statistics*.

Mean An arithmetical average computed by dividing the sum of a group of scores by the total number of scores; a measure of central tendency.

Measures of central tendency Summary statistics that describe what is typical of a distribution of scores.

Median The score that divides a distribution in half so that half the scores in the distribution fall above the median, half below; a measure of central tendency.

Mode The most frequently occurring score in a distribution; a measure of central tendency.

Nondirectional hypothesis A statement that predicts a difference between treatment groups without predicting the exact pattern of results.

Normal curve The distribution of data in a symmetrical, bell-shaped curve.

Null hypothesis (H_0) A statement that the performance of treatment groups is so similar that the groups must belong to the same population; a way of saying that the experimental manipulation had no important effect.

One-tailed test A statistical procedure used when a directional prediction has been made; the critical region of the distribution of the test statistic (t, for instance) is measured in just one tail of the distribution.

Range The difference between the largest and smallest scores in a set of data; a rough indication of the amount of variability in the data.

Raw data Data recorded as an experiment is run; the responses of individual subjects.

Significance level The statistical criterion for deciding whether to reject the null hypothesis or not.

Standard deviation The square root of the variance; measures the average deviation of scores about the mean, thus reflecting the amount of variability in the data.

Statistical inference A statement made about a population and all its samples based on the samples observed.

Statistical significance Meeting the set criterion for significance; the data do not support the null hypothesis, confirming a difference between the groups that occurred as a result of the experiment.

Statistics Quantitative measurements of samples; quantitative data.

Summary data Descriptive statistics computed from the raw data of an experiment, including the measures of central tendency and variability.

Test statistics Statistics that can be used as indicators of what is going on in a population and can be used to evaluate results; also called *inferential statistics*.

Two-tailed test A statistical procedure used when a nondirectional prediction has been made; the critical region of the distribution of the test statistic (*t*, for instance) is divided over both tails of the distribution.

Type 1 error An error made by rejecting the null hypothesis even though it is really true; stating that an effect exists when it really does not.

Type 2 error An error made by retaining the null hypothesis even though it is really false; failing to detect a treatment effect.

Variability Fluctuation in data; can be defined numerically as the range, variance, or standard deviation.

Variance The average squared deviation of scores from their mean; a more precise measure of variability than the range.

REVIEW AND STUDY QUESTIONS

1. What is variability? Give three examples of dependent measures that you would expect to have high variability.

2. Jack is still looking for a shortcut. After running an experiment, he says: "Oh, wow. The difference between my two treatment means is 60 points. I mean, like, that's such a large difference that I'm sure my independent variable had an effect." What is Jack forgetting? Explain how you could account for his findings without assuming that his independent variable produced the difference between his treatment means.

3. What is a null hypothesis?

4. You have run an experiment to test the effects of noise on motor dexterity. It was a three-group experiment. Your three conditions were a control condition with no noise, a low-noise condition, and a high-noise condition. Your three treatment means are different. State the null hypothesis for your experiment.

5. a. Julie is going to run an experiment tomorrow in which her significance level will be $p < .05$. What does that mean?
   b. If she decides to use $p < .01$ as her significance level, will it be easier or harder for her to detect the effect of the independent variable? Why?

6. For each of the following examples, explain whether the researcher has committed a Type 1 or Type 2 error and why.
   a. Dr. G. rejects the null hypothesis although the independent variable had no effect.
   b. Dr. R. rejects the null hypothesis when it is false.
   c. Although the independent variable had an effect, Dr. E. retains the null hypothesis.

7. a. What are the odds that you will make a Type 1 error in an experiment?
   b. How could you reduce those odds?

8. Given what you know about Type 1 and Type 2 errors, explain why it is important to replicate the results of an experiment.

9. Explain why each of the following hypotheses is directional or nondirectional and whether it would require a one-tailed or two-tailed statistical test:
   a. Adversity builds character.
   b. Television viewing can affect children's attention spans.
   c. Recall of nonsense syllables improves with repeated presentations.
   d. Newborns behave differently under bright versus dim lights.

10. Mary is a little discouraged. She says: "If we cannot prove that our independent variable had an effect, why bother doing an experiment?" Explain to Mary what we do accomplish when we evaluate the results of an experiment.

11. What are the three basic steps for analyzing the results of an experiment?

12. What are descriptive statistics? Why do we need them in an experiment?

13. Define each of the following and explain what each tells us about a set of data:
    a. The mean, median, and mode
    b. The range, variance, and standard deviation

14. Two families have the same average income per person. Does this mean that each person in both families earns the same amount of money? Explain.

15. Below are two distributions of scores on a memory test. Find the mean, range, variance, and standard deviation of each group.

Group 1	Group 2
5	3
6	1
8	3
3	2
1	5

REFERENCES

Cohen, J. (1988). *Statistical power analysis for the behavioral sciences* (2nd ed.). Hillsdale, NJ: Lawrence Erlbaum Associates.

Huff, D. (1954). *How to lie with statistics.* New York: Norton.

Reichmann, W. J. (1961). *Use and abuse of statistics.* London: Methuen.

Vesselo, I. R. (1965). *How to read statistics.* London: George G. Harrap.

C H A P T E R   1 3

ANALYZING RESULTS: TWO-GROUP EXAMPLES

In the last chapter, we discussed the logic behind statistical tests, hypothesis testing, and statistical inference. We covered two of the three basic steps in analyzing results: organizing and summarizing the data. By now you may be thinking, "Okay, I have organized and summarized my data, and I still do not know what to do next." In this chapter, you will learn how to *analyze* data: how to select a statistical test and carry it through when you have a two-group experiment. We will begin by looking at the results of experiments with two independent groups. We will trace the process of selecting a statistical test, then we will actually carry out that test. Finally, we will apply some of the same principles to handle a two-condition experiment that was run within subjects.

If you have access to computers, you may wish to obtain packaged software to carry out the statistical procedures covered in this and the next chapter. Minitab, SPSS(X), BMDP, StatView, and SAS are some software programs that are currently used by psychologists. However, you will develop a greater understanding of what the procedures accomplish if you follow the examples in the chapters and work out the practice exercises yourself first.

WHICH TEST DO I USE?

The discussion of how to choose a statistical test was postponed until now so that we could present the various aspects of data analysis first. In practice, however, it is best to select a test (and a significance level) as you plan the design of the experiment.

When we looked at experimental designs, we developed a set of questions to help us choose the best design for an experiment. We can make decisions about which statistical tests to use in much the same way. The number of independent variables is still important. How many do you have? How many treatment groups? Is the experiment within or between subjects? Did you use matching? As you become more familiar with selecting and using statistics, you will not need to go through all these steps. But you will find it much easier to choose the right test if you begin with these questions. Along with the number of independent variables and treatment conditions, we need to consider the *type of data* we are analyzing. The way we measure the dependent variable makes a difference in the way we handle the results. There are different statistical tests for different kinds of data.

Levels of Measurement

Recall from Chapter 6 that the **level of measurement** is the kind of scale used to measure a variable. There are four levels of measurement: ratio, interval, ordinal, and nominal. To review quickly, a **ratio scale** has equal intervals between all its values and an absolute zero point. These attributes enable us to express relationships between values on these scales as ratios: We can say 2 minutes is twice as long as 1 minute.

An **interval scale** also measures magnitude, or quantitative size, and has equal intervals between values. However, it has no true zero point.

An **ordinal scale** reflects differences only in magnitude, where magnitude is measured in the form of ranks. We cannot be sure that the intervals between values are equal, and the scale has no absolute zero.

A **nominal scale** classifies items into distinct categories that have no quantitative relationship to one another. Nominal scaling provides the least information. It tells nothing about magnitude, nor does it have equal intervals between values.

Variables may be measured by using one of these four types of scales. Our examples have used mainly ratio and interval data because these scales yield the most information and researchers tend to prefer them. But remember that different techniques are needed for different types of data.

Selecting a Test for a Two-Group Experiment

To select the appropriate statistical test, first decide which level of measurement is being used to measure the dependent variable and then answer the other questions summarized in Table 13-1. You now have all the information you need to select a statistical test.

Table 13-2 shows the most common statistical tests, organized by the number of independent variables they can handle, the level of measurement of the dependent variable, and whether the experiment is within or between

TABLE 13-1 The parameters of data analysis

1. How many independent variables are there?

2. How many treatment conditions are there?

3. Is the experiment run between or within subjects?

4. Are the subjects matched?

5. What is the level of measurement of the dependent variable?

TABLE 13-2 Selecting a possible statistical test by number of independent variables and level of measurement

Level of measurement of dependent variable	One Independent Variable				Two Independent Variables		
	Two Treatments		More than Two Treatments		Factorial Designs		
	Two independent groups	Two matched groups (or within subjects)	Multiple independent groups	Multiple matched groups (or within subjects)	Independent groups	Matched groups (or within subjects)	Independent groups and matched groups (or between subjects and within subjects)
Interval or ratio	t test for independent groups	t test for matched groups	One-way ANOVA	One-way ANOVA (repeated measures)	Two-way ANOVA	Two-way ANOVA (repeated measures)	Two-way ANOVA (mixed)
Ordinal	Mann-Whitney U test	Wilcoxon test	Kruskal-Wallis test	Friedman test			
Nominal	Chi square test		Chi square test		Chi square test		

NOTE: You can find explanations of these tests in most standard texts on statistics. A good general source is Hurlburt (1994). For within-subjects factorial and mixed designs, see Myer and Well (1991).

subjects, or mixed. We will not discuss all the tests in detail; the table note supplies sources to consult for further information. Other tests not listed are used less often, and you may not need them until you take more advanced courses. Here and in the next chapter we will focus on the tests you are most likely to need for your first experiments.

Table 13-2 indicates "possible" tests; it does not tell us what we will definitely need in all cases. That is because we may be able to use more than one test. As you learn about the tests, you will also learn that each test has its own additional requirements.

Let us consider a simple two-independent-groups experiment that uses nominal data first. Imagine that a researcher wants to test whether subjects can be induced to make errors on a test question by first presenting them with a task designed to *prime,* or elicit, a certain incorrect response. Subjects in the experimental group are asked the following priming question by the experimenter: "What do the letters *T-O-P-S* spell?" Subjects will answer, "Tops." Then they are asked the following test question: "What does a car do at a green light?" Of course, the experimenter hopes subjects will give the wrong answer, "Stop," instead of the correct answer "go," because just seeing the word *tops* should make the rhyming word *stop* more likely to come to mind than the nonrhyming word *go.* Here the experimenter would merely record whether the subject made the error or not. The control group could be asked a different question. One question that would not be expected to produce very much interference with the answer to the test question might be: "What do the letters *C-A-R* spell?" After the subject responds, the same test question is asked, and the subjects' responses, correct or incorrect, are recorded. The data collected are nominal; each subject's answer falls into either the correct or incorrect category. How would we analyze the data from this experiment?

First, let's answer the questions from Table 13-1.

1. There is one independent variable (priming).
2. There are two treatment conditions (priming versus no priming).
3. The experiment is run between subjects. (There are different subjects in each treatment condition.)
4. The subjects are not matched.
5. The dependent variable is measured by a nominal scale.

With this information, we can select a possible test to use for the data from the tests suggested in Table 13-2. Table 13-2 suggests a chi square test for our priming experiment.

THE CHI SQUARE TEST

One type of inferential statistic is the chi square test. Because we make inferences about the population, we use many of the concepts from Chapter 12: testing the null hypothesis, sampling distributions, Type 1 and Type 2 errors, and critical values, for instance. However, the chi square test is a *nonparametric* test; it does not assume that the population has certain parameters, such as a normal (or any other shape) distribution, or that variances in the two groups are approximately equal. Instead of relating differences between treatment means to the amount of variability we would expect to see between any two sets of data drawn from the same population, a chi square compares frequencies (e.g., how many subjects answered correctly; how many incorrectly). A **chi square** (X^2) **test** determines whether the frequencies of responses in our sample represent certain frequencies in the population. The test requires that all responses be sampled independently; this simply means that you cannot test each subject more than once. It is commonly used for nominal data.[1]

In Chapter 12 we pointed out that researchers mostly prefer to use parametric tests (requiring interval and ratio scales of measurement) because they are more powerful. Nevertheless, computed chi squares are frequently seen in the research literature. An interesting published example is a recent experiment by McMinn, Williams, and McMinn (1994; experiment 3). These researchers tested whether identification of sexist language could be improved with training. Subjects in the experimental group received prior training in identifying sexist language; the control group did not. There were nine items in the test that actually contained sexist language. Results of chi square tests showed that the training had a strong effect on all nine items, although at least one subject made errors on each of the items even after training. (We will return to this study in Chapter 16.) You may find that you need to use a X^2 in your first experiment, so we will discuss it briefly here, even though the test tends to be less powerful than the other statistics we will cover.

To conduct a chi square test, data are first organized in the form of a 2×2 contingency table.[2] Frequency counts are tabulated and placed in the appropriate cells. The chi square compares the frequencies obtained in the experiment, called *obtained frequencies* (O), with expected population frequencies, called *expected frequencies* (E), to test the null hypothesis. H_0, here, is that obtained frequencies are not different from expected frequencies, or $O = E$. If the chi square test is significant, we can reject H_0. For a two-group experiment like this one, statisticians recommend that the expected frequency in each cell should be at least 10. Hypothetical data from 20 experimental and 20 control subjects from the priming experiment are shown in Table 13-3.

A chi square for two independent samples is very easy to compute with a hand calculator. First, obtain the expected frequency for each of the four cells in the table. Expected frequencies are computed for each cell from

---

[1]However, when sample data are extremely skewed or large differences exist in the variances of data from different groups in the experiment, assumptions from statistical tests designed for interval, or ratio data may be violated. In these cases, the researcher might switch to a chi square test to avoid inflating the Type 1 error rate.

[2]It is very simple to organize and summarize data for a chi square using frequency counts as data: A 2×2 table that includes both obtained and expected frequencies (as in Table 13-3) serves both to organize and to summarize the data. There is no need to calculate measures of central tendency or variability.

TABLE 13-3 Number of correct and incorrect responses from experimental and control groups

| | Outcome of Study | | |
	Correct Responses	Incorrect Responses	Row Totals
Experimental group	4 (12)	16 (8)	20
Control group	20 (12)	0 (8)	20
Column totals	24	16	

NOTE: Expected frequencies are shown within parentheses.

observed frequencies, using the following formula:

$$E = \frac{(\text{Row Total}) \times (\text{Column Total})}{N}$$

Here, N is the total number of responses (in this case, 40). Each of the expected frequencies has been included in Table 13-3, but let us try to compute one. Let's compute E for the top left cell:

$$E = \frac{(20) \times (24)}{40}$$

$$E = \frac{480}{40}$$

$$E = 12$$

Once you have the expected frequencies, you can calculate X^2, using this formula:

$$X^2 = \Sigma \frac{(O - E)^2}{E}$$

Substituting our data, we would have:

$$X^2 = \frac{(4 - 12)^2}{12} + \frac{(16 - 8)^2}{8} + \frac{(20 - 12)^2}{12} + \frac{(0 - 8)^2}{8}$$

$$X^2 = \frac{(-8)^2}{12} + \frac{8^2}{8} + \frac{8^2}{12} + \frac{(-8)^2}{8}$$

$$X^2 = 5.333 + 8 + 5.333 + 8 = 26.667$$

We have obtained a chi square value of 26.67 (rounded off). Is that enough? To know, we must compare the value we obtained (X^2_{obt}) with the **critical value** needed to reject H_0. The critical value is the minimum value necessary to reject the null hypothesis at our chosen significance level. The critical value can be found in the X^2 table of critical values (Table B2 in Appendix B). To select the appropriate X^2 distribution from the table, however, we need to first understand the concept of degrees of freedom.

Degrees of Freedom

We select the appropriate distribution for test statistics such as X^2 based on **degrees of freedom (df)**. The degrees of freedom tell us how many members of a set of data could vary or change value without changing the value of a statistic we already know for those data. Samples that are the same size can have different degrees of freedom depending on the way the experiment is designed and on the statistic being computed. Let us say we know the mean of the data. Then the degrees of freedom tell us how many members of that set of data could change without altering the value of the mean.

Imagine that a phone number is a set of data. It has seven digits. Suppose that the total of the seven digits in the number is 37 and that the first six digits of the number are 8, 9, 4, 3, 9, and 2. Can you find the last digit? Of course you can. Since you know the total and six of the digits, you can easily compute the value of the last digit, which is *not free to vary*. Different combinations of the first six digits are possible. But once their values have been set, the value of the last digit is also set if the total must equal 37. If we tried to substitute any other value for the seventh digit, the total, or the known statistic, would no longer be correct. The degrees of freedom for this phone number therefore equal 6. If we include an area code in the data—say 2, 1, 2—we would say that the telephone number has 10 digits. It now totals 42, and its degrees of freedom now equal $10 - 1$, or 9. Clearly, the degrees of freedom are related to the number of digits, or data, in a sample.

Similarly, the degrees of freedom in the distribution of a statistic vary in a way related to the number of subjects sampled. However, we compute degrees of freedom differently for different test statistics. For analysis of a 2×2 contingency table, there is only 1 *df*. (The actual formula for computing the degrees of freedom is: number of rows minus 1 × number of columns minus 1; in this case $(2 - 1) \times (2 - 1) = 1$.

Sometimes all but one value of a set of data can change, sometimes many fewer, as is the case with X^2. The way we compute the degrees of freedom can also vary with different applications of the same statistic, as we will see later in the chapter. If we are using different statistics or the same statistic applied in different ways, we may have different degrees of freedom even though sample sizes are identical. That is why the critical values of test statistics are always presented and organized by degrees of freedom rather than by number of subjects.

The Critical Value of X^2

Now that we know that the X^2 test for our experiment has 1 *df*, we can look up the critical value in Appendix B. For a significance level of .05, the critical value needed to reject H_0 is 3.84. If our X^2_{obt} is this large or larger, our effect is statistically significant; we can reject the null hypothesis. In this case, X^2_{obt} is 26.67, which is much larger than the critical value necessary for significance at $p < .05$. Notice that if we had set our significance level at .01, our test would still have been statistically significant. In the priming experiment, it is very likely that the independent variable had an effect! If we were writing up the results of this experiment, we could now say the following:

1. The research hypothesis was supported. (We never say it was "proven." Why?)
2. As predicted by the research hypothesis, there was a significant difference between the experimental and the control condition.
3. Subjects who received the T-O-P-S prime were much more likely to give the incorrect response, "Stop," than were subjects who were given the control prime.

If you are using packaged software for your statistical analyses, you will not need to look up any critical values; instead, the program prints out the actual level of statistical significance obtained by the test. If it is less than the level of significance you selected (typically $p < .05$), your results are considered significant. This is one of the many advantages of using computers to analyze data. Once you have a thorough background in statistics, statistical analysis with computers can be a great time saver and offers tremendous flexibility. But there are disadvantages, too. The program will accept whatever data you have; for example, it will run programs designed for interval or ratio data even if your data are nominal. And the program will not tell you how your results should be interpreted; only a good grounding in statistics will provide those kinds of answers. (Incidentally, it is usually easy for your instructor to tell when a student uses a statistic that she or he does not fully understand.) Figure 13-1 shows a sample StatView printout for the X^2 analysis we just computed. What was the actual significance level obtained?

THE *t* TEST

Now, let us return to our hypothetical time-estimation experiment from the previous chapter and answer the questions from Table 13-1 to select a statistical test.

1. There is one independent variable ("fun").
2. There are two treatment conditions ("fun" versus "no fun").
3. The experiment is run between subjects. (Each treatment condition has different subjects.)

```
                    Contingency Table Analysis
                       Summary Statistics

  DF:                                         1
  Total Chi-Square:                           26.667      p = .0001
  G Statistic:                                   .
  Contingency Coefficient:                     .632
  Phi:                                         .816
  Chi-Square with continuity correction:      23.438      p = .0001
```

NOTE: When StatView analyzes a 2 x 2 contingency table, it automatically computes contingency coefficients and Phi, but it does not explain what they mean. Would you know how to interpret this printout?

FIGURE 13-1 StatView Analysis of Priming Experiment
NOTE: When StatView analyzes a 2 × 2 contingency table, it automatically computes contingency coefficients and Phi, but it does not explain what they mean. Would you know how to interpret this printout?

4. The subjects are not matched.
5. The dependent variable is measured by a ratio scale (time).

For this hypothetical experiment, Table 13-2 suggests the t test for independent groups, a common test statistic. When we want to evaluate interval or ratio data from a two-group experiment, we compute the test statistic t, which is a computational way of relating differences between treatment means to the amount of variability we would expect to see between any two sets of data drawn from the same population. When we introduced the concepts of one- and two-tailed tests in the last chapter, we illustrated these concepts with a figure of a t distribution showing critical regions and critical values for statistical significance. When we evaluate the likelihood of obtaining a particular value of t, we are performing a **t test.**

The exact probabilities of each value of t have been calculated for us. However, the distribution of these values changes depending on the number of subjects in the samples. Before actually computing t for the time-estimation example, let us examine the family of t distributions and the effects of sample size.

Effects of Sample Size

The size of our sample is very important. If we take both small and large samples from the same population, we will generally find that small samples vary more from the mean of the population than large samples do. You already know that parametric test statistics represent a relationship between treatment effects and variability. If sample size affects variability, it also affects the size of the test statistics.

For a test statistic such as t, sample size is critical because the exact shape of the distribution of t changes depending on the size of the samples. The t statistic has a whole family of distributions, some of which are shown

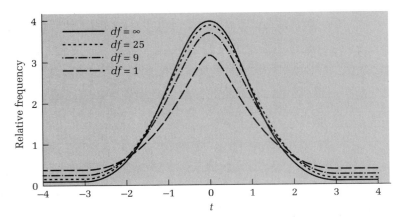

FIGURE 13-2 Some members of the family of *t* distributions.
Adapted from *Quantitative Methods in Psychology*, by D. Lewis. Copyright ©1960 by
McGraw-Hill, Inc. Reprinted by permission.

in Figure 13-2. The *t* distributions resemble the normal curve we looked at
in Chapter 12. They are symmetrical, with the greatest concentration of values around the mean. The shape of the *t* distribution becomes more and
more like the normal curve as the sample size increases. With small samples, the *t* distribution has a flatter and wider shape.

Sample size is also important because of the assumptions we make whenever we apply *t*. One of the requirements of a *t* test is that the data to be analyzed (interval or ratio) come from populations that are normally distributed.
We must be able to assume that if we could somehow measure all the members of the population, their scores on the dependent variable would form a
normal curve. If the data come from populations that are not normally distributed, we have a problem. The odds of getting each individual *t* value have
been worked out for populations that are normally distributed. If the data do
not come from such populations, the odds that have been worked out for *t*
will be wrong for those data. Of course, we can hardly ever measure all the
members of a population. We get around this problem by using large samples
so that the correct odds of each *t* value are very close to what they would be
if the population were normally distributed. This is rarely a problem because
the *t* test is relatively **robust**—the assumption of a normal distribution of population values can be violated without creating serious errors. If there are at
least 15 to 20 subjects in each treatment group, a *t* test is probably safe; with
30 subjects in a group, most researchers would not worry at all.

As we saw earlier with X^2, we select the appropriate *t* distribution based
on degrees of freedom. (Figure 13-2 refers to degrees of freedom [*df*] rather
than number of subjects.) Let us look more closely at two distributions of *t*
to get a clearer idea of how degrees of freedom will affect the critical value of
t. The critical value of *t* is the minimum value necessary to reject the null
hypothesis at our chosen significance level. Figure 13-3 shows distributions

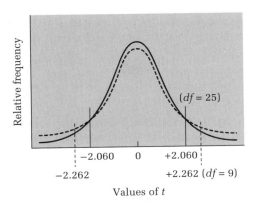

FIGURE 13-3 The t distribution for 25 and 9 degrees of freedom and critical values at $p < .05$.

of t for 25 and 9 degrees of freedom. It also shows the critical values of t for the $p < .05$ significance level using a two-tailed test. What is the relationship between these levels?

As the t distribution changes shape, the critical value of t needed to reject the null hypothesis at our chosen significance level also changes. Remember that the significance level refers to probabilities. We are looking to see whether the value of t that we compute from our data is more or less likely than our chosen critical value. If the experimental manipulation was effective, the computed value of t should be more extreme than the chosen critical value. In terms of probabilities, this means that the computed value of t is so extreme that it could have occurred by chance less than 5% of the time.

It is easy to see that the distribution for 9 degrees of freedom is flatter and wider than the other curve shown. In terms of probabilities, you can see that the most extreme 5% of this distribution falls relatively far out on the curve. Smaller degrees of freedom mean more variability between samples. That means that more and more cases will be far from the mean of the population; large differences between samples can be expected to occur relatively often just by chance. Thus the tails of the t distribution will get fatter as sample size (and degrees of freedom) get smaller. With 25 degrees of freedom, the tails of the t distribution are thinner; the most extreme 5% of the distribution falls closer to the mean.

Can you see how differences in degrees of freedom relate to our decision about the null hypothesis? We will reject the null hypothesis if the computed value of t is more extreme than the most extreme 5% of the distribution. Because the distribution changes shape as the degrees of freedom change, the critical value of t also changes. In fact, the critical value of t (the value needed to reject the null hypothesis) gets larger as the degrees of freedom get smaller. The fewer the subjects, the less likely it is that we will be able to reject the null hypothesis. The fewer the subjects, the higher the critical value of t

needed to demonstrate a statistically significant effect from an experimental manipulation. And with fewer subjects, we also have a greater chance of making a Type 2 error.

Using the *t* Test

Before we can use the *t* test, we have to know how to find the critical values of *t*. Fortunately, they have been worked out for us and organized into tables in which we can find them quickly and easily. To use the statistical tables, we need three pieces of information.

1. Will we use a directional or nondirectional test (that is, a one- or two-tailed test)?
2. What is our significance level?
3. How many degrees of freedom do we have?

In our experiment on fun, we have a directional hypothesis. Our directional hypothesis predicts that the average time estimate of the no-fun group will be greater than the average time estimate of the fun group. That means that we may use a one-tailed test. We chose a $p < .05$ significance level. The degrees of freedom (*df*) for this experiment equal the total number of subjects in both groups minus the number of groups. Here, $df = 5 + 5 - 2$, or 8. Now turn to Table B3 in Appendix B, which shows the critical values of *t* for both one- and two-tailed tests and several degrees of freedom. Find the critical value of *t* for 8 *df*, a one-tailed test, and $p < .05$.

The critical value of *t* is 1.86 for this experiment.[3] If our observed value of *t* (the value we compute) is less than 1.86, we cannot reject the null hypothesis. Computed values of *t* that are less extreme than the critical value indicate that differences between our treatment groups are not large enough to be significant. They were probably caused by chance variations between the samples. If the computed value of *t* is equal to or greater than 1.86, we reject the null hypothesis. If the computed value of *t* is more extreme than the critical value in the table, it is unlikely that the differences between treatment groups can be explained simply by chance. In a well-controlled experiment, the most likely explanation is that differences were produced by the independent variable.

The *t* Test for Independent Groups

We use the **t test for independent groups** when we have two different, randomly selected samples of subjects, randomly assigned to two treatments, and interval or ratio data. Let us use *t* to analyze the results of the time estimation experiment. The hypothetical data from that experiment are summarized

---

[3]You already know that it is easier to get statistical significance with a one-tailed test. If we had not made a directional prediction, the critical value of *t* (two tailed, $p < .05$) would have been 2.306.

in Table 13-4. The table tells us at a glance that the performance of the groups is different: The mean time estimate of subjects in the no-fun group is 14.2 minutes; that of subjects in the fun group is 9.6 minutes. Of course, we know that this absolute difference may not be significant. We have to evaluate the difference in terms of the amount of variability we find between any samples drawn from the population, and we have to decide whether to retain or reject the null hypothesis. To do that, we must compute the observed value of t (t_{obs}) for these data using the formula below:

$$t_{obs} = \frac{\overline{X}_1 - \overline{X}_2}{\sqrt{\left(\dfrac{(N_1 - 1)s_1{}^2 + (N_2 - 1)s_2{}^2}{(N_1 + N_2 - 2)}\right) \cdot \left(\dfrac{1}{N_1} + \dfrac{1}{N_2}\right)}}$$

The computation of t for these data is shown in Table 13-5. The formula is just a shorthand way of writing the steps to get t. If you take it slowly, step by step, you should have no trouble.

When we first talked about parametric test statistics in a general way, we said that they represent a relationship between treatment effects and variability. If you think about what is shown in the formula for t, you will see clearly how that principle is applied. The *numerator* (the top) tells us to find the difference between the means of the two treatment groups. If the independent variable had a large effect, we would expect this difference to be

TABLE 13-4 Summary data for a hypothetical experiment on fun and time estimation

No-Fun Group (Group 1)	Fun Group (Group 2)
$\overline{X}_1 = 14.2$ min	$\overline{X}_2 = 9.6$ min
$s_1{}^2 = 8.6$ min	$s_2{}^2 = 8.8$ min
$N_1 = 5$	$N_2 = 5$

NOTE: Since we predicted that the no-fun group will make larger time estimates, we labeled that group "group 1." Given our prediction, $\overline{X}_1 - \overline{X}_2$ should be a positive number and our computed value of t should be positive. It does not really matter which way the groups are labeled as long as we set up the critical value of t (in a positive or negative direction) consistent with our predictions and our computations of t. We are using hypothetical data here to keep things simple. If you were actually running this experiment, you would want to have more than five subjects in each treatment group.

TABLE 13-5 Computation of t for the data presented in Table 13-4, the hypothetical experiment on fun and time estimation

Step 1. Lay out the formula.	$$t_{obs} = \frac{\overline{X}_1 - \overline{X}_2}{\sqrt{\left(\frac{(N_1 - 1)s_1^2 + (N_2 - 1)s_2^2}{(N_1 + N_2 - 2)}\right) \cdot \left(\frac{1}{N_1} + \frac{1}{N_2}\right)}}$$
Step 2. Put in all the quantities needed.	$$t_{obs} = \frac{14.2 - 9.6}{\sqrt{\left(\frac{(5 - 1)8.6 + (5 - 1)8.8}{(5 + 5 - 2)}\right) \cdot \left(\frac{1}{5} + \frac{1}{5}\right)}}$$
Step 3. Calculate the difference between treatment means; begin simplifying the denominator.	$$t_{obs} = \frac{4.6}{\sqrt{\left(\frac{(4)8.6 + (4)8.8}{(8)}\right) \cdot \left(\frac{1}{5} + \frac{1}{5}\right)}}$$
Step 4. Continue simplifying the denominator.	$$t_{obs} = \frac{4.6}{\sqrt{\left(\frac{34.4 + 35.2}{(8)}\right) \cdot \left(\frac{1}{5} + \frac{1}{5}\right)}}$$
Step 5. Remember to complete all operations inside the parentheses first.	$$t_{obs} = \frac{4.6}{\sqrt{\left(\frac{69.6}{8}\right) \cdot \left(\frac{2}{5}\right)}}$$
Step 6. Convert all fractions in the denominator to decimals.	$$t_{obs} = \frac{4.6}{\sqrt{(8.7) \cdot (.40)}}$$
Step 7. Complete the multiplication.	$$t_{obs} = \frac{4.6}{\sqrt{(3.48)}}$$
Step 8. Remember to take the square root of the denominator.	$$t_{obs} = \frac{4.6}{1.86}$$
Step 9. Divide the numerator by the denominator and you have the computed value of t. Compare it with the critical value.	$$t_{obs} = 2.47$$

NOTE: $df = N_1 + N_2 - 2$; $df = 5 + 5 - 2$, or 8.

relatively large.[4] Notice that the *denominator* of the formula (the bottom) is a collection of terms that represents the variances of the treatment groups and the number of subjects in each group. The denominator is an estimate of variability. If the ratio between the two components is relatively large, we may be able to reject the null hypothesis. Here we will reject it if the computed value of t is more extreme than 1.86. If the value of t_{obs} is more

---

[4]Computed and critical values of t will be negative numbers in cases where the mean of group 2 is larger than the mean of group 1.

extreme than that, the odds are very good that the difference between the groups did not occur by chance.

The computed value of t turns out to be 2.47. Since a value of 2.47 is more extreme than the critical value, we reject the null hypothesis: There is a significant difference between the time estimates of subjects who had fun and subjects who did not. How much importance we wish to attach to these findings depends partly on our assessment of the quality of this experiment. Were control procedures adequate? Were variables defined appropriately? The possibility of a Type 1 error must be considered. Before we can draw any sweeping conclusions from the findings, we should replicate the experiment. (We will return to these issues when we discuss the interpretation of results in Chapter 15.) However, as long as the experiment was conducted properly using appropriate control procedures, we can now say:

1. The research hypothesis was supported.
2. As predicted by the research hypothesis, there was a significant difference between the group that was "having fun" and the group that was "not having fun."
3. Subjects who were "having fun" gave much shorter time estimates than subjects who were "not having fun."

The t Test for Matched Groups

The procedures we have discussed so far assume that the two samples of subjects are independent groups. We need different procedures when we look at the data for matched groups of subjects. If we did statistical tests for these experiments in the same way as for an independent-groups experiment, we would overestimate the amount of variability in the population sampled.

You know that subjects are apt to differ on a dependent variable simply because subjects are not all the same. Even if we are testing cockroaches or rats, we find that some run faster than others. One source of variability is individual differences. Subjects' scores vary because subjects differ from one another. Even the scores of the same subjects measured at different times vary, but they usually do not vary quite as much as the responses of different subjects. Neither do the scores of subjects who are matched on a relevant variable. For these reasons, the way that we compute variability changes when we use matched groups or a within-subjects design. You will get a better sense of how these procedures compare by looking at an example of a within-subjects experiment done with two treatment conditions. The research problem is summarized in Box 13-1.

What statistical test would you use for the Yin experiment? (See Table 13-2.) This experiment is similar to the time estimation example in that we are looking at one independent variable, two treatment conditions, and a ratio scale of measurement (that is, number of correct identifications). However, this experiment was run with only one group of subjects, making it a within-subjects experiment. The appropriate statistical test is therefore a t test for matched groups (also called a *within-subjects* t *test*). Obviously, the treatment groups in

BOX 13-1

A TWO-GROUP, WITHIN-SUBJECTS EXAMPLE

Robert Yin (1969) had already done research showing that people had trouble recognizing photographs of faces they had seen upside down. (Figure 13-4 shows an upside-down example.) Now he wanted to test whether inversion would affect recognition of line drawings as well. Yin showed the same subjects two sets of drawings of faces.* After each set, he showed subjects pairs of drawings and asked them to pick out the drawing they had seen before in each pair. Subjects saw one set of drawings and test pairs in the usual upright position; the other set was shown to them upside down. The order of presentation was counterbalanced across subjects to control for order effects.

FIGURE 13-4 Do you recognize this person? © CBS Photography

*Yin tested for effects on the memory of costumed figures as well as faces. Since he used the same procedures to handle both kinds of pictures, we will focus only on faces. Yin's results for the costumed figures were similar but less dramatic than the results for the inverted faces.

TABLE 13-6 Evaluating data from a within-subjects experiment on memory for inverted faces (scores represent number recalled correctly)

Subject (or Pair)	Upright Faces (X_1)	Inverted Faces (X_2)	Difference Scores $(X_1 - X_2) = D_i$	D_i^2
S_1	5	3	$(5 - 3) = 2$	4
S_2	3	2	$(3 - 2) = 1$	1
S_3	4	3	$(4 - 3) = 1$	1
S_4	5	3	$(5 - 3) = 2$	4
S_5	3	0	$(3 - 0) = 3$	9
			$\Sigma D_i = 9$	$\Sigma D_i^2 = 19$

Computing t

Step 1. This formula for *t* requires difference scores (D_i). The computation of *t* is based on differences between pairs of scores rather than group means. (Note how difference scores were computed above.)

$$t_{obs} = \frac{\Sigma D_i}{\sqrt{\dfrac{N\Sigma D_i^2 - (\Sigma D_i)^2}{N-1}}}$$

Step 2. Put in all the required values. Note that *N* stands for the number of pairs of data.

$$t_{obs} = \frac{9}{\sqrt{\dfrac{5(19) - (9)^2}{5-1}}}$$

Step 3. Simplify the denominator. Remember to take the square root.

$$t_{obs} = \frac{9}{\sqrt{\dfrac{(95) - (81)}{4}}} \text{ or } \frac{9}{\sqrt{\dfrac{14}{4}}}$$

Step 4. Our computed *t*. We are now ready to make a decision on the null hypothesis.

$$t_{obs} = 4.81$$

$df = N - 1$, where *N* is the number of pairs of scores.

NOTE: A *t* test for matched groups, to be used for two matched groups or a two-condition within-subjects design, ratio or interval data only. These hypothetical scores represent the number of drawings correctly recognized out of five presented in each condition.

this experiment were not matched in the usual sense of the term; they were simply the same subjects, and there may be no better match than that.

The ***t* test for matched groups** uses the same family of *t* distributions you have already seen. It also applies to interval and ratio data and requires the assumption that the population sampled is normally distributed on the dependent variable. But because this test is used to evaluate data from an experiment in which the treatment groups are not independent, the computations are handled differently. Table 13-6 shows how data and computations from a within-subjects (or matched-groups) experiment would look, based on the inverted faces experiment. The data are hypothetical and are presented just to illustrate the procedures simply; Yin used many more subjects. The scores for each subject represent the number of correct responses each made under each treatment condition. The table also illustrates the computation of *t* for matched groups: We use exactly the same procedures for within-subjects and matched-groups experiments with two treatment conditions.

From Table 13-6 you can see that we compute *t* for these data by looking at differences between each subject's performance under the two treatment conditions. This procedure reflects the logic behind the design we are using; we are evaluating the effect of the independent variable *within* each subject. Similarly, when we have matched pairs of subjects, we want to look at the effects of our independent variable within each matched pair. The observed value of *t* for these data is $t_{obs} = 4.81$. How does that compare to the critical value of *t*? Can we reject the null hypothesis? Who knows? Unfortunately, we never bothered to figure out what the critical value of *t* would be. Of course, we need to look at Table B3 in Appendix B. Assume that the researcher had decided to use a $p < .05$ significance level. Should we use a one- or a two-tailed test? Although Yin (1969) might have made a directional prediction based on prior evidence, he was simply testing the notion that inversion would affect line drawings of faces. He did not specify the direction of the effect, so a two-tailed test is appropriate.

Since we computed *t* for this experiment with different procedures, we also have to compute *df* differently. Because we are looking at differences between pairs of scores, our *df* is based on the number of pairs. The *df* for two matched groups is $N - 1$, where N is the number of pairs. For this experiment the *df* is $5 - 1$, or 4. If you look at Table B3, you will see that the critical value of *t* for 4 *df* and a two-tailed test ($p < .05$) is 2.776. Since the computed value of *t* (4.81) is more extreme than the critical value, we reject the null hypothesis, which says that these data were sampled from the same population. Assuming the experiment was conducted properly, what three things can we now say about the results? (Incidentally, the actual data from Yin's experiment also yielded a significant difference; subjects had significantly more difficulty recognizing drawings presented upside down.)

Notice that using the within-subjects procedures affects the critical value of *t*. In the last example, we had five subjects in each treatment group for a total of ten scores—just as we have here—but when we use the within-subjects or matched-groups *t*, we end up with many fewer degrees of freedom. Even though we have the same number of actual scores in both examples, we have about half as many degrees of freedom when we use the *t* test for matched groups. Table B3 shows that the critical value of *t* needed to reject the null hypothesis increases as the degrees of freedom get smaller. The fewer degrees of freedom we have, the more difficult it will be to reject the null hypothesis. It takes a more extreme *t* to reach significance in the matched-groups or within-subjects experiment. Compare the two-tailed critical values of *t* ($p < .05$) for 4 *df* and 8 *df* and you will see that you need a larger *t* when you have fewer degrees of freedom.

If we need a larger value of *t* in a within-subjects or matched-groups experiment, why would we bother to match subjects or use a within-subjects design at all? It seems as though an easier task would be to find a significant difference with the independent-groups design. In fact, it would not. We have not yet discussed all the reasons for variability in data, but one thing should be clear: If we measure the responses of *different* subjects, we are likely to get much more variability than if we measure the same subjects, or matched subjects. Using a within-subjects or matched-groups design lowers the amount of variability in the data. Look at the formulas for t: The denominator (the bottom) of each formula reflects variability. When we reduce variability among individual subjects, we make the denominator of the t formula smaller. That in turn makes the computed value of t a great deal larger. To put it more simply, when we use a matched-groups or a within-subjects design, we have a trade-off: We lower the degrees of freedom for the experiment, but we also lower the amount of variability produced by factors other than the independent variable. This trade-off almost always works to make the t test for matched groups a more powerful test than the t test for independent groups and decreases the chance of a Type 2 error.[5]

SUMMARY

As we saw in Chapter 12, analyzing data involves three basic steps: (1) organizing the data; (2) summarizing them; (3) applying the appropriate statistical test.

Five basic questions help us choose an appropriate statistical test: (1) How many independent variables are there? (2) How many treatment conditions are there? (3) Is the experiment run between or within subjects? (4) Are the subjects matched? (5) What is the level of measurement of the dependent variable?

For a two-independent-groups experiment with nominal data, we use a chi square (X^2) test. *Chi square (X^2)* is an inferential statistic that tests whether the frequencies of responses in our sample represent certain frequencies in the population. However, unlike the other tests covered in this text, the chi square is a *nonparametric* test because it does not make assumptions about the population (normal distribution, equal variances, etc.). The appropriate X^2 distribution is selected based on the *degrees of freedom* for the experiment. The degrees of freedom indicate how many members of a set of data could vary or change value without changing the value of a statistic already known for those data.

When the data from two-group experiments are interval or ratio, a common statistical test is the *t test for independent groups*. The t statistic is a computational way of relating differences between treatment means to the amount of variability expected between any two samples of data from the same population. One of the assumptions of the test is that the data come from populations that are normally distributed on the dependent variable; therefore it is a parametric test. A t test is done by computing a t statistic for the data. The computed value of t is compared to the critical value of t based on the chosen significance level (generally $p < .05$). If the computed value of t is more extreme than the critical value, the null hypothesis is rejected; the difference between treatment means is statistically significant.

The t statistic has a whole family of distributions based on the degrees of

---

[5]Don't forget the other benefit of the within-subjects design—you have only used half as many subjects as you did in the matched-groups or independent-groups design.

freedom for the experiment. With two independent groups, the degrees of freedom for t are equal to the total number of subjects minus 2. As the degrees of freedom of t get larger, the critical value of t gets less extreme. Besides the degrees of freedom, the critical value of t also depends on whether the hypothesis is directional or nondirectional.

A within-subjects design or matching in a two-group experiment requires a different statistical procedure, the *t test for matched groups*. The same family of t distributions that apply to the independent-groups procedures are used for this test. However, t for matched or within-subjects data is computed by looking at the differences between each pair of responses. This procedure decreases the degrees of freedom, making it somewhat harder to reject the null hypothesis. However, using the matched-groups procedures to compute t greatly reduces the estimate of variability in the data, and this trade-off generally results in a more powerful test of the effects of the independent variable.

KEY TERMS

chi square (X^2) A nonparametric, inferential statistic that tests whether the frequencies of responses in our sample represent certain frequencies in the population; used with nominal data.

Critical value The minimum value of the test statistic necessary to reject the null hypothesis at the chosen significance level.

Degrees of freedom (df) The number of members of a set of data that can vary or change value without changing the value of a known statistic for those data.

Interval scale The measurement of magnitude, or quantitative size, having equal intervals between values but no true zero point.

Level of measurement The type of scale of measurement—either ratio, interval, ordinal, or nominal—used to measure a variable.

Nominal scale The simplest level of measurement; classifies items into two or more distinct categories on the basis of some common feature.

Ordinal scale A measure of magnitude in which each value is measured in the form of ranks.

Ratio scale A measure of magnitude having equal intervals between values and having an absolute zero point.

Robust A term describing a statistical test that can be used without creating serious errors even though its assumptions (e.g., the population is normally distributed and has equal variances) are violated.

t test A statistic that relates differences between treatment means to the amount of variability expected between any two samples of data from the same population; used to analyze the results of a two-condition experiment with one independent variable and interval or ratio data.

t test for independent groups A statistic that relates differences between treatment means to the amount of variability expected between any two samples of data from the same population; used to analyze the results of a two-group experiment with independent groups of subjects.

***t* test for matched groups** A statistic that relates differences between treatment means to the amount of variability expected between any two samples of data from the same population; used to analyze two-group experiments using matched-subjects or within-subjects designs. Sometimes referred to as a within-subjects *t* test.

REVIEW AND STUDY QUESTIONS

1. What five basic questions must we answer before we can select the appropriate statistical test for an experiment?

2. What is a X^2 test? When is it used?

3. A two-independent-groups experiment was conducted to study the effects of low versus high anxiety on people's desire to affiliate with others. (Assume the procedures were the same as those used in the two-group experiment by Schachter discussed in Chapter 6.) After the anxiety manipulation, each subject could elect to wait either in an empty room or a room where another person was waiting. The data are shown in the 2 × 2 contingency table below.

Desire to Affiliate

	Yes	No
Low anxious subjects	10	20
High anxious subjects	20	10

   a. What is the H_0 in this experiment?
   b. What is the researcher's H_1?
   c. Analyze the data using a X^2. Can the researcher reject the null hypothesis?

4. What is a *t* test? When is it used?

5. Briefly outline the difference between the *t* test for independent groups and the *t* test for matched groups.

6. Our computed value of *t* is more extreme than the critical value. What does that mean? Do we reject the null hypothesis or not?

7. Our computed value of *t* is less extreme than the table value. What does that mean? Do we reject the null hypothesis or not?

8. Our computed value of *t* is +3.28. Our critical value of *t* is +2.048. We have 28 degrees of freedom and we are using a two-tailed (nondirectional) test. Draw a simple figure to illustrate the relationship between the critical and the computed values of *t* for this result.

9. Poor Jack is getting more and more confused. He says: "Anyone can see that my group means are different. Why do I have to go through all the trouble of making all these computations of *t*?" Can you explain to him

why these procedures are necessary? What advantage do they have over simply doing Jack's "eye test"?

10. Our computed value of t is -1.07. We have made a directional prediction and our critical value is -1.734. Make a rough illustration of the relationship between the computed and table values of t in this case. Is there a significant difference between the treatment means?

11. Suppose that we had *not* made a directional prediction in the time estimation experiment. Would the results still have been statistically significant if we had used a two-tailed test?

12. A researcher has studied subjects' ability to learn to translate words into Morse code. He has experimented with two treatment conditions: In one condition, the subjects are given massed practice; they spend 8 full hours working on the task. In the other condition, subjects are given distributed practice; they also spend 8 hours practicing, but their practice is spread over four days; they practice 2 hours each day. After the subjects have completed their practice, they are given a test message to encode. The dependent variable is the number of errors made in encoding the test message. Since intelligence may affect the learning of this new skill, the researcher has matched the subjects on that variable. The results are given below. Decide which statistical test would be appropriate for these data, carry out the test, and evaluate the outcome. Assume that the researcher has chosen a $p < .01$ level of significance and that the direction of the outcome has not been predicted.

Massed Practice		Distributed Practice	
S_1	6	S_1	5
S_2	4	S_2	3
S_3	3	S_3	2
S_4	5	S_4	2
S_5	2	S_5	3

13. Assume that the Morse code researcher did not match the subjects.
    a. Which statistical test would be appropriate? Carry out that test and evaluate the outcome for $p < .01$ and a nondirectional prediction.
    b. Follow the same procedure as in 13a but assume that the researcher has now predicted that the massed-practice group will make more errors.

14. Alice has decided that the procedures for finding t for a matched-groups design are a little easier to do, so she will just make sure she can match her subjects on some variable. That way she can save a little time on the computations. What is wrong with her approach? What is she forgetting?

15. Interpret the results of the t test we conducted on hypothetical data from the upside-down face experiment. (What are the three statements we can make?)

ANALYZING RESULTS: MULTIPLE-GROUPS AND FACTORIAL EXPERIMENTS

So far we have covered some of the techniques for data from experiments with two groups. The X^2 test is used for two-independent-groups experiments in which the dependent variable is measured using a nominal scale. The t tests for matched and independent groups are used when we have interval or ratio data in two-group experiments. Very often, however, we need to test more than two levels of an independent variable. We may need three or more groups to give an adequate idea of the way that a particular variable operates. We may even want to study more than one independent variable at a time. For those experiments, we need other kinds of statistical procedures.

In this chapter we will look at procedures that can be used for interval or ratio data from multiple-group and factorial experiments. These procedures fall under the general heading of analysis of variance. By the end of this chapter, you will know how these procedures work and why they are needed; you will also be ready to carry them out. We will begin by taking a general look at analysis of variance.

ANALYSIS OF VARIANCE

The **analysis of variance (ANOVA)** is a statistical procedure used to evaluate differences among two or more treatment means.[1] The name reflects the basic nature of the test, which divides all of the variance in the data into component parts and then compares and evaluates them for statistical significance. Treatment means are not compared directly. In Chapter 13 the t test was used to evaluate the data from a two-group experiment. You may be wondering why we need another procedure at all; after all, a multiple-group experiment is just a continuation of a two-group design. We could use t tests to compare all the treatment means. We could analyze one pair, then the next, and just keep doing that until we did all the pairs. But computing several t tests for each experiment is a bothersome task. With five treatment levels, you would need ten different t tests to account for all possible pairs of means.

There is also a more serious problem. The more t tests in one experiment, the more apt you are to make a Type 1 error. Remember that when you do a single test, the odds of rejecting the null hypothesis by mistake are equal to your significance level (for example, 5%). Doing many t tests in the same experiment distorts those odds and increases the possibility that you will reject a null hypothesis that is really true. Although it would be inappropriate to use several t tests in a multiple-group experiment, many of the principles of statistical analysis in the last two chapters still apply. We are still testing a null hypothesis. From the samples we have tested, we draw inferences about the

---

[1]In a two-group experiment, a researcher could actually use either a t test or an analysis of variance; both are found in the research literature. When statistics must be calculated by hand, the t test has been preferred because it is somewhat easier to calculate. However, for a two-group experiment, t values and ANOVA values (called Fs) are directly related. In fact, $F = t^2$ when only two groups are being tested.

population. We also use distributions to evaluate the results according to the significance levels we have chosen.

Still, there are many differences between an analysis of variance and a *t* test. When we computed *t*, we calculated differences between treatment groups—differences between treatment means for the independent-groups design and differences between pairs of scores in the matched-groups design. We looked at those differences in relation to our estimates of the amount of variability in the populations sampled. An analysis of variance enables us to test the null hypothesis in a slightly different way. It breaks up the variability in the data into component parts. Each part represents variability produced by a different combination of factors in the experiment.

In the simplest analysis of variance, all the variability in the data can be divided into two parts: within-groups variability and between-groups variability. **Within-groups variability** is the degree to which the scores of subjects in the *same* treatment group differ from one another (that is, how much subjects vary from others in the group). **Between-groups variability** is the degree to which the scores of *different* treatment groups differ from one another (that is, how much subjects vary under different levels of the independent variable). The proportions of the within-groups and between-groups variability differ from one experiment to another. Sometimes between-groups variability is larger than within-groups variability; sometimes the two parts are about the same. Their relative proportions vary depending on the impact of the independent variable. When we carry out an analysis of variance, we are actually evaluating the likelihood that the proportions we observe could occur by chance. To understand how this process works, we need to look more closely at the sources of variability that produce these components.

SOURCES OF VARIABILITY

Ideally, when we run an experiment we would like to be able to show that the pattern of data obtained was caused by the experimental manipulation. However, you already know that if we observe changes in the dependent variable across treatment conditions, those changes may not be entirely caused by the effects of the independent variable. But what else accounts for changes in the dependent variable? What else might produce variability in the scores of subjects across treatment conditions?

One common source of variability is individual differences. Whether we test children or chimps, we find that some subjects do better than others. Within each treatment group, subjects' scores will differ from one another because subjects are different from one another. We use random assignment or matching in each experiment so that these differences do not confound the results of the experiment. We do not want differences between groups to be produced solely by extraneous subject variables. However, no two groups will be identical in every respect, so individual differences may lead to variability between groups as well as within the same group.

There are other sources of variability in data. Some differences between scores will be the result of procedures we did not handle well in the experiment. For instance, we may have made small mistakes in measuring lines that subjects drew or in timing their answers (*experimental error*). Extraneous variables of all kinds can produce more variability, causing changes in subjects' behavior that we may not detect; one subject is tested when the room is cool and so does a little better than the others. As with individual differences, these factors can lead to variability within the same group of subjects as well as between different treatment groups. We can lump all these factors together in a single category called **error:** Individual differences, undetected mistakes in recording data, variations in testing conditions, and a host of extraneous variables are all aspects of error that produce variability in subjects' data both within and between treatment groups.

Another major source of variability in data is the experimental manipulation. We test subjects under different treatment conditions (that is, at various levels of an independent variable). We predict that these conditions will alter subjects' behavior; we expect subjects under different treatment conditions to behave differently from one another. In other words, we expect our treatment conditions to create variability among the responses of subjects who are tested under different levels of an independent variable.

But the experimental manipulation does not operate the same as other sources of variability in the experiment. Error can lead to variability between different treatment groups; it can also produce variability within the same group. Unlike those sources of variability, *treatment conditions produce variability only between the responses of different treatment groups.* Subjects within the same treatment group are all treated in the same manner. Their scores may differ because of individual differences or error but not because they were exposed to different levels of the independent variable: Subjects in the same treatment group all receive the same level of the independent variable.

When we do an analysis of variance, we break the variability in our data into parts that reflect the sources of variability in the experiment: within-groups variability and between-groups variability. *Within-groups variability is the extent to which subjects' scores differ from one another under the same treatment conditions.* The factors that we call error explain the variability that we see within groups. *Between-groups variability is the extent to which group performance differs from one treatment condition to another.* Between-groups variability is made up of error and the effects of the independent variable. These components are summarized in Table 14-1.

We can evaluate the effect of the independent variable by comparing the relative size of these components of variability. The logic behind this is straightforward. The variability within groups comes from error and nothing else; the variability between groups comes from both error and treatment effects. If the independent variable had an effect, the between-groups variability should be larger than the within-groups variability. We compare the

TABLE 14-1 Sources of variability in an experiment with one independent variable

Variability Within Groups	Variability Between Groups
Error	Error
Individual differences	Individual differences
Extraneous variables	Extraneous variables
	Treatment effects

relative sizes of these components by computing a ratio between them called the **F ratio.** Conceptually, it looks like this:

$$F = \frac{\text{Variability from treatment effects } + \text{ error}}{\text{Variability from error}}$$

or

$$F = \frac{\text{Variability between groups}}{\text{Variability within groups}}$$

Theoretically, if the independent variable had no effect, the F ratio should equal 1.[2] There should be just as much variability within groups as there is between them: The same sources of variability would be operating both within and between treatments. However, the larger the effect of the independent variable, the larger the F ratio should be. The independent variable will lead to greater differences between the scores of subjects who receive different levels of the independent variable. Figure 14-1 represents both possibilities graphically.

We use the distribution of F to evaluate the significance of the F ratio that

(a) No treatment effects. Within- and between-groups variability are about equal.

(b) Large treatment effects. Within-groups variability is small relative to between-groups variability.

FIGURE 14-1 The components of variability in an experiment with two possible outcomes.

[2]Theoretically, the error terms in the numerator and denominator are identical, but in practice we expect some "error" in measuring error, so it is possible to obtain F values that are less than 1.

we compute. *F*, like *t*, is actually a whole family of distributions. The shape of the distribution changes as the size of the samples changes. We will use the degrees of freedom to choose the correct distribution and critical value for each experiment. If the *F* ratio is statistically significant, the amount of between-groups variability is large compared to the amount of within-groups variability—so large that it is unlikely that all the group means belong to the same population. If *F* is significant, we reject the null hypothesis that all the treatment means were drawn from the same population: We confirm the existence of differences across the groups that were probably produced by the independent variable.

A ONE-WAY BETWEEN-SUBJECTS ANALYSIS OF VARIANCE

Now that you have a general idea of how ANOVA works, let us turn to an example of a multiple-group experiment. We will look at some hypothetical data obtained from three independent groups of subjects who learned high-, medium-, and low-frequency words. We will proceed step by step through the computation of the *F* ratio. We will test *F* with a *p* < .05 significance level. Since this experiment uses a between-subjects design and has only one independent variable, the statistical test we do is called a **one-way between-subjects analysis of variance.**

Assume that we have done a very simple experiment on learning. We have made up three lists of words that occur with varying frequencies in the English language. We know that frequency is likely to affect subjects' ability to learn lists of words. Words that occur with greater frequencies are apt to be easier to learn because they are more familiar and also more meaningful to us. We have made up lists of high-, medium-, and low-frequency two-syllable nouns. We defined these categories on the basis of Howes's (1966) count of the frequency of words in spoken English. Our high-frequency words occurred at least 50 times in Howes's sample of 250,000 words. Our medium-frequency words occurred more than once but less than 50 times. The low-frequency words occurred only once in Howes's sample. By these criteria, words like *hundred, mother,* and *question* are high frequency; *coffee* and *paper* are medium frequency; *turtle* and *textbook* are low frequency. Our hypothesis is that a list of words that has higher frequency in the spoken language will be recalled with greater accuracy than a list that has lower frequency. We ran the experiment using a between-subjects design: Our subjects were randomly assigned to three different treatment groups, one for each of the three word frequencies. The procedures for presenting the lists and testing recall were identical for all the groups.

This is a three-group experiment. It has one independent variable—the frequency of the words on each list. The dependent variable is the number of words subjects are able to recall, a ratio scale measure. As in any experiment, we will test the null hypothesis: The means of the three groups were sampled from the same population. Let us use a significance level of *p* < .05 for the

TABLE 14-2 Hypothetical data from an experiment on word frequency and learning

	Group 1 (Low Frequency)	Group 2 (Medium Frequency)	Group 3 (High Frequency)
S_1	2	1	3
S_2	2	3	4
S_3	1	3	2
S_4	0	3	3
S_5	1	3	4
	$\overline{X}_1 = 1.2$	$\overline{X}_2 = 2.6$	$\overline{X}_3 = 3.2$
	$s_1^2 = .7$	$s_2^2 = .8$	$s_3^2 = .7$

NOTE: Scores represent the number of words recalled from a list. All subjects saw the same number of items.

data. Table 13-2 (from the previous chapter) indicates that the data from this experiment may be analyzed by using a one-way analysis of variance. Table 14-2 shows some hypothetical data. As you can see, there are three groups. Their scores represent the number of words they recalled from the list they were shown. We have already begun our analysis of the data by organizing and summarizing it in table form.

Certain assumptions about our data must be met if we are to use analysis-of-variance procedures appropriately. First, the procedures we will use here require that treatment groups are independent from each other and that the samples have been selected at random. They also require that the populations from which the groups are sampled are normally distributed on the dependent variable and that the variances of those populations are roughly equal, or *homogeneous*. However, the F test is relatively robust. If we have fairly large groups of subjects, the assumptions can be violated without serious errors. The computations shown here are for illustration only. We are looking at very few subjects so that the procedures will be clear. In practice, of course, it would be better to have larger treatment groups because of the assumptions of the ANOVA procedures.

Within-Groups Variability

To compute an F ratio for these data, we need two pieces of information: the within-groups variability and the between-groups variability. We begin with the procedures for finding within-groups variability because they are a little simpler.

Think about the definition of within-groups variability—the extent to which subjects' scores vary from the scores of other subjects within the same group. If we had only one group, we could measure its variability by computing the variance. We would use the formula

$$s_2 = \frac{\Sigma(X - \overline{X})^2}{N - 1}$$

Begin by finding the sum of squared deviations from the group mean. For each score in the group, we would calculate the difference between that score and the group mean $(X - \overline{X})$. We would square each of those differences $(X - \overline{X})^2$, then add them together (Σ). To get a good estimate of the amount of variability in the population sampled, we would find the variance by dividing the sum of the squared deviations by $N - 1$, the degrees of freedom.

The variance we compute for one group is the average squared deviation from the mean of that group. Of course, when we do an analysis of variance, we are working with several groups at the same time. We need to get an estimate of within-groups variability. That estimate must *pool*, or combine, the variability in all treatment groups. We do that in two stages that are exactly parallel to the way we find the variance of a single group. First, we compute the **sum of squares (SS)**, which is just a shorthand way of talking about the sum of squared deviations from the group mean. To get the sum of squares for within-groups variability, or **SS_W**, we compute the squared deviation of each score from its group mean.[3] Then we simply add them all together.

We can summarize all those steps with the formula

$$\mathbf{SS_W} = \Sigma(X_1 - \overline{X}_1)^2 + \Sigma(X_2 - \overline{X}_2)^2 + \Sigma(X_p - \overline{X}_p)^2$$

The letter p stands for the number of groups in our experiment. Our example has only three groups, but the analysis-of-variance procedures can be used with any number of groups. We simply keep adding up the squared deviations of scores from their group means until we have accounted for all the scores in all the groups.

Once we have the sum of squares within groups, we are ready to find the within-groups variance. With only one group, we know that we get a good estimate of the variance in the population if we divide our sum of squared deviations by $N - 1$, which is actually the degrees of freedom for one group. When we compute within-groups variance for several groups, we also need to divide by the degrees of freedom. For one group, the degrees of freedom are $N - 1$. For more than one group, the degrees of freedom are $N - p$. N is the total number of scores; p is the total number of groups. We divide through by that number (df_W) to get the within-groups variance. The W stands for within groups.

Note that although we are calculating the variance within groups, analysis of variance has its own peculiar terminology. You have learned sum of squares, which is an understandable abbreviation. However, when we finally

---

[3]The formulas throughout this chapter are definitional formulas—direct statements of the operations they define. They are presented to clarify the logic behind the ANOVA procedures. Computational formulas derived from the definitional formulas are shown in Appendix A. Although computational formulas are easier to use, the logic behind them is not as easy to explain.

obtain what we would otherwise call a variance estimate, we change terms rather abruptly. Dividing the SS_W by df_W gives us the mean square. This is actually an abbreviation, too, although its origin is not as clear. The mean is an average. The variance is the average squared deviation from the mean. So the **mean square (MS)** is an average squared deviation. (The existence of a plot to confuse students on this point has been suggested many times, but it has never been confirmed.) The important point is this: We are still talking about variance in the data. The **mean square within groups (MS_W)** is one estimate of the amount of variability in the population sampled. It represents one portion of the variability in the data, the portion produced by the combination of sources that we call "error." The value of MS_W will constitute the denominator, or bottom, of the F ratio. Table 14-3 shows how to compute SS_W and MS_W for our three-group example.

Between-Groups Variability

Once we have MS_W, we are ready to calculate the second component of the F ratio, a measure of the variability between groups of subjects. It is a measure that reflects both error and treatment effects: Between-groups variability is the extent to which group performance differs from one treatment condition to another. Let us look a little more closely at the implications of that definition.

If the independent variable had no effect in this experiment, the subjects in all the groups would have done about equally well. We would not expect to see any dramatic difference in recall from one group to another; the only differences we would see would be those caused by error. If that were the case, the means of the individual treatment groups would all be about the same. We could compute one overall mean, or **grand mean,** an average of all the treatment means. If our independent variable had no effect, the grand mean would describe the data about as well as three separate means, one for each of the three separate groups. But imagine what would happen if the independent variable really did have an effect on subjects' recall. We could still compute an overall grand mean that would represent the average of all the subjects' scores. However, the means of the individual groups would be quite different from the grand mean. They would also be quite different from one another.

You already know that we measure the amount of variability *within* groups by finding the total variance of scores from the individual group means. Similarly, we can measure the variability *between* groups by finding the variance of the group means from their mean, the grand mean of the experiment. Now that you are familiar with the logic behind the procedures, let us compute the between-groups variance. The process is carried out in Table 14-4 for our three-group example. We begin by computing the grand mean, the average of all the treatment means. We then compute deviations of the group means from the grand mean, and then we obtain the squared deviations. Notice, however, that the formula for SS_B (B stands for between groups) is a little different from the one for SS_W.

TABLE 14-3 Computing within-groups variance for a three-group example

Step 1. Compute the deviation of each score from its group mean.	Group 1 (Low Frequency)	$(X_1 - \bar{X}_1)$	$(X_1 - \bar{X}_1)^2$
	S_1 2	.8	.64
	S_2 2	.8	.64
	S_3 1	$-$ .2	.04
	S_4 0	-1.2	1.44
	S_5 1	$-$ .2	.04
	$\bar{X}_1 = 1.2$		$\Sigma(X_1 - \bar{X}_1)^2 = 2.80$
Step 2. Square the deviation of each score from its group mean.	Group 2 (Medium Frequency)	$(X_2 - \bar{X}_2)$	$(X_2 - \bar{X}_2)^2$
	S_1 1	-1.6	2.56
	S_2 3	.4	.16
	S_3 3	.4	.16
	S_4 3	.4	.16
	S_5 3	.4	.16
	$\bar{X}_2 = 2.6$		$\Sigma(X_2 - \bar{X}_2)^2 = 3.20$
Step 3. Total the square deviation scores for each group.	Group 3 (High Frequency)	$(X_3 - \bar{X}_3)$	$(X_3 - \bar{X}_3)^2$
	S_1 3	$-$ .2	.04
	S_2 4	.8	.64
	S_3 2	-1.2	1.44
	S_4 3	$-$ .2	.04
	S_5 4	.8	.64
	$\bar{X}_3 = 3.2$		$\Sigma(X_3 - \bar{X}_3)^2 = 2.80$

Step 4. Add all the group totals together to find SS_w.

$$\boxed{SS_w = \Sigma(X_1 - \bar{X}_1)^2 + \Sigma(X_2 - \bar{X}_2)^2 + \Sigma(X_3 - \bar{X}_3)^2 = 8.80}$$

Step 5. Find df_w.

$$\boxed{df_w = N - p}$$

N = Number of scores

p = Number of groups

$$df_w = 15 - 3$$
$$df_w = 12$$

Step 6. Find MS_w.

$$\boxed{MS_w = \frac{SS_w}{df_w}}$$

$$MS_w = \frac{8.80}{12}$$

$$MS_w = .73$$

NOTE: The same procedures apply when the groups are unequal in size.

TABLE 14-4 Finding the between-groups variance for our three-groups example

	Group 1 (Low Frequency)	Group 2 (Medium Frequency)	Group 3 (High Frequency)

Step 1. Compute the grand mean, the mean of all the group means.

$\bar{X}_1 = 1.2$ $\bar{X}_2 = 2.6$ $\bar{X}_3 = 3.2$

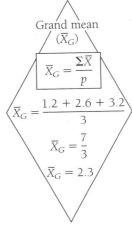

Grand mean $(\bar{X}_G)$

$$\bar{X}_G = \frac{\Sigma \bar{X}}{p}$$

$$\bar{X}_G = \frac{1.2 + 2.6 + 3.2}{3}$$

$$\bar{X}_G = \frac{7}{3}$$

$$\bar{X}_G = 2.3$$

Step 2. Compute the differences between each group and the grand mean.

$\bar{X}_1 - \bar{X}_G =$ $1.2 - 2.3 = -1.1$ $\bar{X}_2 - \bar{X}_G =$ $2.6 - 2.3 = .3$ $\bar{X}_3 - \bar{X}_G =$ $3.2 - 2.3 = .9$

Step 3. Put those differences in the SS$_B$ formula; n is the number of subjects in each group; p is the number of groups—this general formula can handle any number of groups.

$$\boxed{SS_B = n_1(\bar{X}_1 - \bar{X}_G)^2 + n_2(\bar{X}_2 - \bar{X}_G)^2 + n_3(\bar{X}_3 - \bar{X}_G)^2 \cdots n_p(\bar{X}_p - \bar{X}_G)^2}$$

$$SS_B = 5(-1.1)^2 + 5(.3)^2 + 5(.9)^2$$

Step 4. Square all deviations from the grand mean.

$$SS_B = 5(1.21) + 5(.09) + 5(.81)$$

Step 5. Carry out all multiplications.

$$SS_B = 6.05 + .45 + 4.05$$

continued

TABLE 14-4 (continued)

Step 6. Obtain the total SS_B.	$SS_B = 10.55$
Step 7. Calculate the degrees of freedom; p is the number of groups	$\boxed{df_B = p - 1}$ $df_B = 3 - 1$, or 2
Step 8. Divide SS_B by df_B to find the mean square between groups, the second estimate of population variance.	$\boxed{MS_B = \dfrac{SS_B}{df_B}}$ $MS_B = \dfrac{10.55}{2}$ $MS_B = 5.28$

NOTE: At this point you can check your work by computing SS_T, which represents the total sum of squares for the data. Since we are simply dividing the variability into two components. $SS_B + SS_W$ should equal SS_T. You can compute SS_T with this formula: $SS_T = \Sigma(X^2) - \dfrac{(\Sigma X)^2}{N}$. N is the number of scores. For this example,

$SS_T = 101 - \dfrac{(35)^2}{15}$

$SS_T = 101 - \dfrac{1225}{15}$

$SS_T = 101 - 81.67$

$SS_T = 19.33$

Check:

$SS_T = SS_B + SS_W$

$19.33 = 10.55 + 8.80$

(The small discrepancy is due to rounding error.)

Next, we find the variance about the grand mean, the mean square between groups (MS_B). To get MS_B, we divide SS_B by its degrees of freedom. We are now working with group means rather than individual subjects' scores. Hence, our degrees of freedom for SS_B (df_B) are equal to $p - 1$, where p is the number of groups. The MS_B gives us a second estimate of the amount of variability in the population. MS_B reflects the amount of variability produced by error *and* treatment effects in the experiment. This variability estimate will form the numerator, or top, of the F ratio.

Computing and Evaluating the *F* Ratio

We now have both components of variability that we need to compute our F ratio. As you already know, the F ratio represents this relationship:

$$F = \frac{\text{Variability from treatment effects} + \text{error}}{\text{Variability from error}}$$

We have transformed the components of this formula into the numerical terms MS_B and MS_W. Thus the statistical form of the F ratio is as follows:

$$F = \frac{MS_B}{MS_W}$$

If we substitute our computed values into this formula, we find that for our three-group example

$$F = \frac{5.28}{.73} \text{ or } 7.23$$

To test our F ratio for significance, we need to find the critical value. As you know, F is a whole family of distributions. We use our degrees of freedom to locate the appropriate distribution. But is there a problem? As we computed F, we actually calculated two different degrees of freedom, one to get MS_B and another to get MS_W. Which do we use? Since the F test can be used with any number of groups as well as any number of subjects, we need both. The F distribution changes as the size of treatment groups changes; it also changes as the number of treatment conditions changes. If you look in Appendix B, you will find that Table B4 lists critical values of F. The table is organized by the degrees of freedom. The values listed across the top refer to the degrees of freedom of the numerator of the F ratio—here, df_B. Values listed vertically down the side of the table indicate the degrees of freedom of the denominator of the F ratio—here, df_W. To find the appropriate critical value, first locate df_B along the top of the table, then locate df_W along the side. Now find the place in the table where those two lines meet. We are looking for df_B = 2 and df_W = 12. (These are simply the df values we computed to get mean squares.) If we look at a portion of the table, we see this:

The value in light type, 3.88, is the critical value of F at the .05 level; **6.93**, shown in boldface, is the critical value of F at the .01 level. Remember,

(a) The distribution of F with 2 (numerator) and
     12 (denominator) degrees of freedom

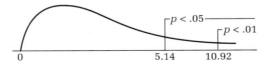

(b) The distribution of F with 2 (numerator) and
     6 (denominator) degrees of freedom

FIGURE 14-2 The distribution of F with varying degrees of freedom.

these values apply *only* to an F test with 2 and 12 degrees of freedom. We
have to look up the critical values for each experiment. Figure 14-2 illustrates
the distribution of F with 2 and 12 degrees of freedom. It also shows the distribution of F with 2 and 6 degrees of freedom. As you can see, the critical
values change dramatically as the degrees of freedom change.

    We chose a significance level of $p < .05$ for our three-group experiment.
To be statistically significant, we need a computed value of F that is greater
than the table value for our level of significance. Our computed value of F
was 7.23. The table value of F is 3.88 at the .05 level; therefore, our computed F is significant. We reject the null hypothesis that the treatment means
came from the same population. Our computed F is large enough, in fact,
that it is also significant at the .01 level: It is greater than 6.93, the critical
value of F at the .01 level.

Preparing a Summary Table

By now it may seem that we have gone through a thousand steps to evaluate
the data from this study. The count is actually slightly less than that, but you
can understand why we need to prepare a simple, comprehensive summary
of the findings. We would not present all the steps and calculations in an
actual report. Instead, we sometimes summarize our computations in a summary table. A summary table for our example is shown in Table 14-5. The
table includes all the basic information needed to compute F, along with the
actual computed value. However, we do not include the table values of F. Since
we have given the degrees of freedom, readers can always consult their own
tables to get the critical value if they need it. The format of the table is used
by convention, and you should follow it exactly; list between-groups variance
first, and so on.

TABLE 14-5 Analysis-of-variance summary table

Source	df	SS	MS	F
Between groups	2	10.55	5.28	$\dfrac{MS_B}{MS_W} = 7.23^*$
Within groups	12	8.80	.73	
Total	14	19.35		

$^*p < .01$

Graphing the Results

Another useful way of summarizing the results of an experiment is graphing. We can transform our findings into a picture that shows the reader the over-all results at a glance. Look closely at Figure 14-3, which presents the results of our experiment as a graph. The figure illustrates several general points you should keep in mind. Notice that the figure is well proportioned; the vertical axis is roughly three-fourths the size of the horizontal axis. Notice also that the independent variable is plotted on the horizontal axis; the dependent variable is plotted on the vertical axis. Finally, note that the data points represent group means. We do not graph the data of individual subjects unless we have a small N design. Of course, the axes are labeled clearly so that readers will know exactly what the figure represents.

Interpreting the Results

We know that the computed F was significant for these data. We will have more to say about interpreting the meaning of significant outcomes in the next

FIGURE 14-3 The mean number of words recalled as a function of word frequency.

chapter. However, there are some points about an ANOVA that should be made before we go further.

From the graph of our results (Figure 14-3), you can see quite clearly that subjects in different groups performed differently from one another in this experiment. Subjects in the high-frequency group recalled the most items; subjects in the low-frequency group recalled the least. You can also see clearly from the figure that the variation between different groups was not uniform. The high- and low-frequency groups differed more from each other than from the medium-frequency group. It is very important to keep in mind that when we compute F, we test only the *overall* pattern of treatment means. Our significant F in this example tells us that across all the group means, there is a significant difference. If we had only two treatment groups, we would know immediately that one group mean was significantly higher than another. But when three or more groups are being compared, as they are in our experiment, the ANOVA does not test the differences between each pair of means, and we do not know exactly where the difference is. From the graph, it *seems* likely that the high and the low groups are significantly different from each other. After all, they differ the most. However, the difference between, say, the low- and the medium-frequency groups may or may not be significant. After a significant F has been obtained, further statistics are needed to determine which groups are really different from each other. (If an F is nonsignificant, we would not need to go any further.) When we need to pinpoint the exact source of the differences across several treatment groups, we need to conduct follow-up tests. There are two basic types of follow-up tests: post hoc tests and a priori comparisons.

There are several different **post hoc tests**—tests done after the overall analysis indicates a significant difference. We will not go into the details of these tests here, but some of the names you will see are the Tukey and the Scheffé tests. These tests have essentially the same function: They can be used to make pair-by-pair comparisons of the different groups to pinpoint the source of a significant difference across several treatments. For instance, by comparing each treatment group with every other group in our word frequency experiment, post hoc tests can tell us whether high-frequency words were significantly easier to recall than medium-frequency words or only easier than low-frequency words. They can also tell us whether medium-frequency words were significantly easier to recall than low-frequency words.

Couldn't we just use a series of t tests to make these pairwise comparisons? No, because (as we mentioned at the beginning of this chapter) we would be increasing our odds of making a Type 1 error. With three treatment groups, our chances of making a Type 1 error could be as high as three times our significance level ($3 \times .05 = .15$). Post hoc tests, however, are more *conservative* statistical tests. They are conservative because they are specifically designed to guard against increasing the chances of rejecting the null hypothesis when it is really true. These kinds of post hoc tests, however, can result in less power to detect treatment effects, and they can increase the chances of making a Type 2 error. One way around this dilemma is to use another statistical procedure—a priori comparisons—for pinpointing significant effects.

A priori comparisons are tests between specific treatment groups that were anticipated, or planned, before the experiment was conducted. For this reason, they are also called *planned comparisons*. A priori comparisons are often used to test specific predictions. For example, in our word frequency experiment, we might have made the following two predictions before we conducted the study: (1) High-frequency words will be easier to recall than medium-frequency words, and (2) medium-frequency words will be easier to learn than low-frequency words. If the overall ANOVA is significant, we would conduct two a priori comparisons. Unlike post hoc tests, a priori comparisons are considered part of the original analysis of variance. Typically, we do not worry about increasing the odds of a Type 1 error as long as the number of planned comparisons is *less than* the number of treatment groups in the experiment. Planned comparisons can also be used to test predictions that one group will be different from all the others in the experiment. For instance, we might have planned to contrast the high-frequency conditions with all others. The manner of computing a priori comparisons is less conservative than post hoc tests, making them more powerful.

Wouldn't we always use planned comparisons, then? Not necessarily. Sometimes we have too many predictions, making the chances of a Type 1 error unacceptable. Other times (particularly when things do not turn out exactly the way we expected) we want to explore group differences that we did not predict in advance. Just as we cannot change our hypotheses or our significance levels to suit the way the data come out, it is always inappropriate to use planned comparisons to pinpoint *unplanned* effects.

Suppose we had predicted in advance that each group would be significantly different from the others. (This prediction would make sense if we believe that the two variables, word frequency and recall, are strongly linked phenomena.) How would we interpret the results of the significant ANOVA along with the planned comparisons that supported our predictions? In the case in which the ANOVA and the a priori comparisons were all significant and predicted in advance, we could now report the following:

1. The research hypothesis was supported.
2. As predicted, there was a significant difference in recall between groups that differed in word frequency.
3. Recall was significantly better for high-frequency words than for medium- or low-frequency words; and recall for medium-frequency words was significantly better than recall for low-frequency words, as predicted before the experiment. (Notice how specific and detailed we are when we describe the effects of statistical analyses.)

Let us briefly summarize what we have accomplished in this chapter so far. We took a multiple-group experiment and selected a suitable statistical test on the basis of three dimensions: the number of independent variables, the number of treatment groups, and the level of measurement. The experiment had one independent variable (word frequency) and three treatment groups (low, medium, and high frequency). The dependent variable (number of words recalled) was measured by a ratio scale. The data therefore required a one-way analysis of variance, which we carried out and evaluated. We also prepared a summary table of our analysis and graphed the group means.

Statistical Control for Differences Between Groups

You are already familiar with the concept of control. You have learned many procedures for controlling extraneous variables that might impact on the dependent variable. You have also learned about controlling for potentially important subject variables by matching subjects on characteristics that are expected to influence subjects' responses to experimental manipulations. You also know that subject variables can be used as factors in an experiment.

At some times, however, researchers want to exert control over extraneous variables, particularly subject variables, that cannot be controlled experimentally. Suppose, for example, that a researcher is worried that scores on the recall measure in the word frequency experiment might be influenced by the size of subjects' vocabulary; some of the low-frequency words, for example, might be used more by subjects with a large vocabulary. The researcher considered matching subjects on scores from the vocabulary part of the SAT but decided against it because she knows that it could work against her if vocabulary size is not an important *moderating variable* (one that can moderate, or change, the influence of the independent variable). Instead, she used random assignment to conditions.

There is a way the researcher can still exert some control over this "uncontrolled" variable. A more complex form of ANOVA, called *analysis of covariance* (ANCOVA), can be used to control statistically for potential moderating variables. ANCOVA works by subtracting the variance produced by scores on the moderating variable, called the *covariate,* from the variance in the ANOVA that was produced by *error.* According to Keppel (1982), ANCOVA can be used to accomplish the following two objectives: "(1) to refine estimates of experimental error and (2) to adjust treatment effects for any differences between the treatment groups that existed before the start of the experiment" (p. 483). ANCOVA is analogous to holding the moderating variable constant or statistically equating subjects before the experiment. It can increase the sensitivity of the experiment to detect the effects of the independent variable. ANCOVA is very difficult to compute by hand, but it is an option in most computer statistics programs. Part of the analysis also calculates whether the covariate was an important influence or not, adding precision to interpretation of statistical results.

ONE-WAY REPEATED MEASURES ANALYSIS OF VARIANCE

The basic principles of the analysis of variance apply in many multiple-group experiments. For example, we can use an ANOVA to analyze the effects in a multiple-group experiment testing one independent variable that uses a within-subjects design. This is called a **one-way repeated measures ANOVA.** Suppose we conducted the word frequency experiment within instead of between subjects by presenting subjects with a mixed list, a list containing words of all three frequencies, and then assessing recall. If we had completely counterbalanced the order of the words in each list, we would not need to use order as a factor in the design, and we would have a three-group within-subjects experiment. In this case, we would analyze the results with a one-way repeated measures ANOVA. Conceptually, the repeated measures ANOVA is the same as the ANOVA for independent groups; however, the denominator is calculated somewhat differently. The principles of analysis of variance can also be extended to handle more complex research designs: between-subjects factorials, within-subjects factorials, and mixed factorial designs. We will carry these principles further in our next example, an experiment with a between-subjects (B/S) factorial design.

ANALYZING DATA FROM A BETWEEN-SUBJECTS FACTORIAL EXPERIMENT

Factorial experiments are designed to look at the effects of more than one independent variable at a time and at the interaction between variables. The impact of one independent variable may differ depending on the values of the other independent variables in the experiment. When we analyze the data from a factorial experiment, we evaluate both kinds of effects. We look at the impact of each independent variable, the main effects produced by each factor. We also evaluate any interaction between the factors. Let us look at an example of a simple between-subjects factorial experiment and see which statistical procedures are used to accomplish these goals.

Assume we have set up and run another experiment to explore the relationship between word frequency and recall. Half the subjects saw high-frequency words, and half saw low-frequency words. This time, though, we have run a factorial experiment. Besides evaluating the effect of frequency, we have manipulated our testing procedures in a 2 × 2 design (diagrammed in Figure 14-4). Half the subjects have been asked simply to recall the words they saw on the original list; the other half have been given cues to aid them in remembering the words they saw. For instance, suppose subjects saw the word *camel* on the original list. If they were in the "no-cue" condition, they were simply asked to recall the word. If they were in the "cue" condition, we provided the name of the category the word belongs to—animal. Category cues were given for all words on the list.

Our hypothesis, which is based on prior research (such as Tulving & Pearlstone, 1966), is that cuing will enhance recall. Frequency will also affect recall, with the more frequent words being easier to recall. We have two independent variables in this experiment—word frequency and category cues. Our dependent variable is the number of words correctly recalled from each list, a ratio measure. We will use $p < .05$ as our significance level. If you consult

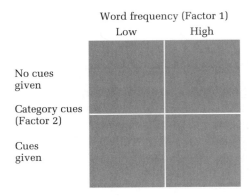

FIGURE 14-4 Diagram of a 2 × 2 factorial experiment on the effects of word frequency and cuing on recall.

Table 13-2, you will find that the statistical test indicated for these data is a two-way analysis of variance between subjects.

You already know how to do the basic, or one-way, ANOVA. The same principles apply to all ANOVA procedures. But when we have a factorial design, additional complexities arise. The procedures for the one-way ANOVA are not designed to give us as much information as we want to get from a factorial experiment. We want to be able to evaluate the main effect of each independent variable; we need to know whether the word frequency and category cues affect ability to recall words. Of course, we also want to know whether there was any interaction between the two variables. We want to know whether the effects of using different frequencies may change depending on whether cues are given—or whether the effect of cues may differ depending on whether the word to be recalled is relatively frequent or infrequent.

To answer all these questions with an analysis of variance, we need to break down the variance in the data into more components than we had before. In the one-way ANOVA, we had one independent variable. We divided all the variability in the data into just two parts: within-groups and between-groups variability. Within-groups variability is created by all those sources of error in the experiment: individual differences, the experimenter's mistakes, and other extraneous variables. Between-groups variability is created by all those sources of error plus the effect of the independent variable.

The same is true in a factorial experiment. We can separate variability into within-groups and between-groups variance. However, the picture is more complex here. Between-groups variability comes from error and treatment effects, but there are several sources of treatment effects in the factorial experiment. Each independent variable may produce its own unique treatment effects; each can produce a portion of the between-groups variability or a main effect. The interaction of the independent variables can produce another portion. This is represented graphically in Figure 14-5, which compares the com-

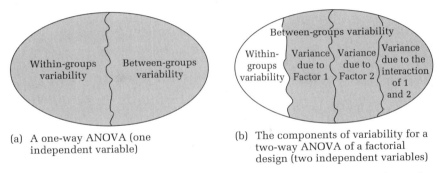

(a) A one-way ANOVA (one independent variable)

(b) The components of variability for a two-way ANOVA of a factorial design (two independent variables)

FIGURE 14-5 The components of variability for (a) a one-way analysis of variance (one independent variable) and (b) a two-way analysis of variance (two independent variables).

ponents of variability for the one-way analysis of variance against a two-way analysis of variance for a two-factor experiment. We can begin our analysis of variance for the between-subjects factorial experiment by finding within- and between-groups variability. However, we will also need to break between-groups variability into its component parts: the variability associated with each of the independent variables and the variability associated with the interaction between them.

When we did the one-way ANOVA, we used a summary table to organize our computations. When we do a two-way ANOVA, it is helpful to plan the summary table in advance because we can use it to keep track of computations as we do them. The outline of the summary table for a two-factor experiment is shown in Table 14-6. You can see that all the sources of variability in the experiment are represented. We must find all these components to compute the F ratios needed to judge significance. We will calculate a different F ratio for every source of between-groups variability in the experiment and use those ratios to decide whether the effects of each independent variable are significant. We will also decide whether there is a significant interaction.

TABLE 14-6 Summarizing the analysis of variance for a two-factor experiment

Source	df	SS	MS	$F = \dfrac{\text{MS}}{\text{MS}_W}$
Between groups				
Factor 1				
Factor 2				
Interaction 1 × 2				
Within groups				
Total				

TABLE 14-7 Hypothetical data from a two-factor experiment: The effects of word frequency and category cues on recall in a list-learning task.

	Word Frequency (Factor 1)	
	Low	High
No cues given	2 3 1 4 5 $\bar{X}_1 = 3$	4 5 4 6 6 $\bar{X}_2 = 5$
Cues given	4 6 5 6 9 $\bar{X}_3 = 6$	7 6 9 8 10 $\bar{X}_4 = 8$

Category Cues (Factor 2)

NOTE: Scores represent number of words correctly recalled from a list.

A TWO-WAY ANALYSIS OF VARIANCE

Table 14-7 presents some hypothetical data from our experiment to test the effect of word frequency and category cues on recall. Since this is a 2 × 2 factorial design, the data are divided into four treatment groups. We have already begun the data analysis by computing the mean number of words correctly recalled by each treatment group. Let us take an overall look at the steps required to complete the analysis of variance. The actual computations are shown in Tables 14-8 through 14-12, which follow our written description.

Assumptions Behind the Two-Way Analysis of Variance

The procedures and formulas for a two-way between-subjects ANOVA are based on the same set of assumptions as the one-way ANOVA procedures we examined earlier. They assume that the treatment groups are independent from each other and that the observations were randomly sampled. They also assume that the population from which each treatment group is sampled is normally distributed on the dependent variable. Finally, they assume that the variances of the populations are homogeneous. The computations here are done just for the sake of illustration, so we have only five subjects per treatment group. However, the assumptions behind the ANOVA procedures are more likely to be met with larger groups of subjects. In addition, the procedures shown here assume an equal number of subjects (*n*) in each group and more than one subject per group. If you have unequal *n*'s, you will need more complicated procedures. The same is true if you have used within-subjects procedures. In either case, consult your instructor or statistics textbook if you need the formulas.

Finally, these procedures are set for fixed models, experiments in which the values of the independent variables are fixed by the experimenter. In other words, the experimenter chooses to run subjects at certain levels of each independent variable. In our example the experimenter has chosen to use high and low word frequencies and two levels of the category-cue variable—cues versus no cues. In experiments with random models (randomly selected values of the independent variables), different statistical procedures are required, however; most experiments follow the fixed model, as we do here.

With the increased accessibility of computers for calculating statistics, the use of complicated analyses of variance has greatly expanded. Thirty years ago, researchers had to do all of their statistics by hand (or they used clunky electric calculators), so the experimental designs they selected tended to be much simpler than they are today. Now it would be difficult indeed to find a researcher who does hand computations. However, even the most sophisticated computer software programs still require the user to select the appropriate ANOVA model to apply to the data, to set up post hoc tests, and, of course, to interpret the results. For these reasons, it is still necessary to understand the logic behind ANOVA and other statistical procedures even if you do not analyze your data by hand. Let us look at how the two-way ANOVA for the data from our factorial experiment is computed.

Step 1: Computing Within-Groups Variability
We begin the ANOVA by filling in the within-groups section of the summary table. We need the degrees of freedom (df), the sum of squares within groups (SS_W), and the mean square within groups (MS_W). To get them, we follow the same basic procedures that we used for the one-way ANOVA. The calculations for our 2×2 experiment are shown in Table 14-8. Remember that the mean square within groups represents variability produced by individual differences, extraneous variables, and other sources of error in the experiment. We will use MS_W to evaluate the impact of the independent variables and their interaction in the experiment.

Step 2: Computing Between-Groups Variability
We continue our ANOVA by finding the total sum of squares between groups, SS_B. We need the SS_B because it represents all the variability we have among treatment groups. To complete our ANOVA, we will have to divide the SS_B into its main components: the parts associated with each of the independent variables and the part associated with the interaction between them. Table 14-9 illustrates the procedures for finding SS_B for our factorial example.

Step 3: Computing Main Effects
As you know, the ANOVA procedures have some special terms associated with them. *Sum of squares* and *mean square* refer to variability in the data. When we want to discuss the variability associated with a single independent variable in a factorial design, we call it a **main effect**, the change in the dependent

TABLE 14-8 Step 1: Computing within-group variability (MS_W) for a 2×2 factorial experiment

		Word Frequency (Factor 1)					
		Low			High		

Category Cues (Factor 2)		X_1	$(X_1 - \bar{X}_1)$	$(X_1 - \bar{X}_1)^2$	X_2	$(X_2 - \bar{X}_2)$	$(X_2 - \bar{X}_2)^2$
No cues given		2	-1	1	4	-1	1
		3	0	0	5	0	0
		1	-2	4	4	-1	1
		4	1	1	6	1	1
		5	2	4	6	1	1
		$\bar{X}_1 = 3$		$\Sigma(X_1 - \bar{X}_1)^2 = 10$	$\bar{X}_2 = 5$		$\Sigma(X_2 - \bar{X}_2)^2 = 4$
		X_3	$(X_3 - \bar{X}_3)$	$(X_3 - \bar{X}_3)^2$	X_4	$(X_4 - \bar{X}_4)$	$(X_4 - \bar{X}_4)^2$
Cues given		4	-2	4	7	-1	1
		6	0	0	6	-2	4
		5	-1	1	9	1	1
		6	0	0	8	0	0
		9	3	9	10	2	4
		$\bar{X}_3 = 6$		$\Sigma(X_3 - \bar{X}_3)^2 = 14$	$\bar{X}_4 = 8$		$\Sigma(X_4 - \bar{X}_4)^2 = 10$

$$SS_W = \Sigma(X_1 - \bar{X}_1)^2 + \Sigma(X_2 - \bar{X}_2)^2 + \Sigma(X_3 - \bar{X}_3)^2 + \Sigma(X_4 - \bar{X}_4)^2 + \cdots + \Sigma(X_{pq} - \bar{X}_{pq})^2$$

$SS_W = 10 + 4 + 14 + 10$

$SS_W = 38$

$\boxed{df_W = N - pq}$ N = Number of scores; pq = Number of rows $\times$ number of columns

$df_W = 20 - 4$, or 16

$$\boxed{MS_W = \frac{SS_W}{df_W}}$$

$MS_W = \dfrac{38}{16}$

$MS_W = 2.38$

variable produced by the various levels of a single independent variable. In our 2×2 example, we are looking for a main effect of word frequency and a main effect of category cues. The number of main effects to be tested in a factorial experiment is determined by the number of independent variables in the experiment.

When we carry out our ANOVA, we evaluate whether each main effect in the experiment is significant: We compute an F ratio to test the impact of each independent variable. When we test for a significant main effect, we are simply asking again whether subjects' scores on the dependent variable differ depending on the levels of one independent variable that we have manipu-

TABLE 14-9 Step 2: Computing the between-groups variability (SS_B) for a 2 × 2 factorial experiment

	Group 1	Group 2	Group 3	Group 4	Grand Mean $(\bar{X}_G)$
Step 1. Compute the grand mean, the mean of all the group means.	$\bar{X}_1 = 3$ $n_1 = 5$	$\bar{X}_2 = 5$ $n_2 = 5$	$\bar{X}_3 = 6$ $n_3 = 5$	$\bar{X}_4 = 8$ $n_4 = 5$	$\bar{X}_G = \dfrac{\text{Total of all group means}}{\text{Number of groups}}$ $\bar{X}_G = \dfrac{3+5+6+8}{4}$ $\bar{X}_G = \dfrac{22}{4}$ $\bar{X}_G = 5.5$
Step 2. Compute the deviation of each group mean from the grand mean.	$\bar{X}_1 - \bar{X}_G =$ $3 - 5.5$ or -2.5	$\bar{X}_2 - \bar{X}_G =$ $5 - 5.5$ or $-.5$	$\bar{X}_3 - \bar{X}_G =$ $6 - 5.5$ or $.5$	$\bar{X}_4 - \bar{X}_G =$ $8 - 5.5$ or 2.5	
Step 3. Put the deviations in the SS_B formula; n is the number of subjects in each group.	$SS_B = n_1(\bar{X}_1 - \bar{X}_G)^2 + n_2(\bar{X}_2 - \bar{X}_G)^2 + n_3(\bar{X}_3 - \bar{X}_G)^2 + \cdots + n_{pq}(\bar{X}_{pq} - \bar{X}_G)^2$ $SS_B = 5(-2.5)^2 + \quad 5(-.5)^2 + \quad 5(.5)^2 + \quad 5(2.5)^2$				
Step 4. Square all deviations from the grand mean.	$SS_B = 5(6.25) +$	$5(.25) +$	$5(.25) +$	$5(6.25)$	
Step 5. Complete all computations.	$SS_B = 31.25 +$ $SS_B = 65$	$1.25 +$	$1.25 +$	31.25	

lated. To measure the total between-groups variability, we calculated the deviation of group means around their grand mean. In effect, we asked how much individual treatment groups differed from the average of all the groups. When we measure a main effect, we want to look only at one portion of the total variability. We want to measure how much variability occurs between groups because of the impact of one independent variable.

We can ask a straightforward question: How much do the means of groups under different levels of one variable—say, word frequency—differ from the grand mean of all the groups? This is like the logic we followed in doing the one-way ANOVA: The larger the effect of the independent variable, the larger

TABLE 14-10 Step 3: Finding the main effect for Factor 1 (word frequency) in a 2 × 2 factorial experiment

		Word Frequency (Factor 1)	
		Low	High
Step 1. Find the mean at each level of Factor 1: Ignore Factor 2 (rows) and find the mean of each column. N is the number of scores.	No cues given	$\bar{X}_1 = 3$ ($N = 5$)	$\bar{X}_2 = 5$ ($N = 5$)
	Cues given	$\bar{X}_3 = 6$ ($N = 5$)	$\bar{X}_4 = 8$ ($N = 5$)
	Column means	$\bar{X}_{\text{col }1} = 4.5$	$\bar{X}_{\text{col }2} = 6.5$
Step 2. Find the difference between each column mean and the grand mean.	Column mean − Grand mean $\bar{X}_G = 5.5$	$\bar{X}_{\text{col }1} - \bar{X}_G =$ $4.5 - 5.5 = -1.0$	$\bar{X}_{\text{col }2} - \bar{X}_G =$ $6.5 - 5.5 = -1.0$

(Left margin label for rows: Category Cues (Factor 2))

Step 3. Put those differences in the SS₁ formula; n is the number of subjects in each group; p is the number of rows; q is the number of columns. This general formula will handle any number of columns.

$$\mathbf{SS_1} = np\,\Sigma[(\bar{X}_{\text{col }1} - \bar{X}_G)^2 + (\bar{X}_{\text{col }2} - \bar{X}_G)^2 + \cdots + (\bar{X}_{\text{col }q} - \bar{X}_G)^2]$$

$$\mathbf{SS_1} = 5(2)\Sigma[(-1.0)^2 + (1.0)^2]$$
$$\mathbf{SS_1} = 10[(1) + (1)]$$
$$\mathbf{SS_1} = 10(2)$$
$$\mathbf{SS_1} = 20$$

Step 4. To get MS₁, divide SS₁ by df₁.

$$\mathbf{MS_1} = \frac{\mathbf{SS_1}}{df_1} \qquad df_1 = q - 1$$
$$\qquad\qquad\qquad df_1 = 2 - 1, \text{ or } 1$$

$$\mathbf{MS_1} = \frac{20}{1}$$
$$\mathbf{MS_1} = 20$$

the differences from the grand mean. In our example a large main effect of word frequency would mean that subjects' recall varied depending on whether the words to be learned were relatively common or uncommon. When we evaluate the main effect of one independent variable, we treat the data as if that variable is the only one in the experiment. We simply ignore all the other experimental manipulations that were done: We say *we collapse the data across the other conditions of the experiment.* In effect, we pretend that those conditions did not exist. Table 14-10 shows how this is done as we compute $\mathbf{SS_1}$ for our first independent variable, word frequency.

We also need to test for a main effect of the second independent variable. We know that this second variable may have contributed to the total variability between treatment groups. We can evaluate the main effect of the sec-

TABLE 14-11 Step 3: Finding the main effect for Factor 2 (category cue) in a 2 × 2 factorial experiment

			Word Frequency (Factor 1)			
			Low	High	Row Means	Row Mean − Grand Mean

Step 1. Find the mean at each level of Factor 2: Ignore Factor 1 (columns) and find the mean of each row.

Step 2. Find the difference between each row mean and the grand mean.

Category Cues (Factor 2)

	Low	High	Row Means	Row Mean − Grand Mean
No cues given	$\bar{X}_1 = 3$	$\bar{X}_2 = 5$	$\bar{X}_{\text{row 1}} = 4$	$\bar{X}_{\text{row 1}} - \bar{X}_G =$ 4 − 5.5 or −1.5
Cues given	$\bar{X}_3 = 6$	$\bar{X}_4 = 8$	$\bar{X}_{\text{row 2}} = 7$	$\bar{X}_{\text{row 2}} - \bar{X}_G =$ 7 − 5.5 or 1.5

$$(\bar{X}_G = 5.5)$$

Step 3. Put those differences in the SS$_2$ formula; n is the number of subjects in each group; q is the number of columns; p is the number of rows. This general formula will handle any number of rows.

$$SS_2 = nq \, \Sigma[(\bar{X}_{\text{row 1}} - \bar{X}_G)^2 + (\bar{X}_{\text{row 2}} - \bar{X}_G)^2 + \cdots + (\bar{X}_{\text{row }p} - \bar{X}_G)^2]$$

$$SS_2 = 5(2)[(-1.5)^2 + (1.5)^2]$$
$$SS_2 = 10[2.25 + 2.25]$$
$$SS_2 = 10(4.50) \text{ or } 45$$

Step 4. To get MS$_2$, divide SS$_2$ by df$_2$.

$$MS_2 = \frac{SS_2}{df_2} \qquad \begin{aligned} df_2 &= p - 1 \\ df_2 &= 2 - 1, \text{ or } 1 \end{aligned}$$

$$MS_2 = \frac{45}{1}$$

$$MS_2 = 45$$

ond variable by using the same basic procedures we followed to get the main effect of word frequency. In effect, we ask whether subjects' recall differed depending on whether they were given category cues or not: Did it differ regardless of whether they were shown high- or low-frequency words? We look at the effects of our second independent variable by simply disregarding the word-frequency manipulation. *We collapse the data across the word-frequency conditions.* Table 14-11 shows the procedures.

Step 4: Computing the Interaction
The variability associated with the interaction of the two independent variables is simply what remains after the main effects of the independent variables have been taken into account. The variability between groups that is not explained by either independent variable can be explained by their **interaction.**

Since we have two independent variables, the **SS$_B$** must be divided into three parts: the variability associated with the first independent variable (SS_1); the variability associated with the second independent variable (SS_2); and the variability associated with the interaction of the two ($SS_{1 \times 2}$). Once we have

TABLE 14-12 Steps 4 and 5: Summary table; analysis of variance for a 2 × 2 factorial experiment and computed F ratios

Source	df	SS	MS	F
Between groups		65^a		
Factor 1 (word frequency)	$q - 1 = 1$	20	20	$F_1 = \dfrac{20}{2.38}$ or 8.40*
Factor 2 (category cues)	$p - 1 = 1$	45	45	$F_2 = \dfrac{45}{2.38}$ or 18.91**
Interaction 1 × 2	$(p - 1)(q - 1) = 1$	0^b	0	$F_{1\times2} = \dfrac{0}{2.38}$ or 0
Within groups	$N - pq = 16$	38	2.38	
Total	$N - 1 = 19$			

*$p < .05$
**$p < .01$
^{a}SS$_B$ is usually not shown in published articles.
^{b}We find the sum of squares for the interaction of our two variables by subtracting:
$$SS_{1\times2} = SS_B - SS_1 - SS_2$$
The $SS_{1\times2}$ represents all the between-groups variability that is not explained by the main effect of either independent variable. Its degrees of freedom depend on the degrees of freedom for the main effects. Here, there is no interaction.

computed the total SS_B, SS_1, and SS_2, the simplest way to find $SS_{1\times2}$ is by subtracting:

$$SS_{1 \times 2} = SS_B - SS_1 - SS_2$$

The sum of squares for the interaction is entered in the summary table, Table 14-12.

Step 5: Computing the F Ratios
We have now completed nearly all the computations that we need to evaluate the results of our experiment. We summarize our calculations in a summary table (Table 14-12). The table is similar to the one we prepared for the simple ANOVA except in the way it represents the sources of variability. Because we have two independent variables in this experiment, we have three sources of variability: factor 1, factor 2, and their interaction. The within-groups variability (MS_W) is used as the denominator of all three F ratios required to evaluate the significance of these sources. The three F ratios have been computed and are also shown in the summary table.

Evaluating the F Ratios

To judge whether the computed F ratios are significant, we compare them to the table values of F. We get those values from our table of F values in Table B4 of Appendix B. The procedures are the same as those used for the simple ANOVA. We locate the proper value of F by using the degrees of freedom of the F ratio. We look across the top of Table B4 to find the degrees of freedom that belong to the top, or numerator, of the F ratio. We look along the side of the table to find the degrees of freedom of the denominator of our F ratio. Each F ratio we compute has its own degrees of freedom. That means that each ratio has its own critical value or table value of F. When we evaluate each F ratio, we must be sure we are using the correct degrees of freedom and the correct critical value.

Practice finding the correct critical value by looking up the table values of F for the F ratios we have computed. The F ratio for factor 1 (word frequency) has 1 degree of freedom for the numerator (MS_1); it has 16 degrees of freedom for the denominator (MS_W). The table value of $F(1, 16)$ is 4.49 at $p < .05$ and 8.53 at $p < .01$. Our computed value of F for factor 1 is 8.40. Therefore the effect of factor 1 is significant at $p < .05$. Our computed value of F is more extreme than the table value at $p < .05$. This means the main effect of word frequency is so large that it is probably not due to chance. Whether the lists contained high- or low-frequency words made a significant difference in subjects' recall. We reject the null hypothesis that the means of the high- and low-frequency groups were sampled from the same population. But does the significant effect support the alternative hypothesis that high-frequency words are easier to recall than low-frequency words? Because there are only two levels of factor 1, we do not need to worry about post hoc or a priori tests to pinpoint the significant difference; we can see that the high-frequency group has a higher mean recall score than the low-frequency group. So, we can now say that the high-frequency group had significantly better recall than the low-frequency group (as predicted by the research hypothesis).

The F ratio for factor 2 (category cues) also has 1 degree of freedom for the numerator (MS_2); it has 16 degrees of freedom for the denominator (MS_W). We know that the table value of $F(1, 16)$ is 4.49 at $p < .05$ and 8.53 at $p < .01$. (They turn out to be the same as they were for factor 1 because we had the same number of treatment levels and subjects for both word frequency and category cues.) Our computed value of F for factor 2 is 18.91. The main effect of factor 2 is significant at $p < .01$; our computed value of F for factor 2 is more extreme (that is, larger) than the table value at $p < .01$. Again, since there are only two groups in this factor, we can interpret the effects simply by comparing the two group means. We can say that subjects who received category cues recalled significantly more items than subjects who did not receive cues (and we can say that the difference was significant at $p < .01$). We can reject the null hypothesis that the means of the groups under the two levels of factor 2 were sampled from the same population. Instead, we can say that the data analysis supports the research hypothesis.

The computed F for the interaction is 0. This value is clearly not significant. In effect, it tells us that the variability between treatment groups can be explained by the effect of either word frequency or category cues acting separately on subjects' scores. The impact of each independent variable was also unrelated to the value of the other independent variable; the effect of word frequency was the same whether or not subjects received category cues. Similarly, the effect of giving category cues was the same whether subjects saw high- or low-frequency words.

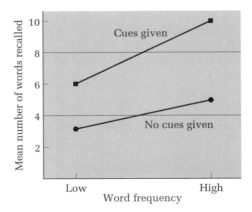

FIGURE 14-6 Graphing the results of a two-factor experiment: Recall of word lists as a function of word frequency and category cues.

If the interaction had been significant, we would be limited in what we could conclude about the main effects in this experiment. Generally, the existence of a significant interaction makes a discussion of simple main effects unnecessary. If there is a significant interaction, it is usually more useful to discuss the impact of the independent variables in combination with each other. A significant interaction means that the impact of one independent variable differs depending on the value of the other. We can make accurate predictions about subjects' performance only when we know the subjects' position with respect to both variables. For instance, in this example a significant interaction would mean that we could accurately predict the approximate number of items the average subject would recall—but only if we knew the subject's position on both variables (for example, if we knew that the subject saw high-frequency words and also received cues). Without a significant interaction, however, we can make a reasonably good prediction if we know the subject's position on only one variable. If we know that Carl was given category cues, we automatically also know that he probably did better than the subjects who did not get cues, regardless of whether he saw high- or low-frequency words.

Graphing the Results

When we had only one independent variable, we had only one line to graph. In a factorial experiment, however, we need to do more. The results of our experiment are presented graphically in Figure 14-6. Notice that the vertical axis still represents the dependent variable. The horizontal axis represents the different levels of one independent variable. Each line that is graphed presents the data from a different level of the other independent variable. One line represents the recall of subjects who were given category cues; the other stands for recall under the no-cues condition. You can see from the location of the

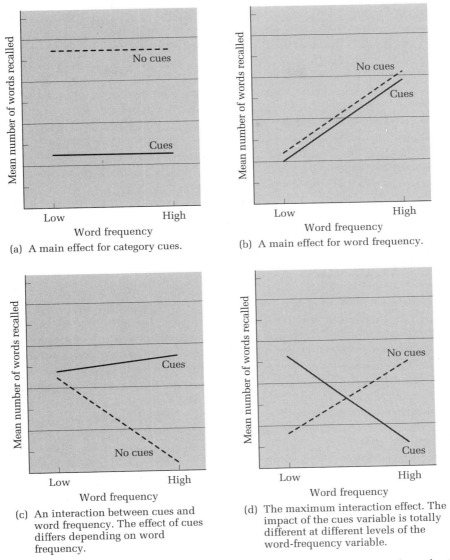

(a) A main effect for category cues.

(b) A main effect for word frequency.

(c) An interaction between cues and word frequency. The effect of cues differs depending on word frequency.

(d) The maximum interaction effect. The impact of the cues variable is totally different at different levels of the word-frequency variable.

FIGURE 14-7 Illustrating other main effects and interactions: Some hypothetical outcomes of an experiment on the effects of word frequency and category cues on list recall.

lines that there are differences between the scores of subjects under the various conditions of this experiment.

Our example yielded two significant main effects. The distance between the two lines (cues versus no cues) reflects the impact of the category cues variable. If giving category cues had no effect on the number of items that subjects recalled, the two lines would fall in the same place on the graph.

Similarly, the impact of the word frequency variable is indicated by the relative position of the data points along the vertical axis. If word frequency had no effect on recall, subjects would recall about the same number of items in both the high- and low-frequency conditions. These and other possible outcomes are illustrated in Figure 14-7.

Notice that interactions appear on the graphs as lines that are not parallel. If the lines converge, diverge, or intersect, we may have a significant interaction effect. Such graphs are useful for summarizing the results of an experiment to give an overall view of the findings, and they are especially useful in constructing summaries of findings for experimental reports. But they are no substitute for statistical analysis. Even though the results look impressive, we need to carry out all the statistical procedures before we can make precise statements about whether we will accept them as significant findings.

REPEATED MEASURES AND MIXED FACTORIAL DESIGNS

There are also ANOVA procedures for within-subjects (repeated measures) factorial designs and mixed factorial designs. The logic behind all of the analysis of variance procedures is similar: Total variability is broken down into component parts representing treatment and error, and an F ratio is computed. The obtained F values for main effects and interactions are compared to critical values needed to reject the null hypothesis. ANOVAs for mixed designs and repeated measures, which are extremely time consuming to calculate by hand, have become much more frequent in the literature as computers have become increasingly available for data analysis. Let us look at a research example of a mixed design.

Siiter and Ellison (1984) were interested in studying stereotypes of a "police personality." As these researchers have reported, there is a commonly held belief that law enforcement officers are a breed apart: "The police, it is said, like the rich, are different from you and me" (p. 334). Many people believe that the police are more suspicious, more cynical, and more *authoritarian* (insisting on strict obedience to rules and authority) than people in general. Actually, there is some evidence that police officers might have somewhat different personality traits than the general population, but little or no support exists for the hypothesis that police officers are more authoritarian than anyone else. Siiter and Ellison tested the stereotype in two groups of male subjects: 62 undergraduates and 62 law enforcement officers. Type of group (a *subject variable*) was the two-level between-subjects (B/S) factor.

All subjects filled out a standard scale of authoritarianism twice: once for their own beliefs and once as they felt a typical member of the other group might respond. Target of the responses (self or other group) was the two-level within-subjects (W/S) factor. This clever design allowed the researchers to assess actual levels of authoritarianism in both groups as well as each group's perceptions of how authoritarian the other group was. The authoritarianism scale data were analyzed with a mixed factorial ANOVA. The sum-

TABLE 14-13 Summary of analyses of variance from Siiter and Ellison's experiment

Source	SS	df	MS	F
Between groups	55,063.50	123	—	—
Groups (G)	8,211.00	1	8,211.00	21.38*
Error$_b$	46,852.50	122	384.04	—
Within subjects	72,290.60	124	—	—
Target (T)	9,725.03	1	9,725.03	30.14*
T × G	23,206.45	1	23,206.45	71.93*
Error$_w$	39,359.12	122	322.62	—
Total	127,354.11	247	—	—

NOTE: Results from Siiter and Ellison (1984).
*$p < .0001$.

mary table is shown in Table 14-13. Notice that results from the B/S factor are tabled first, followed by the results from the W/S factor. You can see by looking at the table that both main effects and the interaction were highly significant.

Interpreting Significant Effects

Interpreting two significant main effects along with a significant interaction can be tricky. Recall that we said earlier in the chapter that whenever a two-way interaction is significant, we are limited in what we can conclude about any significant main effects in the experiment. Generally, the existence of a significant interaction makes a discussion of simple main effects unnecessary because they are *qualified* by an interaction between the factors. If there is a significant interaction, it is more appropriate to discuss effects of the independent variables in combination, since the impact of one independent variable differs depending on the value of the other. Knowing a subject's position on only one of the two factors would not allow us to predict his responses. To interpret the set of results from this study, we would want to say that both main effects and the interaction were significant, but we would focus the interpretation on the significant interaction. The group means are shown in Table 14-14.

TABLE 14-14 Mean authoritarianism scores from Siiter and Ellison's experiment

Group	College Males	Police Officers
Self	87.13	94.97
Others	119.00	88.15

NOTE: Results from Siiter and Ellison (1984).

We cannot interpret the significant interaction, however, until we have conducted post hoc tests to pinpoint differences among the four experimental conditions involved in the interaction. The null hypothesis for this interaction would be that the four groups were sampled from the same population; the significant interaction simply tells us that they probably were not. A significant F value for the interaction does not specify exactly which of the four groups are different from each other. Post hoc tests are necessary to do this. (You will recall that we encountered this problem before when ANOVA was used to analyze a multiple-groups experiment.)

Results of the post hoc tests indicated that the college students' ratings of police ($\overline{X} = 119.00$) were significantly higher than scores of the other three groups ($p < .0001$). The other three groups did not differ from one another; despite small differences among the three means (87.13, 94.97, and 88.15), they were statistically equivalent. Now that we have pinpointed the differences among the four conditions, we can interpret the effects. Let's look at the actual levels of authoritarianism first: Results indicated that the students and the police evidenced similar authoritarianism levels (87.13 and 94.97 were not significantly different mean scores). Next, we can look at how accurate the judgments of the police and students were: The college men rated police officers significantly higher in authoritarianism than they actually were (119.00 vs. 94.97), whereas the police officers' judgments about the students were quite similar to their actual scores (88.15 vs. 87.13). Taken as a whole, the results suggested that the students held a negative stereotype about police, greatly overestimating how authoritarian they were. In the next chapter, we will go into greater detail about interpreting results. We will discuss some problems with interpreting statistical significance. And we will discover a number of other important considerations in interpreting the results of experiments.

SUMMARY

Analysis of variance (ANOVA) procedures are used in experiments having more than two treatment conditions and interval or ratio data. An analysis of variance evaluates the effect of treatment conditions by looking at the variability in data. In the one-way ANOVA for independent groups, all the variability in the data can be divided into two parts: within-groups variability and between-groups variability. *Within-groups variability* is the degree to which the scores of subjects in the same treatment group differ from one another; *between-groups variability* is the degree to which different treatment groups differ from one another.

Variability is caused by all the sources of *error* in the experiment: differences between subjects as well as measurement errors, experimental errors, and other extraneous variables. Error also contributes to within-groups and between-groups variability. Between-groups variability, however, reflects variability caused by error and treatment conditions. If the independent variable had an effect, there should be more variability between treatment groups than there is within them: Between-groups variability should be large relative to the amount of variability within each group.

The relationship of within- and between-groups variability is evaluated by computing the statistic called F, which represents the ratio between the variability observed *between* treatment groups and the variability *within* the groups. The larger the F ratio, the more likely it is that the variability between groups was caused by the independent variable. F is found by computing these quantities: sum of squares between groups ($\mathbf{SS_B}$) and sum of squares within groups ($\mathbf{SS_W}$). Each of these quantities is divided by its respective degrees of freedom (df) to obtain the mean square between groups ($\mathbf{MS_B}$) and mean square within groups ($\mathbf{MS_W}$). The degrees of freedom of the experiment are used to locate the critical values of F in standardized tables. If the computed value of F is more extreme than the table value at the chosen level of significance, the null hypothesis that treatment means were sampled from the same population is rejected.

The analysis of variance tests the overall pattern of means in the different treatment groups. When there are more than two treatment groups tested, the F test does not test for significant differences between each pair of means. To pinpoint the exact location of the differences across several treatment groups, we need to conduct follow-up tests: *post hoc tests* or *a priori comparisons*. A somewhat different one-way ANOVA formula is used to compute F for a within-subjects (or repeated measures) design with a single independent variable, but the concept behind the procedures is very similar.

The basic ANOVA procedures may be extended to handle the data from experiments with more than one independent variable. In factorial experiments the variability in data may be caused by several sources: It can be produced by error; it may also be produced by each independent variable in the experiment. The effects of each independent variable are called *main effects*. Variability may also be the result of the *interaction* or combination of variables in the experiment. There is an interaction when the effect of one independent variable changes across different levels of another independent variable in the experiment. In analyzing data from a factorial experiment, an F ratio is computed to evaluate each main effect and each possible interaction. The basic computational procedures for a two-factor experiment (two-way ANOVA) are similar to those for a one-way analysis of variance. Finally, there are ANOVA formulas for within-subjects (*repeated measures*) and *mixed factorial* designs. These formulas are conceptually similar, but they can be very time consuming to calculate by hand.

KEY TERMS

Analysis of variance (ANOVA) The statistical procedure used to evaluate differences among two or more treatment means by breaking the variability in the data into components that reflect the influence of error and error plus treatment effects.

A priori comparison Statistical test between specific treatment groups that was anticipated, or planned, before the experiment was conducted; also called *planned comparison*.

Between-groups variability The degree to which the scores of *different* treatment groups differ from one another (that is, how much subjects vary under different levels of the independent variable); a measure of variability produced by treatment effects and error.

Error The variability within and between treatment groups that is not produced by changes in the independent variables; variability produced by individual differences, experimental error, and other extraneous variables.

F ratio A test statistic used in the analysis of variance; the ratio between the variability observed *between* treatment groups and the variability observed *within* treatment groups.

Grand mean An average of all the treatment means.

Interaction The effect of one independent variable changes across the levels of another independent variable.

Main effect The action of a single independent variable in an experiment; the change in the dependent variable produced by the various levels of a single independent variable.

Mean square (MS) An average squared deviation; a variance estimate used in analysis-of-variance procedures and found by dividing the sum of squares by the degrees of freedom.

Mean square between groups (MS$_B$) The variance (or average squared deviation) across different treatment groups produced by *error* and treatment effects; also the variance about the grand mean.

Mean square within groups (MS$_W$) The variance (or average squared deviation) within a single treatment group; produced by the combination of sources called *error.*

One-way between-subjects analysis of variance Statistical procedure used to evaluate a between-subjects experiment with three or more levels of a single independent variable.

One-way repeated measures ANOVA Statistical procedure used to evaluate a within-subjects experiment with three or more levels of a single independent variable.

Post hoc test Statistical test performed after the overall analysis indicates a significant difference; used to pinpoint which differences are significant.

Sum of squares (SS) The sum of the squared deviations from the group mean; an index of variability used in the analysis-of-variance procedures.

Sum of squares between groups (SS$_B$) The sum of the squared deviations of the group means from the grand mean.

Sum of squares within groups (SS$_W$) The sum of the squared deviations of subjects' scores from the group mean.

Within-groups variability The degree to which the scores of subjects in the *same* treatment group differ from one another (that is, how much subjects vary from others in the group); an index of the degree of fluctuation among scores that is attributable to error.

REVIEW AND STUDY QUESTIONS

1. When do we use a one-way analysis of variance?
2. What is within-groups variability?

3. What are the sources of within-groups variability?

4. What is between-groups variability?

5. What are the sources of between-groups variability in an experiment with one independent variable?

6. Explain how the one-way analysis of variance works: How do we use within- and between-groups variability?

7. Briefly explain each of these terms:
   a. Sum of squares within groups (SS_W)
   b. Sum of squares between groups (SS_B)
   c. Mean square within groups (MS_W)
   d. Mean square between groups (MS_B)
   e. The F ratio

8. A researcher computed the F ratio for a four-group experiment. The computed F is 4.86. The degrees of freedom are 3 for the numerator and 16 for the denominator.
   a. Is the computed value of F significant at $p < .05$? Explain.
   b. Is it significant at $p < .01$? Explain.

9. Suppose we have done a one-way analysis of variance for a three-group experiment, and our computed value of F is significant.
   a. Without further tests, what can we say about the means of the three treatment groups in our experiment?
   b. Explain why we would need to conduct either post hoc tests or a priori comparisons to interpret these results completely.

10. Explain why $SS_T = SS_W + SS_B$ in the one-way ANOVA.

11. Some of the ANOVA terminology is different from the terms used in earlier chapters. The concepts, however, are similar. Test your understanding of the concepts by matching the following items on the right with the appropriate concepts on the left. (Use each term only once.)

		Choice
a. Within-groups variability	1. A test statistic	_____
b. Mean square	2. Total of squared deviations	_____
c. Null hypothesis	3. A variance estimate	
d. Sum of squares	4. Treatment means sampled from the same population	_____
e. Between-groups variability	5. The table value of the test statistic at the chosen significance level	_____
f. F		
g. Critical value	6. Reflects variability due to error	_____
	7. Reflects variability due to error plus treatment effects	_____

12. Besides the basic requirements for using the analysis of variance, what assumptions must we make about our data to use the test?

13. Jack is still unconvinced. "I'd rather use a bunch of t tests than try to figure out this analysis of variance." Explain to him why the analysis of

variance is more appropriate when we have more than two treatment groups.

14. Practice carrying out the one-way ANOVA procedures by calculating the F ratio for these data. The hypothetical scores below represent the responses of subjects in four treatment groups who were given four different driver-education programs. The dependent variable is the subjects' errors on their state examinations for driver's licenses:

Group 1	Group 2	Group 3	Group 4
3	1	1	2
3	2	1	3
1	1	3	2
3	4	1	5
1	2	2	1

   a. What is the computed value of F for these data?
   b. Is F significant at $p < .05$?
   c. Prepare a summary table for your data.
   d. Graph the results.
   e. Do you need follow-up tests to pinpoint the location of significant group differences? Explain.

15. Using the data from question 14, add 10 to the score of each subject in group 1.
   a. If you now carried through the ANOVA again, would you expect the computed values of SS_B and SS_W to change? Explain.
   b. Would the computed value of F change? If so, how?
   c. Carry out the computations on the new data and see whether your predictions are confirmed.

16. Define these terms:
   a. Main effect
   b. Interaction

17. In the one-way ANOVA, we divide all the variability in our data into just two components. Explain how the ANOVA procedures differ when we are dealing with a factorial experiment.

18. Explain what the components of variability will be in a two-way ANOVA to evaluate the data from a factorial experiment with two independent variables.

19. When we carry out the ANOVA for a factorial experiment, we compute an F ratio for each independent variable and for each possible interaction. Explain why we do not compute F_W, an F ratio to evaluate the size of the within-groups variability.

20. An experimenter has studied the effects of cigarette smoking on learning. Two levels of the smoking variable were used: All the subjects are smokers, but only half are given cigarettes to smoke during the half-hour before the experiment; the other half are not allowed to smoke after they arrive at the laboratory. There are also two levels of the learning variable: Subjects are all given the same materials to study, but half the subjects are

told they will be asked to recall the words they see (intentional learning condition). The remaining subjects are told they will be asked to rate various types of printing for readability. They are *not* told they will be asked to recall the actual words they see (incidental-learning condition).

  a. Here are some hypothetical data from the learning and smoking experiment. Practice the two-way ANOVA on these data.

Factor 1 (Smoking)

	Smoked		Did not smoke	
Intentional	4 3 5 4 4	$\overline{X} = 4$	5 4 4 3 5	$\overline{X} = 4.2$
Incidental	3 2 2 3 2	$\overline{X} = 2.4$	4 3 4 3 2	$\overline{X} = 3.2$

Factor 2 (Learning)

  b. Explain what would happen if we added 10 to the score of each subject in the intentional learning groups.
  c. Explain what would happen if we added 10 to the score of each subject in the incidental learning, no-smoking group.

21. Prepare a simple graph to illustrate each of the following possible outcomes of the experiment in question 21:
  a. There is a main effect for cigarette smoking only: Subjects who smoked remember more. There is no interaction.
  b. There is a main effect for learning: Subjects learned more in the intentional learning condition. There was no main effect for cigarette smoking and no interaction.
  c. There was a strong interaction between smoking and the learning conditions. Illustrate at least two forms this interaction might take.

22. On the next page is a STATVIEW printout of a summary table for a 2 × 2 ANOVA on the data from the learning and smoking experiment. How did your computations fare against the computer's analysis?

23. Interpret the set of effects from the learning and smoking experiment.

ANOVA table for a Two-Factor Analysis of Variance on Y_1: Recall

Source:	df:	Sum of squares:	Mean square:	F-test:	p value:
Smoking (A)	1	1.25	1.25	2.273	.1512
Learning (B)	1	8.45	8.45	15.364	.0012
AB	1	.45	.45	.818	.3791
Error	16	8.8	.55		

There were no missing cells found.

TABLE 14-15 STATVIEW Summary Table

PART IV

DISCUSSION

DRAWING CONCLUSIONS: THE SEARCH FOR THE ELUSIVE BOTTOM LINE

We have now discussed all the major steps for setting up a psychological experiment, running it, and evaluating the results using statistical tests. The goal of an experiment is to establish a cause and effect relationship between an independent and a dependent variable. In this text we have covered a variety of experimental designs and control procedures that enable us to do this in a legitimate way. After the data are analyzed through statistics, however, two questions remain: What does it all mean? Have we accomplished our goal?

Keep in mind that even when a significant treatment effect is present, we have only established a statistical outcome. We have demonstrated that the treatments in our experiment produced differences so large that they could occur by chance only a small percentage of the time—but we have not tested the experimental hypothesis directly. Statistical significance tells us nothing about the quality of the experiment; statistically significant results may or may not have any practical or theoretical implications. You could, in fact, invent data that show significant treatment effects. Of course, we would like to find statistically significant differences that support our research hypothesis. But we would also like findings to be convincing and to have applications in settings outside the experiment. When we interpret the results of experiments, we look beyond the simple question of whether they are statistically significant; we evaluate the pros and cons of accepting these results at face value. A discussion and evaluation of findings are included in all research reports: Besides telling others what we did, we want to tell them what we think it means. We also want to point out any methodological problems or other potential limitations on the findings.

This chapter contains a discussion of some of the problems of drawing conclusions from the results of an experiment. We will review some of the criteria—internal and external validity—used to evaluate the worth of an experiment. We will also focus on some aspects of the generality of particular research findings beyond the context of an experiment. Finally, we will look at the special problems that arise when our predictions are not confirmed.

EVALUATING THE EXPERIMENT FROM THE INSIDE: INTERNAL VALIDITY

When evaluating an experiment, we begin by judging it from the inside: Is the experiment methodologically sound? Is it *internally valid*? An experiment is internally valid when the effects of an extraneous variable—a variable not the focus of the experiment—have not been mistaken for the effects of the independent variable. An internally valid experiment is free of confounding; effects on the dependent variable can be attributed solely to the experimental treatment.

You will not find many obvious examples of internally invalid experiments in the research literature. All the articles published in major journals (for example, those published by the American Psychological Association, the American Psychological Society, or other professional organizations) are carefully reviewed before they are accepted. Only the best are published. An experiment that contained an obvious source of confounding probably would not make it into print. As you read the literature, however, be on the lookout for subtler problems. Perhaps a researcher overlooked something that may be important. Perhaps there is an alternative explanation of the findings if we view them in the context of another theoretical approach. If you can make a good case for your criticism, you may have the beginning of your own study to settle the question. Box 15-1 presents an interesting example of a series of studies undertaken by researchers to explore possible confounding in their own published results.

Of course, the best way to assure internal validity is to plan ahead. As you design experiments, you must be sure that your procedures incorporate the appropriate control techniques. Be sure to use standard techniques like random assignment, constancy of conditions, and counterbalancing throughout your research. But when you are ready to evaluate the outcome of the experiment, do not forget to consider what *actually* happened. You will need to ask yourself whether the experimental setup created the conditions you intended? Did subjects follow instructions properly? Did you manipulate the independent variable successfully? Did the sad film really make the subjects feel sad? Were subjects in the low-anxiety condition really less anxious than subjects in the high-anxiety condition? To be sure, some researchers include such an assessment as part of their experimental procedures. This is called a *manipulation check* because it verifies how successfully the experimenter manipulated the situation he or she intended to produce.

But even the most careful plans can go awry. You may have designed a tight set of procedures before you began testing subjects, but in practice you may have been forced to deviate from the plan. Did these small changes affect the way subjects responded? You want to be certain that all your procedures accomplished what you intended. Did you find that subjects in your control group did not understand directions? Did they keep asking questions to clarify their task in the experiment? Your instructions may have been confusing under that condition. Can you be sure, then, that those subjects really did what you wanted them to do?

B O X   1 5 - 1

ISOLATING VARIABLES IN RECALL

In the first of a series of experiments, Ritchey (1982) reported the findings of a study on children's recall. Age was treated as one independent variable: Third-graders, sixth-graders, and adults were the three levels of this variable. The type of stimulus was another independent variable: words, outline drawings, and detailed drawings, as shown in Figure 15-1.

Ritchey found that, contrary to predictions, children remembered outline drawings better in a subsequent recall task. This outcome was unexpected since the detailed drawings included more features that could be encoded in memory. However, even though outline drawings are less elaborate, they are more distinctive (unusual) because they differ from the drawings we usually see.

In later experiments Ritchey and Armstrong (1982) showed that subjects recalled detailed drawings better than less elaborate drawings—when the degree of distinctiveness was controlled. Distinctiveness, as in the caricature in Figure 15-2, made items easier to recall when the amount of elaboration (detail) was controlled. Thus the original confounding between elaboration and distinctiveness led to further research. This research in turn helped clarify the relationship between the two variables as they influence free recall.

GIRAFFE   GIRAFFE

FIGURE 15-1 Stimuli used to test pictorial detail and recall: detailed (left) and outline (right) drawings. The figure on the right is less elaborate but more distinctive than the figure on the left. Drawings furnished by Gary H. Ritchey. Used with permission.

(continued)

(continued)

FIGURE 15-2 Stimuli used to separate effects of elaboration and distinctiveness. Left to right: detailed, outline, caricature drawings. The figures on the left and the right are equally elaborate, but the right-hand figure is more distinctive. Drawings furnished by Gary H. Ritchey. Used with permission.

Many researchers incorporate an informal interview (or a written questionnaire) at the end of the experiment to get at this kind of information. They ask subjects to talk about their thoughts and feelings during the experiment. They also ask about any questions that subjects might have had during the procedures. If subjects did not follow instructions, the experimental manipulation may not be the best explanation of the findings. In an informal interview, the researcher can also try to get a sense of whether subjects guessed the experimental hypothesis by asking them what they thought the experiment was trying to show. If a group of subjects guessed the hypothesis, their data may be of limited value. You may find it advantageous to spend a little extra time interviewing the first few subjects in depth, so that any potential problems in the procedures can be corrected before you run a large number of subjects through the experiment, wasting your time and theirs.

Some of these validity issues are difficult to resolve because of the demand characteristics of the experiment itself. For instance, Orne (1969) suggested that a *pact of ignorance* forms between subjects and experimenter. Subjects may be aware that if they guess the hypothesis of the experiment, their data will be discarded. If you ask them what they understood about the purpose of the experiment, they may not reveal all they know. Subjects need to believe that you really want a truthful answer. Some researchers have gone as far as offering subjects an incentive for guessing the experimental hypothesis during informal interviews. Orne also pointed out that experimenters may not really press subjects for much information, because it may mean that some data may not be usable. Most researchers do not want to spend unnecessary time testing additional subjects. They may be tempted to accept subjects' reports at face value instead of requesting additional information that might provide a more objective evaluation. Avoid this temptation if you want to be sure your experiment is internally valid.

Always review the experimental procedures after the experiment. Did any extraneous variables change along with the independent variable? Did testing conditions change midstream? Were there any other unplanned changes that might have altered subjects' responses? *When you interpret the results of your experiment, always be open to other potential explanations for your findings.*[1] If something other than the independent variable can explain the results, the experiment is not internally valid. Before concluding that your experiment is internally valid, review the classic threats to internal validity covered in Chapter 6. Remember that it is better if *you* are the one to discover any substantial problems in your experiment; an experienced reader is certain to find them and think even less of your abilities as a researcher if you have missed them. Discuss problems openly in the discussion section of your report. And, do not forget that even the most well-constructed experiment does not *prove* your hypothesis is correct; we never confirm our research hypothesis directly, and we certainly never "prove" it. Statistical tests allow us to make probability statements only, and there is always a chance of Type 1 error. Good scientists are always skeptical about their own results.

Statistical-Conclusion Validity

Let us hope your experiment will be free of such confounding variables as the eight classic threats to internal validity. But confounding is not the only threat to an experiment's internal validity; other kinds of problems can lead to false conclusions about cause and effect relationships between experimental variables. We also need to evaluate the experiment in terms of the results we obtained from statistical tests. We want to be certain that any inferences we make about the relationship between independent and dependent variables have **statistical-conclusion validity**, the validity of drawing conclusions about a treatment effect from the statistical results that were obtained (Cook & Campbell, 1979). Whenever the assumptions of a statistical test are violated, statistical-conclusion validity is in doubt. Clearly, if we used a test statistic inappropriately (a *t* test for nominal data, for example), there would be some doubt about the validity of conclusions we could draw from a "statistically

---

[1]On one hand, we have found that beginning researchers spend *too much time* listing everything imaginable that could have influenced any of the subjects' responses ("Some subjects may have stayed up too late the night before." "Some may have been in a hurry to get to the experiment and did not have time to eat a good breakfast."). As long as these events are infrequent and could occur randomly for subjects in any of the experimental conditions, they are not considered a problem with the experiment (they just add error, making it harder to detect effects). On the other hand, we have found that students spend *too little time* thinking about other potential explanations for their results. Could anything else have changed along with levels of the independent variable? Were high-frequency words shorter than low-frequency words? Could an authoritarianism scale be less valid for police officers than for college students? Could increasing the negative ions in the air also make it less humid? Think carefully about any other effects that could have been produced when you varied the levels of an independent variable.

significant" effect. But less obvious factors can influence statistical-conclusion validity, too. The number of statistical tests computed and the power of the statistical test are two common sources of low validity.

You already know the problem created by too many pairwise comparisons—a higher chance of making a Type 1 error (concluding that your treatment had an effect when it really did not). If the chances of making a Type 1 error have been increased, then statistical-conclusion validity has been lowered. Inferring a cause and effect relationship is much riskier. You also know that it is easier to get statistical significance with a large than with a small sample because small samples reduce the power of statistical tests. If your experimental results were barely significant even though you tested 400 subjects, you probably should be cautious about drawing conclusions. We will return to the notion of statistical power and validity when we discuss null findings later in the chapter.

Sometimes findings can be statistically significant but not very meaningful. Suppose we conducted an experiment to investigate the effect of word frequency on recall. Imagine we used the same three-group design (high-, medium-, or low-frequency words) as the hypothetical word frequency experiment in Chapter 14, but we selected different words. Our results were statistically significant. More high-frequency words ($\overline{X} = 12.3$) were recalled than medium- ($\overline{X} = 12.1$) or low-frequency words ($\overline{X} = 11.9$). Very small mean differences can be statistically significant if there is little variability in the data. Would such small differences really count for much in the broader scheme of things? Probably not.

How can you tell if your effect is meaningful? Here is one good approach. The *Publication Manual of the American Psychological Association,* Fourth Edition (1994) recommends that researchers include a measure of **effect size** along with significant statistical values (*F*s, *t*s, etc.). The effect size is an estimate of the size or magnitude of the treatment effect(s). There are a number of effect size statistics you can compute quite easily from the obtained statistical values and the degrees of freedom. For example, to calculate an effect size η^2 (eta^2) for a significant *F* value, you could use the following formula:

$$\frac{df_1 F}{df_1 F + df_2}$$

Let us calculate an effect size for the word frequency experiment in the last chapter. The obtained value of *F* was 7.23; the numerator (df_1) and denominator (df_2) degrees of freedom were 2 and 14.

$$\frac{2(7.23)}{2(7.23) + 14} = .55$$

The estimated effect size is .55. In the case of an analysis of variance, the effect size represents the proportion of variance in all the scores that can be accounted for, or explained, by the treatment—in this case, .55 or 55% of all of the variability in subjects' scores in the experiment can be accounted for by the treatment. Considering the great number of potential influences on subjects' scores in any psychology experiment, this would be considered a substantial effect. You can consult a statistics book for other formulas for computing effect sizes.

TAKING A BROADER PERSPECTIVE: THE PROBLEM OF EXTERNAL VALIDITY

So far we have talked about evaluating an experiment from the inside. Did extraneous variables contaminate the results? Is the study free of confounding? But we also want to look beyond the experiment to broader questions. We want to know whether the experiment has *external validity:* Do the findings have implications outside the experiment? Can we make any general statements about the impact of the independent variable? An experiment is externally valid if the results can be extended to other situations accurately. However, external validity is not an either/or matter; it is a continuum. Some experiments are more externally valid than others.

Generalizing from the Results

When an experiment has some degree of external validity, we may generalize from the results. We make our findings more universal than they actually are by ignoring the specific details of the experiment. Instead of speaking in terms of a particular sample (for example, 30 female undergraduates) and a specific set of operational definitions (for example, scores on the Manifest Anxiety Scale), we draw broader inferences from the findings through inductive thinking. When we think inductively, we reason from specific facts to more general principles. Early in the text, you saw how we can use induction to formulate research hypotheses. We also use induction when we make generalizations on the basis of a specific set of findings. The accuracy of our generalizations depends on a variety of factors that affect the external validity of an experiment.

An externally valid experiment meets two basic requirements. First, the experiment is internally valid; it demonstrates a cause and effect relationship. The experiment is free of confounding. Second, findings that are externally valid can be *replicated.* We (or other researchers) can replicate or duplicate the original findings in other experiments. If we get statistically significant results again, we can be more sure that the findings were not just flukes of our sampling procedures, or Type 1 errors. Valid experimental findings appear again and again. Similar effects should reappear in similar studies. Findings that appear once and cannot be replicated have limited scientific importance, and any general conclusions that we draw from such findings may be inaccurate.

Of course, when you complete a single experiment, you do not know whether the findings can be replicated unless you are actually replicating some earlier findings. Partly for that reason, you will often see single articles that contain reports of several experiments. These series of experiments typically extend the findings of one principal study. They provide data on alternative explanations and applications of those findings; they also serve to provide evidence that the findings can be replicated. If a researcher consistently obtains confirmation of a hypothesis throughout a series of experiments, the findings have some degree of external validity.

Along with the overall requirements of internal validity and replicability, we can also look at external validity as it applies to several important issues: generalizability across subjects, across procedures, and beyond the laboratory.

Generalizing Across Subjects

How much can we generalize from one group of subjects to another? How much can we generalize from a sample to the population that interests us? These questions have no hard and fast answers. Experiments may have different outcomes when they are run on different samples. For that reason, we try to get samples from the population we want to discuss. If we want to make statements about college students, we ought to sample college students. It makes sense to assume that all college students have some characteristics in common that enable us to speak of them as a group. Nevertheless, we need to be cautious in drawing conclusions about all students on the basis of one study. What is true for students in Kansas may not be true for students in New York.

Practical problems also prevent us from obtaining truly random samples. There is typically *bias* in the way human subjects are chosen, if only in that they are all volunteers. The student (or parent or salesperson) who volunteers may not be typical. You already know that volunteers may be quite different from nonvolunteers (Rosenthal & Rosnow, 1975).

The problem becomes even more acute when we try to extend our findings to a larger group, such as all people. Other writers have commented on the fact that a rather large proportion of research findings in psychology has come from studies of white rats and college students. Of course, many of these findings have been replicated in studies with different species and with a variety of human subjects, too. But the fact remains that the generality of our research is often constrained by practical problems. College students may be intrinsically interesting, but they are also more available for research than the average adult who spends the better part of the day at a regular job. White rats are relatively easy to keep, and they cost less than monkeys. These mundane factors shape the research that we do. When we have trouble finding subjects, we will also have trouble getting samples that are typical of the population we are trying to study, thereby limiting the external validity of the experiment.

How far can we go in generalizing from a study? Clearly, the further from the population actually sampled, the shakier our position becomes, at least until we do more testing. As research findings are replicated in subsequent studies with different types of subjects, their generality is supported. Findings that appeared only with red-headed 19-year-old Stanford University students would not have much generality.

At times, it makes sense to explore some of the questions of generality across subjects *within the same experiment*. For instance, if we suspect that age or social class will alter the impact of an independent variable, we may treat those subject variables as additional independent variables. We might, for example, include several different age groups for testing. When that is not feasible, we may be forced to rely on later studies to clarify the role of those additional variables. However, we may accept the generality of some findings for ethical reasons. Manufacturers often use laboratory animals to test the safety of new products such as drugs, shampoos, and cosmetics. A product that proved harmful to nonhuman subjects would not be marketed, even though there was no *direct* evidence that it was dangerous to humans.

Generalizing from Procedures to Concepts: Research Significance

Ideally, our findings also illustrate the operation of general principles; they are not unique to the particular procedures used in the experiment. For instance, Hess (1975) showed that pupil size affected the ratings men gave to photographs. A picture of the same woman received more favorable ratings when she was shown with larger pupils. If this finding has generality across procedures, we would expect to get similar results with different sets of photographs (as in Neidenthal & Cantor, 1986); we would not expect the findings to be peculiar to the photos of just one person. If the findings also have generality across subjects, we would expect that different types of men would give similar data. We might also expect to see similar responses from women rating photos of men.

Sometimes attempts to generalize across procedures raise theoretical issues that are hard to resolve. These issues arise when we study variables that can have multiple operational definitions. An operational definition, in principle, defines a variable in terms of observable operations, procedures, and measurements. As we saw in an earlier chapter, some variables, like anxiety, may be defined in various ways. When we generalize from the results of an experiment, we face the problem of going from a specific operational definition of a concept to conclusions about the concept itself. We do not want to talk about the number of errors that subjects made; instead, we want to talk about the concept of learning. We may not be interested in the effects of difficult mazes per se; we want to talk about the concept of frustration. Naturally, it is desirable to view findings from this more abstract perspective; we would like to discover principles that explain behavior in general. Ultimately, we would like to use induction to build new theories and to apply our findings to practical problems.

Typically, however, it is risky to generalize from the findings of a single experiment in this way. The reasons are closely related to some of the issues we discussed earlier. We cannot always be certain of how reliable or valid our procedures are. For example, is your definition of learning tapping into the same phenomenon Dr. D. used in his study? One experiment may be suggestive, but we go far beyond our data when we expand our findings to explain all possibilities. For these reasons, researchers hedge a bit when they discuss generalizability. The discussion sections of research reports are dotted with qualifying statements: "These findings suggest . . . ," "It seems reasonable that . . . ," "It appears that. . . ." Such statements often distress new researchers who would prefer to be able to state that something will occur with certainty. But the probabilistic nature of experimentation restricts the kinds of statements we may make about our findings.

Also, as we formulate general conclusions, we move further away from the actual observations that we made. We can make some statements with confidence; we can report exactly what we did and what we observed in the experiment. When we begin to interpret results, we go beyond what we actually did and what we actually observed. As we do so, we are on increasingly shaky ground. Researchers qualify the conclusions they draw because there is no way to be certain their generalizations will always be true. Perhaps the findings describe the effects of the independent variable only under a very specific set of circumstances—namely, those defined in one experiment. Perhaps other operational definitions of the variables would lead to other outcomes. As we know, testing different sorts of subjects might do the same.

Still, if our findings have some degree of generality, we expect them to be consistent with the findings of prior researchers who have studied the same variables. Thus, as we evaluate the generality of our results, we look at them in the context of the work that has already been done in the field.

We have talked about evaluating statistical significance. But findings also have research significance. As we evaluate them, we ask several pertinent questions. First, are they consistent with prior studies? If so, how do they clarify or extend our knowledge? Do they have any implications for broader theoretical issues? At this stage, we are coming full circle on the research process. We began our experimental plan by reviewing the research literature. We used findings of prior researchers as a guide to the important issues and the most suitable procedures for the area we studied. Now, with our results in hand, we consider the place of our findings in the context of prior work in that area.

If our findings do not mesh with earlier findings, our experiment may be suspect. For instance, we know that newborn babies prefer patterns over solid-colored forms (Fantz, 1963). If we have devised a testing system that leads us to conclude that babies actually prefer unpatterned figures, we have a problem. We must be able to reconcile our findings with what has already been shown. Novel findings are suspicious when the prior findings have been replicated; the burden of explanation usually falls on the researcher who claims the novel findings. The possibility of an undetected flaw in the experiment must be evaluated with special caution.

You will occasionally read reports of findings that appear to be conflicting. Often the apparent contradictions result from subtle differences in the operational definitions, the procedures, and the subjects used in various experiments. These inconsistencies may lead researchers into new studies to discover more general principles.

This is part of the process of theory building we discussed in Chapter 1. A theory is meant to make sense of many bits of data. The theory can stand as long as it is adequate to explain observed results. However, as conflicting data appear, more and more supporting assumptions may be needed to explain new findings. Ultimately, the theory may become so burdened by assumptions and exceptions that it must be discarded.

Generalizing Beyond the Laboratory

So far we have talked about using induction to extend the results of specific experiments to other samples, other populations and procedures, and more general concepts. You know by now that we have some difficulty generalizing from one set of experimental procedures to another with accuracy. As you can imagine, we come up against an even greater problem when we extend the results of a laboratory experiment to what we might observe in the real world. Remember that a laboratory experiment is carried out under specific, controlled conditions. Because the laboratory researcher tries to eliminate all the extraneous influences that might affect the outcome of the experiment, the laboratory experiment is the most precise tool we have for measuring the effect of an independent variable as it varies under controlled conditions. The problem in extending laboratory findings is simple in principle: The variables we study usually do not occur under the same controlled conditions in real life. All sorts of extraneous factors may affect the influence of any one variable.

Increasing External Validity

The degree of control we get in a laboratory experiment gives us a great deal of precision. However, some researchers have argued that it may also provide data that have little relevance to our everyday lives; results obtained in the laboratory may not match those obtained in the field. Reviewing the literature on attitudes and behavior, Hanson (1980) found more laboratory than field studies reporting a positive correlation between reported attitudes and behavior. In the laboratory, it seems, people are more likely to think and act consistently. More field than laboratory studies in the literature supported the conclusion that people's reported attitudes do not predict what they will do in their everyday lives.

How safe is it to extend the results of a laboratory experiment to everyday life? There is no clear-cut answer to that question. It is often impossible to know whether the findings of a particular experiment are externally valid until we do additional studies. However, researchers use at least five general approaches to increase and verify the external validity of laboratory findings: aggregation, multivariate designs, nonreactive measurements, field experiments, and naturalistic observation. Let us look at each in turn.

Aggregation

If experiments create a limited, artificial context for behavior, we can begin to increase the generality and external validity of our findings by combining the results of experiments done in different ways. This is the logic behind meta-analysis, discussed in Chapter 5. Meta-analysis uses statistics to combine and quantify data obtained from many similar experiments. For example, meta-analyses by Raudenbush (1984) and Harris and Rosenthal (1985) found that the Rosenthal effect discussed in Chapter 11 was consistently obtained in experiments testing teacher expectancy effects.

Epstein (1980) called this approach **aggregation,** the grouping together and averaging of data gathered in various ways. Epstein described four types of aggregation that can be used to increase the external validity of our data and broaden the scope of our experimental findings.

Aggregation Over Subjects Combining data from several subjects is already typical of psychology studies. Rather than relying on one or two subjects who may be unusual, we sample greater numbers. Their data are pooled and our conclusions are based on group averages, as we saw in the last two chapters. Presumably, the larger sample is more representative of the population. These group data in principle should have greater external validity than smaller samples of the same population.

Aggregation Over Stimuli and/or Situations In addition to generalizing to a population, researchers commonly wish to generalize their results across a range of stimuli. For instance, an experiment on color matching that uses only 20 pairs of colors may be used to draw conclusions about the full range of 7500 different colors. In what sense do the 20 selected colors represent the overall range of 7500?

Epstein argued that stimuli must be sampled as effectively as we sample subjects; so must the context of the experiment. A social psychological experiment on helpfulness, for instance, might yield different results during the holiday season, when subjects may feel especially cooperative and helpful, than at other times of the year. We should not assume that such seemingly irrelevant factors do not alter experimental outcomes. Having sampled in a variety of situations, we can have more confidence in our results.

Aggregation Over Trials and/or Occasions By using many trials and combining multiple testing sessions, we minimize the effects associated with specific trials. If an experimenter unwittingly gives a cue to the correct response on a particular trial, combining data from many trials will cancel out the distortion.[2]

Testing on various occasions also minimizes the effects created by the uniqueness of each testing session. Barber (1976) pointed out that experimental

---

[2]This practice is analogous to the use of grade point averages (GPA) to represent academic achievement. Occasionally, you may feel you received too low a grade; another instructor may surprise you with a grade higher than you expect. These differences tend to cancel out. The more courses you take, the better the chances that your GPA reflects your true level of achievement.

procedures are often not sufficiently standardized. The researcher may be more enthusiastic one time than the next; he or she may use slightly different words to introduce the experiment each time. Aggregating occasions provides data on the replicability of findings obtained in specific testing sessions.

Aggregation Over Measures Finally, Epstein recommended using multiple measuring procedures. When we select a measure, such as one achievement test, we are sampling from all the measures available. But our one selection may not be the best. Measuring in more than one way will offset the errors we may make using one inadequate instrument.

The different forms of aggregation provide converging lines of evidence for an explanation of behavior. The relative importance of the various forms of aggregation is still open to empirical verification. However, it is clear that we can have more confidence in results that can be reproduced using different subjects, in different situations, on different occasions, and measured in more than one way.

Multivariate Designs

In this text we have focused on research designs that have one independent and one dependent variable. However, since variables do not usually occur separately, we also looked at factorial designs in which we explore the effects of more than one independent variable at a time. As complicated as those designs may have seemed at first, there are other designs that are even more elaborate. They are called **multivariate designs** because they deal with multiple dependent variables. These designs have become increasingly important in psychological research as computer technology has become more widely available. Without computers, multivariate statistical analysis is impractical.

Multivariate designs enable us to look at many dependent variables in combination.[3] Measurements may be made on one or several samples (Cooley & Lohnes, 1971). The procedures used to evaluate the results of these studies are extensions of the basic techniques you have already learned. Some of the more common multivariate designs are multiple correlation and factor analysis, which were discussed in Chapter 4, and multivariate analysis of variance. Here we will take a brief look at the multivariate analysis of variance so that you will have some idea of why multivariate procedures are desirable.

The multivariate analysis of variance is an extension of the analysis of variance described in Chapter 14. We used the ANOVA to study the effect of more than one independent variable in a factorial design. However, those designs had only one dependent variable. By using a **multivariate analysis of variance (MANOVA)**, the researcher can measure the effects of independent variables as they affect *sets* of dependent variables. He or she can evaluate whether the independent variables influence subjects' scores on the dependent variables as they occur in combination.

---

[3]Cooley and Lohnes (1971) point out that a factorial design is also "multivariate" in the sense that it has more than one independent variable. However, the term *multivariate* is customarily restricted to designs with multiple dependent variables.

Through this type of design, a researcher interested in improvement after psychotherapy could approach the problem in a more comprehensive way than would be possible through a simpler factorial design. For instance, he or she could explore the effects of several independent variables: type of therapy, type of patient, sex of patient, sex of therapist. He or she could also measure several aspects of improvement instead of just one. The researcher might measure the patients' self-reports, the therapists' reports, and symptoms as rated by objective observers. This combination of measurements could provide a more comprehensive index of "improvement" than any single one. The MANOVA tests the effects of the independent variables on the whole set of measures at once. As with the simpler ANOVA procedures, the researcher would also be able to test for interactions among the independent variables on this set of improvement measures. Type of therapy and type of patient might interact to affect improvement. Higher-order interactions would be possible, too; several independent variables may operate together to affect improvement.

With a MANOVA, the researcher also has the option of analyzing differences in trends among the various dependent measures. Effects produced by independent variables may be stronger on some measures than on others. Perhaps patients' reports show greater improvement than symptom ratings. In short, a MANOVA provides much more information than the simpler analysis of variance.

The advantage of this and other multivariate procedures is that they allow us to look at combinations of variables that can be more representative of reality. Instead of focusing on just one aspect of improvement in therapy, such as self-report, the researcher can evaluate a wider spectrum of behavior. This broader focus provides a perspective on behavior that can have greater external validity than the simpler univariate approach. For that reason, there are now special journals devoted primarily to multivariate research—for example, *Multivariate Behavioral Research* and *Journal of Multivariate Experimental Personality and Clinical Psychology*. We may be able to increase the external validity of some studies by using multivariate rather than univariate approaches. We can also extend earlier findings by applying these new techniques to old questions.

Nonreactive Measurements

We can also increase external validity by working to minimize **reactivity** in an experiment. Subjects react to being subjects. They react to being observed. Their responses may not be the same as the responses of others who are not observed, and thus they may not have external validity.

We dealt with the problem of reactivity when we discussed survey techniques in Chapter 3 and demand characteristics of an experiment in Chapter 11. If an experiment has obvious demand characteristics, the results may not have much generality. They may not reflect what we would see outside the laboratory. When a subject comes into an experiment, the subject assumes an active role. The subject has certain expectations about what will happen in the experiment. If the researcher inadvertently gives cues that tell the subject what to do, the problem is even more serious. Subjects may actively try to generate data that support the reseacher's predictions. The opposite may also happen: A subject may "guess" the hypothesis and then try to produce data to refute it!

We try to control demand characteristics and thus reactivity in part by being careful not to give subjects unnecessary cues. However, as Orne (1969) suggested, it may be difficult to get accurate information about our procedures. The pact of ignorance that forms between subjects and experimenters can affect external as well as internal validity. We can make better assessments of the impact of experimental manipulations through single- and double-blind experiments because the results will be less influenced by subjects' reactivity.

Since some subjects react differently from others, we need controls for other social and personality variables as well. We have to be especially wary of variables like social desirability. We know, for instance, that subjects in interviews are apt to present a more favorable picture of themselves, distorting their responses to "look good" in the eyes of the researcher. Results distorted in this way may have little generality; they may not reflect what is true of behavior outside the laboratory.

Developing unobtrusive measures. As long as subjects know they are being observed and measured, their responses may be distorted in some way. If nothing else, they may be a little nervous. For that reason, researchers have also tried to develop specific procedures to measure subjects' behavior without letting them know they are being measured. These **unobtrusive measures** are not influenced by subjects' reactions. They have greater external validity because they yield data more similar to what we expect to see outside an experiment.

For example, in Chapter 3 we discussed the Bechtol and Williams (1977) study of littering, which was done partly through unobtrusive measures such as counting up cans on a beach to obtain an index of littering. Many unobtrusive measures depend on physical aspects of the environment. We could evaluate the popularity of several attractions in a national park by comparing the condition of the trails leading to those sites; the more popular attractions should have well-worn trails. Similarly, we could judge the seating preferences of patrons of a theater by the condition of the seats.

We can also gather data by observing subjects unobtrusively. For example, Marston, London, Cooper, and Cohen (1977) made unobtrusive observations of obese and thin diners in a restaurant. Without diners' knowledge, they recorded behaviors such as toying with food, size of bites, and rate of eating. They identified a "thin eating" pattern among women: smaller bites, a generally slower rate of eating, and more extraneous behaviors, such as putting down the fork now and then. The unobtrusive approach seems to have greater external validity than bringing subjects into a laboratory to observe their eating behavior.

Field Experiments

Perhaps the most obvious way of dealing with the whole problem of external validity is simply to take the experiment out of the laboratory, where most unobtrusive measures are used. If we suspect that subjects will behave differently under more realistic conditions, we can try it and see. Clearly, some experimental problems do not lend themselves to this approach. But those that do can lead us into fruitful new tests of our hypotheses.

The **field experiment** meets the basic requirements of an experiment: We manipulate antecedent conditions and observe the outcome on dependent measures of behavior. Instead of studying subjects in the laboratory, however, we observe them in a natural setting. This approach has greater external validity. For instance, Mann (1977) studied social influence and line-joining behavior. He conducted his experiment at a bus stop in Jerusalem. Baseline data collected in the control condition showed that people there do not typically form lines to wait for buses. In the experimental condition, confederates of the experimenter took their places at the empty bus stop soon after a bus had stopped there. The experimental manipulations consisted of varying the number of confederates waiting and their positions at the bus stop. Mann found that lines of at least six confederates were required to produce significant levels of line-joining behavior among the first commuters to arrive at the stop.

This approach clearly illustrates the advantages of the field approach. It would be difficult to set up a laboratory situation that would be a credible representation of "waiting for a bus." However, field experiments also have certain limitations. One potential problem is that the researcher often has little control over choice of participants in the experiment: Whoever came to the bus stop during the experiment was included. Thus samples may not be random. We may also have more difficulty specifying the characteristics of these samples than we do in a laboratory experiment, where we are usually able to get more information about subject variables. Assigning subjects in the field to treatment conditions at random provides some control for subject variables, but we are usually less able to control extraneous variables in a field setting.

Field experiments can be used to validate findings obtained in the laboratory. If results under controlled laboratory conditions have some degree of external validity, we should observe similar outcomes when we study behavior in more realistic settings. Doob and Gross (1968) used this approach to verify data obtained through questionnaires. College students were asked to say whether they would be likely to honk sooner at a stalled new car or a stalled old car in the street. Men predicted they would honk sooner at a newer car. Women predicted they would honk sooner at an older car. In a field experiment, drivers were blocked in traffic by either a new expensive car or an old car. Observers recorded the time before honking. They found that, in general, subjects of both genders actually waited longer before honking at the new expensive car.

The inconsistencies in the Doob and Gross data highlight the importance of verifying evidence (particularly evidence based on subject reports) in more realistic settings. The logical extension of this process is evaluating findings in the context of ongoing behavior, without experimental intervention. This takes us back to one of the basic methods of gathering psychological data—naturalistic observation.

Naturalistic Observation

Miller (1977) has advocated for the application of naturalistic observation in psychological research. In particular, he suggested that "naturalistic observation can be used to validate or add substance to previously obtained laboratory findings" (p. 214). Miller also suggested that the process of laboratory research and naturalistic observation may be used in a complementary way. We can use naturalistic observation to suggest specific hypotheses about behavior and then test those hypotheses under the controlled conditions of the laboratory. We can return to the naturalistic setting to verify our findings.

The important implication of Miller's statement is this: Although we often think of the experiment as a unique, perhaps isolated method of research, we can use it to best advantage in combination with other modes of research. Psychologists try to discover principles and applications that will ultimately benefit humanity. Since most of us do not live in laboratories, our research must have some link to everyday life. Psychologists can strengthen that link by using a variety of research methods in combination. In this way they can maintain precision without sacrificing relevance.

HANDLING A NONSIGNIFICANT OUTCOME

Up to this point, we have approached the problems of interpreting data from a fairly optimistic perspective. We have more or less assumed that the results we are trying to evaluate were statistically significant and that they supported the predictions. But suppose we have run a well-planned experiment that did not work: Our predictions were not confirmed; our treatment means are embarrassingly similar. Can anything be gained from such an experiment?

Research journals give the impression that all experiments yield significant results. Unfortunately, we do not see all the studies carried out that did not make it into print. The occasional negative outcome reported in the literature is there because that outcome has implications for a theoretical position that predicts there *should* be significant differences. In reality, many studies do not turn out exactly the way the researcher expected.

If you ran an experiment and your results were not significant, don't be discouraged; even the best researchers have an occasional dud. One of the characteristics of a good researcher is that he or she uses nonsignificant findings in a constructive way. A good researcher asks, "Why didn't things go as expected?" and uses the answers to generate better studies. If your experiment did not support your predictions, you should evaluate it from two perspectives. First, were the procedures right? Second, was the hypothesis reasonable?

Faulty Procedures

We may not confirm our predictions because our procedures were faulty. Of course, we are always on the lookout for confounding. For instance, we may have inadvertently allowed control subjects a little more practice time, which compensated for the effects of the special training procedures used in the experimental condition. Review everything you did. Did you apply all the appropriate control procedures? Did you use random assignment? Counterbalancing? Are there problems with demand characteristics or experimenter bias?

Another possibility is that although there were no confounding variables in the experiment, numerous uncontrolled variables increased the amount of variability between individual subjects' scores. If there was a lot of uncontrolled variability in scores on the dependent measure, treatment effects might not have been detectable. Perhaps your reading of the instructions varied from time to time. Maybe some of the subjects were recruited in the laundromat, whereas others came from a factory. Perhaps your measuring instrument was unreliable. Even though the effects of these variables tend to "randomize out" across treatment conditions, they still have the net effect of increasing the amount of within-groups or error variance. If we happen to be studying an independent variable that has a relatively weak effect, we may be in trouble. Our experimental manipulation may not be powerful enough to override the effect of all the other sources of variation in the experiment. (We may be attempting to find a needle in a haystack.) We may be unable to reject the null hypothesis even though the independent variable had an effect—that is, we may be making a Type 2 error. You can also see that when an experiment produces a large error variance, statistical-conclusion validity is lowered. In this case, a decision not to reject the null hypothesis based on the results of the statistical test may be an invalid conclusion.

When you get null findings, always ask yourself whether your sample was large enough. It can be difficult to get statistically significant effects using very small samples unless your treatment effects are strong. You may simply not have had enough *power* in your statistical test if only a small number of subjects were used. Low power reduces the statistical-conclusion validity and can produce a Type 2 error. The technique for assessing power can be found in Cohen (1988) and many statistics textbooks. Keep in mind that Type 2 errors can occur; *failing to reject the null hypothesis does not mean that the null hypothesis is necessarily correct.* Even if your experiment failed to support your research hypothesis, a subsequent experiment might.

Another possible cause of null results is that the experimental manipulation was inadequate: The independent variable might have had a powerful effect if we had defined treatment levels in a better way. Our "hungry" rats were deprived of food for only 6 hours. Perhaps 24 hours would have been a more effective fast. We instructed our experimental subjects to form mental images of the words on a screen. Perhaps our control subjects did the same even though we told them not to. Better procedures may be needed. Of course, the only way to verify these possibilities is by running new experiments.

We also look for problems in the way we measured the dependent variable. Did we measure what we intended? Was the measure valid? Suppose we are trying to assess the effect of different camera angles on the sexual appeal of photographs. We ask subjects to rate a series of photographs, some of which are mildly erotic. Subjects' ratings may be contaminated by their need to give socially desirable responses. We may end up measuring social desirability rather than the appeal of the photos.

Check to see if subjects used the full range of scores on the dependent variable. If scores on the dependent variable are too restricted, finding significance can be extremely difficult. If most of your subjects use only the top (or bottom) ratings on your scale, there will be little or no variability caused by treatment, so your results are not likely to be significant. Imagine you are an ice cream maker for Ben & Jerry's. You want to compare your new version of chocolate cherry fudge with the old version. You invite people to taste the old or the new version and rate how much they like it on a scale from 0 (not at all) to 10 (very much). The old version gets all 10s (because it is really good). The new version tastes even better, but it gets all 10s, too, because your scale doesn't allow people to discriminate between, say, very good and scrumptious! When subjects tend to "top out" on the scale, it is called a *ceiling effect*. The same thing can occur if people only use the bottom of the range; then it is called a *floor effect*.

If the experimental procedures or measures are faulty, we have not made a valid test of our hypothesis. The best time to deal with faulty procedures is *before* running the experiment. It seems easy enough to formulate after-the-fact explanations: "I did not get significant results because there were flies in the room when I tested my experimental group." Well, maybe.

No one enjoys coming to the end of a data analysis only to find no significant differences between the treatment groups—all that work and so little to show for it! At best, it is disappointing. Perhaps, to save face, we sometimes get caught up in attempts to explain that what we did was fine; we designed sound procedures that were internally valid. Was it our fault that a fire drill was called in the middle of the experiment? Of course not. But few of us like to consider the possibility that the experiment was doomed from the start.

Faulty Hypothesis

When we evaluate the outcome of an experiment, we must look at it from the standpoint of all of the internal components we have discussed. Besides procedural aspects, we want to be sure that the experiment represents good thinking. If we have what seems to be a flawless procedure for studying a hypothesis, if we have executed the experiment carefully and the results are not significant, we must at least consider the possibility that the hypothesis was faulty. We will need to go back and rethink the problem. Perhaps we overlooked some key feature of prior studies; perhaps our reasoning was confused. The good researcher uses this evaluation process to decide where to go next.

Be cautious in drawing conclusions from nonsignificant results. Researchers often find themselves in a quandary when their results are *almost* statistically significant, for instance, when $p < .10$. Claiming the experiment "almost worked" or the data were "almost significant" is simply not convincing, even if the probability value is close to being significant. The null hypothesis may actually be correct. We treat as new knowledge *only* statistically significant disconfirmations of the null hypothesis. Consider the possibility that the hypothesis needs to be reworked. Use what you learned in this experiment to plan a better one the next time.

This chapter has presented the major factors that need to be considered when experimental findings are interpreted and conclusions are drawn. In the final chapter of the text, we will learn how to present these interpretations and conclusions in a research report.

SUMMARY

Some of the problems we encounter in evaluating and drawing conclusions from the results of an experiment have to do with whether or not an experiment is internally and externally valid. An experiment that is *internally valid* is free of confounding. In evaluating the internal validity of an experiment, the researcher needs to consider both the plan for running the experiment and what actually happened. If extraneous variables affected the results, the findings may not be interpretable. The classic threats to internal validity are always potential confounding variables that should be considered. Researchers always need to be open to the possibility of other explanations for their findings. Inferences about the relationship between independent and dependent variables must have *statistical-conclusion validity*, too. Some statistically significant results might not be very meaningful; calculating the *effect size* of significant statistical values is one way to gauge the magnitude of treatment effects.

An experiment is *externally valid* if the results can be extended to other situations with accuracy. Inductive thinking can be used to generalize from the results of the particular experiment to broader principles and implications. To be externally valid, an experiment must first be internally valid. External validity is a continuum rather than an either/or situation; some studies have greater external validity than others. Findings that are externally valid can be replicated. They can be extended to different samples of subjects and to the larger population. Externally valid findings can also be extended to different experimental procedures and, perhaps, to different operational definitions of the variables.

A major part of interpreting research involves placing it in the context of prior work. If findings are consistent with prior work, we discuss how they extend our knowledge. If findings are inconsistent with prior studies, the discrepancy must be explained. These inconsistencies may form the basis of new experiments.

Externally valid results can also have implications outside the experimental setting. However, it is usually difficult to make this determination within the context of a single study. Researchers use at least five approaches to increase as well as verify the degree of external validity of their findings:

aggregation of data, multivariate designs, nonreactive measures, field experiments, and naturalistic observation. Data may be *aggregated,* or combined, over subjects, stimuli, and/or situations (as in a meta-analysis). Findings may also be verified through multiple trials and/or testing occasions and by measuring outcomes through more than one measuring instrument. *Multivariate designs* test multiple dependent variables. Researchers also try to decrease *reactivity* in their studies; they measure behavior in such a way that the outcome will not be affected by subjects' reactions to the experiment. Reactivity is reduced by controlling the demand characteristics of the experiment. *Unobtrusive measures* of behavior can also be used to control reactivity. The *field experiment* is another means of increasing external validity. Finally, researchers may confirm the validity of laboratory findings through *naturalistic observation.* Using research methods in combination is another fruitful way to study behavior.

There is also the practical dilemma of dealing with nonsignificant findings. Experimental procedures must always be reviewed for sources of internal invalidity, such as uncontrolled extraneous variables. Low statistical power or a weak manipulation of the independent variable need to be considered. Finally, the thinking that led to the hypothesis should be reviewed to be sure the predictions were reasonable.

KEY TERMS

Aggregation The grouping together and averaging of data gathered in various ways; including aggregation over subjects, over stimuli and/or situations, over trials and/or occasions, and over measures.

Effect size A statistical estimate of the size or magnitude of the treatment effect(s); one example of an effect size statistic is η^2 (eta^2), which is used to estimate effect sizes from ANOVA values.

Field experiment An experiment conducted outside the laboratory used to increase external validity, verify earlier laboratory findings, and investigate problems that cannot be studied successfully in the laboratory.

Multivariate analysis of variance (MANOVA) The statistical procedure used to study the impact of independent variables on two or more dependent variables; an extension of analysis of variance.

Multivariate design Research design or statistical procedure used to evaluate the effects of many dependent variables in combination; including multiple correlation, factor analysis, and multivariate analysis of variance.

Reactivity The tendency of subjects to alter responses or behaviors when they are aware of the presence of an observer.

Statistical-conclusion validity The degree to which conclusions about a treatment effect can be drawn from the statistical results obtained.

Unobtrusive measure A procedure for assessing subjects' behaviors without their knowledge; used to obtain more objective data.

REVIEW AND STUDY QUESTIONS

1. Discuss three potential sources of internal invalidity in an experiment. How would you control each one?

2. How does internal validity affect the conclusions that may be drawn from the results of an experiment?

3. What are the eight classic threats to internal validity presented in Chapter 6? Why are they potential confounds?

4. What factors influence statistical-conclusion validity?

5. What do we mean when we say that results can be significant but not meaningful? What is a good approach for judging how meaningful an effect is?

6. What is external validity?

7. An experiment that is not internally valid cannot be externally valid. Why?

8. Why is replicability a requirement for external validity?

9. Explain how we use inductive thinking to extend the findings of an experiment beyond the particular study.

10. What issues affect the decision to generalize the findings of an experiment to other samples of subjects? To other populations?

11. The operational definition of a given variable may be changed from one experiment to another. Explain how and why this change of definition affects the generality of research findings.

12. In writing up a research report, a psychologist concluded by saying: "These results prove my hypothesis. They provide conclusive evidence that working crossword puzzles improves vocabulary." Without knowing the details of the researcher's procedures, what could you say about each of the following:
   a. Assuming that the findings are statistically significant, are the researcher's conclusions justified? Explain.
   b. Assume that several researchers have conducted similar experiments. The previous findings have been inconclusive. What can be said about the conclusion in view of prior research?
   c. Given your answers to (a) and (b), reword the experimenter's conclusions appropriately.
   d. If you chose to conduct a similar study, what extraneous variables might affect the internal validity of the experiment?
   e. Explain how aggregation could be used to broaden the implications of these findings.

13. What are multivariate procedures?

14. How can multivariate procedures be used to increase the external validity of an experiment?

15. How does the reactivity of subjects influence the external validity of an experiment? Discuss three techniques for reducing reactivity.

16. Pick one of the laboratory experiments we have discussed in this text and devise a way to confirm the findings of that experiment—either through a field experiment or through naturalistic observation.

17. Deanna is not quite sure how to interpret the results of an experiment she did. She found that her data were almost significant ($p < .07$). What advice would you give her about explaining her findings?

18. Jack is skeptical of this whole chapter: "If we have to put so many limits on what we can say about an experiment, why bother? Let's just talk about what we found and leave it at that." Explain to Jack the purpose of generalizing from our findings. What do we accomplish when we generalize correctly?

CHAPTER 16

WRITING THE RESEARCH REPORT

Report writing is a major part of the research process. For that reason, you may find that your instructor shows little sympathy for your reluctance to write up dull results. Most likely, you will be required to write a report whether or not your findings will change the direction of psychology. In this chapter we will discuss the purpose and structure of psychological **research reports.** As you know, the overall structure of this text parallels the general structure of these reports. In each report we find an *introduction,* a *method* section, a section on *results,* and a *discussion.* Each report also has an *abstract* or summary and a list of *references.* We will begin by reviewing the basic content of each section. Then we will look at an example of a published research article to see how these ideas are put into practice. We will also focus on specific aspects of preparing the manuscript of a report and on points that often cause problems for beginners.

THE WRITTEN REPORT: PURPOSE AND FORMAT

The primary purpose of a written report is *communication.* Through our report we tell others what we did and what we found. In addition to reporting findings, we should also provide enough information to enable other researchers to make a critical evaluation of procedures and a reasonable judgment about the quality of the experiment. In addition, we want to provide enough information to enable others to replicate and extend the findings.

Research reports are written in a **scientific writing style.** You have probably noticed that the writing style in published articles seems fact-filled, highly structured, and more concise than other kinds of writing. It is supposed to be. The goal of an experimental report is to provide objective information, not to entertain the reader, express opinions, or talk about personal life experiences. You already know that all facts need to be documented by citing the published sources where you read about them. When you write a research report, you must also avoid seeming opinionated about your topic. Try to keep your personal feelings out of the report; it is a scientific document for public communication, not an essay or personal statement. Most authors will avoid personal pronouns like *I* or *we* whenever possible (their occasional use is acceptable to avoid awkward sentences).

The scientific style is also *parsimonious*—the author attempts to give complete information in as few words as possible. Because the amount of publication space in journals is limited, authors write as concisely as possible, selecting their words carefully. Each word is chosen for its precision. (Yes, scientific writers use the dictionary a lot.) Do not be surprised if your instructor crosses out many words (particularly adjectives and adverbs) or even whole sentences in your report; beginning writers typically use many more words than necessary. Most of us need practice to write scientifically because it is very different from more common writing styles. If you can avoid writing any sentences that seem flowery, you will be on your way to a scientific writing style. Always avoid slang; it lacks exact meaning and may not be universally familiar.

When you write your research report, be careful to use unbiased language. The American Psychological Association (APA) and other journal publishers are committed to encouraging language free of gender and ethnic bias in their publications. There are several techniques for avoiding bias: When writing about ethnic groups, for example, use the term that is currently preferred by most members of that group. Always use nonsexist language. Whenever you are writing about individuals (research participants, people in general), select words that are free of gender bias. Because some sexist words are so embedded in our language, this can seem awkward at first.[1] For example, do not talk about the benefits of psychological research for "man" or "mankind" when you really mean "all people"—say "people" instead. Don't refer to a subject as "he" (unless all your subjects really were male); use "he or she" or "they" instead. If you use "he or she" (or "she or he"), however, do so sparingly or the usage becomes distracting. Never use contrived contractions, like "s/he," or "he/she," which suggest that the genders are interchangeable. When discussing people of both genders, most experienced researchers try to construct gender-free sentences instead. Often, just pluralizing the sentence can take care of the problem. Instead of saying, "When a subject arrived, he was . . . "; say instead, "When subjects arrived, they . . . ," and so forth. Never assume that a researcher is male; 50% of those currently graduating with Ph.Ds in psychology are women.

Avoid other kinds of language that have negative overtones. Do not call lesbians and gay men "homosexuals." Use "nonhandicapping" language when referring to people with mental or physical disabilities. Referring to your subjects as "20 people with obsessive-compulsive disorder" is much better than saying "20 obsessive-compulsives." Similarly, don't use the name of a disability to characterize a person. Saying "a person living with paraplegia" is much better than saying "a paraplegic."

---

[1] You might recall that McMinn, Williams, and McMinn (1994; experiment 3) found that identification of sexist language was improved after training. Psychologists feel that it is important to make these language changes because a number of experiments have demonstrated that gender-biased language reinforces sexist attitudes and behaviors (e.g., Gastil, 1990; Silveira, 1980).

One of the most common pitfalls of a first report is taking too much for granted. After you have worked on a study for some time, what you did may seem completely obvious. The problem is that an element that seems obvious to you may not be obvious to your readers unless you explain it. Remember that the whole point of writing a report is to communicate information. A reader should be able to understand what you did and why simply by reading the report.

Psychological reports are expected to follow the format set by APA. It is presented in detail in the fourth edition of the *Publication Manual of the American Psychological Association* (1994), which was prepared to make the job of reporting easier for researchers as well as readers. As early as 1928, psychologists and other social scientists recognized the need for standards for presenting research data. The first "manual" was a seven-page article that appeared in *Psychological Bulletin* in 1929. The present manual spans over 350 pages and contains material on all aspects of appropriate content as well as detailed explanations of specific layout and style requirements. Our presentation here will be brief; if you have questions about specific problems, you should refer to the manual.

The need for a standard format for reports becomes clear when you consider the tremendous volume of research going on today. The APA alone publishes over 20 journals, which translates to about 1500 articles per year. Even more are published in the many non-APA psychology journals. Many thousands more are reviewed and not accepted for publication.[2] If everyone used a different format for writing reports, reviewers would have a hard time evaluating the work; writers would agonize over its presentation; and readers would have trouble locating the information they need. The place for creativity is the design of your experiment, not the format of your report, which should conform to APA standards. Although some details of format vary slightly from one journal to another, most follow the overall structure outlined here.

When you prepare the manuscript of your research report, some of the format requirements will seem strange at first. That is because the format has been designed with publishers, as well as readers, in mind. It simply makes the job of translating a written report into a published article easier. In the last section of this chapter, you will learn these procedural details. You will see that the manuscript version of a research report does not look exactly like the published version. But let us first look at what goes into the major sections of the report.

MAJOR SECTIONS

Every research report must contain these major components: a descriptive title, an abstract, an introduction, a method section, a results section, a discussion section, and a list of references. We will look at each section in turn

---

[2]Most high-quality journals reject 70% to 85% of all the articles that are submitted (a few reject even more).

so that you will have a clear idea of the basic requirements of each. Many reports contain additional features such as footnotes, tables, or figures (graphs, pictures, or drawings). For now we will focus on the content of the major sections. Try to develop a feel for what each section accomplishes. Later, we will look at layout requirements and additional components.

Descriptive Title

Reports need a **descriptive title** that gives readers an idea of what the report is about. The simplest way to achieve this goal is by including both the independent and dependent variables of the study in the title, stating the relationship between them. Here are some examples from articles we have discussed in previous chapters: "Negative Ions and Behavior: Impact on Mood, Memory, and Aggression Among Type A and Type B Persons" (Baron et al., 1985); "Anxiety, Fear, and Social Affiliation" (Sarnoff & Zimbardo, 1961); "Social Enhancement and Impairment of Performance in the Cockroach" (Zajonc et al., 1969); "Effect of Initial Selling Price on Subsequent Sales" (Doob et al., 1969). Titles like "A Psychological Experiment" or "An Experiment on Rock Music Videos" are far too vague to be of much use to a reader who is trying to track down specific information. The recommended title length, however, is about 10 to 12 words; leave *something* to be said in the body of the report.

Abstract

An **abstract** is a summary of the report. It should not exceed 960 characters and spaces (about 120 words) for an empirical study. Write the abstract in the same general style you use in the report, and write it in the past tense (because the research has already happened). The abstract should be a concise synopsis of the experiment, written so that it makes sense and can stand by itself. It should contain a statement of the problem studied, the method, the results, and the conclusions. Unless you are replicating a specific published experiment, leave out citations. Tell your readers what sorts of subjects you used (for example, 30 adult macaque monkeys). Describe the design (for example, a 2×2 between-subjects factorial design). Summarize the procedures used in the experiment and state the results briefly. You should also state the important and interesting conclusions you reached.

At this point you may be thinking, "All that in 120 words or less? You must be kidding!" Actually, we're quite serious. But it may help you to know that abstracts are notoriously difficult to write; they require a technique few of us practice very often. For that reason, many people find it easiest to write the abstract after they write the report. You may want to do the same. The abstract is an important part of the research report because it will appear in publications such as *Psychological Abstracts,* in PsycLIT, and in all the other abstract sources that are the guides to the literature in psychology. You will recall that we discussed these sources in Chapter 5 when you learned how to conduct a literature search.

The abstract is probably the most frequently read portion of any article. If the abstract is poor, uninteresting, or uninformative, readers may not go on to read the entire article. That is why it is especially important to include all the pertinent facts of an experiment in the abstract. Good abstracts make our research more accessible to our readers. Good titles do the same, since the title determines the way that an article will be indexed in *Psychological Abstracts* and other sources. When you are using abstracts in your review of the research literature, you are also preparing for the next major section of your research report, the Introduction.

Introduction

The **introduction** of your research report sets the stage for what follows. A good introduction tells readers what you are doing and why: It introduces your hypothesis and how you will test it. As you write your introduction, think about what readers should get out of it. Your focus should be the experiment's hypothesis. After reading the introduction, readers should have answers to the following questions: What problem are you studying? What does the prior literature in the area say about the problem? What is your hypothesis? What thinking led up to that hypothesis? What is the overall plan for testing the hypothesis? Do you make any specific predictions about the outcome of the study?

The introduction is the proper place to include a review of the research literature that led to your hypothesis or that lends support to it. For instance, you might show how prior findings have been inconsistent or ambiguous; explain how your experiment may clarify the problem. It is not necessary to cite every bit of research that has ever been done in an area; cite *only* what is most essential to understanding the nature of the problem. Be careful to show how you got to your hypothesis; readers should be able to follow the thinking that took you there. Do not assume that anything is obvious. Remember that you are writing for an audience that is probably already familiar with your research area, so an exhaustive review of the literature is unnecessary. Be careful about citations. Cite all articles that the background experiments for your hypothesis came from as well as any source from which you obtained your ideas.

State your hypothesis explicitly in the introduction. Usually it should appear toward the end, after you have explained the research and the thinking behind it. Identifying independent and dependent variables is appropriate. You may then want to say something about general procedures if that seems warranted. You may also want to include a sentence or two about operational definitions to prepare readers for what follows in the report. If you have made predictions about the outcome of the study, by all means say so. Be sure you explain why you expect these results; do not expect readers to guess what you are thinking. The introduction should leave readers prepared for the method section. As Rosnow and Rosnow (1995) explain:

> The introduction provides the rationale for your study and prepares the reader for the methods you have chosen. . . . If you can get readers to think when they later see your method section, "Yes, of course, that's what this researcher had to do to answer this question," then you will have succeeded in writing a strong introduction. (p. 44)

Method

The **method section** tells readers how you went about doing the experiment. It should be detailed enough to allow another researcher to replicate your experiment. It is customary to subdivide the method section into several labeled subsections: participants, apparatus (or materials), and procedure. However, you will find that authors deviate from the customary subheadings when they feel it is appropriate. Complicated research designs, unusual manipulations or experimental stimuli, and complex dependent measures or scoring procedures are sometimes placed in separately labeled subsections. Participants, apparatus (or materials), and procedure subsections are standard, but you should adjust the format according to the kind of study you are presenting.

Participants

The subsection on participants (sometimes called subjects) should give readers the important characteristics of your sample. It should answer these key questions: How many subjects did you have? What are their relevant characteristics (age, sex, species, weight, and so on)? How were subjects recruited and/or selected? Were they paid or given course credit? Give any additional information that may be important to understanding your experiment. Remember that the reader will need to know the characteristics of your sample in order to assess the external validity of your results. (If you need to, refer back to the detailed section on samples in Chapter 3.) If any subjects dropped out of the study, report that, too, and explain the circumstances.

Apparatus

This is sometimes called the materials section when the experiment uses very little equipment beyond paper and pencils. Use your judgment to decide which label is more appropriate for your study. In this subsection you should provide readers with a description of the equipment used. Unless they are unusual in some way, standard items like stopwatches, pencils, or tables and chairs do not have to be described in detail. However, refer to any ready-made, specialized equipment by name, manufacturer, size, and model number—for example, "The film clip was presented on an RCA 19-inch color monitor, model #318482." Identify standardized tests by name and include a citation—for instance, "Subjects filled out the Social Desirability Scale (Crowne & Marlowe, 1964)." If you built your own equipment or prepared your own stimulus figures or questionnaire, give the details. Sometimes an illustration or sample items need to be included. If your equipment is *extremely* complex, you can include a complete description in an appendix at the end of the report. Be sure to provide all the information essential for replication, including physical dimensions like length, width, and color if appropriate. Unless another measure is standard (as in TV screens), give measurements in metric units.

Procedure

This section should provide readers with a clear description of all the procedures followed in your experiment. Include information on how subjects were assigned to the different groups in the experiment (random assignment, selected by scores on a personality test, etc.). Explain the experimental manipulation and the procedures you used for controlling extraneous variables (counterbalancing, and so forth). After reading this section, a person should know how to carry out the experiment just as you did. "Subjects were seated in a chair located approximately 2.85m from the television monitor." Any special control procedures you used should be identified here—for instance, "To control for order effects, the film clips were presented in counterbalanced order." You may want to include the exact instructions you gave to subjects, particularly if the instructions constituted your experimental manipulation. Otherwise, simply summarize them.

One easy way to write a procedure section is to report everything step by step in chronological order. Use some discretion in reporting commonplace details; the reader does not need to be told the obvious. For instance, if you gave subjects a written test, it would be unnecessary to report that they were provided with pencils and were seated during the test. However, do report anything unusual about your procedures. (Having to use the experimenter's back as a writing surface would be unusual, and you would need to report it.) Be sure to identify your experimental manipulations carefully. Spell out the way you measured the dependent variable. Always ask yourself whether someone could replicate your experiment based on what you have said. By the end of the Procedure section, readers should be able to identify the kind of research design you have.

Unless your design is very simple and easily constructed from the written procedures, consider the option of including a subsection called Design. If you have chosen a complex factorial design, for instance, it can be very helpful to the reader if you include a design statement with the factor labels (as you learned in Chapter 8). For instance, in a $6 \times 4 \times 3$ factorial design, write out the factor names along with the design. Specify whether the design was between subjects, within subjects, or mixed—for example, "The experiment was a 6 × 4 × 3 (Reinforcement × Food Deprivation × Age) between-subjects factorial design." In mixed designs, specify the within- and between-subjects factors, because they may not be obvious to the reader. For example, if reinforcement had been a within-subjects factor in this experiment, you could say instead, "Level of reinforcement was a within-subjects factor; food deprivation and age were between-subjects factors." As the design becomes more complicated, readers usually need more explicit help in structuring the plan of the experiment.[3] Do what makes the most sense to clarify your study. Finally, specify the dependent variable: "The dependent variable was the amount of time it took to learn the maze."

Results

The **results section** of a report should tell readers what statistical procedures you used and what you found. Findings are easier to understand if you begin with a brief summary of your principal findings stated *in words*. Then report the results of your statistical tests (F or t values, results from post hoc tests, and so on) and summary data (for example, an ANOVA summary table or a table that includes means and standard deviations. Remember that we usually do not report individual scores unless we have a small N design. Tell readers what statistical tests you used to evaluate the data, along with the obtained values of test statistics. Indicate degrees of freedom and significance levels. Be sure that you have stated all group means included in important findings.[4] Some measure of group variability (typically the standard deviation, or SD) is required whenever you are reporting values of F or t. You should also state the significance level you selected, typically $p < .05$. (Some of these requirements are new to the fourth edition of the APA *Publication Manual*, so you will not find all of this information in every study you read.)

Here is an example. Suppose a student researcher replicated a prior finding from the literature (Greeson & Williams, 1986) that violent music videos can increase people's acceptance of violent behavior. The student conducted an experiment testing the effects of watching either violent or nonviolent music videos on subjects' attitudes toward violence. She designed a questionnaire to measure attitudes toward violence; the higher the score, the more accepting an individual was of violent behavior. A between-subjects t test showed that the prediction was confirmed by her experiment, and she was

---

[3]If the design is fairly straightforward from a written description of the procedures, some researchers prefer to state the design factors in the first paragraph of the results section as part of the description of the statistical analysis. For example, you might find a statement like this: "A 6 × 4 × 3 (Reinforcement × Food Deprivation × Age) between-subjects ANOVA was conducted on the maze running data."

[4]When reporting means, we use the abbreviation M instead of $\bar{X}$; for example, a group mean would be reported as $M = 7.89$ (see the example later in this section).

able to reject the null hypothesis at $p < .05$. Her results section might begin by stating, in words, what she found:

> As predicted, subjects expressed more positive attitudes toward violence after viewing violent music videos than after viewing nonviolent videos.

Then she could report the results of her statistical tests and relevant summary data—for example,

> With an alpha level of .05, a t test indicated that attitude scores were significantly different after violent videos than after nonviolent ones, $t(34) = 3.12$, $p < .01$. Subjects shown a violent music video were more accepting of violence ($M = 7.89$, $SD = 2.10$) than subjects who watched a nonviolent video ($M = 4.20$, $SD = 1.89$).

As we mentioned in the preceding chapter, an estimate of the *effect size* is strongly recommended in the *Publication Manual*. It is usually reported right after the obtained statistical value and probability level, like this:

> A t test indicated that attitude scores were significantly different after violent videos than after nonviolent ones, $t(34) = 3.12$, $p < .01$ ($\eta^2 = .22$).

There are no hard and fast rules for presenting statistics—as long as the presentation is complete and the results are clear to the reader.

In a simple two-group experiment, the results section would probably not be very long. But if you have a factorial design, you will have more results to report (main effects, interactions, post hoc tests, and the like). If you have more than one dependent measure, you may wish to present the results for each measure separately. (This is the approach the author took in the sample journal article explained in the next section of the chapter.) As with the simpler experiment, begin by stating, in words, what you found. Then report all the effects produced by your statistical tests and relevant summary data for each kind of effect. Typically, we report main effects first, then go on to the interaction(s). Finally, give the results of post hoc tests or other group comparisons if you used them. If the number of subjects in each group was not equal, report the cell sizes. Be sure that the reader can understand one effect completely before going on to the next. If you have presented many statistics, it is helpful to the reader if you summarize the effects in words at some point.

Sometimes results can be summarized most easily through figures or tables, but these should be used sparingly (because they take up a lot of valuable journal space). A figure or table should enhance what you have to say about the data. Avoid reporting the same statistics or summary data in the text *and* in a table or graph. If your *F* values, means, and *SD*s are in a table, simply refer the reader to the table at the appropriate time—for instance, "Results of the statistical tests and group means are shown in Table 1." Never duplicate the same information in a table *and* a figure. Figures and tables must be referred to within the text and should be an integral part of the presentation, not ornaments dangling in space. (Later in the chapter, you will learn how to include them in your written report.) The results section is used only to present the objective data as they appeared in the experiment. Interpretation of the results belongs in the next section.

Discussion

The overall purpose of the **discussion section** is to evaluate your experiment and interpret the results. As you learned in the previous chapter, the discussion should tie things together for readers. In the introduction you reviewed the literature and showed readers how you arrived at your hypothesis and predictions. In the method section, you described the details of what you did. In the results section, you presented what you found. Now in the discussion you need to pull everything together. You need to explain what you have accomplished: How do your findings fit in with the original problem stated in the introduction? Was your hypothesis supported? How do the findings fit in with prior research in the area? Are they consistent? If not, can any discrepancies be reconciled? The discussion section is also the place to talk about what you think your results mean: What are the implications of the research? Can you generalize from the findings? Does further research suggest itself?

Begin the discussion section with a clear summary sentence or two restating your results (in words only). Any sources of *confounding* or problems with the experiment that might influence the interpretation of the data should be reported. But be reasonable; it is not necessary to mention things that are probably irrelevant. Whether or not all subjects had breakfast probably is not critical, especially if you assigned them to conditions at random. However, if half the experimental subjects walked out on the experiment before it was over because they were faint from hunger, your readers should know that, as well as how that may have affected the data.

Do not get caught up in offering excuses for why your results were not significant. Rethink both your procedures and your hypothesis if necessary. Apologies for small samples often lead to this common error: "If more subjects had been tested, the results would have been significant." Avoid being tempted to make something out of nonsignificant findings, even if they go in the direction you predicted. *A trend in the right direction does not guarantee a significant outcome with a larger sample.* Very small samples are unreliable; the trend could easily reverse itself if you had a larger sample! Running the experiment with more subjects is the only way to validate your hunch.

If you believe your study suggests a new theoretical model or has practical, real-world implications, you may say so here, but be humble about it. The results of a single study are rarely earth shattering. If another study would clarify the findings, you can propose your idea for future research.

Keep in mind that when readers finish the discussion section, they should have a sense of closure. They should know where you were going and why.

They should know how you got there, what you found, and where it fits in the context of what was already known about the problem.

References

Any articles or books mentioned in the report should be listed in your **references** at the end. This list enables readers to go back and make their own evaluation of the literature. Be sure that the references are accurate and that they follow the new APA procedures for listing them.

LOOKING AT A JOURNAL ARTICLE

Now let us take a detailed look at the requirements of a research report by going through an actual journal article. We have selected an article that is relatively short; many journal articles are considerably longer. First, we will examine the basic content of the article; then we will look at the procedures to follow when preparing the manuscript. We will do this in separate steps just as you should when writing your own manuscript. Work on the content first, then put in the procedural details as you create your final draft. Keeping these stages separate will simplify your task. The article will appear on the following righthand pages with our comments on the lefthand pages so that you may shift back and forth easily between the two.

General Orientation

Journal articles are usually written for informed audiences. They are also written with strict constraints on the amount of space that can be devoted to any single topic. That is why you may find some articles difficult to follow unless you have already read somewhat extensively in the field. Therefore, before we launch into our examination of the article, let us review some general concepts you need in order to understand it.

The article (Davis, 1995) is a published report of an experiment testing differences in how girls and boys manage their expressions of negative emotions after they receive a gift they do not really like. Past research has generally (but not always) found that girls are better than boys at presenting affective, or emotional, displays that mask their negative feelings with a positive facial expression after they receive a disappointing gift. Three explanations for the gender difference have been offered: (1) differences in knowledge about how people are supposed to manage their impressions when they are disappointed (this is similar to the social desirability response set); (2) differences in the ability to mask negative feelings with a positive expression (girls may be better at producing facial expressions); and (3) differences in the motivation to cover up negative feelings with a positive expression (girls may be socialized to do this more than boys are).

The first explanation has not been supported by prior research, but there is some evidence to support both remaining explanations (2 and 3). Davis set up a very clever experiment to discover which of the two remaining explanations was the most likely cause of the gender difference. She first had children rank ten small gift items from most to least preferred. During the first half of the experiment, a situation was set up in which each child "helped" an experimenter evaluate the difficulty of two different workbook problems. After helping with the first, the child received a "good" gift (one that the child previously rated as a first or second choice, like a "smelly marker"). After the second problem, the child received a "disappointing" gift (like a teething ring, that had previously been ranked as one of the two least desirable items). The workbook task was set up so that each child's reaction to an attractive and a disappointing gift (one they liked, and one they did not) could be videotaped.

Then, during the second half of the experiment, the children were asked to play a game with the experimenter: Prizes (actually another attractive and another disappointing item) were placed inside two different boxes, set up so that only the child could see into the boxes. The children were told to try to trick the experimenter into believing that they liked both items equally well. To heighten the children's motivation, the experimenter told them that they could keep both prizes if they were able to trick her into believing that they liked both prizes very much. The children's reactions were, again, videotaped.

By using the two different tasks, Davis was able to compare the ability explanation for gender differences with the motivation explanation. She predicted that in task 1 girls would be better at masking their disappointment (as past research has found). Clearly, however, either explanation could explain why girls would be better than boys: Girls might have greater ability, or they might be more motivated to dissemble because it is the socially desirable thing to do. The competing explanations are tested in the second experiment by a task designed to rule out the motivation explanation: If motivation is the most likely explanation, then the gender differences should disappear if both girls and boys are equally highly motivated. Task 2 was designed explicitly to place both boys and girls in a high-motivation situation.

The dependent variable was the children's behavior after receiving each gift or prize. The children's videotaped behavior was scored by judges using a behavior coding system (If you want to refresh your memory about techniques for coding dependent measures, refer back to our discussion in Chapter 3). Four categories of behaviors were coded: positive displays, negative displays, social monitoring behaviors, and tension behaviors. In terms of Davis's hypothesis, we are most interested in the effects of the task manipulations on how well boys and girls masked their *negative behaviors*. Statistical analyses showed that when girls and boys were both highly motivated to mask negative behaviors, the gender difference was much smaller than usual, but it did not disappear completely. Girls were still somewhat better than boys.

This pattern of effects suggested that *both* ability and motivation probably play a role in the greater ability of girls to hide their disappointment. Davis explains the findings in terms of (1) differences in how little boys and little girls are socialized, (2) possible gender differences in biological aspects of temperament, and (3) how these two important factors might interact to produce the effects demonstrated in the experiment. Now that you have some background, let us look at the actual article.

A Sample Journal Article[5]

(1) ### Descriptive Title

Note that the title, "Gender Differences in Masking Negative Emotions: Ability or Motivation?" identifies the main focus of the study. Without reading farther, we know that the researcher studied gender differences in masking negative emotions and the ways in which ability or motivation influences the difference.

(2) ### Names and Affiliation

The author's name is given as it would ordinarily be written; titles (Dr., Mr., Ms.) are not stated. The university, agency, or business affiliation of the author (or authors) is also listed.

(3) ### Abstract

In the published article, the abstract is usually not labeled. It is conspicuously indented and set off by smaller type. (Your typed manuscript, of course, will not look like this. Your abstract will be typed on its own page and labeled, as you will see a little later.) Notice that the abstract summarizes what was done and what was found; all the main points of the article are presented.

(4) ### Author Notes

Notes are included to provide information about special circumstances surrounding the study—for instance, if the results were presented elsewhere or were part of a dissertation or thesis project. (However, when you type your manuscript, author notes will go on a separate page.) Author notes are also used to acknowledge special contributions from individuals or granting organizations who facilitated the research. Author notes always include a correspondence address where readers can write for a copy of the experiment (called a "reprint") or for further information.

(5) ### Introduction

In a published article, the introduction begins immediately after the abstract. (In your typed manuscript, it begins on a new page.) The introduction is never labeled. Notice how the author presents the logic and background research that suggested this study. The general problem area is mentioned in the first paragraph, followed by a brief review of the *relevant* published findings. Davis leads into her hypothesis by describing first several possible explanations for the gender difference. Supporting research is clearly cited.

---

[5]From "Gender Differences in Masking Negative Emotions: Ability or Motivation?" by T. L. Davis, 1995, *Developmental Psychology, 31,* 660–667. Copyright ©1995 American Psychological Association. Reprinted with permission.

Developmental Psychology
1995, Vol. 31, No. 4, 660–667

(1)

Gender Differences in Masking Negative Emotions: Ability or Motivation?

(2) Teresa L. Davis
University of Florida

(3) Research has demonstrated that boys display greater negative affect than girls when they receive a disappointing gift. In this study, ability and motivation were investigated as possible reasons for the gender differences. First- and 3rd-grade children's emotion dissimulation in a disappointing gift task was compared with their degree of dissimulation in a highly motivating game task that required the same ability (masking disappointment with a positive expression) but involved a self-gain motive. If boys are motivated, can they hide their disappointment as well as girls? Boys reduced their expression of negative affect in the game task; however, they still showed higher levels of negativity than did the girls. Perhaps because of socialization experiences, girls have more practice in hiding disappointment and, therefore, are better skilled. Girls also showed higher levels of social monitoring behaviors than boys, and younger girls demonstrated the greatest number of tension behaviors.

(5) Adults and children are capable of presenting to others affective displays that differ from the emotions they are really experiencing. Studies of the development of spontaneous regulation of emotional displays suggest that this ability develops early, being demonstrated even by preschool children (Cole, 1986; Reissland & Harris, 1991), and may improve with age (Saarni, 1984). The degree of emotion dissimulation demonstrated, at least in some situations, also seems to be related to the gender of the child (Cole, 1986; Saarni, 1984).

Children's spontaneous use of display rules or the principles that guide the expression of emotion has been examined primarily through a *disappointing gift* paradigm developed by Saarni (1984). This paradigm evokes a culturally defined display rule. "You should look pleased when you receive a gift even if you don't like it," requiring the masking of the child's true emotion. In Saarni's (1984) study, first-, third-, and fifth-grade children received an attractive gift for their participation in the evaluation of workbooks, and then, in a later session, they received a disappointing "baby gift." The number of positive, negative, and transitional behaviors (those that were minimally positive or were suggestive of uncertainty) was measured.

Saarni (1984) found a marginally significant age effect, with older children, especially girls, expressing more positive facial and vocal behaviors on receipt of the disappointing gift compared with younger children. The other major finding was a gender difference in response to the disappointing gift, with girls' behaviors appearing less negative than boys'. The older two age groups of girls responded equally positively to the attractive and unattractive gifts. Third- and fifth-grade boys also displayed more transitional behaviors than girls of the same age.

In a similar study using preschool, first-grade, and third-grade children, Cole (1986) did not find an age effect. She did, however, replicate Saarni's (1984) gender finding. In a follow-up study, Cole further explored whether the preschool girls were actually feeling disappointment by comparing the expressions of preschool girls who opened a disappointing gift in the presence of an experimenter with girls who opened the gift while the experimenter was absent. More disappointment was expressed when the experimenter was absent, suggesting that these young girls were indeed hiding their feelings of unhappiness.

The purpose of the present study was to investigate the possible reasons for the effects of gender found in this type of task. Saarni (1984) has suggested three possible explanations. These explanations are linked to the three components necessary to effectively use a display rule: The children must have knowledge of the rule, must be able to produce the expression, and must be motivated to hide their true emotions.

The first explanation for the gender effect, differences in knowledge, is not supported by the literature. Studies using picture story tasks find that although the understanding of display rules increases between the ages of 4 and 10 years for both boys and girls, there are no differences in knowledge on the basis of gender (Friend & Davis, 1993; Gnepp & Hess, 1986; Harris, Donnelly, Gabriell, & Pitt-Watson, 1986; Saarni, 1979). In addition, these studies suggest that hiding disappointment in a gift situation is one of the earliest understood display rules and should be well known by the older children in the disappointing gift studies.

A second plausible reason for the gender effect could be a difference in the abilities of boys and girls to produce the positive expression (Saarni, 1984) or perhaps prevent the negative emotion from showing. Although research on adults suggests that women may be better encoders (or producers) of emotional cues than men (Buck, Miller, & Caul,

(4) This research was supported by a National Institute of Child Health and Human Development traineeship awarded to the Department of Psychology, University of Florida (National Research Service Award 1T32HD07318).

I wish to thank Scott A. Miller and Patricia H. Miller for their valuable comments on earlier versions of this article and James Algina for statistical consultation. I am also grateful to Janice Wachtel, Yonette Hassell, Mindy Yoskin, and Barbara Quinones for assisting with data collection and to the children of Stephen Foster elementary school for their participation in this project.

Correspondence concerning this article should be addressed to Teresa L. Davis, who is now at Department of Psychology, Box 87, Middle Tennessee State University, Murfreesboro, Tennessee 37132.

Introduction (*continued*)

Notice the format for citing prior research illustrated by this sentence from the first paragraph: "Studies of the development of spontaneous regulation of emotional displays suggest that this ability develops early, being demonstrated even by preschool children (Cole, 1986; Reissland & Harris, 1991), and may improve with age (Saarni, 1984)." Factual statements must always carry citations of this type. Full credit must be given to the source of ideas, procedures, or phrases to avoid any form of plagiarism. Note that the full references for all citations are given in the references section at the end of the article; we rarely use footnotes to cite references.

In the introduction, Davis tells us (1) the problem area she is studying, (2) the pertinent facts about the field, and (3) how these facts relate to the hypotheses of the experiment. Then she states the hypotheses: H_1 relates to the first "disappointing gift task"; two competing hypotheses, H_2 and H_3, are presented for the second "game task."

Hypothesis 1: "It was expected that the results of the disappointing gift task would replicate those of previous studies. Girls . . ."

Hypothesis 2: "It was also expected that if the primary difference between the two sexes is the ability to pose the positive expression and suppress the negative one, then . . ."

Hypothesis 3: "However, if motivation is the important difference, one would expect to see girls . . ."

Notice that by the end of the introduction the author has given us enough information to prepare us for the description of the experiment in the method section.

(6) Running Head for Publication

A **running head** is an abbreviated title (with a maximum of 50 characters) that is printed above pages of the article to help readers identify it in a journal containing other articles. (In your typed version, this marker will go on the title page.)

(7) Method

This section describes in detail how the experiment was carried out. Notice that the author has adapted the format of the subsections to fit the kind of information she needs to present; each subsection is clearly labeled. In this article, the participants subsection contains information about the children's ages, genders, ethnicity, and socioeconomic status. This information gives the reader a clear picture of the sample for purposes of assessing external validity and comparing results across different experiments. Recruitment procedures are also described.

1974; Hall, 1979; Rotter & Rotter, 1988), studies with children as encoders often find that the identification of emotions based on facial expressions is not affected by the gender of the child displaying the feeling (Felleman, Barden, Carlson, Rosenberg, & Masters, 1983; Morency & Krauss, 1982).

Posing the positive expression is only one part of masking disappointment. The child must also prevent the real emotion from showing. Shennum and Bugental (1982) asked 6- to 12-year-olds to hide their emotions. When the task was to mask dislike with happy expressions, no sex differences were found. In contrast to these results, Feldman, Jenkins, and Popoola (1979) found that girls were better able to look pleased while drinking sour fruit juice than boys. These studies indicate that there is some question about whether girls are better at masking negative emotions.

A third possible explanation for gender differences involves differing levels of motivation between boys and girls. For example, Saarni (1984) suggested that there may be more social pressure for girls to act nice. Consistent with this view, Banerjee and Eggleston (1993) found that parents of preschoolers expect girls to be more restricted in their emotional displays than boys and also expect girls to use more sophisticated mentalistic strategies to control their emotions. Because of these different cultural expectations, girls may be more motivated to hide their disappointment than boys.

Of the three components necessary for display rule use—knowledge, ability to pose facial expressions, and motivation—the gender differences noted in the disappointing gift paradigm are most probably related to ability and motivation. Both of these possibilities are investigated.

In the present study, children's ability to mask disappointment with happiness was compared on two tasks. Each child participated in a disappointing gift task that was modeled after the Saarni (1984) and Cole (1986) studies and also in a game task. The game required the same ability as the disappointing gift task (immediately masking disappointment with happiness), but the motivation for doing so was self-interest (winning the game). The game was designed to discover whether gender differences appear in a situation in which boys and girls are highly motivated to hide their disappointment. As in the gift task, the children received a positive item and then a disappointing one. To keep the attractive prize, the child had to appear to like the second, unattractive one. This game differs from most of the emotion-masking research in which a child is simply asked to act and has little to explicitly gain or lose by his or her actions. In this game, the child could win or lose an attractive prize depending on his or her ability to mask disappointment.

It was expected that the results of the disappointing gift task would replicate those of previous studies. Girls would demonstrate less negativity than boys when receiving a disappointing gift and would respond equally positively to the positive and negative gifts. It was also expected that if the primary difference between the two sexes is the ability to pose the positive expression and suppress the negative one, then the same pattern of performance would appear in both tasks (game and disappointing gift)—girls would show fewer negative and more positive behaviors than boys. However, if motivation is the important difference between the performance of girls and boys, one would expect to see girls masking negative emotions more successfully than boys on the prosocial gift task but both sexes performing equally well on the self-interest game task.

In addition, two other behavior categories were explored in this study. Saarni (1992) extended her previous scoring system (Saarni, 1984) to include social monitoring and tension behaviors. Behaviors indicating that the children were attempting to control their expressions but were not entirely successful (such as a mumbled "thank you") were coded as social monitoring behaviors. The tension behavior category included indicators of anxiety (such as twisting in chair). This study is the first to investigate these two separate behavior categories in a situation involving the masking of disappointment.

 Method

Participants

The participants were 64 children: 32 first graders (16 girls and 16 boys; M = 6 years 11 months) and 32 third graders (16 girls and 16 boys; M = 9 years 3 months). The children were predominantly from middle-class families and were recruited through the public school system by means of a letter to the parents. Seven of the children were members of ethnic minority groups. First and third graders were selected to be consistent with the age groups in the previous two studies that demonstrated the gender difference. Younger children were considered; however, pilot testing indicated that they had difficulty understanding the game task.

Materials

Various segments of the interview were videotaped by using a camera in view of the children. The children were not aware of when they were being taped and when the camera was off. The camera was introduced to the children at the beginning of the interview, and most of them paid little attention to it after showing some initial interest.

Procedure

The children were interviewed individually in a four-part session at their elementary school by one of two pairs of female experimenters used in the study. Each pair interviewed an equal number of children of each gender and at each grade level. Within each pair, the experimenters alternated between the role of Experimenter 1 and Experimenter 2 (counterbalanced across grade and gender). The order of presentation of the gift and game tasks was also counterbalanced.

At the beginning of the testing session, the child was introduced to Experimenter 1, who asked the child to rank order 10 items. The items included a range of desirable (e.g., "smelly" Magic Markers and glow-in-the-dark Super Balls) and the less desirable (e.g., plastic spoons and teething rings) objects. The children were told that the experimenter wanted to see what types of items children of different ages liked. The children's two lowest-ranked and two highest-ranked items were used in the study. The highest-ranked item was always paired with the 9th-ranked item, and the 2nd-ranked item was always paired with the lowest-ranked item. The pairs of items used in each task (1st and 9th, 2nd and 10th) were counterbalanced across tasks (gift and game) and gender and grade. The child was then escorted to a different part of the room and was given the game and gift tasks.

Disappointing gift task. Experimenter 2 explained that she was interested in how children liked different types of workbooks. The children were told that if they would work a problem and help evaluate the workbook, they would receive a gift for their effort and help. The child was then told that the session would be videotaped so that the

Method (*continued*)

Random selection is not mentioned; Davis probably used a convenience sample. The reader can assume that the sample was representative of the population of similar students—or, at least, representative of those students whose parents believe that psychological research is valuable. If this were not the case, the author would have mentioned the problem here. Information about how subjects were assigned to conditions is not necessary because the task variable was a within-subjects factor.

Notice that the author chose a materials subsection (rather than apparatus) because the only equipment used was a video camera. She could have stated the make and model, but since video cameras are pretty much interchangeable this was not really necessary. The procedure used in this study, however, was described in detail, beginning with a description of control procedures. Both the experimenters and the order of the two tasks were carefully counterbalanced to eliminate the possibility that the results might be confounded by these two extraneous variables (experimenter and task order). Next, the procedure used to select the "gifts" and "prizes" for each child was described.

All independent and dependent variables are described fully in the method section. Each of the two tasks was carefully described; notice that enough detail is given to permit replication. The wording of statements made to subjects was a critical component of the experimental manipulation in the game task, so the spoken instructions were reported verbatim. Both tasks were explained, and a complete description of the positive gift and negative gift conditions was provided. This information enables the reader to see how the different tasks and the "gift" and "prize" conditions constituted within-subjects manipulations.

The number of negative displays shown by each child was the primary dependent measure, but Davis also measured positive displays, social monitoring behaviors, and tension behaviors. These measures required special scoring procedures, so the author chose to describe them in a separate subsection labeled Scoring.

Subjects were also asked about their feelings about the "gifts" or "prizes" after each task was completed, and they were allowed to trade their "prizes" for others after the game task if they wished. This allowed Davis to check whether the gift/prize manipulation successfully produced positive and negative feelings in the children. To verify that the children were masking negative feelings after the disappointing gift, she needed to be certain that the children really did not like the negative items as much as they did the positive ones.

A design subsection was not included in the method section because the design was restructured for different statistical analyses. Instead, the design structure is given in the next section, results, where each analysis can be completely explained.

experimenter could see how children work on problems. The experimenter helped the child pick out a problem to work. After the child finished the problem, the experimenter asked a few questions regarding difficulty of the workbook and comparison to classroom work. The child was then thanked and given a gift. The child was asked to unwrap the gift at the table.

The first gift was always either the child's first or second choice. For the next 10 s, the examiner made eye contact with the child but did not stare, maintained a neutral expression, and did not interact with the child to avoid leading the child's facial expression. The children were then asked to help with a second workbook problem. The procedure was repeated except that the gift the child received was one of his or her least favorite items. Experimenter 2 then thanked the child and exited the room.

Experimenter 1 (who had been taping) then interviewed the child about the gifts that were received. This interview was based on the method used in Cole's (1986) study. The children were first asked which gift they liked better. They were then asked if they felt more happy or more sad when they unwrapped each gift. If they indicated that they felt happy about the disappointing gift, they were prompted: "I thought that ___ was your last choice. Some children would feel sad about receiving this prize and some would not. I want to know how you really feel."

Game task. Experimenter 1 told the children that she wanted to play a new game with them to see if it was the kind of game children their age like to play. The children were told they were being videotaped to see how children play the game. Experimenter 2 brought in two boxes, set them in front of the child, and then operated the camera. The boxes opened toward the child, and Experimenter 1 could not see what was in them. The rules were explained to the child as follows:

> Inside each box is a prize. I cannot see the prize from here, so only you know what is in the box. The way this game works is that you will look into the blue box first and then you will look up at me. Then you will look into the red box and look at me. OK? To win the game, you want to try to trick me. If you trick me then you get to keep both prizes. If you don't then I get both prizes back. This is how you trick me: There may be two prizes that you really like in the boxes or there may be one prize you like a little better. To win the game, you want to act like you like both of the prizes very much. You want to look happy when you look at me. If you look like you like both prizes very much, then you get to keep both of the prizes. But, if I can tell you don't like one of the prizes in the box, then I get both the prizes back and you don't get to keep any. OK, let's make sure you understand. What are you going to do first? How do you want to look when you look at me? And if I can tell that you don't like a prize, what happens?

When the children indicated that they understood, the game began. The children were told to look in the first box and then look up at the experimenter. They were also told they could say anything that they wanted to as long as they did not mean the item in the box. The children looked at the experimenter for 10 s before being told to proceed to the next box.

The first box the children opened contained an attractive prize. The second box contained a least-favorite item. The children needed to look happy in spite of this to win the game and keep the first prize. At the end of the game, all of the children were told that they did very well and would get to keep both prizes. Experimenter 1 then asked the children the same questions about the prizes that were asked about the gifts (i.e., which the child liked better and how the child felt about receiving each). The children were then allowed to trade in the prizes that they did not want for others. They were told that we might not be able to trade in prizes for all of the children but today we happened to have extras. We asked them not to tell the others that they got to trade in their prizes. They were then asked if they had heard about the experiment from any of the other children and what specifically they had heard.

Scoring

A behavior coding system developed by Saarni (1992) was used. This system is similar to the one used in Saarni's 1984 study and involves observing behaviors such as facial expressions, vocalizations, gazing, and selected body movements. In Saarni's 1984 coding system, behaviors were coded as positive, negative, or transitional. The behaviors coded into the first two categories were obvious positive or negative displays. Behaviors coded into the transitional category were those that seemed to indicate an understanding that some degree of expressive control was required, but the children were not yet executing the control properly. Some of these behaviors suggested that the children felt anxious, such as shifting in their seats; other behaviors appeared to be attempts at expressive control, such as fake smiles. In Saarni's (1992) new system, transitional behaviors have been further divided into two types: social monitoring behaviors and tension behaviors. The responses coded into the social monitoring category are minimally positive in affect or suggestive of attempts at control, and those in the tension category indicate uneasiness and stress. The Appendix lists the types of behaviors that were coded into each category.

The 10 s following the exposure to each gift and prize were scored (four 10-s segments per child). The time interval began when the child first made eye contact with the prize or gift and was analyzed with a frame-by-frame technique. Each child received a score for each dimension (positive, negative, social monitoring, and tension) for each of the four segments (16 scores for each child). Two taped segments had to be dropped from the analysis. One first-grade boy dropped his disappointing gift on the floor when he opened it and thus was under the table retrieving it during the 10-s taping period. A third-grade boy looked into the first box in the game task before he was given the instructions.

The scores consisted of a frequency count of the number of behaviors on each dimension the observer counted. Repeated instances of the same behavior were not counted toward the frequency totals (Saarni, 1984, 1992). Two individuals who were unaware of the methodology and purpose of the study coded each tape. Using the Spearman-Brown formula, the interrater reliability was $r = .87$ for the positive dimension, $r = .77$ for the negative dimension, $r = .78$ for the social monitoring dimension, and $r = .76$ for the tension dimension. Disagreements were resolved by discussion.

 Results

Preliminary analyses indicated that there were no main effects or interactions involving task order or experimenter pair. Therefore, these variables were not included. All analysis of variance (ANOVA) results were calculated using the PROC/GLM procedure in SAS.

Disappointing Gift Task

The results of the positive and negative behaviors were first analyzed for the gift condition only in order to explore the replication of previous findings on disappointing gift tasks. Preliminary analyses indicated that there was no effect of grade on the number of positive or negative behaviors; therefore, this variable was dropped from further analyses. A 2×2 (Sex $\times$ Valence: positive gift/disappointing gift) ANOVA on the number of positive expressions indicated a main effect of valence, $F(1, 61) = 14.90, p < .001$. The children responded more positively to the attractive gift ($M = 2.05$) than they did to the disappointing gift ($M = 1.34$).

Because specific predictions were made regarding gender, planned pairwise comparisons were made contrasting positive expressions in the attractive and disappointing gift conditions for boys and girls separately. There was a significant

⑧ **Results**

Notice that the author conducted a preliminary analysis to demonstrate that counterbalancing procedures used to control potential experimenter and order effects were successful. As you know, both of these extraneous variables can influence the results of experiments. The experimenters and the task orders were used as factors in an ANOVA; this analysis showed that neither variable produced any effects on the dependent measures.

The primary statistical analyses that followed were constructed to test the three hypotheses. H_1 required an analysis of data for the "disappointing gift" task *only,* so type of task was not included as a factor. Instead, the author begins by using a 2 × 2 (Sex × Valence: positive gift, disappointing gift) mixed ANOVA to test the first hypothesis that girls would display fewer negative emotional behaviors after the disappointing gift than boys would. (Notice that this hypothesis requires a different design structure than tests of the other two hypotheses, which require including the task factor in the ANOVA, as you will see shortly.)

As you read the results of the "disappointing gift" task, notice that hypothesis 1 is supported by the presence of a significant Sex × Valence interaction on the number of negative displays. The significant interaction was tested further by a series of planned comparisons. As predicted, these tests showed that girls and boys did not differ in negative displays after an attractive gift, but boys showed significantly more negative displays than girls after a disappointing gift. (Notice that Davis reported the test results for the main effects produced by the individual factors first.)

Statistical analyses to test hypotheses two and three required a 2 × 2 × 2 (Sex × Valence × Task) ANOVA on each of the four dependent measures. As you know already, whenever a three-way ANOVA is used, many significant effects are possible. Reporting the results can be very cumbersome if a number of effects are statistically significant. (Davis did not state her alpha level, as you will need to do to follow the new APA format, but we can assume it was set at .05.) To help the reader see the overall picture, the author presents Table 1, showing the group means and *SD*s in all eight experimental conditions for the two dependent measures (positive and negative displays) related to tests of hypotheses 2 and 3. Then she takes the reader through the statistical analyses—one dependent measure at a time.

Hypotheses 2 and 3 are centered around effects on the positive and negative displays, so let us look more closely at how the author treated significant effects on these two dependent measures.

Positive displays Only the main effects for task and for valence were significant for positive displays. Information about each significant main effect is given in the text (*F* values, *df*s, *p* levels, and *M*s). These effects are fairly straightforward and easy to report. Results on the negative displays, however, are much more complicated.

decrease in positive behaviors expressed by boys in the disappointing ($M = 1.23$) versus the attractive ($M = 2.13$) gift condition, $F(1, 30) = 12.10$, $p < .002$. However, for the girls the difference was not significant (disappointing gift condition, $M = 1.44$; attractive gift condition, $M = 1.97$).

The same ANOVA on negative emotions also indicated a main effect of valence, $F(1, 61) = 27.83$, $p < .001$. Children expressed a greater number of negative behaviors when they received a disappointing gift ($M = 2.71$) than when they received an attractive gift ($M = 1.76$). The valence main effect was qualified by a Sex × Valence interaction, $F(1, 61) = 4.52$, $p < .04$. In the attractive gift condition, there was no difference in the negative expressions of boys ($M = 1.77$) and girls ($M = 1.75$); however, when the children received a disappointing gift, the number of negative expressions did differ, $F(1, 61) = 5.60$, $p < .02$, with boys ($M = 3.10$) demonstrating a greater number than girls ($M = 2.31$).

These results are consistent with those found in other studies using this paradigm. The girls in this study showed the same degree of positivity when receiving either a disappointing gift or an attractive gift. The boys, however, showed a decrease in positive behaviors in the disappointing gift situation and also demonstrated more negative behaviors than girls when receiving a disappointing gift.

A Comparison of the Disappointing Gift and Game Tasks

Performance in the game task was compared to performance on the disappointing gift task to investigate the influence of ability and motivation on children's masking of negative emotions. Because the children never said "thank you" in the game task, the children's scores on the gift task were recalculated excluding this item. The adjusted scores were used in all analyses comparing the gift and game tasks. The means for the game task and the adjusted means for the gift task are presented in Table 1. The four dimensions of emotional expression were analyzed separately. Preliminary analyses indicated no main effects or interactions involving grade for the positive and negative dimensions; therefore, grade was not included in the analyses on these two dimensions.

A 2 × 2 × 2 (Sex × Valence × Task: game/gift) ANOVA on the number of positive expressions indicated a main effect of task, $F(1, 60) = 8.31$, $p < .005$. Children were more positive in the game task ($M = 2.20$) than in the gift task ($M = 1.69$). There was also a valence main effect, $F(1, 60) = 12.59$, $p < .001$, with a greater number of positive expressions when the gift/prize was attractive ($M = 2.19$) than when the gift/prize was disappointing ($M = 1.70$).

The same analysis on the number of negative expressions indicated three significant main effects: task, valence, and sex. The task main effect, $F(1, 60) = 32.31$, $p < .001$, indicated that a greater number of negative behaviors were expressed in the gift task ($M = 2.23$) than in the game task ($M = .69$). For valence, $F(1, 60) = 15.17$, $p < .001$, more negativity was expressed when a disappointing gift/prize was received ($M = 1.74$) than when an attractive gift/prize was received ($M = 1.18$). The gender main effect, $F(1, 60) = 7.41$, $p < .008$, showed that boys expressed more negativity ($M = 1.66$) than did girls ($M = 1.26$).

These main effects were qualified by two interactions (see Figure 1). Follow-up t tests on a Task × Valence interaction,

Table 1

Mean Numbers of Positive and Negative Behaviors Expressed as a Function of Task, Gender, and Valence

| | Sex of child | | | |
| | Male | | Female | |
Condition	M	SD	M	SD
	Positive behaviors			
Gift				
Attractive	2.06	1.57	1.84	1.72
Disappointing	1.23	1.27	1.41	1.50
Game				
Attractive prize	2.10	1.26	2.53	1.34
Disappointing prize	1.93	1.52	2.21	1.54
	Negative behaviors			
Gift				
Attractive	1.10	0.71	1.06	1.07
Disappointing	2.23	1.47	1.53	0.95
Game				
Attractive prize	.73	0.83	.50	0.67
Disappointing prize	1.06	1.11	.50	0.84

$F(1, 60) = 11.80$, $p < .001$, indicated that on the gift task there were more negative behaviors expressed when receiving the disappointing gift ($M = 1.76$) than when receiving the attractive gift ($M = 2.71$), $t(61) = 4.50$, $p < .001$. However, in the game task, there was no difference in the number of negative behaviors expressed when either the attractive or disappointing gift was received ($Ms = .61$ and $.78$, respectively).

A significant Sex × Valence interaction was also found, $F(1, 60) = 4.03$, $p < .05$. There was no difference in the negative behavior of boys and girls when an attractive gift/prize was received ($Ms = 1.24$ and 1.12, respectively). There was a significant difference in the number of negative

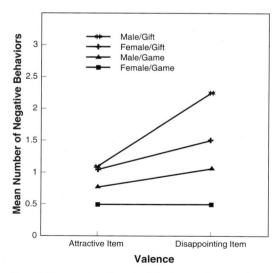

Figure 1. Mean number of negative behaviors as a function of gender, task, and valence.

Results (*continued*)

Negative displays There were a number of significant effects on negative displays. Significant main effects were produced by all three factors, and these are reported first. Because each main effect is qualified by a significant two-way interaction, however, the author does not focus on the main effects; instead, the major focus is on the significant interactions.

Davis reports each significant interaction and all planned comparisons (in this case, follow-up *t* tests) in the text. Before presenting the complicated results of the analyses of variance, however, she refers us first to Figure 1, which organizes the findings clearly and quickly. Notice that the figure adds to the information presented in the text by depicting the means for each of the eight conditions of the experiment.[6] The figure also allows us to more easily visualize the results of the planned comparisons. You can see that the figure is well proportioned and pleasing to look at. The lines are clearly labeled by a legend that appears within the figure. Each axis is also clearly labeled and marked off, and units of measurement are given.

After the major analyses on positive and negative displays are reported, Davis presents the results on social monitoring and tension behaviors. She refers us to Table 2 before presenting the ANOVA results. You will notice that this table includes an additional factor (the child's grade level).[7]

When multiple measures are used, effects are considerably easier to understand when shown in tables. For instance, the reader can easily compare effects obtained on both kinds of displays just by looking at Table 2. Tables can also eliminate the need for a wordier presentation of the findings.

Note the format used to report the test statistics. The statistic (for example, *F*) is indicated first, in italics. (All test statistics and the letter *p* to represent significance levels should be italicized; however, you should indicate italics in your typed manuscript by underlining instead of changing the font to italics.) Degrees of freedom are shown in parentheses. Then the computed value and the significance level that was obtained are given:

$$F(1,30) = 6.65, p < .02$$

(For *F* values, it is customary to show the *df* for the numerator first.) Note that we never give the critical values from the statistical tables—the reader can look them up if necessary. The null hypothesis is not stated, either. However, you should indicate any time you have used a one-tailed test.

---

[6]The figure allows us to see all eight group means at once, something we could not see if we only look at the group means for each of the two-way interactions (Task × Valence, Sex × Valence) separately.

[7]The only influence of child's grade level was found in a Sex × Grade interaction ($p < .08$) on tension behaviors; however, it was only *marginally significant* ($p > .05$, but $< .10$). The reason that the interaction was considered important in this experiment is that planned comparisons showed that grade level made a significant difference for the number of tension behaviors exhibited by girls, although not by boys. (If Davis had not planned this comparison ahead of time, she would not have included grade level in the table at all.)

Table 2
Mean Numbers of Social Monitoring and Tension Behaviors Expressed as a Function of Task, Valence, Grade, and Gender

| | Grade 1 | | | | Grade 3 | | | |
| | Male | | Female | | Male | | Female | |
Task	M	SD	M	SD	M	SD	M	SD
	Social monitoring behaviors							
Gift								
Attractive	1.07	0.80	1.62	0.96	1.47	0.74	1.75	1.24
Disappointing	1.13	0.83	1.37	0.89	1.40	1.35	1.81	1.11
Game								
Attractive prize	1.86	0.63	2.31	0.70	1.73	0.96	2.12	1.02
Disappointing prize	1.46	0.92	2.37	0.89	2.20	0.68	2.38	0.62
	Tension behaviors							
Gift								
Attractive	2.06	1.79	3.12	1.75	2.13	1.24	2.69	1.30
Disappointing	2.80	1.47	3.81	2.34	2.53	0.99	3.31	2.30
Game								
Attractive prize	2.40	1.68	4.25	2.05	2.80	2.07	2.37	1.45
Disappointing prize	2.47	1.96	4.06	1.65	2.20	1.21	3.06	1.65

behaviors expressed by boys and girls when a negative gift/prize was received, $F(1, 60) = 9.16, p < .004$, with girls expressing fewer negative behaviors ($M = 1.40$) than boys ($M = 2.08$). The negative behavior of girls did not differ based on whether a negative or positive item was received. However, boys were significantly more negative when they received a disappointing versus an attractive gift/prize, $t(30) = 3.32, p < .002$. These findings indicate that girls were better than boys at suppressing negative expressions not only in the gift task but also in the game task.

The means for the social monitoring and tension behaviors are presented in Table 2. Preliminary analyses indicated that grade was not significant for the social monitoring behaviors; therefore, this variance was not included. A 2 × 2 × 2 (Sex × Valence × Task: game/gift) ANOVA on the number of social monitoring behaviors indicated a main effect of task, $F(1, 60) = 23.15, p < .001$. The number of social monitoring behaviors was higher in the game task ($M = 2.05$) than in the gift task ($M = 1.45$). There was also a significant effect of sex, $F(1, 60) = 8.59, p < .005$, with girls showing a higher degree of social monitoring ($M = 1.97$) than boys ($M = 1.54$).

A 2 × 2 × 2 × 2 (Sex × Valence × Grade × Task: game/gift) ANOVA on the number of tension behaviors indicated main effects of valence and sex. The valence main effect, $F(1, 58) = 4.63, p < .04$, showed that tension behaviors were higher when the children received a disappointing gift/prize ($M = 3.03$) than when they received a positive gift/prize ($M = 2.72$). The sex main effect, $F(1, 58) = 11.89$, $p < .001$, indicated that girls ($M = 3.33$) demonstrated more tension behaviors than boys ($M = 2.42$). A marginal Sex × Grade interaction, $F(1, 58) = 3.14, p < .08$, suggests that for girls there is a significant difference between first ($M = 3.81$) and third ($M = 2.86$) graders, $F(1, 30) = 6.65, p < .02$. For boys, there was no significant difference based on grade (first-grade boys: $M = 2.43$; third-grade boys: $M = 2.42$). The youngest girls demonstrated the greatest number of tension behaviors.

Trading of Gifts and Statements of Positive and Negative Feelings

The children's trading behavior and their descriptions of their feelings about receiving the gifts and prizes suggested that they were more disappointed with the unattractive items than with the attractive ones. When allowed to trade their gifts and prizes at the end of the session, all of the children except 3 kept their attractive items. Most of the children, however, decided to trade the negative gifts and prizes they had been given. A categorical modeling analysis (CATMOD in SAS) indicated that there were no significant differences in the percentage of boys (84%) who traded and the percentage of girls (90%) who traded their disappointing gifts. For the negative prizes in the game task, all of the boys traded the prize and all but 7 of the girls traded.

The children all stated that they felt happy about receiving the attractive gifts and prizes. More children stated that they felt sad (70%) rather than happy (30%) when they received the unattractive items. Using the children's responses after their answer had been probed, a 2 × 2 (Sex × Task: game vs. gift) CATMOD analysis on the children's probed responses indicated that there were no effects of sex or task. Although not all of the children were willing to admit that they felt sad when they received the disappointing item, there were no sex or task differences that would suggest one gender was more disappointed than the other or that the items in one task were more or less disappointing than the items in the other.

⑨ Discussion

Consistent with previous research, gender differences in emotional expression were found in the disappointing gift task. The girls expressed fewer negative behaviors than the boys on receipt of an unattractive gift. The two groups did not differ in the degree of positive and negative expressiveness when receiving an attractive gift. Consistent with Cole (1986), no age differences were found.

Results (*continued*)

Finally, in a separate subsection, Davis reports analyses conducted to check whether the children reported being sad when they received the "disappointing gifts" and how many children traded them for other items.

(9)   **Discussion**

Note that the author begins by restating her major findings. First, she restates the results on the disappointing gift task that related to the first hypothesis. Next, she restates succinctly the findings that related to hypotheses 2 and 3. Then she offers her explanations for the findings, referring back to the theories that formed the basis for the experiment. Notice that she relates her findings to the broader theoretical issues of gender socialization, gender expectations, and the interaction between individual biology and the social environment. There are no obvious problems with the experiment that might limit the conclusions that can be drawn, so these are not discussed. (This is not surprising because *Developmental Psychology* is a highly selective journal that publishes well-conducted research.) Notice that Davis does not make vast leaps from her data to grand conclusions, but she does explain the implications of her experimental findings for children's emotional development. Finally, she provides a number of good suggestions for using the same design in future research on related topics.

The present study extended the previous findings in several ways. First, this study explored the importance of motivation and ability as possible explanations for the gender differences in emotional expression found in a disappointing gift situation. When the children's dissimulation in the disappointing gift task was compared with their performance in a motivating game task, two interesting findings emerged. First, negativity was reduced a great deal for both boys and girls in the game task, suggesting that motivation was playing a role in the degree of emotion dissimulation. Second, and perhaps more interestingly, even though the absolute level of negativity expressed was greatly depressed in the game task, the boys still were not as capable of suppressing negative expressions in response to a disappointing item as were the girls. Girls may be more skilled at this type of emotion dissimulation.

The two tasks, gift and game, did differ in that the children needed to spontaneously access the display rule in the gift condition whereas they were told the rule in the game condition. However, of interest was the ability to hide spontaneously felt disappointment with happiness. The game task seemed an adequate elicitor of that ability.

Gender differences were also found for social monitoring and tension behaviors. The girls in this study seemed to be more involved in social monitoring than the boys, regardless of whether they were receiving a positive or negative item. There was also a higher degree of social monitoring for both genders in the game task. The tension behaviors were higher when children received negative gifts and prizes. The girls showed more tension behaviors than the boys, but this was found primarily for the younger girls.

There are several possible explanations for the gender differences found in this study. Some explanations emphasize a biological basis for differences. For example, there may be differences in brain structure that may affect emotional expressiveness, or women could be endowed with a greater innate capacity for learning to communicate nonverbally (see Blanck, Buck, & Rosenthal, 1986; Hall, 1979). Other explanations have focused primarily on socialization practices. If society exerts more pressure on girls to "act nice," then perhaps girls have spent more time hiding certain negative feelings and this experience has led to increased ability. Boys, even when trying hard, cannot do as well because they have had less practice than girls. Greater pressure for girls to be compliant and act nice may also have led to higher levels of social monitoring and to greater levels of tension behaviors, especially for the younger girls who may have less confidence in their abilities to regulate their negative feelings.

There is some evidence that parents socialize their children's emotional expressiveness differently depending on the gender of the child. Malatesta and Haviland (1982) found that mothers responded to the emotional displays of boys and girls differently beginning in the first year of life. Mothers showed more contingent smiling to the smiles of infant boys and were more likely to match the emotional behavior of boys than girls. As previously discussed, Banerjee and Eggleston (1993) have demonstrated that parents of preschool children expect girls to show more control of their emotions than boys, and they expect girls to use more sophisticated emotional control strategies. Other studies, however, have indicated that parents believe they encourage their sons to control their feelings to a greater degree than

their daughters (Block, 1979), and parents are more emotionally responsive to their daughters in negative emotion-eliciting situations (Fabes et al., 1994).

In addition, boys and girls have different expectations about how their genuine displays of emotion will be responded to by adults. Boys expect more disapproval for expressing sadness than girls and expect less disapproval than girls for expressing anger (Fuchs & Thelen, 1988; Perry, Perry, & Weiss, 1989). It is clear that more research is needed to further investigate the socialization patterns of parents regarding their children's control of emotional displays.

The biosocial interactionist view suggests that perhaps biological differences in male and female individuals interact with factors in the social environment leading to gender differences (Kenrick, 1987). For example, research suggests that sex differences may exist on the approach–avoidance dimension of temperament (Rothbart, 1989). This difference may affect social–emotional development. If girls are more likely to show inhibition of approach, then parents may be more successful in their attempts to socialize impulsive actions, such as emotional displays (see Rothbart, 1989). In another type of interactive effect, Fabes et al. (1994) have demonstrated that socialization practices may also be influenced by the mother's perception of the child's level of emotional responsiveness.

The interaction of child characteristics and socialization could be further explored by investigating children's spontaneous masking of emotions other than disappointment. An emotional display difference that is based on differences in temperament between boys and girls would lead to the expectation that boys would have more difficulty masking other types of emotions at least in the early years. However, a finding that gender differences vary across different kinds of emotions would be consistent with the socialization practices explanation. Also consistent with the socialization explanation are findings that gender differences in emotion dissimulation in a disappointing gift context are not found in all cultures (Josephs, 1993). Even within American culture, Gross and Richardson (1993) have demonstrated that emotion dissimulation in a disappointing gift task differs on the basis of whether the children are in the presence of a same-sex or opposite-sex peer.

The joint influence of child characteristics and socialization may lead to different developmental patterns in emotional dissimulation. For example, if socialization pressures are the same for both genders but one gender is more sensitive to these pressures (e.g., because of temperamental differences), then one may see the gender difference decreasing as children get older. However, if socialization pressures are different for boys and girls for certain emotional displays such as sadness, then one may see gender differences widening in older children. There is also the possibility that socialization processes may lead eventually to less global but more context-specific differences in emotion dissimulation. For example, Saarni (1988) found that older girls more than younger girls or boys prefer to express their true emotions to peers rather than to adults.

The present study begins to explore the roles of motivation and skill in an emotion dissimulation situation. The design used in this study to examine the contributions of motivation and skill could be applied to the masking of other

(10) **References**

Here the author cites all the sources mentioned in the article. Note that the references follow a set format. However, when you type your manuscript, you will use a different format. Here are examples of how your references need to be typed. Notice that the first line has a 5–7 space paragraph indent; remaining lines start at the left margin (the opposite of the published version shown). The general format is provided first, followed by examples.

For journal articles

Author(s) surname(s), and initial(s). The year of publication (in parentheses). Title of the article with only the first word capitalized. The Name of the Journal, Volume number, page numbers.

Saarni, C. (1988). Children's understanding of the interpersonal consequences of dissemblance of nonverbal emotional expressive behavior. Journal of Nonverbal Behavior, 12, 275–294.

Gnepp, J. & Hess, D. L. (1986). Children's understanding of verbal and facial display rules. Developmental Psychology, 22, 103–108.

For books

Author(s) surname(s), and initial(s). The year of publication (in parentheses). Title of the book with only the first word capitalized (volume number, if any, in parentheses). City of publication:[8] Publisher's name.

Rosnow, R. L., & Rosnow, M. (1995). Writing papers in psychology. Pacific Grove, CA: Brooks/Cole.

Myers, A., & Hansen, C. (1996). Experimental psychology (4th ed.). Pacific Grove, CA: Brooks/Cole.

For chapters from edited books

Chapter author(s) surname(s), and initial(s). The year of publication (in parentheses). Title of the chapter with only the first word capitalized. In book author(s) initial(s), and surname(s) (Ed[s].), Title of the book with only the first word capitalized (chapter pages in parentheses). City of publication: Publisher's name.

Shennum, W. A., & Bugental, D. B. (1982). The development of control over affective expression in nonverbal behavior. In R. S. Feldman (Ed.), Development of nonverbal behavior in children (pp. 101–122). New York: Springer-Verlag.

Other references listed in Davis's article illustrate additional procedures for other sources. For more unusual problems, see the APA *Publication Manual* (1994), Appendix 3.

---

[8]If the city is well known (e.g., New York), just name the city; if it is not, include both the name of the city, and the abbreviation for the state (e.g., Pacific Grove, CA).

emotions or even reported gender differences in other behavioral domains. In addition, it is clear that within each gender there is a great deal of variability in emotion dissimulation. As discussed, various individual difference variables may be interacting with the socialization process. This paradigm could be used to explore a variety of variables potentially important to children's masking of emotions including degree of empathy, temperament, level of social monitoring, and family expressiveness.

(10) References

Banerjee, M., & Eggleston, R. (1993, March). *Preschoolers' and parents' understanding of emotion regulation.* Paper presented at the meetings of the Society for Research in Child Development, New Orleans, LA.

Blanck, P. D., Buck, R., & Rosenthal, R. (Eds.). (1986). *Nonverbal communication in the clinical context.* University Park: Pennsylvania State University Press.

Block, J. H. (1979). Another look at sex differentiation in the socialization behaviors of mothers and fathers. In J. Sherman & F. L. Denmark (Eds.), *Psychology of women: Future directions in research* (pp. 29–87). New York: Psychological Dimensions.

Buck, R., Miller, R. E., & Caul, W. F. (1974). Sex, personality, and physiological variables in the communication of affect via facial expression. *Journal of Personality and Social Psychology, 30,* 587–596.

Cole, P. M. (1986). Children's spontaneous control of facial expression. *Child Development, 57,* 1309–1321.

Fabes, R. A., Eisenberg, N., Karbon, M., Bernzweig, J., Speer, A. L., & Carlo, G. (1994). Socialization of children's vicarious emotional responding and prosocial behavior: Relations with mothers' perceptions of children's emotional reactivity. *Developmental Psychology, 30,* 44–55.

Feldman, R., Jenkins, L., & Popoola, O. (1979). Detection of deception in adults and children via facial expressions. *Child Development, 50,* 350–355.

Felleman, E. S., Barden, R. C., Carlson, C. R., Rosenberg, L., & Masters, J. C. (1983). Children's and adults' recognition of spontaneous and posed emotional expressions in young children. *Developmental Psychology, 19,* 405–413.

Friend, M., & Davis, T. L. (1993). The appearance–reality distinction: Children's understanding of the physical and affective domains. *Developmental Psychology, 29,* 907–914.

Fuchs, D., & Thelen, M. (1988). Children's expected interpersonal consequences of communicating their affective state and reported likelihood of expression. *Child Development, 59,* 1314–1322.

Gnepp, J., & Hess, D. L. (1986). Children's understanding of verbal and facial display rules. *Developmental Psychology, 22,* 103–108.

Gross, D., & Richardson, A. (1993, March). *Emotional–expressive behavior in children: Social context effects.* Paper presented at the meetings of the Society for Research in Child Development, New Orleans, LA.

Hall, J. A. (1979). Gender, gender roles and nonverbal communication skills. In R. Rosenthal (Ed.), *Skill in nonverbal communication* (pp. 32–67). Cambridge, MA: Oelgeschlager, Gunn & Hain.

Harris, P. L., Donnelly, K., Gabriell, R. G. & Pitt-Watson, R. (1986). Children's understanding of the distinction between real and apparent emotion. *Child Development, 57,* 895–909.

Josephs, I. E. (1993, March). *The development of display rules: Do you understand what you already do?* Paper presented at the meetings of the Society for Research in Child Development, New Orleans, LA.

Kenrick, D. T. (1987). Gender, genes, and the social environment: A biosocial interactionist perspective. In P. Shaver & C. Hendrick (Eds.), *Sex and gender: Review of personality and social psychology* (Vol. 7, pp. 14–43). London: Sage.

Malatesta, C. Z., & Haviland, J. M. (1982). Learning display rules: The socialization of emotion expression in infancy. *Child Development, 53,* 991–1003.

Morency, N. L., & Krauss, R. M. (1982). Children's nonverbal encoding and decoding of affect. In R. S. Feldman (Ed.), *Development of nonverbal behavior in children* (pp. 181–199). New York: Springer-Verlag.

Perry, D., Perry, L., & Weiss, R. (1989). Sex differences in the consequences that children anticipate for aggression. *Developmental Psychology, 25,* 312–319.

Reissland, N., & Harris, P. (1991). Children's use of display rules in pride-eliciting situations. *British Journal of Developmental Psychology, 9,* 431–435.

Rothbart, M. K. (1989). Temperament and development. In G. A. Kohnstamm, J. E. Bates, & M. K. Rothbart (Eds.), *Temperament in childhood* (pp. 187–247). New York: Wiley.

Rotter, N. G., & Rotter, G. S. (1988). Sex-differences in the encoding and decoding of negative facial emotions. *Journal of Nonverbal Behavior, 12,* 139–148.

Saarni, C. (1979). Children's understanding of display rules for expressive behavior. *Developmental Psychology, 15,* 424–429.

Saarni, C. (1984). An observational study of children's attempts to monitor their expressive behavior. *Child Development, 55,* 1504–1513.

Saarni, C. (1988). Children's understanding of the interpersonal consequences of dissemblance of nonverbal emotional expressive behavior. *Journal of Nonverbal Behavior, 12,* 275–294.

Saarni, C. (1992). Children's emotional–expressive behaviors as regulators of others' happy and sad emotional states. In N. Eisenberg & R. A. Fabes (Eds.), *New directions for child development: Vol. 55. Emotion and its regulation in early development* (pp. 91–106). San Francisco: Jossey-Bass.

SAS Institute Inc. (1985). *SAS® user's guide: Statistics* (5th edition). Cary, NC: Author.

Shennum, W. A., & Bugental, D. B. (1982). The development of control over affective expression in nonverbal behavior. In R. S. Feldman (Ed.), *Development of nonverbal behavior in children* (pp. 101–122). New York: Springer-Verlag.

(11)   **Appendix**
The author presented the dimensions of expressive behavior used for scoring
positive, negative, social monitoring, and tension behaviors in an appendix at
the end of the article. An appendix is used *only* when the material (1) is necessary for readers to evaluate or replicate the study, and (2) would be very
distracting if presented in the body of the manuscript.

Appendix

Dimensions of Expressive Behavior

Postive Behaviors

Relaxed broad smile (teeth showing),
closed lip smile
Enthusiastic "Thank you"
Arched brows as in positive surprise
Smiling eye contact with experimenter
Eye crinkle while smiling
Positive verbal comments
Positive tone of voice
Giggling, laughing
Leans forward
Uses expressive hand gestures while talking

Negative Behaviors

Tense, square-looking smile (lips open, teeth may show)
Down-turned mouth (as in frown or grimace)
Avoids eye contact
Knit brows
Leans backward
Sharp breath exhalation, snorting, groaning
Sighing
Omitted "Thank you"
Negative verbal comments
Negative tone of voice

Social Monitoring Behaviors

Slight and/or closed lip smile
Staring at experimenter
Tilts head
Faint or mumbled "Thank you"

Questioning vocalization
Abrupt onset/offset of smile
Rapid glances at experimenter when neither is speaking

Tension Behaviors

Pressing, pursing, biting, or sucking of lips
Bites or mouths clothing
Cheek puffing
Prolonged tongue protrusions
Jaw wiggling, rotating, thrusting, etc.
Nose wrinkle
Rapid, nervous blinking
Looking around room or at ceiling in a scanning fashion
Face, nose touching or scratching
Finger(s) in mouth, on lips, or nail biting
Touches/scratches hair, scalp, ears, etc.
Touches/scratches upper or lower torso
Hides hands (in pockets, sleeves, sits on)
Rubs eyes
Finger rubbing or scratching
Holds or folds hands or arms together
Hand wringing, twisting
Covers face (or part of face with hand(s)
Stands up during session
Shrugs
Twisting, shifting, sinking in chair
Pumps up/down in seat
Stretching

Received June 21, 1993
Revision received July 5, 1994
Accepted July 11, 1994 ■

PREPARING YOUR MANUSCRIPT: PROCEDURAL DETAILS

By now you have a good idea of what we accomplish through a research paper. You have also seen some of the specific techniques used to achieve these goals. Now that we understand the content of each section, let us look at the details of setting up the typed copy. Journal articles are printed in special typefaces, and some journals use a two-column layout that you cannot create easily on your typewriter or word processor. Thus your actual written report will not look like a published article. Your job is to put together a draft that could easily be turned into the published form. A typed version of the Davis article is reproduced for you in Appendix C so that you can refer to it as you prepare your own report.

Be careful to follow the format for spacing and underlining precisely. Double space everything in the manuscript. Leave margins of at least 1 inch all the way around. Let the right margin "float"; do not use the word processing function that alters word spacing to create a uniform right margin. Here we will look at the layout of sections and headings as shown in Figure 16-1. Your manuscript should be laid out exactly like the sample pages shown.

On the first page, give the title, your name, and your affiliation. Also show a **running head** above the title, beginning at the left margin. As we saw earlier, the running head is a brief version of your title, typed in capital letters. (Davis used the running head: GENDER DIFFERENCES IN MASKING NEGATIVE EMOTIONS.) The head should take no more than 50 characters, including spaces between words. If your full title is short, your running head may be the same as your full title.

The first page is numbered at the top right with the number 1. You also need to create a **page header.** The page header is the first few words of your title (e.g., Gender Differences); it is used to identify manuscript pages during the editorial process in case your pages get separated. The page header is positioned to the left of (or above) the page number, with five spaces between the end of the header and the page number, and it will go on every page of your manuscript except the figure pages. If you are using a word processor, create a single header instruction that includes the page header and page number.

Type the word *Abstract* as a centered heading on the next page. Type the abstract in block form (no paragraph indent) and use double spacing. The abstract is always page 2.

Type the complete title, centered, at the top of page 3. Then type the introduction in paragraph form, using 5–7 space paragraph indents. Do not label it "title"; everyone will know what it is. Continue to use double spacing throughout the report.

You do not need a new page to start the method section; begin it wherever the introduction ends. Type the word *Method* as a centered heading. Label each subsection of the method section with the appropriate subheading. Start each subheading (such as *Participants*) flush with the margin of the page. Underline the subheadings. Type the information in paragraph form.

Your results section may also be started within a page. Start it where the Method section ends and simply type the word *Results* as a centered heading. Be sure to follow the correct format for reporting statistical data.

FIGURE 16-1 The general layout of a research report. Use uniform margins of at least 1 inch (2.54 cm) on all sides. Double space throughout.

Graphs, drawings, or pictures are called *figures*. Rows and columns of numbers are called *tables*. If you wish to use a table or figure, be sure to refer to it in words in the text—for instance: "See Table 1"; "The group means are shown in Table 1"; or "Figure 1 illustrates the significant interaction." Tables are numbered consecutively: Your first table is called "Table 1"; your second table is called "Table 2," and so on. Figures are numbered the same way: Your first figure is always called "Figure 1," your second is "Figure 2," and so forth. Use the *centered insert format* (below) to tell the printer where each table or figure would go in the body of the report for publication:

Insert Table 1 about here

Follow the same procedure for inserting figures. Prepare each table and each figure on a separate page. Notice that figure pages do not have a page number or page header on the front. Instead, write the figure number and page header lightly on the back of each figure in pencil; also indicate the top of each figure by writing the word *top* at the top of the page (lightly on the back). Figure captions do not go on the figures themselves; the captions to all figures go on a separate page labeled "Figure captions." With tables, all written information (including the title) is typed right in the table. Notice that tables do not have any vertical lines. Remember that everything is double spaced—even tables and figure captions.

Continue on to the discussion. Type the word *Discussion* as a centered heading after the results section ends, then type your discussion in paragraph form.

Begin your reference list on a new page. Type the centered heading *References*. List all your references in alphabetical order by the last name of the first author. Start each reference with a paragraph indent, and begin other lines at the left margin of the page. Begin the next reference again with a paragraph indent.

The author note, containing acknowledgments and your corresponding address, goes on a new page after the references. Any footnotes will go on the following page. Center these headings as in Figure 16-1.

Now put in all pages of tables in the order they will appear in the text. Put in the page of figure captions next. Be sure the captions are in order according to the way they will appear in the text. Last, put in all the figures. Remember that all pages except those containing a figure need a page header and page number. (Refer to Appendix C to see how all these details come together in an actual manuscript.)

We follow the procedures outlined here so that our reports can be turned into published versions fairly easily. Although they may seem somewhat arbitrary and unnecessarily rigid, the alternative is a chaotic situation in which no one knows what to do or what to expect. The value of having standard procedures is that in the long run they make our work easier.

MAKING REVISIONS

Now that we understand most of the major reporting principles, we should spend a bit more time looking at the overall picture. Remember that your task in writing a report is to communicate exactly what you did in the experiment. You need to do that as clearly and concisely as possible. Often authors are asked to cut articles down to save expensive journal space.

At first, you may feel overwhelmed by the many procedural details of report writing, but, with practice, you will find that they actually make the task of communicating a complicated experiment easier by providing you with a readymade structure for presenting your work. In your first report, strive to present your ideas clearly and in a logical sequence. Use well-written journal articles, such as the one in this chapter, as a guide. Scientific writing is eco-

"OH, HOW I HATE THE RE-WRITING!"

nomical, clear, and precise—you will need to choose your words carefully—but it does not have to be dull. Use the active voice whenever possible. For example, it sounds more compelling if you say, "The experimenter read the instructions to each subject," rather than "The instructions were read to each subject by the experimenter."

The job of presenting a great many facts and details can be accomplished smoothly with the careful use of transitional words (such as *then, next, furthermore, therefore,* or *besides*). Try not to pack too much information into a single sentence; when possible, keep your sentences short. Avoid unusual syntax and technical jargon—it is distracting and makes your report more difficult to read. Never use euphemisms for everyday words: Don't say "financially challenged" when you really mean "poor." Check your spelling and punctuation carefully. If any grammatical or typographical errors are present, they will detract greatly from your research report.

Try to model your writing style after the precise language of a journal article. Try to say exactly what you mean. That is not as simple as it sounds. One technique some students use is reading aloud. How does it sound? Your own ear can be a guide. Would you be able to understand it if you had not written it? Try to put yourself in your reader's place. Better yet, try to get the opinion of a reader who is not already familiar with your experiment. Can your reader follow what you did? Can you make it clearer? Then revise your report.

Many people are surprised to learn that when researchers sit down to write reports, they do not usually stop at a first draft. They may continue to revise and rework the same paper several times before they feel it is acceptable. Though the thought of rewriting may seem unnerving, the fact is that even the best writers make revisions. Good writing takes work. The first draft of your report should be just that—a first draft. Work on improving it, polishing it, refining it. Put as much care into writing your report as you put into doing the study itself. A good study merits a good presentation. Evaluate your draft to make sure you have accomplished the goals of each section of the report. Make the necessary changes or additions.

As you work on revisions, be aware of some common errors that can detract from your report. First, be sure you understand the difference between *affect* and *effect*. Both of these words can be either a noun or a verb. *Affect* can be a verb ("The powerful heat *affected* their thinking"). *Affect* can be a noun meaning *emotion* ("Davis's article demonstrated gender differences in masking negative *affect*"). *Effect* can be a noun ("The *effect* of food deprivation was transient—but food deprivation *affects* learning"). Finally, *effect* can be a verb meaning *to bring about* or *cause to happen* ("The goal of therapy is to *effect* a positive behavior change").

Be careful of other spelling errors, too. If your word processor has a spell-checker, be sure to use it. Note that the word *data* is a plural noun ("The data *are* convincing"). Double-check for biased or sexist language. As with any writing, try to form each paragraph around a single main idea, but avoid paragraphs that are composed of only one or two sentences. If an idea is important enough for a report, it probably deserves at least three sentences. You can often combine several points in the same paragraph (as we did in this one).

It is inaccurate as well as disappointing to say, "I got no results in this experiment." You *always* get results, although they may not be what you predicted. Conversely, do not make grand statements based on the data of one experiment. Your results may enable you to reject the null hypothesis. However, you have not "proven" anything; you simply confirmed your predictions. You could be making a Type 1 error. Remember your statistics are only making probability statements. Use words like *probably, likely,* and *might;* avoid words like *proven, true,* and *absolutely.*

Finally, keep in mind that this process is part of a scientific venture. We are looking for observable data that can be evaluated on the basis of objective criteria. This is not the place to talk about personal experiences, popular knowledge, or common sense. All your statements need to be documented. Stick to the literature and facts that can be documented. Present and discuss data. Pay particular attention to your Discussion section. Remember that your discussion should wrap things up; readers should finish your report with an understanding of what the study was about and where it fits. You may offer suggestions for future research, but try to view each report as a document that has a beginning, a middle, and an end.

SUMMARY

The purpose of a *research report* is communication. A *scientific writing style* is used in research reports. Through a report we tell others what we did and what we found. A report should contain enough information to permit other researchers to evaluate the findings and replicate them if they choose. The language used is objective, unbiased, and nonsexist.

The *Publication Manual of the American Psychological Association,* fourth edition, includes detailed information regarding the format, content, and layout of reports. We follow these standards by convention so that writers as well as readers will have a consistent model for dealing with psychological research.

The psychological research report has these main components: a *descriptive title,* an *abstract,* an *introduction,* a *method* section, a *results* section, a *discussion,* and a list of *references.* Additional components include author notes, footnotes, and tables or figures.

There are many specific procedural details for carrying out the goals of each section of the report. Each section must contain certain kinds of information. There is a set format for typed manuscripts, which must be followed exactly. The published and typed versions of the report contain the same information, but they look quite different. Reports are written in stages; the first stage is a draft, which is then revised and polished to give the experiment the best possible presentation.

KEY TERMS

Abstract A brief summary (approximately 120 words or 960 characters) of the report, which precedes the four major sections.

Descriptive title The title of the report, which describes what the report is about; typically includes the variables tested and the relationship between them.

Discussion section The final major section of the report; evaluates and interprets results and discusses implications of the research.

Introduction The first major section of the report; explains the research, what led up to it, and states the research hypothesis.

Method section The second major section of the report; explains in detail how the research was conducted and who the subjects were.

Page header A header made up of the first few words of your title; used to identify manuscript pages during the editorial process in case the pages get separated.

References A list of books and articles cited in the research report; placed at the end of the report.

Research report Written report of psychological research, which contains four major sections: introduction, method, results, and discussion.

Results section The third major section of the report; describes the findings and presents results of statistical tests and summary data.

Running head A short version of the title, which will appear at the top of pages of the published report.

Scientific writing style A concise, impersonal, and unbiased form of writing used in research reports.

REVIEW AND STUDY QUESTIONS

1. What is the purpose of a research report?

2. What is a scientific writing style? How is it different from writing a letter to a friend?

3. What are the major sections that should be included in each report?

4. Think of three terms that are ethnically biased, three that are sexist, and three that "handicap" people mentally or physically. Think of some alternative unbiased terms and practice them in everyday conversation.

5. What do we mean when we say a title should be descriptive? What is the importance of using a descriptive title?

6. Practice writing report titles by suggesting a good descriptive title that might be used for a report on each of the following sets of independent and dependent variables:
   a. Food deprivation; the speed of maze running
   b. Practice; time required to solve a word problem
   c. Maturation; fear of strangers
   d. Printer's type; reading rate
   e. Gender and grade level; masking negative emotions

7. What is the function of the abstract of a research report? What basic information should it contain?

8. What is the *Publication Manual of the American Psychological Association*?

9. What is the function of the Introduction of a report? What basic information should you include in an Introduction?

10. What is the function of the Method section of a report? What basic information should you include in the Method section?

11. You want to divide a Method section into subsections. What subsections are commonly used? What information would you include in each?

12. What information would you include in the Results section?

13. The Discussion section of a report serves several functions. What are they?

14. Why do we need to include a References section at the end of a report?

15. Jack is not pleased with this chapter. He says: "If I have to follow all these silly rules for writing a report, I won't have any chance to be creative." Tell him why a standard format for writing reports is important.

16. Explain how you would show each of the following in a report:
    a. The results of a t test with 38 degrees of freedom, where the obtained value of t was 1.38, and the significance level was $< .20$.
    b. The results of an ANOVA with 1 and 12 degrees of freedom, where the computed value of F was 6.26, and the significance level was $< .01$.
    c. The proper placement of a figure within the text.
    d. The proper placement of a table within the text.
    e. The proper reference for this book.

17. Explain the major differences between the manuscript version of an article and the printed version we might see in a journal.

COMPUTATIONAL FORMULAS

TABLE A-1 A one-way analysis of variance for a three-group example: Computational formulas

	Group 1	X_1^2	Group 2	X_2^2	Group 3	X_3^2
Step 1. Square each score.	2	4	1	1	3	9
	2	4	3	9	4	16
	1	1	3	9	2	4
	0	0	3	9	3	9
	1	1	3	9	4	16
Step 2. Total the scores and squared scores of each group.	$\Sigma X_1 = 6$ $N_1 = 5$	$\Sigma X_1^2 = 10$	$\Sigma X_2 = 13$ $N_2 = 5$	$\Sigma X_2^2 = 37$	$\Sigma X_3 = 16$ $N_3 = 5$	$\Sigma X_3^2 = 54$

Step 3. Total all scores.

$$\Sigma X = 6 + 13 + 16$$
$$= 35$$

Step 4. Total all squared scores.

$$\Sigma X^2 = 10 + 37 + 54$$
$$= 101$$

Step 5. Find sum of squares total. N is the total number of scores.

$$\boxed{SS_T = \Sigma X^2 - \frac{(\Sigma X)^2}{N}}$$

$$= 101 - \frac{(35)^2}{15}$$

$$= 101 - \frac{(1225)}{15}$$

$$= 101 - 81.67$$

$$= 19.33$$

Step 6. Find sum of squares between groups (p is the number of groups).

$$SS_B = \frac{(\Sigma X_1)^2}{N_1} + \frac{(\Sigma X_2)^2}{N_2} + \cdots + \frac{(\Sigma X_p)^2}{N_p} - \frac{(\Sigma X)^2}{N}$$

$$= \frac{(6)^2}{5} + \frac{(13)^2}{5} + \frac{(16)^2}{5} - \frac{(35)^2}{15}$$

$$= 7.20 + 33.80 + 51.20 - 81.67$$

$$= 92.20 - 81.67$$

$$= 10.53$$

Step 7. Find sum of squares within groups.

$$SS_W = SS_T - SS_B$$
$$= 19.33 - 10.53$$
$$= 8.80$$

Step 8. Complete the summary table and compute F.

Source	df	SS	MS	F
Between groups	$(p-1) = 2$	10.53	5.26	7.21*
Within groups	$(N-p) = 12$	8.80	.73	
Total	14	19.33		

$$*p < 0.1$$

NOTE: Table 14-3 in this text shows the analysis using definitional formulas. Discrepancies between the computed values found through the two methods are due to rounding errors. The two approaches are mathematically equivalent.

TABLE A-2 A two-way analysis of variance: Computational formulas

		Factor 1 (Word Frequency)				Row Totals	Row Means
		Low		**High**			
		X_1 X_1^2		X_2 X_2^2			
Step 1. Total scores in each treatment group.							
Step 2. Find row and column totals and means.	**Factor 2 (Category cues)** No cues	2 4 3 9 1 1 4 16 5 25 $\Sigma X_1 = 15$ $\Sigma X_1^2 = 55$ $N_1 = 5$		4 16 5 25 4 16 6 36 6 36 $\Sigma X_2 = 25$ $\Sigma X_2^2 = 129$ $N_2 = 5$		40	20
	Cues	X_3 X_3^2 4 16 6 36 5 25 6 36 9 81 $\Sigma X_3 = 30$ $\Sigma X_3^2 = 194$ $N_3 = 5$		X_4 X_4^2 7 49 6 36 9 81 8 64 10 100 $\Sigma X_4 = 40$ $\Sigma X_4^2 = 330$ $N_4 = 5$		70	35
Step 3. Total all scores and compute grand mean. N is the total number of scores.	Column Totals Column means	45 22.5		65 32.5		Grand total $\Sigma X = 110$ Grand mean $\dfrac{\Sigma X}{N} = 5.5$	

Step 4. Find the total of all squared scores.

$$\Sigma X^2 = 55 + 129 + 194 + 330$$
$$= 708$$

Step 5. Find the sum of squares total.

$$SS_T = \Sigma X^2 - \frac{(\Sigma X)^2}{N}$$
$$= 708 - \frac{(110)^2}{20}$$
$$= 708 - 605$$
$$= 103$$

Step 6. Find sum of squares between groups (p is the number of levels of Factor 2; q is the number of levels of Factor 1; pq is the number of groups).

$$SS_B = \frac{(\Sigma X_1)^2}{N_1} + \frac{(\Sigma X_2)^2}{N_2} + \cdots + \frac{(\Sigma X_{pq})^2}{N_{pq}} - \frac{(\Sigma X)^2}{N}$$
$$= \frac{(15)^2}{5} + \frac{(25)^2}{5} + \frac{(30)^2}{5} + \frac{(40)^2}{5} - \frac{(110)^2}{20}$$
$$= 45 + 125 + 180 + 320 - 605$$
$$= 670 - 605$$

Step 7. Find sum of squares within groups.

$$\boxed{SS_W = SS_T - SS_B}$$
$$= 103 - 65$$
$$= 38$$

Step 8. Find sum of squares for Factor 1; total (Σ) across all columns.

$$\boxed{SS_1 = \Sigma \left[\frac{(\text{Total of each column})^2}{(N \text{ in each column})} \right] - \frac{(\Sigma X)^2}{N}}$$
$$= \Sigma \left(\frac{(45)^2}{10} + \frac{(65)^2}{10} \right) - \frac{(110)^2}{20}$$
$$= (202.5 + 422.5) - 605$$
$$= 625 - 605$$
$$= 20$$

Step 9. Find sum of squares for Factor 2; total (Σ) across all rows.

$$\boxed{SS_2 = \Sigma \left[\frac{(\text{Total of each row})^2}{(N \text{ in each row})} \right] - \frac{(\Sigma X)^2}{N}}$$
$$= \Sigma \left(\frac{(40)^2}{(10)} + \frac{(70)^2}{(10)} \right) - \frac{(110)^2}{20}$$
$$= (160 + 490) - 605$$
$$= 650 - 605$$
$$= 45$$

Step 10. Find sum of squares for the interaction.

$$\boxed{SS_{1\times2} = SS_B - SS_1 - SS_2}$$
$$= 65 - 20 - 45$$
$$= 0$$

Step 11. Complete the summary table and compute F (p is the number of levels of Factor 2; q is the number of levels of Factor 1).

Source	df	SS	MS	F
Between groups				
Factor 1	$q - 1 = 1$	20	20	$F_1 = \dfrac{20}{2.38}$ or 8.40*
Factor 2	$p - 1 = 1$	45	45	$F_2 = \dfrac{45}{2.38}$ or 18.91**
Interaction 1×2	$(p-1)(q-1) = 1$	0	0	$F_{1\times2} = \dfrac{0}{2.38}$ or 0
Within groups	16	38	2.38	
Total	$N - 1 = 19$	65		

*$p \le .05$
**$p \le .01$

NOTE: Tables 14-3 through 14-11 in this text illustrate the definitional formulas for these procedures. The two approaches are mathematically equivalent.

STATISTICAL TABLES

TABLE B-1 Random numbers

03 47 43 73 86	36 96 47 36 61	46 98 63 71 62	33 26 16 80 45	60 11 14 10 95
97 74 24 67 62	42 81 14 57 20	42 53 32 37 32	27 07 36 07 51	24 51 79 89 73
16 76 62 27 66	56 50 26 71 07	32 90 79 78 53	13 55 38 58 59	88 97 54 14 10
12 56 85 99 26	96 96 68 27 31	05 03 72 93 15	57 12 10 14 21	88 26 49 81 76
55 59 56 35 64	38 54 82 46 22	31 62 43 09 90	06 18 44 32 53	23 83 01 30 30
16 22 77 94 39	49 54 43 54 82	17 37 93 23 78	87 35 20 96 43	84 26 34 91 64
84 42 17 53 31	57 24 55 06 88	77 04 74 47 67	21 76 33 50 25	83 92 12 06 76
63 01 63 78 59	16 95 55 67 19	98 10 50 71 75	12 86 73 58 07	44 39 52 38 79
33 21 12 34 29	78 64 56 07 82	52 42 07 44 38	15 51 00 13 42	99 66 02 79 54
57 60 86 32 44	09 47 27 96 54	49 17 46 09 62	90 52 84 77 27	08 02 73 43 28
18 18 07 92 46	44 17 16 58 09	79 83 86 19 62	06 76 50 03 10	55 23 64 05 05
26 62 38 97 75	84 16 07 44 99	83 11 46 32 24	20 14 85 88 45	10 93 72 88 71
23 42 40 64 74	82 97 77 77 81	07 45 32 14 08	32 98 94 07 72	93 85 79 10 75
52 30 28 19 95	50 92 26 11 97	00 56 76 31 38	80 22 02 53 53	86 60 42 04 53
37 45 94 35 12	83 39 50 08 30	42 34 07 96 88	54 42 06 87 98	35 85 29 48 39
70 29 17 12 13	40 33 20 38 26	13 89 51 03 74	17 76 37 13 04	07 74 21 19 30
56 62 18 37 35	96 83 50 87 75	97 12 25 93 47	70 33 24 03 54	97 77 46 44 80
99 49 57 22 77	88 42 95 45 72	16 64 36 16 00	04 43 18 66 79	94 77 24 21 90
16 08 15 04 72	33 27 14 34 09	45 59 34 68 49	12 72 07 34 45	99 27 72 95 14
31 16 93 32 43	50 27 89 87 19	20 15 37 00 49	52 85 66 60 44	38 68 88 11 80
68 34 30 13 70	55 74 30 77 40	44 22 78 84 26	04 33 46 09 52	68 07 97 06 57
74 57 25 65 76	59 29 97 68 60	71 91 38 67 54	13 58 18 24 76	15 54 55 95 52
27 42 37 86 53	48 55 90 65 72	96 57 69 36 10	96 46 92 42 45	97 60 49 04 91
00 39 68 29 61	66 37 32 20 30	77 84 57 03 29	10 45 65 04 26	11 04 96 67 24
29 94 98 94 24	68 49 69 10 82	53 75 91 93 30	34 25 20 57 27	40 48 73 51 92
16 90 82 66 59	83 62 64 11 12	67 19 00 71 74	60 47 21 29 68	02 02 37 03 31
11 27 94 75 06	06 09 19 74 66	02 94 37 34 02	76 70 90 30 66	38 45 94 30 38
35 25 20 16 20	33 32 51 26 38	79 78 45 04 91	16 92 53 56 16	02 76 59 95 98
38 23 16 86 38	42 38 97 01 50	87 75 66 81 41	40 01 74 91 62	48 51 84 08 32
31 96 25 91 47	96 44 33 49 13	34 86 82 53 91	00 52 43 48 85	27 55 26 89 62
66 67 40 67 14	64 05 71 95 86	11 05 65 09 68	76 83 20 37 90	57 16 00 11 66
14 90 84 45 11	75 73 88 05 90	52 27 41 14 86	22 98 12 22 08	07 52 74 95 80
68 05 51 18 00	33 96 02 75 19	07 60 62 93 55	59 33 82 43 90	49 37 38 44 59
20 46 78 73 90	97 51 40 14 02	04 02 33 31 08	39 54 16 49 36	47 95 93 13 30
64 19 58 97 79	15 06 15 93 20	01 90 10 75 06	40 78 78 89 62	02 67 74 17 33
05 26 93 70 60	22 35 85 15 13	92 03 51 59 77	59 56 78 06 83	52 91 05 70 74
07 97 10 88 23	09 98 42 99 64	61 71 62 99 15	06 51 29 16 93	58 05 77 09 51
68 71 86 85 85	54 87 66 47 54	73 32 08 11 12	44 95 92 63 16	29 56 24 29 48
26 99 61 65 53	58 37 78 80 70	42 10 50 67 42	32 17 55 85 74	94 44 67 16 94
14 65 52 68 75	87 59 36 22 41	26 78 63 06 55	13 08 27 01 50	15 29 39 39 43

(continued)

TABLE B-1 Random numbers (continued)

17 53 77 58 71	71 41 61 50 72	12 41 94 96 26	44 95 27 36 99	02 96 74 30 83
90 26 59 21 19	23 52 23 33 12	96 93 02 18 39	07 02 18 36 07	25 99 32 70 23
41 23 52 55 99	31 04 49 69 96	10 47 48 45 88	13 41 43 89 20	97 17 14 49 17
60 20 50 81 69	31 99 73 68 68	35 81 33 03 76	24 30 12 48 60	18 99 10 72 34
91 25 38 05 90	94 58 28 41 36	45 37 59 03 09	90 35 57 29 12	82 62 54 65 60
34 50 57 74 37	98 80 33 00 91	09 77 93 19 82	74 94 80 04 04	45 07 31 66 49
85 22 04 39 43	73 81 53 94 79	33 62 46 86 28	08 31 54 46 31	53 94 13 38 47
09 79 13 77 48	73 82 97 22 21	05 03 27 24 83	72 89 44 05 60	35 80 39 94 88
88 75 80 18 14	22 95 75 42 49	39 32 82 22 49	02 48 07 70 37	16 04 61 67 87
90 96 23 70 00	39 00 03 06 90	55 85 78 38 36	94 37 30 69 32	90 89 00 76 33
53 74 23 99 67	61 32 28 69 84	94 62 67 86 24	98 33 41 19 95	47 53 53 38 09
63 38 06 86 54	99 00 65 26 94	02 82 90 23 07	79 62 67 80 60	75 91 12 81 19
35 30 58 21 46	06 72 17 10 94	25 21 31 75 96	49 28 24 00 49	55 65 79 78 07
63 43 36 82 69	65 51 18 37 88	61 38 44 12 45	32 92 85 88 65	54 34 81 85 35
98 25 37 55 26	01 91 82 81 46	74 71 12 94 97	24 02 71 37 07	03 92 18 66 75
02 63 21 17 69	71 50 80 89 56	38 15 70 11 48	43 40 45 86 98	00 83 26 91 03
64 55 22 21 82	48 22 28 06 00	61 54 13 43 91	82 78 12 23 29	06 66 24 12 27
85 07 26 13 89	01 10 07 82 04	59 63 69 36 03	69 11 15 83 80	13 29 54 19 28
58 54 16 24 15	51 54 44 82 00	62 61 65 04 69	38 18 65 18 97	85 72 13 49 21
34 85 27 84 87	61 48 64 56 26	90 18 48 13 26	37 70 15 42 57	65 65 80 39 07
03 92 18 27 46	57 99 16 96 56	30 33 72 85 22	84 64 38 56 98	99 01 30 98 64
62 95 30 27 59	37 75 41 66 48	86 97 80 61 45	23 53 04 01 63	45 76 08 64 27
08 45 93 15 22	60 21 75 46 91	98 77 27 85 42	28 88 61 08 84	69 62 03 42 73
07 08 55 18 40	45 44 75 13 90	24 94 96 61 02	57 55 66 83 15	73 42 37 11 61
01 85 89 95 66	51 10 19 34 88	15 84 97 19 75	12 76 39 43 78	64 63 91 08 25
72 84 71 14 35	19 11 58 49 26	50 11 17 17 76	86 31 57 20 18	95 60 78 46 75
88 78 28 16 84	13 52 53 94 53	75 45 69 30 96	73 89 65 70 31	99 17 43 48 76
45 17 75 65 57	28 40 19 72 12	25 12 74 75 67	60 40 60 81 19	24 62 01 61 16
96 76 28 12 54	22 01 11 94 25	71 96 16 16 88	68 64 36 74 45	19 59 50 88 92
43 31 67 72 30	24 02 94 08 63	38 32 36 66 02	69 36 38 25 39	48 03 45 15 22
50 44 66 44 21	66 06 58 05 62	58 15 54 35 02	42 35 48 96 32	14 52 41 52 48
22 66 22 15 86	26 63 75 41 99	58 42 36 72 24	58 37 52 18 51	03 37 18 39 11
96 24 40 14 51	23 22 30 88 57	95 67 47 29 83	94 69 40 06 07	18 16 36 78 86
31 73 91 61 19	60 20 72 93 48	98 57 07 23 69	65 95 39 69 58	56 80 30 19 44
78 60 73 99 84	43 89 94 36 45	56 69 47 07 41	90 22 91 07 12	78 35 34 08 72
84 37 90 61 56	70 10 23 98 05	85 11 34 76 60	76 48 45 34 60	01 64 18 39 96
36 67 10 08 23	98 93 35 08 86	99 29 76 29 81	33 34 91 58 93	63 14 52 32 52
07 28 59 07 48	89 64 58 89 75	83 85 62 27 89	30 14 78 56 27	86 63 59 80 02
10 15 83 87 60	79 24 31 66 56	21 48 24 06 93	91 98 94 05 49	01 47 59 38 00
55 19 68 97 65	03 73 52 16 56	00 53 55 90 27	33 42 29 38 87	22 13 88 83
34				

SOURCE: From *Statistical Tables for Biological, Agricultural and Medical Research,* Sixth Edition, by Fisher and Yates (1963), Addison Wesley Longman Ltd.

TABLE B-2 χ^2 Critical Values

df	.99	.98	.95	.90	.80	.70	.50	.30	.20	.10	.05	.02	.01	.001
1	$.0^3157$	$.0^3628$	.00393	.0158	.0642	.148	.455	1.074	1.642	2.706	3.841	5.412	6.635	10.827
2	.0201	.0404	.103	.211	.446	.713	1.386	2.408	3.219	4.605	5.991	7.824	9.210	13.815
3	.115	.185	.352	.584	1.005	1.424	2.366	3.665	4.642	6.251	7.815	9.837	11.345	16.266
4	.297	.429	.711	1.064	1.649	2.195	3.357	4.878	5.989	7.779	9.488	11.668	13.277	18.467
5	.554	.752	1.145	1.610	2.343	3.000	4.351	6.064	7.289	9.236	11.070	13.388	15.086	20.515
6	.872	1.134	1.635	2.204	3.070	3.828	5.348	7.231	8.558	10.645	12.592	15.033	16.812	22.457
7	1.239	1.564	2.167	2.833	3.822	4.671	6.346	8.383	9.803	12.017	14.067	16.622	18.475	24.322
8	1.646	2.032	2.733	3.490	4.594	5.527	7.344	9.524	11.030	13.362	15.507	18.168	20.090	26.125
9	2.088	2.532	3.325	4.168	5.380	6.393	8.343	10.656	12.242	14.684	16.919	19.679	21.666	27.877
10	2.558	3.059	3.940	4.865	6.179	7.267	9.342	11.781	13.442	15.987	18.307	21.161	23.209	29.588
11	3.053	3.609	4.575	5.578	6.989	8.148	10.341	12.899	14.631	17.275	19.675	22.618	24.725	31.264
12	3.571	4.178	5.226	6.304	7.807	9.034	11.340	14.011	15.812	18.549	21.026	24.054	26.217	32.909
13	4.107	4.765	5.892	7.042	8.634	9.926	12.340	15.119	16.985	19.812	22.362	25.472	27.688	34.528
14	4.660	5.368	6.571	7.790	9.467	10.821	13.339	16.222	18.151	21.064	23.685	26.873	29.141	36.123
15	5.229	5.985	7.261	8.547	10.307	11.721	14.339	17.322	19.311	22.307	24.996	28.259	30.578	37.697
16	5.812	6.614	7.962	9.312	11.152	12.624	15.338	18.418	20.465	23.542	26.296	29.633	32.000	39.252
17	6.408	7.255	8.672	10.085	12.002	13.531	16.338	19.511	21.615	24.769	27.587	30.995	33.409	40.790
18	7.015	7.906	9.390	10.865	12.857	14.440	17.338	20.601	22.760	25.989	28.869	32.346	34.805	42.312
19	7.633	8.567	10.117	11.651	13.716	15.352	18.338	21.689	23.900	27.204	30.144	33.687	36.191	43.820
20	8.260	9.237	10.851	12.443	14.578	16.266	19.337	22.775	25.038	28.412	31.410	35.020	37.566	45.315
21	8.897	9.915	11.591	13.240	15.445	17.182	20.337	23.858	26.171	29.615	32.671	36.343	38.932	46.797
22	9.542	10.600	12.338	14.041	16.314	18.101	21.337	24.939	27.301	30.813	33.924	37.659	40.289	48.268
23	10.196	11.293	13.091	14.848	17.187	19.021	22.337	26.018	28.429	32.007	35.172	38.968	41.638	49.728
24	10.856	11.992	13.848	15.659	18.062	19.943	23.337	27.096	29.553	33.196	36.415	40.270	42.980	51.179
25	11.524	12.697	14.611	16.473	18.940	20.867	24.337	28.172	30.675	34.382	37.652	41.566	44.314	52.620
26	12.198	13.409	15.379	17.292	19.820	21.792	25.336	29.246	31.795	35.563	38.885	42.856	45.642	54.052
27	12.879	14.125	16.151	18.114	20.703	22.719	26.336	30.319	32.912	36.741	40.113	44.140	46.963	55.476
28	13.565	14.847	16.928	18.939	21.588	23.647	27.336	31.391	34.027	37.916	41.337	45.419	43.278	56.893
29	14.256	15.574	17.708	19.768	22.475	24.577	28.336	32.461	35.139	39.087	42.557	46.693	49.588	55.302
30	14.953	16.306	18.493	20.599	23.364	25.508	29.336	33.530	36.250	40.256	43.773	47.962	50.892	59.703

SOURCE: From Table IV of Fisher and Yates: *Statistical Tables for Biological, Agricultural and Medical Research*, Sixth Edition (1963), published by Addison Wesley Longman Ltd. Reprinted with permission.

TABLE B-3 Critical Values of t

	Level of Significance for One-tailed Test			
	.05	.025	.01	.005
	Level of Significance for Two-tailed Test			
df	.10	.05	.02	.01
1	6.314	12.706	31.821	63.657
2	2.920	4.303	6.965	9.925
3	2.353	3.182	4.541	5.841
4	2.132	2.776	3.747	4.604
5	2.015	2.571	3.365	4.032
6	1.943	2.447	3.143	3.707
7	1.895	2.365	2.998	3.499
8	1.860	2.306	2.896	3.355
9	1.833	2.262	2.821	3.250
10	1.812	2.228	2.764	3.169
11	1.796	2.201	2.718	3.106
12	1.782	2.179	2.681	3.055
13	1.771	2.160	2.650	3.012
14	1.761	2.145	2.624	2.977
15	1.753	2.131	2.602	2.947
16	1.746	2.120	2.583	2.921
17	1.740	2.110	2.567	2.898
18	1.734	2.101	2.552	2.878
19	1.729	2.093	2.539	2.861
20	1.725	2.086	2.528	2.845
21	1.721	2.080	2.518	2.831
22	1.717	2.074	2.508	2.819
23	1.714	2.069	2.500	2.807
24	1.711	2.064	2.492	2.797
25	1.708	2.060	2.485	2.787
26	1.706	2.056	2.479	2.779
27	1.703	2.052	2.473	2.771
28	1.701	2.048	2.467	2.763
29	1.699	2.045	2.462	2.756
30	1.697	2.042	2.457	2.750
40	1.684	2.021	2.423	2.704
60	1.671	2.000	2.390	2.660
120	1.658	1.980	2.358	2.617
∞	1.645	1.960	2.326	2.576

SOURCE: From *Statistical Tables for Biological, Agricultural and Medical Research*, Sixth Edition, by Fisher and Yates (1963), Addison Wesley Longman Ltd.

TABLE B-4 Critical values of F (.05 level in roman type, .01 level in **boldface**)

Each cell lists the .05-level critical value (roman, top) and the .01-level critical value (boldface, bottom) as "05 / **01**".

	\multicolumn{24}{c}{Degrees of Freedom for Greater Mean Square (numerator)}

df (denom.)	1	2	3	4	5	6	7	8	9	10	11	12	14	16	20	24	30	40	50	75	100	200	500	∞
1	161 / **4,052**	200 / **4,999**	216 / **5,403**	225 / **5,625**	230 / **5,764**	234 / **5,859**	237 / **5,928**	239 / **5,981**	241 / **6,022**	242 / **6,056**	243 / **6,082**	244 / **6,106**	245 / **6,142**	246 / **6,169**	248 / **6,208**	249 / **6,234**	250 / **6,261**	251 / **6,286**	252 / **6,302**	253 / **6,323**	253 / **6,334**	254 / **6,352**	254 / **6,361**	254 / **6,366**
2	18.51 / **98.49**	19.00 / **99.00**	19.16 / **99.17**	19.25 / **99.25**	19.30 / **99.30**	19.33 / **99.33**	19.36 / **99.36**	19.37 / **99.37**	19.38 / **99.39**	19.39 / **99.40**	19.40 / **99.41**	19.41 / **99.42**	19.42 / **99.43**	19.43 / **99.44**	19.44 / **99.45**	19.45 / **99.46**	19.46 / **99.47**	19.47 / **99.48**	19.47 / **99.48**	19.48 / **99.49**	19.49 / **99.49**	19.49 / **99.49**	19.50 / **99.50**	19.50 / **99.50**
3	10.13 / **34.12**	9.55 / **30.82**	9.28 / **29.46**	9.12 / **28.71**	9.01 / **28.24**	8.94 / **27.91**	8.88 / **27.67**	8.84 / **27.49**	8.81 / **27.34**	8.78 / **27.23**	8.76 / **27.13**	8.74 / **27.05**	8.71 / **26.92**	8.69 / **26.83**	8.66 / **26.69**	8.64 / **26.60**	8.62 / **26.50**	8.60 / **26.41**	8.58 / **26.35**	8.57 / **26.27**	8.56 / **26.23**	8.54 / **26.18**	8.54 / **26.14**	8.53 / **26.12**
4	7.71 / **21.20**	6.94 / **18.00**	6.59 / **16.69**	6.39 / **15.98**	6.26 / **15.52**	6.16 / **15.21**	6.09 / **14.98**	6.04 / **14.80**	6.00 / **14.66**	5.96 / **14.54**	5.93 / **14.45**	5.91 / **14.37**	5.87 / **14.24**	5.84 / **14.15**	5.80 / **14.02**	5.77 / **13.93**	5.74 / **13.83**	5.71 / **13.74**	5.70 / **13.69**	5.68 / **13.61**	5.66 / **13.57**	5.65 / **13.52**	5.64 / **13.48**	5.63 / **13.46**
5	6.61 / **16.26**	5.79 / **13.27**	5.41 / **12.06**	5.19 / **11.39**	5.05 / **10.97**	4.95 / **10.67**	4.88 / **10.45**	4.82 / **10.29**	4.78 / **10.15**	4.74 / **10.05**	4.70 / **9.96**	4.68 / **9.89**	4.64 / **9.77**	4.60 / **9.68**	4.56 / **9.55**	4.53 / **9.47**	4.50 / **9.38**	4.46 / **9.29**	4.44 / **9.24**	4.42 / **9.17**	4.40 / **9.13**	4.38 / **9.07**	4.37 / **9.04**	4.36 / **9.02**
6	5.99 / **13.74**	5.14 / **10.92**	4.76 / **9.78**	4.53 / **9.15**	4.39 / **8.75**	4.28 / **8.47**	4.21 / **8.26**	4.15 / **8.10**	4.10 / **7.98**	4.06 / **7.87**	4.03 / **7.79**	4.00 / **7.72**	3.96 / **7.60**	3.92 / **7.52**	3.87 / **7.39**	3.84 / **7.31**	3.81 / **7.23**	3.77 / **7.14**	3.75 / **7.09**	3.72 / **7.02**	3.71 / **6.99**	3.69 / **6.94**	3.68 / **6.90**	3.67 / **6.88**
7	5.59 / **12.25**	4.74 / **9.55**	4.35 / **8.45**	4.12 / **7.85**	3.97 / **7.46**	3.87 / **7.19**	3.79 / **7.00**	3.73 / **6.84**	3.68 / **6.71**	3.63 / **6.62**	3.60 / **6.54**	3.57 / **6.47**	3.52 / **6.35**	3.49 / **6.27**	3.44 / **6.15**	3.41 / **6.07**	3.38 / **5.98**	3.34 / **5.90**	3.32 / **5.85**	3.29 / **5.78**	3.28 / **5.75**	3.25 / **5.70**	3.24 / **5.67**	3.23 / **5.65**
8	5.32 / **11.26**	4.46 / **8.65**	4.07 / **7.59**	3.84 / **7.01**	3.69 / **6.63**	3.58 / **6.37**	3.50 / **6.19**	3.44 / **6.03**	3.39 / **5.91**	3.34 / **5.82**	3.31 / **5.74**	3.28 / **5.67**	3.23 / **5.56**	3.20 / **5.48**	3.15 / **5.36**	3.12 / **5.28**	3.08 / **5.20**	3.05 / **5.11**	3.03 / **5.06**	3.00 / **5.00**	2.98 / **4.96**	2.96 / **4.91**	2.94 / **4.88**	2.93 / **4.86**
9	5.12 / **10.56**	4.26 / **8.02**	3.86 / **6.99**	3.63 / **6.42**	3.48 / **6.06**	3.37 / **5.80**	3.29 / **5.62**	3.23 / **5.47**	3.18 / **5.35**	3.13 / **5.26**	3.10 / **5.18**	3.07 / **5.11**	3.02 / **5.00**	2.98 / **4.92**	2.93 / **4.80**	2.90 / **4.73**	2.86 / **4.64**	2.82 / **4.56**	2.80 / **4.51**	2.77 / **4.45**	2.76 / **4.41**	2.73 / **4.36**	2.72 / **4.33**	2.71 / **4.31**
10	4.96 / **10.04**	4.10 / **7.56**	3.71 / **6.55**	3.48 / **5.99**	3.33 / **5.64**	3.22 / **5.39**	3.14 / **5.21**	3.07 / **5.06**	3.02 / **4.95**	2.97 / **4.85**	2.94 / **4.78**	2.91 / **4.71**	2.86 / **4.60**	2.82 / **4.52**	2.77 / **4.41**	2.74 / **4.33**	2.70 / **4.25**	2.67 / **4.17**	2.64 / **4.12**	2.61 / **4.05**	2.59 / **4.01**	2.56 / **3.96**	2.55 / **3.93**	2.54 / **3.91**
11	4.84 / **9.65**	3.98 / **7.20**	3.59 / **6.22**	3.36 / **5.67**	3.20 / **5.32**	3.09 / **5.07**	3.01 / **4.88**	2.95 / **4.74**	2.90 / **4.63**	2.86 / **4.54**	2.82 / **4.46**	2.79 / **4.40**	2.74 / **4.29**	2.70 / **4.21**	2.65 / **4.10**	2.61 / **4.02**	2.57 / **3.94**	2.53 / **3.86**	2.50 / **3.80**	2.47 / **3.74**	2.45 / **3.70**	2.42 / **3.66**	2.41 / **3.62**	2.40 / **3.60**
12	4.75 / **9.33**	3.88 / **6.93**	3.49 / **5.95**	3.26 / **5.41**	3.11 / **5.06**	3.00 / **4.82**	2.92 / **4.65**	2.85 / **4.50**	2.80 / **4.39**	2.76 / **4.30**	2.72 / **4.22**	2.69 / **4.16**	2.64 / **4.05**	2.60 / **3.98**	2.54 / **3.86**	2.50 / **3.78**	2.46 / **3.70**	2.42 / **3.61**	2.40 / **3.56**	2.36 / **3.49**	2.35 / **3.46**	2.32 / **3.41**	2.31 / **3.38**	2.30 / **3.36**
13	4.67 / **9.07**	3.80 / **6.70**	3.41 / **5.74**	3.18 / **5.20**	3.02 / **4.86**	2.92 / **4.62**	2.84 / **4.44**	2.77 / **4.30**	2.72 / **4.19**	2.67 / **4.10**	2.63 / **4.02**	2.60 / **3.96**	2.55 / **3.85**	2.51 / **3.78**	2.46 / **3.67**	2.42 / **3.59**	2.38 / **3.51**	2.34 / **3.42**	2.32 / **3.37**	2.28 / **3.30**	2.26 / **3.27**	2.24 / **3.21**	2.22 / **3.18**	2.21 / **3.16**

Row label (side): Degrees of Freedom for Lesser Mean Square (denominator)

NOTE: Find the critical value of F for each of your F ratios. Locate the degrees of freedom associated with the numerator of your F ratio along the top of the table. Locate the degrees of freedom associated with the denominator of your F ratio along the side of the table. The place where the correct row and column meet indicates the appropriate critical values. The numbers in light type give you the values at the .05 level; the numbers in dark type give you the values at the .01 level. Reject the null hypothesis when the computed value of F is equal to or greater than the table value.

(continued)

TABLE B-4 Critical values of F (continued)

Degrees of Freedom for Greater Mean Square (numerator) — top value = .05 level, bottom value = .01 level

Degrees of Freedom for Lesser Mean Square (denominator) shown in first column.

df	1	2	3	4	5	6	7	8	9	10	11	12	14	16	20	24	30	40	50	75	100	200	500	∞
14	4.60 / 8.86	3.74 / 6.51	3.34 / 5.56	3.11 / 5.03	2.96 / 4.69	2.85 / 4.46	2.77 / 4.28	2.70 / 4.14	2.65 / 4.03	2.60 / 3.94	2.56 / 3.86	2.53 / 3.80	2.48 / 3.70	2.44 / 3.62	2.39 / 3.51	2.35 / 3.43	2.31 / 3.34	2.27 / 3.26	2.24 / 3.21	2.21 / 3.14	2.19 / 3.11	2.16 / 3.06	2.14 / 3.02	2.13 / 3.00
15	4.54 / 8.68	3.68 / 6.36	3.29 / 5.42	3.06 / 4.89	2.90 / 4.56	2.79 / 4.32	2.70 / 4.14	2.64 / 4.00	2.59 / 3.89	2.55 / 3.80	2.51 / 3.73	2.48 / 3.67	2.43 / 3.56	2.39 / 3.48	2.33 / 3.36	2.29 / 3.29	2.25 / 3.20	2.21 / 3.12	2.18 / 3.07	2.15 / 3.00	2.12 / 2.97	2.10 / 2.92	2.08 / 2.89	2.07 / 2.87
16	4.49 / 8.53	3.63 / 6.23	3.24 / 5.29	3.01 / 4.77	2.85 / 4.44	2.74 / 4.20	2.66 / 4.03	2.59 / 3.89	2.54 / 3.78	2.49 / 3.69	2.45 / 3.61	2.42 / 3.55	2.37 / 3.45	2.33 / 3.37	2.28 / 3.25	2.24 / 3.18	2.20 / 3.10	2.16 / 3.01	2.13 / 2.96	2.09 / 2.98	2.07 / 2.86	2.04 / 2.80	2.02 / 2.77	2.01 / 2.75
17	4.45 / 8.40	3.59 / 6.11	3.20 / 5.18	2.96 / 4.67	2.81 / 4.34	2.70 / 4.10	2.62 / 3.93	2.55 / 3.79	2.50 / 3.68	2.45 / 3.59	2.41 / 3.52	2.38 / 3.45	2.33 / 3.35	2.29 / 3.27	2.23 / 3.16	2.19 / 3.08	2.15 / 3.00	2.11 / 2.92	2.08 / 2.86	2.04 / 2.79	2.02 / 2.76	1.99 / 2.70	1.97 / 2.67	1.96 / 2.65
18	4.41 / 8.28	3.55 / 6.01	3.16 / 5.09	2.93 / 4.58	2.77 / 4.25	3.66 / 4.01	2.58 / 3.85	2.51 / 3.71	2.46 / 3.60	2.41 / 3.51	2.37 / 3.44	2.34 / 3.37	2.29 / 3.27	2.25 / 3.19	2.19 / 3.07	2.15 / 3.00	2.11 / 2.91	2.07 / 2.83	2.04 / 2.78	2.00 / 2.71	1.98 / 2.68	1.95 / 2.62	1.93 / 2.59	1.92 / 2.57
19	4.38 / 8.18	3.52 / 5.93	3.13 / 5.01	2.90 / 4.50	2.74 / 4.17	2.63 / 3.94	2.55 / 3.77	2.48 / 3.63	2.43 / 3.52	2.38 / 3.43	2.34 / 3.36	2.31 / 3.30	2.26 / 3.19	2.21 / 3.12	2.15 / 3.00	2.11 / 2.92	2.07 / 2.84	2.02 / 2.76	2.00 / 2.70	1.96 / 2.63	1.94 / 2.60	1.91 / 2.54	1.90 / 2.51	1.88 / 2.49
20	4.35 / 8.10	3.49 / 5.85	3.10 / 4.94	2.87 / 4.42	2.71 / 4.10	2.60 / 3.87	2.52 / 3.71	2.45 / 3.56	2.40 / 3.45	2.35 / 3.37	2.31 / 3.30	2.28 / 3.23	2.23 / 3.13	2.18 / 3.05	2.12 / 2.94	2.08 / 2.86	2.04 / 2.77	1.99 / 2.69	1.96 / 2.63	1.92 / 2.56	1.90 / 2.53	1.87 / 2.47	1.85 / 2.44	1.84 / 2.42
21	4.32 / 8.02	3.47 / 5.78	3.07 / 4.87	2.84 / 4.37	2.68 / 4.04	2.57 / 3.81	2.49 / 3.65	2.42 / 3.51	2.37 / 3.40	2.32 / 3.31	2.28 / 3.24	2.25 / 3.17	2.20 / 3.07	2.15 / 2.99	2.09 / 2.88	2.05 / 2.80	2.00 / 2.72	1.96 / 2.63	1.93 / 2.58	1.89 / 2.51	1.87 / 2.47	1.84 / 2.42	1.82 / 2.38	1.81 / 2.36
22	4.30 / 7.94	3.44 / 5.72	3.05 / 4.82	2.82 / 4.31	2.66 / 3.99	2.55 / 3.76	2.47 / 3.59	2.40 / 3.45	2.35 / 3.35	2.30 / 3.26	2.26 / 3.18	2.23 / 3.12	2.18 / 3.02	2.13 / 2.94	2.07 / 2.83	2.03 / 2.75	1.98 / 2.67	1.93 / 2.58	1.91 / 2.53	1.87 / 2.46	1.84 / 2.42	1.81 / 2.37	1.80 / 2.33	1.78 / 2.31
23	4.28 / 7.88	3.42 / 5.66	3.03 / 4.76	2.80 / 4.26	2.64 / 3.94	2.53 / 3.71	2.45 / 3.54	2.38 / 3.41	2.32 / 3.30	2.28 / 3.21	2.24 / 3.14	2.20 / 3.07	2.14 / 2.97	2.10 / 2.89	2.04 / 2.78	2.00 / 2.70	1.96 / 2.62	1.91 / 2.53	1.88 / 2.48	1.84 / 2.41	1.82 / 2.37	1.79 / 2.32	1.77 / 2.28	1.76 / 2.26
24	4.26 / 7.82	3.40 / 5.61	3.01 / 4.72	2.78 / 4.22	2.62 / 3.90	2.51 / 3.67	2.43 / 3.50	2.36 / 3.36	2.30 / 3.25	2.26 / 3.17	2.22 / 3.09	2.18 / 3.03	2.13 / 2.93	2.09 / 2.85	2.02 / 2.74	1.98 / 2.66	1.94 / 2.58	1.89 / 2.49	1.86 / 2.44	1.82 / 2.36	1.80 / 2.33	1.76 / 2.27	1.74 / 2.23	1.73 / 2.21
25	4.24 / 7.77	3.38 / 5.57	2.99 / 4.68	2.76 / 4.18	2.60 / 3.86	2.49 / 3.63	2.41 / 3.46	2.34 / 3.32	2.28 / 3.21	2.24 / 3.13	2.20 / 3.05	2.16 / 2.99	2.11 / 2.89	2.06 / 2.81	2.00 / 2.70	1.96 / 2.62	1.92 / 2.54	1.87 / 2.45	1.84 / 2.40	1.80 / 2.32	1.77 / 2.29	1.74 / 2.23	1.72 / 2.19	1.71 / 2.17
26	4.22 / 7.72	3.37 / 5.53	2.98 / 4.64	2.74 / 4.14	2.59 / 3.82	2.47 / 3.59	2.39 / 3.42	2.32 / 3.29	2.27 / 3.17	2.22 / 3.09	2.18 / 3.02	2.15 / 2.96	2.10 / 2.86	2.05 / 2.77	1.99 / 2.66	1.95 / 2.58	1.90 / 2.50	1.85 / 2.41	1.82 / 2.36	1.78 / 2.28	1.76 / 2.25	1.72 / 2.19	1.70 / 2.15	1.69 / 2.13

TABLE B-4 Critical values of F (continued)

Degrees of Freedom for Greater Mean Square (numerator)

df	1	2	3	4	5	6	7	8	9	10	11	12	14	16	20	24	30	40	50	75	100	200	500	∞	df
27	4.21 7.68	3.35 5.49	2.96 4.60	2.73 4.11	2.57 3.79	2.46 3.56	2.37 3.39	2.30 3.26	2.25 3.14	2.20 3.06	2.16 2.98	2.13 2.93	2.08 2.83	2.03 2.74	1.97 2.63	1.93 2.55	1.88 2.47	1.84 2.38	1.80 2.33	1.76 2.25	1.74 2.21	1.71 2.16	1.68 2.12	1.67 2.10	27
28	4.20 7.64	3.34 5.45	2.95 4.57	2.71 4.07	2.56 3.76	2.44 3.53	2.36 3.36	2.29 3.23	2.24 3.11	2.19 3.03	2.15 2.95	2.12 2.90	2.06 2.80	2.02 2.71	1.96 2.60	1.91 2.52	1.87 2.44	1.81 2.35	1.78 2.30	1.75 2.22	1.72 2.18	1.69 2.13	1.67 2.09	1.65 2.06	28
29	4.18 7.60	3.33 5.42	2.93 4.54	2.70 4.04	2.54 3.73	2.43 3.50	2.35 3.33	2.28 3.20	2.22 3.08	2.18 3.00	2.14 2.92	2.10 2.87	2.05 2.77	2.00 2.68	1.94 2.57	1.90 2.49	1.85 2.41	1.80 2.32	1.77 2.27	1.73 2.19	1.71 2.15	1.68 2.10	1.65 2.06	1.64 2.03	29
30	4.17 7.56	3.32 5.39	2.92 4.51	2.69 4.02	2.53 3.70	2.42 3.47	2.34 3.30	2.27 3.17	2.21 3.06	2.16 2.98	2.12 2.90	2.09 2.84	2.04 2.74	1.99 2.66	1.93 2.55	1.89 2.47	1.84 2.38	1.79 2.29	1.76 2.24	1.72 2.16	1.69 2.13	1.66 2.07	1.64 2.03	1.62 2.01	30
32	4.15 7.50	3.30 5.34	2.90 4.46	2.67 3.97	2.51 3.66	2.40 3.42	2.32 3.25	2.25 3.12	2.19 3.01	2.14 2.94	2.10 2.86	2.07 2.80	2.02 2.70	1.97 2.62	1.91 2.51	1.86 2.42	1.82 2.34	1.76 2.25	1.74 2.20	1.69 2.12	1.67 2.08	1.64 2.02	1.61 1.98	1.59 1.96	32
34	4.13 7.44	3.28 5.29	2.88 4.42	2.65 3.93	2.49 3.61	2.38 3.38	2.30 3.21	2.23 3.08	2.17 2.97	2.12 2.89	2.08 2.82	2.05 2.76	2.00 2.66	1.95 2.58	1.89 2.47	1.84 2.38	1.80 2.30	1.74 2.21	1.71 2.15	1.67 2.08	1.64 2.04	1.61 1.98	1.59 1.94	1.57 1.91	34
36	4.11 7.39	3.26 5.25	2.86 4.38	2.63 3.89	2.48 3.58	2.36 3.35	2.28 3.18	2.21 3.04	2.15 2.94	2.10 2.86	2.06 2.78	2.03 2.72	1.98 2.62	1.93 2.54	1.87 2.43	1.82 2.35	1.78 2.26	1.72 2.17	1.69 2.12	1.65 2.04	1.62 2.00	1.59 1.94	1.56 1.90	1.55 1.87	36
38	4.10 7.35	3.25 5.21	2.85 4.34	2.62 3.86	2.46 3.54	2.35 3.32	2.26 3.15	2.19 3.02	2.14 2.91	2.09 2.82	2.05 2.75	2.02 2.69	1.96 2.59	1.92 2.51	1.85 2.40	1.80 2.32	1.76 2.22	1.71 2.14	1.67 2.08	1.63 2.00	1.60 1.97	1.57 1.90	1.54 1.86	1.53 1.84	38
40	4.08 7.31	3.23 5.18	2.84 4.31	2.61 3.83	2.45 3.51	2.34 3.29	2.25 3.12	2.18 2.99	2.12 2.88	2.07 2.80	2.04 2.73	2.00 2.66	1.95 2.56	1.90 2.49	1.84 2.37	1.79 2.29	1.74 2.20	1.69 2.11	1.66 2.05	1.61 1.97	1.59 1.94	1.55 1.88	1.53 1.84	1.51 1.81	40
42	4.07 7.27	3.22 5.15	2.83 4.29	2.59 3.80	2.44 3.49	2.32 3.26	2.24 3.10	2.17 2.96	2.11 2.86	2.06 2.77	2.02 2.70	1.99 2.64	1.94 2.54	1.89 2.46	1.82 2.35	1.78 2.26	1.73 2.17	1.68 2.08	1.64 2.02	1.60 1.94	1.57 1.91	1.54 1.85	1.51 1.80	1.49 1.78	42
44	4.06 7.24	3.21 5.12	2.82 4.26	2.58 3.78	2.43 3.46	2.31 3.24	2.23 3.07	2.16 2.94	2.10 2.84	2.05 2.75	2.01 2.68	1.98 2.62	1.92 2.52	1.88 2.44	1.81 2.32	1.76 2.24	1.72 2.15	1.66 2.06	1.63 2.00	1.58 1.92	1.56 1.88	1.52 1.82	1.50 1.78	1.48 1.75	44
46	4.05 7.21	3.20 5.10	2.81 4.24	2.57 3.76	2.42 3.44	2.30 3.22	2.22 3.05	2.14 2.92	2.09 2.82	2.04 2.73	2.00 2.66	1.97 2.60	1.91 2.50	1.87 2.42	1.80 2.30	1.75 2.22	1.71 2.13	1.65 2.04	1.62 1.98	1.57 1.90	1.54 1.86	1.51 1.80	1.48 1.76	1.46 1.72	46
48	4.04 7.19	3.19 5.08	2.80 4.22	2.56 3.74	2.41 3.42	2.30 3.20	2.21 3.04	2.14 2.90	2.08 2.80	2.03 2.71	1.99 2.64	1.96 2.58	1.90 2.48	1.86 2.40	1.79 2.28	1.74 2.20	1.70 2.11	1.64 2.02	1.61 1.96	1.56 1.88	1.53 1.84	1.50 1.78	1.47 1.73	1.45 1.70	48

Degrees of Freedom for Lesser Mean Square (denominator)

(continued)

TABLE B-4 Critical values of F (*continued*)

Degrees of Freedom for Lesser Mean Square (denominator) — rows; Degrees of Freedom for Greater Mean Square (numerator) — columns. Each cell lists two values.

den \ num	1	2	3	4	5	6	7	8	9	10	11	12	14	16	20	24	30	40	50	75	100	200	500	∞
50	4.03 / 7.17	3.18 / 5.06	2.79 / 4.20	2.56 / 3.72	2.40 / 3.41	2.29 / 3.18	2.20 / 3.02	2.13 / 2.88	2.07 / 2.78	2.02 / 2.70	1.98 / 2.62	1.95 / 2.56	1.90 / 2.46	1.85 / 2.39	1.78 / 2.26	1.74 / 2.18	1.69 / 2.10	1.63 / 2.00	1.60 / 1.94	1.55 / 1.86	1.52 / 1.82	1.48 / 1.76	1.46 / 1.71	1.44 / 1.68
55	4.02 / 7.12	3.17 / 5.01	2.78 / 4.16	2.54 / 3.68	2.38 / 3.37	2.27 / 3.15	2.18 / 2.98	2.11 / 2.85	2.05 / 2.75	2.00 / 2.66	1.97 / 2.59	1.93 / 2.53	1.88 / 2.43	1.83 / 2.35	1.76 / 2.23	1.72 / 2.15	1.67 / 2.06	1.61 / 1.96	1.58 / 1.90	1.52 / 1.82	1.50 / 1.78	1.46 / 1.71	1.43 / 1.66	1.41 / 1.64
60	4.00 / 7.08	3.15 / 4.98	2.76 / 4.13	2.52 / 3.65	2.37 / 3.34	2.25 / 3.12	2.17 / 2.95	2.10 / 2.82	2.04 / 2.72	1.99 / 2.63	1.95 / 2.56	1.92 / 2.50	1.86 / 2.40	1.81 / 2.32	1.75 / 2.20	1.70 / 2.12	1.65 / 2.03	1.59 / 1.93	1.56 / 1.87	1.50 / 1.79	1.48 / 1.74	1.44 / 1.68	1.41 / 1.63	1.39 / 1.60
65	3.99 / 7.04	3.14 / 4.95	2.75 / 4.10	2.51 / 3.62	2.36 / 3.31	2.24 / 3.09	2.15 / 2.93	2.08 / 2.79	2.02 / 2.70	1.98 / 2.61	1.94 / 2.54	1.90 / 2.47	1.85 / 2.37	1.80 / 2.30	1.73 / 2.18	1.68 / 2.09	1.63 / 2.00	1.57 / 1.90	1.54 / 1.84	1.49 / 1.76	1.46 / 1.71	1.42 / 1.64	1.39 / 1.60	1.37 / 1.56
70	3.98 / 7.01	3.13 / 4.92	2.74 / 4.08	2.50 / 3.60	2.35 / 3.29	2.23 / 3.07	2.14 / 2.91	2.07 / 2.77	2.01 / 2.67	1.97 / 2.59	1.93 / 2.51	1.89 / 2.45	1.84 / 2.35	1.79 / 2.28	1.72 / 2.15	1.67 / 2.07	1.62 / 1.98	1.56 / 1.88	1.53 / 1.82	1.47 / 1.74	1.45 / 1.69	1.40 / 1.62	1.37 / 1.56	1.35 / 1.53
80	3.96 / 6.96	3.11 / 4.88	2.72 / 4.04	2.48 / 3.56	2.33 / 3.25	2.21 / 3.04	2.12 / 2.87	2.05 / 2.74	1.99 / 2.64	1.95 / 2.55	1.91 / 2.48	1.88 / 2.41	1.82 / 2.32	1.77 / 2.24	1.70 / 2.11	1.65 / 2.03	1.60 / 1.94	1.54 / 1.84	1.51 / 1.78	1.45 / 1.70	1.42 / 1.65	1.38 / 1.57	1.35 / 1.52	1.32 / 1.49
100	3.94 / 6.90	3.09 / 4.82	2.70 / 3.98	2.46 / 3.51	2.30 / 3.20	2.19 / 2.99	2.10 / 2.82	2.03 / 2.69	1.97 / 2.59	1.92 / 2.51	1.88 / 2.43	1.85 / 2.36	1.79 / 2.26	1.75 / 2.19	1.68 / 2.06	1.63 / 1.98	1.57 / 1.89	1.51 / 1.79	1.48 / 1.73	1.42 / 1.64	1.39 / 1.59	1.34 / 1.51	1.30 / 1.46	1.28 / 1.43
125	3.92 / 6.84	3.07 / 4.78	2.68 / 3.94	2.44 / 3.47	2.29 / 3.17	2.17 / 2.95	2.08 / 2.79	2.01 / 2.65	1.95 / 2.56	1.90 / 2.47	1.86 / 2.40	1.83 / 2.33	1.77 / 2.23	1.72 / 2.15	1.65 / 2.03	1.60 / 1.94	1.55 / 1.85	1.49 / 1.75	1.45 / 1.68	1.39 / 1.59	1.36 / 1.54	1.31 / 1.46	1.27 / 1.40	1.25 / 1.37
150	3.91 / 6.81	3.06 / 4.75	2.67 / 3.91	2.43 / 3.44	2.27 / 3.14	2.16 / 2.92	2.07 / 2.76	2.00 / 2.62	1.94 / 2.53	1.89 / 2.44	1.85 / 2.37	1.82 / 2.30	1.76 / 2.20	1.71 / 2.12	1.64 / 2.00	1.59 / 1.91	1.54 / 1.83	1.47 / 1.72	1.44 / 1.66	1.37 / 1.56	1.34 / 1.51	1.29 / 1.43	1.25 / 1.37	1.22 / 1.33
200	3.89 / 6.76	3.04 / 4.71	2.65 / 3.88	2.41 / 3.41	2.26 / 3.11	2.14 / 2.90	2.05 / 2.73	1.98 / 2.60	1.92 / 2.50	1.87 / 2.41	1.83 / 2.34	1.80 / 2.28	1.74 / 2.17	1.69 / 2.09	1.62 / 1.97	1.57 / 1.88	1.52 / 1.79	1.45 / 1.69	1.42 / 1.62	1.35 / 1.53	1.32 / 1.48	1.26 / 1.39	1.22 / 1.33	1.19 / 1.28
400	3.86 / 6.70	3.02 / 4.66	2.62 / 3.83	2.39 / 3.36	2.23 / 3.06	2.12 / 2.85	2.03 / 2.69	1.96 / 2.55	1.90 / 2.46	1.85 / 2.37	1.81 / 2.29	1.78 / 2.23	1.72 / 2.12	1.67 / 2.04	1.60 / 1.92	1.54 / 1.84	1.49 / 1.74	1.42 / 1.64	1.38 / 1.57	1.32 / 1.47	1.28 / 1.42	1.22 / 1.32	1.16 / 1.24	1.13 / 1.19
1000	3.85 / 6.66	3.00 / 4.62	2.61 / 3.80	2.38 / 3.34	2.22 / 3.04	2.10 / 2.82	2.02 / 2.66	1.95 / 2.53	1.89 / 2.43	1.84 / 2.34	1.80 / 2.26	1.76 / 2.20	1.70 / 2.09	1.65 / 2.01	1.58 / 1.89	1.53 / 1.81	1.47 / 1.71	1.41 / 1.61	1.36 / 1.54	1.30 / 1.44	1.26 / 1.38	1.19 / 1.28	1.13 / 1.19	1.08 / 1.11
∞	3.84 / 6.64	2.99 / 4.60	2.60 / 3.78	2.37 / 3.32	2.21 / 3.02	2.09 / 2.80	2.01 / 2.64	1.94 / 2.51	1.88 / 2.41	1.83 / 2.32	1.79 / 2.24	1.75 / 2.18	1.69 / 2.07	1.64 / 1.99	1.57 / 1.87	1.52 / 1.79	1.46 / 1.69	1.40 / 1.59	1.35 / 1.52	1.28 / 1.41	1.24 / 1.36	1.17 / 1.25	1.11 / 1.15	1.00 / 1.00

SOURCE: From *Statistical Methods*, Sixth Edition, by G. W. Snedecor and W. G. Cochran, Iowa State University Press, 1967.

A JOURNAL ARTICLE

IN MANUSCRIPT

FORM*

Note:

Some procedures for preparing and submitting a manuscript vary from journal to journal. Consult the correct APA publication manual and the specific journal before submitting any manuscript for publication.

*From "Gender Differences in Masking Negative Emotions: Ability or Motivation" by Teresa L. Davis, 1995, *Developmental Psychology, 31(4),* pp. 660–667. Copyright ©1995 by the American Psychological Association. Reprinted by permission.

Running head: GENDER DIFFERENCES IN MASKING NEGATIVE EMOTIONS

Gender Differences in Masking Negative Emotions:

Ability or Motivation?

Teresa L. Davis

University of Florida

Gender Differences   2

Abstract

Research has demonstrated that boys display greater negative affect than girls when they receive a disappointing gift. In this study, ability and motivation were investigated as possible reasons for the gender differences. First- and 3rd-grade children's emotion dissimulation in a disappointing gift task was compared with their degree of dissimulation in a highly motivating game task that required the same ability (masking disappointment with a positive expression) but involved a self-gain motive. If boys are motivated, can they hide their disappointment as well as girls? Boys reduced their expression of negative affect in the game task; however, they still showed higher levels of negativity than did the girls. Perhaps because of socialization experiences, girls have more practice in hiding disappointment and, therefore, are better skilled. Girls also showed higher levels of social monitoring behaviors than boys, and younger girls demonstrated the greatest number of tension behaviors.

Gender Differences in Masking Negative Emotions:

Ability or Motivation?

Adults and children are capable of presenting to others affective displays that differ from the emotions they are really experiencing. Studies of the development of spontaneous regulation of emotional displays suggest that this ability develops early, being demonstrated even by preschool children (Cole, 1986; Reissland & Harris, 1991), and may improve with age (Saarni, 1984). The degree of emotion dissimulation demonstrated, at least in some situations, also seems to be related to the gender of the child (Cole, 1986; Saarni, 1984).

Children's spontaneous use of display rules or the principles that guide the expression of emotion has been examined primarily through a disappointing gift paradigm developed by Saarni (1984). This paradigm evokes a culturally defined display rule. "You should look pleased when you receive a gift even if you don't like it," requiring the masking of the child's true emotion. In Saarni's (1984) study, first-, third-, and fifth-grade children received an attractive gift for their participation in the evaluation of workbooks, and then, in a later session, they received a disappointing "baby gift." The number of positive, negative, and transitional behaviors (those that were minimally positive or were suggestive of uncertainty) was measured.

Saarni (1984) found a marginally significant age effect, with older children, especially girls, expressing more positive facial and vocal behaviors on receipt of the disappointing gift compared with younger children. The other major finding was a gender difference in response to the disappointing gift, with girls' behaviors appearing less negative than boys'. The older two age groups of girls responded equally positively to the attractive and unattractive gifts. Third- and fifth-grade boys also displayed more transitional behaviors than girls of the same age.

In a similar study using preschool, first-grade, and third-grade children, Cole (1986) did not find an age effect. She did, however, replicate Saarni's (1984) gender finding. In a follow-up study, Cole further explored whether the preschool girls were actually feeling disappointment by comparing the expressions of preschool girls who opened a disappointing gift in the presence of an experimenter with girls who opened the gift while the experimenter was absent. More disappointment was expressed when the experimenter was absent, suggesting that these young girls were indeed hiding their feelings of unhappiness.

The purpose of the present study was to investigate the possible reasons for the effects of gender found in this type of task. Saarni (1984) has suggested three possible explanations. These explanations are linked to the three components necessary

to effectively use a display rule: The children must have
knowledge of the rule, must be able to produce the expression,
and must be motivated to hide their true emotions.

The first explanation for the gender effect, differences in
knowledge, is not supported by the literature. Studies using
picture story tasks find that although the understanding of
display rules increases between the ages of 4 and 10 years for
both boys and girls, there are no differences in knowledge on
the basis of gender (Friend & Davis, 1993; Gnepp & Hess, 1986;
Harris, Donnelly, Gabriell, & Pitt-Watson, 1986; Saarni, 1979).
In addition, these studies suggest that hiding disappointment in
a gift situation is one of the earliest understood display rules
and should be well known by the older children in the
disappointing gift studies.

A second plausible reason for the gender effect could be a
difference in the abilities of boys and girls to produce the
positive expression (Saarni, 1984) or perhaps prevent the
negative emotion from showing. Although research on adults
suggests that women may be better encoders (or producers) of
emotional cues than men (Buck, Miller, & Caul, 1974; Hall, 1979;
Rotter & Rotter, 1988), studies with children as encoders often
find that the identification of emotions based on facial expressions is not affected by the gender of the child displaying the
feeling (Felleman, Barden, Carlson, Rosenberg, & Masters, 1983;

Morency & Krauss, 1982).

Posing the positive expression is only one part of masking disappointment. The child must also prevent the real emotion from showing. Shennum and Bugental (1982) asked 6- to 12-year-olds to hide their emotions. When the task was to mask dislike with happy expressions, no sex differences were found. In contrast to these results, Feldman, Jenkins, and Popoola (1979) found that girls were better able to look pleased while drinking sour fruit juice than boys. These studies indicate that there is some question about whether girls are better at masking negative emotions.

A third possible explanation for gender differences involves differing levels of motivation between boys and girls. For example, Saarni (1984) suggested that there may be more social pressure for girls to act nice. Consistent with this view, Banerjee and Eggleston (1993) found that parents of preschoolers expect girls to be more restricted in their emotional displays than boys and also expect girls to use more sophisticated mentalistic strategies to control their emotions. Because of these different cultural expectations, girls may be more motivated to hide their disappointment than boys.

Of the three components necessary for display rule use—knowledge, ability to pose facial expressions, and motivation—the gender differences noted in the disappointing gift paradigm are most probably related to ability and

motivation. Both of these possibilities are investigated.

In the present study, children's ability to mask

disappointment with happiness was compared on two tasks. Each

child participated in a disappointing gift task that was modeled

after the Saarni (1984) and Cole (1986) studies and also in a

game task. The game required the same ability as the

disappointing gift task (immediately masking disappointment with

happiness), but the motivation for doing so was self-interest

(winning the game). The game was designed to discover whether

gender differences appear in a situation in which boys and girls

are highly motivated to hide their disappointment. As in the

gift task, the children received a positive item and then a

disappointing one. To keep the attractive prize, the child had

to appear to like the second, unattractive one. This game

differs from most of the emotion-masking research in which a

child is simply asked to act and has little to explicitly gain

or lose by his or her actions. In this game, the child could win

or lose an attractive prize depending on his or her ability to

mask disappointment.

It was expected that the results of the disappointing gift

task would replicate those of previous studies. Girls would

demonstrate less negativity than boys when receiving a

disappointing gift and would respond equally positively to the positive and negative gifts. It was also expected that if the primary difference between the two sexes is the ability to pose the positive expression and suppress the negative one, then the same pattern of performance would appear in both tasks (game and disappointing gift)—girls would show fewer negative and more positive behaviors than boys. However, if motivation is the important difference between the performance of girls and boys, one would expect to see girls masking negative emotions more successfully than boys on the prosocial gift task but both sexes performing equally well on the self-interest game task.

In addition, two other behavior categories were explored in this study. Saarni (1992) extended her previous scoring system (Saarni, 1984) to include social monitoring and tension behaviors. Behaviors indicating that the children were attempting to control their expressions but were not entirely successful (such as a mumbled "thank you") were coded as social monitoring behaviors. The tension behavior category included indicators of anxiety (such as twisting in chair). This study is the first to investigate these two separate behavior categories in a situation involving the masking of disappointment.

Method

Participants

The participants were 64 children: 32 first graders (16

girls and 16 boys; $\underline{M}$ = 6 years 11 months) and 32 third graders

(16 girls and 16 boys; $\underline{M}$ = 9 years 3 months). The children were

predominantly from middle-class families and were recruited

through the public school system by means of a letter to the

parents. Seven of the children were members of ethnic minority

groups. First and third graders were selected to be consistent

with the age groups in the previous two studies that

demonstrated the gender difference. Younger children were

considered; however, pilot testing indicated that they had

difficulty understanding the game task.

Materials

   Various segments of the interview were videotaped by using

a camera in view of the children. The children were not aware of

when they were being taped and when the camera was off. The

camera was introduced to the children at the beginning of the

interview, and most of them paid little attention to it after

showing some initial interest.

Procedure

   The children were interviewed individually in a four-part

session at their elementary school by one of two pairs of female

experimenters used in the study. Each pair interviewed an equal

number of children of each gender and at each grade level.

Within each pair, the experimenters alternated between the role of Experimenter 1 and Experimenter 2 (counterbalanced across

grade and gender). The order of presentation of the gift and

game tasks was also counterbalanced.

At the beginning of the testing session, the child was

introduced to Experimenter 1, who asked the child to rank order

10 items. The items included a range of desirable (e.g.,

"smelly" Magic Markers and glow-in-the-dark Super Balls) and the

less desirable (e.g., plastic spoons and teething rings)

objects. The children were told that the experimenter wanted to

see what types of items children of different ages liked. The

children's two lowest-ranked and two highest-ranked items were

used in the study. The highest-ranked item was always paired

with the 9th-ranked item, and the 2nd-ranked item was always

paired with the lowest-ranked item. The pairs of items used in

each task (1st and 9th, 2nd and 10th) were counterbalanced

across tasks (gift and game) and gender and grade. The child was

then escorted to a different part of the room and was given the

game and gift tasks.

Disappointing gift task. Experimenter 2 explained that she

was interested in how children liked different types of

workbooks. The children were told that if they would work a

problem and help evaluate the workbook, they would receive a

gift for their effort and help. The child was then told that the session would be videotaped so that the experimenter could see how children work on problems. The experimenter helped the child pick out a problem to work. After the child finished the problem, the experimenter asked a few questions regarding difficulty of the workbook and comparison to classroom work. The child was then thanked and given a gift. The child was asked to unwrap the gift at the table.

The first gift was always either the child's first or second choice. For the next 10 s, the examiner made eye contact with the child but did not stare, maintained a neutral expression, and did not interact with the child to avoid leading the child's facial expression. The children were then asked to help with a second workbook problem. The procedure was repeated except that the gift the child received was one of his or her least favorite items. Experimenter 2 then thanked the child and exited the room.

Experimenter 1 (who had been taping) then interviewed the child about the gifts that were received. This interview was based on the method used in Cole's (1986) study. The children were first asked which gift they liked better. They were then asked if they felt more happy or more sad when they unwrapped each gift. If they indicated that they felt happy about the disappointing gift, they were prompted: "I thought that ___ was your last choice. Some children would feel sad about receiving

this prize and some would not. I want to know how you really
feel."

Game task. Experimenter 1 told the children that she wanted
to play a new game with them to see if it was the kind of game
children their age like to play. The children were told they
were being videotaped to see how children play the game. Experimenter 2 brought in two boxes, set them in front of the child,
and then operated the camera. The boxes opened toward the child,
and Experimenter 1 could not see what was in them. The rules
were explained to the child as follows:

Inside each box is a prize. I cannot see the prize from
here, so only you know what is in the box. The way this game
works is that you will look into the blue box first and then
you will look up at me. Then you will look into the red box
and look at me. OK? To win the game, you want to try to trick
me. If you trick me then you get to keep both prizes. If you
don't then I get both prizes back. This is how you trick me:
There may be two prizes that you really like in the boxes or
there may be one prize you like a little better. To win the
game, you want to act like you like both of the prizes very
much. You want to look happy when you look at me. If you look
like you like both prizes very much, then you get to keep
both of the prizes. But, if I can tell you don't like one of

the prizes in the box, then I get both the prizes back and
you don't get to keep any. OK, let's make sure you
understand. What are you going to do first? How do you want
to look when you look at me? And if I can tell that you don't
like a prize, what happens?

When the children indicated that they understood, the game
began. The children were told to look in the first box and then
look up at the experimenter. They were also told they could say
anything that they wanted to as long as they did not name the
item in the box. The children looked at the experimenter for 10
s before being told to proceed to the next box.

The first box the children opened contained an attractive
prize. The second box contained a least-favorite item. The
children needed to look happy in spite of this to win the game
and keep the first prize. At the end of the game, all of the
children were told that they did very well and would get to keep
both prizes. Experimenter 1 then asked the children the same
questions about the prizes that were asked about the gifts
(i.e., which the child liked better and how the child felt about
receiving each). The children were then allowed to trade in the
prizes that they did not want for others. They were told that we
might not be able to trade in prizes for all of the children but
today we happened to have extras. We asked them not to tell the
others that they got to trade in their prizes. They were then

asked if they had heard about the experiment from any of the other children and what specifically they had heard.

Scoring

A behavior coding system developed by Saarni (1992) was used. This system is similar to the one used in Saarni's 1984 study and involves observing behaviors such as facial expressions, vocalizations, gazing, and selected body movements. In Saarni's 1984 coding system, behaviors were coded as positive, negative, or transitional. The behaviors coded into the first two categories were obvious positive or negative displays. Behaviors coded into the transitional category were those that seemed to indicate an understanding that some degree of expressive control was required, but the children were not yet executing the control properly. Some of these behaviors suggested that the children felt anxious, such as shifting in their seats; other behaviors appeared to be attempts at expressive control, such as fake smiles. In Saarni's (1992) new system, transitional behaviors have been further divided into two types: social monitoring behaviors and tension behaviors. The responses coded into the social monitoring category are minimally positive in affect or suggestive of attempts at control, and those in the tension category indicate uneasiness and stress. The Appendix lists the types of behaviors that were coded into each category.

The 10 s following the exposure to each gift and prize were scored (four 10-s segments per child). The time interval began when the child first made eye contact with the prize or gift and was analyzed with a frame-by-frame technique. Each child received a score for each dimension (positive, negative, social monitoring, and tension) for each of the four segments (16 scores for each child). Two taped segments had to be dropped from the analysis. One first-grade boy dropped his disappointing gift on the floor when he opened it and thus was under the table retrieving it during the 10-s taping period. A third-grade boy looked into the first box in the game task before he was given the instructions.

The scores consisted of a frequency count of the number of behaviors on each dimension the observer counted. Repeated instances of the same behavior were not counted toward the frequency totals (Saarni, 1984, 1992). Two individuals who were unaware of the methodology and purpose of the study coded each tape. Using the Spearman-Brown formula, the interrater reliability was r = .87 for the positive dimension, r = .77 for the negative dimension, r = .78 for the social monitoring dimension, and r = .76 for the tension dimension. Disagreements were resolved by discussion.

Results

Preliminary analyses indicated that there were no main
effects or interactions involving task order or experimenter
pair. Therefore, these variables were not included. All analysis
of variance (ANOVA) results were calculated using the PROC/GLM
procedure in SAS.

Disappointing Gift Task

The results of the positive and negative behaviors were
first analyzed for the gift condition only in order to explore
the replication of previous findings on disappointing gift
tasks. Preliminary analyses indicated that there was no effect
of grade on the number of positive or negative behaviors;
therefore, this variable was dropped from further analyses.
A 2 × 2 (Sex × Valence: positive gift/disappointing gift) ANOVA
on the number of positive expressions indicated a main effect of
valence, $\underline{F}(1, 61) = 14.90$, $\underline{p} < .001$. The children responded
more positively to the attractive gift ($\underline{M} = 2.05$) than they did
to the disappointing gift ($\underline{M} = 1.34$).

Because specific predictions were made regarding gender,
planned pairwise comparisons were made contrasting positive
expressions in the attractive and disappointing gift conditions
for boys and girls separately. There was a significant decrease
in positive behaviors expressed by boys in the disappointing ($\underline{M}$

= 1.23) versus the attractive (M = 2.13) gift condition, F(1, 30) = 12.10, p < .002. However, for the girls the difference was not significant (disappointing gift condition, M = 1.44; attractive gift condition, M = 1.97).

The same ANOVA on negative emotions also indicated a main effect of valence, F(1, 61) = 27.83, p < .001. Children expressed a greater number of negative behaviors when they received a disappointing gift (M = 2.71) than when they received an attractive gift (M = 1.76). The valence main effect was qualified by a Sex $\times$ Valence interaction, F(1, 61) = 4.52, p < .04. In the attractive gift condition, there was no difference in the negative expressions of boys (M = 1.77) and girls (M = 1.75); however, when the children received a disappointing gift, the number of negative expressions did differ, F(1, 61) = 5.60, p < .02, with boys (M = 3.10) demonstrating a greater number than girls (M = 2.31).

These results are consistent with those found in other studies using this paradigm. The girls in this study showed the same degree of positivity when receiving either a disappointing gift or an attractive gift. The boys, however, showed a decrease in positive behaviors in the disappointing gift situation and also demonstrated more negative behaviors than girls when receiving a disappointing gift.

A Comparison of the Disappointing Gift and Game Tasks

Performance in the game task was compared to performance on the disappointing gift task to investigate the influence of ability and motivation on children's masking of negative emotions. Because the children never said "thank you" in the game task, the children's scores on the gift task were recalculated excluding this item. The adjusted scores were used in all analyses comparing the gift and game tasks. The means for the game task and the adjusted means for the gift task are presented in Table 1. The four dimensions of emotional expression were analyzed separately. Preliminary analyses indicated no main effects or interactions involving grade for the positive and negative dimensions; therefore, grade was not included in the analyses on these two dimensions.

Insert Table 1 about here

A 2 × 2 × 2 (Sex × Valence × Task: game/gift) ANOVA on the number of positive expressions indicated a main effect of task, $F(1, 60) = 8.31$, $p < .005$. Children were more positive in the game task ($M = 2.20$) than in the gift task ($M = 1.69$). There was also a valence main effect, $F(1, 60) = 12.59$, $p < .001$, with a greater number of positive expressions when the gift/prize was attractive ($M = 2.19$) than when the gift/prize was disappointing ($M = 1.70$).

The same analysis on the number of negative expressions indicated three significant main effects: task, valence, and sex. The task main effect, $F(1, 60) = 32.31$, $p < .001$, indicated that a greater number of negative behaviors were expressed in the gift task ($M = 2.23$) than in the game task ($M = .69$). For valence, $F(1, 60) = 15.17$, $p < .001$, more negativity was expressed when a disappointing gift/prize was received ($M = 1.74$) than when an attractive gift/prize was received ($M = 1.18$). The gender main effect, $F(1, 60) = 7.41$, $p < .008$, showed that boys expressed more negativity ($M = 1.66$) than did girls ($M = 1.26$).

These main effects were qualified by two interactions (see Figure 1).

Insert Figure 1 about here

Follow-up t tests on a Task × Valence interaction, $F(1, 60) = 11.80$, $p < .001$, indicated that on the gift task there were more negative behaviors expressed when receiving the disappointing gift ($M = 1.76$) than when receiving the attractive gift ($M = 2.71$), $t(61) = 4.50$, $p < .001$. However, in the game task, there was no difference in the number of negative behaviors expressed when either the attractive or disappointing gift was received ($Ms = .61$ and $.78$, respectively).

A significant Sex × Valence interaction was also found,

$F(1, 60) = 4.03$, $p < .05$. There was no difference in the negative behavior of boys and girls when an attractive gift/prize was received ($Ms = 1.24$ and 1.12, respectively). There was a significant difference in the number of negative behaviors expressed by boys and girls when a negative gift/prize was received, $F(1, 60) = 9.16$, $p < .004$, with girls expressing fewer negative behaviors ($M = 1.40$) than boys ($M = 2.08$). The negative behavior of girls did not differ based on whether a negative or positive item was received. However, boys were significantly more negative when they received a disappointing versus an attractive gift/prize, $t(30) = 3.32$, $p < .002$. These findings indicate that girls were better than boys at suppressing negative expressions not only in the gift task but also in the game task.

The means for the social monitoring and tension behaviors are presented in Table 2. Preliminary analyses indicated that grade was not significant for the social monitoring behaviors; therefore, this variance was not included. A $2 \times 2 \times 2$ (Sex $\times$ Valence $\times$ Task: game/gift) ANOVA on the number of social monitoring behaviors indicated a main effect of task, $F(1, 60) = 23.15$, $p < .001$. The number of social monitoring behaviors was higher in the game task ($M = 2.05$) than in the gift task ($M = 1.45$). There was also a significant effect of sex, $F(1, 60) = 8.59$, $p < .005$, with girls showing a higher degree of social monitoring (M = 1.97) than boys (M = 1.54).

_____

Insert Table 2 about here

_____

A 2 × 2 × 2 × 2 (Sex × Valence × Grade × Task: game/gift) ANOVA on the number of tension behaviors indicated main effects of valence and sex. The valence main effect, F(1, 58) = 4.63, p < .04, showed that tension behaviors were higher when the children received a disappointing gift/prize (M = 3.03) than when they received a positive gift/prize (M = 2.72). The sex main effect, F(1, 58) = 11.89, p < .001, indicated that girls (M = 3.33) demonstrated more tension behaviors than boys (M = 2.42). A marginal Sex × Grade interaction, F(1, 58) = 3.14, p < .08, suggests that for girls there is a significant difference between first (M = 3.81) and third (M = 2.86) graders, F(1, 30) = 6.65, p < .02. For boys, there was no significant difference based on grade (first-grade boys: M = 2.43; third-grade boys: M = 2.42). The youngest girls demonstrated the greatest number of tension behaviors.

Trading of Gifts and Statements of Positive and Negative

Feelings

The children's trading behavior and their descriptions of their feelings about receiving the gifts and prizes suggested that they were more disappointed with the unattractive items than with the attractive ones. When allowed to trade their gifts and prizes at the end of the session, all of the children except 3 kept their attractive items. Most of the children, however, decided to trade the negative gifts and prizes they had been given. A categorical modeling analysis (CATMOD in SAS) indicated that there were no significant differences in the percentage of boys (84%) who traded and the percentage of girls (90%) who traded their disappointing gifts. For the negative prizes in the game task, all of the boys traded the prize and all but 7 of the girls traded.

The children all stated that they felt happy about receiving the attractive gifts and prizes. More children stated that they felt sad (70%) rather than happy (30%) when they received the unattractive items. Using the children's responses after their answer had been probed, a 2×2 (Sex $\times$ Task: game vs. gift) CATMOD analysis on the children's probed responses indicated that there were no effects of sex or task. Although not all of the children were willing to admit that they felt sad when they received the disappointing item, there were no sex or task differences that would suggest one gender was more disappointed than the other or that the items in one task were more or less disappointing than the items in the other.

Discussion

Consistent with previous research, gender differences in

emotional expression were found in the disappointing gift task.
The girls expressed fewer negative behaviors than the boys on
receipt of an unattractive gift. The two groups did not differ
in the degree of positive and negative expressiveness when
receiving an attractive gift. Consistent with Cole (1986), no
age differences were found.

The present study extended the previous findings in several
ways. First, this study explored the importance of motivation
and ability as possible explanations for the gender differences
in emotional expression found in a disappointing gift situation.
When the children's dissimulation in the disappointing gift task
was compared with their performance in a motivating game task,
two interesting findings emerged. First, negativity was reduced
a great deal for both boys and girls in the game task,
suggesting that motivation was playing a role in the degree of
emotion dissimulation. Second, and perhaps more interestingly,
even though the absolute level of negativity expressed was
greatly depressed in the game task, the boys still were not as
capable of suppressing negative expressions in response to a
disappointing item as were the girls. Girls may be more skilled
at this type of emotion dissimulation.

The two tasks, gift and game, did differ in that the
children needed to spontaneously access the display rule in the
gift condition whereas they were told the rule in the game

condition. However, of interest was the ability to hide

spontaneously felt disappointment with happiness. The game task

seemed an adequate elicitor of that ability.

Gender differences were also found for social monitoring

and tension behaviors. The girls in this study seemed to be more

involved in social monitoring than the boys, regardless of

whether they were receiving a positive or negative item. There

was also a higher degree of social monitoring for both genders

in the game task. The tension behaviors were higher when

children received negative gifts and prizes. The girls showed

more tension behaviors than the boys, but this was found

primarily for the younger girls.

There are several possible explanations for the gender

differences found in this study. Some explanations emphasize a

biological basis for differences. For example, there may be

differences in brain structure that may affect emotional expres-

siveness, or women could be endowed with a greater innate

capacity for learning to communicate nonverbally (see Blanck,

Buck, & Rosenthal, 1986; Hall, 1979). Other explanations have

focused primarily on socialization practices. If society exerts

more pressure on girls to "act nice," then perhaps girls have

spent more time hiding certain negative feelings and this

experience has led to increased ability. Boys, even when trying

hard, cannot do as well because they have had less practice than girls. Greater pressure for girls to be compliant and act nice may also have led to higher levels of social monitoring and to greater levels of tension behaviors, especially for the younger girls who may have less confidence in their abilities to regulate their negative feelings.

There is some evidence that parents socialize their children's emotional expressiveness differently depending on the gender of the child. Malatesta and Haviland (1982) found that mothers responded to the emotional displays of boys and girls differently beginning in the first year of life. Mothers showed more contingent smiling to the smiles of infant boys and were more likely to match the emotional behavior of boys than girls. As previously discussed, Banerjee and Eggleston (1993) have demonstrated that parents of preschool children expect girls to show more control of their emotions than boys, and they expect girls to use more sophisticated emotional control strategies. Other studies, however, have indicated that parents believe they encourage their sons to control their feelings to a greater degree than their daughters (Block, 1979), and parents are more emotionally responsive to their daughters in negative emotion-eliciting situations (Fabes et al., 1994).

In addition, boys and girls have different expectations about how their genuine displays of emotion will be responded to by adults. Boys expect more disapproval for expressing sadness than girls and expect less disapproval than girls for expressing anger (Fuchs & Thelen, 1988; Perry, Perry, & Weiss, 1989). It is clear that more research is needed to further investigate the socialization patterns of parents regarding their children's control of emotional displays.

The biosocial interactionist view suggests that perhaps biological differences in male and female individuals interact with factors in the social environment leading to gender differences (Kenrick, 1987). For example, research suggests that sex differences may exist on the approach-avoidance dimension of temperament (Rothbart, 1989). This difference may affect social-emotional development. If girls are more likely to show inhibition of approach, then parents may be more successful in their attempts to socialize impulsive actions, such as emotional displays (see Rothbart, 1989). In another type of interactive effect, Fabes et al. (1994) have demonstrated that socialization practices may also be influenced by the mother's perception of the child's level of emotional responsiveness.

The interaction of child characteristics and socialization could be further explored by investigating children's spontaneous masking of emotions other than disappointment. An emotional display difference that is based on differences in temperament between boys and girls would lead to the expectation that boys would have more difficulty masking other types of emotions at least in the early years. However, a finding that gender differences vary across different kinds of emotions would be consistent with the socialization practices explanation. Also consistent with the socialization explanation are findings that gender differences in emotion dissimulation in a disappointing gift context are not found in all cultures (Josephs, 1993). Even within American culture, Gross and Richardson (1993) have demonstrated that emotion dissimulation in a disappointing gift task differs on the basis of whether the children are in the presence of a same-sex or opposite-sex peer.

The joint influence of child characteristics and socialization may lead to different developmental patterns in emotional dissimulation. For example, if socialization pressures are the same for both genders but one gender is more sensitive to these pressures (e.g., because of temperamental differences), then one may see the gender difference decreasing as children get older. However, if socialization pressures are different for boys and girls for certain emotional displays such as sadness, then one may see gender differences widening in older children. There is also the possibility that socialization processes may lead eventually to less global but more context-specific differences in emotion dissimulation. For example, Saarni (1988) found that older girls more than younger girls or boys prefer to express their true emotions to peers rather than to adults.

The present study begins to explore the roles of motivation and skill in an emotion dissimulation situation. The design used in this study to examine the contributions of motivation and skill could be applied to the masking of other emotions or even reported gender differences in other behavioral domains. In addition, it is clear that within each gender there is a great deal of variability in emotion dissimulation. As discussed, various individual difference variables may be interacting with the socialization process. This paradigm could be used to explore a variety of variables potentially important to children's masking of emotions including degree of empathy, temperament, level of social monitoring, and family expressiveness.

References

Banerjee, M., & Eggleston, R. (1993, March). Preschoolers' and parents' understanding of emotion regulation. Paper presented at the meetings of the Society for Research in Child Development, New Orleans, LA.

Blanck, P. D., Buck, R., & Rosenthal, R. (Eds.). (1986). Nonverbal communication in the clinical context. University Park: Pennsylvania State University Press.

Block, J. H. (1979). Another look at sex differentiation in the socialization behaviors of mothers and fathers. In J. Sherman & F. L. Denmark (Eds.), Psychology of women: Future directions in research (pp. 29-87). New York: Psychological Dimensions.

Buck, R., Miller, R. E., & Caul, W. F. (1974). Sex, personality, and physiological variables in the communication of affect via facial expression. Journal of Personality and Social Psychology, 30, 587-596.

Cole, P. M. (1986). Children's spontaneous control of facial expression. Child Development, 57, 1309-1321.

Fabes, R. A., Eisenberg, N., Karbon, M., Bernzweig, J., Speer, A. L., & Carlo, G. (1994). Socialization of children's vicarious emotional responding and prosocial behavior: Relations with mothers' perceptions of children's emotional reactivity. Developmental Psychology, 30, 44-55.

Feldman, R., Jenkins, L., & Popoola, O. (1979). Detection of deception in adults and children via facial expressions. Child Development, 50, 350-355.

Felleman, E. S., Barden, R. C., Carlson, C. R., Rosenberg, L., & Masters, J. C. (1983). Children's and adults' recognition of spontaneous and posed emotional expressions in young children. Developmental Psychology, 19, 405-413.

Friend, M., & Davis, T. L. (1993). The appearance-reality distinction: Children's understanding of the physical and affective domains. Developmental Psychology, 29, 907-914.

Fuchs, D., & Thelen, M. (1988). Children's expected interpersonal consequences of communicating their affective state and reported likelihood of expression. Child Development, 59, 1314-1322.

Gnepp, J., & Hess, D. L. (1986). Children's understanding of verbal and facial display rules. Developmental Psychology, 22, 103-108.

Gross, D., & Richardson, A. (1993, March). Emotional-expressive behavior in children: Social context effects. Paper presented at the meetings of the Society for Research in Child Development, New Orleans, LA.

Hall, J. A. (1979). Gender, gender roles and nonverbal communication skills. In R. Rosenthal (Ed.), Skill in nonverbal communication (pp. 32-67). Cambridge, MA: Oelgeschlager, Gunn & Hain.

Harris, P. L., Donnelly, K., Gabriell, R. G. & Pitt-Watson, R. (1986). Children's understanding of the distinction between real and apparent emotion. Child Development, 57, 895-909.

Josephs, I. E. (1993, March). The development of display rules: Do you understand what you already do? Paper presented at the meetings of the Society for Research in Child Development, New Orleans, LA.

Kenrick, D. T. (1987). Gender, genes, and the social environment: A biosocial interactionist perspective. In P. Shaver & C. Hendrick (Eds.), Sex and gender: Review of personality and social psychology (Vol. 7, pp. 14-43). London: Sage.

Malatesta, C. Z., & Haviland, J. M. (1982). Learning display rules: The socialization of emotion expression in infancy. Child Development, 53, 991-1003.

Morency, N. L., & Krauss, R. M. (1982). Children's nonverbal encoding and decoding of affect. In R. S. Feldman (Ed.), Development of nonverbal behavior in children (pp. 181-199). New York: Springer-Verlag.

Perry, D., Perry, L., & Weiss, R. (1989). Sex differences in the consequences that children anticipate for aggression. Developmental Psychology, 25, 312-319.

Reissland, N., & Harris, P. (1991). Children's use of display rules in pride-eliciting situations. British Journal of Developmental Psychology, 9, 431-435.

Rothbart, M. K. (1989). Temperament and development. In G. A. Kohnstamm, J. E. Bates, & M. K. Rothbart (Eds.), Temperament in childhood (pp. 187-247). New York: Wiley.

Rotter, N. G., & Rotter, G. S. (1988). Sex-differences in the encoding and decoding of negative facial emotions. Journal of Nonverbal Behavior, 12, 139-148.

Saarni, C. (1979). Children's understanding of display rules for expressive behavior. Developmental Psychology, 15, 424-429.

Saarni, C. (1984). An observational study of children's attempts to monitor their expressive behavior. Child Development, 55, 1504-1513.

Saarni, C. (1988). Children's understanding of the interpersonal consequences of dissemblance of nonverbal emotional expressive behavior. Journal of Nonverbal Behavior, 12, 275-294.

Saarni, C. (1992). Children's emotional—expressive behaviors as regulators of others' happy and sad emotional states. In N. Eisenberg & R. A. Fabes (Eds.), New directions for child development: Vol. 55. Emotion and its regulation in early development (pp. 91-106). San Francisco: Jossey-Bass.

SAS Institute Inc. (1985). SAS® user's guide: Statistics (5th edition). Cary, NC: Author.

Shennum, W. A., & Bugental, D. B. (1982). The development of control over affective expression in nonverbal behavior. In R. S. Feldman (Ed.), Development of nonverbal behavior in children (pp. 101-122). New York: Springer-Verlag.

Appendix

Dimensions of Expressive Behavior

Positive Behaviors

Relaxed broad smile (teeth

showing), closed lip smile

Enthusiastic "Thank you"

Arched brows as in positive

surprise

Smiling eye contact with

experimenter

Eye crinkle while smiling

Positive verbal comments

Positive tone of voice

Giggling, laughing

Leans forward

Uses expressive hand gestures

while talking

Social Monitoring Behaviors

Slight and/or closed lip

smile

Staring at experimenter

Tilts head

Negative Behaviors

Tense, square-looking smile

(lips open, teeth may show)

Down-turned mouth (as in

frown or grimace)

Avoids eye contact

Knit brows

Leans backward

Sharp breath exhalation,

snorting, groaning

Sighing

Omitted "Thank you"

Negative verbal comments

Negative tone of voice

Tension Behaviors

Pressing, pursing, biting, or

sucking of lips

Bites or mouths clothing

Cheek puffing

(appendix continued)

Appendix (Cont.)

Social Monitoring Behaviors	Tension Behaviors
Faint or mumbled "Thank you"	Prolonged tongue protrusions
Questioning vocalization	Jaw wiggling, rotating, thrusting, etc.
Abrupt onset/offset of smile	Nose wrinkle
Rapid glances at experimenter when neither is speaking	Rapid, nervous blinking
	Looking around room or at ceiling in a scanning fashion
	Face, nose touching or scratching
	Finger(s) in mouth, on lips, or nail biting
	Touches/scratches hair, scalp, ears, etc.
	Touches/scratches upper or lower torso
	Hides hands (in pockets, sleeves, sits on)
	Rubs eyes
	Finger rubbing or scratching
	Holds or folds hands or arms together

<u>Tension Behaviors</u> (continued)

Hand wringing, twisting

Covers face (or part of face)

  with hand(s)

Stands up during session

Shrugs

Twisting, shifting, sinking

  in chair

Pumps up/down in seat

Stretching

Author Note

This research was supported by a National Institute of Child Health and Human Development traineeship awarded to the Department of Psychology, University of Florida (National Research Service Award 1T32HD07318).

I wish to thank Scott A. Miller and Patricia H. Miller for their valuable comments on earlier versions of this article and James Algina for statistical consultation. I am also grateful to Janice Wachtel, Yonette Hassell, Mindy Yoskin, and Barbara Quinones for assisting with data collection and to the children of Stephen Foster elementary school for their participation in this project.

Correspondence concerning this article should be addressed to Teresa L. Davis, who is now at Department of Psychology, Box 87, Middle Tennessee State University, Murfreesboro, Tennessee 37132.

Table 1

Mean Numbers of Positive and Negative Behaviors Expressed as a

Function of Task, Gender, and Valence

	Sex of child			
Condition	Male		Female	
	$\underline{M}$	$\underline{SD}$	$\underline{M}$	$\underline{SD}$
Positive behaviors				
Gift				
Attractive	2.06	1.57	1.84	1.72
Disappointing	1.23	1.27	1.41	1.50
Game				
Attractive prize	2.10	1.26	2.53	1.34
Disappointing prize	1.93	1.52	2.21	1.54
Negative behaviors				
Gift				
Attractive	1.10	0.71	1.06	1.07
Disappointing	2.23	1.47	1.53	0.95
Game				
Attractive prize	.73	0.83	.50	0.67
Disappointing prize	1.06	1.11	.50	0.84

Table 2

Mean Numbers of Social Monitoring and Tension Behaviors

Expressed as a Function of Task, Valence, Grade, and Gender

| | Grade 1 | | | | Grade 3 | | | |
| | Male | | Female | | Male | | Female | |
Task	M	SD	M	SD	M	SD	M	SD
Social monitoring behaviors								
Gift								
Attractive	1.07	0.80	1.62	0.96	1.47	0.74	1.75	1.24
Disappointing	1.13	0.83	1.37	0.89	1.40	1.35	1.81	1.11
Game								
Attractive prize	1.86	0.63	2.31	0.70	1.73	0.96	2.12	1.02
Disappointing prize	1.46	0.92	2.37	0.89	2.20	0.68	2.38	0.62
Tension behaviors								
Gift								
Attractive	2.06	1.79	3.12	1.75	2.13	1.24	2.69	1.30
Disappointing	2.80	1.47	3.81	2.34	2.53	0.99	3.31	2.30
Game								
Attractive prize	2.40	1.68	4.25	2.05	2.80	2.07	2.37	1.45
Disappointing prize	2.47	1.96	4.06	1.65	2.20	1.21	3.06	1.65

Figure Caption

Figure 1. Mean number of negative behaviors as a function of

gender, task, and valence.

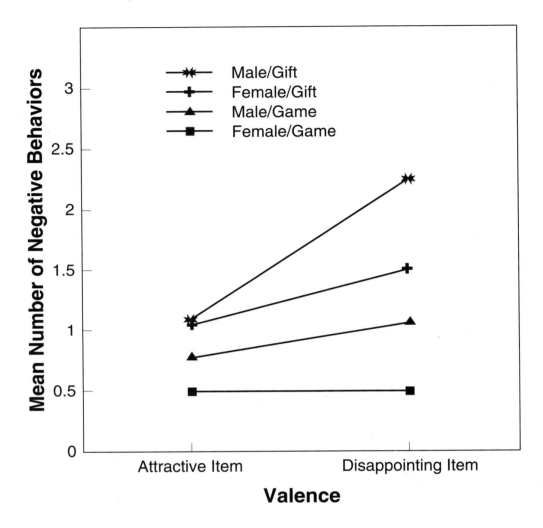

GLOSSARY

***AB* design** A design in which a baseline condition (*A*) is measured first, followed by measurements during the experimental intervention (*B*); there is no return to the baseline condition.

***ABA* design** A design in which a baseline condition (*A*) is measured first, followed by measurements during the experimental condition (*B*), followed by a return to the baseline condition (*A*) to verify that the change in behavior is linked to the experimental condition; also called a reversal design.

***ABAB* design** A design in which a baseline condition (*A*) is measured first, followed by measurements during a treatment condition (*B*), followed by a return to the baseline condition (*A*) to verify that the change in behavior is linked to the experimental condition, followed by a return to the treatment condition (*B*).

***ABABA* design** A small *N* design in which a baseline condition (*A*) is measured first, followed by measurements during a treatment condition (*B*), followed by a return to the baseline measurement condition (*A*), followed by a return to the treatment condition (*B*) and a final baseline measurement condition (*A*) to verify that the change in behavior is linked to the experimental condition.

Abstract A brief summary (approximately 120 words or 960 characters) of the report, which precedes the four major sections.

Across-subjects counterbalancing A technique for controlling progressive error that pools all subjects' data together to equalize the effects of progressive error for each condition.

Aggregation The grouping together and averaging of data gathered in various ways; including aggregation over subjects, over stimuli and/or situations, over trials and/or occasions, and over measures.

Alternative hypothesis (H_1) A statement that the data came from different populations; the research hypothesis, which cannot be tested directly.

Analysis of variance (ANOVA) The statistical procedure used to evaluate differences among two or more treatment means by breaking the variability in the data into components that reflect the influence of error and error plus treatment effects.

Analytic statement A statement that is always true.

Animal rights The concept that all sensate species who feel pain are of equal value and have rights.

Animal welfare The humane care and treatment of animals.

Antecedent conditions All circumstances that occur or exist before the event or behavior to be explained; also called *antecedents*.

A priori comparison Statistical test between specific treatment groups that was anticipated, or planned, before the experiment was conducted; also called *planned comparison*.

At minimal risk The subject's odds of being harmed are not increased by the research.

At risk The likelihood of a subject's being harmed in some way because of the nature of the research.

Balancing A technique used to control the impact of extraneous variables by distributing their effects equally across treatment conditions.

Baseline A measure of behavior as it normally occurs without the experimental manipulation; a control condition used to assess the impact of the experimental condition.

Between-groups variability The degree to which the scores of *different* treatment groups differ from one another (that is, how much subjects vary under different levels of the independent variable); a measure of variability produced by treatment effects and error.

Between-subjects design A design in which different subjects take part in each condition of the experiment.

Block randomization A process of randomization that first creates treatment blocks containing one random order of the conditions in the experiment; subjects are then assigned to fill each successive treatment block.

Carryover effect The persistence of the effect of a treatment condition after the condition ends.

Case study The descriptive record of an individual's experiences and/or behaviors kept by an outside observer.

Causal modeling Creating and testing models that may suggest cause and effect relationships among behaviors.

Cause and effect relationship The relation between a particular behavior and a set of antecedents that always precedes it—whereas other antecedents do not—so that the set is inferred to *cause* the behavior.

Chi square (χ^2) A nonparametric, inferential statistic that tests whether the frequencies of responses in our sample represent certain frequencies in the population; used with nominal data.

Cluster sampling A form of probability sampling in which a researcher samples entire *clusters*, or naturally occurring groups, that exist within the population.

Commonsense psychology Everyday, nonscientific collection of psychological data used to understand the social world and guide our behavior.

Complete counterbalancing A technique for controlling progressive error that uses all possible sequences that can be formed out of the treatment conditions and uses each sequence the same number of times.

Confounding An error that occurs when the value of an extraneous variable changes systematically along with the independent variable in an experiment; an alternative explanation for the findings.

Constancy of conditions A control procedure used to avoid confounding; keeping all aspects of the treatment conditions identical except for the independent variable that is being manipulated.

Construct validity The degree to which an operational definition accurately represents the construct it is intended to manipulate or measure.

Content analysis A system for quantifying responses to open questions by categorizing them according to objective rules or guidelines.

Content validity The degree to which the content of a measure reflects the content of what is measured.

Context variable Extraneous variable stemming from procedures created by the environment, or context, of the research setting.

Continuous dimension The concept that traits, attitudes, and preferences can be viewed as continuous dimensions, and each individual may fall at any point along each dimension; for example, sociability can be viewed as a continuous dimension ranging from very unsociable to very sociable.

Contradictory statement A statement that is always false.

Control condition The determination of the value of a dependent variable without the presence of the independent variable.

Control group The subjects in a control condition.

Convenience sampling A convenience sample is obtained by using any groups who happen to be convenient; considered a weak form of sampling because the researcher exercises no control over the representativeness of the sample (also called *accidental sampling*).

Correlation The degree of relationship between two traits, behaviors, or events, represented by *r*.

Correlational study A study designed to determine the correlation between two traits, behaviors, or events.

Counterbalancing A technique for controlling order effects by distributing progressive error across the different treatment conditions of the experiment; may also control carryover effects.

Cover story A plausible but false explanation of the procedures in an experiment

told to disguise the actual research hypothesis so that subjects will not guess what it is.

Critical region Portion(s) of the distribution of a test statistic extreme enough to satisfy the researcher's criterion for rejecting the null hypothesis—for instance, the most extreme 5% of a distribution where $p < .05$ is the chosen significance level.

Critical value The minimum value of the test statistic necessary to reject the null hypothesis at the chosen significance level.

Cross-lagged panel design A method in which the same set of behaviors or characteristics are measured at two separate points in time (often years apart); six different correlations are computed, and the pattern of correlations is used to infer the causal direction.

Cross-sectional study A method in which different groups of subjects who are at different stages are measured at a single point in time; a method that looks for time-related changes.

Data Facts and figures gathered from observations in research. (*Data* is the plural form of the Latin word *datum*.)

Debriefing The principle of full disclosure at the end of an experiment; that is, explaining to the subject the nature and purpose of the study.

Deductive model The process of reasoning from general principles to specific instances; most useful for testing the principles of a theory.

Degrees of freedom (df) The number of members of a set of data that can vary or change value without changing the value of a known statistic for those data.

Demand characteristics The aspects of the experimental situation itself that demand or elicit particular behaviors; may lead to distorted data by compelling subjects to produce responses that conform to what subjects believe is expected of them in the experiment.

Dependent variable (DV) The specific behavior that a researcher tries to explain in an experiment; the variable that is measured.

Descriptive method Research method in which characteristics of situations can be identified, and relationships between behaviors can be documented through carefully constructed observations.

Descriptive statistics The standard procedures used to summarize and describe data quickly and clearly; also summary statistics reported for an experiment, including mean, range, and standard deviation.

Descriptive title The title of the report, which describes what the report is about; typically includes the variables tested and the relationship between them.

Deviant case analysis An extension of the evaluative case study in which deviant individuals are compared with those who are not to isolate the significant variations between them.

Directional hypothesis A statement that predicts the exact pattern of results that will be observed, such as which treatment group will perform best.

Discrete trials design A design that relies on presenting and averaging across many, many experimental trials; repeated applications result in a reliable picture of the effects of the independent variable.

Discussion Concluding section of the research report, used to integrate the experimental findings into the existing body of knowledge; showing how the current research advances knowledge, increases generalizability of known effects, or contradicts past findings.

Discussion section The final major section of the report; evaluates and interprets results and discusses implications of the research.

Double-blind experiment An experiment in which neither the subjects nor the experimenter knows which treatment the subjects are in; used to control experimenter bias.

Effect size A statistical estimate of the size or magnitude of the treatment effect(s); one example of an effect size statistic is η^2 (eta squared) which is used to estimate effect sizes from ANOVA values.

Elimination A technique to control extraneous variables by removing them from an experiment.

Environmental variable Aspects of the physical environment that the experimenter can bring under direct control as an independent variable.

Error The variability within and between treatment groups that is not produced by changes in the independent variables; variability produced by individual differences, experimental error, and other extraneous variables.

Experimental condition A treatment condition in which the researcher applies a particular value of an independent variable to subjects and then measures the dependent variable; in an experimental group–control group design, the group that receives some value of the independent variable.

Experimental design The general structure of an experiment (but not its specific content).

Experimental error Variation in subjects' scores produced by uncontrolled extraneous variables in the experimental procedure, experimenter bias, or other influences on subjects not related to effects of the independent variable.

Experimental group The subjects in an experimental condition.

Experimental hypothesis A statement that predicts the effects of specified antecedent conditions on a measured behavior.

Experimental operational definition The explanation of the meaning of independent variables; defines *exactly* what was done to create the various treatment conditions of the experiment.

Experimentation The process undertaken to discover something new or to demonstrate that events that have already occurred will occur again under a specified set of conditions; a principal tool of the scientific method.

Experimenter bias Any behavior of the experimenter that can create confounding in an experiment.

Explanatory method Research method that explains observed differences in behavior; the experimental method.

Ex post facto study A study in which a researcher systematically examines the effects of preexisting subject characteristics (often called subject variables) by forming treatment groups based on these naturally occurring differences between subjects.

External validity How well the findings of an experiment generalize or apply to people and settings that were not tested directly.

Extraneous variable A variable other than an independent or dependent variable; a variable that is not the main focus of an experiment and that may confound the results if not controlled.

F **ratio** A test statistic used in the analysis of variance; the ratio between the variability observed *between* treatment groups and the variability observed *within* treatment groups.

Face validity The degree to which a manipulation or measurement technique is self-evident.

Factor An independent variable in a factorial design.

Factorial design An experimental design in which more than one independent variable is manipulated.

Falsifiable statement A statement that is worded so that it is falsifiable, or disprovable.

Falsification To challenge an existing explanation or theory by testing a hypothesis that follows logically from it and demonstrating that this hypothesis is false.

Fatigue effects Changes in performance caused by fatigue, boredom, or irritation.

Field experiment An experiment conducted outside the laboratory used to increase external validity, verify earlier laboratory findings, and investigate problems that cannot be studied successfully in the laboratory.

Field study A nonexperimental research method used in the field or in a real-life setting, typically employing a variety of techniques including naturalistic observation and unobtrusive measures or survey tools, such as questionnaires and interviews.

Fraud The unethical practice of falsifying or fabricating data; plagiarism is also a form of fraud.

Fruitful statement A statement that leads to new studies.

Good thinking Organized and rational thought, characterized by open-mindedness and objectivity, and including application of the principle of parsimony; a principal tool of the scientific method.

Grand mean An average of all the treatment means.

Higher-order interaction An interaction effect involving more than two independent variables.

History threat A threat to internal validity in which an outside event or occurrence might have produced effects on the dependent variable.

Hypothesis The thesis, or main idea, of an experiment consisting of a statement that predicts the relationship between at least two variables.

Hypothetical construct Concepts used to explain unseen processes, such as hunger or learning; postulated to explain observable behavior.

Independent variable (IV) The variable (antecedent condition) that the experimenter intentionally manipulates.

Inductive model The process of reasoning from specific cases to more general principles to form a hypothesis.

Inferential statistics Statistics that can be used as indicators of what is going on in a population; also called *test statistics.*

Informed consent A subject's voluntary agreement to participate in a research project after the nature and purpose of the study have been explained.

Institutional review board (IRB) An institutional committee that reviews proposed research to safeguard the safety and rights of subjects.

Instrumentation threat A threat to internal validity produced by changes in the measuring instrument itself.

Interaction The effect of one independent variable changes across the levels of another independent variable; can only be detected in factorial designs.

Interitem reliability The degree to which different items measuring the same variable attain consistent results.

Internal validity The determination that the changes in behavior observed across treatment conditions in the experiment were actually caused by the independent variable.

Interrater reliability The degree of agreement among different observers or raters.

Interval scale The measurement of magnitude, or quantitative size, having equal intervals between values but no true zero point.

Introduction Beginning section of a research report that guides the reader toward your research hypothesis; includes a selective review of relevant, recent research.

Intuition The development of ideas from hunches; knowing directly without reasoning from objective data.

Large N design A design in which the behavior of groups of subjects is compared.

Latent content The "hidden meaning" behind a question.

Latin square counterbalancing A partial counterbalancing technique in which a matrix, or square, of sequences of treatment conditions is constructed to which subjects are assigned at random.

Laws General scientific principles that explain our universe and predict events.

Level of measurement The type of scale of measurement—either ratio, interval, ordinal, or nominal—used to measure a variable.

Levels of the independent variable The two or more values of the independent variable manipulated by the experimenter.

Longitudinal study A method in which the same group of subjects is followed and measured at different points in time; a method that looks for changes across time.

Main effect The action of a single independent variable in an experiment; the change in the dependent variable produced by the various levels of a single independent variable.

Manifest content The plain meaning of the words or questions that actually appear on the page.

Maturation threat A threat to internal validity produced by internal (physical or psychological) changes in subjects.

Mean An arithmetical average computed by dividing the sum of a group of scores by the total number of scores; a measure of central tendency.

Mean square (MS) An average squared deviation; a variance estimate used in analysis-of-variance procedures and found by dividing the sum of squares by the degrees of freedom.

Mean square between groups (MS$_B$) The variance (or average squared deviation) across different treatment groups produced by *error* and treatment effects; also the variance about the grand mean.

Mean square within groups (MS$_W$) The variance (or average squared deviation) within a single treatment group; produced by the combination of sources called *error*.

Measured operational definition The description of *exactly* how a variable in an experiment is measured.

Measurement The systematic estimation of the quantity, size, or quality of an observable event; a principal tool of the scientific method.

Measures of central tendency Summary statistics that describe what is typical of a distribution of scores.

Median The score that divides a distribution in half so that half the scores in the distribution fall above the median, half below; a measure of central tendency.

Method The section of a research report in which the subjects and experiment are described in enough detail that the experiment may be replicated by others; it is typically divided into subsections, such as Participants, Apparatus or Materials, and Procedures.

Methodology The scientific techniques used to collect and evaluate psychological data.

Method section The second major section of the report; explains in detail how the research was conducted and who the subjects were.

Mixed design A factorial design that combines within-subjects and between-subjects factors.

Mode The most frequently occurring score in a distribution; a measure of central tendency.

Multiple-baseline design A small *N* design in which a series of baselines and treatments are compared within the same person; once established, however, a treatment is not withdrawn.

Multiple correlation Statistical intercorrelations among three or more behaviors, represented by *R*.

Multiple-groups design A between-subjects design with one independent variable, in which there are more than two treatment conditions.

Multiple-independent-groups design The most commonly used multiple-group design in which the subjects are assigned to the different treatment conditions at random.

Multiple regression analysis A correlation-based technique (from multiple correlation) that uses a regression equation to predict the score on one behavior from scores on the other related behaviors.

Multivariate analysis of variance (MANOVA) The statistical procedure used to study the impact of independent variables on two or more dependent variables; an extension of analysis of variance.

Multivariate design Research design or statistical procedure used to evaluate the effects of many dependent variables in combination; including multiple correlation, factor analysis, and multivariate analysis of variance.

Naturalistic observation A descriptive, nonexperimental method of observing behaviors as they occur spontaneously in natural settings.

Nay-sayers People who are apt to disagree with a question regardless of its manifest content.

Negative correlation The relationship existing between two variables such that an increase in one is associated with a decrease in the other; also called an *inverse relationship*.

Nominal scale The simplest level of measurement; classifies items into two or more distinct categories on the basis of some common feature.

Nondirectional hypothesis A statement that predicts a difference between treatment groups without predicting the exact pattern of results.

Nonexperimental hypothesis A statement of predictions of how events, traits, or behavior might be related, but not a statement about cause and effect.

Nonprobability sampling Sampling procedures in which subjects are not chosen at random; two common examples are quota and convenience samples.

Normal curve The distribution of data in a symmetrical, bell-shaped curve.

Null hypothesis (H_0) A statement that the performance of treatment groups is so similar that the groups must belong to the same population; a way of saying that the experimental manipulation had no important effect.

Observation The systematic noting and recording of events; a principal tool of the scientific method.

One-tailed test A statistical procedure used when a directional prediction has been made; the critical region of the distribution of the test statistic (t, for instance) is measured in just one tail of the distribution.

One-way between-subjects analysis of variance Statistical procedure used to evaluate a between-subjects experiment with three or more levels of a single independent variable.

One-way repeated measures (ANOVA) Statistical procedure used to evaluate a within-subjects experiment with three or more levels of a single independent variable.

Operational definition The specification of the precise meaning of a variable within an experiment; defines a variable in terms of observable operations, procedures, and measurements.

Order effects Change in subjects' performance that occurs when a condition falls in different positions in a series of treatments.

Ordinal scale A measure of magnitude in which each value is measured in the form of ranks.

Page header A header made up of the first few words of your title; used to identify manuscript pages during the editorial process in case the pages get separated.

Parsimonious statement A statement that is simple and does not require many supporting assumptions.

Partial counterbalancing A technique for controlling progressive error by using some subset of the available sequences of treatment conditions.

Participant-observer study A special kind of field observation in which the researcher actually becomes part of the group being studied.

Path analysis An important correlation-based method in which subjects are measured on several related behaviors; the researcher creates (and tests) models of possible causal sequences using sophisticated correlational techniques.

Personality variables The personal characteristics that an experimenter or volunteer subject brings to the experimental setting.

Phenomenology A nonexperimental method of gathering data by attending to and describing one's own immediate experience.

Physical variables Aspects of the testing conditions that need to be controlled.

Pilot study A miniexperiment using only a few subjects to pretest selected levels of an independent variable before conducting the actual experiment.

Placebo effect The result of giving subjects a pill, injection, or other treatment that actually contains none of the independent variable but elicits a change in subjects' behavior regardless.

Placebo group In drug testing, a control condition in which subjects are treated exactly the same as subjects who are in the experimental group, except for the presence of the actual drug; the prototype of a good control group.

Plagiarism The representation of someone else's ideas, words, or written work as one's own; a serious breach of ethics that can result in legal action.

Population All people, animals, or objects that have at least one characteristic in common.

Position preference When in doubt about answers to multiple-choice questions, some people always select a response in a certain position, such as answer *b*.

Positive correlation The relationship between two measures such that an increase in the value of one is associated with an increase in the value of the other; also called a *direct relationship*.

Post hoc test Statistical test performed after the overall analysis indicates a significant difference; used to pinpoint which differences are significant.

Power The chance of detecting a genuine effect of the independent variable.

Practice effect Change in subjects' performance resulting from practice.

Precision matching Creating pairs whose subjects have identical scores on the matching variable.

Predictive validity The degree to which a measure, definition, or experiment yields information that allows prediction of actual behavior or performance.

Pretest/posttest design A research design used to assess whether the occurrence of an event alters behavior; scores from measurements made before and after the event (called the *pretest* and *posttest*) are compared.

Principle of parsimony An aspect of good thinking, stating that the simplest explanation is preferred until ruled out by conflicting evidence; also known as *Occam's razor.*

Probability sampling Selecting samples in such a way that the odds of any subject being selected for the study are known or can be calculated.

Progressive error Fatigue, practice, and other extraneous sequence effects producing changes in subjects' responses during within-subjects experiments.

Psychological journal A periodical that publishes individual research reports and integrative research reviews, which are up-to-date summaries of what is known about a specific topic.

Psychology experiment A controlled procedure in which at least two different treatment conditions are applied to subjects whose behaviors are then measured and compared to test a hypothesis about the effects of the treatments on behavior.

Quasi-experimental designs Nonexperimental designs that "almost seem like" experiments (as the prefix *quasi-* implies) but are not because subjects are not randomly assigned to treatment conditions.

Quota sampling Selecting samples through predetermined quotas that are intended to reflect the makeup of the population; they can reflect the proportions of important population subgroups, but the particular individuals are not selected at random.

Random assignment The technique of assigning subjects to treatments so that each subject has an equal chance of being assigned to each treatment condition.

Randomized counterbalancing The simplest partial counterbalancing procedure in which the experimenter randomly selects as many sequences of treatment conditions as there are subjects for the experiment.

Random number table A table of numbers generated by a computer so that every number has an equal chance of being selected for each position in the table.

Random selection An unbiased method for selecting subjects such that the outcome of the sampling procedure cannot be predicted ahead of time by any known law.

Range The difference between the largest and smallest scores in a set of data; a rough indication of the amount of variability in the data.

Range matching Creating pairs of subjects whose scores on the matching variable fall within a previously specified range of scores.

Rank-ordered matching Creating matched pairs by placing subjects in order of their scores on the matching variable; subjects with adjacent scores become pairs.

Ratio scale A measure of magnitude having equal intervals between values and having an absolute zero point.

Raw data Data recorded as an experiment is run; the responses of individual subjects.

Reactivity The tendency of subjects to alter their behavior or responses when they are aware of the presence of an observer.

References A list of books and articles cited in the research report; placed at the end of the report.

Regression analysis A correlation-based technique that uses a regression equation to estimate a score on one measured behavior from a score on another behavior.

Regression line The line of best fit; represents the equation that best describes the mathematical relationship between two variables measured in a correlational study.

Repeated-measures design A design in which subjects are measured more than once on the dependent variable; same as a within-subjects design.

Replication The process of repeating research procedures to verify that the outcome will be the same as before; a principal tool of the scientific method.

Representativeness The extent to which the sample responses we observe and measure reflect those we would obtain if we could sample the entire population.

Research report Written report of psychological research, which contains four major sections: Introduction, Method, Results, and Discussion.

Response set A tendency to answer questions based on their latent content with the goal of creating a certain impression of ourselves.

Response style Tendency for subjects to respond to questionnaire items in a specific way, regardless of the content.

Results section The third major section of the report; describes the findings and presents results of statistical tests and summary data.

Retrospective data Data collected in the present based on recollections of past events. Such data is apt to be inaccurate because of faulty memory, bias, mood, and situation.

Risk/benefit analysis A determination, made by an institutional review board, that any risks to the individual are outweighed by potential benefits or the importance of the knowledge to be gained.

Robust A term describing a statistical test that can be used without creating serious errors even though its assumptions (e.g., the population is normally distributed and has equal variances) are violated.

Rosenthal effect The phenomenon of experimenters treating subjects differently depending on what they expect from the subjects; also called the *Pygmalion effect*.

Running head A short version of the title, which will appear at the top of pages of the published report.

Sample of subjects A selected subset of the population of interest.

Sampling Deciding who or what the subjects will be and selecting them.

Scatterplot A graph of data from a correlational study, created by plotting pairs of scores from each subject; the value of one variable is plotted on the X (horizontal) axis and the other variable on the Y (vertical) axis.

Science The systematic gathering of data to provide descriptions of events taking place under specific conditions, enabling researchers to explain, predict, and control events.

Scientific method Steps scientists take to gather and verify information, answer questions, explain relationships, and communicate findings.

Scientific writing style A concise, impersonal, and unbiased form of writing used in research reports.

Selection interactions A family of threats to internal validity produced when a selection threat combines with one or more of the other threats to internal validity; when a selection threat is already present, other threats can affect some experimental groups but not others.

Selection threat A threat to internal validity that can occur when nonrandom procedures are used to assign subjects to conditions or when random assignment fails to balance out differences among subjects across the different conditions of the experiment.

Serendipity The knack of finding things that are not being sought.

Shorthand notation A system that uses numbers to describe the design of a factorial experiment.

Significance level The statistical criterion for deciding whether to reject the null hypothesis or not.

Simple random sampling The most basic form of probability sampling whereby a portion of the whole population is selected in an unbiased way.

Single-blind experiment An experiment in which subjects are not told which of the treatment conditions they are in; a procedure used to control demand characteristics.

Small N design A design in which just one or two subjects are used; typically, the experimenter collects baseline data during an initial control condition; applies the experimental treatment; then reinstates the original control condition to verify that changes observed in behavior were caused by the experimental intervention.

Social variables The qualities of the relationships between subjects and experimenters that may influence the results of an experiment.

Standard deviation The square root of the variance; measures the average deviation of scores about the mean, thus reflecting the amount of variability in the data.

Statistical-conclusion validity The degree to which conclusions about a treatment effect can be drawn from the statistical results obtained.

Statistical inference A statement made about a population and all its samples based on the samples observed.

Statistical regression threat A threat to internal validity that can occur when subjects are assigned to conditions on the basis of extreme scores on a test; upon retest, the scores of extreme scorers tend to regress toward the mean even without any treatment.

Statistical significance Meeting the set criterion for significance; the data do not support the null hypothesis, confirming a difference between the groups that occurred as a result of the experiment.

Statistics Quantitative measurements of samples; quantitative data.

Stratified random sampling A form of probability sample obtained by randomly sampling from people in each important population subgroup in the same proportions as they exist in the population.

Subject The scientific term for an individual who participates in research.

Subject-by-subject counterbalancing A technique for controlling progressive error for each individual subject by presenting all treatment conditions twice, first in one order, then in reverse order.

Subject mortality threat A threat to internal validity produced by differences in dropout rates across the conditions of the experiment.

Subject variable The characteristics of the subjects in an experiment or quasi-experiment that cannot be manipulated by the researcher; used to select subjects into groups.

Sum of squares (SS) The sum of the squared deviations from the group mean; an index of variability used in the analysis-of-variance procedures.

Sum of squares between groups (SS_B) The sum of the squared deviations of the group means from the grand mean.

Sum of squares within groups (SS_W) The sum of the squared deviations of subjects' scores from the group mean.

Summary data Descriptive statistics computed from the raw data of an experiment, including the measures of central tendency and variability.

Survey research A useful way of obtaining data about people's opinions, attitudes, preferences, and experiences that are hard to observe directly; data may be obtained using questionnaires or interviews.

Synthetic statement A statement that can be either true or false, a condition necessary to form an experimental hypothesis.

Systematic observation A system for recording observations; each observation is recorded using specific rules or guidelines, so observations are more objective.

_t_ test A statistic that relates differences between treatment means to the amount of variability expected between any two samples of data from the same population; used to analyze the results of a two-condition experiment with one independent variable and interval or ratio data.

_t_ test for independent groups A statistic that relates differences between treatment means to the amount of variability expected between any two samples of data from the same population; used to analyze the results of a two-group experiment with independent groups of subjects.

_t_ test for matched groups A statistic that relates differences between treatment means to the amount of variability expected between any two samples of data from the same population; used to analyze two-group experiments using matched-subjects or within-subjects designs. Sometimes referred to as a within-subjects _t_ test.

Testable Capable of being tested; typically used in reference to a hypothesis. Two requirements must be met in order to have a testable hypothesis: procedures for manipulating the setting must exist, and the predicted outcome must be observable.

Testable statement A statement that can be tested because the means exist for manipulating the antecedent conditions and for measuring the resulting behavior.

Testing threat A threat to internal validity produced by a previous administration of the same test or other measure.

Test statistics Statistics that can be used as indicators of what is going on in a population and can be used to evaluate results; also called *inferential statistics*.

Theory A set of general principles that attempts to explain and predict behavior.

Treatment A specific set of antecedent conditions created by the experimenter and presented to subjects to test its effect on behavior.

Two-experimental-groups design A design in which two groups of subjects are exposed to different levels of the independent variable.

Two-factor experiment The simplest factorial design, having two independent variables.

Two-group design The simplest experimental design, used when only two treatment conditions are needed.

Two-independent-groups design An experimental design in which subjects are placed in each of two treatment conditions through random assignment.

Two-matched-groups design An experimental design with two treatment conditions and with subjects who are matched on a subject variable thought to be highly related to the dependent variable.

Two-tailed test A statistical procedure used when a nondirectional prediction has been made; the critical region of the distribution of the test statistic (t, for instance) is divided over both tails of the distribution.

Type 1 error An error made by rejecting the null hypothesis even though it is really true; stating that an effect exists when it really does not.

Type 2 error An error made by retaining the null hypothesis even though it is really false; failing to detect a treatment effect.

Unobtrusive measure A procedure for assessing subjects' behaviors without their knowledge; used to obtain more objective data.

Variability Fluctuation in data; can be defined numerically as the range, variance, or standard deviation.

Variance The average squared deviation of scores from their mean; a more precise measure of variability than the range.

Willingness to answer People differ in their style of responding to questions they are unsure about; some people will leave these questions blank, whereas others will take a guess.

Within-groups variability The degree to which the scores of subjects in the *same* treatment group differ from one another (that is, how much subjects vary from others in the group); an index of the degree of fluctuation among scores that is attributable to error.

Within-subjects design A design in which each subject takes part in more than one condition of the experiment.

Yea-sayers People who are apt to agree with a question regardless of its manifest content.

REFERENCES

American Association for Laboratory Animal Science (1984). Policy statement on bio-medical research (news release, October 26).

American Psychological Association (1992). Ethical principles of psychologists and code of conduct. *American Psychologist, 47,* 1597–1611.

American Psychological Association (1994). *Publication manual of the American Psychological Association* (4th ed.). Washington, DC: Author.

Anastasi, A. (1958). *Differential psychology* (3rd ed.). New York: Macmillan.

Barber, T. X. (1976). *Pitfalls in human research.* New York: Pergamon Press.

Baron, R. A., Russell, G. W., & Arms, R. L. (1985). Negative ions and behavior: Impact on mood, memory, and aggression among Type A and Type B persons. *Journal of Personality and Social Psychology, 48,* 746–754.

Baumeister, R. F., & Steinhilber, A. (1984). Paradoxical effects of supportive audiences on performance under pressure: The home field disadvantage in sports championships. *Journal of Personality and Social Psychology, 47(1),* 85–93.

Bechtol, B. E., & Williams, J. R. (1977). California litter. *Natural History, 86(6),* 62–65.

Boring, E. G. (1950). *A history of experimental psychology* (2nd ed.). New York: Appleton-Century-Crofts.

Bower, G. H. (1972). Mental imagery and associative learning. In L. W. Gregg (Ed.), *Cognition in learning and memory.* New York: Wiley.

Bower, G. H. (1981). Mood and memory. *American Psychologist, 36(2),* 129–148.

Bowman, P. J. (1992). Coping with provider role strain: Adaptive cultural resources among Black husband-fathers. In A. Burlew, W. Banks, H. McAdoo, & D. Azibo (Eds.), *African American psychology: Theory, research, and practice* (pp. 135–154). Newbury Park, CA: Sage Publications.

Brady, J. V. (1958). Ulcers in "executive" monkeys. *Scientific American, 199(4),* 95–100.

Bramel, D. (1963). Selection of a target for defensive projection. *Journal of Abnormal and Social Psychology, 66,* 318–324.

Breuer, & Freud, S. (1957). *Studies in hysteria.* New York: Basic Books.

Broadhurst, P. L. (1959). The interaction of task difficulty and motivation: The Yerkes-Dodson Law revived. *Acta Psychologica, 16,* 321–328.

Burt, C. (1966). The genetic determination of differences in intelligence: A study of monozygotic twins reared together and apart. *British Journal of Psychology, 57,* 137–153.

Burt, C. (1972). Inheritance of general intelligence, *American Psychologist, 27,* 174–190.

Byrne, G. (1988). Bruening pleads guilty. *Science, 242,* 27–28.

Campbell, D. T. (1957). Factors relevant to the validity of experiments in social settings. *Psychological Bulletin, 54,* 297–312.

Campbell, D. T., & Stanley, J. T. (1966). *Experimental and quasi-experimental designs for research.* Chicago: Rand McNally.

Campbell, D., Sanderson, R. E., & Laverty, S. C. (1964). Characteristics of a conditioned response in human subjects during extinction trials following a single traumatic conditioning trial. *Journal of Abnormal and Social Psychology, 68,* 627–639.

Carter, D. B., & Levy, G. D. (1988). Cognitive aspects of early sex role development: The influence of gender schemas on preschoolers' memories and preferences for sex-typed toys and activities. *Child Development, 59,* 786–792.

Cattell, R. B. (1946). *Description and measurement of personality.* New York: World Book.

Christensen, L. (1988). Deception in psychological research: When is its use justified? *Personality and Social Psychology Bulletin, 14,* 664–675.

Churchill, W. (1930). *My early life.* New York: Scribners.

Cleckley, J. (1976). *The mask of sanity* (5th ed.). St. Louis, MO: C. V. Mosby.

Cohen, J. (1988). *Statistical power analysis for the behavioral sciences.* Hillsdale, NJ: Lawrence Erlbaum Associates.

Coile, D. C., & Miller, N. E. (1984). How radical animal activists try to mislead humane people. *American Psychologist, 39,* 700–701.

Conway, J. C., & Rubin, A. M. (1991). Psychological predictors of television viewing motivation. *Communication Research, 18(4),* 443–463.

Cook, T. D., & Campbell, D. T. (1979). *Quasi-experimentation: Design and analysis issues for field settings.* Boston: Houghton Mifflin.

Cooley, W. W., & Lohnes, P. R. (1971). *Multivariate data analysis.* New York: Wiley.

Crano, W. D., & Brewer, M. B. (1986). *Principles and methods of social research.* Newton, MA: Allyn & Bacon.

Cronbach, L. J. (1950). Further evidence on response sets and test design. *Educational and Psychological Measurement, 10,* 3–31.

Crowne, D. P., & Marlowe, D. (1964). *The approval motive.* New York: Wiley.

Cunningham, M. R. (1989). Reactions to heterosexual opening gambits: Female selectivity and male responsiveness. *Personality and Social Psychology Bulletin, 15(1),* 27–41.

Davis, T. L. (1995). Gender differences in masking negative emotions: Ability or motivation? *Developmental Psychology, 31(4),* 660–667.

Davison, G. C., & Neale, J. M. (1986). *Abnormal psychology: An experimental clinical approach.* New York: Wiley.

Diagnostic and statistical manual of mental disorders, fourth edition (1994). Washington, DC: American Psychiatric Association.

Dillman, D. A. (1978). *Mail and telephone surveys: The total design method.* New York: Wiley.

Donnerstein, E., & Berkowitz, L. (1981). Victim reactions in aggressive erotic films as a factor in violence against women. *Journal of Personality and Social Psychology, 41,* 710–724.

Donnerstein, E., Linz, D., & Penrod, S. (1987). *The question of pornography: Research findings and policy implications.* New York: Free Press.

Doob, A. N., Carlsmith, J. M., Freedman, J. L., Landauer, T. K., & Tom, S. (1969). Effect of initial selling price on subsequent sales. *Journal of Personality and Social Psychology, 11,* 345–350.

Doob, A. N., & Gross, A. N. (1968). Status of frustrator as an inhibitor of horn-honking responses. *Journal of Social Psychology, 76(2),* 213–218.

Dunning, D., Griffin, D. W., Milojkovic, J., & Ross, L. (1990). The overconfidence effect in social prediction. *Journal of Personality and Social Psychology, 58,* 568–581.

Ekman, P., Friesen, W., & Ancoli, S. (1980). Facial signs of emotional experience. *Journal of Personality and Social Psychology, 39(6),* 1125–1134.

Elmes, D. G., Kantowitz, B. H., & Roediger, H. L. (1995). *Research methods in psychology.* St. Paul, MN: West.

Epstein, S. (1980). The stability of behavior. II. Implications for psychological research. *American Psychologist, 35(9),* 790–806.

Eron, L. D., Huesmann, L. R., Lefkowitz, M. M., and Walder, L. O. (1972). Does television violence cause aggression? *American Psychologist, 27,* 253–263.

Evans, E. P. (1898). *Evolutional ethics and animal psychology.* New York: D. Appleton.

Fantz, R. L. (1963). Pattern vision in newborn infants. *Science, 140,* 296–297.

Favreau, O. E. (1977). Psychology in action: Disillusioned. *American Psychologist, 32(7),* 568–571.

Fazio, R. H. (1990). Multiple processes by which attitudes guide behavior: The mode model as an integrative framework. In M. P. Zanna (Ed.), *Advances in experimental social psychology* (Vol. 23, pp. 75–109). New York: Academic Press.

Ferster, C. B., & Skinner, B. F. (1957). *Schedules of reinforcement.* New York: Appleton-Century-Crofts.

Fisher, R. A. (1935). *The design of experiments.* London: Oliver & Boyd.

Franklin, K. M., Janoff-Bulman, R., & Roberts, J. E. (1990). Long-term impact of parental divorce on optimism and trust: Changes in general assumptions or narrow beliefs? *Journal of Personality and Social Psychology, 59(4),* 743–755.

Freud, S. (1933). Analysis of a phobia in a five-year-old boy. In *Collected Papers* (Vol. 3). London: Hogarth Press.

Fridlund, A. J. (1989). *The sociality of solitary smiling: Potentiation by an implicit audience.* Paper presented at the 29th Annual Meeting of the Society for Psychophysiological Research, New Orleans.

Fridlund, A. J., Ekman, P., & Oster, H. (1987). Facial expressions of emotion. In A. W. Siegman & S. Feldstein (Eds.), *Nonverbal behavior and communication* (2nd Ed.), pp. 143–224.

Gastil, J. (1990). Generic pronouns and sexist language: The oxymoronic character of masculine generics. *Sex Roles, 23(11/12),* 629–643.

Gibbons, E. (1970). *Stalking the wild asparagus.* New York: David McKay.

Green, B. F. (1992). Exposé or smear? The Burt affair. *Psychological Science, 3,* 328–331.

Greenwald, A., Spangenbert, E., Pratkanis, A., and Eskenazi, J. (1991). Double-blind tests of subliminal self-help audiotapes. *Psychological Science, 2(2),* 119–122.

Greeson, L. E., & Williams, R. A. (1986). Social implications of music videos for youth. *Youth and Society, 18,* 177–189.

Haas, A., & Sherman, M. (1982). Reported topics of conversation among same-sex adults. *Communication Quarterly, 30(4),* 332–342.

Hall, E. T. (1966). *Hidden dimensions.* Garden City, NY: Doubleday.

Hall, R. V., Alley, S. J., & Cox, L. (1971). *Managing behavior. 3: Applications in school and home.* Austin, TX: PRO-ED, Inc.

Hamilton, D. L., & Rose, T. L. (1980). Illusory correlations and the maintenance of stereotypic beliefs. *Journal of Personality and Social Psychology, 39(5),* 832–845.

Hanson, D. J. (1980). Relationship between methods and findings in attitude-behavior research. *Psychology, 17,* 11–13.

Harris, M. J., & Rosenthal, R. (1985). Mediation of interpersonal expectancy effects: 31 meta-analyses. *Psychological Bulletin, 97,* 363–386.

Heider, F. (1958). *The psychology of interpersonal relations.* New York: John Wiley & Sons.

Herzog, H. A. (1991). Conflicts of interests: Kittens and boa constrictors, pets and research. *American Psychologist, 46,* 246–248.

Hess, E. (1975). Role of pupil size in communication. *Scientific American, 233(5),* 110ff.

Holloway, S. M., & Hornstein, H. A. (1976, July). How good news makes us good. *Psychology Today,* pp. 76ff.

Howes, D. (1966). A word count of spoken English. *Journal of Verbal Learning and Verbal Behavior, 5,* 572–604.

Huff, D. (1954). *How to lie with statistics.* New York: Norton.

Hurlburt, R. T. (1994). *Comprehending behavioral statistics.* Pacific Grove, CA: Brooks/Cole.

Irwin, O. C., & Weiss, L. A. (1934). Differential variations in the activity and crying of newborn infants under different intensities of light: A comparison of observational with polygraph findings. *University of Iowa Studies in Child Welfare, 9,* 139–147.

Isen, A. (1987). Positive affect, cognitive processes, and social behavior. In L. Berkowitz (Ed.), *Advances in experimental social psychology* (Vol. 20, pp. 203–253). New York: Academic Press.

Ivry, R. B., & Lebby, P. C. (1993). Hemispheric differences in auditory perception are similar to those found in visual perception. *Psychological Science, 4(1),* 41–45.

Jacobson, E. (1971). *Depression.* New York: International Universities Press.

James, W. (1950). *Principles of psychology.* New York: Dover. (Original work published 1890.)

Jenkins, C. D., Zyzanski, S. J. & Rosenman, R. H. (1979). *Jenkins Activity Survey.* New York: Psychological Corporation.

Johnson, D. (1990). Animal rights and human lives: Time for scientists to right the balance. *Psychological Science, 1(4),* 213–214.

Jones, M. C. (1924). A laboratory study of fear: The case of Peter. *Pedagogical Seminary, 31,* 308–315.

Jones, S. S., Collins, K., & Hong, H-W. (1991). An audience effect on smile production in 10-month-old infants. *Psychological Science, 2(1),* 45–49.

Judd, C., Smith, E., & Kidder, L. (1991). *Research in social relations.* Fort Worth, TX: Holt, Rinehart, & Winston, Inc.

Judd, D. B., & Kelly, K. L. (1965). The ISCC-NBS method of designating colors and a dictionary of color names. *U.S. National Bureau of Standards Circular, 553* (2nd ed.).

Kazdin, A. E. (1992). *Research design in clinical psychology* (2nd ed.). Needham Heights, MA: Allyn & Bacon.

Keehn, J. D. (1977). In defence of experiments with animals. *Bulletin of the British Psychological Society, 30,* 404–405.

Kelley, H. H. (1950). The warm-cold variable in the first impressions of persons. *Journal of Personality, 18,* 431–439.

Kelley, H. H. (1971). *Attribution in social interaction.* Morristown, NJ: General Learning Press.

Kelly, J. A., St. Lawrence, J. S., Hood, H. V., & Brashfield, T. L. (1989). Behavioral intervention to reduce AIDS risk activities. *Journal of Consulting and Clinical Psychology, 50,* 60–67.

Keppel, G. (1982). *Design and analysis: A researcher's handbook* (2nd ed.). Englewood Cliffs, NJ: Prentice-Hall.

Kerlinger, F. N. (1973). *Foundations of behavioral research* (2nd ed.). New York: Holt, Rinehart & Winston, Inc.

Kolb, L. C. (1973). *Modern clinical psychiatry* (8th ed.). Philadelphia: Saunders.

Kunda, Z., & Nisbett, R. E. (1986). The psychometrics of everyday life. *Cognitive Psychology, 18,* 195–224.

Lassen, C. L. (1973). Effect of proximity on anxiety and communication in the initial psychiatric interview. *Journal of Abnormal Psychology, 81,* 226–232.

Latané, B., & Darley, J. M. (1970). *The unresponsive bystander: Why doesn't he help?* New York: Appleton-Century-Crofts.

Leavitt, P. (1974). *Drugs and behavior.* Philadelphia: Saunders.

Lehman, R. S. (1991). *Statistics and research design in the behavioral sciences.* Belmont, CA: Wadsworth.

Lewis, M. (1978). A new response to stimuli. In *Readings in psychology 78/79, Annual Editions.* Guilford, CT: Dushkin. (Original work published 1977.)

Likert, R. (1932). A technique for the measurement of attitudes. *Archives of Psychology,* No. 140.

Lonner, W. J. (1990). An overview of cross-cultural testing and assessment. In R. W. Brislin (Ed.), *Applied cross-cultural psychology* (pp. 56–76). Newbury Park, CA: Sage Publications.

Lutey, C. L. (1977). *Individual intelligence testing: A manual and sourcebook.* Greeley, CO: Carol L. Lutey Publishing.

Mann, L. (1977). The effect of stimulus queues on queue-joining behavior. *Journal of Personality and Social Psychology, 35(6),* 437–442.

Marsh, H. W., & Parker, J. W. (1984). Determinants of student self-concept: Is it better to be a relatively large fish in a small pond even if you don't learn to swim as well? *Journal of Personality and Social Psychology, 47(1),* 213–231.

Marston, A. R., London, P., Cooper, L., & Cohen, N. (1977). In vivo observation of the eating behavior of obese and nonobese subjects. *Journal of Consulting and Clinical Psychology, 45,* 335–336.

McBeath, M. K., Morikawa, K., & Kaiser, M. K. (1992). Perceptual bias for forward-facing motion. *Psychological Science, 3(6),* 362–367.

McGuigan, F. J. The experimenter: A neglected stimulus object. In J. Jung (Ed.), *The experimenter's dilemma* (pp. 182–195). New York: Harper & Row.

McMinn, M. R., Williams, P. E., & McMinn, L. C. (1994). Assessing recognition of sexist language: Development and use of the Gender-Specific Language Scale. *Sex Roles, 31(11/12),* 741–755.

McNemar, Q. (1946). Opinion-attitude methodology. *Psychological Bulletin, 43,* 289–374.

Mednick, S. A. (1969). A longitudinal study of children with a high risk for schizophrenia. In M. Zax & G. Stricker (Eds.), *The study of abnormal behavior.* London: Macmillan.

Mednick, S. A., Schulsinger, F., & Venables, P. H. (1981). The Mauritius project. In S. A. Mednick, A. Baert, & B. P. Bachmann (Eds.), *Prospective longitudinal research* (pp. 314–316). Oxford: Oxford University Press.

Mehrabian, A., & Piercy, M. (1993a). Differences in positive-negative connotations of nicknames and given names. *Journal of Social Psychology, 133(5).*

Mehrabian, A., & Piercy, M. (1993b). Affective and personality characteristics inferred from length of first names. *Personality and Social Psychology Bulletin, 19(6),* 755–758.

Miller, D. (1977). Roles of naturalistic observation in comparative psychology. *American Psychologist, 32(3)*, 211–219.

Miller, D. L., & Kelley, M. L. (1994). The use of goal setting and contingency contracting for improving children's homework performance. *Journal of Applied Behavior Analysis, 27*, 73–84.

Miller, H. B., & Williams, W. H. (1983). *Ethics and animals.* Clifton, NJ: Humana Press.

Mori, D., Chaiken, S., & Pliner, P. (1987). "Eating lightly" and the self-presentation of femininity. *Journal of Personality and Social Psychology, 53*, 693–702.

Myer, J. L., & Well, A. D. (1991). *Research design and statistical analyses.* New York: HarperCollins.

National Geographic Atlas of the World, 6th Edition. (1990). Washington, DC: National Geographic Society.

Neidenthal, P. M. , & Cantor, N. (1986). Affective responses as guides to category-based inferences. *Motivation and Emotion, 10*, 217–232.

Niedenthal, P. M., & Setterlund, M. B. (1994). Emotion congruence in perception. *Personality and Social Psychology Bulletin, 20(4)*, 401–411.

Nisbett, R. E., & Wilson, T. E. (1977). Telling more than we can know: Verbal reports on mental processes. *Psychological Review, 84*, 231–259.

Orne, M. T. (1969). Demand characteristics and the concept of quasicontrols. In R. Rosenthal & R. L. Rosnow (Eds.), *Artifact in behavioral research.* New York: Academic Press.

Orne, M. T. (1972). On the social psychology of the psychological experiment: With particular reference to demand characteristics and their implications. In A. G. Miller (Ed.), *The Social Psychology of Psychological Research* (pp. 233–246). New York: The Free Press.

Orne, M. T., & Scheibe, K. E. (1964). The contribution of nondeprivation factors in the production of sensory deprivation effects: The psychology of the "panic button." *Journal of Abnormal and Social Psychology, 68*, 3–12.

Osgood, C. E., Suci, D. J., & Tannenbaum, P. H. (1957). *The measurement of meaning.* Urbana, IL: University of Illinois Press.

Partington, J. R. (1964). *A history of chemistry: Vol. IV.* London: Macmillan.

Pavlov, I. (1927). *Conditioned reflexes* (G. V. Anrep, Trans.). London: Oxford University Press.

Pedalino, E., & Gamboa, V. (1974). Behavior modification and absenteeism: Intervention in one industrial setting. *Journal of Applied Psychology, 59*, 694–698.

Pedersen, N. L., Plomin, R., Nesselroade, J. R., & McClearn, G. E. (1992). A quantitative genetic analysis of cognitive abilities during the second half of the life span. *Psychological Science, 3(6)*, 346–353.

Piaget, J. (1954). *The construction of reality in the child.* New York: Basic Books.

Pliner, P., & Chaiken, S. (1990). Eating, social motives, and self-presentation in women and men. *Journal of Experimental Social Psychology, 26(3)*, 240–254.

Plous, S. (1991). An attitude survey of animal rights activists. *Psychological Science, 2(3)*, 194–196.

Pogliano, C. (1991). Between form and function: A new science of man. In P. Corsi (Ed.), *The enchanted loom: Chapters in the history of neuroscience* (pp.144–157). New York: Oxford University Press.

Popper, K. R. (1963). Science: Conjectures and refutations. In G. Radnitzky & W. W. Bartley, III, (Eds.), *Evolutionary epistemology, rationality, and the sociology of knowledge* (pp. 139–157). La Salle, IL: Open Court.

Pritchard, R. D., Dunnette, M. D., & Jorgenson, D. O. (1972). Effects of perceptions of equity and inequity on worker performance and satisfaction. *Journal of Applied Psychology, 56*, 75–94.

Raudenbush, S. W. (1984). Magnitude of teacher expectancy effects on pupil IQ as a function of the credibility of expectancy induction: A synthesis of findings from 18 experiments. *Journal of Educational Psychology, 76(1),* 85–97.

Regan, T. (1983). *The case for animal rights.* Berkeley, CA: University of California Press.

Reichmann, W. J. (1961). *Use and abuse of statistics.* London: Methuen.

Ritchey, G. H. (1982). Pictorial detail and recall in adults and children. *Journal of Experimental Psycholoy: Learning, Memory, and Cognition, 8(2),* 139–141.

Ritchey, G. H., & Armstrong, E. L. (1982). *Elaboration, distinctiveness, and recognition time in free recall.* Paper presented at the meeting of the Psychonomic Society, Minneapolis, MN.

Robinson, P. W. (1976). *Fundamentals of experimental psychology.* Englewood Cliffs, NJ: Prentice-Hall.

Rorer, L. G. (1965). The great response-style myth. *Psychological Bulletin, 63,* 129–156.

Rosenthal, R. (1969). Interpersonal expectations: Effects of the experimenter's hypothesis. In R. Rosenthal & R. L. Rosnow (Eds.), *Artifact in behavioral research* (pp. 182–277). New York: Academic Press.

Rosenthal, R. (1973, September). The Pygmalion effect lives. *Psychology Today,* pp. 56–63.

Rosenthal, R. (1976). *Experimenter effects in behavioral research* (2nd ed.). New York: Halsted.

Rosenthal, R. (1978). How often are our numbers wrong? *American Psychologist, 33(11),* 1005–1008.

Rosenthal, R. (1994). Science and ethics in conducting, analyzing, and reporting psychological research. *Psychological Science, 5(3),* 127–134.

Rosenthal, R., & Fode, K. L. (1963). The effect of experimenter bias on the performance of the albino rat. *Behavioral Science, 8,* 183–189.

Rosenthal, R., & Jacobson, L. (1966). Teachers' expectancies: Determinants of pupils' IQ gains. *Psychological Reports, 19,* 115–118.

Rosenthal, R., & Rosnow, R. L. (1975). *The volunteer subject.* New York: Wiley.

Rosnow, R. L., & Rosnow, M. (1995). *Writing papers in psychology.* Pacific Grove, CA: Brooks/Cole.

Rosnow, R., & Rosenthal, R. (1976). The volunteer subject revisited. *Australian Journal of Psychology, 28,* 97–108.

Ross, L., & Nisbett, R. E. (1991). *The person and the situation: Perspectives of social psychology.* New York: McGraw-Hill, Inc.

Rowan, A. N., & Andrutis, K. A. (1990). Animal numbers: Up, down and swing them all around. *Psychologists for the Ethical Treatment of Animals Bulletin, 9(2),* 3–5.

Russell, B. (1945). *A history of western philosophy.* New York: Simon & Schuster.

Sackett, G. P. (1978). *Observing behavior (Vol. II): Data collection and analysis methods.* Baltimore: University Park Press.

Sadker, M., & Sadker, D. (1982). *Gender equity handbook for schools.* New York: Longman Press.

Sarnoff, I., & Zimbardo, P. G. (1961). Anxiety, fear, and social affiliation. *Journal of Abnormal and Social Psychology, 62,* 356–363.

Scanlon, T. J., Luben, R. N., Scanlon, F. L., & Singleton, N. (1993, 18–25 December). Is Friday the 13th bad for your health? *British Medical Journal, 307,* 1584–1586.

Schachter, S. (1959). *The psychology of affiliation.* Stanford, CA: Stanford University Press.

Schieber, F. (1988). Vision assessment technology and screening older drivers: Past practices and emerging techniques. In National Research Council (Eds.),

Transportation in an Aging Society, Vol. 2 (pp. 270–293). Washington, DC: Transportation Research Board.

Schlegel, R. (1972). *Inquiry into science: Its domain and limits.* New York: Anchor.

Schwartz, M. D., Lerman, C., Miller, S. M., Daly, M., & Masny, A. (1995). Coping disposition, perceived risk, and psychological distress among women at increased risk for ovarian cancer. *Health Psychology, 14(3),* 232–235.

Schweigert, W. A. (1994). *Research methods & statistics.* Pacific Grove, CA: Brooks/Cole.

Serbin, L. A., Zelkowitz, P., Doyle, A., Gold, D., & Wheaton, B. (1990). The socialization of sex-differentiated skills and academic performance: A mediational model. *Sex Roles, 23(11/12),* 613–628.

Siiter, R., & Ellison, K. W. (1984). Perceived authoritarianism in self and others by male college students and police officers. *Journal of Applied Social Psychology, 14,* 334–340.

Silveira, J. (1980). Generic masculine words and thinking. In C. Kramarae (Ed.), *The voice of women and men.* New York: Pergamon Press.

Simon, H. A. (1967). Motivational and emotional controls of cognition. *Psychological Review, 74,* 29–39.

Singer, P. (1975). *Animal liberation.* New York: New York Review, Random House.

Stewart, R. B., Mobley, L. A., Van Tuyl, S. S., & Salvador, L. A. (1987). The firstborn's adjustment to the birth of a sibling: A longitudinal assessment. *Child Development, 58,* 341–355.

Stoneman, Z., & Brody, G. H. (1983). Immediate and long-term recognition and generalization of advertized products as a function of age. *Developmental Psychology, 19(1),* 56–61.

Suls, J., & Rosnow, J. (1988). Concerns about artifacts in behavioral research. In M. Morawski (Ed.), *The rise of experimentation in American psychology* (pp. 163–187). New Haven, CT: Yale University Press.

Tate, B. G., & Baroff, G. S. (1966). Aversive control of self-injurious behavior in a psychotic boy. *Behavior Research and Therapy, 4,* 281–287.

Taylor, J. A. (1953). A personality scale of manifest anxiety. *Journal of Abnormal and Social Psychology, 48,* 285–290.

Thurstone, L. L. (1928). Attitudes can be measured. *American Journal of Sociology, 33,* 529–554.

Tuchman, B. W. (1984). *The march of folly: From Troy to Vietnam.* New York: Knopf.

Tulving, E., & Pearlstone, Z. (1966). Availability versus accessibility of information in memory for words. *Journal of Verbal Learning and Verbal Behavior, 5,* 381–391.

Underwood, B. J. (1966). *Experimental psychology.* New York: Appleton-Century-Crofts.

U. S. Department of Health, Education, and Welfare (1975, March 13). Protection of human subjects. *Federal Register, 40(50),* Part II.

U. S. Department of Health, Education, and Welfare (1978). Guide for the use and care of laboratory animals. Washington, DC: U.S. Government Printing Office.

Velten, H. V. (1943). The growth of phonemic and lexical patterns in infant language. *Language, 19,* 281–292.

Vesselo, I. R. (1965). *How to read statistics.* London: George G. Harrap.

Vineberg, R., & Joyner, J. N. (1983). Performance measurement in the military services. In F. Landy, S. Zedeck, & J. Cleveland (Eds.), *Performance measurement and theory* (pp. 233–250). Hillsdale, NJ: Erlbaum.

Wall Street Journal Report. March 3, 1984. New York: WPIX-TV.

Walster (Hatfield), E., Walster, G., & Berscheid, E. (1978). *Equity: Theory and research.* Boston: Allyn & Bacon.

Ward, S. E., Leventhal, H., & Love, R. (1988). Repression revisited: Tactics used in coping with a severe health threat. *Personality and Social Psychology Bulletin, 14(4),* 735–746.

Warwick, D. P., & Lininger, C. A. (1975). *The sample survey: Theory and practice.* New York: McGraw-Hill.

Wasson, J. H., Sauvigne, A. E., Mogielnicki, R. P., Gaudette, C., & Rockwell, A. (1984). Continuity of outpatient medical care in elderly men. *Journal of the American Medical Association, 252(17),* 2413–2417.

Watanabe, S., Sakamoto, J., & Wakita, M. (1995). Pigeons' discrimination of paintings by Monet and Picasso. *Journal of the Experimental Analysis of Behavior, 63,* 165–174.

Watson, J. B., & Rayner, R. (1920). Conditioned emotional reactions. *Journal of Experimental Psychology, 3,* 1–14.

Weiss, J. M. (1972). Psychological factors in stress and disease. *Scientific American, 226(6),* 104–113.

Wells, G. L., & Petty, R. E. (1980). The effects of overt head-movements on persuasion: Compatibility and incompatibility of responses. *Journal of Basic and Applied Social Psychology, 1,* 219–230.

Wheeler, L. (1988). My year in Hong Kong: Some observations about social behavior. *Personality and Social Psychology Bulletin, 14(2),* 410–420.

Which are the safest vehicles? (1994, November 27). *Parade Magazine,* p. 16. (Sunday supplement magazine of the Oakland Press). New York: Parade Publications.

Whitehead, A. N. (1925). *Science and the modern world.* New York: Free Press.

Willems, E. P. (1969). Planning a rationale for naturalistic research. In E. P. Willems & H. L. Raush (Eds.), *Naturalistic viewpoints in psychological research.* New York: Holt, Rinehart, & Winston, Inc.

Windle, C. (1954). Test-retest effect on personality questionnaires. *Educational Psychology Measurement, 14,* 617–633.

Winer, B. J. (1971). *Statistical principles in experimental design* (2nd ed.). New York: McGraw-Hill.

Wolff, P., & Levin, J. R. (1972). The role of overt activity in children's imagery and production. *Child Development, 43,* 537–548.

Yepez, M. E. (1994). An observation of gender-specific teacher behavior in the ESL classroom. *Sex Roles, 30(1/2),* 121–133.

Yin, R. (1969). Perception of inverted faces. *Journal of Experimental Psychology, 81,* 141–145.

Zajonc, R. B. (1966). Attitudinal effects of mere exposure. *Journal of Personality and Social Psychology, 9,* 1–27.

Zajonc, R. B. (1968). Cognitive theories in social psychology. In G. Lindzey & E. Aronson (Eds.), *The handbook of social psychology* (2nd ed., Vol. 1, pp. 320–411). Reading, MA: Addison-Wesley.

Zajonc, R. B., Heingartner, A., & Herman, E. M. (1969). Social enhancement and impairment of performance in the cockroach. *Journal of Personality and Social Psychology, 13,* 83–92.

INDEX*

*Page numbers in italics designate the page on which a key term is defined. Key terms also appear in the glossary.

TO THE OWNER OF THIS BOOK:

We hope that you have found *Experimental Psychology,* Fourth Edition, useful. So that this book can be improved in a future edition, would you take the time to complete this sheet and return it? Thank you.

School and address: _____

Department: _____

Instructor's name: _____

1. What I like most about this book is: _____

_____

_____

2. What I like least about this book is: _____

_____

_____

3. My general reaction to this book is: _____

_____

4. The name of the course in which I used this book is: _____

_____

5. Were all of the chapters of the book assigned for you to read? _____

   If not, which ones weren't? _____

6. In the space below, or on a separate sheet of paper, please write specific suggestions for improving this book and anything else you'd care to share about your experience in using the book.

_____

_____

_____

_____

_____

Optional:

Your name: _____ Date: _____

May Brooks/Cole quote you, either in promotion for *Experimental Psychology,*
Fourth Edition, or in future publishing ventures?

Yes: _____ No: _____

Sincerely,

Anne Myers and Christine Hansen